The Art and Craft of Computing

The Art and Craft of Computing

S. Ceri
D. Mandrioli
L. Sbattella

 **Addison-Wesley**

Harlow, England • Reading, Massachusetts • Menlo Park, California • New York
Don Mills, Ontario • Amsterdam • Bonn • Sydney • Singapore • Tokyo • Madrid
San Juan • Milan • Mexico City • Seoul • Taipei

Addison Wesley Longman Limited
Edinburgh Gate
Harlow
Essex CM20 2JE
England

and Associated Companies throughout the World.

A first version of this book by Stefano Ceri, Dino Mandrioli and Licia Sbattella
was originally published in Italian by McGraw Hill, Italia, 1994 with the title
'Informatica Istituzioni'

Cover designed by Designers & Partners, Oxford
and printed by The Riverside Printing Co. (Reading) Ltd.
Translated and typeset by 46
Printed and bound in Great Britain by Biddles Ltd., Guildford and King's Lynn

First printed 1997

ISBN 0–201–87698–1

British Library Cataloguing-in-Publication Data
A catalogue record for this book is available from the British Library

Preface

Computer science is an essential ingredient of modern education, with the potential to raise great interest and enthusiasm in young students. It is also an evolving discipline, with technological revolutions occurring every few years, forcing even computer science experts to re-educate themselves, or otherwise quickly become out of date. Thus, writing an introductory book in computer science is a great challenge.

Approach

In spite of its relative youth, computer science has reached a degree of richness and complexity comparable to more mature disciplines, such as physics, chemistry, or biology; like them, it is internally structured into very different fields, each with its own abstractions, technologies and methodologies. However, the newness of computer science is seen in the way it is approached in introductory textbooks. There is strong disagreement between educators; as a result, introductory books on computer science may emphasize either concepts and theory, or programming practice, or computer architectures, or software engineering and so on.

Students who specialize in computer science or computer engineering will sooner or later be exposed to all these topics and approaches and find some balance between them. However, computer science courses are also offered to students who specialize in many scientific disciplines, such as mathematics, physics, or engineering; and it is also becoming widespread in the curricula of some humanistic studies, such as communication sciences. These students typically take only one or two computer science courses; thus, they are likely to have an unbalanced view of the subject as a result of their limited experience. They may learn how to program a computer, but remain uncertain about how the computer works; or they may understand the internals of chips, but not be able to bridge this knowledge to high-level programming or to advanced, distributed architectures. The absence of a 'global view' leaves students with the impression that many unexplained features of computer science are simply 'magic'; this may encourage them to consider this discipline only as instrumental to their instruction, but not really as a scientific discipline in its own right. One of our educational objectives is to help students who do not specialize in computer science to view computer science as a well-organized scientific discipline.

In many successful books introducing scientific disciplines, such as physics, or chemistry, or biology, authors are often driven by an idea, a unifying paradigm that inspires and permeates the entire educational project. For instance, in a book on biology, many authors take 'the cell' as the central idea; they may start with a description of its structure, then of the chemical transformations that occur within cells, then of the functionalities that the cells may perform in different tissues, then of the physiology of these tissues and so on.

Our educational program is also based on a unitary idea, a driving paradigm that can be found in all the chapters and parts of this book. In the same way as biology is explained from the inside of the cell reaching out towards its functions, we are driven by an operational approach, which explains computer science from inside (that is, from the computer structure and from basic programming concepts) to outside (that is, to applications of computers which are visible to users).

This 'bottom-up' approach starts with descriptions of basic ingredients and then describes the functionalities that these ingredients can offer; increasingly complex functionalities are described, based on the functionalities described previously. Our readers will have to learn about algorithms, the structure of the machine and the general structure of computer programs, before running their first program. However, when eventually they type a message and see its effect on the screen, they will have a good understanding of what happened in the machine to produce that effect. We want to make students see that computer science is not magic (in the same way that the cell's physiology is not magic), but is built up progressively from fundamental principles.

Contents and modular organization

Another objective in designing the structure of our book has been to balance theory and practice, software and hardware architectures, technologies and methodologies. This objective has forced us to work out a modular architecture for our book. The book starts with two introductory chapters giving an overview of computer science, stressing two fundamental concepts: the notion of the algorithm, exemplified by means of several narrative examples, and basic computer organization, represented by the von Neumann machine. Describing computer organization so early in the book is rather unusual and some lecturers may choose to postpone Chapter 2 until later in the course. However, the proposed organization has the advantage of introducing an operational model of the computer quite early and this can help students understand programming concepts.

After these introductory chapters, the book follows an apparently traditional manner, by devoting Part I to 'Programming', Part II to 'Hardware and Software Architecture' and Part III to 'Software Development'. Although these three parts correspond to three classical computer science courses, note that they are very rarely covered by the same book. Thus, we cover a broader spectrum than many other introductory textbooks in computer science.

Modularity is further reflected by the way in which the parts are divided into chapters. In general, each chapter deals with a well-defined topic; the first chapters of each part present the foundations and the later chapters further develop previously discussed topics by introducing new features. The last chapters of each part are dedicated to advanced topics, which need not necessarily be covered; these optional chapters allow lecturers to stress the direction most appropriate to the needs of the particular audience to which the book is directed. Advanced chapters and sections are marked with an asterisk.

The programming part starts with the specification of algorithms using simple programs which initially are not executable. Each succeeding chapter introduces one ingredient: from program structures, to types, to control structures, to functions and procedures, to recursion, to file management. At this point, the classical 'ingredients' constituting a first programming course have been covered. The final chapters cover dynamic data structures, discussing classical data structures and algorithms for their manipulation; and complexity analysis, discussing a classical problem which is fairly theoretical in nature but has a strong impact in practice.

The architecture part is where the bottom-up approach is most evident. We start with the representation of information in the computer, then we describe computer instructions, their symbolic description in assembler language and their execution by a simple hardware architecture. Next, we move to the operating system and describe its layered architecture and the functionalities offered by each layer. We then turn to data management and describe file and database organization. Next, we turn to distributed computing architectures supported by either local or geographic networks. Finally, we reach the levels where applications are mostly visible to everyday users; we describe the Internet in terms of the services that it can provide and the look and technology of modern user interfaces.

The third part on software development is more traditional, with an initial description of the software life cycle that offers a broad view of all activities involved in software production, followed by a description of the main phases: requirement analysis (focusing on models for describing reality), design (focusing on modularization techniques) and verification (focusing on programming errors and the techniques for finding and removing them). Modern software engineering is supported by computer-based tools, so one chapter is dedicated to classifying and describing them.

The final chapters of this part are optional and deal with subjects that cross the boundaries represented by the part structure of the book; they are placed in Part III for convenience. One chapter is dedicated to object orientation, an increasingly important approach to programming and design, here presented in comparison with the procedure-oriented approach, used in Part I and in the first chapters of Part III. Another chapter is dedicated to innovative language paradigms, in particular to functional or logic languages.

One could ask why we are concerned with software engineering and not with the equally challenging problem of hardware engineering, that is, of how hardware systems are developed. The reason is that hardware development is really a task for the computer expert, while students or professionals are more likely to encounter software development in the course of their careers, since most applications require some software production or adaptation. However, an extended example of VLSI design – a particular hardware design technology – is provided in Part II.

The last chapter in the book, which stands alone, gives an historical introduction to computer science and describes its impact on society. A further reading section provides suggestions for readers interested in extending their knowledge of the discipline. Several appendices provide various technical details, such as the full syntax of the C language and solutions to selected exercises.

Critical choices

Anyone teaching computer science faces two critical choices concerning the selection of the programming language and the computer architecture.

Trying to select a programming language that satisfies all needs is a hopeless task. Many lecturers prefer Pascal or Pascal-like languages (such as Modula-2), being most influenced in their choice by the clean and pure language organization, which has obvious didactic merits. In the original Italian edition of this textbook we chose Pascal. Yet, Pascal or Pascal-like languages, with very few exceptions, are not used in practice; their role is confined to introductory courses in computer science. So, we have felt increasing pressure from students and colleagues to choose a real programming language, one that students could actually use for writing programs related to their studies or to their profession.

Needless to say, some colleagues pushed for Fortran, which is still widely used in engineering schools; but in the past few years, all these requests have turned to C (or C++, its object-oriented evolution), probably because of the widespread use of C and C++ in nearly all the fields of application of computer science. So, we have accepted this viewpoint and have chosen C. However, we are aware of the risks of using C and have decided to teach C but to keep a Pascal-like didactic approach. Thus, we follow a classical Pascal-like progression in the presentation of the arguments and we omit the programming tricks which have made C popular, but which have also caused many errors, at least for beginners. We considered our choice of C, and our approach to the teaching of the language, as another challenge. C++ is briefly introduced in Part III, in the chapter describing the object-oriented approach to programming. While we have decided to move from Pascal to C, we have resisted from the temptation of moving further, for example to Java or Telescript: although languages for mobile computing are very much 'in fashion', we believe that they still need to be assessed as vehicles for introducing programming concepts to beginners.

Another critical choice concerns the use of real computer architectures, such as the Pentium, the Alpha, or the Motorola 68000, to illustrate the architecture of computers. Here, we have chosen to use simplified architectures rather than real ones. Thus, throughout Part II, we rely on simplified, abstract machines, rather than on concrete ones; otherwise, the amount of detail required would be overwhelming.

But this does not mean that our descriptions lack depth. Readers may not have details of a real architecture, such as the Pentium, but they will still be able to understand the Internet on the personal computer in terms of the instructions executed by the chip inside the computer itself, data transmission along the telephone line and modem connecting to a host, or the interface technology provided by Netscape or Explorer. All these technologies are explained by a simplified but realistic model.

Necessarily, topics that are closely linked to technology evolution are likely to become outdated very soon. For instance, during the writing of this book Windows 95 came onto the market: it caused a small revolution in the PC world, making the MS-DOS operating system and traditional Windows outdated. We believe that it is almost impossible for a text such as this to keep pace with technological evolution, no matter how many efforts the authors make to revise the material. Nevertheless, thanks to the emphasis we put on fundamental principles, the reader should gain an understanding of not only today's technology but also its evolution: thus, not much effort should be required if, for instance, in a few years' time, Netscape and Explorer are replaced by new tools for navigating the Internet.

Examples, exercises and other supporting material

As in any introductory book on computer science, examples and exercises play a major role. Examples are of different types and lengths and of different depths. They are sometimes technical (for example, programs) and sometimes descriptive (for example, user interfaces). A few examples in the programming part require some mathematical background (such as matrices and trigonometric functions); in most cases we make them self-contained by defining the necessary mathematical notation. A few other examples with heavy mathematical notation are not on the 'critical path' of the book, so they can simply be skipped by readers without the necessary mathematical background; however, they are included because they can be didactically very instructive. Examples range from short ones, illustrating simple and fundamental concepts, to long and detailed ones. The latter, mainly consisting of programs, serve to show how to move from fictional cases to more realistic cases. In the laboratories of introductory courses, students must write nontrivial programs: long examples help them bridge the gap between programming theory and practice.

Some examples are explicitly labelled as extended examples; they either go deeper into some critical issue (such as object-oriented design or the UNIX operating system) or provide a state-of-the-art view of some technological or application field (such as advanced computer architectures or virtual reality). They are not on the critical path and thus can be easily skipped or postponed to a second reading.

Exercises too are of different types and levels, ranging from less difficult applications or repetitions of mechanisms illustrated in the text to fairly challenging and complex tasks. Difficult exercises are marked by an asterisk (*). Some exercises suggest elaboration and deepening of concepts raised at specific points of the text. To avoid disturbing the flow of the text, these exercises are postponed to the end of the relevant chapter. However, the special marker '☞' in the margin indicates that the given topic is the subject of a related exercise, so that the reader is warned that the topic under discussion can be examined in more detail and this will be suggested by an appropriate exercise. Solutions to selected exercises are given in Appendix E. Some are fully detailed whereas others are just briefly sketched.

The book is also equipped with an Instructor's Manual. This will be available to teachers adopting the text. It includes:

- solutions to other exercises in the main text, either in detail or in outline;
- further exercises (possibly with suggested solutions) which can be given as complementary homework;
- more suggestions on how to organize courses based on this text.

Mapping contents to courses

Each part of this book is self-contained; lecturers may focus on each part separately (an obvious prerequisite to software engineering is some programming background). The entire textbook is suitable for use in one complete course, as is done at the Politecnico di Milano and in many engineering faculties in Italy, where the Italian version of this book is adopted for courses which are about 80–100 hours long. But this textbook is also particularly suited for two or three coordinated 'modularized' courses, of about 30–50 hours each, which are commonly taught in most countries. Indeed, references between parts help students build a complete overview, which could be emphasized by lecturers or left to the independent and spontaneous work of the readers. And, of course, this book could be used in one course module whose teacher will concentrate on one part and cover only a few chapters of the other parts, perhaps suggesting the remaining chapters as further reading.

Thanks to its structure, the book imposes only a partial order on topics; that is, the teacher and the reader are not compelled to follow the linear flow of the text exactly: only a few basic and natural precedences must be fulfilled.

For example, one lecturer could concentrate on the first chapters of the 'Programming' part and complement them with aspects of computer architecture and operating systems (to explain the operational model of the computer) and with aspects of software design and verification (to explain modularization and removal of errors from programs). Another could approach programming in greater depth, by adding data structures and algorithms and/or complexity analysis, and then continue with software engineering; in this case, the architectural chapters could be left as further reading, or approached only for software-related aspects such as operating systems and databases. A third lecturer could concentrate on 'hardware and software architectures', thus stressing the organization of complex computer-based systems and presenting programming concepts only where required for basic algorithms using a reduced version of the language, with a more descriptive style. These examples indicate just a few of the very many course organizations allowed by our textbook. Obviously, courses based on 'architectures' could be coordinated with courses based on 'programming', such as the first and last example given above.

We are aware that this book cannot cover the needs of hands-on courses with intense experimental activity – and we do believe that experimental activities should indeed be present in any introductory computer science course. Students need to complement this textbook with other material, such as programming manuals or the description of a specific hardware architecture. For instance, in Italy a programming project is compulsory and students typically complement our textbook with manuals describing the specific programming environments. We consider it quite natural that hands-on courses require device-specific complements and we believe that it is good to expose students to two radically different sources of information, such as a 'global' textbook and a 'specific' manual.

More suggestions on how to base university courses on this textbook are given in the Instructor's Manual.

In conclusion, this textbook offers many ways of organizing the teaching of introductory computer science; we provide more material than is typically covered by introductory courses, but we give it a modular organization and divide it into fundamental and optional chapters. Lecturers can then make their own selection of the material and the level at which it should be covered. And students, in turn, may complement this material with further reading, or follow the 'logical pointers' that connect the arguments together. Hopefully, they may be able to develop a bottom-up, operational answer to their most recurrent problem and satisfy their curiosity about 'how and why computers work'.

Acknowledgements

The authors would like to acknowledge the cooperation of several colleagues in the preparation of the first Italian edition of this book, including Roberto Bisiani, Franco Bombi, Augusto Celentano, Stefano Crespi-Reghizzi, Fausto Distante, Pierluigi Della Vigna, William Fornaciari, Alfonso Fuggetta, Gabriele Longoni, Luca Mainetti, Renato Martucci, Rosamaria Morpurgo, Antonio Natali, Giuseppe Pelagatti, Fabio Salice, Donatella Sciuto, Michele Ursino, and Giovanni Vigna. The thoroughly revised, present international edition has benefited from a number of suggestions from the (Venetian, anonymous) translator and from competent anonymous reviewers. Special thanks are due to Carlo Bellettini, who has followed the entire process with dedication and care and helped in program verification.

All examples included in this book were executed using the Turbo C/C++ programming environment.

Stefano Ceri
Dino Mandrioli
Licia Sbattella
Milan, October 1997

Contents

An introduction to computer science

1

In this chapter, we introduce computer science as a scientific discipline which, in spite of its ancient roots, developed only in the second half of the twentieth century with the arrival of computers.

1.1 What is computer science?

When different people are asked this question, they often give vague and contradictory answers – many critical voices argue that computer science is really more an art than a science, as it cannot even be properly defined. This is not really surprising, as computer science has grown to include many diverse fields, from scientific and engineering calculus to business administration, from artificial intelligence to geographic and environmental data management.

To start with, we must make the point that computer science is not only the science and technology of electronic computing machines: we regard the computer as a tool which allows computer scientists to operate in practice. Similarly, computer science cannot be confused with any one of its numerous applications, although many professionals are typically very focused on their application and regard it as the essence of computer science.

Our definition attempts to be broad but accurate: we regard computer science as the *science of information representation and management*. This definition stresses that information is the main product of computer technology and that computer science includes not only the technology of computers, but also the way in which information is structured and managed. The emphasis on 'information' provides an explanation as to why computer science is fast becoming an integral part of all human activities: almost all human activities involve some form of information management and would therefore benefit from using computers as a support tool. On the other hand, the term 'science' emphasizes the fact that, in computing, information management is handled rigorously and systematically and can therefore be made automatic. This is different from what happens in less formalized types of activity, such as journalism, which also deal with information.

The Association for Computing Machinery (ACM), the main body representing researchers and professional operators in the computing field, has put forward a definition of computer science which is slightly more complex, but totally compatible with the one just mentioned. According to this definition, computer science is the *systematic study of those algorithms which describe and transform information: the underpinning theory, analysis, planning, efficiency, realization and application*. Such a definition brings into play the term **algorithm**, which can be informally defined as a precise sequence of operations that are clearly stated and therefore can be executed in automatic mode. Furthermore, the definition itself puts the accent on the planning and realization aspects which are such a prominent part of computer scientists' activity.

It should be noted that, according to the two given definitions, it is perfectly possible to have an activity which is conceptually definable as falling within the realm of computer science even without actually using a computer, for example in planning and applying specific rules for computing arithmetic operations using only pen and paper. The computer is simply a more powerful computing tool, compared to the abacus, for example: its greater power is such that it allows management of an otherwise unmanageable quantity of information.

This chapter introduces a number of fundamental concepts of computer science, which will be dealt with in more depth at a later stage: algorithms, programming languages, computer systems architecture, the main computer applications and the breakdown of the discipline into several areas.

1.2 The concept of the algorithm

As already stated, an algorithm can informally be described as 'a sequence of precisely defined steps which lead to the accomplishment of a task'. For example, the assembly instructions for an electrical appliance contain algorithms which guide us step by step through the assembly procedure. We also use simple algorithms when we calculate the greatest common divisor of several natural numbers and each time we get cash out of an automated teller machine. In this latter case, some of the steps of the algorithm are: inserting a magnetic card into the machine, entering a PIN code and specifying the amount.

It is essential that an algorithm should be *understandable* to the person who needs to implement it. Let us go back to the assembly instructions for our electrical appliance: if these are printed only in the language of its country of origin, there is obviously a fair chance that the buyer in a different country will not understand them. In computer science, there is a fundamental link between algorithms and computers: computers can in fact be described as performers of algorithms. Algorithms are described by means of **programs**, that is, sequences of instructions written in an appropriate language that is understood by the computer. It is the task of the computer scientist to produce algorithms (that is, to understand the sequence of steps that lead to the solution of a problem) and to code them into programs (that is, to make them understandable to the computer).

The computer executes the programs step by step, precisely, fast and powerfully, but without alterations or deviations even when their implementation is obviously wrong: the computer cannot bring into play any form of 'common sense'. Indeed, total precision is one basic feature of computer science's management of information: the rule 'in order to make an apple pie, one needs three kilograms of apples, three eggs and 500 grams of flour' is sufficiently precise to be considered a computer science rule, whereas the rule 'truss the roast joint with a piece of string and rub with salt' is not, because it relies, for its execution, on the cook's knowledge of how much salt will be needed for that particular joint and of how to use the string for trussing the joint.

Here we are informally introducing two essential features of algorithms, *correctness* and *efficiency*, which will be extensively discussed in the following chapters. An algorithm is correct if it arrives at the solution of the task for which it has been designed, without missing any of the fundamental steps. If, in the algorithm for assembling an electrical appliance, the step of checking the voltage is missed out and we plug the appliance in without using our own common sense, this may lead to a short circuit or the melting of a fuse; the assembly will then have to be stopped until appropriate repairs have been made.

Efficiency is another desirable feature of algorithms, that is, the algorithm must reach the solution to the problem in the shortest possible time and/or by using the smallest possible quantity of physical resources, as long as this is compatible with correctness. For example, an assembly algorithm is not efficient if it first adjusts a device and then, in a further step, does something which will lead to the need to readjust it, thereby leading to a repetition of the same step. A good computer scientist will always seek out the most efficient algorithm, within the set of those which correctly solve a given problem.

Let us now illustrate in more detail the fundamental characteristics of the algorithm concept, with the aid of some examples. Examples 1.1 and 1.2 are extremely simple and show how an algorithm is a sequence of operations which can be easily mechanized. Example 1.3 introduces the discussion of the efficiency of algorithms. The subsequent extended example illustrates how to construct an algorithm by breaking down a rather complex problem into many simpler subproblems, identifying the solution of each individual subproblem and then reassembling the individual solutions into the solution of the original problem.

EXAMPLE 1.1 Adding two numbers using an abacus

We want to calculate the sum of two numbers using an abacus. In order to simplify the problem even further, let us assume that the first addendum is represented by

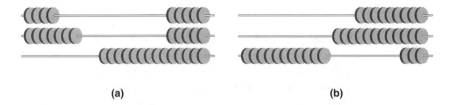

(a)   (b)

Figure 1.1 Configuration of the abacus (a) before and (b) after executing the sum operation.

the first row of the abacus, the second by the second row and the result is in the third row, as shown in Figure 1.1. We further assume that each row of the abacus contains a sufficiently large number of digits to accommodate the three numbers.

Before describing the algorithm that executes the sum operation, let us take another look at the abacus. This represents numerical information in an extremely simple and primitive way: the number indicated by each row of the abacus is represented by a corresponding number of digits aligned to the left of the row, whereas the unused digits are aligned to the right.

As we all know, the following operations are required in order to obtain the sum of two figures using an abacus:

(1) On the first row, one digit is shifted from left to right and at the same time, on the third row, one digit is shifted from right to left.

(2) The above operation is repeated until the left-hand side of the first row is empty.

(3) On the second row, one digit is moved from left to right and at the same time, on the third row, one digit is moved from right to left.

(4) The above operation is repeated until the left-hand side of the second row is empty.

The number of digits on the left-hand side of the third row is the desired result; the final configuration is shown in Figure 1.1(b).

The above procedure is an algorithm. It consists of the iterative execution of an extremely simple and limited set of elementary operations: selecting a row, shifting a digit from left to right or vice versa, checking whether a row is empty. Anybody who is capable of executing these basic operations is capable of adding two numbers with an abacus. This shows why the concept of an algorithm is fundamental to the automatic manipulation of data: once we have constructed a mechanical executor of the elementary operations, we can use it to solve any problem whatsoever, as long as we can describe its solution in terms of an algorithm that uses those operations.

EXAMPLE 1.2   Operating a portable CD player

Let us consider a portable CD player, with a number of control buttons and a display which indicates whether the CD player is operational and in particular the track which is currently being played. We want to listen to the thirteenth track, a pop song; the operations required for achieving this result constitute a small algorithm which is described below:

(1)   If we are at home and an electric outlet is available, plug the power adapter into the outlet.

(2)   If no outlet is available, verify that the CD player includes the right number of batteries and that these are sufficiently charged; otherwise, insert or replace the batteries with new ones.

(3)   Switch the CD player on.

(4)   Insert the CD in the CD player; the display indicates 'No Disk'.

(5)   Push the 'Start' button and wait until the display indicates 'Disk OK'.

(6)   Repeatedly push the 'Forward' button until the display indicates track 13.

(7)   Put on the headphones.

Finally, we get to listen to our chosen track. Again, in this example, we have built our algorithm using a suitable combination of a few elementary operations: inserting the disk, pushing several buttons, checking the content of the display, putting headphones on. Notice also that the sequence of execution of such elementary operations may depend on the (partial) results of the execution itself. For instance, we must plug in the power adapter *if* we verify the availability of an outlet; we must repeat the pushing of a button *until* a certain condition is verified (the fact that display indicates 13). The possibility of deciding which operation to perform on the basis of the inspection of the state of execution is a crucial feature of any nontrivial algorithm.

The above algorithm is a simplified version of what we do in practice and does not take into account several variants. For instance, the decision whether to plug in the adapter or to use the batteries may depend on several other factors than those exemplified here; if the CD is not correctly inserted in the CD player, then even after pushing the 'Start' button the disk does not spin properly and the indication 'Disk OK' does not show up on the display. If this happens, we need to repeat step 5, as follows:

(5)   Push the 'Start' button; while the display indicates 'No Disk',
      repeat:

      (a) Insert the CD into the CD player again.

      (b) Push the 'Start' button.

This new version of the algorithm is probably also too much of a simplification. In reality, even the biggest music fanatic will give up after several attempts and perhaps will conclude that the CD player is out of order. This discussion shows that people are good executors of algorithms but can also decide to abandon them (for example, in exceptional conditions) using their common sense. Computers, on the other hand, have no common sense and no intuition; all exceptional situations must be described to them first in order to enable appropriate reactions.

EXAMPLE 1.3   Reference search in a library

Let us consider a small library which contains a certain number of shelves full of books. Each book is in a precise and unvarying position: if a volume is taken off the shelf, the position of those surrounding it does not change (let us assume, for simplicity's sake, that a book, even when isolated, does not fall over or change its position); when, later, the volume is returned, it is put back into its original position. The library possesses a card-index catalogue. Each card contains, in this order:

- surname and first name of the author (if the book has more than one author, all surnames and first names are inserted in the order in which they are printed on the book cover);
- book title;
- publication date;
- number of the shelf where it is placed;
- number of the position on the shelf assigned to the book.

```
AUTHOR(S):
GHEZZI CARLO,
JAZAYERI MEHDI.

TITLE:
PROGRAMMING LANGUAGE CONCEPTS.
1981.

SHELF 35
POSITION 21
```

Figure 1.2   An example of a library card.

A sample card is shown in Figure 1.2. The cards are arranged in alphabetical order by author and title; that is, their order depends on the first author, then for books with the same first author, on the second author and so on; books with the same author(s) are ordered by title. A simple algorithm to access a book in the library, assuming you know author and title, is as follows.

(1)   Look for the book's card in the catalogue.

(2)   Once you have found it, write the shelf number and book position number on a piece of paper.

(3)   Look for the indicated shelf.

(4)   Once you have identified the shelf, access the position of the book, take it out and, if required, write on the card the date of the loan and the name of the borrower.

In this case, too, the most difficult step of the algorithm is step 1; let us therefore look at it in detail. The simplest catalogue-searching technique is:

(1)   Check the first card of the catalogue.

(2)   If the author's name and book title are the ones you are looking for, the search has terminated successfully, otherwise check the next card.

(3)   Proceed card by card until you find the card you are looking for. If you arrive at the last card without finding the author and title, the search terminates unsuccessfully and you will have to look for this book in a different library.

The above (sub)algorithm is very simple but requires an excessive number of operations. Just think how long it would take to execute it in a library with only 1000 books! Fortunately, this is not the algorithm we use in real life; the operations we execute in a more efficient search for our book look more like the following algorithm:

(1)   Take the middle card of the catalogue.

(2)   If this is the card you are looking for, the search is terminated.

(3)   If not, then if the card you are looking for follows in alphabetical order the one you have just checked, the search continues in the second half of the catalogue, otherwise the search proceeds in the first half of the catalogue. The search is conducted by repeating steps 1, 2 and 3; more precisely, if the search is in the second half of the catalogue, then the next card to be taken is positioned three-quarters of the way through, while if the search is in the first half of the catalogue, then the next card to be taken is positioned one-quarter of the way through the catalogue.

The above algorithm is incomplete, as another condition for terminating its execution is to determine that the search zone is empty; thus, step 2 of the algorithm can be revised as:

(2)   If this is the card you are looking for or if the portion of the catalogue that you are searching is empty, then the search is terminated.

When the search terminates because the portion of the catalogue being examined is empty, you may conclude that the book you are looking for is not in the catalogue.

The second search method is better than the first: this should be sufficiently obvious even without a rigorous analysis of the two algorithms (such analyses will be discussed in Chapter 12). It also shows that often it is not enough to identify an algorithm for the solution of a problem, but that it is also necessary to make it as efficient as possible.

EXTENDED EXAMPLE: Consulting a road map

As a last, extended example of an algorithm, consider the problem of consulting a road map, normally used to plan a journey by car.

First of all, we need to analyse the way information is represented on a map. Counties, seas, lakes and mountains are defined in outline by their boundaries, reproduced to a given scale. Some visual aids help us to understand the map better, such as the choice of background colours for surfaces: blue is used for seas and lakes, green for plains, brown for hills and mountains. Towns are represented by small circles and the roads that connect the various towns are indicated by lines which approximately reproduce their course. The actual thickness of the line is selected from a finite set that denotes the type of road (motorway, highway, secondary road and so on). Finally, the distance between two points on the road is indicated by a number next to the line that represents the road.

Maps may be consulted to solve various types of problem. However, the way in which the information on the map is handled does not always correspond to the execution of an algorithm. If, for example, we consult a map before going on holiday, the map tells us the distance between our home town and our chosen destination and whether, during our journey, we will drive near large cities, alongside lakes or up mountains. Usually, though, selecting a holiday resort does not obey strict algorithmic rules – rather, it is influenced by subjective considerations and factors not found on a map, such as the availability of hotels and restaurants, previous experience, or the recommendation of friends.

On the other hand, the problem of how to find the shortest route to drive from one town to another can be solved by an algorithm. The solution to this problem allows us, for example, to choose the best route for a holiday journey. This problem lends itself to a precise – or *algorithmic* – description, because it can be expressed in terms which do not contain elements linked to subjective judgement; at the same time, the map described contains all the elements required to solve the problem, if we go along with the hypothesis that the shortest route is in fact shown on the map. In this case, we can formulate the solution to the problem by drawing up a precise sequence of steps, as follows:

(1) Find all the sequences of towns which define a route between the two given towns. More precisely, let us take c_d and c_a as the departure and the arrival town, respectively: let us identify and note, each on a different sheet of paper, all sequences $\{c_0, c_1, c_2, ..., c_k\}$ of names of towns, such that:

   (a) No town appears in the sequence twice.

   (b) The first element of the sequence, c_0, coincides with c_d and the last, c_k, coincides with c_a.

   (c) For each pair of contiguous elements, $<c_i, c_{i+1}>$, there is a stretch of road connecting them; this stretch of road obviously cannot pass through any town.

(2)   For each sequence, calculate the sum of the distances covered by the various stretches of road and note it next to the sequence.

(3)   Identify the sequence whose total distance is shortest and choose it as the shortest route. If there is more than one route with the same distance between c_d and c_a, select one of them arbitrarily (for example, the first one found). If, however, no route is found, for example where c_d and c_a are separated by the sea, the algorithm terminates by stating that there is no solution.

You will have noticed that the operations used in the above steps (identify sequences of stretches of road, calculate the sum of various distances and so on) are rather complex and, maybe, not sufficiently detailed. However, it should not be too difficult to formulate at least steps 2 and 3 more precisely, using more elementary operations, in order to arrive at a final formulation which is precise enough to be executed.

Step 1, on the other hand, requires a more in-depth analysis. Finding all the routes which lead from one town to another is a problem in its own right, which has to be solved through an appropriate algorithm: we may call it a subproblem of the main problem, because its solution is needed to construct the overall solution. The algorithm for providing a solution to this subproblem could be based on the following reasoning.

If n is the number of towns shown on the map, a route that connects c_d to c_a cannot have a constituent number of elements (stretches of road) higher than $n-1$: any route with a higher number of elements would have to pass through the same town more than once, a situation which we have explicitly excluded. It is therefore sufficient to construct all routes that start from c_d and have a number of elements lower than or equal to $n-1$ and then select those that end in c_a.

In order to construct all the routes that start in c_d and have a generic number of elements r, we can use the following reasoning. Let us suppose that we have already found all the routes starting in c_d with a length of $r-1$ elements. We can now obtain routes of length r by creating many copies of the routes with length $r-1$ and adding to each copy one more element which connects the last town c_{r-1} to all towns directly connected to it, excluding those towns that are already part of the sequence $r-1$.

In order to start, it is sufficient to consider a route of length 0, a fictitious route that starts and ends in c_d. At this point, routes of length 1 are those that connect c_d to its neighbouring towns, that is, to all towns that are directly connected to c_d by a road. Thus, we have defined the first two steps of an algorithm which, in n steps, generates all routes of length $n-1$ that start in c_d and therefore provides a solution to step 1 of the main algorithm. This type of reasoning is a first example of **induction**, a very powerful procedure in mathematics and computer science, which we will use to solve all sorts of different problems.

The reasoning that we have seen can be expressed in synthesis with an algorithm as follows:

(1.1) We start with an initial sequence, transcribed on a sheet of paper, which includes only town c_d; this sequence has length 0.

(1.2) We analyse the sequences of length $r-1$ constructed so far. Let us call S a generic sequence $\{c_d, c_1, c_2, ..., c_{r-1}\}$. For each sequence S we construct new sequences of length r as follows:

(a) Let c_{r-1} be the last town of the sequence S. Find all towns connected to c_{r-1} by a road: we call these the set of towns $\{a_1, a_2, ..., a_s\}$.

(b) Exclude from the set $\{a_1, a_2, ..., a_s\}$ all the towns which are already part of S. We are thus left with $\{a_1, a_2, ..., a_t\}$ towns, with $t \le s$.

(c) Construct t sequences of length r, obtained by adding to S a different town a_i chosen from the t towns identified in the previous step.

(1.3) Repeat the execution of the previous step until the condition $r = n$ is met. At this point, extract (from all constructed sequences of length $< n$) those sequences that have c_a as the last town, and the algorithm which identifies all possible routes terminates. If none are found, we can terminate the whole algorithm, stating that 'there is no solution to the problem'.

Figure 1.3 shows the identification of the best road between town E and town D obtained by applying the described algorithm for consulting a map.

Several important observations can be made with regard to this example:

- The way we normally consult road maps to solve the same problem is (luckily for us) quite different from the way described here. Does this mean that we use a better algorithm or that we do not use an algorithm at all? Indeed, when we consult maps, we quite often identify the best road very quickly, just at a glance. Also, we know that the best road between two towns is probably somewhere around the straight line between them, which allows us to focus our research on a limited section of the map. It has to be said, though, that this kind of knowledge, which can help us to find quick solutions in many cases, can also become a source of errors in critical cases, for example where the towns are separated by mountains or areas with difficult driving conditions.

- The algorithm we have found is quite clearly not the only solution to the problem and definitely not the best one. There exists, indeed, a much more efficient solution to it, even assuming that the performer of the algorithm cannot see things 'at a glance' and has no inventiveness whatsoever. As an exercise, you may want to invent new algorithms by going back to this problem at a later stage and checking if your solution improves the proposed one.

- It is not yet very clear at which point an algorithm may be considered to be sufficiently specific to be executed by the 'prototype executor': obviously, an expert will be capable of understanding, and if necessary executing, a rough outline of an algorithm, whereas a beginner will need a lot more details. The only way to give a rigorous definition of an algorithm is to give a rigorous definition of its executor, as will be discussed in Chapters 2 and 3.

- However, the solution that we have described cannot yet be executed by a computer. Our hypothetical executor has lost some typically human features

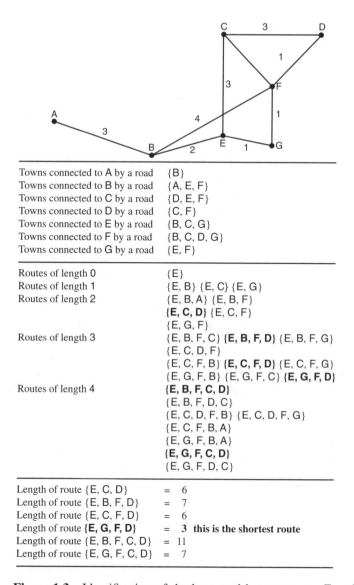

Towns connected to A by a road	{B}
Towns connected to B by a road	{A, E, F}
Towns connected to C by a road	{D, E, F}
Towns connected to D by a road	{C, F}
Towns connected to E by a road	{B, C, G}
Towns connected to F by a road	{B, C, D, G}
Towns connected to G by a road	{E, F}

Routes of length 0	{E}
Routes of length 1	{E, B} {E, C} {E, G}
Routes of length 2	{E, B, A} {E, B, F}
	{E, C, D} {E, C, F}
	{E, G, F}
Routes of length 3	{E, B, F, C} **{E, B, F, D}** {E, B, F, G}
	{E, C, D, F}
	{E, C, F, B} **{E, C, F, D}** {E, C, F, G}
	{E, G, F, B} {E, G, F, C} **{E, G, F, D}**
Routes of length 4	**{E, B, F, C, D}**
	{E, B, F, D, C}
	{E, C, D, F, B} {E, C, D, F, G}
	{E, C, F, B, A}
	{E, G, F, B, A}
	{E, G, F, C, D}
	{E, G, F, D, C}

Length of route {E, C, D}	= 6
Length of route {E, B, F, D}	= 7
Length of route {E, C, F, D}	= 6
Length of route **{E, G, F, D}**	= 3 **this is the shortest route**
Length of route {E, B, F, C, D}	= 11
Length of route {E, G, F, C, D}	= 7

Figure 1.3 Identification of the best road between town E and town D obtained by applying the defined algorithm.

such as common sense and view-at-a-glance, but has preserved others such as the capability of 'reading' a road map, for example to find towns adjacent to each other. There remains therefore the problem of representing the map, or at least the information that it contains, in such a way that this information can be understood by a computer.

1.3 Languages for programming algorithms

Let us now briefly introduce the languages for the description of algorithms: the so-called **programming languages**. An important activity of computer scientists is to define the languages for the coding of algorithms, that is, languages which allow algorithms to be written as programs that can be understood by the computer – the executor. Even though this activity has been in existence for only 50 years, computer scientists have managed, in this short span of time, to imitate the behaviour of the human race which has created, throughout the centuries, a very large number of different languages. The presence of so many programming languages has, on the one hand, the advantage of allowing us to choose the most appropriate language for coding particular algorithms; on the other, it causes quite a few problems, owing to the necessity of learning different languages and 'communicating' information between programs written in different languages.

At the dawn of computer science, people were forced, in order to communicate their algorithms to a computer, to learn machine language, that is, the set of instructions and commands that the machine was capable of executing. During the second half of the 1950s, the level of the languages used to communicate algorithms to computers began to rise, becoming, firstly, more appropriate for coding algorithms, and secondly, more comprehensible; the tiresome task of translating a program into machine language was assigned to the machine itself. As we will see in Section 1.4.5, this was made possible by the invention of other programs capable of translating high-level languages into machine code.

In those days, computers were mainly used to solve problems of numerical calculus; thus, the first high-level programming language to be introduced was Fortran (an acronym for FORmula TRANslator), particularly suitable for describing the manipulation of mathematical formulae and still widely used for this purpose.

Shortly after Fortran came Cobol (COmmon Business Oriented Language), the first language oriented towards business applications, particularly suitable for storing and manipulating data. Cobol and Fortran are still among the most widely used programming languages. This might come as a surprise, because they have some features which are rather 'out of date'; their success is due to the resistance to change which we find in many corporations who have invested enormous resources in their programs and are therefore reluctant to change languages.

Then there is a category of languages more rigorously based on a study of the principles of programming. The 'progenitor' of these languages is Algol 60 and therein lies its real importance, even though it has not found much practical application. Presently better known and actually applied languages in this family are:

- Pascal, widely used in the teaching of computer science;

- C, which we will use in this book, maybe the most successful language for the construction of computer applications at the present time;

- Ada, selected by the American Department of Defense (DoD) and supported by vast industrial investments.

More recently, a new programming style, called *object-oriented programming*, has established itself; it tries to maintain the correspondence between the objects that characterize an application and their coding. This has naturally led to the development of languages based on this style: *object-oriented languages*. Object-oriented programming and object-oriented languages are introduced in Chapter 25. With the advent of the Internet, new languages have been developed with the purpose of enabling the programming of applications on networks of inter-connected computers, such as Java and Telescript.

Finally, let us mention the existence of nonconventional languages that want to avoid a programming style conditioned by the characteristics of the computer and adopt, instead, a way of thinking nearer to the language of mathematics. The most well known among these are:

- Lisp, based on the mathematical concept of *function*;

- Prolog, based on the formalism of *mathematical logic*.

The key features of nonconventional languages are described in Chapter 26.

1.4 Architecture of computer systems

In this section, we deal with the executors of algorithms, that is, computer systems, giving an outline of their components, their organization and their behaviour. Chapter 2 and the second part of this book describe these concepts in greater detail.

The term 'computer system' is used throughout this book to denote a range of quite varied objects, from the smallest personal computer notebook to multi-user computer systems with huge quantities of programs and data. Between these two extremes, there is a continuous line of systems of growing complexity. Nevertheless, it is possible to identify elements which are common to all these systems and study their characteristics.

A computer system is a complex object consisting of many parts that interact with each other. Studying the architecture of a computer system means identifying each of its parts, understanding its general functioning principles and comprehending how the various parts interact with one another. The first big subdivision we have to make is between **hardware**, the physical components of the computer, and **software**, the programs executed by the computer. This distinction, which is apparently very clear, becomes a lot less clear at second glance, when we consider that the same functions can be executed by hardware circuits and devices or by particular programs, called microprograms, which are defined by the computer manufacturer. Nevertheless, as a first approximation, this distinction is very useful.

1.4.1 Hardware

The hardware of a computer is made up of a set of functional elements present in every computer, though in various quantities and with rather different characteristics.

- The **processor** (often called the CPU – Central Processing Unit) is the part of the system that does the computing and coordinates data transfer inside the whole computer. The processor has the task of 'executing the programs', that is, interpreting and executing the various instructions of which the programs are composed.

- The **central memory** (often called RAM – Random Access Memory) is used to store the data and programs needed to make the computer work. The central memory normally has a limited capacity and therefore contains only a small quantity of programs and data; also, it is volatile, that is, its contents are lost when the computer is switched off, or when there is a system breakdown or an interruption in electricity supply. On the other hand, access to information stored in central memory is very fast.

- The **secondary** or **mass storage** is used to store large quantities of data and programs. The information stored in mass storage is persistent, that is, it is not lost when the computer is switched off. On the other hand, access to mass storage is quite a lot slower than RAM access.

- The system **bus** connects all the functional elements described above and serves to exchange data between them.

- The **peripheral units** are used to make the computer communicate with the outside world. The most common peripherals include **terminals**, with screen, keyboard and a pointing device (normally a mouse), and **printers** which produce output (hard copy) on paper.

When the outside world is not human (for example, an industrial plant, a robot, or an aircraft to be controlled), communication occurs through sensors and actuators. **Sensors** perceive external phenomena, measuring physical values or detecting images and sounds; **actuators** translate appropriate commands into actions that can influence the outside world, such as movements, sound and adjustments.

1.4.2 Personal computers

All the functional elements listed in the previous section are present in a personal computer, as shown in Figure 1.4. Generally, a personal computer consists of a box which contains the CPU, the RAM memory and the mass storage; this box is connected to a keyboard, a pointing device (normally a mouse) and a monitor. A personal computer is completely dedicated to a single user.

The mass storage of a personal computer normally consists of two elements: a hard disk and one or more floppy disk drives. The **hard disk** is fixed and has a higher capacity, that is, it can contain large quantities of data and programs. The

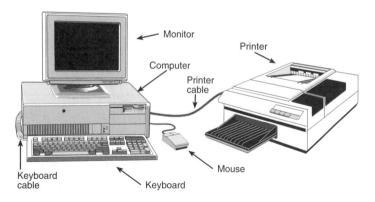

Figure 1.4   Elements of a personal computer.

floppy disks have a lower storage capacity, can be removed from their drives and are used to store data and programs and exchange them between various users.

The information contained in the mass storage, whether on hard disks or on floppy disks, is organized in archives or files; each **file** has its own name (which allows it to be identified within the mass storage) and contains data which can be organized in various ways. For example, some files may contain text, others executable programs, others appropriately coded images. Compact disks (CD-ROM), based on optical (laser) technology, are commonly used as read-only mass memory as support of software packages and of multimedia products for education and entertainment.

1.4.3   Other computer systems

Personal computers have a rather simple structure, a rather limited performance and a very low cost. Complexity, performance and price increase when we pass from personal computers to workstations; these generally possess big screens on which text can appear in a wide variety of typefaces or images can be shown in great detail, and a CPU capable of high performance, especially when dedicated to a single user. We go on to minicomputers, capable of serving several dozen users, each of them connected to the minicomputer through a terminal. Finally, there are systems of vast dimensions, or mainframe computers, capable of handling hundreds of users, with several processors and huge mass storage. Mainframe computers may have hundreds or even thousands of terminals; think, for example, of systems for booking air travel, or for handling bank accounts.

The processing power of a computer system can grow by adding memory, processors, terminals and printers. Another, maybe more important, way of increasing processing power can be obtained by joining various computers into a so-called computer network. In the current state of computer system development, it has become quite rare to find isolated computers: most computers are part of a network (Figure 1.5).

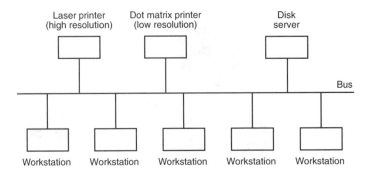

Figure 1.5 A local area network.

A **computer network** is a collection of computers which are connected by means of some media enabling data transfer between them. Computer networks fall into two principal categories: local area networks (LANs) and geographical, wide area networks (WANs). **Local area networks** connect computers and terminals which are physically near to each other, for example situated in the same office or building; they are very fast (that is, they transmit large quantities of data in little time). In a local area network, some 'services' are made available to the computers connected to the network, for example high-performance printers or computers with large mass storage for large amounts of data. Figure 1.5 shows a typical local area network which connects several workstations, situated in different offices in the same building; the network also includes a computer with large mass storage (or disk server) and two printers dedicated to bulk printing and high-quality printing, respectively.

A **wide area network** connects computers, generally of medium to large size, which are quite distant from each other; data transfer in wide area networks is slower and more onerous than in LANs. Figure 1.6 schematically shows a complex computer system with various large computers (so-called host computers), some of which are at the centre of a network of minicomputers. The host computers communicate with each other across a WAN, whereas they communicate with the minicomputers through direct connections or a LAN. Moreover, there are various terminals connected to the computers either directly or via telephone lines (using modems). In this system, the computers communicate with each other by exchanging messages; these messages transfer from one computer to another the data or instructions needed to activate or control the execution of remote programs, thus constructing distributed applications.

In this quick overview, the dimensions of the computer systems and, consequently, their complexity have been constantly increasing. This growth, though, concerns not only the hardware, devices and connections which characterize the various machines and their interaction, but also, and in an ever more significant measure, the software, that is, the set of programs which guarantee that the computer system does its job (performs its task). We start again with the simplest computer system, the PC, and concentrate on its software.

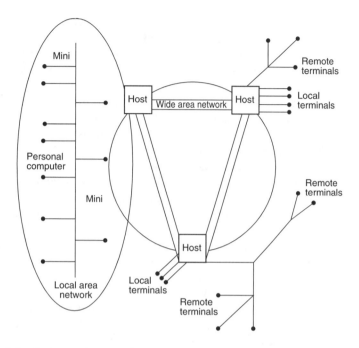

Figure 1.6   Scheme of a complex computer system.

1.4.4 Software

We have already said that the border between hardware and software is rather fuzzy. The 'no-man's-land' is occupied by a layer of microprograms (or **firmware**) which are written into permanent memory by the computer manufacturer; these programs act directly above the hardware layer and may perform tasks of varying degrees of complexity.

The software of a computer system is generally classified as follows:

- **Basic software**, dedicated to the management of the computer, operates directly on top of the hardware or firmware.

- **Application software**, dedicated to the realization of specific application requirements, operates on top of the basic software.

The principal program of the basic software is the operating system, which manages the various hardware resources of the computer, performing different functions according to the complexity of the computer system under its control.

In a personal computer, the **operating system** is quite simple and principally performs two tasks: it interprets and executes elementary commands and it organizes the structure of the mass storage. In its first function, the operating system can, for example, start the execution of a program, print the contents of a file or show it on screen; in the second function, it organizes and manages the mass storage space (hard and floppy disks), allowing, for example, files to be read, written, copied and deleted (erased).

The complexity of operating systems grows with the increasing complexity of the computer system. In a multi-user system in which a multitude of users are connected to the computer system via terminals the operating system has to manage the available resources, that is, it has to distribute the various 'parts' of the computer to the various users. In particular, it has to manage the processing unit, starting the execution of the different programs requested by the individual users; it has to manage the central memory, making sure that programs and data requested by the various users can be loaded into memory. In the course of executing these functions, the operating system tries to satisfy as far as possible all requests of all users. Furthermore, the operating system shows a computer system apparently 'dedicated' to each user, in which all resources are accessed by each user as if the other users did not exist.

The operating system can be part of the computer system as sold by its manufacturer or may be implemented by a specialized software firm. In any case, in practice a normal user cannot modify the instructions of the operating system and cannot use the physical machine without it.

Another important component of the software architecture, which is typically available on most computer systems, is a **database management system**. This software is used to access and manipulate large amounts of data, which are typically shared between several users of the computer system. Examples of large databases are reservation systems, financial systems (such as account management systems within banks), or systems managing environmental data. The database management system provides a software layer that makes data access and sharing much easier, by providing several functionalities to application programs; thus it is typically classified as basic software.

Software is also largely responsible for the management of data transfer and computer networks. In particular, while the transmission channels are responsible for transporting (typically electrical) signals, the **communication protocols** (software) are responsible for guaranteeing correct communication on the transmission channels, guaranteeing the transfer of data from terminals to computer and vice versa, and guaranteeing the transfer of messages between two computers connected in a network.

Above the operating system and the communication software, we find the application programs which are written to solve specific problems, using high-level programming languages, such as those introduced in Section 1.3. It is important to note that application programs are hardly or not at all aware of the architectural characteristics of the underlying system; this allows application programs to be ported from one computer system to another with little difficulty.

1.4.5 Programming environment

Even though programming languages may differ greatly, each is characterized by its own programming environment, that is, a set of programs that facilitate writing programs and verifying their correctness. Programming environments, although different, have many common aspects. In particular, nearly all of them include an editor, a compiler or an interpreter, a linker and a debugger:

- The **editor** is used to construct text files, that is, files which contain sequences of characters. In particular, in a programming environment, the editor is used to write the *source programs*, that is, programs written in a high-level programming language.

- The **compiler** translates the source program into an *object* (executable) *program*, written in a language that can be directly executed by the computer. In the course of the translation, the compiler may find errors, that is, discover that the program is not correct. In this case, the object program is not generated, and the programmer is informed of the nature of the errors found by the compiler and is assisted in correcting the source program.

- Sometimes an interpreter is used in place of a compiler. The **interpreter** directly executes the source code without translating it into the language of the hardware machine. Thus, the interpreter is a kind of high-level processor that is able to execute high-level source code directly. For normal languages such as C, Pascal, Fortran and Ada, execution by means of an interpreter is less efficient than compiling source code and then executing the object code. Thus, compilation is usually preferred.

- A specific application problem may be tackled by a single program or by several coordinated programs (or modules). In this case, each module can be compiled separately; a **linker** puts together the various object programs produced by the compiler into one single *executable program* which can then be run.

- The **debugger** is used to find errors which may be present in a program. The debugger allows the program's behaviour to be checked during its execution, for example by stopping its normal progress and showing the contents of the memory; this control helps discover errors that occur at run time, which have not been found by the compiler.

1.4.6 Personal and productivity software

Some software systems do not require any knowledge of programming and assist in typical functions of everyday life (writing and communicating); they are in common use by a large number of computer users and are often referred to as **personal software**. They include:

- **Word-processing systems** for constructing texts and formatting them for printing. Text processing has become one of the commonest computer applications (especially on personal computers), not least because of the existence of sophisticated printers, based on laser technology, which produce high-quality printouts.

- **Electronic agendas** for storing a work schedule or a personal address book; these systems can notify their users of imminent deadlines via messages.

- **Hypertexts** for constructing complex network-like structures containing 'pieces' of text (lists of words, phrases, paragraphs, chapters, references); the network allows these 'pieces' to be arranged in various ways and can be used both to compose documents and to retrieve information within documents.

- **Electronic mail** for exchanging messages between any two users of computer systems connected through one or more networks; this tool, at least in the scientific community, tends to be used instead of the telephone for interpersonal communications.

- **Spreadsheets**, which allow accounting data to be processed efficiently.

- **Database management systems**, besides being elements of the basic software, can also be regarded as personal software systems when used on a personal computer or for personal use.

In these systems, ease of user interaction is paramount, as the user is usually not a computer specialist. The interaction occurs via **user-friendly interfaces**, which allow the user to control the tools' performance by using **menus** (a fixed list of possible choices); the user confirms choices by selecting a number or a combination of keys which corresponds to the desired command. Occasionally commands are associated with areas on the screen; in this case the user can express commands by moving the **cursor** (a pointer to a specific position on the screen) above an area and keying in a command on the keyboard. As well as the menu commands used to control the tools, there are also some **masks** (also called **dialog boxes**: areas on the screen where the user can provide data) associated with the operations carried out automatically; the masks are meant to store data exchanged with the user in the most user-friendly format possible, in order to foster the interaction. A more comprehensive view of the most common interfaces will be provided in Chapter 19.

1.5 Computer science applications

Since computer science deals with the representation and processing of information, it is obvious that it has potential applications in almost all human activities: from computing numbers, to games, to sport, to the judiciary. This range of applications remained unchanged for a long time, because of power and cost constraints imposed by the state of technological development: it was obviously unthinkable that a computer costing several million dollars could be used for handling the family accounts or producing documents for a small professional outfit.

More recently, however, the picture has changed drastically: the continuous increase in computing power and in data transmission (which every four or five years has increased several times over) and the ensuing vast reduction in cost have made the computer accessible to practically anybody, at least in the more technologically advanced parts of the world.

In parallel with the increase in computing and transmission power, technological progress has brought about improvements in human–computer interaction: this was necessary to make computers available to a wide range of users as opposed to just a few specialists. Today we have a large number of interfaces available for the human–machine dialogue. As well as the more traditional screens, printers and keyboards, we now have tools, such as the mouse, which allow the transfer of graphic information (lines and surfaces) rather than only textual information.

Multimedia technology has allowed new and previously unimaginable applications. This term describes the ability to represent, manage and transfer information which may come from different physical media and be perceived by different human senses, such as sight and hearing. Today it is possible to manage, through information technology, not simply traditional texts, but also visual representations (including those that evolve rapidly and dynamically and have three-dimensional effects), sound and mechanical movements, with such coordination that they seem very close to real life.

These recent technological developments are the reason for the amazing increase, both quantitative and qualitative, in computer applications; we shall look at a few representative examples.

1.5.1 'Number-crunching' applications

The first application of computing was numerical in nature. This activity is now technically and scientifically mature and has a satisfactory cost–benefit ratio in terms of return on investment. From a technological standpoint, the issues linked with number crunching, whether for demographic statistics, weather forecasting or locating oil fields, refer mainly to the level of precision in the approximation. Consequently, this type of application mainly requires vast number-crunching power and dedicated hardware; many numerical algorithms, namely those operating on matrices, are highly complex in computational terms. On the other hand, number-crunching applications are usually relatively easy to produce, since the algorithms involved are fairly simple and straightforward to program.

1.5.2 Management applications

This sector is also fairly well established and has formed the largest part of the computer market for some time now. The classical management applications operate on large databases, building up integrated information systems; among the most typical environments are banking, insurance and financial institutions, transport businesses (involving booking systems), telephone companies, public utilities and bodies (such as registry offices, motor taxation offices and income tax offices), as well as accounting, human resources, customers and stock management within the vast majority of modern companies.

It should also be noted that these applications can fruitfully be employed for the production of socially useful services, such as the management of blood banks or for matching unemployed people to available jobs.

More recently a new application field has been developed. With the so-called **office automation systems** (also called **workflow management systems**), we have witnessed the development of services aimed at improving the quality of work and the personal interaction between employees, who are increasingly reliant on the computer to carry out their daily tasks. While traditional management systems handle specialized and repetitive functions, such as computing salaries and deductions, managing over-the-counter operations and so on, which are usually applied to a considerable amount of data, office automation tends to provide high-quality, easy-to-use services, addressed to nonspecialized users (anybody must be able to interact with the system, from managers to secretaries, without having to learn special procedures) and with a high level of integration.

For example, in every office there are a number of different activities, from business planning to document production to administration. Each of these activities can benefit from the use of computing tools: spreadsheets, word processors, databases and other more traditional application programs. In many cases, a degree of specialization in the use of these tools may substantially increase productivity; for example, an office where a large number of documents incorporating textual and graphic information are produced and where sophisticated presentation techniques are required will find it very useful to employ specific graphic-handling packages which will improve productivity in this area.

1.5.3 Telematic applications

If giant steps have recently been made in computer science, the same applies to telecommunications. To give just one example, the use of optical fibres has allowed very fast transmission of a large quantity of information.

Obviously, in a science dedicated to information processing there are many opportunities for linking up with a science dedicated to transmission of the same information. In many cases, information relevant to one activity is physically stored in different places, perhaps at some considerable distance from each other. This may apply to inter-bank transactions, possibly between different countries, or to reciprocal use of scientific programs by different universities, or even to access to large public centralized archives, such as registry offices, police records and so on.

A new discipline, called **telematics**, addresses the successful marriage between computer science and telecommunications. Telematics already guarantees a large number of services for the general public as well as the ability to access practically any application from stations located anywhere.

Some well-known examples of telematic services are automated bank teller machines, travel booking services, remote access to public archives and so on. In practice, almost all computing information could be shared, that is, could be processed in the various business locations instead of being 'centralized', that is, concentrated at one central computing point.

A very important telematic service which practically covers the whole world is the Internet service, which allows scientific and industrial establishments to share a great variety of information. This will be described in Chapter 18.

1.5.4 Industrial automation

The automation of a factory has some features in common with office automation, but it also has some substantial differences. While the office mainly produces and manages documents, a factory is geared towards manufacturing output. However, the production of a car makes use of a large amount of data which should be optimized. The data may be used, for example, to manage a robot used for the physical assembly of the manufactured item.

The main application of computers in industrial automation concerns **robotics**, an interdisciplinary activity, which brings together mechanical, electronic and computing techniques. To realize the importance of computer science within robotics, consider that the robot's movements are defined through sophisticated algorithms which need to solve problems of vision (for instance, recognizing obstacles and identifying their features) and planning in order to compute optimized paths.

Furthermore, there is a planning activity in industry involved in equipment or component manufacture, which is supported by computer-based tools, usually defined as **CAD** (Computer Aided Design) and **CIM** (Computer Integrated Manufacturing). CAD often requires number-crunching applications for solving mathematical equations, though these are only one of many significant components: the project handler also receives support in the actual drawing of graphics or other types of visual aids, in searching for tool descriptions within catalogues or 'libraries', and so on.

1.5.5 Control of industrial plants and embedded applications

In many cases the computer is used to control automatically a process which takes place within an industrial plant, such as energy production plants, chemical or manufacturing plants. In such applications the computer tool either is a substitute for human intervention or it integrates the human activity in the task of monitoring and controlling the plant, for example to guarantee its safety.

Sometimes the computer system is still under human supervision: this applies, for instance, to the control room of a nuclear production plant and even, perhaps stretching the point a bit, to air traffic control systems. In other cases it is completely enclosed in the overall product so that the user interacts with it without being aware of the presence of the computer tool. Such applications are defined as **embedded** because the computer component of the product is not visible to the user; they can be found almost anywhere, within cars (for example the ABS, or the automatic control of fuel distribution), electrical appliances, air navigation support systems (on-board computers) and so on.

1.5.6 Virtual reality and advanced user interfaces

Virtual reality is one of the most recent and significant frontiers opened up by the computer's evolution. This term refers to the use of computers to give a simulated but maximally realistic presentation of a real-life scenario.

From the user's point of view, this type of application can be deployed in a large number of areas: from training pilots on sophisticated flight simulators (Figure 1.7), to games, to the simulation of buildings, for example for evaluating interior decoration schemes.

Other applications use technologies and methods which are similar to virtual reality, but whose aims and objectives are to reshape reality to improve living conditions, rather than simply to reproduce real life. For example, computer science can help disabled people to interact with other people and with the surrounding environment providing multimedia interfaces. People who have limited use of their hands can interact with workstations through mechanical sensors which detect the movement of their head and eyes and sound sensors which detect voice commands. Special touch screens on portable computers can be designed to help mentally handicapped children to improve their communication opportunities and their

Figure 1.7 A modern flight simulator.

Figure 1.8 A multimedia interface for disabled children.

linguistic capabilities, as shown in Figure 1.8. In a multimedia interface of this kind, text and pictorial symbols are integrated with full-motion video and sound.

From a technological point of view, virtual reality applications almost always require the use of multimedia. It is a fact that our interaction with the world around us takes place through the simultaneous and integrated use of all our senses: when we drive a car, we do not simply need to see what is happening around us, we also need to hear what is going on. It is also evident that better results in simulating reality will be obtained by stimulating our senses as realistically as possible.

EXTENDED EXAMPLE: Car racing simulator

A typical example of virtual reality is the game that simulates car racing. It is interesting to look at the evolution of such a game, which has been available in arcades for ages.

Originally this consisted purely of a moving track (at most one could control the speed) with a drawn road environment and the representation of a car connected to a piece of string which could be activated by using the steering wheel (Figure 1.9).

All the user could do was to 'drive' the car by using the steering wheel, which was connected to the piece of string, and by using a foot pedal to accelerate, thus controlling the speed of the track. The single computer component in this game was the sensors which determined the position of the car on the track and signalled whether the car itself was within or outside the track.

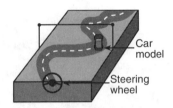

Figure 1.9   An old car racing simulator.

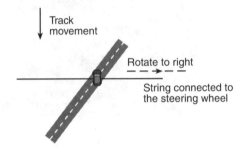

Figure 1.10   Part of the track in the simulator shown in Figure 1.9. The string is pulled by turning the steering wheel.

Obviously the level of approximation of reality provided by this version of the game was crude. The worst effect was that caused by the steering wheel which was very different from what happens in real life. Let us look at a track such as the one shown in Figure 1.10.

We must remember that in real life a driver will need to rotate the steering wheel in order to drive round a bend; coming out of the bend, the driver will need to get the steering wheel back to the straight position. However, the player must carry on rotating the steering wheel synchronously with the speed of the track so long as the track itself is not at 90 degrees to the landscape; this is because the steering wheel does not determine the *direction* of the car in the simulation, but rather its horizontal *position* on the track. Therefore, so long as the track is not at 90 degrees, the driver will need to continue turning the steering wheel.

Subsequently the game was much improved by the introduction of an electronic screen to represent the landscape and by a more realistic simulation of the steering and accelerator performance. Such improvement was made possible because of the increasingly low cost of wide colour screens and of the computing power required to simulate movement in real time, that is, with a more realistic dynamic representation.

The more up-to-date versions (Figure 1.11) of this game now use all the multimedia resources available, as they provide a landscape integrated with sound effects, a complete range of commands (as well as steering and accelerating, brakes, gears and clutch are available) and a flexible interior which in some ways simulates

Figure 1.11   A modern game of car racing simulation.

the performance of a real-life vehicle (for example, by turning the steering wheel the car shifts to a horizontal angle which is proportional to the speed of the vehicle, in order to simulate centripetal acceleration). In many versions, the user can select a view from inside the car as well as from outside: even though this latter option is less realistic, it does offer some advantages because virtual reality should not always be simply confined to reproducing real life to the best of its abilities!

1.6 Disciplines within computer science

A recent collection of articles[1], describing the perspectives in computer science at the fiftieth anniversary of the Association for Computing Machinery, broke down computer science into ten identified disciplinary areas; these are reproduced here as a useful reference point.

(1) *Algorithms and data structures*: studies the representation and manipulation of information; specifically, it deals with the theory of algorithms and their formal properties (including the study of their complexity, which provides some estimate of their execution times) and of the data organization which is best suited to represent the required information. This is a fundamental and interdisciplinary activity, which finds its application in all the other disciplinary areas.

[1] Tucker A. and Wegner P., eds (1996). **ACM Computer Surveys**, 28:1 (March).

(2)   *Architecture*: studies the design and production of the various hardware components of a computer system; specifically, its objectives are to build more and more reliable and efficient functional elements, as well as more and more complex systems and interconnections.

(3)   *Artificial intelligence and robotics*: studies the automation of tasks which are usually executed by human beings by simulating their intelligence and the computer-related aspects of robots. Some examples of classical applications of artificial intelligence include: natural language understanding, knowledge representation and the design of expert systems (systems which deploy a degree of knowledge of their application domain). Robotics is concerned with all the aspects of controlling the behaviour of robots (for example, their vision, motion control and decision-making processes).

(4)   *Computational science*: studies the solution of numerical problems, with an emphasis on the efficiency of the solution technique and the accuracy of the results. Classical numerical problems include the solution of differential equations, applicable to many scientific disciplines (for example electro-magnetism and fluid dynamics).

(5)   *Databases and information retrieval*: studies the storage and retrieval of large quantities of data for management applications. Efficient, reliable and secure data management is nowadays an essential ingredient in any business activity (for example, the financial or administrative management of companies). Information retrieval is specifically concerned with selecting relevant information from large data collections (for example, by means of keywords).

(6)   *Computer graphics*: studies the techniques for representing and manipulating two- and three-dimensional images on the computer's screen. This discipline is becoming more and more important with the increasing use of multimedia documents (which include texts, sounds, images and videos) and computer animation (that is, creation of the illusion of movement by displaying sequences of images representing the states of a scene).

(7)   *Human–computer interaction*: deals with the efficient transfer of information between humans and computers, not only by means of classical interfaces (such as the screen and the keyboard), but also by means of various sensors and actuators, that is, devices for detecting inputs and producing outputs which are most effective in given contexts. It is also concerned with the psychological study of modes of interaction that increase productivity and/or acceptance of computers.

(8)   *Operating systems and networks*: studies the building and management of operating systems and of the software dedicated to the control of computer networks; that is, of the system software which stands between the physical devices and the high-level programs, hiding the physical features of such devices and enabling users to share all the resources within the system.

(9)   *Programming languages*: studies programming languages and techniques, identifying features common to the various languages and accurately defining

their properties. It also studies the issues linked to the translation of high-level languages into object languages, that is, languages which are directly executable by the computer.

(10) *Software engineering*: studies the methods and tools which can support the building of programs and software systems. Its objectives are to increase productivity for programmers and to optimize efficiency, reliability and ease of use for applications *vis-à-vis* the user.

In practice, the breakdown of computer science into disciplinary areas is a controversial issue and the structure we have followed here is not above criticism; we have decided to use it because there are no alternative classifications which are more widely accepted. Such a breakdown of computer science into disciplinary branches gives an initial orientation regarding the structure of the contents of this book and provides a foundation for understanding the main themes in the realm of computer science.

The book does not intend to cover all the disciplinary areas which make up computer science; such an encyclopaedic objective does not match our desire to focus on a few important concepts. We provide several suggestions for further reading at the end of the book.

Exercises

1.1 Consider the following two prototypes of instructions you normally get when you ask someone the way. Which of these can be considered as an algorithm and why?

(a) 'Turn right at the next roundabout, then left at the second set of traffic lights; after three hundred metres you get to another roundabout; take the road indicated by the sign 'Rotherham' and follow it straight on until you reach the city limits; there you turn left immediately: that's the road you are looking for.'

(b) 'Go for about two kilometres in this direction (the sentence is accompanied by a vague indication with the hand); you'll find a large road; follow this large road, ignoring all secondary roads; after you've driven past a very high building turn right, then after about three hundred metres turn left: at that point you've arrived.'

1.2 In the context of Exercise 1.1, consider the following answer: 'Turn right at the first roundabout, then left at the second set of traffic lights; after three hundred metres you'll find another roundabout: at this point ask again.' Can we consider this answer an algorithm?

1.3 Change the algorithm of Example 1.2 to favour a 'lazy user': the user must use the power adapter only if strictly necessary.

1.4   With a library organized as in Example 1.3, find a search algorithm suitable for readers who know only the title of the book they are looking for.

1.5   On the basis of Exercise 1.4, discuss why libraries normally have different catalogues: by author, title, category, date and so on.

1.6   How would you change the structure of the cards if the library consisted of a number of rooms, each with several shelves and in each room the numbering of the shelves started with 1?

1.7   What would change in the algorithm of Example 1.3 if each time a book is taken out the rest of the books are moved up in order not to leave empty space? Assume that the returned books are put back in the relative position they occupied before being borrowed: in other words, the order of the books on the shelves remains the one determined by their initial position, but their absolute position depends on how many other books are present.

1.8   Consider again the extended example of Section 1.2 concerning the problem of consulting a road map. Suppose we want to identify any route that connects c_d with c_a, not necessarily the shortest one: find an algorithm to solve this problem. Discuss whether the problem given in this exercise is a simpler one and if so, whether this greater simplicity leads to the construction of an intuitively simpler algorithm.

1.9   Suppose that you want to determine a connection between c_d and c_a by a route that can be driven as fast as possible by car. Suppose that the speed on motorways is double the speed on normal highways and that all other types of road are excluded. Which steps of the algorithm described have to be changed and how?

1.10   Consider the following problem: let c_d be a town in the United States and c_a a town in Canada; road maps of the USA and Canada are available, but not of the whole of North America. Is it possible to find the shortest route between c_d and c_a? Which hypotheses have to be formulated? How is the proposed algorithm to be modified?

1.11   Construct an algorithm that solves the problem of going from one place to another in a town, using a street map like the ones you find in phone books, where the map of the whole town is broken up into several sectors which fit together perfectly. Discuss the characteristics of the solution.

Computer architecture

2

In Chapter 1 we presented a broad introduction to computer science, with special emphasis on the concept of the algorithm; in this chapter we introduce the fundamental concepts at the roots of computer architecture. We consider these two notions (algorithms and computer architecture) as preliminaries to programming, which will be covered by Part I.

The architecture of most computers follows the model of the so-called **von Neumann machine**, named after the American researcher who, with others, dedicated his studies to the realization of the first computers during the Second World War; one of the first applications of computers was the coding and decoding of messages to be exchanged within the US Army.

The aim of this chapter is to make the reader aware that nothing 'magical' happens within a machine that executes a program (a coded algorithm), by showing how the von Neumann machine can execute a program.

Section 2.1 illustrates the main components of the von Neumann architecture. Section 2.2 describes through examples how data and instructions constituting a program are represented inside the machine to allow a correct execution of the program itself. In the following sections we analyse the behaviour of each functional unit of the von Neumann architecture and we show the global functioning of the machine with reference to the execution of a simple program. An in-depth treatment of the binary coding of data and instructions, and of the structure and the behaviour of traditional and advanced architecture, is provided in Chapters 13 and 14.

2.1 Elements of the von Neumann machine

The von Neumann machine is composed of four basic functional elements: processor (or CPU), main memory, peripherals and system bus; these were briefly mentioned in Section 1.4.1. Figure 2.1 illustrates their interaction.

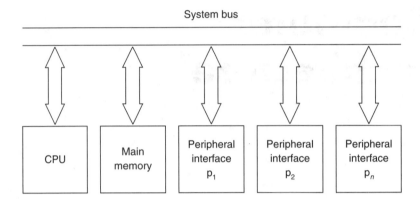

Figure 2.1 Architecture of the von Neumann machine.

The **processor** contains the electronic devices capable of fetching, interpreting and executing the program's instructions. The **main memory** contains the information needed to execute a program: instructions and data. The **peripherals** allow the exchange of information between the computer and the outside world, via input (from the outside world to the computer) and output (from the computer to the outside world) operations. Only the **interfaces** to the peripherals are considered to be part of the computer, the peripherals themselves being considered as separate devices. In the von Neumann architecture, the peripherals also include the **mass storage devices** which, from the point of view of interaction with the computer, functionally behave in the same way as terminals, printers and other devices connected to the outside world. Finally, the **system bus** connects these functional elements. This simple architecture is an abstraction of a real machine, where additional components may be present; however, such abstraction is sufficiently close to reality to give a good idea of the functional elements of a computer.

The functioning of the von Neumann machine can be schematically characterized as follows. The processor coordinates the various activities; in particular, it **fetches** instructions by bringing them from the memory into the processor, **decodes** them by understanding their meaning and finally **executes** them by performing suitable activities within the von Neumann architecture. Instructions may involve operations for *manipulating* information (for example, addition of numbers) or operations for *transferring* information (for example, reading data from a peripheral interface into main memory).

Transfers between different functional elements always occur via the system bus which provides a logical connection between specific functional elements of the von Neumann architecture; logical connections are established when needed, whereas the physical connections are always there. In the von Neumann machine, the processing phases are synchronized by a **system clock**. During each time interval, a part of the processor called the **control unit** coordinates the timely execution of the functions which are to be carried out in the processor itself and in the other functional elements.

The von Neumann model, even though it is nearly 50 years old, is still adopted by computers, but its main limitation is that all operations are carried out in strict sequence, determined by the processor. Thus, many computers now differ from the von Neumann architecture because they introduce various forms of **parallelism**, that is, simultaneous execution of instructions.

2.2 Coding data and program instructions

In a computer, data and program instructions are coded in **binary** form, that is, as finite sequences of ones and zeros. The most basic unit of data in a computer corresponds to the state of a physical device which is interpreted as either 1 or 0. This unit is called a **bit**. Another important unit of data is the **byte**, which is a sequence of eight bits. Eight bits (one byte) can be used to produce 2^8 different sequences of ones and zeros (00000000, 00000001, 00000010, ..., 11111111).

Different kinds of data can be treated by a computer: numbers (natural, integer, real, fractional), texts, images, sounds and so on. All data, no matter how complicated, has to be transformed into a sequence of bits in order to be managed by a computer. Different conventions are used to code natural numbers, integers, reals, fractions, characters, images and so on. We do not aim to give a full account of binary representation of information here, instead postponing it to Chapter 13; but we shall show, by means of examples, that such binary representation is indeed possible:

- Eight bits are enough to represent *natural numbers* from 0 to 255 (= 2^8-1). 0 is represented in eight bits as 00000000; 8 as 00001000; 255 as 11111111.

- *Integer numbers* include negative numbers as well as zero and positive numbers, therefore the sign of the number must be represented, as well as the value. In practice, the first bit of the byte is used as the sign bit; by convention, 0 indicates a positive number, 1 a negative number. Thus, eight bits can represent integer numbers from –127 to 127 , that is from $-(2^{(8-1)}-1)$ to $(2^{(8-1)}-1)$.

- *Real numbers* are considered to be rational numbers containing an integer part and a fractional part which approximate the real number with arbitrary precision. If a *fixed point notation* is adopted, a real number could be represented by coding separately the integer part of the number and its fractional part. In this case, for example, the number 8.345 could be represented using two bytes as follows:

   first byte (the representation of the integer 8) = 00001000

   second byte (the representation of the fractional part 0.345) = 01011000

- The *characters* that make up a text are coded in bit sequences using a translation code. The most widely used code is ASCII (American Standard Code for Information Interchange); it uses seven bits and thus allows a maximum of 128 characters to be represented. The ASCII code assigns to each letter (upper case from A to Z, lower case from a to z), digit (from 0 to 9) or separator (used as punctuation or arithmetic operator) a natural number which can be represented in binary form. For instance, the letter 'A' is coded in ASCII as number 65 and its binary form in a byte is 01000001; the separator ';' is coded in ASCII as number 59 and its binary form in a byte is 00111011.

As we said before, instructions in the so-called object (executable) code may denote operations for manipulating information (for example, numerical operations) or operations for transferring information through the elements of the machine. A coded instruction generally presents two parts, an operational code and one or more operands. The **operational code** specifies the operation to be executed; the **operands** specify in various modes where the machine can find data to be involved in the transfer or in the manipulation. The operational code and operands are coded in binary form using particular conventions.

2.3 Behaviour of the von Neumann machine

This section describes the behaviour of each functional unit of the von Neumann architecture shown in Figure 2.1. Particular attention is paid to the central role of the processor and to the exchange of information between different units involved in the execution of programs.

2.3.1 Main memory

Main memory is designed to receive the 'working material' on which the computer operates: data and programs, that is, sequences of instructions. Using the human brain as an analogy, the main memory contains short- and medium-term information, whereas long-term information is stored in the mass storage. The main memory is generally limited in size and can thus accept only part of the available information. However, it is a 'necessary condition': before it can be processed, information has to be in main memory. This generally involves an input/output operation in which information is transferred from mass storage to main memory or vice versa. We will discuss the characteristics of these operations in Chapter 15.

From a conceptual point of view, the main memory is a sequence of memory cells; each cell contains a word. **Words**, therefore, are sequences of bits; each word in memory assumes a particular value during a computation (for instance, the number 4327 or the character string 'mi') represented as a sequence of zeros and ones inserted into the corresponding memory cells. The memory cells of a computer all have the same capacity (and, consequently, the words of one computer all have the same length, although different computers can have words of different length). The most typical lengths of words are the first few multiples of a byte (8 bits) and therefore we have computers with words of 8, 16, 32 and 64 bits.

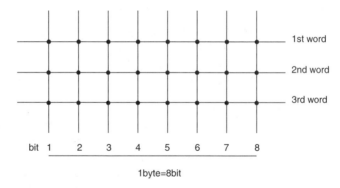

Figure 2.2 Memory structure.

Technologically, memories are realized as semiconductor devices; a memory can be ideally seen as a big 'table' whose rows are the various cells; the columns identify each bit. Information is present in memory as a state (high or low) of voltage in the memory positions identified at the intersections of rows and columns. Let us associate a low voltage value with the value zero and a high voltage value with the value one. Figure 2.2 gives a schematic representation of the memory structure.

Generally, main memory is *volatile*, that is, its contents are lost when the computer is switched off (or, for example, when there is a power failure); after restarting, the values of the zeros and ones in memory are not meaningful. Mass storage, on the other hand, is *permanent* and therefore the information stored is not lost when the computer is switched off. However, some main memories of recent design are powered by autonomous batteries and thus become permanent in their turn; this allows the 'robustness' of some applications to be improved, making them less susceptible to failures and malfunctions.

Each memory cell can be *addressed*, which means that the computer can select a particular memory cell. The **address** of a memory cell is simply its relative position (or ordinal number) with respect to the first memory cell, which normally is attributed position zero. Memory addressing is carried out via a specific register, called an **address register**, inside the processor. A register is an electronic device capable of storing a sequence of bits. As we have seen in the previous section, sequences of bits can be interpreted as numbers; in particular, bits contained in registers are interpreted as natural numbers. If the address register has k bits, we can address up to 2^k memory cells whose addresses go from 0 to $2^k - 1$.

This mechanism is the reason why the memory size, that is, the number of available words, is generally some power of 2. In particular, if the address register is 10 bits long, $2^{10} = 1024$ cells are addressed; we refer to this number of cells as a 'kiloword' (in computing, the term 'kilo' is commonly associated with 2^{10}, unlike its usual meaning). If the address register is 20 bits long, $2^{20} = 1048\,576$ cells can be addressed; in this case we have a 'megaword' (and the term 'mega' is associated with 2^{20}). Note, however, that the capacity of main memory is normally expressed as the number of bytes available (and therefore the number of kilobytes or megabytes) and not the number of words, because the size in bytes is independent of the word length of a specific computer and, therefore, a more general unit of measure.

Thus, it is possible to select one specific memory cell by loading the address register with a sequence of bits which indicates the relative position of the cell in memory. At this point, we can carry out two operations, *get* from and *put* into memory.

Both operations use another processor register, the so-called **data register**, which has the same length as a memory word. The get operation causes the contents of the memory cell to be copied into the data register; it **loads** the data register with a memory word. The put operation copies the contents of the data register into a memory cell; it **stores** the contents of the data register in a memory word. These operations can be visualized by imagining that the values (zero and one) are copied from the addressed cell to the data register or vice versa. In reality, the electronic circuits of the memory are connected to each other in an appropriate way so that the voltage values (high or low) are transmitted in order.

The behaviour of the memory is summarized in Figure 2.3. Note the address register (k bits long), the memory (with 2^k cells, each containing a word of h bits) and the data register (h bits long). Available operations are: loading the data register (indicated by the letter 'L'), which reads a memory cell, and storing the data register in memory (indicated by the letter 'S'), which writes a memory cell. These operations are carried out under the control of the processor (which also coordinates loading the address register) and involve the bus, as described in the next section.

The memory described so far, which can be read from and written to via program instructions, is called **RAM** (Random Access Memory); this term is not the most appropriate one, but indicates the possibility of selecting any of the memory cells for a get or put operation. By contrast, computers generally have one or more areas of memory that cannot be written to; these memories are called **ROM** (Read Only Memory); they are initialized by the manufacturer of the computer with the programs and data that make the system run.

At first sight, the fact that ROMs can only be read may seem a limitation; in reality, the contents of the ROM are thus protected, that is, shielded from failures or

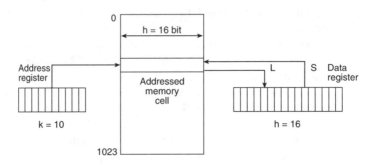

Figure 2.3 Memory function scheme.

write operations by incorrect programs. Furthermore, the contents of ROMs are permanent. Because of these characteristics, ROMs are used in the microprocessors built into various kinds of control devices, for example in dishwashers or systems installed in cars or aeroplanes.

2.3.2 System bus

The system bus is composed of a set of elementary connections, or lines, along which information is transferred. It connects the processor, the main memory and the various input/output interfaces. Topologically, the bus is normally an open connection (that is, not closed at one end) to which the various functional units are connected. At any moment, the bus is dedicated to connecting two functional units: one transmits data and the other receives it. Possible interconnections are between the processor and memory, or between the processor and the interface of a specific peripheral. Usually the bus is controlled by the processor, which selects the interconnection to be activated and indicates the operation to be carried out; the other functional units connected to the bus are activated only when selected by the processor. In such cases the processor plays the role of **master**, whereas the other functional units assume the role of **slave**. During each operation, the bus is assigned to a specific connection for a certain time; the shorter this time, the higher the transmission speed of the bus.

In an informal way, we can think of the passage of data along the bus as a flow of data from one point to another. The lines of the bus are, in their turn, functionally specified and divided into three categories, depending on the type of information transferred. The system bus therefore consists of a data bus, an address bus and a control bus:

- The **data bus** transfers data from master to slave or vice versa. If, for example, the slave unit is main memory, data is transferred from a memory cell into the data register as the result of a get operation, or from the data register into a memory cell as the result of a put operation.

- The **address bus** serves, for example, to transmit the contents of the address register to main memory; in this way, a specific memory cell can be selected for a get or a put operation. To allow this operation, the information transfer takes place from the processor to the memory.

- The **control bus** transfers from the master to the slave unit a code corresponding to the instruction to be executed and from the slave to the master unit information regarding the completion of the required operation.

In order to carry out a get operation from main memory, the processor must therefore:

(1) load the address of the requested memory word into the address register and transmit it to the main memory via the address bus;

(2) request a get operation, by sending the command via the control bus.

The memory then:

(3)   performs the get operation, which moves via the data bus the contents of the addressed word into the data register;

(4)   signals to the processor, via the control bus, that the operation has been completed and the required data is available in the data register.

In order to carry out a put operation into main memory, the processor must:

(1)   load the address of the requested memory word into the address register and transmit it to the main memory via the address bus;

(2)   load the data to be put into memory into the data register (the contents of the data register are transmitted to the main memory via the data bus);

(3)   request a put operation, by sending the command via the control bus.

The memory then:

(4)   performs the put operation, which moves the contents of the data register received via the data bus, into the addressed word;

(5)   signals to the processor that the operation has been completed.

The presence of many lines in a bus allows data to be transferred 'in parallel'; generally, all bits of the same memory word are transmitted on the bus at the same instant by dedicating one line to each of them. Alternatively, transmission may require more than one transfer for the same memory word; this becomes necessary when the number of lines in the data bus is smaller than the length of the memory words.

2.3.3 Processor

The processor, also called the CPU (Central Processing Unit), contains the circuit elements that control the functioning of the computer. Its function is to execute the programs contained in memory, by fetching, decoding and executing the instructions of which they are composed one after the other. The circuit elements that constitute a CPU are illustrated in Figure 2.4:

- The **control unit** is responsible for fetching and decoding the instructions and for sending control signals which cause the processing needed to execute the decoded instruction.

- The **system clock** synchronizes the operations with respect to a set frequency.

- The **arithmetic and logic unit** (ALU) realizes the manipulation of data needed for the execution of the instruction (such as the arithmetic operations to be carried out on data when required by the program).

In addition, the CPU has several registers. As already mentioned, a **register** is a memory element which can be read from or written to very quickly, and is used to store partial results or control information. The principal CPU registers are as follows:

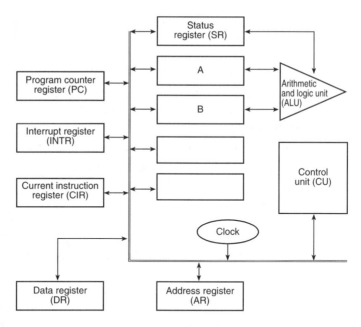

Figure 2.4 Components of the processor.

- The **data register** (DR) and the **address register** (AR), already described in Section 2.3.1. Remember that the AR is k bits long and the DR h bits, that is, equal to the length of a word.

- The **current instruction register** (CIR), h bits long, contains the instruction that is being executed by the computer.

- The **program counter** (PC), k bits long, stores the address of the next instruction of the program being executed.

- The **interrupt register** (INTR) contains information about the functional state of the peripherals; the use of this register is discussed in Chapter 15.

- The registers which contain the operands and the result of the operations carried out by the ALU, conventionally called **A** and **B.**

- A rather large number of **working registers** which are very much like memory cells but which can be read from and written to very quickly without using get or put operations; these registers contain frequently used data or instructions or the intermediate results of processing.

The ALU can also be highly sophisticated and capable of complex operations. In this book, we describe a simple ALU with only two operands and capable of executing the classic numerical operations (addition, subtraction, multiplication, division). The ALU is activated by the control unit which specifies an operational code corresponding to the operation to be carried out. Beforehand, the A and B registers are loaded with the values of the two operands. The execution of an operation requires a certain amount of time, measured by the system clock, after which the A register is loaded with the result of the operation; in the case of an integer division, the remainder is loaded into the B register, but for the other operations the contents of the B register are not defined.

● A particular register, called the **status register** (SR), contains in some of its bits information regarding the result of the operations carried out by the ALU. These include:

– the **carry bit**, which indicates the presence of a carry-over;

– the **zero bit**, which indicates that the A register contains the value 'zero';

– the **sign bit**, which indicates the sign of the result of an arithmetic operation;

– the **overflow bit**, which allows an overflow condition to be detected when the result of the last arithmetic operation executed by the ALU overwhelms the value 2^h that can be represented as the maximum value in the A register supposed to be h bits long.

When an overflow condition occurs, the overflow bit indicates that register A contains a wrong result with respect to the last arithmetic operation executed by the ALU. The previous bits also allow comparison operations between two operands to be carried out. These comparisons can be done by subtracting the second operand from the first and testing the result, as shown in Example 2.2 at the end of this chapter.

It should again be stressed that the *control unit* has the task of coordinating the entire system: it interprets the instructions of the program being executed and ensures that execution is carried out in the right sequence. Under its direction, information is transferred or processed by the ALU inside the CPU, got from or put into memory and exchanged with the outside world.

2.3.4 Input/output interfaces

The input/output interfaces constitute the circuit elements that allow the connection of the computer to the various peripherals. An interface contains registers to send commands to the peripheral, exchange data and control the functioning of the peripheral. The interfaces are very different, depending on the type of peripheral (terminals, printers, mass storage devices, measuring instruments, optical readers, plotters, sensors and actuators of robots and so on). Furthermore, peripherals can be more or less 'intelligent', that is, they can possess their own control units capable of converting and processing data; intelligent interfaces can relieve the CPU of some tasks. For example, a typical evolution of the von Neumann architecture consists in dedicating some processors exclusively to input/output operations. In the following, we limit ourselves to describing an elementary standard interface. Such an interface generally contains the following elements:

- A **peripheral data register** (PDR) to exchange data with the peripheral. Data can be sent to the peripheral (for example, to a printer) or to the computer (for example, from an optical reader). A terminal has two distinct data registers, one that allows the computer to get data from the keyboard and one that accepts data to be visualized on the screen.

- A **peripheral command register** (PCR) which contains the command that the peripheral has to execute.

- **Status information** about the peripheral (for a printer, for example, the status could be: ready to receive new data, busy printing data, or an error condition, such as 'no paper' or 'no ink').

The data register is connected to the data bus and the command register to the control bus; the status information can be transferred into a special **peripheral status register** (PSR) and read 'on command' by the processor (using the bus), or connected via special electronic circuits to the processor (in which case the information is transferred to the interrupt register, INTR). In Chapter 15, we will see how input/output operations are managed.

2.4 Executing programs

We have introduced von Neumann architecture in this chapter in order to present an operational model of the computer, that is, to illustrate how the computer can execute simple algorithms. In this chapter we shall only show a few examples, without defining a machine language precisely; discussion of machine language is postponed to Chapter 14.

To begin the execution of a program, the von Neumann machine needs the binary form of the program to be loaded in main memory. The **binary form** of a program, shown in Figure 2.5, is of course a sequence of binary words (like all information in computer memories). The figure also shows the location of the program in main memory, assuming that it is loaded from cell number zero (the first cell of main memory). To execute a program, the von Neumann machine gets the program instructions from main memory and executes them by repeating a sequence of operations in the CPU. Note that the program is made up of two different parts: the first one containing coded instructions and the second one containing data (input, output, computed and temporary). The two parts are divided by the special instruction 'halt'. When the machine executes the special instruction 'halt' the execution of the program stops.

Each instruction is executed in three phases: acquisition from main memory, interpretation (decoding) and execution.

The acquisition phase, also called the **fetch phase,** is carried out in four steps. Each step corresponds to a data transfer between CPU registers and/or specific main memory locations. The fetch phase is executed as follows:

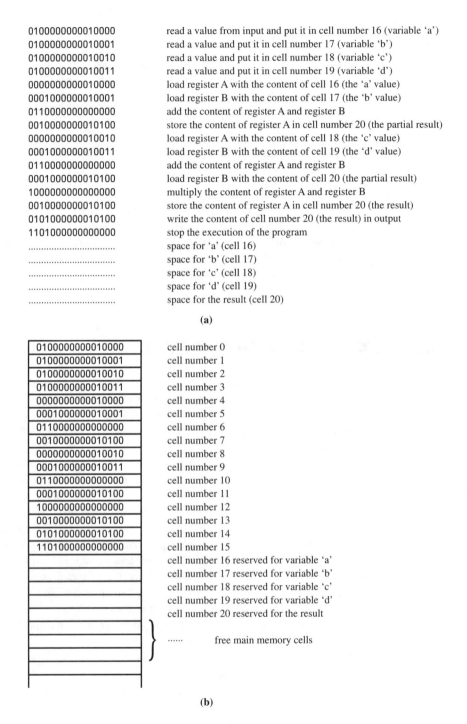

0100000000010000	read a value from input and put it in cell number 16 (variable 'a')
0100000000010001	read a value and put it in cell number 17 (variable 'b')
0100000000010010	read a value and put it in cell number 18 (variable 'c')
0100000000010011	read a value and put it in cell number 19 (variable 'd')
0000000000010000	load register A with the content of cell 16 (the 'a' value)
0001000000010001	load register B with the content of cell 17 (the 'b' value)
0110000000000000	add the content of register A and register B
0010000000010100	store the content of register A in cell number 20 (the partial result)
0000000000010010	load register A with the content of cell 18 (the 'c' value)
0001000000010011	load register B with the content of cell 19 (the 'd' value)
0110000000000000	add the content of register A and register B
0001000000010100	load register B with the content of cell 20 (the partial result)
1000000000000000	multiply the content of register A and register B
0010000000010100	store the content of register A in cell number 20 (the result)
0101000000010100	write the content of cell number 20 (the result) in output
1101000000000000	stop the execution of the program
....	space for 'a' (cell 16)
....	space for 'b' (cell 17)
....	space for 'c' (cell 18)
....	space for 'd' (cell 19)
....	space for the result (cell 20)

(a)

0100000000010000	cell number 0
0100000000010001	cell number 1
0100000000010010	cell number 2
0100000000010011	cell number 3
0000000000010000	cell number 4
0001000000010001	cell number 5
0110000000000000	cell number 6
0010000000010100	cell number 7
0000000000010010	cell number 8
0001000000010011	cell number 9
0110000000000000	cell number 10
0001000000010100	cell number 11
1000000000000000	cell number 12
0010000000010100	cell number 13
0101000000010100	cell number 14
1101000000000000	cell number 15
	cell number 16 reserved for variable 'a'
	cell number 17 reserved for variable 'b'
	cell number 18 reserved for variable 'c'
	cell number 19 reserved for variable 'd'
	cell number 20 reserved for the result
	...... free main memory cells

(b)

Figure 2.5 (a) The binary form of the program of Example 2.1. (b) The program of Example 2.1 loaded in main memory.

(1)   The contents of the program counter register (PC) are transferred into the address register (AR). Note that PC contains the address of the next instruction to be executed, which usually is the instruction immediately following the last one executed.

(2)   A get from main memory operation is executed. The contents of the memory cell that corresponds to the address contained in the AR are transferred into the data register (DR) via the system bus.

(3)   The contents of the DR are transferred into the current instruction register (CIR).

(4)   The value of register PC is incremented by 1, so that PC contains the address of the instruction immediately after the instruction currently loaded in the CIR. Thus, the execution of the next fetch phase is prepared. However (as we will see in Example 2.2), it is possible that during execution of the current instruction a different address is stored in the PC, thus changing the 'sequential' execution of the program. This kind of instruction is called a **branch**.

Figure 2.6(a) shows the behaviour of the von Neumann machine during the fetch phase of the first instruction of the program in Example 2.1.

The next phase, called the **interpretation phase**, decodes the instruction. This involves analysing the contents of the CIR register to find out which operation is to be executed. In this phase, only the operational code of the current instruction is analysed. Looking at Figure 2.6(b), the operational code of the instruction contained in cell number 0 of the program in Example 2.1 is interpreted by the machine as a read operation, that is as: 'transfer the data available in the peripheral data register into a main memory cell'.

Finally, the **execution phase**, which is different for each operation, consists in executing the operation itself. Operations supported by each computer are different; they involve data transfer from or into memory and peripherals and operations supported by the ALU and the various machine registers. Figure 2.6(c) shows the behaviour of the von Neumann machine during the execution phase of the first instruction of the program in Example 2.1. This part of the figure can be better understood by reading Example 2.1.

*EXAMPLE 2.1

We want to compute the value of the expression $(a + b)*(c + d)$, reading variable values from an input device and writing the result of the evaluation on the output device.

A general algorithm that performs such an operation is the following:

(1)   Read from the input device into memory the 'a', 'b', 'c' and 'd' values.

(2)   Add the values of 'a' and 'b'.

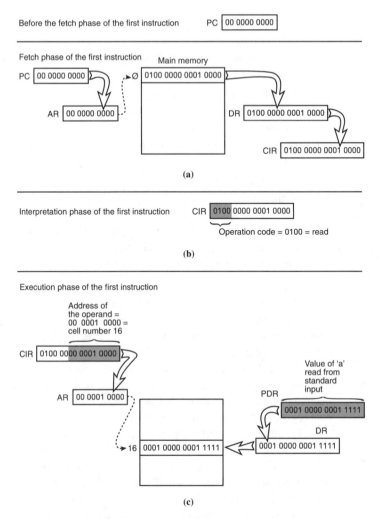

Figure 2.6 The behaviour of the von Neumann machine during the processing of the first instruction of the program of Example 2.1.

(3)   Save the partial result into memory.

(4)   Add the values of 'c' and 'd'.

(5)   Multiply the partial result just obtained and the one previously saved.

(6)   Write the final result of the evaluation on the output device.

(7)   Stop the execution of the program.

This program requires the use of memory cells; these are normally allocated to programs. Suppose that cells number 16, 17, 18 and 19 have been respectively reserved for 'a', 'b', 'c' and 'd' values, and that cell 20 is also available. The von Neumann machine just described will be able to solve the problem through the following algorithm (note that each step of the previous algorithm may require more than one step in the algorithm below):

(1)   Put into main memory, in cell number 16 (reserved for the 'a' value), the value read from the input device (the value is present in the PDR register); do the same for 'b', 'c' and 'd' values putting them respectively in cells number 17, 18 and 19.

(2)   Perform the addition of 'a' and 'b':

    (2.1)   load the contents of cell number 16 corresponding to 'a' into register A;

    (2.2)   load the contents of cell number 17 corresponding to 'b' into register B;

    (2.3)   add the contents of the two registers (the operation is carried out by the ALU).

(3)   Store the partial result, now available in register A, in cell number 20.

(4)   Perform the addition of 'c' and 'd':

    (4.1)   load the contents of cell number 18 corresponding to 'c' into register A;

    (4.2)   load the contents of cell number 19 corresponding to 'd' into register B;

    (4.3)   add the contents of the two registers.

(5)   Perform the multiplication of (a+b) and (c+d):

    (5.1)   load into register B the contents of cell 20, containing the partial result (a+b) previously obtained;

    (5.2)   multiply the contents of the two registers; note that register A still contains the value (c+d).

(6)   Write the result on the output device:

    (6.1)   store the result, now available in register A, in cell number 20 (the cell prepared to store the result);

    (6.2)   write the result of the computation on the output device, by getting it from cell number 20 in main memory and writing it into the data register of the proper peripheral.

(7)   Halt (stop the execution of the program).

Note that during the execution phase, data manipulation and data transfer operations are realized:

- Steps 2.3, 4.3 and 5.2 involve a data manipulation operation whereas the other steps involve the following data transfer operations.
- Step 1 is a data transfer from a peripheral interface to the main memory.
- Steps 2.1, 2.2, 4.1, 4.2 and 5.1 are data transfers from the main memory to the processor.
- Steps 3 and 6.1 are data transfers from the processor to the main memory.
- Step 6.2 is a data transfer from the main memory to a peripheral interface.

*EXAMPLE 2.2

This presents an algorithm to manipulate data stored in memory cells 'x', 'y' and 'm' in the following way: 'if 'x' is greater than 'y' then store the value of 'x' in 'm', otherwise store the value of 'y' in 'm''. The following general algorithm performs this operation:

(1)   Subtract the contents of cell 'y' from the contents of cell 'x'.

(2)   If the difference is greater than 0 then branch to instruction 5.

(3)   Move the contents of cell 'y' into cell 'm'.

(4)   Stop the execution of the program.

(5)   Move the contents of cell 'x' into cell 'm'.

(6)   Stop the execution of the program.

This algorithm takes into account the fact that in our machine it is possible to test the sign of the result of an operation performed by the ALU.

The von Neumann machine will be able to solve the problem through the following algorithm:

(1)   Subtract 'y' from 'x':

   (1.1) load the contents of the cell corresponding to 'x' into register A;

   (1.2) load the contents of the cell corresponding to 'y' into register B;

   (1.3) execute the difference between the contents of the two registers.

(2)   If the result is greater than 0 branch to 5 else continue.

(3)   Transfer 'y' into 'm':

   (3.1) load the contents of the cell corresponding to 'y' into register A;

   (3.2) store the contents of register A in the cell corresponding to 'm'.

(4)   Halt.

(5)   Transfer 'x' into 'm':

   (5.1) load the contents of the cell corresponding to 'x' into register A;

   (5.2) store the contents of register A in the cell corresponding to 'm'.

(6)   Halt.

As shown in Example 2.1, the von Neumann machine can easily execute data manipulations (statement 1.3) or data transfers between the functional elements of the machine (statements 1.1, 1.2, 3.1, 3.2, 5.1 and 5.2). Let us now focus our attention on the execution of step 2. First, note that the execution phase of step 1.3 has set the sign bit of the status register in agreement with the sign of the result obtained by subtracting the contents of registers A and B. The execution of step 2 tests the value of the sign bit in the status register; if the value of the sign bit indicates a result greater than 0, it puts the address in main memory of step 5.1 into register PC, otherwise it leaves in PC the existing value (referring to statement 3.1).

The value of the PC register after the execution of step 2 determines which statement is fetched, decoded and executed after step 2 (statement 5.1 in the first case, statement 3.1 otherwise). In this way the von Neumann machine executes a choice between different instructions to be executed, as required by algorithms.

We have now completed our first description of the computer and are now ready to turn to its high-level programming in C. More information about computer organization and architecture will be given in Chapters 13 and 14.

Exercises

2.1 Illustrate the relationship between the number of lines in the data bus and the length of a word.

2.2 Describe the characteristics (connections, type and length of registers, bus dimensions) of a machine consisting of a screen display, a keyboard, 256-kbyte memory of 16-bit words and two types of mass storage (floppy disk and hard disk).

2.3 Explain how, in the architecture described in this chapter, it is possible to compare two numbers and say when they are equal.

2.4 Describe an algorithm for the evaluation of the expression x = a + b, 'a' and 'b' being the input variables and 'x' the output variable of the program. The algorithm must be executable by the von Neumann machine described in this chapter.

2.5 Consider the following general algorithm:

(1)   read the values of two variables 'n' and 'm' from the standard input device;

(2)   write the value of variable 'n' on the standard output, repeating the writing operation a number of times as indicated by the value of variable 'm';

and describe an algorithm executable by the von Neumann machine presented in this chapter.

2.6 Describe the fetch phase, the interpretation phase and the execution phase of all the instructions of the two examples presented in this chapter as shown in Figure 2.6 for the first instruction of Example 2.1.

PART I
Programming

This part is dedicated to high-level language programming, beginning with the invention of an algorithm for the automatic solution of a given problem and ending with the production of executable code written in some high-level language. We introduce algorithm coding by using the C language. The accent, however, is on explaining the language as a means of achieving the goal of algorithm description rather than as a complete description of all language features. Thus, we first illustrate a programming concept, and then how this concept is implemented in C. Occasionally, we shall make some observations concerning certain peculiarities of the language and outline some of the alternatives offered by other widely used languages.

To help focus attention on essential principles without the distraction of a mass of technical details, in Chapter 3 we first present a simplified kernel of C. In particular we use a simplified set of I/O operations and avoid the explicit declaration of the items that are used in the program. As a consequence, the programs presented in this chapter are not truly executable; however, programs will be executable from Chapter 4 onwards.

In subsequent chapters we systematically present fundamental programming techniques and the way they are supported by the C language: Chapter 4 illustrates the structure of a complete C program and allows the writing of the first truly executable programs; Chapter 5 deals with organizing complex information into suitable **data structures**; Chapter 6 presents **control structures**, that is, the various ways to select and to repeat the execution of sequences of statements during program execution; Chapters 7 and 8 introduce **subprograms**, that is, a way of coding algorithms devoted to the solution of the subproblems of a given problem once and for all, so that whenever we need to solve a particular subproblem, we just use the corresponding subprogram without rewriting it; in particular, Chapter 8 is devoted to the recursive use of subprograms, a powerful technique that makes use of a subprogram during the execution of the subprogram itself. Chapter 9 deals with the management of files; Chapters 10 and 11 introduce more sophisticated techniques to realize data structures; finally, Chapter 12 introduces the analysis of algorithm complexity in a rigorous way.

It must be noted that programming is only a part of the whole activity of software design, which includes various phases that can be schematically summarized as follows:

(1) analysis of the problem;

(2) specification of the characteristics that the system must possess to solve the problem satisfactorily;

(3) formulation of the project as an architecture composed of different components whose cooperation and integration lead to the solution of the problem;

(4) realization or implementation of the system by coding the various components in a programming language and integrating them;

(5) verification that the realized system behaves as expected and correction of any defects.

Normally, introductory computer science textbooks do not focus on the process of software design; in some cases they introduce a few software design techniques intertwined with the teaching of a programming language. However, we believe that a systematic overview of this issue is important, even in an introductory book, but that it can be best appreciated *after* gaining enough knowledge of programming paradigms. Thus, we dedicate the whole of Part III to the topic of software design.

Coding algorithms in a high-level language

3

In Chapter 1 we introduced the fundamental concept of the algorithm as a sequence of elementary operations defined so precisely that they can be executed by a machine. In Chapter 2 we described the fundamental characteristics of a typical machine for executing algorithms: a computer. A program, indeed, is nothing more than an algorithm coded in the language of a particular computer.

However, even the simplest examples presented in Chapters 1 and 2 raised the problem of how to formulate an algorithm. On the one hand the natural language used in Chapter 1 is easily understandable but cannot be executed by a computer; on the other hand the operations described in Chapter 2 are machine executable, but an algorithm coded by using them is difficult to understand. Think, for example, of how tedious and error prone it would be to code the algorithm of the extended example of Section 1.2 as a program, that is, a sequence of operations, of the von Neumann machine as described in Chapter 2. No doubt, such an endeavour could be carried out, in principle, but at what price? Also, once we had such a program, imagine trying to read and understand it!

The above discussion highlights two fundamental requirements of any language for describing algorithms: on the one hand, the language must be *precise*, in order to remove any doubts about the interpretation and meaning of the operations to be executed; on the other, the language also has to be *concise*, in order to avoid making the interpretation of programs extremely difficult. Note that the first requirement is dictated by the automatic executor, whereas the second derives from the needs of human comprehension. It is no surprise, therefore, to find that machine language and natural language are diametrically opposed, each satisfying one of the requirements to the detriment of the other.

High-level programming languages are explicitly designed to bridge such a gap. In this chapter we introduce the core of the C language using a simplified set of I/O operations and avoiding the explicit declaration of the items that are used in the program. With respect to low-level programming using machine instructions such as those illustrated in Chapter 2, the main features that are offered by this initial subset of C are the following:

- The possibility of referring to program items (memory cells, statements, constant values) in a *symbolic* way, that is, by giving them a name, or **identifier**, which is much easier to understand and to remember for human beings. Think of the effort required to remember the meaning of a memory cell if we refer to it as 'cell 1001001100'.

- The possibility of expressing statements and the control of their execution sequence in a way that is closer to natural language than to machine language.

  Consider, for instance, the computation of the expression $(a + b)*(c + d)$ described in Example 2.1: the sequence of machine instructions that execute that simple algorithm considerably obscures its meaning. Such a meaning is expressed in an equally precise, but much more understandable, way by the original mathematical formulation.

  Similarly, Example 2.2 motivates the need for a more natural way to describe, during algorithm formulation, selection between two different alternatives based on the result of the evaluation of some condition, say a comparison between different values.

3.1 The core of the C language

To describe the C language, let us refer to an abstract machine – the C machine – which is able to 'understand' and to execute the programs coded in its language. It is strongly based on the von Neumann machine described in Chapter 2. However, it is even more abstract in the sense that various details of its structure are omitted in order to simplify its use. As we stated in Chapter 1, it is the job of the compiler to allow the user to 'see' the abstract high-level machine and to forget the details of the underlying, real, machine.

The C machine possesses a central processing unit, a main memory and a bus, like the von Neumann architecture. Unlike the von Neumann machine, however, it has only one input unit, called **Standard Input**, and one output unit, called **Standard Output**. This is an ideal way to indicate input and output interfaces that can be realized by very different physical devices (video terminals, printers, magnetic tapes and so on).

As Figure 3.1 suggests, Standard Input, Standard Output and memory are divided into elementary cells, each containing one datum. Data contained in the various cells can be either numerical or characters. For the time being, however, we do not impose any physical limits either on the memory size or on the input/output devices: they have an unlimited number of cells and each cell may contain any numerical value (whether integer or real), or any character value, which requires a variable number of bits. We will also use string values. A **string** is a finite sequence of characters, such as 'George, yesterday, alpha-beta, …'. To stay close to reality we will assume that a string is stored in consecutive cells, each one containing a

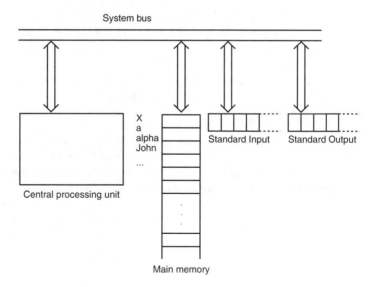

Figure 3.1 The C abstract machine.

single character of the string. Thus, the notion of a memory cell is more abstract than in the case of the von Neumann machine.

Memory cells are also called **variables** to emphasize the fact that their contents may change during program execution.

Variables, instructions and other program items that will be introduced later are denoted through symbolic identifiers defined by the programmer. A **symbolic identifier** is a sequence of alphabetic letters and digits headed by a letter. The special character '_' is treated as an honorary digit. (Examples of C identifiers are: a, x, alpha, fool, a1, xy23, Barry, TheDayAfterTomorrow, The_Day_After_Tomorrow, ...) Notice that uppercase letters are different from lowercase letters (Var1, var1 and VAR1 are identifiers of three different variables).

To avoid ambiguity the same identifier cannot be used to indicate different items, nor can different identifiers be used for the same item.

Some identifiers are **predefined** and **reserved**, that is, they are associated a priori with some language item and, therefore, they cannot be used by the programmer for a different meaning. For instance, scanf and printf denote elementary input/output operations: thus they cannot be used in a C program to identify, say, a variable.

The term **keyword** denotes other predefined words of the programming language. They are also reserved and thus cannot be used as normal identifiers by the programmer.

To enhance readability, in this text all program items are written using a special font; keywords are written in boldface to help highlight the syntactic structure of a program.

A C program consists of a header followed by a sequence of statements enclosed in the symbols { and }. The **header** consists of the predefined identifier main followed by a pair of parentheses () (the role of this pair of parentheses, which, for the time being, are empty, will become clear later). **Statements** are sentences of the programming language; each statement is concluded by the symbol ;. C statements are of the following three types.

1. The assignment statement

This fundamental statement is used to assign the value of an expression to a variable and consists of the symbol = preceded by the identifier of a memory cell and followed by an expression that defines a value. The **expression** may consist of constant values, variable identifiers or a combination thereof obtained through the normal **arithmetic operators** (+, -, *, /) and parentheses, as in traditional arithmetic expressions. Simple examples of assignment statements are the following:

```
x = 23;
w = 'a';
y = z;
alpha = x + y;
r3 = (alpha*43 - xgg) * (delta - 32*ijj);
x = x + 1;
```

The execution of an assignment statement consists of evaluating the expression, by replacing the variable identifiers with the values of the corresponding memory cells at the instant of evaluation and storing the result in the variable to the left of the = symbol. For example, if cell a contains the value 45 and cell z the value 5, the statement

```
x = (a - z)/10;
```

causes the value 4 to be stored in cell x.

2. Input and output statements

These consist of the predefined identifiers scanf or printf, followed by a pair of parentheses enclosing a variable identifier. They allow the value of a variable to be read from the Standard Input or written to the Standard Output in the same way as the corresponding machine language instructions.

For ease of use, the printf statement also has an extended form in which an entire expression may appear within the pair of parentheses. For instance, the statement

```
printf((a - z)/10);
```

can be seen as an abbreviation for the pair of statements:

```
temp = (a - z)/10;
printf(temp);
```

where temp denotes a variable not otherwise used within the program.

In particular, the `printf` statement can also be used to print a character. In this case, in order to avoid ambiguities between a 'character value' to be printed directly and a variable identifier which is the same as that character, the character is enclosed in single quotes. Thus,

```
printf('a');
```

causes the character 'a' to be written into the Standard Output cell corresponding to the current print position, not the printing of the contents of cell a. Note the difference between the statements `printf (2)` and `printf ('2')`. Finally, for the sake of brevity, the `printf` statement's argument may be a value consisting of a whole string. In this case, it is enclosed in double quotes. For example, the statement

```
printf("alpha");
```

is an abbreviation of the sequence

```
printf('a');
printf('l');
printf('p');
printf('h');
printf('a');
```

3. Compound statements

These produce various effects depending on the verification of certain conditions on the values of variables. A **condition**, also called a **Boolean expression**, is an expression whose value can be either true or false. The expression is constructed using the normal arithmetic operators, the **relational operators** (==, !=, <, >, <=, >=) corresponding, respectively, to the relations equal, not equal, less than, greater than, less than or equal, greater than or equal, and the **logical operators** (||, &&, !) corresponding, respectively, to the logical operations OR, AND, NOT. The OR and AND operations apply to two operands, the NOT operation to only one. The OR operation result is true if either or both of its operands are true; the AND operation result is true if both its operands are true; and the NOT operation result is the opposite of its operand. Their meaning is described by Table 3.1 which is an example of a **truth table**, that is, a table which describes the value of the result of an operation as a function of the value of its operands, assuming that both the operands and the result of the operation can be either the value 'true' or the value 'false'. The following are examples of conditions:

```
x == 0
alpha > beta && x != 3
!((a + b)*3 > x || a < c)
```

If we assume that variables x, alpha, beta, a, b and c store, respectively, the values 0, 1, 2, 3, 4 and 5, the evaluation of the three above conditions yields the results T, F and F, respectively.

Notice that the evaluation of a Boolean expression is subject to certain precedence rules between logical operators: for instance in the expression

Table 3.1 The definition of the logical operators: (a) NOT, (b) OR, (c) AND.

A		A\B	F	T	A\B	F	T
F	T	F	F	T	F	F	F
T	F	T	T	T	T	F	T
(a): NOT(A)			(b): A OR B			(c): A AND B	

T means 'true'; F means 'false'

```
x > 0 || y == 3 && z > w
```

the **&&** operator must be executed before the **||**, in the same way as in the expression

```
a + b * c
```

the ***** operation must be executed before the **+**.

A complete table of precedence rules for arithmetic and logical operators is given in Appendix B.

There are two types of compound statements:

(1) **The conditional statement.** This allows one of two different sequences of statements to be executed, depending on the truth value of a condition. It consists of the keyword **if**, followed by a condition enclosed in parentheses, the first sequence of statements enclosed in braces, the keyword **else** and, finally, the second sequence of statements enclosed in braces. The so-called '**else** branch' of the statement, that is, the keyword **else** and the following sequence of statements, can be omitted. Also, for the sake of brevity, enclosing braces are normally omitted when the sequence of statements reduces to a single statement. The following are examples of conditional statements:

```
if (x == 0) z = 5; else y = z + w*y;
if (x == 0) {z = 5;} else {y = z + w*y;}
if ((x + y)*(z - 2) > (23 + v)) {z = x + 1; y = 13 + x;}
if ((x == y && z > 3) || w != y) z = 5; else {y = z + w*y; x = z;}
```

The following statements are constructed incorrectly:

```
if (x == 0) else y = z; y = 34;
if (x == 0) a; else b + c;
```

The execution of a conditional statement by the machine is simple and intuitive: it evaluates the condition, that is, it establishes whether its value is true or false. If true, it executes only the first sequence of statements; if false, only the second one. If the latter does not exist and the condition is false, the machine continues with the next statement following the conditional statement.

(2) **The iterative statement (or loop).** This allows the execution of a sequence of statements to be repeated every time a certain condition is true. It consists of the keyword **while**, followed by the condition enclosed in parentheses (as for the conditional statement) and by a sequence of statements enclosed in braces (called the **body of the loop**). As for conditional statements, enclosing braces can be omitted when the sequence of statements reduces to a single statement. The following are examples of loop statements:

```
while (x >= 0) x = x - 1;
while (z != y) {y = z - x; x = x*3;}
```

The execution of a loop statement by the machine starts with the evaluation of the condition. If it is false, the body of the loop is not executed at all and the program proceeds with the following statement. Otherwise, the body of the loop is executed for the first time; then the condition is evaluated again and, if it is true, the body of the loop is executed again. When the condition becomes false, the loop is exited, that is, execution continues with the statement following the loop statement. In other words, the loop is repeated as long as the condition is true: that is why this statement is called 'iterative.'

Conditional and iterative statements are called **compound statements** because they are constructed by joining simpler statements together; they therefore contain other statements within themselves. This is not a characteristic shared by the statements of the von Neumann machine, but, as we shall see, it is very useful for constructing complex programs. It is important to note that the possibilities for constructing compound statements using the two mechanisms described above are unlimited: a compound statement can contain any other statement, including compound statements.

3.2 First examples of C programs

The first three examples of C programs in this section are quite simple and illustrate the use of compound statements. Subsequent examples are of increasing complexity to show how the combination of basic instructions of the language naturally suits the specification of various parts of an algorithm.

The programs are often given a name by using comments. **Comments** are pieces of text enclosed between the symbols /* and */ and, strictly speaking, are not part of the program. They can be written freely and are simply ignored by the abstract machine. Comments can take more than one line and can appear at any point: their only purpose is to help the human reader understand the meaning of the program and algorithm. To help further distinguish comments from real code, comments, in this book, will be set towards the right-hand side of the page.

The reader will notice that algorithms, expressed in C, are not too far from a natural language formulation, yet they are now executable by a machine, because the compiler, itself a software program, translates them into sequences of operations such as those described in Chapter 2, which are eventually understood by the machine.

EXAMPLE 3.1

The following programs read two numbers and print the greater of them. They illustrate a simple use of the conditional statement.

```
                                    /*Program GreaterNumber - first version*/
main()
{
    scanf(x);
    scanf(y);
    if (x > y) z = x; else z = y;
    printf(z);
}
```

```
                                    /*Program GreaterNumber - second version*/
main()
{
    scanf(x);
    scanf(y);
    if (x > y) printf(x); else printf(y);
}
```

EXAMPLE 3.2

The following program reads a sequence of numbers greater than, or equal to, 0, that contains at least one 0 and prints a 1 as soon as it finds the first 0. This is a first example of the use of the iterative statement.

```
                                                    /*Program SearchFirstZero*/
main()
{
    one = 1;
    scanf(datum);
    while (datum != 0) scanf(datum);
    printf(one);
}
```

EXAMPLE 3.3

Consider the problem of calculating the sum of a sequence of nonzero numbers; the sequence is terminated by a 0. The following program is a simple solution of the problem: it initializes variable sum to 0; then it starts reading data and, while the number read is different from 0, it keeps adding it to the current value of variable sum; eventually, when the number read is 0, it prints the value of sum on the Standard Output.

```
                                                    /*Program SequenceSum*/
main()
{
   sum = 0;
   scanf(number);
   while (number != 0)
   {
      sum = sum + number;
      scanf(number);
   }
   printf(sum);
}
```

EXAMPLE 3.4

We want to write a program that simulates the following simple game between two players: each player selects a colour (out of, say, 'black', 'white' and 'red'). Then the two colours are compared: black defeats white, white defeats red and red defeats black.

The program must read two characters from the Standard Input. The first one gives the choice of the first player, the second the choice of the second player ('b' denotes 'black', 'w' denotes 'white', 'r' denotes 'red'). Then, it must write the winner on the Standard Output, or indicate that the game is a draw (both players chose the same colour).

The following program produces the desired result:

```
                                                   /*Program ColourPlayers*/
main()
{
   scanf(FirstColour);
   scanf(SecondColour);
   if (FirstColour == SecondColour)
     printf("The game is a draw");
   else
     if ((FirstColour == 'b' && SecondColour == 'w') ||
         (FirstColour == 'w' && SecondColour == 'r') ||
         (FirstColour == 'r' && SecondColour == 'b'))
       printf("The winner is player # 1");
     else
       printf("The winner is player # 2");
}
```

Notice the use of nested compound statements: once we realize that the two players did not choose the same colour, we must establish who is the winner; thus, within the **else** branch of the first conditional statement, we put another conditional statement. Also, notice the use of appropriate indentation in the layout of the program to enhance readability. This is a matter of style; indentation does not affect correct execution of the program, but does have an impact on human understanding.

Remark

The use of nested conditional statements produces the risk of ambiguity when some of them lack the **else** branch. Consider, for instance, a statement like the following:

```
if (C1) if (C2) S1; else S2;
```

It contains two nested conditional statements, only one of them including the **else** branch: with which of the two **if**s should the only **else** branch be associated? In principle both the following interpretations, clarified by appropriate indentation, should be possible:

```
if (C1)
    if (C2) S1;
else S2;
```

and

```
if (C1)
    if (C2) S1;
    else S2;
```

The two interpretations have different meanings. To solve this problem, C adopts the convention that the first **else** branch is attributed to the last **if**. In the above example, this means choosing the second alternative.

If the desired meaning is different, we must make explicit use of braces. Therefore, if we want the first interpretation of the previous statement, we have to write the following statement:

```
if (C1) {if (C2) S1;} else S2;
```

Somewhat similarly, when we write $a + b * c$ we mean $a + (b * c)$; if we want a different precedence relation between multiplication and sum, we must explicitly write $(a + b) * c$.

EXAMPLE 3.5

The next example has an algorithmic structure quite similar to the previous one, but it is applied to a problem of a mathematical nature. We want to write a program that: reads three numbers from the input; checks whether they can be the lengths of the three sides of a triangle (the length of each side must be less than the sum of the other two); and finally determines whether the triangle is scalene, isosceles or equilateral.

An algorithm to solve this problem could be worded as follows:

(1)   Read the three data items, called X, Y and Z, respectively.

(2)   Check that each data item is less than the sum of the other two; if not, output the following message: 'the data read does not correspond to a triangle: be more careful'; otherwise proceed as follows:

(2.1) check whether X, Y and Z are all equal: in this case, print the message: 'the data read corresponds to an equilateral triangle';

(2.2) in the negative case, check whether at least two of the sides are equal: if so, print the message: 'the data read corresponds to an isosceles triangle';

(2.3) otherwise, print the message; 'the data read corresponds to a scalene triangle'.

This algorithm can be reformulated quite easily in C, as the following program shows:

```
                                    /*Program for evaluation of a triangle*/
main()
{                                                      /*read input data*/
    scanf(X); scanf(Y); scanf(Z);
        /*check that the data can be lengths of the sides of a triangle*/
if ((X < Y + Z) && (Y < X + Z) && (Z < X + Y))
                        /*distinction between various types of triangle*/
    if (X == Y && Y == Z)
        printf("the data read corresponds to an equilateral triangle");
    else
        if (X == Y || Y == Z || X == Z)
            printf("the data read corresponds to an isosceles triangle");
        else
            printf("the data read corresponds to a scalene triangle");
    else
        printf("the data read does not correspond to a triangle:
            be more careful")¹;
}
```

EXAMPLE 3.6

Consider the algorithm presented in Example 1.1 to execute the sum operation by means of an abacus. Recall that an abacus represents numerical information in an extremely simple and primitive way: the number indicated by each row of the abacus is represented by a corresponding number of digits. This is also called **unary numbering**. Even though C presents numbers to the user in the more comfortable and efficient way based on Arabic arithmetic (see the description of number systems in Chapter 13), it may be instructive to solve the problem of addition through unary numbering using C.

First, we have to establish an appropriate conversion to represent the unary coding of numbers in terms of the C alphabet. A natural choice is the following: the Standard Input contains a space followed by n Is (the symbol I encodes a single abacus counter), followed by another space, m Is and a final space. Standard

---

¹ To simplify the writing of printf instructions including a string which occupies more than one line we always omit to close double quotes at the end of each text line and to open them again at the beginning of the following indented one (as required by the syntax of C).

Output will contain, at the end of program execution, a blank followed by a sequence of $n + m$ Is and a final blank.

This can be easily obtained by the following program:

```
                                            /*Program for Unary Sum*/
main()
{
  scanf(CurrentChar);
  printf(CurrentChar);
                    /*the first character, that is, a space, is read and
                    immediately rewritten. Subsequently, the sequence of
                    'I's that follow the first character is read and
                    rewritten via a loop that is repeated until the next
                    space is encountered.*/
  scanf(CurrentChar);
                    /*this operation most likely executes reading in the
                    first 'I' of the first addendum.*/
  while (CurrentChar == 'I')
                    /*note that each reading of an 'I' character
                    corresponds to the movement of a counter from left to
                    right in the first row of the abacus, referring to the
                    algorithm illustrated in Example 1.1; symmetrically,
                    each writing of the same character corresponds to the
                    movement of one counter from right to left in the third
                    row.*/
  {
    printf(CurrentChar);
    scanf(CurrentChar);
  }
  scanf(CurrentChar);
                    /*when the next space is encountered, the next character
                    is read without writing the space. From now on, reading
                    the 'I' character spells out the second addendum, and
                    therefore corresponds to the movement of a counter from
                    left to right in the second row of the abacus.*/
  while (CurrentChar == 'I')
  {
    printf(CurrentChar);
    scanf(CurrentChar);
  }
  printf(CurrentChar);
                    /*the last character read is the space that delimits the
                    second addendum and is written to the Standard Output as
                    the delimiter of the result.*/
☛ 1                }
```

EXAMPLE 3.7

We now introduce a nontrivial and famous algorithm to solve a classic mathematical problem. We want to calculate the greatest common divisor of two positive integers, *n* and *m*. A first, simple solution to the problem is given in the following algorithm which strictly applies the definition of the greatest common divisor. The algorithm is:

'Scan all numbers between 1 and the minimum of *m* and *n*. For each number, establish if it is a common divisor of *m* and *n* (to find out if *x* is a divisor of *y*, execute the integer division *y/x* – which produces a truncated integer as a result – and multiply the result by *x*: if you obtain *y* again, then *x* is a divisor of *y*). Whenever the number under analysis is a divisor of both *m* and *n*, store it as the current greatest common divisor (initially, this variable is set to 1). When all the numbers have been scanned, this variable contains the desired result.'

This algorithm can be immediately coded into the following program:

```
                                        /*Program GreatestComDivisor*/
main()
{
    scanf(n); scanf(m);
    gcd = 1;
    if (n <= m) min = n; else min = m;
    counter = 1;
    while (counter <= min)
    {
        if ((n/counter)*counter == n && (m/counter)*counter == m)
        gcd = counter;
        counter = counter + 1;
    }
    printf(gcd);
}
```

A less trivial way to solve the problem is the famous Euclid's algorithm (which shows how some fundamental concepts of computer science were known long before electronic computers were invented). It is based on the remark that, if *m* = *n*, then the greatest common divisor of *m* and *n*, abbreviated here as gcd(*m,n*), is trivially *m* or *n* itself; if *m* ≠ *n* (for example, *m* > *n*) then they share the same gcd with the value of their difference, *m* − *n*. Let us look more closely at this claim: its analysis will in fact drive the derivation of the algorithm:

(1) If *m* > *n* and *k* is a common divisor of *m* and *n*, then *k* is also a divisor of *m* − *n*. In fact, being a common divisor of *m* and *n* means *m* = *k* · *d* and *n* = *k* · *r* for some positive integers *d* and *r*. Therefore *m* − *n* = *k* · (*d* − *r*), where *d* − *r* is again a positive integer and, therefore, *k* is a divisor of *m* − *n* too.

(2) Symmetrically, it is possible to prove that if *k* is a common divisor of *m* − *n* and *n*, it is also a divisor of *m*.

(3) Therefore, all common divisors of *m* and *n* coincide with the common divisors of *m* − *n* and *n*; therefore, the greatest common divisors of the two pairs of numbers also coincide.

Now, let us call s the value of $m - n$. The above reasoning can again be applied to the pair of numbers s and n, that is, either $s = n$ and they coincide with their gcd, or they share the gcd with their difference.

By proceeding in this way, eventually the two numbers under consideration will be equal (maybe they become 1) and are therefore the greatest common divisor we are looking for.

At this point, we can translate the above reasoning into the following program:

```
                                                    /*Program Euclid's Algorithm*/
main()
{
    scanf(m); scanf(n);
    while (m != n)
      if (m > n)
        m = m - n;
      else                        /*in this case certainly n > m because
                                     the loop is executed only if m != n*/

      n = n - m;
    gcd = n; printf(gcd);
}
```

Note how the new algorithm is more elegant and concise than the previous one. It is also interesting to compare the two algorithms from an efficiency point of view, that is, the time taken by the machine to execute them. Even without executing the two algorithms on a real machine, we can immediately state that in some cases the first one is to be preferred (for example, if $m = 1000\,000\,001$ and $n = 2$), whereas in other cases it is the second one (for example, if $m = 100$ and $n = 500$).

☛ 2   The important problem of evaluating the efficiency of algorithms is treated systematically in Chapter 12.

The above examples have shown that C is a more natural tool for describing algorithms than machine language. Indeed, programs written in C are far more similar to a formulation of the corresponding algorithms in natural language than to a coding in machine language. C's keywords are words from the English vocabulary with a well-defined meaning.

3.3 Array data

In many cases, the information to be processed is grouped into higher level components made up of simpler data. This is the case, for example, with lists of names, invoices, personnel archives in a company organized in a department structure, vectors and matrices in mathematics and so on.

High-level languages allow us to treat this type of information in a way that reflects its logical organization, through the use of **structured variables**, that is, variables that store various information elements. In the following chapters we examine in detail the different ways of treating structured data in high-level programming. Here, we limit ourselves to examining the simplest and most necessary one: the array.

An **array** is a sequence of consecutive and homogeneous memory cells, that is, cells containing uniform data (for example, all integers, all reals or all characters). Each sequence is given a unique name or identifier, whereas a single cell in a sequence is identified by the name of the sequence and an index, that is, an integer greater than or equal to zero that indicates the ordinal number of the cell within the sequence. The index number of the first cell is 0, that of the second cell is 1 and so on. The index value is enclosed in a pair of brackets written immediately to the right of the array identifier. For example, if s is the identifier of the sequence and the sequence is composed of 10 elements, the index assumes values between 0 and 9 and the third cell of the sequence is indicated by the notation s[2]. For the time being, we do not care about possible bounds to the number of cells occurring in an array: to be as simple and abstract as possible we view an array as an unbounded sequence of cells, as Figure 3.2 suggests. We shall be more precise in this respect in Chapter 5.

Notice that, since it is impossible to use the same identifier with different meanings, writing s[3] demands that s within one program corresponds to one unique array. Consequently, a statement that treated s as a simple variable (for example, s = 5) would be an error.

A memory cell identified using this mechanism can be used in the same way as other memory cells. Thus, we can write statements such as

```
scanf(s[2]);
```

to read a datum and store it in the third cell of array s

```
a[3] = s[1] + x;
```

to execute the sum of the contents of the second cell of array s and the contents of cell x and assign the result to the fourth cell of a

```
if (a[4] > s[1] + 3) s[2] = a[2] + a[1];
```

and so on.

The index of an array can also be denoted by the contents of another variable; in fact, it is the value of an expression which can be calculated during program execution. Thus, it is possible to write:

```
x = a[i];
```

to cause the value of the cell of array a, whose ordinal number +1 is the value contained in variable i, to be assigned to variable x. Similarly, we can write statements such as:

```
a[i] = a[i + 1];
a[i*x] = s[a[j + 1] - 3]*(y - a[y]);
```

and so on.

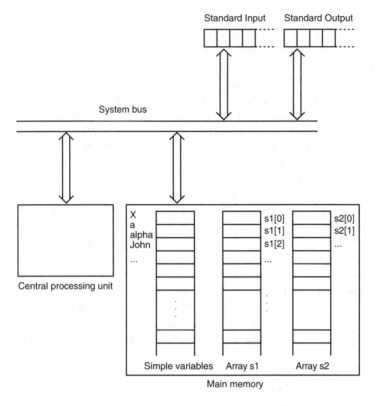

Figure 3.2 A view of the C abstract machine displaying array variables.

To access any cell of an array, all that the abstract machine has to do is:

- Compute the value of the index.
- Add the computed value to the address of the first cell of the array (the 0th one).

We will see in Chapter 14 that modern hardware architectures can execute such a sequence of operations in an extremely efficient way.

The usefulness of arrays is shown by the following examples.

EXAMPLE 3.8

Consider the problem of reading a sequence of characters and writing them out in reverse order. This problem could be easily solved without using arrays only if the items in the sequence were not too many and known a priori: for instance, we could write in reverse order a sequence of three characters using the following program:

```
                                    /*Program TrivialSequenceInversion*/
main()
{
   scanf(x1); scanf(x2); scanf(x3);
   printf(x3); printf(x2); printf(x1);
}
```

Clearly such a program does not scale up to a generic sequence of any number of elements. Let us assume that the end of the sequence is marked by the special character % which otherwise does not occur within the sequence and which must not be written in the output sequence. In such a case, the problem can easily be solved by storing all input data in the cells of an array in order and then by writing them in the Standard Output starting from the last element and going backwards to the first one.

This is obtained by a reading loop which, at each iteration, reads a character, stores it in an element of the array which has a given index and increments the value of the index by 1. Subsequently, a writing loop passes through the array, 'sliding' the index backwards, that is, starting from the last value taken by the index and decrementing it by 1 at each iteration. This simple algorithm is precisely defined by the following C code:

```
                                          /*Program SequenceInversion*/
main()
{
   index = 0;
   scanf(x);
   while (x != '%')
   {
      sequence[index] = x;
      index = index + 1;
      scanf(x);
   }
   while (index > 0)
   {
      index = index - 1;
      printf(sequence[index]);
   }
}
```

EXAMPLE 3.9

Suppose we have on the Standard Input a series of data regarding invoices: for each invoice, one cell of the Standard Input contains the amount and the next three give the date of issue in the European form 'day' (a number between 1 and 31), 'month' (a number between 1 and 12) and 'year'. To be precise, the first cell of the input contains the amount of the first invoice, the second its day of issue, the third the month, the fourth the year, the fifth the amount of the second invoice and so on.

The special character % is put after the year of the last invoice to denote the end of the sequence.

We want to print on the Standard Output the following rearrangement of the input data:

(1) the words AMOUNTS OF ISSUED INVOICES;

(2) the sequence of all amounts, in the same order as the input, preceded by the character $;

(3) the words TOTAL ISSUED INVOICES;

(4) the total of the invoices, preceded by the character $;

(5) the words DATES OF ISSUE;

(6) the sequence of issue dates, in the same order as the input. The three elements of each date, however, must be separated by a / and must be given in the American form, that is, 'month / day / year'; at the end of each date the character # is written.

A simple algorithm to solve this problem is the following:

(1) A first loop reads in the data, four values at a time (as each invoice is described by four elements). Each of the four values read is stored, respectively, in a cell of four different arrays, called `invoice`, `day`, `month` and `year`, respectively. The index of each of these arrays is incremented by 1 at each iteration of the loop. This loop also calculates the total amount of the various invoices.

(2) The words AMOUNTS OF ISSUED INVOICES are printed via a single `printf` statement.

(3) A first writing loop prints, in order, all elements of the `invoice` array, each one preceded by the $ symbol.

(4) The words TOTAL ISSUED INVOICES are printed, followed by the character $ and by the value of the previously calculated total.

(5) The words DATES OF ISSUE are printed.

(6) A second writing loop prints the various triples of 'month, day, year', fetching them in order from their corresponding arrays and putting the character / between month and day and between day and year, and the character # between the year of the current date and the day of the next date.

The above algorithm coded in C is as follows:

```
                                                  /*Program Invoices*/
main()
{
   counter = 0; total = 0; scanf(input);
   while (input != '%')
   {
      invoice[counter] = input;
      total = total + input;
```

```
      scanf(input); day[counter] = input;
      scanf(input); month[counter] = input;
      scanf(input); year[counter] = input;
      scanf(input);
      counter = counter + 1;
   }
   printf("AMOUNTS OF ISSUED INVOICES");
   InvoiceNum = counter;
   counter = 0;
   while (counter < InvoiceNum)
   {
      printf('$'); printf(invoice[counter]);
         counter = counter + 1;
   }
   printf("TOTAL ISSUED INVOICES"); printf('$'); printf(total);
   printf("DATES OF ISSUE");
   counter = 0;
   while (counter < InvoiceNum)
   {
      printf(month[counter]); printf('/');
      printf(day[counter]); printf('/');
      printf(year[counter]); printf('#');
      counter = counter + 1;
   }
}
```

3.4 Incremental development of programs

To be executed mechanically, an algorithm must be formulated as a program, that is, written in an appropriate high-level or low-level programming language.

It is easy to imagine the potential difficulties of developing and comprehending algorithms when we want to tackle the solution of far more complex problems than the ones discussed so far. In this section we present the derivation of programs using a technique of developing different versions of an algorithm, gradually raising the level of detail and formality of the code: we start with very compact formulations which we refine step by step, specifying the meaning of the operations we use. Also, the language we use to describe the various formulations will be transformed, passing from plain English to C, through 'mixed' versions. Such a 'semi-formal' language is often called **pseudocode**.

We would like to stress, however, that the proposed method is intended as a general guideline, not as a prescription. Experience shows that attempting to constrain a strongly creative process such as writing programs with a set of excessively rigid rules can be counterproductive.

EXAMPLE 3.10

We want to develop a text processor that systematically replaces one word with another one. More precisely, suppose that the Standard Input has the following contents.

In the first position (written character by character) we find a word (by 'word' we mean a sequence of alphabetic characters); this is followed by the character $, then another word, followed by the character #; next comes a sequence of words separated from each other by a space and terminated by a % (that is, after the last word there is a space followed by the terminator %).

The program has to write the sequence of words after the # to the Standard Output, replacing each occurrence of the first word of the Standard Input with the second word. If the first word is missing, the program prints a message that informs the user of the error and stops execution. The second word may be omitted: in that case, each occurrence of the first word will just be deleted; also, it is possible that there is no text to rewrite, in which case nothing is produced on the Standard Output.

The solution of this problem requires an algorithm that cannot be formulated in a couple of lines, whatever language we use for its description. It is therefore convenient to create it gradually, so that we do not have to tackle the analysis of too many details at a time. Let us begin with a very compact formulation in English.

(1)   Check that there is a word before the character $. If not, print the message THE WORD TO BE REPLACED IS MISSING. If the word is present, proceed as follows.

(2)   Store the first word of the text in an array of characters.

(3)   Store the second word in another array.

(4)   At this point, scan the whole text word by word (until you find the character %).

  (4.1) Store each word in an array.

  (4.2) Compare each word read with the first word. If the words match, write the second word to the Standard Output, otherwise write the word just read.

The formulation of the algorithm, although precise enough, cannot be immediately translated into C; it makes use of expressions such as 'store a word in an array' which do not directly correspond to statements of the language; in fact, they also need an algorithm in order to be realized. It might therefore be useful to write an intermediate version of the algorithm that uses pseudocode composed of a mixture of C and English. To avoid confusion, the informal parts not written in pure C are enclosed in brackets. The following pseudoprogram is an example:

```
                                     /*Program WordSubstitution*/
main()
{
  scanf(character);
  if (character == '$')
    printf("THE WORD TO BE REPLACED IS MISSING");
```

```
else
{
    [store in array FirstWord the sequence of characters up to '$'];
    [store in array SecondWord the sequence of characters
    following the '$' up to '#'];
    scanf(character);
    while (character != '%')
    {
        [store in array CurrentWord the sequence of characters
        up to the following space];
        [compare FirstWord with CurrentWord];
        if ([FirstWord == CurrentWord])
            [printf(SecondWord)];
        else
            [printf(CurrentWord)];
        printf(' ');
                        /*whether we wrote the word just read
                        (CurrentWord), or the second word instead of the
                        first one, we write a space to separate it from
                        the following word*/
        scanf(character);
                        /*we begin to read the next CurrentWord, unless
                        the character read in is %*/
    }
}
}
```

To transform the above pseudocode into a program, we first have to write the statements needed to store a word in an array, to write a word and to compare two words. Each of these operations requires a 'subalgorithm'. Let us consider the least trivial of the three: the comparison.

A simple way to decide if two words (stored in the two arrays FirstWord and CurrentWord, respectively) are the same is the following:

(1) If the two words are of different lengths, they are definitely different. Otherwise:

(2) Scan the two arrays character by character until you find two different characters or until the index of the array exceeds the word length.

(3) In the first of the above two cases, we conclude that the two words are different; in the second case we conclude that they are the same.

This algorithm can be easily coded in C as follows:

```
if (LengthFirstWord == LengthCurrentWord)
{
    counter = 0;
    while ((counter < LengthFirstWord) &&
            (FirstWord[counter] == CurrentWord[counter]))
        counter = counter + 1;
    if (counter >= LengthFirstWord)
        printf("The two words are the same");
```

```
          else
              printf("The two words are different");
      }
      else
          printf("The two words are different");
```

Now we have to integrate the code for comparing two words (and that for storing and writing single words) into the first pseudocode. Obviously, the result of the comparison will not yield messages to be printed, but either CurrentWord or SecondWord to be written to the Standard Output. It will also be necessary to register the lengths of the various words as they are read and stored, as this information is needed for the comparison. The final result is the following program:

```
                                              /*Program WordSubstitution*/
main()
{
    scanf(character);
    if (character == '$')
       printf("THE WORD TO BE REPLACED IS MISSING");
    else
    {
       counter = 0;
       while (character != '$')                    /*store the first word*/
       {
          FirstWord[counter] = character;
          counter = counter + 1;
          scanf(character);
       }
       LengthFirstWord = counter;
       scanf(character); counter = 0;
       while (character != '#')                    /*store the second word*/
       {
          SecondWord[counter] = character;
          counter = counter + 1;
          scanf(character);
       }
       LengthSecondWord = counter;
                  /*we begin the actual scanning phase of the whole text*/
       scanf(character);
       while (character != '%')
       {
          counter = 0;
          while (character != ' ')                 /*store the current word*/
          {
             CurrentWord[counter] = character;
             counter = counter + 1;
             scanf(character);
          }
          LengthCurrentWord = counter;
                      /*compare the first word with the current word*/
          if (LengthFirstWord == LengthCurrentWord)
          {
             counter = 0;
```

```
        while (counter < LengthFirstWord &&
               FirstWord[counter] == CurrentWord[counter])
          counter = counter + 1;
        if (counter >= LengthFirstWord)    /*we copy the second word*/
        {
          counter = 0;
          while (counter < LengthSecondWord)
          {
            printf(SecondWord[counter]);
            counter = counter + 1;
          }
        }
        else                                 /*we copy the current word*/
        {
          counter = 0;
          while (counter < LengthCurrentWord)
          {
            printf(CurrentWord[counter]);
            counter = counter + 1;
          }
        }
      }
      else
              /*we copy the current word: in this case the two words
              are different because their lengths are different*/
      {
        counter = 0;
        while (counter < LengthCurrentWord)
        {
          printf(CurrentWord[counter]);
          counter = counter + 1;
        }
      }
      printf(' ');
              /*whether we wrote the current word or the second word
              instead of the first one, we write a space to separate
              it from the following word*/
      scanf(character);
              /*we start to read the next CurrentWord, unless the
              character read is %*/
    }
  }
}
```

*EXAMPLE 3.11

The final example of this chapter assumes a little mathematical background on the part of the reader. Suppose that the Standard Input contains the coordinates of four points on a plane, stored in the following order: $<x_1, y_1>$, $<x_2, y_2>$, $<x_3, y_3>$, $<x_4, y_4>$. Indicate with P_i the point of coordinates $<x_i, y_i>$, with $1 \leq i \leq 4$. We want to know whether the two segments $<P_1, P_2>$ and $<P_3, P_4>$ intersect.

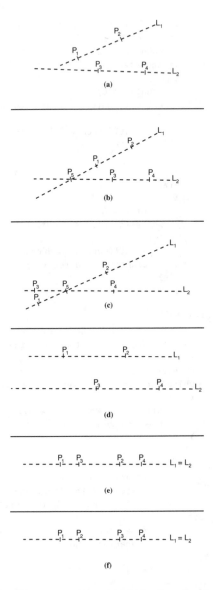

Figure 3.3 The steps of the algorithm that checks whether two segments intersect or not.

A first formulation of an algorithm to solve this problem can be immediately derived from a geometric analysis of its definition. It is formulated in the following pseudocode with the help of Figure 3.3 which illustrates the important steps of the algorithm:

```
                                              /*Program VerifyIntersection*/
main()
{
   [read 8 data items from the Standard Input and store them in the
   variables x1, y1, x2, y2, x3, y3, x4, y4, respectively];
   if ([P1 coincides with P2 or P3 coincides with P4])
      printf("The problem is ill-defined because the given points do not
            define two segments");
   else
   {
      [construct the straight line L1 that passes through P1 and P2
      and the straight line L2 that passes through P3 and P4];
                                              /*Figure 3.3(a)*/
      if ([L1 is not parallel to L2])
      {
         [calculate the intersection between L1 and L2, called P5];
                                              /*Figure 3.3(b)*/
         if ([P5 belongs to <P1, P2> and P5 belongs to <P3, P4>])
            printf("The two segments intersect");        /*Figure 3.3(c)*/
         else
            printf("The two segments do not intersect");
                                              /*Figure 3.3(b)*/
      }
      else
         if ([L1 does not coincide with L2])
            printf("The two segments do not intersect");
                                              /*Figure 3.3(d)*/
         else
            if ([the two segments overlap, even though only partially])
               printf("The two segments overlap");       /*Figure 3.3(e)*/
            else
               printf("The two segments do not intersect");
                                              /*Figure 3.3(f)*/
   }
}
```

The pseudocode is now refined by transforming the phrases written in English into executable code. Ignoring the reading of the input data, the other operations can be realized as follows:

(1) Check if P_1 coincides with P_2 or if P_3 coincides with P_4.

Two points coincide if and only if their coordinates are identical. Thus, the code executing the preliminary verification is the following:

```
if ((x1 == x2 && y1 == y2) || (x3 == x4 && y3 == y4))
   printf("The problem is ill-defined because the given points do not
         define two segments");
else ...
```

(2) Construct a straight line passing through two points.

A standard way to represent a generic straight line L of the plane is by means of an equation of the type $a \cdot x + b \cdot y + c = 0$ that must be satisfied by the

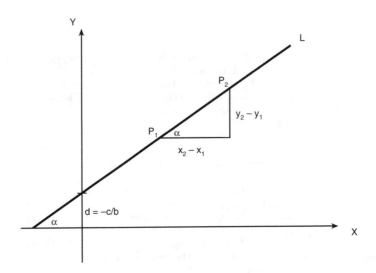

Figure 3.4   Construction of the coefficients that define a straight line in a plane. α is the angle whose tangent m is $(y_2-y_1)/(x_2-x_1)$. m is also called the **angular coefficient** of L. $d = -c/b$ is the value of y when L intersects the Y-axis.

coordinates $<x, y>$ of all and only those points that belong to L. Thus, the calculus of the straight line passing through two generic points of coordinates $<x_1, y_1>$, $<x_2, y_2>$ is carried out by the following assignments, whose geometrical meaning is recalled in Figure 3.4:

```
a = y2 - y1;
b = x1 - x2;
c = (y2 - y1)*x1 + (x2 - x1)*y1;
```

(3)   Check if the two straight lines are parallel.

Given two straight lines L_1 and L_2, described by the equations $a_1 \cdot x + b_1 \cdot y + c_1 = 0$ and $a_2 \cdot x + b_2 \cdot y + c_2 = 0$, respectively, L_1 is parallel to L_2 if and only if the two angular coefficients, m_1 and m_2, are equal, that is, if:

$$(y_2-y_1)/(x_2-x_1) = (y_4-y_3)/(x_4-x_3) \tag{3.1}$$

To avoid the risk of division by 0 in particular cases (when one of the two lines is parallel to one of the two axes), it is better to restate condition (3.1) as:

$$(y_2-y_1)\cdot(x_4-x_3) = (y_4-y_3)\cdot(x_2-x_1)$$

that is,

$$a_1 \cdot b_2 = a_2 \cdot b_1$$

Such a condition can be immediately formulated as a C code Boolean expression.

(4) Calculate the intersection of two straight lines.

Given two nonparallel straight lines L_1 and L_2, the coordinates of the point of intersection P_5 between L_1 and L_2 are the solution of the system

$$a_1 \cdot x + b_1 \cdot y + c_1 = 0$$
$$a_2 \cdot x + b_2 \cdot y + c_2 = 0$$

Again using a little knowledge of linear algebra, we can derive the following values for the coordinates of P_5:

$$x_5 = (b_1 \cdot c_2 - b_2 \cdot c_1)/(a_1 \cdot b_2 - a_2 \cdot b_1)$$
$$y_5 = (c_1 \cdot a_2 - a_1 \cdot c_2)/(a_1 \cdot b_2 - a_2 \cdot b_1)$$

The above equations are transformed into suitable assignments to variables x5 and y5 which store the coordinates of P_5.

(5) Check if P_5 is included within a segment of a given straight line.

We know that P_5 lies on the straight line to which the segment $<P_1, P_2>$ belongs; thus, P_5 is included within the segment if and only if

$$(x_1 \le x_5 \wedge x_5 \le x_2) \vee (x_1 \ge x_5 \wedge x_5 \ge x_2)$$

(6) Coincidence of two parallel straight lines.

Given two straight lines L_1 and L_2, described by the equations $a_1 \cdot x + b_1 \cdot y + c_1 = 0$ and $a_2 \cdot x + b_2 \cdot y + c_2 = 0$, respectively, L_1 and L_2 coincide if and only if their coefficients a_1, b_1, c_1 and a_2, b_2, c_2 are pairwise proportional, that is,

$$a_1/a_2 = b_1/b_2 = c_1/c_2$$

Again, to avoid the risk of division by 0, it is more convenient to restate the above conditions as

$$(b_1 \cdot c_2 = b_2 \cdot c_1) \text{ and } (c_1 \cdot a_2 = a_1 \cdot c_2)$$

(7) Partial overlapping of two segments.

Two segments $<P_1, P_2>$ and $<P_3, P_4>$ which lie on the same straight line overlap, or partially overlap, if and only if

$$((x_1 \le x_3) \wedge (x_3 \le x_2)) \vee$$
$$((x_2 \le x_3) \wedge (x_3 \le x_1)) \vee$$
$$((x_1 \le x_4) \wedge (x_4 \le x_2)) \vee$$
$$((x_2 \le x_4) \wedge (x_4 \le x_1))$$

Conditions 5, 6 and 7 are immediately translated into corresponding C Boolean expressions. Finally, putting the different portions of code that correspond to the various operations into the 'skeleton' of our initial pseudo-code, we obtain the following program:

```
                                              /*Program VerifyIntersection*/
main()
{
                                                      /*reading of data*/
    scanf(x1); scanf(y1); scanf(x2); scanf(y2);
    scanf(x3); scanf(y3); scanf(x4); scanf(y4);
    if                      /*P1 coincides with P2 or P3 coincides with P4*/
      ((x1 == x2 && y1 == y2) || (x3 == x4 && y3 == y4))
      printf("The problem is ill-defined");
    else
    {
                          /*construction of the straight line L1 that passes
                          through P1 and P2 and the straight line L2 passing
                          through P3 and P4*/
      a1 = y2 - y1;
      b1 = x1 - x2;
      c1 = (y1 - y2)*x1 + (x2 - x1)*y1;
      a2 = y4 - y3;
      b2 = x3 - x4;
      c2 = (y3 - y4)*x3 + (x4 - x3)*y4;
      if (!(a1*b2 == b1*a2))                     /*L1 is not parallel to L2*/
                    /*calculate the intersection between L1 and L2, P5*/
      {
        x5 = (b1*c2 - b2*c1)/(a1*b2 - a2*b1);
        y5 = (c1*a2 -a1*c2)/(a1*b2 - a2*b1);
        if           /*P5 belongs to <P1, P2> and P5 belongs to <P3, P4>*/
          (((x1 <= x5 && x5 <= x2) || (x1 >= x5 && x5 >= x2)) &&
          ((x3 <= x5 && x5 <= x4) || (x3 >= x5 && x5 >= x4)))
          printf("The two segments intersect");
        else
          printf("The two segments do not intersect");
      }
      else
        if                                /*L1 does not coincide with R2*/
            (!((b1*c2 == b2*c1) && (c1*a2 == a1*c2)))
          printf("The two segments do not intersect");
        else
          if              /*the two segments overlap, even partially*/
              (((x1 <= x3) && (x3 <= x2)) ||
              ((x2 <= x3) && (x3 <= x1)) ||
              ((x1 <= x4) && (x4 <= x2)) ||
              ((x2 <= x4) && (x4 <= x1)))
            printf("The two segments overlap");
          else
            printf("The two segments do not intersect");
    }
}
```

Note that it is often useful to keep part or a slight variation of the informal portions of the pseudocode in the final version of the code, in the form of comments.

Exercises

3.1 Write a program that reads a number and prints its absolute value or modulo. Use a conditional statement without the **else** branch.

3.2 Check, through careful reading and working out the execution by hand, that the following program prints the sums of all sequences of numbers greater than 0 enclosed between two 0s, ignoring all negative numbers and that the sums are separated by a 0. The whole data sequence starts with a 0 and ends with two consecutive 0s.

```
main()
{
    scanf(x);
    scanf(y);
    while (y != 0)
    {
        sum = 0; z = y;
        while (z != 0)
        {
            if (z > 0) sum = sum + z;
                scanf(z);
        }
        printf(sum); printf(z); scanf(y);
    }
}
```

3.3 Write a program that, after reading a number, prints the value 1 if it is odd, 0 if it is even.

3.4 Write a program that reads three numbers and prints the greatest of them.

3.5 Write a program that reads a number n from Standard Input and executes the sum of the next n numbers in an even position and the sum of the next n numbers in an odd position; more precisely, assuming that the number n occupies the first position of the Standard Input, we want the sum of the second, fourth, sixth, ... numbers and the sum of the third, fifth, ...

3.6 Write a program to calculate the smallest common multiple of two numbers.

3.7 Write a program to calculate the greatest common divisor and another to calculate the smallest common multiple of a sequence of positive numbers, terminated, as always, by a 0.

3.8 Write a program that, given a number different from 0 and a sequence of numbers terminated by a 0, outputs 1 if the first number exists in the sequence, 0 otherwise.

3.9 Verify that the following program is equivalent to that of Example 3.10. Specify exactly how the two algorithms differ, though producing the same result.

```
                                                    /*New Program WordSubstitution*/
main()
{
   scanf(character);
   if (character == '$')
      printf("THE WORD TO BE REPLACED IS MISSING");
   else
   {
      count = 0;
      while (character != '$')
      {
         FirstWord[count] = character;
         count = count + 1;
         scanf(character);
      }
      FirstWord[count] = character;
                       /*in this way, the array FirstWord contains n+1
                       characters, n being the number of characters of
                       the first word: the last one of these characters
                       is the '$'*/
      scanf(character); count = 0;
      while (character != '#')
      {
         SecondWord[count] = character;
         count = count + 1;
         scanf(character);
      }
      SecondWord[count] = character;
      LengthSecondWord = count;
                       /*we store the length of the second word: this
                       will be useful when it has to be written back*/
                       /*now we begin the phase of actually scanning
                       the text*/
      scanf(character);
      while (character != '%')
      {
         count = 0;
         while (character != ' ')
         {
            CurrentWord[count] = character;
            count = count + 1;
            scanf(character);
         }
         LengthCurrentWord = count; count = 0;
                    /*we compare the first word with the word just read*/
         while (FirstWord[count] != '$' && count < LengthCurrentWord
               && FirstWord[count] == CurrentWord[count])
            count = count + 1;
                    /*if the word just read is the same as the first word*/
         if (FirstWord[count] == '$' && count == LengthCurrentWord)
                                             /*we copy the second word*/
```

```
        {
            count = 0;
            while (count < LengthSecondWord)

            {
                printf(SecondWord[count]);
                count = count + 1;
            }
        }
        else
                                            /*we copy the current word*/
        {
            count = 0;
            while (count < LengthCurrentWord)
            {
                printf(CurrentWord[count]);
                count = count + 1;
            }
        }
        printf(' ');
                    /*whether we wrote the current word or the second
                    word instead of the first one, we write a space to
                    separate it from the following word*/
    }
  }
}
```

3.10   Think about the behaviour of the program given in Example 3.10 if words are
separated from each other by more than one space. Write a program that behaves
in the same way as the previous one, but eliminates the superfluous spaces, so that
in the output text there is never more than one space between two words.

3.11   Write a new version of the program of Example 3.10 in which the comparison
between the first word and the current word of the text is done, in order to save
time, during the reading operation: if at a certain point in the comparison we realize
that the two words are different, we output the part of the current word scanned up
to that point and then proceed with a simple copy from the input to the output up to
the end of the word; if the comparison is successful, we copy the second word.
Think about the payoff gained in terms of time, that is, how many machine
operations have been saved.

3.12   Write a C program that realizes the following 'cut and paste' operation: the input
text is composed of a sequence of words separated by single spaces and terminated
by %, as in Example 3.10. After the %, there are three positive numbers, n, m, p, with
n <= m. The output text is obtained from the input text by placing the portion
between the nth and mth positions, inclusive, into the pth position.

3.13   In the Standard Input, we find two series of numbers separated by a & and
terminated by a %. Write a program that writes to the output a series containing

all and only those numbers that are present in both input series. Even if a number is contained more than once in a series, it must be present only once in the output series, provided that it also appears at least once in the second series of input numbers.

3.14 Write a program that calculates the integer square root of an input positive integer n. The result m must be such that $m^2 <= n$ and $(m + 1)^2 > n$.

3.15 Write a program that, given a sequence of words separated from each other by a space and followed by a $ and a final word, counts how many times the final word occurs in the sequence.

☞ 1. Consider the program of Example 3.6. Check what happens in the particular case that there are no Is between the first and the second space.

2. The formulation of Euclid's algorithm given in Example 3.7 is rather inefficient if one of the two numbers is much greater than the other (think of the case $m = 1000\,000\,001$ and $n = 2$). Improve the program using the feature that, if m is a multiple of n, then gcd(m,n) = n; otherwise, calling r the remainder of the division of m and n, gcd(m,n) = gcd(m,r). Write a program that exploits this property (see Table 5.2 for the corresponding C operator).

Running C programs on real machines
4

The programs in Chapter 3 are written in C but cannot be compiled by a C compiler and therefore cannot be executed. One reason is that they are missing some important ingredients, such as variable declarations. The other reason is that we adopted simplified I/O statements with respect to the real language. This was done to avoid any distraction which might have been caused by the many details that are needed to write complete C programs; we wanted instead to concentrate on the core of algorithm programming. For instance, consider the program of Example 3.3 which executes the sum of a sequence of numbers different from zero, terminated by a zero. Once coded in 'full C' it becomes the following program:

```
                                              /*Program SumSequence*/
#include <stdio.h>
main()
{
   int   datum, sum;
   sum = 0;
   scanf("%d", &datum);
   while (datum != 0)
   {
      sum = sum + datum;
      scanf("%d", &datum);
   }
   printf("The sum of the numbers typed in is: %d\n", sum);
}
```

Clearly, the essential features of this program already existed in the simplified version of Example 3.3. The full C program, however, contains some new symbols and special words that do not contribute to algorithm description but are necessary for the compiler.

This brief chapter fills up the remaining 'gaps'. First, in Section 4.1, we describe the syntactic structure of a complete C program: this will allow us to include those few points that were lacking in Chapter 3 and a few more besides. Many other important language features, however, will be described systematically in subsequent chapters. Then, in Section 4.2, we will eventually be able to write our first 'running' C programs, such as the one just exemplified.

4.1 The structure of C programs

At the very minimum a C program must contain, in order:

- A **directives** part, which contains directives for the compiler. A very limited use of this part will be illustrated in Section 4.1.2.
- The predefined identifier `main` followed by the pair `()`; so far, the meaning of the reserved identifier `main` and of the pair `()` has remained rather obscure. It will become clear in Chapter 7.
- Two parts, syntactically enclosed by the pair `{ }`:
  - the **declarative** part
  - the **executable** part

The declarative part of a program lists all the elements that are part of the program together with their principal characteristics. The executable part consists of a sequence of statements as described in Chapter 3. Let us first focus our attention on the declarative part.

4.1.1 The declarative part of a program

The declarative part is placed before the code of the algorithm and contains, besides other declarations that will be explained in the following chapters, the following items:

- the **constant declaration** section
- the **variable declaration** section

At first sight, forcing programmers to list the objects they are going to use in the executable part of their programs seems a pointless exercise. However, experience has shown that the extra effort required in the program development phase is more than compensated by the better **diagnostics** (or *signalling of errors*) allowed by this rule. For example, consider two instructions such as

```
x = alpha;
aloha = alpha + 1;
```

where the o of `aloha` is written instead of `p` by mistake. If we do not compel the programmer to list all variables used in the program, the abstract machine of the language cannot do anything other than interpret `aloha` as a new variable and, obviously, produce an erroneous result. In C, instead, the compiler would immediately identify aloha as a variable not present in the declarative part and signal this error to the programmer, who could then correct the program in a much more efficient way.

In the following subsections, we discuss in more depth the rules for declarations of variables and constants in C, although, generally, in a C program the declaration of constants precedes the declaration of variables.

Variable declaration

The aim of variable declaration is to list all the variables used in the executable part and to attribute to each of them a **type**, that is, to specify the characteristics that govern their use.

The variable declaration section of a program consists of a list of variable declarations. Each variable declaration, in turn, consists of a **type specifier**, followed by a list of one or more variable identifiers separated by a `,`; each variable declaration ends with a `;`.

Thus, a variable declaration associates a list of identifiers with a type. All identifiers in the same list are declared of the same type. The type of a variable is understood as the set of values that the variable can take (the concept of type is discussed in more depth in Chapter 5). For the time being, we use only the three simple types already introduced in Chapter 3: integers, real numbers and characters. Thus, a type specifier can be one of the keywords **int**, **float** or **char**.

For instance, if, in a program, we use the variables x and y of real type, i and j of integer type and symb of character type, the corresponding declarative part might be as follows:

```
float    x,y;
int      i,j;
char     symb;
```

Note that the following declaration would also be correct:

```
float    x;
int      i,j;
char     symb;
float    y;
```

If a variable identifier x is declared as **int**, it can only be used as such in the executable part. Consequently, it will never contain a real value, say, 3.14.

Constant declaration

A constant declaration *permanently* associates a value with an identifier. As for variables, the constant declaration section consists of a list of constant declarations. Each constant declaration, in turn, consists of:

- The keyword **const**.
- The type specifier, which specifies the type of the constant.

- The identifier of the constant.
- The symbol =.
- The value of the constant. This can be, among other things, an integer number, with or without sign, a real number or a character.
- The usual 'terminator' ;.

Examples of constant declarations are the following:

```
const    float    Pi = 3.14;
const    float    Pi = 3.1415, e = 2.718;
const    int      N = 100, M = 1000;
const    char     CHAR1 = 'A', CHAR2 = 'B';
```

Notice that, for the sake of brevity, we can group the declaration of several constants of the same type into a single list.

The declaration of a constant must not be confused with the assignment statement even though the effect of this declaration is equivalent to assigning a value to a variable which will remain unchanged throughout the execution of the program (indeed, any attempt to assign a value to a constant would be signalled as an error by the compiler).

For instance, the statement

```
CircleArea = Pi*CircleRadius*CircleRadius;
```

is equivalent to:

```
CircleArea = 3.14*CircleRadius*CircleRadius;
```

if it occurs in a program that contains the first of the above declarations. It is equivalent to:

```
CircleArea = 3.1415*CircleRadius*CircleRadius;
```

instead, if the second declaration of Pi has been given.

The above examples should emphasize the usefulness of constant declarations. First, the use of an identifier for a constant instead of its effective value allows the information it represents to be treated in a symbolic way, which immediately helps us to perceive its meaning when reading the program.

It should be noted that, in geometry books, we read that 'the surface area of a circle is the product of its squared radius multiplied by π' and not by '3.14', '3.1415', or '3.14159'. Here, because the Greek letter π is not part of the alphabet of C, we had to write it as Pi, but the fact remains that we preferred to use *a symbolic notation of an abstract value instead of a concrete approximation.*

Even more important is the fact that the use of constants allows programs to be parametrized; this makes them easily reusable when certain external circumstances change.

The case of the number π can help us to explain this assertion. The value 3.14 is the 'normal' approximation for π. Sometimes, a higher precision might be needed, for example with four decimal digits instead of two. In this case, adapting a program that uses π without a constant declaration would require us to change the value 3.14 into 3.1415 everywhere it is used. If, instead, the declaration:

```
const    float    Pi = 3.14;
```

is used properly (this implies: 'if in the executable part of the program *only* the identifier `Pi` is used and *never* its value 3.14'), then the program can be adapted to the new precision requirements simply by changing the above declaration into:

```
const    float   Pi = 3.1415;
```

Further advantages of constant declarations will be illustrated later. In Chapter 5 we will also see a different means for the declaration of constants.

4.1.2 The executable part of a program: the input/output statements

As we already anticipated, the structure of the executable part of a C program consists of a sequence of statements as described in Chapter 3: the only things we need to make it really executable are appropriate input/output statements.

Strictly speaking, the C language does not possess statements for input and output, but a C programmer can use a set of **predefined functions** (**subprograms**) to realize particular operations. These functions (among them the input/output functions) belong to the **standard library** whose functions are made available in each ANSI C programming environment. Thus, the `printf` and `scanf` identifiers are the names of two functions (called **library functions**) which, when called properly within the code of a C program, write to the Standard Output (for example, on a screen) and read from the Standard Input (for example, from the keyboard), respectively.

Since we have not, as yet, defined the concept of function in a C program, for the time being we shall consider (with much approximation) `printf` and `scanf` as normal instructions whose use is defined here more precisely, with respect to the simplified version given in Chapter 3.

`printf` requires the presence of a control string and a set of elements to be printed. The statement in a C program that causes a set of elements to be displayed on the screen is constructed as follows:

```
printf(control string, set of elements to be printed);
```

The **control string** is a string that is written to the output. It contains so-called **conversion** or **format characters** preceded by the symbol % and certain other symbols. The format characters %d, %f, %c, %s used in the following examples cause the output on Standard Output of an integer decimal number, a real (floating point) number, a character and a string of characters, respectively (they are called 'conversion characters' because they cause the conversion into characters that is needed to print on the Standard Output device). The symbol \n can also be present in the control string; it causes a carriage return/line feed so that writing continues from the beginning of a new line. Thus, the control string allows the output format to be specified. The set of elements to be printed is a list of correctly identified variables, constants or compound expressions with variables and constants. Two simple examples clarify the use of `printf`.

EXAMPLE 4.1

Consider the statement

```
printf("The annual salary of employees in category %d is $ %f", empl_cat,
       aver_sal);
```

- If empl_cat is a variable of **int** type which represents the category of employees, the printf statement is executed using its current value, say 6.
- If aver_sal is a variable of **float** type which represents the average salary calculated for the group of employees, the printf statement is executed using its current value, say 157 058.0.

The execution of the printf statement causes the following sentence to be displayed on the screen:

```
The annual salary of employees in category 6 is $ 157058.0
```

EXAMPLE 4.2

The following statement has a somewhat complex control string: it best explains why we decided to simplify I/O statements in Chapter 3):

```
printf("%s\n%c%c\n\n%s\n", "This program has been written by",
       first_init, name_init, "Enjoy working with it!");
```

- If first_init is a variable of **char** type which represents the initial of the programmer's first name, the printf statement is executed using its current value, say G.
- If name_init is a variable of **char** type which represents the initial of the programmer's surname, the printf statement is executed using its current value, say M.

The execution of the printf statement causes the following sentences to be displayed on the screen:

```
This program has been written by
GM

Enjoy working with it!
```

Note the effect of the \n symbols in the control string: the first \n causes the new line between the string 'This program has been written by' and the two characters 'GM', the second \n causes a new line after the two characters 'GM' and the third \n, causing another new line, produces the blank line between the two characters 'GM' and the string 'Enjoy working with it!'

scanf, too, requires the specification of a control string and a set of elements to be read. The statement in a C program that reads a set of elements from the keyboard looks like this:

```
scanf(control string, set of elements to be read);
```

The control string contains conversion or format characters preceded by the symbol %. Thus, the control string specifies how the characters read from the keyboard are to be interpreted (%d for decimal integers, %f for real numbers, %c for characters or %s for strings). The list of elements to be read gives the names of the variables to which the values read are to be assigned. The variable names are preceded by the unary operator &. The meaning of this operator will become clear only in Chapter 9, but a simple example can clarify the use of scanf right now.

EXAMPLE 4.3

Consider the following statement:

```
scanf("%c%c%c%d%f", &c1, &c2, &c3, &i, &x);
```

If, when the scanf statement is executed, the user types the following data:

ABC 3 7.345

then:

- the variable c1 (of **char** type) assumes the value 'A' as a consequence of the execution of the scanf statement. The character A is stored by scanf in the memory cell whose address is the address of the variable c1 (&c1 should be read as ' the address of variable c1');
- variable c2 (of type **char**) assumes the value 'B';
- variable c3 (of type **char**) assumes the value 'C';
- variable i (of type **int**) assumes the value 3;
- variable x (of type **float**) assumes the value 7.345.

To write simple but compilable C programs we must briefly return to the fact that printf and scanf are not true statements of the C language, but functions available in the standard library.

The code of library functions is resident in the ANSI C programming environment (and therefore available to be included in the code of the source program). It is the programmer's responsibility, though, to declare which library functions are going to be used within a program. Without going into the detail that we will in Chapter 7, it is enough to state here that *each program that uses the functions* printf *and* scanf *must declare the use of these functions in the directives part which precedes the main program.* The easiest way to do this is to put the following statement before the header main():

```
#include <stdio.h>
```

where the term 'stdio' is an abbreviation for 'Standard Input/Output'. This directive is given to a part of the compiler, called the preprocessor, which includes a copy of the contents of the file stdio.h. Among the function definitions contained in stdio.h we find those of printf and scanf. This allows the correct compilation of a program that uses printf and scanf in its executable part and the correct production of the executable code, thanks to the use of the code that the C system makes available for printf and scanf.

4.2 First examples of executable C programs

We are now ready at last to write our first 'real' C programs: the first examples are given in this section. Chapters 5–9 will continue the systematic exposition of the most relevant features of C, their syntax, their semantics (that is, their meaning) and their use. Appendix D provides a full description of the syntax of C. It also introduces a standard formal notation that is particularly suited to describing precisely all the details of the syntax of a programming language.

EXAMPLE 4.4

The following program is perhaps the simplest program one can ever write in C: it writes, on the Standard Output, the sentence 'This is my first C program':

```
                                                        /*FirstCProgram*/
#include <stdio.h>
main()
{
    printf("This is my first C program/n");
}
```

Note that there is no declarative part in the program FirstCProgram, as it does not use any variable or constant.

EXAMPLE 4.5

The following program shows the use of variable declarations and the organization of the Standard Output into lines: it reads two integer values from the Standard Input and writes their sum to the Standard Output:

```
                                                      /*Program TwoIntegerSum*/
#include <stdio.h>
main()
{
   int a, b, sum;
   scanf("%d%d", &a, &b);
   sum = a + b;
   printf("The sum of a+b is:\n%d \nBye!\n", sum);
}
```

If the numbers 3 and 5 are typed in, executing the program produces the following message on the Standard Output:

```
The sum of a+b is:
8
Bye!
```

If we had omitted the first two \n symbols in the control string of the `printf` statement, the effect of executing the program would have been:

```
The sum of a+b is:8 Bye!
```

If a variable declaration had been missing, the compiler would have signalled an error.

The program `TwoIntegerSum` is also our first example of an interactive program, if the Standard Input and the Standard Output are the keyboard and screen display, respectively. Indeed, during its execution a simple 'dialogue' takes place between the user and the computer: the user supplies the addenda to the computer which 'replies' by displaying the sum on the screen.

You should now be ready to write your own programs and to run them on your own machine. The following exercises suggest a path to achieve such a goal.

Exercises

4.1 Go back to the programs given in the examples and exercises of Chapter 3. Rewrite them in full C, then compile and execute them on a computer available to you (the programs that use arrays should be postponed until you have read Chapter 5).

4.2 Modify the program `TwoIntegerSum` given in Example 4.5 in such a way that the user–computer dialogue takes place as shown in the following:

Computer: `Type the value of a (must be integer)`

User: `...`

Computer: `Type the value of b (must be integer)`

User: `...`

> *Computer:*   The sum of a + b is:
>
> ...
>
> Bye!

4.3   Write a program that reads a real number r and outputs the value of the area of the circle whose radius is of length r. The user–computer dialogue should resemble the following:

> *Computer:*   Type the value of r (must be a real number)
>
> *User:*   ...
>
> *Computer:*   Assuming that the value of Pi is 3.14 the area of the circle whose radius is of length r is:
>
> ...
>
> Bye!

Then modify your program in such a way that the adopted approximation of Pi is 3.1415 instead of 3.14.

Data types

5

We have already seen that a C program manipulates data of different types. In the examples of Chapter 4 we introduced variable and constant declarations as parts of the program which associate each variable and constant with its type. In Chapter 3 we showed that it may be convenient to aggregate or group various logically correlated elements into sequences called arrays. This chapter is a systematic introduction to the concept of a data type and the use of types in C.

A sufficiently general and rigorous idea of the concept of a data type is given by the following definition: a **data type** is a set of values and a set of operations that can be applied to that set of values.

For example, integers consist of the set $\{\ldots, -2, -1, 0, +1, +2, \ldots\}$ and the usual arithmetic operations (sum, difference, ...).

Each data type has its own representation in memory, that is, it is represented by an appropriate coding which uses a certain number of memory cells. In Chapter 2, we looked at the modes of representing numbers (distinguishing between positive integers, signed integers, fractions and real numbers) and characters, and more will be said about this subject in Chapter 13. Each piece of information is coded by an appropriate sequence of bits; fortunately though, in high-level programming languages it is possible to treat information in an *abstract* manner[1], that is, without worrying about how it is represented inside the machine. Just to show how important such abstraction is, imagine having to read the Bible coded as a sequence of bits corresponding to the ASCII representation of each single letter!

In C, all the variables in a program have a type associated with them; this type is fixed, once and for all, in the declaration. This fact has the following important consequences:

---

[1] In this text we strive for as abstract a use of data types as possible. C, however, like most practical programming languages does not completely support the construction and use of really *abstract data types*, as occasionally it allows – or even imposes – the use of data types assuming some knowledge of their internal – or concrete – representation. At critical points we will explicitly point out whether or not the use of a data type is really abstract.

- For each variable it is possible to determine, a priori, the set of admissible values, that is, the values that the variable can take during the execution of the program and the set of operations that can be applied to the variable.

- For each variable it is possible to determine, a priori, the necessary amount of memory (which may vary from machine to machine). This can be calculated on the basis of the representation of that variable's data type. A **char** variable, for example, generally requires 1 byte (8 bits) for its representation and an **int** variable generally requires one memory word (16 bits on some machines, 32 on others), whereas some machines allocate 4 bytes to **float** type variables. Consequently, the memory needed to execute a program can be calculated and allocated during compilation without influencing the efficiency of the execution itself. (We will see in Chapters 8 and 10 that there is an exception to this rule.)

- During the compilation of the program, it is possible to detect errors in the use of variables. It should always be remembered that the C language requires a type definition for each variable and constant involved in an expression or an assignment and that the defined type determines the set of operations that can be applied to them. The C compiler can therefore detect the presence of expressions or assignments that involve variables or constants of heterogeneous types.

  - If the terms are homogeneous, the operation that is executed is the one associated with the particular type.

  - If the terms are heterogeneous, the compiler can evaluate these expressions and assignments, automatically applying a set of rules (called implicit conversion rules) aimed at transforming the expression or assignment into an expression or assignment involving variables and constants of homogeneous type.

  - If the transformation is successful, the execution of the expression or assignment can be carried out correctly (the type of the result is defined correctly and the operation is executed correctly).

  - If the transformation is unsuccessful, an error is signalled during the compilation phase.

The remainder of this chapter is organized as follows: first we present a classification of C data types. These will then be examined in a systematic way, without going into too many non-essential and specialized features of the language. Finally, we briefly discuss the organization of data types in other languages.

5.1 Classification of data types

Variables in a program can represent simple information, such as a speed or a temperature; in these cases, the use of a numeric variable is a natural solution. Data types used to represent this kind of information are therefore called **simple types**.

But a program may need to deal with more complex information, such as a date (composed of three elementary pieces of data: day, month and year) or the data sheet for a client of a surgery (composed of personal data, illnesses and their dates, treatments, analyses and so on). It is possible to represent this information using separate variables: for example, we can represent a date using three integers. However, the programmer must then remember that the three integers are not independent, but only make sense when interpreted as the three components of a date. Anyone with experience of mail correspondence between the USA and Europe knows that it is easy to get dates confused because of the different order in which the three elements of a date are written (month, day, year or day, month, year). This shows how convenient it is to treat information in an abstract rather than a concrete manner: it is less equivocal to refer to the day of a date than to the first integer that codes it. Thus, something like a type 'date', provided with adequate operations, would allow the programmer to treat date information in a more abstract manner than would be possible when referring to a concrete representation in memory.

When information consists of an aggregation of various components, the corresponding data types are called **structured types**.

In Chapter 3, we saw a first way of building structured data: an array can represent complex information consisting of a sequence of homogeneous elements such as a list of invoices. We will deal with various modes of structuring data in more depth in Section 5.5.

The fundamental difference between simple and structured types is not so much in the amount of memory required as in the fact that the information contained in a simple type variable is logically indivisible, whereas the information contained in a structured type variable can be decomposed into its components. Consequently, one can access the third element of the array `invoices`, but not the third digit of an integer variable, even though it can be represented as a sequence of digits in the machine.

A quick survey of possible computer applications shows an almost infinite range of data types (both simple and structured) for the various abstract concepts that can be used in a program: for example, 'employee', 'colour', 'car', 'insurance policy' and so on. However, it would be impossible for a programming language to provide all the types of information that correspond to the various abstractions necessary to describe reality.

The C language, like almost all modern languages, provides us with a simple and powerful solution to this problem: the possibility of defining and constructing new types, called **user-defined types**, to be used alongside those **built-in** to the language. Consequently, we can define a new data type for each 'category of information' (dates, invoices, employees, salaries) and treat the variables of each type in an abstract manner.

Let us recapitulate what we have learnt in this section about the characteristics of data types:

(1) To deal with the potentially infinite number of abstract data types, the C language allows the user to define new data types to be used alongside those already existing in the language. From this viewpoint, types can be divided into two categories:

(a)   predefined or pre-existent or built-in types

(b)   user-defined types

(2)   On the basis of their structure, types can be divided into another two categories:

(a)   simple types

(b)   structured types

The following section presents the simple predefined types available in C; subsequent sections show how simple and structured user-defined types can be declared in C.

5.2 Simple predefined types

The C language has four simple and predefined basic types: **char** (characters), **int** (integers), **float** (real numbers), **double** (double precision real numbers). The type 'qualifiers' **signed** or **unsigned** can be applied to **char** and **int**, **short** or **long** to **int**, and **long** to **double**. This generates the 12 simple predefined types listed in Table 5.1.

Table 5.1 C's predefined simple data types.

Predefined type	Alternative denominations
char	
signed char	
unsigned char	
signed short int	signed short, short
signed int	signed, int
signed long int	long int, signed long, long
unsigned short int	unsigned short
unsigned int	unsigned
unsigned long int	unsigned long
float	
double	
long double	

The type qualifiers **short** and **long** determine the space allocated by the compiler to store the typed variables (the allocated space depends on the machine used).

The type qualifiers **signed** and **unsigned**, **short** and **long** (in their possible combinations) determine the set of values that the typed variable can take, together with its maximum and minimum values.

It is not necessary to declare built-in types: their identifiers and representations are already defined a priori.

Let us now examine the main features of the various types.

5.2.1 The int type

Recalling the definition of type given at the beginning of this chapter, the type 'integer' is not just the set $\{\ldots, -1, 0, 1, 2, \ldots\}$, but this same set 'equipped' with sum, difference, multiplication and so on.

Obviously, the mathematical 'integer' type has infinite values and also infinite operations defined on those values. The position of the **int** type is slightly different in C, where the set of possible values and the corresponding operations are limited a priori. The built-in type is, therefore, an *approximation* of the corresponding mathematical type.

The space allocated to an **int** and the set of values it may take depend on the particular machine on which the program is going to be executed, but we can state the following.

Normally, an **int** is stored in one word (the most widely used machines have 16-bit or 32-bit words). A compiler can allocate less memory to a **short int** (normally 16 bits), but does not necessarily do so. A compiler can allocate more memory to a **long int** (normally 32 bits), but again does not necessarily do so. Regardless of the machine on which a program is executed, the following property holds:

allocated space (**short int**) <= allocated space (**int**)

<= allocated space (**long int**)

The binary representation of a **signed int** in n bits uses one bit to represent the sign, whereas the binary representation of an **unsigned int** uses all n bits to represent the integer value which is assumed to be positive.

For a **signed int** represented in a 16-bit word, the set of values is $\{-2^{15}, \ldots, 2^{15} - 1\}$. (More details can be found in Chapter 13.) The implementation of the language, therefore, influences the maximum representable value of a signed integer. The minimum and maximum integer values have a predefined symbolic denotation, named INT_MIN and INT_MAX, respectively. INT_MIN and INT_MAX are predefined constant identifiers, exactly as **int** is a predefined type identifier; their values, too, are predefined, with the difference that they are predefined *by the implementation, not by the definition* of the language. The definition is contained in the file <limits.h> of the standard library. The inclusion of this file (via the directive #include <limits.h>) allows the use of the constants defined in it.

For an **unsigned int** represented in a 16-bit word, the set of values is $\{0, \ldots, 2^{16} - 1\}$. The implementation of the language, therefore, also influences the maximum representable value of an unsigned integer.

Regardless of the machine on which a program is executed, the following property holds:

allocated space (**signed int**) = allocated space (**unsigned int**)

The operations that can be applied in C to **int** type data (and to a type derived through type qualifiers) are shown in Table 5.2.

Table 5.2   Built-in operations for **int** type data.

=	Assignment of an **int** value to an **int** variable
+	Sum (between **int** has an **int** as result)
−	Difference (between **int** has an **int** as result)
*	Multiplication (between **int** has an **int** as result)
/	Division truncating the fractional part (result **int**)
%	Remainder of the integer division
==	'Equal' relation
!=	'Not equal' relation
<	'Less than' relation
>	'Greater than' relation
<=	'Less or equal' relation
>=	'Greater or equal' relation

Note: A relation operation on two int type values produces as its result the integer value 0 if the relation is false, and a nonzero value if the relation is true.

If an operation produces a result which does not belong to the set of allowed values (for example, if the result of a multiplication is greater than INT_MAX), the result is an error message (*Integer Overflow*) to inform the user that the concrete result does not correspond to the expected abstract value.

Let us now further familiarize ourselves with the **int** type through a simple example.

EXAMPLE 5.1

The following program reads a sequence of positive integer numbers representing different years (the input sequence ends with a number less than or equal to 0). The program checks which numbers refer to a leap year. The algorithm takes into account that the number representing a leap year is a multiple of 4.

```
                                                  /*Program Leap Years*/
#include <stdio.h>
main()
{
   int     year, remainder;
   printf("Insert a positive integer number to check if it corresponds
           to a leap year - a negative number or the 0 value ends the
           program\n");
   scanf("%d", &year);
   while (year > 0)
   {
                      /*when a number is a multiple of 4 the remainder of
                        its integer division by 4 equals 0*/
      remainder = year % 4;
      if (remainder == 0) printf("The year %d is a leap year\n", year);
```

```
        else printf("The year %d is not a leap year\n", year);
        printf("Insert a positive integer number to check if it
               corresponds to a leap year - a negative number or
               the 0 value ends the program\n");
        scanf("%d", &year);
    }
☛ 1           }
```

5.2.2 The `float` and `double` types

Types **float** and **double** are obviously an approximation of mathematics' real numbers, not only from the point of view of their limits, but also from the point of view of precision of representation: it is clear that it will never be possible to represent (the exact value of) every real number in the memory of a computer.

We have already seen in Chapter 2 one way of representing a real type value. This is the normal decimal, or fixed point, notation in which we could write:

    3.14
    1 234.543 328
    543.
    0.000 076

This method becomes extremely wasteful, in terms of memory capacity and graphical representation, for very big and very small (absolute) values. For example, to represent 10^{900} or 10^{-900} in this way would require an enormous number of digits and therefore memory cells, all containing 0s.

In these cases it is preferable to use floating point notation which, in fact, uses the base and exponent representation that we have just used for 10^{900} and 10^{-900}.

Syntactically, in C, the **floating point notation** consists of two parts: a **mantissa** and an **exponent**, that is, two numbers, separated by the character 'e'. If a number n has mantissa m and exponent e, its value is $n = m \cdot 10^e$.

For instance, the number 1780 000.000 0023 can be represented in the following ways:

    178 000.000 000 23e1
    17 800 000 000 023e−7
    1.780 000 000 0023e +6

and so on.

Note that possible rounding off due to the loss of less significant digits could transform the above number into 1.780e6, that is 1780 000., which does not constitute a serious error. More details on floating point notation, with particular attention to its use *inside* the computer, are given in Chapter 13.

Both notations, fixed and floating point, can be used both in the computer's memory (in this case numbers are represented in binary form) and externally, that is, when a user types a real number on a terminal or the computer prints it out to be read. If the contents of two real variables are represented in both ways and we have to add them, for example, we do not have to worry because the machine automatically performs the format conversion.

The space allocated to variables of **float** type and **double** type, and the set of values these variables may take, depend on the particular machine on which the program is going to be executed; however, the following holds.

A C compiler normally allocates more memory to a **double** type variable than to a **float** type one (although it need not necessarily do so). On many machines, a **float** is stored in 4 bytes and a **double** in 8 bytes. This gives a precision of 6 decimal digits for a **float** and 15 decimal digits for a **double**, and a set of values approximately between 10^{-38} and 10^{+38} for a **float** and between 10^{-308} and 10^{+308} for a **double**.

A C compiler can allocate more memory for a **long double** type variable than for a **double** one, although it need not necessarily do so (many compilers, though not all, allocate the same memory space to **double** and **long double** type variables). Regardless of the machine on which a program is executed, however, the following holds:

allocated space (**float**) <= allocated space (**double**)

<= allocated space (**long double**)

The operations that can be applied in C to **float**, **double** or **long double** type variables are listed in Table 5.3. The standard library, moreover, provides many useful predefined mathematical functions (**sqrt**, **pow**, **exp**, **sin**, **cos**, **tan**, ...) usually dealing with **double** type variables; for this reason in the following programs we will often use the type **double** rather than **float** to refer to real numbers (more information about this subject can be found in Chapter 7 and Appendix C).

The following examples will help familiarize us with the real type.

Table 5.3 Built-in operations for **float**, **double** and **long** type data.

=	Assignment
+	Sum
−	Difference
*	Multiplication
/	Division (with real result –the symbol is identical to that used for integer division)
==	'Equal' relation
!=	'Not equal' relation
<	'Less than' relation
>	'Greater than' relation
<=	'Less or equal' relation
>=	'Greater or equal' relation

Note: A relation operation on two float (double or long) type values produces as its result the integer value 0 if the relation is false, and a nonzero value if the relation is true.

EXAMPLE 5.2

The following program reads a temperature in degrees Fahrenheit (F) and returns the corresponding temperature in degrees Celsius (C) using the formula $C = (5/9)(F - 32)$. Note that the algorithm applies the formula expressing numbers 5 and 9 as real numbers (with the decimal point and a fractional digit). In this way the symbol / involving two real operands correctly produces as a result a real number, which is needed to avoid a mistake: an expression involving two integer numbers (5 and 9) would produce a 0 result owing to the integer division of two integer numbers. The expression involved in this program will be discussed in more depth in Section 5.7.1.

```
                                    /*Program from Fahrenheit to Celsius*/
#include <stdio.h>
main()
{
   int     FTemp,
   float   CTemp;
   printf("Insert the temperature in degrees Fahrenheit to be converted
          into degrees Celsius\n");
   scanf("%d", &FTemp);
   CTemp = (5.0 / 9.0) * (FTemp - 32);
   printf("%d degrees Fahrenheit correspond to %f degrees Celsius\n",
          FTemp, CTemp);
}
```

EXAMPLE 5.3

The following program reads the radius (r) of a sphere and computes its volume using the formula $V = (4/3)\pi r^3$.

```
                                    /*Program volume of a sphere*/
#include <stdio.h>
main()
{
   const   float   Pi = 3.1415;
   float   volume, radius;
   printf("Insert the radius of the sphere\n");
   scanf("%f", &radius);
   volume = (4.0/3.0) * Pi * radius * radius * radius;
   printf("The volume of the sphere having radius %f is %f\n",
          radius, volume);
}
```

Notes on the use of reals

In line with the fundamental mathematical characteristics of real numbers, the techniques used for their representation and processing can introduce approximation errors. For example, in certain circumstances, the number 1 could be replaced by the value 0.999 999. Consequently, it is extremely dangerous, although not formally prohibited, to execute exact 'equal' comparisons between real values. For example, the expression

```
(x/y) * y == x
```

might produce the result `false` (the equal relation between real values is verified simply by checking that the bit sequences that represent them are identical, using the same representation technique).

It is therefore recommended to 'include an acceptable margin of error' when comparing two real values.

For example, instead of writing

```
if (x==y) ...
```

write

```
if (x<=y + .000001 && y<=x + .000001)...
```

We will not go more deeply into the automatic processing techniques for real numbers, since those techniques belong to the field of numeric calculus, not programming.

5.2.3 The `char` type

Another simple C language type we already know is **char**, an abbreviation of the word 'character'. The obviously finite set of characters, that is, of **char** type data, is, for the most part, the set of ASCII characters and must in any case contain all the letters, digits and symbols that are available on normal keyboards. The ASCII coding allows each character to be represented by an appropriate integer value. The set of ASCII characters, like any encoding, defines the order of the values, in the sense that for each pair of characters x and y, $x < y$ if and only if x precedes y in the list of characters.

Some characters are **control characters**, in the sense that writing them does not print a symbol on paper or on the screen, but executes an operation concerned with the visualization of the data: one example we have already encountered is the 'newline' character, written in C as \n, which causes a new line to be started when the data is visualized (other particularly important control characters are \b = 'backspace', \t = 'horizontal tab', \r = 'carriage return').

The ANSI C compiler allocates one byte to a **char** type variable and one byte to a variable of **signed char** or **unsigned char** type. One byte can represent 256 different binary values. For a **signed char**, the set of values is from −128 to +127, for an **unsigned char**, from 0 to 255. The type **char** is equivalent to either **signed char** or **unsigned char**, depending on the compiler.

Operations defined for the **char** type are the assignment (=), the arithmetic (+, −, *, /, %) and the relational (==, !=, < and so on) operations listed in Table 5.1. The fact that **char** and **int** share the same operations is a natural consequence of the representation of characters as integer numbers. To analyse the relationship between characters and integers in C, let us consider the following example.

EXAMPLE 5.4

The following program reads a sequence of characters (the character # ends the sequence); for each character read the program prints its ASCII code and, in the case of a lowercase alphabetic letter, transforms it into the uppercase one.

```
                                          /*Program handling characters*/
#include <stdio.h>
main()
{
    char      C, UC;
    printf("insert a character - # to end the program\n");
    scanf("%c", &C);
    while (C != '#')
    {
        printf("The ASCII code of character %c is %d\n", C, C);
                            /*if the character is a lowercase letter*/
        if (C >= 'a' && C <= 'z')
        {
            /*the difference 'a' - 'A' is the offset between the ASCII
            representation of uppercase and lowercase alphabetic letters*/
            UC = C - ('a' - 'A');
            printf("The uppercase letter for %c is %c and its ASCII code is
                    %d\n", C, UC, UC);
            scanf("insert a character - # to end the program\n");
            scanf("%c", &C);
        }
    }
}
```

The standard library provides various predefined functions for character manipulation; refer to Appendix C for further information.

Note that, in a rather intuitive manner, we have used some operational symbols in the same way for different data types (for example, <): formally, they denote different operations for different data types, even though their meaning is clearly inspired by the symbol used to denote the operations. Thus, not only 2 < 34, but also 'A' < 'R', '(' < '3' and '5' < 'A' hold.

5.2.4 Classification of basic C data types

Let us summarize and complement the essential features of C's basic types. A character type variable (**char**, **signed char**, or **unsigned char**) is represented in memory by an integer number. The same goes for integer type variables (whether **short**, **int**, **long**, **unsigned short**, **unsigned** or **unsigned long**). This fact justifies the classification of predefined types in C given in Table 5.4.

Table 5.4 Classification of C's predefined simple types.

Integral types:		
char	signed char	unsigned char
short	int	long
unsigned short	unsigned	unsigned long
Floating types:		
float	double	long double
Arithmetic types:	integral types + floating types	

Characters are indeed treated as short integers, and short integers can be treated as characters. Each expression that has an integral type result can be printed in character or integer format. This conversion is possible using, in the printf 'command', the format descriptors %c or %d, respectively, as shown in Example 5.4.

All arithmetic types in C share some important characteristics:

- They are totally ordered, that is, for each pair of values x and y, with x != y, either x < y or y < x.

- They are limited, in the sense that they possess a maximum and a minimum value. In the case of integers and real numbers, this is due to the limits of their concrete representation, whereas the mathematical type would be unlimited. Thanks to the floating point representation, however, the limits of real numbers can often be ignored.

Furthermore, the integral types, as opposed to the floating types, are **discrete sets**. This means that they can be enumerated, that is, put into one-to-one correspondence with a subset of the natural numbers, maintaining their ordering. In other words, it would be possible to refer to: the first integer value, the smallest (greatest) integer value which follows (precedes) another integer value, the first character value, the second integer value and so on. This property does not hold for the **dense set** of real numbers insofar as, between two real values, there is (in the mathematical type) an infinite number of values. Rigorously speaking, the concrete representation of floating types is still discrete, since they represent anyway a finite set of possible values. However, using the floating point representation it is possible to denote an enormous number of values between, say, 3.0 and 4.0; thus we obtain a good approximation of the mathematical set of real numbers.

5.3 The definition of new types: syntactic rules

Let us now look at how user-defined types are built. First, we shall discuss general syntactic rules, and then present several of C's type constructors. From a syntactic point of view, all non-predefined data types used in a program must be declared, like any other element of the program. The type declaration is given in the declarative part of the program, between the declaration of constants and the declaration of variables (which we saw in Section 4.1.1).

A **type declaration** consists of the keyword **typedef**, followed by the specification of the new type (that is, how it is constructed from already existing types), the identifier of the new type and the symbol **;** which closes the declaration.

This means, for example, that a new type could be defined as follows, simply by renaming an already existing type:

```
typedef    int    year;
```

Once a new type has been defined and identified (named) through the keyword **typedef**, any variable can be declared of this type in the same way as it can be declared of any already existing type. For example:

```
char   x;
year   y;
```

In C new types can also be defined without using the keyword **typedef**. To be more precise we should say that the keyword **typedef** simply allows us to associate an identifier (a name) with a type (either a predefined type or a new one). But this construction allows a uniform style of defining types and associating them with appropriate identifiers. Therefore, in this book, we use it rather often, in an effort to achieve program generality.

Notice also that **typedef** does not allow us to define new operations applicable to the set of values specific to the new type. This somewhat hampers the use of new data types in an abstract way since knowledge of their internal structure – defined through the type declaration – is required to manage them. We shall consider this in more depth in Chapter 7, where we shall present a major tool to help the abstract use of data types.

Let us now systematically present the various modes for building the representation of a new type.

5.4 Simple user-defined types

The programmer can define new simple types by redefinition or by applying the explicit value enumeration constructor. These two mechanisms are illustrated in the following sections.

5.4.1 Redefinition

As we stated earlier, a new type can be created by simply renaming an existing type using a declaration such as the following:

```
typedef      ExistingType      NewType;
```

`ExistingType` can be either a built-in (predefined) type, for example, **int**, or a previously defined user-defined type. For example, we can write:

```
typedef      int       type1;
typedef      char      type2;
typedef      type1     type3;
typedef      type2     type4;
```

This is the first example of an extremely important characteristic of the construction of a new type: a new type can be constructed on the basis of a type already defined by the user; in turn, the new type can be used to define yet another new type and so on. We shall see shortly how important this feature is.

5.4.2 Explicit enumeration of values

A new type can also be constructed by enumerating all its values, enclosed in a pair of braces and separated by commas. Here are some examples which also clarify their meaning:

```
typedef enum {sun, mon, tue, wed, thu, fri, sat} WeekDay;
typedef enum {red, green, yellow, orange, purple, brown, black,
             ochre} colours;
typedef enum {John, Claudia, Carla, Simon, Serafino} persons;
typedef enum {jan, feb, mar, apr, may, jun, jul, aug, sep, oct,
             nov, dec} YearMonth;
```

Given the following variable declaration

```
persons individual, individual1, individual2;
```

it is possible to write statements such as

```
individual = John;
if (individual1 == individual2) individual = Claudia;
```

without enclosing the values `John` and `Claudia` in quotes (they are not string type values!).

For the sake of convenience and clarity the values of a new type are frequently represented by names. We have to keep in mind, though, that the compiler associates ascending integer values with these names and that these integer values are used for the evaluation of expressions, relations and assignments that involve variables of enumerated type. For example, a variable x declared of `month` type which, during program execution, takes the value `jan`, really takes the value 0 and it becomes 3 when it is assigned the value `apr`. Owing to this particular treatment of the enumerated type, it is often said that the definition of a new type via the enumeration constructor is nothing more than a redefinition of the **int** type. This is an example of lack of abstraction in C: in fact we are allowed to use the 'internal knowledge' of what the value of jan concretely is in the computer memory. We recommend, however, that this possibility *should not be abused*. The use of the new declared type, in fact, makes the program code much more readable, as shown in Example 5.7.

The particular relationship between integers and enumerated types also implies that the operations applicable to integers can be applied to enumerated values: the arithmetic operations (+, −, *, /, %), the operations of assignment (=), comparisons for 'equal' (==), 'not equal' (!=) and strict and weak precedence (<, <=, >, >=). In particular, the precedence relation is defined by the order in which the values of the type are listed. Thus, with regard to the above examples, the evaluation of each of the following relations yields a nonzero integer result (corresponding to the logical value 'true'):

```
apr < jun
red < orange
```

whereas the evaluation of each of the following relations yields as a result the integer value 0 (corresponding to 'false'):

```
sat < mon
Simon < John
```

From this we can deduce that a type constructed through enumeration is, in analogy to the integral types, a totally ordered, limited and enumerable type.

It is important to note that via the **enum** type constructor it is possible to define in C a type that in other languages, such as Pascal, exists as a predefined type: the type **boolean**. In Pascal, the boolean type contains only the two logical values true and false. On these, the classic logical operations AND, OR and NOT are defined.

In C, the definition of variables that can take the values true or false requires the declaration of a type using the **enum** type constructor:

```
typedef    enum {false, true} boolean;
boolean        flag, ok;
```

flag and ok can thus be defined as variables that can take the values true or false during the execution of a program in which they are involved. Their involvement in logical operations will become clear through the examples presented in Chapter 6.

5.5 Structured types

In Chapter 3, we introduced array variables as sequences of homogeneous elements, that is, as structured variables. Strictly speaking, however, C does not possess built-in structured data types. It does have, though, four type constructors that allow the definition of even highly complex structured types (array, **struct**, **union** and pointer). Three of these, array, **struct** and pointer, are described in the following subsections. The remaining one is omitted as it is little used.

5.5.1 **The array constructor**

The C language allows the declaration of array variables as follows:

```
int         list[20];
```

list is an array of 20 elements homogeneous in type (the type of each element is **int**). The 20 elements are ordered and accessible via an index whose value defines the position of the element we want to consider.

The above variable declaration also contains an *implicit declaration of a new type*; indeed, we could *explicitly* declare a new type named anArray in the following way:

```
typedef     int   anArray[20];
```

and then declare one or more variables of type anArray:

```
anArray           list1, list2;
```

The array in C is a mechanism that allows the construction of data types whose elements are *homogeneous sequences of values belonging to one single type*. Each element of a sequence is identified via an index which itself also belongs to a certain type.

Syntactically, the explicit declaration of a type obtained through the array constructor consists of:

- the keyword **typedef**, followed by
- the identifier of the type of the array's elements; it can be *any type* (pre-defined or user-defined, simple or structured), followed by
- the identifier of the new type obtained through the array constructor
- the array's dimension; this must be an integer constant enclosed within the pair [].

As shown in our example, once an array type has been constructed and has been given an identifier according to the above rule (anArray in the given example), one or more variables of that type can be declared in the variable declaration section by simply writing the name anArray followed by the (list of) variable(s) which is (are) attributed that type. If such a list contains more than one variable (list1 and list2 in the given example), its elements are separated by a *,*; the list is then ended by the usual *;*.

Instead, the abbreviated declaration of a single variable of a type obtained through the array constructor (normally, but wrongly, called an array type variable) consists of:

- the identifier of the type of the array's elements, followed by
- the identifier of the variable, followed by
- the array's dimension which, as in an explicit type definition, must be an integer constant enclosed within the pair `[]`.

This allows the declaration shown at the beginning of this section:

```
int        list[20];
```

The variable that will be used as an index to refer to the elements of the array must be an integral type (**int**, **char** or a type derived from them using type qualifiers). The index ranges from 0 up to the value enclosed within `[]` – 1.

Let us now examine various features of array declarations.

First, we observe that *the array is a type constructor, not a type*. The structured type obtained through a declaration such as the following:

```
typedef    int      anArray[20];
```

is not the generic type `anArray`, but rather the type 'array of 20 elements of **int** type', which is named `anArray` and whose index can take the integer values between 0 and 19. Analogously, the declaration:

```
typedef    double   NewList[30];
```

defines the type `NewList` as 'array of 30 **double** type elements whose index can take the integer values between 0 and 29'. This type is different from the preceding one.

Nevertheless, for the sake of brevity, it is often said that 'a certain variable is of array type' meaning that 'it is of a type obtained by using the array constructor'.

Next, we observe that *the declaration of an array can be implicit in the declaration of a variable*.

The above rules allow, as we have already seen, a declaration such as the following:

```
int             list[20];
```

or, alternatively, the following pair of declarations:

```
typedef    int   anonymous[20];
anonymous        list;
```

Obviously, any other identifier given to the type would have produced the same effect, as long as it did not interfere with other identifiers of the program.

When there is no reason to make the type identifier explicit, the first declaration is preferred to the second because it does not force the programmer to waste time inventing useless names.

For example, when coding numerical algorithms, it is generally both useless and tedious to write declarations such as:

```
typedef double   VectorOfReals[20];
VectorOfReals    v1, v2, v3;
```

instead of the simpler and just as clear:

```
double           v1[20], v2[20], v3[20];
```

On the other hand, the following declaration:

```
typedef double       MonthlyRain[12];
typedef double       ShareIndex[12];
MonthlyRain          Rain87, Rain88, Rain89;
ShareIndex           Index87, Index88, Index89;
```

would certainly be preferred to the shorter :

```
double               Rain87[12], Rain88[12], Rain89[12], Index87[12],
                     Index88[12], Index89[12];
```

The examples proposed in this book, experience and personal taste will guide readers towards their own good type declaration style.

Next, we observe that *array elements can be given arbitrary types* (built-in or user-defined, simple or structured). This feature allows a powerful programming style. It is therefore possible to have 'arrays of arrays', that is, arrays whose elements are, in their turn, arrays. Here are some new examples of the use of the array constructor:

```
typedef int          Vector[20];
typedef Vector       IntegerMatrix20By20[20];
```

and we can declare the variable `matrix1` as follows:

```
IntegerMatrix20By20   matrix1;
```

An alternative and more synthetic declaration for the type 'integer matrix 20 by 20' is:

```
typedef int          Matrix20By20[20][20];
```

and an alternative and more synthetic declaration for the variable `matrix1` is:

```
int                  matrix1[20][20];
```

A variable of tri-dimensional matrix type could be declared as:

```
int                  matrix3d1[10][20][30];
```

To access an element of `matrix3d1` we could write:

```
matrix3d1[2][8][15]
```

Referring back to the `colours` type defined in Section 5.4.2, we could define the variable `ColourList` as:

```
colours    ColourList[10];
```

Finally, note that *an array has fixed dimensions*. As a consequence of the fact that array dimensions must be an integer constant, the limits of an array's indices cannot change during program execution.

This rule can create some inconvenience. In many cases, while coding an algorithm, we do not know how many elements a structured variable will have to contain. Just look again at the examples you have seen so far: beginning with the problem of writing a list of data in reverse order, we needed to store an a priori unknown number of data items in an array. Also, the number of invoices issued by a company in a certain period of time cannot be known beforehand, nor the length of a word and so on.

Nevertheless, C and many other languages require the programmer to specify, in the type and variable declaration, how many elements each array and, in general, each structured variable contains.

The reason for this restriction is linked to the problems of implementing language compilers. If a language's abstract machine knows how much memory is needed before the execution of a program starts, the program can be executed more efficiently. This is because the abstract memory cells have to be mapped onto the physically available memory of the machine: if this operation can be carried out before starting the program, there will be no time lost, during program execution, as a result of having to find new physical cells to assign to structured variables that grow in an unforeseeable way. Thus, the most widely used programming languages still restrict the possibility of allocating new memory space during program execution to exceptional situations.

Consequently, whenever the number of elements of an array is not known beforehand, the programmer is forced to make an a priori estimate, trying to mediate between the risk of 'wasting' cells and the risk of overflow, that is, that the number of cells actually needed is higher than the number available. Clearly, the second risk is worse than the first.

A classical example of such a situation is given by character strings. We often have to group a text, that is, a sequence of characters, into words which by nature do not have a fixed length. Some trivial examples of this kind have already been examined: as long as they were treated in the small subset of C – which, however, was not executable – given in Chapter 3, we deliberately did not worry about the length of the arrays destined to store a word. But now we want to build compilable and executable C programs, thus we have to define the type string with a declaration such as the following:

```
typedef char      String[30];
```

and then declare variables such as:

```
String            FirstName, LastName;
```

It is clear that short words stored in these variables leave rather a large quantity of (physical) memory unused; on the other hand, very long names could occur which could not be stored in the declared variables. In such a case, it is the programmer's task to make sure that the lack of correspondence between abstract and concrete variable is at least appropriately signalled; in this case, any word that is longer than the above declaration. For example, while a word is being read in character by character, a counter WordLength could be updated and before each new character is read, the following statement could be executed:

```
if (WordLength == 30)
   printf("Word too long");
```

A greater flexibility in the use of arrays can be obtained, even though only partially, through an appropriate use of constant declarations, as suggested by the following example which also introduces an alternative mechanism offered by C to define constants.

EXAMPLE 5.5

Consider any program that processes an array, for example the following program which inverts the sequence of a fixed number of integers:

```
                                              /*Program Sequence Inversion*/
#include <stdio.h>

main()
{
    int     Counter;
    int     Storage[100];

    Counter = 0;
    while (Counter < 100)
                              /*recall that the value of the index of a
                              100 element array varies from 0 to 99*/
    {
        scanf("%d", &Storage[Counter]);
        Counter = Counter + 1;
    }
    Counter = Counter - 1;
    while (Counter >= 0)
    {
        printf("%d\n", Storage[Counter]);
        Counter = Counter - 1;
    }
}
```

This program needs to know from the start that the sequence to be inverted is composed of exactly 100 integers.

Let us suppose that we want to apply the program to sequences of 1000 integers: obviously, we have to modify it because it is based on the assumption that the length of the sequence is known a priori. The required modification is trivial but tedious and also dangerous: we have to replace all occurrences of the number 100 with the number 1000.

It is all too likely that in programs a trifle less trivial than this one, there will be many substitution points and one or two will be forgotten.

Even worse, it could be that in some places the number 100 is used with a different meaning, for example as a change of scale: in the rush, 100 could be replaced by 1000 even where its meaning is the latter one!

To manage such a change, a much better solution consists of declaring once and for all that a given identifier, say, SequenceLength, represents (is the same thing as) a particular value, say, 100. This cannot be obtained through the **const** declaration introduced in Chapter 4 but the directive #define, offered by C, can properly be used.

In our case, the directive

```
#define SequenceLength    100
```

added after the #include <stdio.h> directive and before the main would associate the identifier SequenceLength with the constant value 100. Unlike the **const** declaration, this constant declaration *does not allocate memory space* and the substitution of the constant value for the identifier is carried out by the preprocessor at compile time: this is fundamental to allow the allocation of needed memory cells at compile time.

Thus, consider the following new version of the program and see how much easier, and above all safer, the necessary modification is:

```
                                        /*Program Sequence Inversion*/
#include <stdio.h>
#define SequenceLength    100

main()
{
    int      Counter;
    int      Storage[SequenceLength];

    Counter = 0;
    while (Counter < SequenceLength)
    {
        scanf("%d", &Storage[Counter]);
        Counter = Counter + 1;
    }
    Counter = Counter - 1;
    while (Counter >= 0)
    {
        printf("%d\n", Storage[Counter]);
        Counter = Counter - 1;
    }
}
```

Note that the use of constants – realized in the case of array declarations through the #define directive – does not prevent the compiler from knowing exactly how many elements there are in an array before the execution of the program, which is the requirement that imposes limits on the construction of arrays. Obviously, a change in the declaration of a constant causes the compiler to re-examine the entire program: but now it is the machine, and not the programmer, that is landed with the job!

The elements of an array can be involved individually in all *operations* defined for the type that characterizes them. The array as a whole, however, cannot be involved in global comparison or assignment operations merely by using its identifier. (The reasons for this limitation will be discussed in Section 5.6 where we consider the close relationship that exists in C between the name of an array and the memory address of its first element.) Global assignment and comparison operations have to be carried out by going through the elements one by one, carrying out the assignment or comparison on each of them.

If `Array1` and `Array2` are two variables defined as follows:

```
typedef    int     AnArray[10];
AnArray            Array1, Array2;
```

an attempt to assign the values of the individual elements of `Array1` to the elements of `Array2` via the statement:

```
Array2 = Array1;
```

will not produce the expected result. The assignment has to be realized through a loop statement whose body involves the individual elements of the arrays identified through an appropriate value of their index (as shown in the previous example). The same happens if a string contained in `Array1` and a string contained in `Array2` have to be compared and concatenated to form a third string contained in `ArrayConc,` as shown in Example 5.6.

EXAMPLE 5.6

The following program reads two strings composed of exactly 50 characters each and builds a third string concatenating them in alphabetical order. The program returns the created string.

```
                                        /*Program String Concatenation*/
#include <stdio.h>
#define ArrayLength    50

main()
{
   int   i, j, k;
   char  TempChar;
   char  Array1[ArrayLength]; Array2[ArrayLength];
                /*in the following declaration the value ArrayLength*2
                is a constant value computed at compile time*/
   char  ArrayConc[ArrayLength*2];
                /*read the first string ensuring that it does not exceed
                the dimension of the array - 50 characters*/
   i = 0;
   scanf("%c", &TempChar);
   while (i < ArrayLength)
                /*recall that the value of the index of an array of
                ArrayLength elements varies from 0 to ArrayLength -1*/
```

```
{
   Array1[i] = TempChar;
   i = i + 1;
   scanf("%c", &TempChar);
}
                           /*read the second string ensuring that it
                           does not exceed the dimension of the array
                           - 50 characters*/
i = 0;
scanf("%c", &TempChar);
while (i < ArrayLength)
{
   Array2[i] = TempChar;
   i = i + 1;
   scanf("%c", &TempChar);
}
                           /*compare the two strings to understand which
                           one precedes the other in alphabetic order*/
i = 0;
while (i < ArrayLength && Array1[i] == Array2[i])
   i = i + 1;
if (i == ArrayLength || Array1[i] < Array2[i])
                           /*the two strings are equal or the first one
                           precedes the second in alphabetic order*/
{
   k = 0; j = 0;
   while (j < ArrayLength)
   {
      ArrayConc[k] = Array1[j];
      k = k + 1;
      j = j + 1;
   }
   j = 0;
   while (j < ArrayLength)
   {
      ArrayConc[k] = Array2[j];
      k = k + 1;
      j = j + 1;
   }
}
else
                           /*if the second string precedes the first
                           one in alphabetic order - if (Array2[i] <
                           Array1[i])*/
{
   k = 0; j = 0;
   while (j < ArrayLength)
   {
      ArrayConc[k] = Array2[j];
      k = k + 1;
      j = j + 1;
   }
   j = 0;
```

```
        while (j < ArrayLength)
        {
           ArrayConc[k] = Array1[j];
           k = k + 1;
           j = j + 1;
        }
     }
                        /*print the string obtained through concatenation*/
        k = 0;
        while (k < (ArrayLength * 2)) printf("%c", ArrayConc[k]);
     }
```

At the end of Chapter 7 we will present another solution to Example 5.6 using predefined functions provided by the C standard library for the global manipulation of strings. We will use predefined functions to copy, compare or concatenate strings conventionally defined as arrays of characters in which the element immediately following the last one is set to the special character \0 (ASCII 0).

5.5.2 The struct constructor

The type constructor **struct** in C allows the definition of structures, grouping together heterogeneous information: an example might be a variable *employee* that contains information such as *first* and *last name*, *social security number*, *address*, *phone number*, *salary*, *employment date* and so on. Similarly, the description of a *family* contains a certain set of *persons*, an *estate*, constituted in its turn by a set of *possessions*, each with its *value*, a yearly *income*, various *expenses* for the members of the family and so on.

In these cases, trying to structure the information via the array mechanism would be unnatural or even completely impossible, because an array requires that all its elements are homogeneous.

The type constructor **struct**, however, allows heterogeneous elements, that is, elements of different types, to be aggregated into one single structure. These elements are called **fields** of the structure. The values of the types constructed through the type constructor **struct** are sequences of other values (the field values) belonging to any other types.

The fact that **struct** is a type constructor implies that it can be used, exactly like an array, in explicit type declarations or directly in declarations of variables which thus implicitly construct an anonymous type.

Syntactically, the explicit declaration of a type obtained through the **struct** constructor consists of:

- the keywords **typedef struct**, followed by
- the list of the structure's fields enclosed within the pair **{ }**; the elements of the field list are separated from each other by a **;**. Each one in turn consists of:
  - the type of the field, followed by

- – the identifier of the field. As a particular case a whole (sub)list of field identifiers can receive the same type. In such a case all elements of the list can be listed together, separated by a ,
- the identifier of the new type obtained through the **struct** constructor
- as usual the declaration is terminated by a ;.

Some examples of structure explicit declarations are the following:

(1)
```
typedef struct  { int      Day;
                  int      Month;
                  int      Year;
                } Date;
```

(2)
```
typedef struct  { String   Addressee;
                  int      Amount;
                  Date     IssueDate;
                } InvoiceDescription;
```

Obviously, it is assumed that the types String and Date have been defined beforehand, as illustrated above.

(3)
```
typedef struct  { int      Channel;
                  PowType  PowerSwitch;
                  double   BrightnessControl, ColourControl,
                           VolumeControl;
                } TVChannels;
```

where PowType is defined as:

```
typedef enum {On, Off} PowType;
```

(4)
```
typedef struct  { String   FirstName;
                  String   LastName;
                  int      Salary;
                  char     SSN[16];
                  Date     EmploymentDate;
                  CatType  Category;
                } Staff;
```

where CatType is defined as:

```
typedef enum {Manager, Employee, Labourer} CatType;
```

Once a type has been constructed through the type constructor **struct** and has been given an identifier, say, Staff, according to (4) above, one or more variables of type Staff can be declared in the variable declaration section by simply writing the name Staff followed by the (list of) variable(s) which is (are) attributed that type. If such a list contains more than one variable, its elements are separated by a ,; the list is then ended by the usual ;.

```
Staff   Staff1, Staff2;
```

The abbreviated declaration of variables of a type obtained through the **struct** constructor consists of:

- the keyword **struct** followed by
- the list of the structure's fields which is constructed in the same way as in the explicit type definition
- the variable identifier(s) (if there is more than one they are separated by **,**)
- the usual terminator **;**.

The abbreviated declaration of the previously used Staff1 and Staff2 variables is the following:

```
struct          { String  FirstName;
                  String  LastName;
                  int     Salary;
                  char    SSN[16];
                  Date    EmploymentDate;
                  CatType Category;
                } Staff1, Staff2;
```

Each structured variable requires a mechanism to access its individual elements. Whereas in order to access individual elements of an array we write the array's identifier, followed by the index of the element enclosed in brackets, to access the individual fields of a structure we write the structure's identifier, followed by a full stop (or **dot**, from where the term **dot notation** is derived to indicate the present syntax rule) and the identifier of the required field.

Referring to the previous declaration, if we wanted to increase by 10% the salary of a staff member whose description is stored in the variable Staff1, it would be sufficient to write the statement:

```
Staff1.Salary = Staff1.Salary + (Staff1.Salary*10) /100;
```

The access mechanisms for elements of structured variables can be combined, just as type constructors can be combined. Thus, if we want to establish that the staff member whose description is contained in the variable Staff1 was employed on 8 January 1988, we can write the following code:

```
Staff1.EmploymentDate.Day = 8;
Staff1.EmploymentDate.Month = 1;
Staff1.EmploymentDate.Year = 1988;
```

Similarly, if we want to know if the first letter of the last name of Staff1 is A, we can write the following condition:

```
if (Staff1.LastName [0] == 'A') ...
```

Finally, suppose we have created a variable InvoiceArchive as:

```
InvoiceDeclaration    InvoiceArchive[1000];
```

In order to find out whether invoice number 500 was issued not later than 1986 and, if so, for what amount, we can write the following code:

```
if (InvoiceArchive[500].IssueDate.Year <= 1986)
    printf("%d",InvoiceArchive[500].Amount);
else
    printf("The invoice under consideration was issued after 1986\n");
```

Note how, although it is an artificial and formally defined language, C allows us to write code that is quite similar to the normal sentences we would use to express the same meaning in a natural language (preferably in English, to be consistent with the English keywords). In any case, it is easily understandable if appropriate identifiers are used. This also encourages the practice suggested in Section 3.4 of deriving a program via successive refinements of pseudocode, which starts with a description of the algorithm in 'quasi-natural' language and arrives at executable code.

The elements of a structure can be involved individually in all operations of the type that characterizes them. Unlike an array, the structure as a whole can be involved, through its identifier, in global operations of comparison (==, !=) or assignment.

Suppose that Staff1 and Staff2 are variables declared as follows:

```
Staff    Staff1, Staff2;
```

It is possible to assign the Staff1 information to Staff2 via the statement:

```
Staff2 = Staff1;
```

Note that this is also possible when fields of the Staff type are of String type (and therefore arrays).

The reason for the nonuniform treatment of arrays and structures in C with respect to global operations lies in the different treatment that the C system applies to identifiers of arrays and structures, as we will see in Section 5.6.

A final example shows how to handle structures.

EXAMPLE 5.7

The following program fragment handles information about the teaching, researching and managing activities of a university professor during a particular year. The information referring to the duration of different jobs done during the year is supposed to be already available to the shown piece of code through a variable named Agenda which is an array of structured data. The number of jobs done during the year is supposed to be available through the variable named NumberOfJobs. The program returns the total numbers of hours devoted to teaching, researching and managing activities by the professor during the year under consideration.

```
                                                      /*Program Agenda*/
#include <stdio.h>
main()
{
   typedef  enum {teaching, researching, managing} Job;
   typedef  struct  {  int      Day;
                       int      Month;
                       int      Year;
                    } Date;
```

```
typedef struct  { Job      TypeOfJob;
                  Date     DateOfJob;
                  int      Duration;
                } JobDescription;

JobDescription      Agenda[1000];
int                 counter, NumberOfJobs;
int                 TeachingHours, ResearchHours, ManagingHours;

..............................
                    /*omitted parts of the program containing the input
                    of values stored in Agenda and in NumberOfJobs*/

counter = 0;
TeachingHours = 0; ResearchHours = 0; ManagingHours = 0;
while (counter < NumberOfJobs)
{
   if (Agenda[counter].TypeOfJob == teaching)
          TeachingHours = TeachingHours + Agenda[counter].Duration;
   else if (Agenda[counter].TypeOfJob == researching)
          ResearchHours = ResearchHours + Agenda[counter].Duration;
   else if (Agenda[counter].TypeOfJob == managing)
          ManagingHours = ManagingHours + Agenda[counter].Duration;
   counter = counter + 1;
}
printf("Summary of jobs done during the current year\n");
printf("Hours devoted to: teaching = %d;researching = %d;
       managing = %d\n", TeachingHours, ResearchHours,
       ManagingHours);
}
```

5.5.3 The pointer constructor

So far, a constant characteristic of programming in a high-level language has been the fact that each variable can be accessed via its name: x = a means 'take the value contained in the cell whose *name* is a and store it in the cell whose *name* is x'.

We now introduce the concept of a **pointer** to a variable. This term indicates the *address* of the variable it refers to. Precisely, the declaration:

```
typedef    DataType    *PointerType;
```

defines the type named PointerType as a pointer to a cell that contains a value of type DataType: thus, the value of a variable P of type PointerType is the address of

Figure 5.1   Graphical representation of a pointer.

another variable whose type is `DataType`. Very often, a situation like this is described graphically as shown in Figure 5.1.

Access to a variable 'pointed' to by pointer `P` occurs through the **indirection** or **dereferencing operator** `*` put in front of the pointer's identifier. Precisely, `*P` indicates the memory cell whose address is contained in `P`. It can be used in exactly the same way as any other variable of type `DataType`. Consequently, on the basis of the following declarations:

```
typedef    DataType    *PointerType;
PointerType            P;
DataType               x;
```

the following statements are allowed:

```
*P = x;
x = *P;
```

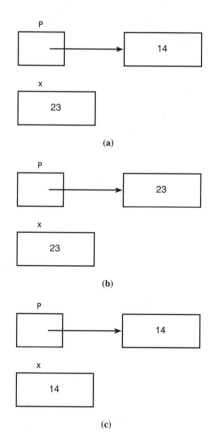

(a)

(b)

(c)

Figure 5.2   (a) The memory before executing the statements. (b) Effect of executing the statement `*P = x` (with the memory initially as in part (a)). (c) Effect of executing the statement `x = *P` (with the memory initially as in part (a)).

Figure 5.2 shows the effect of the above two statements, assuming that `DataType` is **int**.

Pointers can be assigned values, since they are themselves variables. The first example of pointer assignment involves the unary operator & (address of) which we encountered in Section 4.1.2 where the predefined function `scanf` was introduced.

Given the following type and variable declarations:

```
typedef DataType    *PointerType;
PointerType         P, Q;
DataType            y, z;
```

it is possible to assign to pointer P and pointer Q the addresses of the variables y and z, respectively, via the following statements:

```
P = &y;
Q = &z;
```

Note that, in this way, the limit imposed by typing 'pointed' variables is verified: x and y are of type `DataType`, whereas P and Q are both pointers to variables of type `DataType`.

Still referring to the above declarations, it is also possible to execute the following assignment:

```
P = Q;
```

The effect of the three assignments is shown in Figure 5.3. After the last assignment, P also points to the variable z if executed from the state produced by

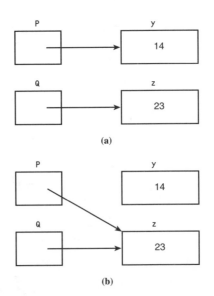

(a)

(b)

Figure 5.3 (a) State of the machine memory after the execution of the statements P = &y; Q = &z. (b) Effect of the execution of the statement P = Q (starting from the state of part (a)).

the first two assignments. Note the difference between the statements P = Q and
*P = *Q: its importance will be highlighted shortly, when we discuss some of the
risks of programming using pointers.

The construction denoted by the symbol * is, in every respect, a type constructor; that is, it produces a new type (the pointer to an object) on the basis of the
type of the object pointed to, in exactly the same way as the array mechanism is a
type constructor which produces a new type on the basis of the types of the elements and the index. Consequently, the following declarations are allowed:

```
typedef  DataType       *PointerType;
typedef  OtherDataType  *OtherPointerType;
DataType                *Pointer;
                        /*note that such a declaration is considered as
                        an abbreviated form that unifies a type
                        declaration and a variable declaration. The
                        variable Pointer points to a variable of type
                        DataType*/;
DataType                **DoublePointer;
                        /*the variable DoublePointer points to a
                        variable which in its turn points to a variable
                        of type DataType*/
PointerType             P, Q;
OtherPointerType        P1, Q1;
DataType                x, y;
OtherDataType           z, w;
```

On the basis of these declarations, we can write statements such as:

```
Pointer = &y;
DoublePointer = &P;
Q1 = &z;
P = &x;
P = Q;
*P = *Q;
*Pointer = x;
P = *DoublePointer;
z = *P1;
Pointer = P;
```

It could be incorrect to write statements such as the following, because they
could violate the rules of compatibility between types (the compiler would issue a
warning – a message to pay attention – or an error message).

```
P1 = P;                 (warning)
w = *P;                 (error)
*DoublePointer = y;     (error)
Pointer = DoublePointer;  (warning)
*P1 = *Q;               (error)
```

Let us consider the case of DataType declared as follows:

```
typedef  struct  { int    FirstField
                   char   SecondField;
                 } DataType;
```

The programmer could refer to the `FirstField` of the variable pointed to by `P` through the following notation

```
(*P).FirstField
```

but C also provides a more synthetic notation perfectly equivalent to the previous one:

```
P->FirstField
```

This notation uses the `->` operator provided by the language to access a member of a structure via a variable that points to the structure itself.

To assign the integer value 12 to the field named `FirstField` the programmer can write either

```
P->FirstField = 12
```

or

```
(*P).FirstField = 12
```

The pointer mechanism thus offers the possibility of referring to a variable in a way other than through its name. Note that the notation `*P` may indicate different cells of memory during program execution as a consequence of an assignment to the variable `P`, similarly to a reference of the kind `a[i]` as a consequence of an assignment to the index `i`; in both cases the flexibility of the mechanism exposes us to a greater risk of error, as we will point out in the next section.

The operations that can be applied to pointers are the following:

- The assignment of the address of a variable via the operator `&` followed by the name of the variable.

- The assignment of the value of another pointer.

- The assignment of the special value `NULL`. If a pointer variable has value `NULL`, `*P` is undefined: in other words, `P == NULL` means that `P` does not point to any meaningful information. Graphically, `P == NULL` is often indicated by a notation as shown in Figure 5.4.

- The assignment of memory addresses following operations of explicit memory allocation (this assignment will be discussed in Chapter 10).

- The dereferencing operation, indicated by the operator `*`.

- Comparison based on the relations `==`, `!=`, `>`, `<`, `<=`, `>=`;

- Arithmetic operations (see Section 5.6).

Note that, in order to avoid errors during the execution of the program, it is always a good idea to *assign each pointer variable explicitly* (possibly initializing it with the special `NULL` value), even though some implementations of the C language might implicitly assign the value `NULL` to each new pointer. This guarantees that the program will run properly under *any* implementation of the language.

The C language is particularly characterized by the ample and flexible use of the pointer type constructor it allows; and the arithmetic operations executable on

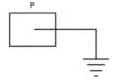

Figure 5.4 Graphical representation of the NULL value for pointers.

pointers are certainly one of the characteristic aspects of this language (but a difficult topic for the beginner).

The importance of the pointer type constructor in the C language will become
clear only after having considered:

- the close relationship between arrays and pointers (Section 5.6),
- the treatment of functions (in Chapter 7),
- the possibility of dynamic memory allocation and explicit reference to it (see
  Chapter 10),
- the possibility of defining dynamic data structures (see Chapter 10).

For this reason you will find meaningful programs involving pointer variables
in those chapters; nevertheless, let us try to exemplify some initial uses of pointer
variables in two simple programs.

EXAMPLE 5.8

The following program fragment assumes that an array containing 100 integer
numbers is available in the memory and assigns a value to two variables pointing to
the element of the array containing, respectively, the lowest and the highest value.

```
                                    /*Program pointers to the lowest and
                                    the highest element of an array*/

#define ArrayLength    100
main()
{
    int     i;
    int     ArrayOfInt[ArrayLength];
    int     *PointToLowest;
    int     *PointToHighest;

    ........................

    PointToLowest = &ArrayOfInt[0];
    i = 1;
    while (i < ArrayLength)
```

```
{
    if (ArrayOfInt[i] < *PointToLowest)
        PointToLowest = & ArrayOfInt[i];
    i = i+1;
}
PointToHighest = &ArrayOfInt[0];
i = 1;
while (i < ArrayLength)
{
    if (ArrayOfInt[i] > *PointToHighest)
        PointToHighest = & ArrayOfInt[i];
    i = i+1;
}
}
```

EXAMPLE 5.9

The following program manages information referring to people working in a factory using data contained in two variables: the first one, named WorkerData, contains information about different workers (managers, employees and labourers); the second one, named Management, allows quick access to data referring to managers contained in the first data structure. Suppose that we want to print the last names and the salary of all managers who earn more than $5000: rather than selecting all elements of the whole array WorkerData on the basis of the worker's category, we store in the – probably much shorter – array Management the pointers to all elements of WorkerData who are managers (this, of course, will make the updating of the two arrays more complex when, for instance, a new person is hired). The following fragment of code assumes that data contained in variables WorkerData and Management are already available and returns the last name and the salary of the managers having a salary greater than $5000.

```
                                              /*Program Managers*/
#include <stdio.h>
main()
{
    typedef enum  { manager, employee, labourer} WorkCat;
    typedef struct{ char            FirstName[30];
                    char            LastName[30];
                    WorkCat         Category;
                    int             Salary;
                    char            SSN[16];
                  } Worker;

    Worker          WorkerData[300];
    Worker          * Management[10];
    ...
    i = 0;
    while (i < 10)
    {
        if (Management[i]->Salary > 5000)
```

```
        {
            j = 0;
            while (j < 30)
            {
                printf("%c", Management[i]->LastName[j]);
                j = j + 1;
            }
            printf("%d \n", Management[i]->Salary);
        }
    }
    i = i+1;
}
```

5.5.4 Some 'risks' of programming with pointers

Pointers are a flexible and powerful tool for handling data characterized by a certain dynamic behaviour. This will be illustrated in detail in Chapter 10, where we refer to some classic and widely used data structures. However, their flexibility also exposes the programmer to some risks, mostly related to the possibility of determining side-effects which are not easily and not entirely foreseeable during the programming phase. Consider, for example, the following sequence of operations with reference to two compatible pointers P and Q:

```
*P = 3;
*Q = 5;
P = Q;                              /*at this point *P = 5*/
*Q = 7;;
```

At this point, *Q = 7, but also, in a more 'deceitful' way, *P = 7. However, a superficial analysis based on the analogy with regard to the following sequence of statements:

```
x = 3;
y = 5;
x = y;
y = 7
```

would have led us to conclude that *P = 5. We are, therefore, in the presence of a side-effect, because an explicit assignment to the variable pointed to by Q causes a hidden assignment (and thus with the risk of not being wanted) to the variable pointed to by P. (Note that this type of risk cannot be completely excluded even from a programming style that does not use pointers. It is a consequence of *aliasing*, that is, the fact that the same object is identified in two different ways.) Side-effects should always be avoided!

Further risks, related to the fact that during execution the references determined by the pointers change, will be illustrated in Chapter 10. In general, we recommend limiting the use of pointers to their essential goals which will be illustrated in Chapters 7 and 10. Even cases such as the one illustrated in Example 5.9 should be considered as examples of 'tricky programming' often used – and *abused* – by experienced programmers with the aim of building more efficient code.

5.6 Arrays, pointers and pointer arithmetic

In order to understand the 'kinship' existing in C between arrays and pointers, it is necessary to consider the way in which an array is located in memory:

- the elements of an array occupy a number of words that depends on their type,
- the elements of the array are allocated consecutive words in memory.

In C, it is possible to use the operator **sizeof** to determine the number of bytes occupied by each element of an array or by the array as a whole.

Assuming that we are working on a machine that reserves four bytes to store an **int** value, and supposing that we have declared:

    int   a[5];

then

    sizeof(a[2])

returns the value 4 and

    sizeof(a)

returns the value 20, equal to the space of the whole array which is composed of 5 elements of 4 bytes each.

The name of an array type variable (a, in the above example) is considered by the C system as the address of the first word in memory that contains the first element of the array type variable (or, shorter, as the address of the first element of the array type variable).

Owing to this fact, we can state that:

- a 'points' to a memory word, exactly like a variable declared of pointer type;
- a always points to the first element of the array type variable (it is a 'fixed' pointer which cannot be assigned the address of another memory word).

The C language allows sum and difference operations to be performed on pointers. The possibility of expressing and carrying out arithmetic operations on pointers allows the programmer great flexibility with respect to the explicit addressing of memory space. If a variable p points to a particular data type, p + 1 supplies the memory address for correctly addressing or storing the next variable of this type.

If p and a supply the memory address of elements of appropriate types, then p+i and a+i supply the memory address of the ith element of this type, after the one pointed to by p and a.

Considering again the array a declared in this section, we can state the following:

- if i is an integer variable, the notation a[i] is equivalent to *(a+i).

    a[i] refers to the ith+1 element of the vector a; similarly, given that a+i 'points' to the ith element of this type after a, the application of the dereferencing operator * allows the value of the ith+1 element of vector a to be retrieved.

Similarly, if p is declared as a pointer to an **int** type variable, it is possible to index p:

- if i is an integer variable, the notation p[i] is equivalent to *(p+i).
  p[i] refers to the ith offset of the value of p. This offset depends on the data type that p points to.

  From what we have stated, it follows that:

  p = a is equivalent to p = &a[0];
  p = a+1 is equivalent to p = &a[1];

  whereas assignments such as:

  a = p;
  a = a +1;

  are not allowed. If p and q point to two different elements of an array, then p – q returns an integer value equal to the number of elements that are between the element pointed to by p and the element pointed to by q. Attention should be paid to the fact that *this difference is not the same as the difference between the values of the pointers.* Supposing that the result of p – q is 3 (that is, there are three elements separating the element pointed to by p from the element pointed to by q) and supposing that each element of the array is stored in 4 bytes, the difference between the address contained in p and the address contained in q is 12.

5.7 C and strong typing

We have seen that assigning types to variables also helps to check that the operations on the corresponding data are used correctly.

In many cases the rules to apply this kind of verification are extremely clear and simple. For instance, it would not make sense to assign the value of a variable declared as **int** to a structured variable considered as a whole. There are, though, more delicate cases in which the correctness of using certain operations is not intuitively that evident. One could, for example, consider whether it makes sense to assign the value of a variable declared as **int** to a variable declared as **float**, or whether the reverse operation (assigning a **float** variable to an **int** variable) should be allowed. If so, one would like to know what will really happen in the execution phase. Is the operation carried out the one defined on the **float** set or the one defined on **int**? How is the result going to be treated?

These issues are handled by different languages in quite different ways. In this section we summarize the main features of C's typing rules (type system). In

Section 5.8 we provide a few hints on the type systems of other major programming languages. C's typing rules are based on the following guidelines:

- It is possible to execute expressions and assignments involving variables heterogeneous in type if all types referred to are compatible, that is, they can be made homogeneous by the application of the implicit conversion rules made available by the system.

- It is not possible to execute expressions and assignments involving variables that remain heterogeneous in type even after application of the implicit conversion rules made available by the system.

The rules for handling the type of variables in C are presented in Section 5.7.1. An important feature is that these rules can all be verified at compile time without requiring program execution. This allows us to say that C pursues the aim of **strong typing.**

The usefulness of this property is obvious: rule violations can be identified before executing the program, therefore increasing its reliability and saving on the cost of its verification[1].

The objective of strong typing is generally achieved in C because it is, thanks to type and variable declarations, normally possible to check during compilation that a statement is compatible with the variables involved.

Finally, it has to be said that in some practical cases, especially in systems programming (that is, the construction of the base software), the type compatibility rules constitute an obstacle. For example, certain data, 'seen' by the operating system, is nothing but a set of bytes; but 'seen' from inside a program it may represent abstract information such as 'employee', 'invoice' and so on. Therefore, practically all programming languages allow, in certain circumstances, their own type rules to be violated. This is very dangerous, especially if it is not precisely documented in the manuals. C is the best-known example of a language with strong typing and precise rules for implicit and explicit type conversion. The rules for implicit type conversion are treated in the next section. It is also possible, for the C programmer, to manage explicit type conversion via **cast** operators. This possibility, however, is not discussed in this text.

5.7.1 Type compatibility rules

To understand more fully the rules for implicit conversion which guide the analysis and execution of expressions and assignments involving variables heterogeneous in type, it is useful to recall the 'kinship' that exists, on the level of representation in memory, between characters and integers, as described in Section 5.2.4.

---

[1] Verification of the type usage rules is a particular case of a general principle: it is desirable that the greatest possible number of errors should be identified as soon as possible and it is even better if they are found before executing the program. Obviously, this aim cannot be pursued for all types of errors. The problem of error checking will be treated in more depth in Chapter 23.

Expressions involving elements heterogeneous in type

An arithmetic expression such as x + y is characterized by the value and the type of the result. The type of the operands determines the operation that has to be executed. (For **int** type operands, the sum operation of this type is applied; a different sum operation is applied to operands of **float** type and so on.) If x and y are of **int** type, the operation executed belongs to the **int** type: it returns an **int** value.

If x is of **short** and y of **int** type, it is necessary to try to convert one of the two variables to make the expression homogeneous and apply the correct operation. In this case, the variable x is temporarily converted into **int** and the sum operation between integers is invoked which returns an integer result.

The following rules are applied to arithmetic expressions of the kind

```
x operator y
```

They are called **implicit,** or **automatic** or **conversion rules,** or also **coercion, promotion** or **widening rules**. They can easily be extended to expressions with several operands:

(1)   Each **char** or **short** type variable (including the respective **signed** or **unsigned** versions) is converted into an **int** type variable.

(2)   If, after execution of step 1, the expression is still heterogeneous with regard to the operands involved, then, taking into account the following hierarchy:

```
int < long < unsigned < unsigned long < float < double < long double
```

the operand of inferior type is temporarily converted into its superior type.

(3)   If, after execution of step 2, the expression is homogeneous with respect to the type of operands, the appropriate operation is invoked. The result of the expression has the same type as the highest one used out of the above hierarchy.

Assignments involving elements heterogeneous in type

The above rules of implicit conversion are also used in the evaluation of assignments between variables heterogeneous in type. Consider, for example, the following declarations:

```
double  d;
int     i;
```

Then, the statement

```
d = i;
```

causes a temporary conversion of the value of the integer i into **double** and, subsequently, the assignment of this **double** value to d.

The execution of the statement

```
i = d;
```

on the other hand, normally yields a loss of information. The value d is truncated to an integer, losing its decimal part.

Another assignment involving elements heterogeneous in type was shown in Example 5.2:

```
CTemp = 5.0 / 9.0 * (FTemp - 32)
```

Since 5.0 and 9.0 are two real constants, the result of the division is a real number; since FTemp and 32 are, respectively, an integer variable and an integer constant, the result of the difference is an integer number. The evaluation of the expression involving elements heterogeneous in type follows the implicit conversion rules previously described: the operand of inferior type (the **int** result of the difference) is temporarily converted into its superior type (the **float** type of the result of the division) and the multiplication is therefore executed producing the **float** result assigned to variable CTemp.

Pointers and the typing of pointed variables

An attempt to combine pointers declared to point to data of different type in an expression or assignment is signalled by the compiler.

5.8 Organization of type structures in other languages

Many of the characteristics regarding the organization of types we have seen in the C language were originally introduced by the Pascal language: they are widely adopted, with changes only in details, in the majority of modern programming languages, such as Ada, Modula-2 and so on (the rules of compatibility between types, though, are different in the different languages).

There are, however, less conventional languages with greatly different features. In particular, several languages (for example, original Lisp and Prolog, Snobol, Smalltalk) allow *dynamic typing*: in these languages the type of a variable can vary during program execution. This often makes type and variable declarations useless. Such a characteristic generally makes programming more flexible (for example, it is often possible to increase the cardinality of a structure during execution) at the price of a greater risk of errors and less efficiency in memory management. Recently, even unconventional languages aimed at advanced and sophisticated uses (for example ML, widely adopted in the world of artificial intelligence and theoretical computer science) tend to adopt strong typing.

We should also recall that the concept of user-defined types was introduced by Pascal, in conjunction with less well-known languages such as Algol-68 and

Simula-67. Previous languages lacked them and thus provided the user only with predefined types.

Fortran, for example, was the first language to introduce the concept of arrays. At first, they were limited to one-dimensional arrays; later, they were extended to two, three and more dimensions. Each change, however, was brought about by a modification of the language. A greatly improved generality was offered by Pascal with its concept of a general type constructor.

Exercises

5.1   Is it possible to write a declaration such as the following? Explain your answer.

```
typedef enum {2, 3, 7, 17, 13, 31} SomePrimeNumbers;
```

5.2   Declare the following types:

(a)   `TrafficLight`

(b)   `MultiWayLight` (one of those traffic lights used in complex crossroads, with directional arrows of various types)

(c)   `MusicalInstruments`

5.3   Establish whether, on the basis of the declarations given in Section 5.5.1, the following statements are correct:

```
ColourList[5] = red;
ColourList[15] = white;
```

5.4   Complete the declaration of the `Staff` type given in Section 5.5.2 with fields for the description of date of birth, monthly working hours and address.

5.5   Assuming that the following variable declarations have been made, with reference to the type declarations of Section 5.5.1, establish whether the following statements are correct:

```
IntegerMatrix20By20    X;
TridimensionalMatrix   Y;
X[3][2] = 34;
Y[2][5][12] = 3;
X[-12] = 33;
```

Does X[1] denote a variable? Of which type?

5.6   Rewrite, in fully executable C, the programs of Chapter 3 that use arrays.

5.7   Describe a variable `Company` made up of a certain number of `Departments`. Each department consists of a certain number of `Employees` and a certain number of various resources. A `Resource` can be a `Computer`, a `Desk`, a `Chair`, a `Printer`, a `Telephone`, or a `TapeRecorder`. Each `Department` has a `HeadOfDepartment` who is an employee, but does not belong to the list of employees of the department itself.

5.8 Write a sequence of statements (it is not necessary to write a complete program) that calculates the overall cost of salaries in a department (for the description of information contained in a variable of `Department` type, see Exercise 5.7). The cost must also include the salary of the `HeadOfDepartment`.

Assume that the time unit used to measure the cost is the same for all employees and for the overall cost (if the salary is monthly, the overall cost of the department should also be given monthly).

5.9 Modify Exercise 5.8, assuming that the cost of each employee is determined by the sum of two elements: salary and contributions. Note that, before you start to modify the statements for the calculation of the overall cost of the department, you will have to modify the declaration of the `Employee` type.

☛ **1.** The reader who knows well the rules defining leap years will have noticed that the program of Example 5.1 contains a small error: 'Century years' whose first two digits are not a number multiple of 4 (for example, 1900) are not leap years. Fix this error in the program.

Control structures

6

From earlier chapters, we have seen that one essential characteristic of an algorithm is the possibility of deciding on the operations to be applied during the execution of the algorithm, based on the state of the execution itself. This possibility was acquired by the von Neumann machine by testing the contents of a register and modifying the contents of another register – typically the PC – according to the result of the test. Since the PC is the register that determines the next instruction to be executed, this testing and modifying operation results in a 'jump' to another instruction conditioned by the contents of some register. We will illustrate such mechanisms in more detail in Chapter 14. The subset of C considered so far has used **if-else** and **while** statements to satisfy this requirement.

Other languages, whether high level or low level, use other mechanisms. The mechanisms used to control the sequence of operations to be applied in the execution of an algorithm are called **control structures**.

It is therefore natural to compare the control structures of C with those of other languages. Two types of questions emerge:

(1) From a theoretical point of view:

    (a) Which types of control structures are more powerful, that is, are there algorithms that can be coded via one type and not via another?

    (b) Are there more powerful control structures than those we have examined so far?

    (c) Are there control structures capable of coding any algorithm whatsoever?

(2) From the point of view of practical utility:

    (a) Which type of control structure is the easiest and most comfortable to use for coding algorithms?

    (b) Are there other control structures that would make the coding of algorithms seem even more smooth and natural?

The first set of questions finds a simple and complete answer in the following statement, which is a simplified formulation of the fundamental **Boehm–Jacopini theorem**.

STATEMENT (Boehm–Jacopini theorem)

The C control structures examined so far (**if-else** and **while** statements) are *equivalent* to machine-level control structures based on direct, conditional manipulation of the PC register; that is, all algorithms that can be coded with one can also be coded with the other and vice versa. They are also equivalent to the control structures of any other programming language. Furthermore, they are *complete*, in the sense that they are sufficient to code any algorithm whatsoever.

The fact that C's structures can be simulated by those of machine language can be understood by noting that compilers must provide an automatic translation from high-level structures to those based on the jump mechanism typical of the von Neumann machine. The compiler's task will be better understood in Chapter 14, when we will go into the analysis of the von Neumann architecture and its language in more detail.

A discussion of the completeness part of the Boehm–Jacopini theorem requires a more in-depth theoretical investigation and is therefore omitted.

Let us now consider the second set of questions. Since we have to answer questions about naturalness and ease of use, it is evident that the answers will be more subjective.

Beginning in Chapter 3, we expressed a clear preference for the control structures of C as opposed to those of machine language. However, there are cases where it could be preferable to express the instructions to be executed in an algorithm via different mechanisms (easily translatable into the ones already discussed thanks to what is guaranteed a priori by the Boehm–Jacopini theorem).

For this reason, the majority of modern programming languages include, together with the basic **if-else** and **while** structures, other control structures intended to facilitate the coding of algorithms. In this chapter, we examine further control structures of the C language and briefly present some control structures of other languages. Another fundamental control structure will be presented independently in Chapter 8.

6.1 Selection statements

The conditional **if-else** statement is designed to select the execution of one instruction in preference to another according to the value of a certain condition. In many cases, however, there may be several (more than two) alternatives to choose from: for example, in an interactive system the user can choose between alternatives by typing different characters on the keyboard; for each of the possible characters, different actions must be carried out. Treating such cases via the **if-else** construct can be tedious and unnatural. C therefore offers another selective control structure, which we now describe.

6.1.1 The switch construct

The **switch** statement is used to select one of a number of alternatives on the basis of the value of a particular variable or expression.

Syntactically, the statement consists of the following:

- the keyword **switch** followed by
- an expression enclosed within a pair ( ), followed by
- a sequence of **case statements** enclosed within a pair {}. Each **case** statement, in turn, consists of:
  - a sequence of **case clauses** separated from each other by a : and terminated by a :. Each **case** clause consists of the keyword **case** followed by a constant expression; that is, an expression that yields a constant value. The **case** clause is followed by one or more statements (separated from each other by a ; and terminated by a ;).

Instead of a **case** statement a **default** statement may occur. The **default** statement consists of just the keyword **default** followed by one or more statements (separated from each other by a ; and terminated by a ;).

The meaning of the **switch** statement is as follows: the machine evaluates the expression indicated after the keyword **switch**; this must be of integral type. The sets of constants specified in each **case** clause are then examined sequentially; for each of them, if it includes the value of the expression, the instructions following the set of constants are executed. Then, the subsequent **case** branches are treated similarly. In order to avoid this phenomenon of 'cascaded execution', a **break** instruction must be inserted; this instruction (which consists of just the keyword **break** followed by a ;) has the effect of 'skipping' the instructions of the subsequent **case** branches and passing execution to the instruction immediately following the **switch** statement (more will be said about the use of the **break** instruction in Section 6.4). If the evaluation of the expression yields a value that does not belong to any of the sets of constants specified, the **default** instruction is executed. If the **default** instruction is omitted, the system does not execute anything *within* the **switch** statement, but continues execution with the first statement *following* the **switch** statement.

The following examples illustrate the use of the **switch** construct:

```
(1)   switch   (CharacterRead)
      {
         case 'A': case 'G': case 'H' : printf("The character read is A or G or
                                                H\n");
```

```
                                            break;
         case 'F' :                         printf("The character read is F\n");
                                            break;
    }


(2)  switch  (CharacterRead)
     {
       case 'A': case 'G': case 'H'  : printf("The character read is A or G or
                                                H\n");
                                        break;
         case 'F' :                     printf("The character read is F\n");
                                        break;
         default :                      printf("The character read is wrong\n");
                                        break;
     }
```

(3)   (The reader can easily imagine the type and variable declarations correspond-
       ing to the identifiers used here.)

```
switch  (Employee.Qualification)
{
    case  ProjectLeader:    Employee.Salary = (Employee.Salary * 11)/10;
                            break;
    case  SalesPerson:      Employee.Salary = (Employee.Salary * 12)/10;
                            break;
    case  Secretary:        Employee.Salary = (Employee.Salary * 12)/10;
                            break;
}
```

The following should be noted to ensure correct use of the **switch** construct:

- To avoid ambiguities, the values of the expressions in the **case** clauses must
  be constant and different from each other (the *exclusiveness* of the cases
  treated must be respected).

- The presence of the **default** statement can ensure the *complete* treatment of
  different cases.

- The **break** instruction at the end of the last **case** statement is not strictly
  necessary but it makes the code more easily extensible if additional **case**
  statements need to be added later.

EXAMPLE 6.1

The following program reads the characters of the name of the user (the character #
ends the sequence) and transforms each character in the name into a musical note. The
aim of the program is to suggest that a name can be used to compose a simple melody
(many composers used a more complex version of this algorithm to create the main
melody of a score and to dedicate it to a famous friend!). For simplicity the program
considers only seven notes (A, B, C, D, E, F and G). The program reads each

character, divides the ASCII code representing it by 7 and looks at the remainder (an integer greater than or equal to 0 and less than 7). If the remainder is 0 the note associated with the character read is A, if it is 1 the associated note is B and so on.

```
                                            /*Program: A melody from your name*/
#include <stdio.h>
main()
{
    char    C;
    int     remainder;
    printf("Insert the first character of your name\n");
    scanf("%c", &C);
    while (C != '#')
    {
        remainder = C % 7;
        switch (remainder)
        {
            case 0: printf("Character %c corresponds to note 'A'\n", C);
                    break;
            case 1: printf("Character %c corresponds to note 'B'\n", C);
                    break;
            case 2: printf("Character %c corresponds to note 'C'\n", C);
                    break;
            case 3: printf("Character %c corresponds to note 'D'\n", C);
                    break;
            case 4: printf("Character %c corresponds to note 'E'\n", C);
                    break;
            case 5: printf("Character %c corresponds to note 'F'\n", C);
                    break;
            case 6: printf("Character %c corresponds to note 'G'\n", C);
                    break;
        }
        printf("Insert the next character of your name -
                # ends the program");
        scanf("%c", &C);
    }
}
```

6.1.2 Other types of multiple alternatives

In C, the selection statements **if-else** and **switch** are also used when there are several actions to choose from, but the selection criterion cannot be expressed in terms of the value of an expression. This can create some trouble. In such cases, the use of a particular programming style can improve the readability of the program. Example 6.2 suggests a graphical structure to represent multiple alternatives.

EXAMPLE 6.2

Suppose that, in a program to calculate various tax operations, we had to calculate the amount of tax based on progressive rates which divide taxpayers' income into different bands.

Remember that in progressive taxation each tax rate is applied in its corresponding band: therefore, with a gross income of 50 000, a taxpayer would have to pay 10% on the first 15 000, 15% on the income between 15 001 and 25 000, 20% between 25 001 and 35 000, and 25% on the income band higher than 35 000, that is, for the remaining 15 000.

Without supplying the complete program, let us focus our attention on the following declarations and statements:

```
                                /*significant portions of the program TaxMan*/

#define  FirstRate          10
#define  FirstLimit       15000
#define  SecondRate         15
#define  SecondLimit      25000
#define  ThirdRate          20
#define  ThirdLimit       35000
#define  FourthRate         25
#define  FirstBand    FirstLimit*FirstRate/100
#define  SecondBand   FirstBand + (SecondLimit - FirstLimit)*SecondRate/100
#define  ThirdBand    SecondBand + (ThirdLimit - SecondLimit)*ThirdRate/100
main()
{
                                                    /*declarative part*/
    typedef  struct  { ...
                            /*various fields that do not interest us
                            in this context: for example, first name,
                            last name, SSN and so on*/
                    double        GrossIncome;
                    double        Tax;
                }TaxPayer;
    TaxPayer    SingleTaxPayer;
    ...

                                                    /*executable part*/
    if (SingleTaxPayer.GrossIncome <= FirstLimit)
        SingleTaxPayer.Tax = SingleTaxPayer.GrossIncome*FirstRate/100;
    else
        if                  /*SingleTaxPayer.GrossIncome > FirstLimit AND*/
            (SingleTaxPayer.GrossIncome <= SecondLimit)
            SingleTaxPayer.Tax = FirstBand +
            (SingleTaxPayer.GrossIncome - FirstLimit)*SecondRate/100;
        else
            if              /*SingleTaxPayer.GrossIncome > SecondLimit AND*/
                (SingleTaxPayer.GrossIncome <= ThirdLimit)
                SingleTaxPayer.Tax = SecondBand +
                (SingleTaxPayer.GrossIncome - SecondLimit)*ThirdRate/100;
```

```
    else                    /*in this case, certainly the relation holds:
                            SingleTaxPayer.GrossIncome > ThirdLimit*/
        SingleTaxPayer.Tax = ThirdBand +
        (SingleTaxPayer.GrossIncome - ThirdLimit)*FourthRate/100;
}
```

This portion of program shows that when we have to consider multiple alternatives, the **if-else** construct forces us to select a first case to oppose to all remaining ones (in our example, the first band of income); subsequently, from the remaining cases, we select another one and so on. Imagine what the code would look like if we had to treat ten income bands instead of four! On the other hand, the inadequacy of the **switch** construct for handling this kind of case is rather obvious.

In the absence of more adequate constructs (a hint that these exist is given in Section 6.5) we suggest changing the layout of the various parts of instructions slightly, in a way that displays alternatives of the *same logical level* with the *same graphical indentation* (remember that the layout of elements of the vocabulary is not part of the C syntax, but only a consequence of stylistic considerations which can be rather subjective). For example, the executable part of the above program could be better written in the following way:

```
                    /*reformulation of the executive part of tax calculus*/
if      (SingleTaxPayer.GrossIncome <= FirstLimit)
        SingleTaxPayer.Tax = SingleTaxPayer.GrossIncome*FirstRate/100;
else if                 /*SingleTaxPayer.GrossIncome > FirstLimit AND*/
        (SingleTaxPayer.GrossIncome <= SecondLimit)
        SingleTaxPayer.Tax = FirstBand +
        (SingleTaxPayer.GrossIncome - FirstLimit)*SecondRate /100;
else if                 /*SingleTaxPayer.GrossIncome > SecondLimit AND*/
        (SingleTaxPayer.GrossIncome <= ThirdLimit)
        SingleTaxPayer.Tax = SecondBand +
        (SingleTaxPayer.GrossIncome - SecondLimit)*ThirdRate/100;
else                    /*in this case, certainly the relation holds:
                        SingleTaxPayer.GrossIncome >ThirdLimit*/
        SingleTaxPayer.Tax = ThirdBand +
        (SingleTaxPayer.GrossIncome - ThirdLimit)*FourthRate/100;
```

In this way, we have given a 'cascade' of **if-else** statements, each nested inside the other, the graphical appearance of a single construct divided into various alternatives.

6.2 Loop statements

For the cyclic repetition of a group of operations – a fundamental element in the construction of algorithms – the **while** control structure used so far is sufficiently general to cover all possible requirements, but is sometimes awkward or unnatural to use. Therefore, it has been complemented by other structures which we describe in this section.

6.2.1 **The** for **loop**

The **for** loop is a special loop that can advantageously replace the **while** construct in the numerous cases where its structure is of the following kind:

```
CounterVariable = InitialValue;
while (CounterVariable <= FinalValue)
{
    [Sequence of statements to be repeated];
    CounterVariable = CounterVariable + 1;
}
```

The term `[Sequence of statements to be repeated]` stands for the **body of the loop**, that is, the statements that have to be executed before incrementing the counter variable and rechecking its value.

Situations of this kind often occur, for example, when we have to scan an array completely and in order (in this case, the `CounterVariable` normally coincides with the index of the array and `InitialValue` and `FinalValue` coincide, respectively, with the lower bound 0 and the upper bound – dimension of the array minus 1 – of the index itself). As such situations occur rather frequently, the **for** loop allows them to be coded in a simpler and more compact form.

Syntactically, the **for** statement consists of:

- the keyword **for** followed by
- a pair of ( ) including three expressions separated from each other by a ;. The second expression must be a boolean expression. They are followed by
- any statement or a sequence of statements enclosed in a pair of { }.

The first expression normally expresses the assignment of an initial value to the variable used as the counter variable; the second expression expresses the condition that determines the execution of the body of the loop (the statements belonging to the body of the loop are executed if the condition evaluates to 'true'); the third expression is executed as the last instruction of the body of the loop and normally increments or decrements the variable used as the counter variable; the final statement or sequence of statements (in the latter case it is enclosed within the pair { } as usual) is repeated at each execution of the loop. Consequently, the above **while** loop can be written more concisely as:

```
for   (CounterVariable = InitialValue;
       CounterVariable <= FinalValue;
       CounterVariable = CounterVariable + 1)
{
       [Sequence of statements to be repeated]
}
```

The expression

```
CounterVariable = CounterVariable + 1
```

can be more concisely expressed as:

```
CounterVariable++.
```

This syntax notation is widely used in **for** loops; it uses the **auto-incrementation operator ++**, which follows the identifier of the variable to which it is applied and causes the variable's value to be incremented by 1. Similarly, the unary **auto-decrementation operator --** may be useful.

The following examples illustrate the use of the **for** construct (for more sophisticated – and less advised – uses, the reader is referred to specialized texts).

EXAMPLE 6.3

The program `InvertSequence`, described in Example 5.5, can be coded, using the **for** loop, in the following way:

```
                                                   /*Program InvertSequence*/
#include <stdio.h>
#define SequenceLength     100

main()
{
    int     Counter;
    int     Storage[SequenceLength];
    for (Counter = 0; Counter < SequenceLength; Counter++)
        scanf("%d", &Storage[Counter]);
    for (Counter = SequenceLength - 1; Counter >= 0; Counter--)
        printf("%d", Storage [Counter]);
}
```

EXAMPLE 6.4

The following program counts how many times each letter of the alphabet occurs in a text composed of a sequence of words separated from each other by one or more spaces (without punctuation marks) and terminated by the special character \0.

```
                                                   /*Program CharacterCount*/
#include <stdio.h>
#define FrequencyVectorDim 123

main()
{
    char    Datum, Cursor;
    int     CharacterFrequency[FrequencyVectorDim];

            /*initialization of the counter array CharacterFrequency.
            Only letters of the alphabet are taken into consideration,
            because the program is applied to a text consisting of
            words*/

    for  (Cursor = 'A'; Cursor <= 'Z'; Cursor++)
        CharacterFrequency[Cursor] = 0;
```

```
for  (Cursor = 'a'; Cursor <= 'z'; Cursor++)
   CharacterFrequency[Cursor] = 0;
scanf("%c", &Datum);                            /*start reading text*/
while   (Datum == '\n' || Datum == '\r')
   scanf("%c", &Datum);
                            /*the above loop allows newline and carriage
                            return characters to be skipped*/
while (Datum != '\0')
{
   if (!(Datum == ' '))
            /*if the character read is a space, it is simply ignored*/
      if (Datum < 'A' || Datum > 'z' || (Datum > 'Z' && Datum < 'a'))

            /*this checks that the character read in is a letter of
            the alphabet, and not some other illegal character*/

         printf("The text contains illegal characters\n");
      else
         CharacterFrequency[Datum] = CharacterFrequency[Datum] + 1;
      scanf("%c", &Datum);
      while (Datum == '\n' || Datum == '\r')
         scanf("%c", &Datum);
}
for (Cursor = 'A'; Cursor <= 'Z'; Cursor++)
                              /*start of the loop for printing the
                              totals of uppercase letters*/
{
   printf("The number of times the character %c occurs in the text
         is: %d\n", Cursor, CharacterFrequency[Cursor]);
}
for (Cursor = 'a'; Cursor <= 'z'; Cursor++)
                              /*printing of totals of lowercase letters*/
{
   printf("The number of times the character %c occurs in the text
         is: %d\n", Cursor, CharacterFrequency[Cursor]);
}
}
```

6.2.2 The do-while **loop**

A further alternative to the **while** loop is provided by the **do-while** construct. It consists of the following elements:

- the keyword **do** followed by
- any statement (or statement sequence enclosed within the pair ❨ ❩), followed by
- the keyword **while** followed by
- a boolean expression enclosed within a pair ❨ ❩ and terminated by a **;**.

As suggested by the syntax itself, the body of a loop of this type is always *executed at least once* and repeated until the condition indicated after **while** *becomes false*. In some cases this convention is preferable to that of the **while** loop.

Suppose, for example, that we have to read a sequence of characters that does not contain a newline and is terminated by the character %, and that we have to store it, last character included, in the array Text. This can be realized via the usual **while** loop in the following way:

```
Counter = 0;
scanf("%c", &Datum);
while (Datum == '\n' || Datum == '\r') scanf("%c", &Datum);
                            /*the above loop skips newline characters*/
Text[Counter] = Datum;
while (Datum != '%' && Counter < MaxLength)
{
   Counter = Counter + 1;
   scanf("%c", &Datum);
   while (Datum == '\n' || Datum == '\r') scanf("%c", &Datum);
   Text[Counter] = Datum;
}
if (Counter == MaxLength && Datum != '%')
     printf("The sequence is too long");
```

The **do-while** loop allows us to obtain the same result more easily:

```
Counter = 0;
do
{
   do
      scanf("%c", &Datum);
   while (Datum == '\n' || Datum == '\r');
                            /*the above loop skips newline characters*/
   Text[Counter] = Datum;
   Counter = Counter + 1;
} while (Datum != '%' && Counter < MaxLength);
if (Counter == MaxLength && Datum != '%')
     printf("The sequence is too long\n");
```

6.3 The goto **statement**

Many high-level languages – including C – have maintained, among their control structures, jump instructions directly inspired by low-level language instructions. They are often called '**goto** statements', from the keyword most often used to denote them.

The syntax of the **goto** statement in C is simply the keyword itself followed by an identifier. This identifier must be used as the label of another statement and precede it, separated from it by a :, as shown in the following code:

```
scanf("%d%d", &x, &y);
if (y == 0)
    goto error;
printf("%f\n", x/y);
...
error: printf("y cannot be equal to 0\n");
```

It must be said, however, that such a control structure is completely inadequate with respect to the principles of a good high-level programming style, often called **structured programming** and its use is therefore strongly discouraged.

6.4 **The** break **and** continue **statements**

Two particular statements in C are capable of interrupting the control flow:

> break; and continue;

The **break** statement (introduced in Section 6.1.1) causes an exit from the body of a loop or from a **switch** statement.

The **continue** statement causes the interruption of the current iteration of the loop and starts the next iteration of it. The **continue** statement can only be used in a **while**, **do-while** or **for** loop.

The following examples illustrate the use of the two constructs:

```
(1)  while (true)                                   /*infinite loop*/
     {
        scanf("%d%d", &x, &y);
        if (x == 0)
            break;                    /*exit from the read loop if x is equal to 0*/
        printf("%f\n", x/y);
     }                                        /*break causes the instruction that follows
                                               this comment to be executed*/

(2)                                       /*code that processes all characters in a text
                                           except lowercase and uppercase letters*/
     for (i=0; i<NumData; i++)
     {
        do
            scanf("%c", &Datum);
        while (Datum == '\n' || Datum == '\r');
                                        /*the above loop skips newline characters*/
        if ((Datum >= 'A' && Datum <= 'Z') || (Datum >= 'a' && Datum <= 'z'))
            continue;
        [Statements that process the other characters]

                                        /*continue transfers control to this point so that
                                         the next iteration of the loop can start. It is
                                         important to note that i++ is also executed in
                                         this case*/

     }
```

6.5 Control structures in other languages

Control structures have reached a good level of stability and standardization, so it is easy to find the structures of C almost unaltered in all modern programming languages.

From a historical point of view, it should be said that the first high-level languages – Fortran and Cobol in particular – preceded the advent of structured programming from which the structures that we have presented here originated and therefore were provided with mechanisms more similar to those of machine languages. Fortran, in particular, had various selection statements that could be described as halfway between the **if-else** statement of C and the low-level selection mechanisms of machine languages. It also had a statement for the cyclic repetition of a sequence of statements similar to the **for** loop, but, in order to realize more general loops, the **goto** statement had to be used directly. More recent versions of Fortran, however, have introduced most of the mechanisms of structured programming.

Among more modern languages (for example, Ada and Modula-2) it has become normal for the control structures to be enriched by an **elseif** construct that allows conditional statements with multiple alternatives to be realized in the style proposed in Example 6.2.

The **goto** statement remains as historical baggage in practically all languages, although attempts are made to limit and discourage its use in order to avoid the risks connected with it (difficult-to-understand control flow, as will be shown more clearly in Chapter 14). Some languages (Ada and Modula-2) possess highly general cyclic instructions (identified by the keyword **loop**) where the programmer can specify the exit at any point in the body. This has been introduced to avoid one of the most frequent reasons for using **goto** even in high-level programming (the immediate exit from a loop as soon as it becomes clear that further processing is superfluous). Whereas in Ada such a mechanism is used alongside the other control structures, Modula-2 is the only reasonably widespread modern language that has eliminated the **goto** altogether.

Finally, we should mention that nearly all modern programming languages provide another powerful control mechanism: *recursion*. This will be discussed in Chapter 8.

Exercises

6.1 Re-examine the various programs discussed in the previous chapters and determine in which cases, and how, the loops contained in these programs could be usefully recoded using the **for** construct.

6.2 Imagine that in C only the **do-while** loop exists. How could we obtain the effect of the other types of loop using the only available tool?

6.3 Would it be possible to obtain the effect of the **if-else** construct via the **switch** construct?

6.4 Write a sequence of statements that calculates the 'norm' of a square matrix, that is, the sum of the squares of its individual elements. We suggest using two nested **for** loops.

Functions and procedures

7

In Chapter 5 we defined a data type as a set of possible values associated with a set of operations applicable to them and presented mechanisms for constructing new data types via type declarations. However, types obtained in this way are somewhat limited in the operations that can be applied to them. Indeed, given a generic definition of a type, only the operations equal, not equal and assignment are automatically defined for it in most cases; sometimes, the ordering operations (<, >) are also defined.

This is obviously rather limiting. Think, for example, of the following data types:

```
typedef  struct  {  int               InvoiceNum;
                    InvoiceDescription  Sequence[MaxInvoiceNum];
                 }  InvoiceList;

typedef  struct  {  int               CostNum;
                    CostDescription   Sequence[MaxCostNum];
                 }  CostList;
```

MaxInvoiceNum and MaxCostNum are constants assumed to have been previously declared and the types InvoiceDescription and CostDescription are defined as follows:

```
typedef  struct  {  String    Addressee;
                    int       amount;
                    Date      IssueDate;
                 }  InvoiceDescription;

typedef  struct  {  String    Addressee;
                    int       amount;
                    Date      DateOfExpense;
                 }  CostDescription;
```

It is clear that when using variables of `InvoiceList` or `CostList` type, we will need operations such as 'Calculate gross turnover', 'Turnover in period x', 'Calculate the sum of overall costs' and so on.

Similarly, we have already mentioned the fact that, when using various built-in types, we might need further abstract operations, such as the square root and trigonometric operations for real numbers and so on.

Certainly, each of the desired operations can be coded fairly easily using the instructions of the language. It is clear, though, that it would be preferable to write a statement such as the following:

```
ManagementResult = GrossTurnover(InvoiceArchive) - SumOfCost(CostArchive);
```

where `InvoiceArchive` and `CostArchive` are declared as follows:

```
InvoiceList    InvoiceArchive;
CostList       CostArchive;
```

rather than the code:

```
GrossTurnover = 0;
for   (Count = 0; Count < InvoiceArchive.InvoiceNum; Count++)
{
   GrossTurnover = GrossTurnover +
                   InvoiceArchive.Sequence[Count].Amount;
}
SumOfCost = 0;
for   (Count = 0; Count < CostArchive.CostNum; Count++)
{
   SumOfCost = SumOfCost +
               CostArchive.Sequence[Count].Amount;
}
ManagementResult = GrossTurnover - SumOfCost;
```

The first example is certainly more *abstract* than the second because it shows just the desired result and hides the operations executed by the machine to obtain it. Its advantages become even more evident when such operations have to be repeated many times.

However, it is clear that an infinite number of abstract operations of this kind may be needed: it would be unrealistic to expect to find predefined in a language all the operations that might ever be needed. Therefore we need mechanisms to create new operations on any data type, define their meaning and apply them.

Such mechanisms are available in all languages (even in those that have no tools for defining new data types); they are generally called **subprograms** or **subroutines**, because they resemble whole programs, but act as 'slaves' for the main program.

First of all, a subroutine has to be *defined*, by listing its name and its input and output parameters (the concept of input and output parameters will become clear shortly). Both the type and the identifier of each input and output parameter have to be specified. Once a subroutine has been defined, it can be *used* within the main program in the same way as any other operation available for the data types used, both predefined and user defined. Using a subroutine in this way is known as 'calling' the routine.

In C, as well as in most programming languages, there are two types of subroutine, each used in a different way: **functions** and **procedures**. This chapter deals with the construction and use of subprograms in C and is organized as follows. First, in Section 7.1, the whole structure of a C program is revised and enriched to include the new items that are the object of this chapter; Section 7.2 deals with subroutines of the 'function' category and Section 7.3 with subroutines belonging to the 'procedure' category; Section 7.4 presents a new technique, besides those already examined in previous sections, for 'communicating' between calling subprograms and called subprograms; Section 7.5 goes into slightly more detail about some technical aspects of the subprogram mechanism. Finally, Section 7.6 deals with predefined subprograms, that is, those subprograms that are already available to the programmer in suitable libraries with no need to redefine them.

7.1 The complete structure of a C program

We saw in Chapter 4 that the minimal structure of a C program must include the following:

- a directives part,
- a main program, which, in turn, consists of a declarative and an executable part.

We now add two new items to the above structure:

- A **global declarative part** is included between the directive part and the main program. It contains the declaration of all items that are *shared* – that is, used in common – by the main program and subprograms. These may be constants, types, variables and other elements that will be explained later. For instance, if in the global declarative part we find the declaration

    ```
    int     x;
    ```

    this means that variable x can be accessed by main and by all subprograms.
- A sequence of subprogram – either function or procedure – definitions follows the main program. We will explain the rules for their definition and use in the following sections.

The above new structure of C programs introduces an important novelty: several items (variables, types, etc.) can be declared in different places; we will see, in fact, that not only main but also subprograms can have their own declarative parts. This immediately raises some nontrivial questions:

- Why do we need to declare different items in different places?
- Are there any rules about which items can be used by which subprograms?

The above questions will receive answers in a stepwise fashion throughout this chapter, leaving their more sophisticated aspects to Section 7.5. Here, we simply state that the `main` program and each subprogram can use all and only the items that are declared within their own declarative part and the items declared in the global declarative part.

We are now ready to examine the various types of subprograms, their goals and their rules.

7.2 Functions

From a mathematical point of view, all the abstract operations considered so far are functions. `Sum`, `Product`, `GrossTurnover` and so on are all functions with a well-defined domain (the type of the input parameters) and a well-defined range (the type of the output parameter). Strictly speaking, some of them represent a family of 'similar functions' with different domains and ranges: the sum operation, for example, can be defined on integers, on real numbers and on other domains. We need tools to construct and use as subroutines those operations that are not available in the language. Our first tools are the definition and call of functions in C.

7.2.1 Function definition

A subroutine of function type is generally referred to as a 'function'[1]. The *structure* of a function is very similar to that of a program; its *definition* (simplified with respect to the complete syntax of the C language) consists of:

- a **header**,
- two parts, syntactically enclosed by the pair {}
  - the declarative part (called the **local declarative part**), and
  - the executable part (called the **body** of the function).

The header contains the most important information for the correct use of the function: it consists of the type of the result, the identifier of the function and the **list of parameters** to which the function is applied, with their corresponding types; in more mathematical terms, the parameter list constitutes the function's domain, and the type of its result is its range.

The parameter list is enclosed in a pair of parentheses and consists of a sequence of declarations of **formal parameters**, separated from each other by a `,`. Each formal parameter declaration consists of a type identifier which can be either built in or user defined and an identifier. The formal parameters represent the

---

[1] In Section 7.5 we will see that this type of subroutine can also realize abstract operations that do not correspond to the purely mathematical meaning of the term. Till then, however, it will be used exclusively with this meaning.

arguments to which the function is applied. The arguments are called formal parameters because they do not have a value of their own, but are simply symbolic references to indicate the arguments of the function.

The result of a function can be of built-in or user-defined type. In particular, a function cannot return arrays or functions, but it can return a pointer to any type.

The following are examples of function headers:

```
int      GrossTurnover(InvoiceList  par)

boolean Precedes(CharacterString par1, CharacterString par2)
                        /*the boolean type was defined
                        in Section 5.4.2 using the type
                        constructor enum*/

boolean Exists(int  par1, IntegerSequence par2)
                        /*establishes whether the first parameter, of
                        integer type, belongs to the set of integers
                        contained in the second parameter:
                        a sequence of integers*/

RealMatrix10By10 *ReverseMatrix(RealMatrix10By10 *par)
                        /*this function receives as input parameter
                        and returns as output parameter  the pointer
                        to an array variable, that is, the address
                        of the first element of a variable of type
                        RealMatrix10By10*/
```

The header is followed by the **local declarations**. These define all the objects needed to realize the abstract operation and obey the same laws as the construction of the declarative part of a program: consequently, in this part we may find new declarations of types, constants, further directives or other subroutines (we shall see in Section 7.2.3 how this is possible using prototypes). For the sake of simplicity, we limit ourselves initially to local declarations containing only variables, called **local variables**. We shall see how they are used shortly. The rules for exploiting the complete generality offered by the syntax of the language will be explained in Section 7.5.1.

After the declarations comes the body of the function, constructed using the same syntax rules as the main program. Inside the body, however, we normally find a **return statement** whose syntax is defined by the keyword **return** followed by an expression.

The **return** statement assigns the variable result (which can be thought of as being identified by the identifier of the function itself) the value of the expression involved in the **return** statement and causes the execution of the function to be terminated. The expression involved in the **return** statement is therefore of the type of the range of the function; its value when the **return** statement is executed is the result of the function.

There may be several **return** statements in the body of a function (obviously, only the first one encountered during function execution is actually executed). If there is no **return** statement in the function's body or if none of those present is executed, the subroutine terminates at the key symbol **}** that closes the function's body. In this case, the result of the function is undefined and causes an error to be signalled.

The following are examples of function definitions:

(1)
```
int  GrossTurnover(InvoiceList parameter)
{
   int  Total, Count;

   Total = 0;
   for (Count = 0; Count < parameter.InvoiceNum; Count++)
      Total = Total + parameter.Sequence[Count].Amount;
   return  Total;
}
```

This function supplies the total value of invoice amounts belonging to a list of the type declared at the beginning of this chapter. Note the use of the local variables Total and Count which are used exclusively inside the function. Further explanations of the use of local declarations are given in Section 7.5.1.

(2)
```
int  IntegerRoot(int par)
{
   int  cont;

   cont = 0;
   while (cont * cont <= par)
      cont =  cont + 1;
   return (cont - 1);
}
```

This supplies the integer square root of the parameter, that is, the largest integer whose square is not greater than the value of the argument. Note that if the argument is negative, the result is '–1' and could be used to signal an improper use of the function.

7.2.2 Function calls

As the principal aim of a subroutine of function type is to realize a function in the mathematical sense of the term, it is only natural that the syntax of function calls is inspired by the mathematical notation. A function applied to an argument value belonging to its domain returns a value belonging to its range. Inside a program, the values of the various types are denoted by the elements that compose expressions. Consequently, a function call takes place inside an expression and consists of the function's identifier followed by the list of actual parameters, enclosed in a pair of parentheses. The **actual parameters** indicate the values of the arguments with which the function is to be calculated. Each parameter can therefore be any kind of expression, including those containing another function call. The correspondence between parameters follows the order of declaration: the first formal parameter is assigned the first actual parameter of every call and so on. It follows that the number of actual parameters in every call must be the same as the number of formal parameters. Furthermore, the type of the actual parameter must be compatible with the type of its corresponding formal parameter. The type of a parameter is fixed in the definition of the function. Consequently, it is not repeated in the call itself.

Obviously, the same function can be called at different points of the same program with different actual parameters.

The following statements or sequences of statements exemplify the use of function calls. They make use of specially defined or universally known functions, such as the trigonometric functions, or functions whose meaning can be immediately understood from the name of their identifier. Furthermore, the identifier Pi indicates, as before, the constant value π.

```
x = sin(y) - cos(Pi - alpha);

x = cos(atan(y) - beta);

x = sin(alpha);
y = cos(alpha) - sin(beta);
z = sin(Pi) + sin(gamma);

ManagementResult = GrossTurnover(InvoiceArchive) -
                            SumOfCost(CostArchive);

Det1 = Determinant(Matrix1);
Det2 = Determinant(ReverseMatrix(Matrix2));

Total = Sum(List1) + Sum(List2);
OrderedList = Order(List);

AlphabeticallyOrdered = Precedes(name1, name2);
```

7.2.3 Function prototypes

A function can be called inside a C program provided that it is *defined* or *declared*. Here the two terms are not synonyms: the declaration of a function (normally called the **prototype** of the function) just repeats the function header, as previously defined. It serves the following purpose.

Sometimes the call of a function precedes the definition of the function in the code; or the functions used by a program are defined in files belonging to the C system (the library functions are examples of functions that can be called by various programs: their definition is contained in files made available by the C system and it is not necessary to redefine these functions within the program that calls them). If the prototype of a function precedes the call of that function in the code, compiling is made easier. The compiler can immediately check the number and type of parameters used in the call and the type of the result returned by the function. If the prototype is inserted after the directive part and before the keyword main of the program or in the local declarative part of the code that calls the function, the compiler does not have to make assumptions about the nature of the parameters and the result, assumptions which would then have to be verified when the definition of the function is encountered. We think it is good programming style to exploit the possibility offered by ANSI C of inserting prototypes of the functions used after the directive part of a program, in the declarative part of `main` or in the declarative part of the various functions that make up the program.

Reconsidering what was said in Section 7.2.1, referring to the declarative part of a C program and taking into account what has been introduced in the meantime, we can say that the global declarative part of a C program, the declarative part of `main` and the declarative part of a function contain the following items:

- constant declarations
- type declarations
- variable declarations
- function prototypes

7.2.4 Function execution and parameter passing

To get a more precise idea of the effect of function type subroutines, we have to examine the behaviour of the abstract machine during their execution.

We will illustrate this behaviour by referring to the function `GrossTurnover`, described in Section 7.2.1. Imagine a program that contains the definition of the `GrossTurnover` function and the definition of a `main` containing, in its executable part, various calls of this function. We outline the essential points of such a program (the dots stand either for declarations already seen or for parts of the program that are of no interest to us).

```
                                                        /*AccountingProgram*/
                                                        /*Directive Part*/
        #include <stdio.h>
        #define  MaxInvoiceNum       1000
                                                    /*Global Declarative Part*/
        typedef  char     String[30];
        typedef  struct  { String               Addressee;
                           int                   amount;
                           Date                  IssueDate;
                         } InvoiceDescription;
        typedef  struct  { int                   InvoiceNum;
                           InvoiceDescription  Sequence[MaxInvoiceNum];
                         } InvoiceList;

    main()
    {
        InvoiceList    InvoiceArchive1, InvoiceArchive2;
        int            Inv1, Inv2, Inv;

        int            GrossTurnover(InvoiceList  parameter);
                                    /*prototype of function GrossTurnover*/
        ...
```

```
Inv1 = GrossTurnover(InvoiceArchive1);
Inv2 = GrossTurnover(InvoiceArchive2);
Inv = Inv1 + Inv2;
...
}                              /*end of the main of AccountingProgram*/

int  GrossTurnover(InvoiceList  parameter)
{
int     Total, Count;
...
return Total;
...
}
```

This shows, in the declarative part of main, the prototype of the GrossTurnover function which is used in the executable part. It also shows the use of the global declarative part: InvoiceDescription and InvoiceList are types that must be known both by main and by the function.

To describe the execution of the program, let us imagine two different abstract machines: a main one, dedicated to the execution of the main part of the AccountingProgram, and a 'slave', dedicated to the execution of the function. Both possess their own set of variables, called their **environment** or **state of execution**.

The environment of the main machine contains, among others, two variables of type InvoiceList, namely InvoiceArchive1 and InvoiceArchive2, and three variables of type int, Inv1, Inv2 and Inv.

The environment of the slave machine, called the **local environment** of the function, consists of a variable of type InvoiceList whose identifier is the formal parameter, two integer variables, Total and Count, and a further variable for communicating the result to the main program: this variable is not explicitly referred to within the body of the function (and therefore does not need an identifier), but it can be thought of as being characterized by the identifier of the function itself and by the type of the returned result. In the example, this variable is assigned, via the **return** statement, the value of the variable Total, used in the function body to calculate the value of the gross turnover. Generally speaking, the environment of any function type subroutine consists of all the variables declared inside itself, its formal parameters and a variable 'identified' by the name of the function, which cannot be directly referred to within the body of the function.

Let us now follow the execution of the main program as carried out by its abstract machine. At a certain point, it reaches the statement:

```
Inv1 = GrossTurnover (InvoiceArchive1);
```

which contains the function call.

When it evaluates the expression to the right of the assignment operator =, the main machine discovers that it needs a value which can be supplied by the slave machine: therefore, *the slave machine is called*. The call first passes the parameters (in our case, one parameter) from the main machine to the slave machine.

Passing the parameters involves copying the value of each actual parameter into the cell of the corresponding formal parameter: in our case, the complete value of InvoiceArchive1 is copied into the parameter cell. Copying does not create any problems, because both parameters are of the same type.

At this point, *control is passed* to the slave machine; that is, the execution of the main machine is suspended and execution of the slave machine begins, obviously starting with the first statement.

Execution proceeds, exactly as for a normal program, until it encounters a **return** statement or the symbol **}** which closes the body of the function. In particular, each reference to the formal parameter causes an access to the corresponding local variable. At the end of execution, the cell GrossTurnover contains either a defined or an undefined value, depending on whether termination was caused by a **return** statement or the key symbol **}**. At this point, control is passed back to the main machine which picks up the value of the GrossTurnover cell and uses it as the value of the expression:

```
GrossTurnover(InvoiceArchive1)
```

which is then assigned to Inv1.

Figure 7.1 summarizes the salient phases of the call to the function, its execution and the resumption of the execution of the main program.

When we come to the next statement in the main program, the sequence of operations just described is repeated, the only difference being that, when the parameters are passed, the value copied into the parameter is that of InvoiceArchive2 instead of InvoiceArchive1; similarly, after having picked up the value of the GrossTurnover cell (the same cell as before!), it is assigned to Inv2.

Sometimes, in order to evaluate an actual parameter, a further function call is necessary, as in the case:

```
x = sin(atan(y)-acos(z));
```

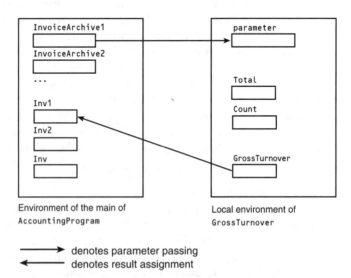

Figure 7.1 Effect of the call Inv1 = GrossTurnover(InvoiceArchive1).

Without going into too much detail, we can say that the overall effect of the computation is the same as that of the following code:

```
temp1 = atan(y); temp2 = acos(z);
x = sin(temp1-temp2);
```

where it is obviously assumed that the variables `temp1` and `temp2` are not used elsewhere.

7.3 Procedures

The abstract operations we need cannot always be naturally described in terms of mathematical functions. Suppose, for example, that we want to print a list of invoices in an easily readable form. This has to be done using parameters, because we might want to print different lists at different times: we therefore need an operation `PrintInvoices` which has many elements in common with the previous examples, but is different insofar as its purpose is not to calculate a value to be assigned to a variable or to be used in the evaluation of an expression, but to produce a printout.

There are other cases in which the *effect* of an abstract operation is not as well described as the calculation of a mathematical function. Here are some examples.

(1)   We want to insert a new invoice into an existing `InvoiceArchive`: in general, the result we expect is not a value of a suitable type to be assigned to a new variable, but an update of a variable that already exists.

(2)   Suppose we have a variable `TrafficLight`, described as follows:

```
typedef enum     { GreenLeft, GreenRight } StateType;
typedef struct   { StateType    State;
                   int          LeftQueue;
                   int          RightQueue;
                 } TrafficLightType;
TrafficLightType               TrafficLight;
```

We want to describe an operation `UpdateTrafficLight` which:

(a)   decrements by a constant value the field `LeftQueue` or `RightQueue`, depending on whether the state of the traffic light is `GreenLeft` or `GreenRight`;

(b)   reads from a terminal the values `NewArrivalsLeft` and `NewArrivalsRight` and adds them to `LeftQueue` and `RightQueue`, respectively;

(c)   assigns the `State` field the value `GreenLeft` if `LeftQueue > RightQueue` and vice versa.

Again, the desired effect is not a value of type `TrafficLightType`, but a change in the contents of the variable `TrafficLight`.

(3) We want to order an array of integers. The effect of a call `Order(a)`, where a is an array of 10 integers, must not be the value of type 'array of 10 integers' obtained by ordering the elements contained in a. Instead, we want the contents of a itself to be ordered by the operation `Order(a)`. In other words, if `ConstructOrderedValue(a)` were a function that produced as its result a permutation of the array a whose elements are ordered, the desired effect of `Order(a)` would be that of the statement a = `ConstructOrderedValue(a)`.

In summary, often the task of an abstract operation is not (or not only) to produce a value of a certain type, but to *modify the state*, that is, the contents of some cell, of the program that uses it.

In these cases, we can use a different type of subroutine, called a **procedural subroutine** or **procedure**.

A procedure in C is defined as a function that has as its result the special type **void** (meaning the absence of a returned value). The **void** type can also be used as the type of the formal parameters in cases where there are no parameters to be passed to the function or procedure.

The call of a procedure is a statement and consists of the procedure's identifier followed by the list of actual parameters, enclosed in a pair of parentheses. The actual parameters indicate the values of the arguments with which the procedure is to be executed. Each parameter can therefore be any kind of expression. The correspondence between parameters follows the order of declaration: the first formal parameter is assigned the first actual parameter of every call and so on. It follows that the number of actual parameters in every call must be the same as the number of formal parameters. Furthermore, the type of the actual parameter must be compatible with the type of its corresponding formal parameter. The type of a parameter is fixed in the definition of the procedure. Consequently, it is not repeated in the call itself.

The following example uses this form of subroutine.

EXAMPLE 7.1

Let us consider the operation `InsertInvoice` referred to in item 1 above.

The program contains, after its directive part, the declarations of type `InvoiceList` and a variable `InvoiceArchive` of type `InvoiceList` already used several times. The variable and the type declarations are shared by `main` and the procedure `InsertInvoice`. This is a new instance of the use of the global environment. This time, not only types but also the global variable `InvoiceArchive` are shared. The desired operation can be realized via the procedure `InsertInvoice` as follows:

```
                                              /*Accounting Program*/
#include <stdio.h>
#define  MaxInvoiceNum    1000
   ...
```

```
typedef  struct  {  String              Addressee;
                    int                 amount;
                    Date                IssueDate;
                 } InvoiceDescription;
typedef  struct  {  int                 InvoiceNum;
                    InvoiceDescription  Sequence[MaxInvoiceNum];
                 } InvoiceList;
InvoiceList      InvoiceArchive;

main()
{
   Date                 TodaysDate;
   InvoiceDescription   Invoice1, Invoice2;
   void     InsertInvoice(InvoiceDescription   Invoice);
   boolean  Precede(Date   Num1, Date   Num2);
   ...
                                /*sequence of statements that read the
                                data of an invoice setting Invoice1*/
   InsertInvoice(Invoice1);
   ...
                                /*sequence of statements that read the
                                data of an invoice setting Invoice2*/
   if (Precede(Invoice2.IssueDate, TodaysDate))
      InsertInvoice(Invoice2);
   ...
}

void     InsertInvoice(InvoiceDescription    Invoice)
{

   if (InvoiceArchive.InvoiceNum == MaxInvoiceNum)
      printf("The archive is full.\n");
   else
   {
      InvoiceArchive.InvoiceNum = InvoiceArchive.InvoiceNum + 1;
      InvoiceArchive.Sequence[InvoiceArchive.InvoiceNum-1] = Invoice;
   }
}
```

7.3.1 Procedure execution

Let us now examine the behaviour of the abstract main and slave machines when a procedure call occurs, referring to Example 7.1. We still consider two abstract machines: one main and one slave, dedicated to the execution of the main program and the procedure, respectively. Both have their own environments or states of execution. Furthermore, the presence of declarations in the global declaration part of the program generates a **global environment** for the program. In the example, the global environment is composed of a variable InvoiceArchive of type InvoiceList. Figure 7.2 displays the global environment and the local environments of main and of the procedure.

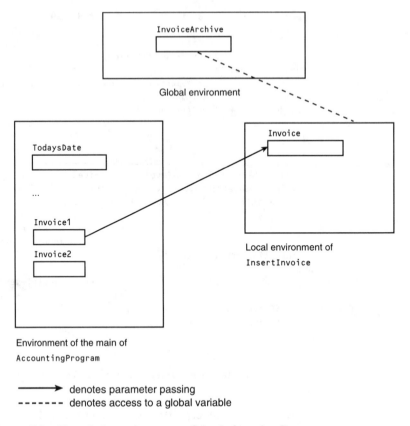

Global environment

Environment of the main of
`AccountingProgram`

Local environment of
`InsertInvoice`

⟶ denotes parameter passing
------ denotes access to a global variable

Figure 7.2 The whole environment of the Accounting Program.

Initially, both machines behave exactly as they did in the case of functions. But now, the machine that executes `InsertInvoice` *accesses the global environment*, which is available to both the main and the slave machine, and *modifies it*. The variable `InvoiceArchive` which it modifies is neither a parameter nor one of its local variables: it is a **global variable** of the `Accounting Program`. At the end of procedure execution, the slave machine just returns control to the main machine, without producing any result (the desired effect having already been obtained by the modification of the global variable `InvoiceArchive` which can also be seen, and therefore accessed, by the main machine).

To understand the difference somewhat better, consider the following analogy: the relationship between the main program and the subprogram is similar to the relationship between master and servant. A 'functional' type servant is given tasks such as 'go and buy three kilos of potatoes with this money'; a 'procedural' type servant is given tasks such as 'put this book in the library': the second task clearly requires more trust because it involves access to a resource owned by the master.

To summarize the difference between procedures and functions, imagine you want to assign the variable x a value to be calculated as a function of the variable z.

This effect can be obtained either by a function or by a procedure by writing statements such as:

```
x = ValueFunctionOf(z);
```

or

```
ModifyValueOfxInFunctionOf(z);
```

7.4 Passing parameters by reference

The examples of subroutines seen so far produce their effects in two different ways:

(1) Supplying a value as the result of calculating a function.
(2) Modifying the state, that is, the contents of the variables, of the global environment of a program. These variables are called global variables with regard to the subroutine.

These two modes, however, do not cover all the needs of the various abstract operations that may be applied during the execution of an algorithm, as shown in the following example.

EXAMPLE 7.2

Consider again the procedure InsertInvoice described in Example 7.1. Suppose now that we want to insert new invoices in *different archives*, always referring to variables of the types previously specified.

As a first try, it would seem quite natural to make the variable to be modified a parameter, too: we would therefore obtain the following version of the InsertInvoice procedure:

```
void  InsertInvoice( InvoiceDescription   Invoice,
                     InvoiceList          InvoiceArchive)
              /*in this version of the procedure, both the
                invoice to be inserted and the archive in which
                to insert it are parameters*/;
{
   if (InvoiceArchive.InvoiceNum == MaxInvoiceNum)
      printf("The archive is full.");
   else
   {
      InvoiceArchive.InvoiceNum = InvoiceArchive.InvoiceNum + 1;
      InvoiceArchive.Sequence[InvoiceArchive.InvoiceNum - 1 ] = Invoice;
   }
}                                     /*end of procedure InsertInvoice*/
```

Let us now examine the effect of the call:

```
InsertInvoice(Invoice1, InvoiceArchive5);
```

At the time of the call, the values of `Invoice1` and `InvoiceArchive5` are *copied* into the cells of the formal parameters `Invoice` and `InvoiceArchive`, respectively. At this point, execution of the procedure starts; it has the effect of inserting the value of `Invoice` into `InvoiceArchive`, but not into `InvoiceArchive5` which remains exactly as it is! Indeed, the abstract operation of the procedure is executed on the formal parameter, not on the corresponding actual parameter. This is a consequence of the way parameters are passed from the calling routine to the called routine.

This method is adequate as long as the parameters to be passed are the values of arguments of functions, but when the aim of a subroutine is to modify the parameters themselves (the actual ones, obviously), it reveals itself to be completely useless.

To obtain the effect of modifying the value of an actual parameter, some languages, such as Pascal, offer the programmer a different way of passing parameters: **passing parameters by reference.** The mode we have used so far is called **passing by value.**

When a parameter is passed by reference, instead of copying the value of the actual parameter into the corresponding cell of the formal parameter, the *address* of the cell containing the actual parameter is copied into a suitable cell attributed to the formal parameter.

Figure 7.3 shows the difference between the two techniques of parameter passing.

When, during execution, the slave machine finds a reference to the formal parameter, it accesses the cell of the actual parameter (not that of the formal parameter!) via the address that was passed to it. In the example of Figure 7.3, it accesses memory cell 1004 whose address is stored in B and therefore accesses the variable Y.

In C, the modality of passing a parameter to a function is always passing by value. However, it is possible to obtain the effect of parameter passing by reference in the following way:

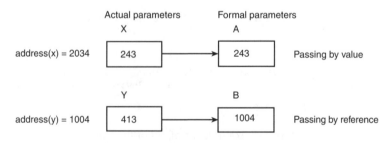

Figure 7.3 Parameter passing by value and by reference.

- using the pointer type constructor to define the formal parameters of the function;
- using the pointer dereferencing operator (***** operator or **->** operator) inside the function body;
- passing the address of a variable as the actual parameter when the function is called (using the **&** operator).

Returning to Example 7.2, the desired effect is obtained as follows:

```
                                              /*Accounting Program*/
#include <stdio.h>
...
main()
{
    InvoiceList          InvoiceArchive5;
                             /*note that in this case InvoiceArchive5 is
                             a variable local to main. It belongs to the
                             environment of the calling program*/
    Date                 TodaysDate;
    InvoiceDescription   Invoice1, Invoice2;
    void    InsertInvoice(InvoiceDescription    Invoice,
                          InvoiceList   *PointToInvoiceArchive);
                             /*prototype of the procedure InsertInvoice*/
    boolean  Precede(Date   Num1, Date    Num2);
                                 /*prototype of the function Precede*/
    ...
                             /*sequence of statements that read the data
                             of an invoice into Invoice1*/
    InsertInvoice(Invoice1, &InvoiceArchive5);
                             /*call of the procedure InsertInvoice: the
                             procedure is passed the value of Invoice1
                             and the address of InvoiceArchive5*/
    ...
                             /*sequence of statements that read the data
                             of an invoice into Invoice2*/
    if (Precede(Invoice2.IssueDate, TodaysDate))
        InsertInvoice(Invoice2,&InvoiceArchive5);
                             /*new call of procedure InsertInvoice: the
                             procedure is passed the value of Invoice2
                             and the address of InvoiceArchive5*/
    ...
}
                             /*definition of procedure InsertInvoice*/
void  InsertInvoice (  InvoiceDescription   Invoice;
                       InvoiceList  *PointToInvoiceArchive)
                       /*in this version of the procedure, the
                       invoice to be inserted and the address of
                       the archive in which to insert it are
                       parameters*/
{
    if (PointToInvoiceArchive->InvoiceNum == MaxInvoiceNum)
                             /*PointToInvoiceArchive is a variable which
                             points to a structure that has a field named
```

```
                              InvoiceNum. The notation
                              PointToInvoiceArchive->InvoiceNum refers to
                              the field InvoiceNum of the structured
                              variable pointed to by
                              PointToInvoiceArchive*/
          printf("The archive is full.\n");
        else
        {
          PointToInvoiceArchive->InvoiceNum =
              PointToInvoiceArchive->InvoiceNum + 1;
          PointToInvoiceArchive->
              Sequence [PointToInvoiceArchive->InvoiceNum - 1] = Invoice;
        }
      }
```

In this way, each statement involving `PointToInvoiceArchive->` (or `*PointToInvoiceArchive`) refers to the variable `InvoiceArchive5` if the procedure has been called with the actual parameter equal to the address of variable `InvoiceArchive5`, and a different variable of type `InvoiceList` each time it is called with a different actual parameter (as long as it is equal to the address of another variable of type `InvoiceList`). Thus, the desired effect of modifying the state of the calling program in a parametric manner is obtained.

7.5 Advanced features in the use of subroutines

The properties of subroutines examined so far allow a sufficiently efficient and general use. There are, however, some characteristics and usage techniques not yet mentioned that allow more sophisticated and sometimes more powerful programming. Although particularly sophisticated programming techniques do not fall within the scope of this book, it nevertheless seems opportune to give some hints about at least the best known of them.

The first issue that we want to treat in more detail are the rules that regulate access to program items, called **scope** or **visibility rules**, and the duration or **lifetime** of variables during the execution of a C program. For instance: can a subprogram access variables that are declared in the main program? Does a variable declared in a subprogram exist while the main program is executed? To address these questions thoroughly we must first go back to analyse the structure of C programs again.

7.5.1 More on the structure of a C program

Recall that the general structure of a C program consists of the following:

- a directive part

- a global declarative part involving
  - constant declarations
  - type declarations
  - variable declarations
  - function and procedure prototypes
- a main program
- function or procedure definitions

More generally, a C program can also be described as a set of functions and variables belonging to the global environment of that program. *One of these functions must be identified as* main. In fact:

- Procedures and main can be considered as particular cases of functions. We discussed the similarities between procedures and functions, so let us now underline the similarities between main and functions. The header of the main program is, in all respects, the header of a function that may involve the special type **void** as the type of the result and of the input parameters. The header of the main program could, indeed, be written as **void** main (**void**). In general, main can have input parameters like any other function: these allow the programmer to define some modes of communication between the program and the operating system environment (for more information on this subject refer to specialized texts).

- A main *must* exist: the execution of the global program begins with the first statement of the executable part of main.

By analysing what happens when a function is executed, we have been able to show the difference between the *global program environment* and the *local function environment*. Everything declared in the global declarative part goes into the *global environment* of the program (everything that could be visible to, and used by, the statements that constitute the executable part of main, and the functions and procedures that constitute the program). Each individual function, each procedure and main also has a *local environment*, made up of what is declared in its declarative part, the received parameters and the result. A further generalization of the notion of main, functions and their environments can be obtained through the notion of 'block'.

The concept of a block

In C a **block** is composed of two parts syntactically enclosed by the pair **{}**:

- a (optional) declarative part
- a sequence of statements

Various blocks can appear internally to main or to the functions that constitute a C program. Blocks can be parallel or nested. Parallel and nested blocks can be combined into arbitrarily complex schemes. The main itself and the individual functions that constitute the program have, after their header, a block (the declarative part and the executable part of the main program or of a function are, indeed, enclosed in braces) and sometimes main and functions are looked upon as blocks provided with an identifier, input parameters and, possibly, a result.

Let us now look at an example that will also serve as a guideline in the following sections. Here, we just state that the executable part of main includes two nested blocks (block1 and block2) and that the executable part of function f1 includes two parallel blocks (block3 and block4).

EXAMPLE 7.3

```
                                          /*Program ComplexInStructure*/

                                                     /*directive  part*/
     #include <stdio.h>

                                              /*Global declarative part*/
     int          g1, g2;
     char         g3;
     int          f1(int  par1, int  par2);      /*prototype of function f1*/

                                                  /*definition of main*/
     main()
     {
        int     a, b;
        int     f2(int      par3, int  par1);    /*prototype of function f2*/
        ...

                                                             /*block1*/
        {
           char    a, c;
           ...

                                              /*block2 nested into block1*/
           {
              float    a;
              ...
           }                                             /*end of block2*/
        }                                                /*end of block1*/
     }                                                   /*end of main*/

                                              /*definition of function f1*/
     int     f1(int      par1, int      par2)
     {
        int     d;
        ...

                                                             /*block3*/
        {
           int     e;
           ...
        }                                                /*end of block3*/
```

```
                                                                  /*block4*/
    {
        int      d;
        ...
    }                                                         /*end of block4*/
  }                                                           /*end of f1*/

                                                   /*definition of function f2*/
  int      f2(int      par3, int      par4)
  {
      int   f;
      ...
  }                                                           /*end of f2*/
```

7.5.2 Scope of variables

The complex structure that a C program can take via the use of subroutines causes problems in regulating the use of the various objects – variables, types, constants and functions – declared in the various declarative parts: for example, we have already seen that a local variable of a subroutine cannot be used – conceptually, it does not exist – outside the subroutine itself.

In this section, we provide the general rules for the usage of the various objects defined within a program, a function and a block. We first rigorously define the various environments that exist for a C program. Note that main and procedures can be considered as particular types of function from the point of view of the analysis and definition of their scope environment.

DEFINITION 7.1

The set of all elements declared in a program's global declarative part is the **global environment of a program**.

DEFINITION 7.2

The set of all elements declared in a function's declarative part and in its header is the **local environment of a function**.

DEFINITION 7.3

The set of all elements declared in a block's declarative part is the **block environment**.

For example, the local environment of the function `InsertInvoice` of Example 7.1 is the sole formal parameter `Invoice`, because the variable `InvoiceArchive` that it accesses belongs to the global environment of the program. However, the local environment of the homonymous procedure of Example 7.2 also includes the variable `InvoiceArchive`, which is one of its parameters.

It is quite natural and convenient to represent the different environments of a program, its `main` and its functions in graphical form, using a model called a **contour model**. In this model, each environment is represented by a box containing the identifiers of the elements that constitute it. Figure 7.4 shows the contour model of the program of Example 7.3.

The concept of environment allows great flexibility in the use of identifiers. Indeed, *the same identifier may be declared several times, even with different meanings, as long as this is done in different environments.*

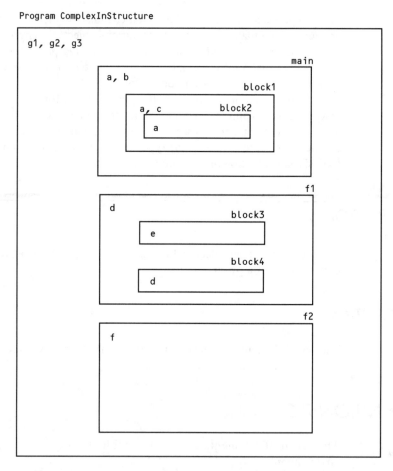

Figure 7.4   The contour model of the C program given in Example 7.3.

This rule, on the one hand, avoids the unnecessary proliferation of identifiers, especially in programs above a certain size: a variable `index` could be an integer in one procedure and a character in another. On the other hand, it introduces the problem of the **scope of identifiers**: at which points in the program can an identifier declared at another point be used? If an identifier is declared at two different points with two different meanings (for example, `x` is a variable in procedure `p` and a type in function `f`), which meaning do we assume for it at any given point in the program?

These questions are answered in the following rule, called the scope rule of environments.

Scope rule of C environments

The elements that constitute the *global program environment* can be 'seen', that is, used and referred to by their identifiers, by all functions (remember that the term 'function', for the purpose of this discussion, includes the particular 'function' `main` and the procedures) and the blocks that constitute the program. If there is more than one definition of the same identifier inside a function or block, the definition nearest to the point of usage is the valid one. The predefined identifiers of the language are considered as being defined in the global program environment.

The elements that constitute the *local environment of a function* can be 'seen' by the statements belonging to the function and the statements belonging to the executable parts of blocks contained in it. If, inside a block, there is more than one definition of the same identifier, the definition of the environment nearest to the point of usage is the valid one.

The elements that constitute the *environment of a block* can be 'seen' by the statements belonging to the block and the statements belonging to the executable parts of blocks contained in it. If, inside a block, there is more than one definition of the same identifier, the definition of the environment nearest to the point of usage is the valid one.

In general, the scope of a variable is determined by the position of its declaration: variables declared inside a block have a block-level scope; variables declared inside a function or in its header have a function-level scope; variables declared outside a function or `main` have a program-level scope[2]. A variable with a program-level scope can be accessed by all functions and by the blocks that constitute the program. A variable with a function-level scope can also be accessed by all blocks contained in the function. The block-level scope is the most limited case. Another rule, typical of C, requires that a variable identifier must not be used prior to its declaration.

The concept of environment and the scope rules concern not only the variables, but also the functions and the identifiers associated with them. The C language has

---

[2] This is true if the word **static** has not been specified before the declaration itself. In this case, the variable has file-level scope, a case not considered in this chapter; it will be considered in Chapter 22 together with techniques for program modularization.

very simple scope rules for functions and their identifiers. Each function defined as a component of a C program can be seen (and therefore called) at any point in the program. If the prototype or the complete definition of the function precedes the calling point, the compiler can check that the types of the parameters passed and the result returned are correct. If the call is not preceded by the declaration of the function header or the definition of the function, the compiler is forced to formulate hypotheses about the types of the parameters and result, which then have to be verified at a later stage. For this reason, it is useful to get into the habit of placing the prototypes of functions called in the various environments (program, function or block) in the declarative parts (the global declarative part of the program and those of main, the functions and the blocks). In this way, each function call is preceded by the specification of its header. This allows freedom of choice in positioning the complete function definition and a better overall structure of the program.

Let us consider Example 7.3 as an example of the application of these rules, with reference to Figure 7.4. We can see that:

- main can access the global variables g1, g2 and g3 and the local variables a and b. main can also call both functions f1 and f2.

- block1 can access the global variables g1, g2 and g3, the variable b local to main and the variables a and c of its own environment (a has been redefined in block1). block1 can also call both f1 and f2.

- block 2 can access the global variables g1, g2 and g3, the variable b local to main, the variable c of block1 and the variable a of its own environment (a has been redefined by block2). block2 can also call both f1 and f2.

- The function f1 can access the global variables g1, g2 and g3, the formal parameters par1 and par2 and the local variable d. It can also call the function f2 or itself (the possibility of calling a function recursively is discussed in Chapter 8) but it cannot access the variables a, b, c and f.

- block3 can access the global variables g1, g2 and g3, the variable d, local to f1, and the variable e of its own environment. block3 can also call both f1 and f2.

- block4 can access the global variables g1, g2 and g3 and the variable d of its own environment (d has been redefined in block4). block4 cannot access the variable e belonging to block3. block4 can also call both f1 and f2.

- The function f2 can access the global variables g1, g2 and g3, the formal parameters par3 and par4 and the local variable f. It can call the function f1 or itself, but it cannot access the variables a, b, c, d and e.

7.5.3 Lifetime of variables

As well as the scope, it is possible to analyse the lifetime of each variable of a program. This characteristic takes into account when the variable is 'created' at execution time and when it is 'destroyed'. The creation of a variable involves allocating in memory the space necessary to represent it and its destruction releases the previously allocated memory.

Without going into more detail of the C language, we can identify two categories of variable with respect to the lifetime of a program's variables. On the one hand, there are variables that are allocated only once and are destroyed only when the execution of the program terminates: they are often called **fixed** or **static variables**, and their values are maintained even when they are not in scope. On the other, there are variables that are created every time their scope is entered and are destroyed on exit from that environment: these variables are often called **automatic variables**, and their values are not maintained outside their own scope. The two terms 'static' and 'automatic' allude to the storage classes `static` and `auto` defined in C. In this text, the storage class `static` is not used explicitly.

The global variables of a program (those declared in the global declarative part) are fixed variables. Independently of the life of function or block environments which can use them, they remain allocated in memory, holding the values taken during program execution (and thus enabling communication between the various environments).

Automatic variables are generally those declared at function level (including the input parameters and the result variable) and those declared at block level. When control is passed to a particular function, space for the local variables is allocated in memory, and this space is released when control is returned to the calling environment. This also holds for the execution of a block. When the execution encounters a declaration of a variable belonging to the declarative part of a block, the space needed for its representation is allocated in memory; it is released on exit from the block.

It is important, in the presence of automatic variables and blocks and functions executed more than once, to note the following:

- different memory cells can be occupied each time for the representation of the same variable;

- the values produced by the previous execution of the function or block are not preserved, given that on exit from the block or function the space allocated for the representation of the variables is released.

In Example 7.3, g1, g2 and g3 are the only fixed variables. The variables a and b of main, a and c of block1, a of block2, d of f1, e of block3, d of block4 and f of f2 are automatic variables. (The lifetime of a and b of main is obviously the same as the global lifetime of the program, given that global execution starts with the execution of main and ends with the main environment still alive.)

Variables belonging to function or block environments can be declared of fixed lifetime if their declaration is preceded by the keyword `static`. By modifying function f1 of Example 7.3 as follows:

```
                                         /*definition of function f1*/
int     f1(int     par1, int  par2)
{
    static int     d;
```

```
                                                                   /*block3*/
    {
       int      e;


       ...
    }                                                          /*end of block3*/
                                                                   /*block4*/
    {
       int      d;


       ...
    }                                                          /*end of block4*/
}                                                         /*end of function f1*/
```

it is possible to hypothesize a use of the variable d (of fixed lifetime) as a counter of
the number of calls to function f1 during execution of the global program. The
variable d is allocated in memory when f1 is called for the first time, but it is not
destroyed when the function execution terminates. When f1 is called again, the
space allocated previously for the representation of the variable d still contains the
value assigned to it by the previous execution. Thus, the variable could act as a
'counter of the number of calls'. It should also be noted that the declaration of an
automatic variable d with a scope inside block4 does not interfere with such a role.
The variable at block level is allocated a different position in memory and has
nothing whatsoever to do with the variable d at the function f1 level.

7.5.4 Use of array type parameters

When an array is passed to a function as a formal parameter, the base address of the
array is passed to the function 'by value'. Therefore, the parameter is, in fact,
passed 'by reference'. The elements of the array are not copied into the formal
parameter. The formal parameter declared in the header of the function is treated as
a pointer. This is a natural consequence of what we saw in Section 5.6 with regard
to the 'kinship' between the identifier of an array type variable and a pointer.
Supposing that ArrayType is defined as:

```
    typedef double    ArrayType[MaxNumElem]
```

the three following function headers are equivalent in C:

```
    double   sum(ArrayType a, int  n)   /*n is the size of the passed array*/
    double   sum(double *a, int  n)
    double   sum(double a[ ], int  n)
```

In the last header, note that the specification of a formal parameter of array type
does not require the specification of the array's dimensions (therefore, nothing
appears inside the brackets in this notation).

Let us now consider, as an example, a function that multiplies the elements of
an array whose elements are of type **double**:

```
double  mul(double  a[ ], int  n)   /*n is the size of the passed array*/
{
   int     i;
   double  result;

   result = 1.0;
   for (i=0; i < n; i = i+1)
      result = result * a[i];
   return result;
}
```

Suppose that in main we have declared a variable v of type array of 50 elements, each of type **double**; after assigning a value to the elements of the array, it is possible to call the function to multiply some number of elements of the array passed as a parameter.

Here are some examples of calls to the function, together with the values calculated and returned:

Call	Calculated and returned value
mul(v, 50)	v[0]*v[1] * ... *v[49]
mul(v, 30)	v[0]*v[1] * ... *v[29]
mul(&v[5], 7)	v[5]*v[6] * ... *v[11]
mul(v+5, 7)	v[5]*v[6] * ... *v[11]

The third call passes as the 'base of the array' the address of the element whose index value is 5. The last call exploits the possibility of performing arithmetic operations on pointers, in order to pass, as in the previous case, the address of the element whose index is 5.

It is important to note that in the function body the vector a is normally referred to as a[i]. Modification operations involving the element referred to as a[i] act, because of passing 'by reference', on the vector v.

Finally, let us note that a C function can never return an array but just a pointer to it.

7.5.5 Use of structure type parameters

A C function can involve a structure as a formal parameter. The structure can be passed by value or by reference. It is important to note that a structure can be passed by value even when it contains an array type component.

A C function can also return a structure by value or by reference (even when it contains an array type component).

Independently of the fact that passing by value a very large structure or a structure containing an array can be particularly inefficient and wasteful in using up memory, it should be stated that the C language offers 'dishomogeneous' possibilities with respect to two widely used structured types.

In the following sections, various examples involving arrays passed by reference and structures passed and returned by reference or by value are presented.

7.5.6 Side-effects

So far, we have neatly distinguished between the use of procedures and the use of functions, using the latter only in the rigorously mathematical sense of the term.

Even though we recommend using the powerful means of abstraction offered by subroutines of function type in this way, the reader should be aware that the programming language allows some licence.

Mathematically speaking, a 'pure' function returns a value that depends exclusively on the value of its arguments. Thus, for any function f, $f(x,y)$ yields a unique value for each pair of values of x and y.

However, a subroutine of function type demonstrating some of the typical characteristics of procedures can be used in C (and in practically any other programming language). In particular, it is possible for the parameters of a function to be passed by reference and it is also possible for such a subroutine to access, that is, refer to – on either side of the = symbol – a nonlocal variable; in other words, it accesses the global environment of the program.

These features mean that a function type subroutine will not necessarily behave exactly like a function in strictly mathematical terms. The following examples illustrate this fact:

(1)
```
int   FirstExample(int  par)
{
    return  (par + x);
}
```

FirstExample is not a function of par in the mathematical sense of the term. Indeed, during execution of the following program fragment:

```
x = 1;
x = FirstExample(1);
x = FirstExample(1);
```

its call produces, the first time, the result '2', the second time, '3'.

(2)
```
int   SecondExample(int   *par)
{
    *par = *par + 1;
    return *par;
}
```

The effect of a call to SecondExample is not only to produce a result that equals the value of the input parameter incremented by 1, but also to increment by 1 the value of the actual parameter. For example, the code:

```
y = SecondExample(&z)
```

assigns to the variable y the value of z + 1, but z also takes the same value. The function call therefore produces, apart from the result of the expression, a side-effect not explicitly made evident by the instruction used, which suggests that its sole effect is to attribute a new value to y.

```
(3)   int   ThirdExample(int    par)
      {
         x = par + 2;
         return  (par + 1);
      }
```

The call to ThirdExample also produces a side-effect:

```
z = ThirdExample(4)
```

assigns the value '5' to z, but also the value '6' to x.

As already recommended, a subroutine of function type should normally be used to realize 'pure' functions. Therefore, its parameters should be passed by value (apart from a consideration that will be made in Section 7.5.7) and it should not access nonlocal variables. However, there are some cases in which a side-effect can simplify writing a program, as shown in Example 7.4.

EXAMPLE 7.4

Suppose we want to examine the last invoice inserted in the variable InvoiceArchive, which we have used several times already, and we want to delete it if its issue date does not correspond to the desired one. This can be obtained via the following function (other parts of the program are omitted insofar as they are either obvious or similar to previous examples):

```
InvoiceDescription   ExamineDelete(Day    ParDay)
{
   InvoiceDescription    LocalInvoice;

   LocalInvoice = InvoiceArchive.Sequence[InvoiceArchive.InvoiceNum - 1];
   if (LocalInvoice.IssueDate.Day == ParDay)
      InvoiceArchive.InvoiceNum = InvoiceArchive.InvoiceNum - 1;
   return   LocalInvoice;
}                                              /*ExamineDelete*/
```

7.5.7 Choosing a parameter passing technique

So far, we have distinguished the two different ways of passing parameters between the calling routine and the called routine exclusively on the basis of the fact that passing by value can only be used to supply input values to the subroutine, whereas passing by reference makes it possible to modify the value of the actual parameter.

Remember, however, that passing by value a structure of vast proportions requires copying a large number of physical memory cells, whereas passing the same structure by reference only requires copying a number of cells sufficient to represent the physical address of a memory area, usually one or two cells, independently of the size of the data that constitutes the parameter. Therefore, we are naturally tempted to use the *by reference* technique, even though, conceptually, *by value* would be more appropriate, in order to save the time and space it would take to copy the whole parameter. We do not oppose the use of passing parameters by reference for efficiency reasons, but the programmer must be conscious that this can cause side-effects. To exemplify this, let us recall that, in C, passing an array of one or more dimensions to a function is always done by reference; thus, if we pass a square matrix to a function that calculates its determinant, and if that function internally executes assignments to some elements of the variable pointed to by the formal parameter (and thus, to some elements of the actual parameter), the call to the subroutine will produce probably unwanted side-effects on the actual parameter. Example 8.5 will show the definition of a structure which has a square matrix as one of its components and a function that calculates the determinant, receiving the structure as a formal parameter passed by value.

7.5.8 Interchangeable use of procedures and functions

We saw, in Section 7.3.1, that a function can sometimes be used to obtain the typical effects of a procedure. However, there are circumstances in which one might wish to use a procedure where it would be natural to use a function. The simplest way to transform a function into a procedure is to make its result a parameter, obviously passed by reference. Suppose, for example, that we have declared a function such as:

```
int   f(int  par1)
{
   ...
   return  result;
}
```

This can be transformed into the following procedure:

```
void    f(int  par1, int  *par2)
{
   ...
   *par2 = result;
}
```

Subsequently, a call such as:

```
y = f(x)
```

is transformed into:

```
f(x, &y)
```

7.6 Predefined procedures and functions: the C standard library

As well as predefined types and constants (**int**, **float** and so on) in C, there are also many predefined commonly used subroutines. This relieves programmers of the task of defining for themselves a number of operations that are necessary in a multitude of cases.

The ANSI version of the language has standardized the set of predefined functions available to the programmer. This set constitutes the **standard library** of the C programming language. The existence of this rich and standardized library for C has made the language particularly compact, powerful and flexible, and has facilitated its increased usage.

The principal functions of the standard library are listed in Appendix C. They cover the following operations:

- *Input/output operations.* Some of these have already been seen in Chapter 4 and others will be discussed in more depth in Chapter 9. Here, we just state that they are interpreted as predefined subroutines, not as elementary operations. This explains why their identifiers are not keywords, but predefined identifiers. Note that some are functions, while others are procedures. Also note that with respect to parameter passing to these subroutines and to compatibility between their types, the conversion rules illustrated in Section 5.7.1 hold. Furthermore, for formatted I/O, more type conversions can be applied based on the type descriptors that are involved in the call of a specific subroutine (for example, the descriptors %d and %f, briefly illustrated in Section 4.1.2 for the function printf).

   The input/output operations include: *operations on files* (renaming a file, opening and closing it, positioning within a file and so on), *operations for the I/O of strings and characters* (reading and writing a character or a string of characters and so on), *operations for formatted I/O*, *operations for nonformatted I/O*, and *operations for handling errors* that can occur during the I/O operations.

- *Mathematical and arithmetic operations*, such as *trigonometric operations* (including inverse and hyperbolic functions), *exponential and logarithmic operations* and the *operation to calculate the absolute value*.

- *Memory management operations* which allocate and release memory (these functions will be discussed in Chapter 10).

- *Character handling* (character recognition or conversion) and *string handling operations* (which include, among others, string copy, concatenation and comparison operations, searching for characters in a string and determining the length of a string as shown in Example 7.5).

- *Search and ordering operations*, applicable to arrays, *date and time management operations* and *general utilities*, such as random number generation.

- *Communication operations for interacting with the operating system environment* and an *error handling operation* for errors that cause a failure in the execution of a function.

EXAMPLE 7.5

The following program uses string handling functions belonging to the C standard library in order to read two strings and build a third string by concatenating the two input strings in lexicographic order; this problem was also considered in Example 5.6.

The program uses different functions presented here through their prototypes which are included in the file `string.h`. The string handling functions assume strings to be arrays of characters terminated, by convention, by the **end-of-string character** \0 (the null character).

The arguments of these functions are pointers to characters. Remember that a string is an array of characters and the name of an array is treated in C as the pointer to the first element of the array. Thus the following functions can be called by passing them the name of the arrays involved as actual parameters:

- `int      strcmp(char *s1, char *s2);`

  Two strings are passed as arguments. An integer is returned that is less than, equal to or greater than zero, depending on whether s1 is lexicographically less than, equal to or greater than s2.

- `char      *strcpy(char *s1, char *s2);`

  The string s2, up to and including \0, is copied into s1. Whatever exists in s1 is overwritten. It is assumed that s1 has enough space to hold the result. The value s1 is returned.

- `char      *strcat(char *s1, char *s2);`

  This function takes two strings as arguments, concatenates them and puts the result in s1. The programmer must ensure that s1 points to enough space to hold the result. The string s1 is returned.

- `unsigned      strlen(char *s);`

  A count of the number of characters before \0 is returned.

The program is listed below:

```
                                    /*Program String Concatenation*/
#include <stdio.h>
#include <string.h>
#define  ArrayLength 50

main()
{
    char      FirstString[ArrayLength], SecondString[ArrayLength];
              ConcString[2*ArrayLength];
    unsigned  ConcLength;
```

```
      scanf("%s", FirstString);
                                /*the previous use of scanf supposes
                                string characters different from space*/
      scanf("%s", SecondString);
                                /*if FirstString is lexicographically less
                                than SecondString is copied as first
                                string in ConcString*/
      if (strcmp(FirstString, SecondString) <= 0)
      {
         strcpy(ConcString, FirstString);
         strcat(ConcString, SecondString);
      }
      else
      {
         strcpy(ConcString, SecondString);
         strcat(ConcString, FirstString);
      }
      ConcLength = strlen(ConcString);
      printf("The string obtained by concatenating the two read strings
            is %s. It is %d characters long\n", ConcString, ConcLength);
   }
```

7.6.1 Header files

It is important to note that the definition of the functions that constitute the library are available in C as compiled code files, not directly readable by the programmer. *It is, however, the programmer's task to insert into the program the prototypes of the functions that are going to be used* (the point of insertion determines, as we saw earlier, the scope of the function and therefore its ability to be called by the program code). In order to facilitate this task, the C library includes some files, called **header files**, that contain the prototypes of a set of library functions. In Appendix C, the name of the corresponding header file is listed for each group of functions. (For example, the file stdio.h contains, among others, the prototypes of formatted I/O handling operations – and thus, among others, the prototype of the printf and scanf functions).

The statement

```
#include <stdio.h>
```

which appears at the beginning of all C programs quoted in this book, is interpreted by the C preprocessor: it copies the contents of the file stdio.h into the program, inserting the prototypes of the functions belonging to the group of which stdio.h is the header file at the point of declaration.

This explains why, in Chapter 4, in order to be able to write compilable C programs using I/O operations, we had to use the obscure statement:

```
#include <stdio.h>
```

It guaranteed the presence of the prototypes of `printf` and `scanf` in the global declarative part of the program and thus allowed us to call these functions from within `main`.

7.6.2 Use of `scanf` function

The syntax of calling the predefined function `scanf` merits a comment. To be able to read something from an input device, the `scanf` function requires a parameter passed 'by reference'. The `scanf` function, therefore, has a variable of pointer type as a formal parameter, and the call to this function passes the function the address of the variable we wish to read. The code of `scanf` therefore modifies (via an instruction that exploits the dereferencing operator of the formal parameter) the variable that belongs to the calling environment. It is assigned the value read from the input device.

The call of `scanf`, which we have already encountered several times, therefore has the form:

```
scanf("%d", &datum);
```

Parameters to the `printf` function have no need to be 'passed by reference'. The datum to be printed can be passed by value to the predefined function.

Exercises

7.1 Simulate the execution of the following statements:

(a) `z = IntegerRoot(27);`

(b) `z = 5; x = z*z ; z = IntegerRoot(x);`

(c) `y = 10; w = 4; z = 14 + IntegerRoot(y - w);`

where x, z, y and w are generic variables of **int** type and `IntegerRoot` is the function declared in Section 7.2.1.

7.2 Write a procedure `DeleteInvoice(x)` that deletes invoice x from the archive of invoices specified in Example 7.1. If x is not found in the list, the procedure should print an appropriate message.

7.3 Write a procedure `ReadInvoice` that reads from the input terminal the description data of an invoice, assigning it to a variable of type `InvoiceDescription`. This variable must be a parameter. Note that this parameter must be 'passed by reference', as the desired effect is to assign it a value, via input operations.

7.4 With reference to the second version of the function f presented in Section 7.5.8, explain how a statement such as the following should be transformed:

```
y = z + f(x);
```

7.5   Describe a type `CostDescription` and a type `CostList`. Then, in a similar manner to our calculation of `GrossTurnover` described in Section 7.2.1, write a procedure `SumOfCost`, such that the user can later use the two procedures in conjunction via calls such as:

```
ManagementResult = GrossTurnover(InvoiceArchive) -
                   SumOfCost(CostArchive);
```

7.6   Write functions to calculate the following operations on integers:

```
Exponentiation: Exp(x,y) = xʸ,
Square,
Factorial,
PrimeNumber = PrimNum(x) = true
```
if x is a prime number, `false` otherwise.

7.7   Write a procedure `UpdateTrafficLight` following the requirements outlined in item 2 of Section 7.3. Note that the procedure is completely parameter free, because the variable `TrafficLight` is a global variable, that is, declared in the global declarative part of the program and the data `NewArrivalsLeft` and `NewArrivalsRight` are read directly by the procedure.

7.8   Modify the procedure `UpdateTrafficLight` of Exercise 7.7 so that the traffic light to be updated is a parameter.

7.9   Write a procedure that orders any array of integers (you must obtain the effect of ordering the actual parameter itself, not that of generating a new array containing the result of ordering the parameter).

7.10 Write a procedure that orders a list of invoices by issue date. If several invoices were issued on the same day, they should be ordered alphabetically by the addressee's last name and first name.

7.11 Write subroutines for the comparison of strings, for searching for a string in a text and for the substitution of one string with another, making use of array type parameters.

Introduction to recursive programming

8

In nearly all modern high-level programming languages, recursive calls to subroutines are allowed: during execution of a subroutine P, the same P can be called again.

This can happen either *directly*, that is, the body, or executable part, of P contains the call to P, or *indirectly*, for example, P executes a call to another subroutine Q which contains a call to P.

At first sight, this might look a bit surprising. Indeed, considering that, generally, a subroutine is a part of the complete program dedicated to the solution of a particular subproblem of the original problem, it seems strange that, in order to solve subproblem S, we have to ... solve subproblem S itself! For example, if we want to construct a subroutine that orders a list of elements, the fact that this subroutine calls itself recursively seems to imply that to order a list it is necessary to order a list first. Such a process seems destined a priori to cause an infinite sequence of subroutine calls.

In reality, recursive programming (or rather, the exploitation of recursion offered by modern programming languages) has deep conceptual roots deriving from the fact that, for a large number of problems, *the solution of a problem can be obtained by solving another, generally simpler, case of the same problem.*

This chapter introduces this powerful programming technique. First, we show how recursion is a natural way of describing problems and their solutions, even independently of a programming language. Subsequently, we show how C supports this programming style and the implications that it has for the implementation of languages.

This chapter, however, is only an introduction. The power and generality of this tool will be fully appreciated and understood by reading Chapters 10–12.

8.1 Formulation of problems and algorithms in recursive terms

Recursion, understood as the formulation of a concept of any type in terms of the concept itself, is 'hidden' in many forms of human reasoning. Let us explain this claim by using some examples and exercises.

EXAMPLE 8.1

Assume a group of marbles of identical shape and weight, with the exception of one, which is heavier than the others. Consider the problem of finding the heaviest marble by using a 'balance scale', that is, a pair of scales equipped with two dishes and only capable of establishing whether the objects put on them are the same weight, or which of the two objects is the heavier.

A classical algorithm to solve this problem by performing the smallest number of 'weighing' tests is as follows. (For simplicity, we assume that the number of marbles is a power of 3, leaving it as an exercise for the reader to solve the general case.)

Weighing algorithm:

(1) Divide the marbles into three groups each containing the same number of marbles. Put two of these groups on the two dishes of the scales and compare their weights.

(2) If the two groups are of equal weight, discard them, because the marble we are looking for is definitely in the remaining group. Otherwise, discard the group that has not been weighed and the lighter of the other two, because the marble we are looking for is in the heavier group.

(3) Divide the remaining group into three and repeat the above process until the groups are reduced to one marble each. The last weighing identifies the heavy marble.

We note that step 3 does nothing more than apply the weighing algorithm to the remaining group of marbles, specifying that reapplication of the algorithm stops when each group consists of one marble. Thus, the algorithm makes *recursive* use of itself. This fact becomes more evident if we reformulate the same algorithm as follows.

New version of the Weighing algorithm:

(1) If the group of marbles consists of one single marble, then this is the marble we are looking for. Otherwise, proceed as follows:

(2) Divide the marbles into three, put two of the three groups on the two dishes of the scales and compare their weights.

(3) If the two groups are of equal weight, discard both. Otherwise, discard both the lighter and the unweighed group and keep the heavier.

(4) Apply the Weighing algorithm to the remaining group.

A careful analysis shows that recursion is present in a large number of concepts, especially mathematical ones. For example, the sum operation on two natural numbers can be defined in the following way, based on the elementary 'successor' operation that yields as its result the number that follows its argument:

```
x + 0 = x          and
x + y = x +  Successor(y-1) = Successor(x + (y-1))
```

In other words, the sum of x and 0 is defined in a trivial way; the sum of x and a number that is a successor to another number is defined by computing the successor of the sum of x itself and that other number. For instance, the sum

```
1+3 = Successor(1+2) = Successor(Successor(1+1)) =
      Successor(Successor(Successor(1+0))) =
      Successor(Successor(Successor(1))) =
      Successor(Successor(2)) = Successor(3) = 4
```

The following are further examples of fundamental mathematical definitions formulated in a recursive way:

(1) The sequence of Fibonacci numbers, $F = \{f_0, ..., f_n\}$, was defined by that mathematician to model the growth of animal species through several generations. It is built as follows:

$$f_0 = 0$$
$$f_1 = 1$$
$$\text{For } n > 1, f_n = f_{n-1} + f_{n-2}$$

We can, then, calculate the first five Fibonacci numbers as follows:

$$f_0 = 0$$
$$f_1 = 1$$
$$f_2 = f_1 + f_0 = 1 + 0 = 1$$
$$f_3 = f_2 + f_1 = 1 + 1 = 2$$
$$f_4 = f_3 + f_2 = 2 + 1 = 3$$

(2) The sum of a sequence of numbers

$$\sum_{i=1}^{n} a_i$$

is intuitively defined as the sum of all elements of the sequence $\{a_1,...,a_n\}$. A simple and clear recursive formulation of the sum is:

$$\sum_{i=1}^{0} a_i = 0$$

$$\sum_{i=1}^{n+1} a_i = a_{n+1} + \sum_{i=1}^{n} a_i$$

For instance, the sum of all elements of the sequence {2,5,7,9}, composed of four elements ($n = 4$), can be obtained by computing

$$9 + \Sigma_{i=1,3} a_i = 9 + (7 + \Sigma_{i=1,2} a_i)$$
$$= 9 + (7 + (5 + \Sigma_{i=1,1} a_i))$$
$$= 9 + (7 + (5 + (2 + \Sigma_{i=1,0} a_i)))$$
$$= 9 + (7 + (5 + (2 + 0)))$$
$$= 9 + (7 + (5 + 2))$$
$$= 9 + (7 + 7) = 9 + 14 = 23$$

(3)   The reverse list L^{-1} of a list of elements $L = \{a_1,\ldots,a_n\}$ is defined as follows:

If $n = 1$, $L^{-1} = L$, otherwise $L^{-1} = \{a_n, (L_{n-1})^{-1}\}$,
where L_{n-1} indicates the list obtained from L by deleting
the last element a_n.

For instance the reverse list L^{-1} of the list $L = \{2,7,5,4\}$ can be obtained as follows:

$$\{2, 7, 5, 4\}^{-1} = \{4, \{2, 7, 5\}^{-1}\}$$
$$= \{4, 5, \{2, 7\}^{-1}\}$$
$$= \{4, 5, 7, \{2\}^{-1}\}$$
$$= \{4, 5, 7, 2\}$$

8.2 Recursion as a programming tool

The possibility offered by many programming languages of calling subroutines recursively allows a recursive formulation of the solution to a problem to be translated, in an immediate and natural way, into an executable program. This is illustrated, for some simple cases, by the following examples.

EXAMPLE 8.2

The factorial of a number n can easily be calculated without making use of recursion. Since $n!$ is the product of the first n numbers > 0, it can be calculated by the following subroutine:

```
int    fact(int  n)
{
    int   i, result;
    result = 1;
    for (i = 1; i <= n; i = i+1)
        result = result * i;
    return   result;
}
```

However, we can immediately verify that, similarly to the sum of n elements, the product of the first n integers enjoys the property $n! = n*(n - 1)!$

Using this property and remembering that $0! = 1$ by convention, we can immediately construct the following function which also calculates the factorial of a number ≥ 0:

```
int    RecFact(int   n)
{
    int      result;

    if (n == 0) result = 1;
    else result = n * RecFact(n - 1);
    return   result;
}
```

The function RecFact is executed by the interpreter of the language following the same fundamental steps that a person would follow. For instance, if we had to calculate RecFact(3), we would use the following chain of computations:

(1) $3 = 0$? No. Therefore, we have to calculate the factorial of 2 and multiply it by 3.

(2) $2 = 0$? No. Therefore, we have to calculate the factorial of 1 and multiply it by 2.

(3) $1 = 0$? No. Therefore, we have to calculate the factorial of 0 and multiply it by 1.

(4) $0 = 0$? Yes. Therefore, the factorial of 0 is 1.

(5)   According to step 3, the factorial of 1 is 1 multiplied by the factorial of 0, that is, $1 * 1 = 1$.

(6)   According to step 2, the factorial of 2 is 2 multiplied by the factorial of 1, that is, $2 * 1 = 2$.

(7)   According to step 1, the factorial of 3 is 3 multiplied by the factorial of 2, that is, $3 * 2 = 6$.

In the following section we will see that the practical realization of such a computation causes some far-from-trivial problems. For the moment, however, we will be satisfied with the intuitive evidence of the examples considered. Other examples of subroutines obtained in a natural way from the formulations of the previous section are the following:

(1) Program *Fibonacci*

```
int     fibonacci(int   n)
{
   int   result;

   if (n == 0) result = 0;
   else if (n == 1) result = 1;
   else result = fibonacci(n - 1) + fibonacci(n - 2);
   return     result;
}
```

(2) Program *Summation*

```
int    sum(int    L[ ])
{
   int       result;

   if (empty(L) == true) result = 0;
   else result = head(L) + sum(tail(L));
   return       result;
}
```

where the sequence of integer numbers contained in the array L is supposed to end with the integer constant EOL – defined below – and the functions empty, head, tail – are also defined below:

```
#define EOL   -1000;
typedef enum {false, true} boolean;
                            /*the function empty returns the value true
                            or false depending on whether the list is
                            empty or not*/
boolean     empty(int     L[ ])
{
   boolean    result;

   if (L[0] == EOL) result = true;
   else result = false;
   return       result;
}
                            /*the function head returns the value of the
                            first element*/
int       head(int    L[ ])
{
   return     L[0];
}
                            /*the function tail returns the address of
                            the part following the first element*/
int       *tail(int     L[ ])
{
   return     L+1;
}
```

(3)   Program *List Inversion*

```
void    InvertList(int  L[ ])
{
                                          /*if the list is not empty*/
   if (empty (L) == false)
   {
      InvertList(tail(L));
      ShiftLeft(L);
   }
}
```

```
                        /*through the function ShiftLeft the first
                        element of the list becomes the last, the
                        second element of the list becomes the
                        first, the third becomes the second and so
                        on ...*/
```

```
void    ShiftLeft(int  L[ ])
{
   int      i, temp;

   temp = L[0];
   i = 1;
   while (empty(L+i) == false)
   {
      L[i-1] = L[i];
      i = i + 1;
   }
   L[i-1] = temp;
}
```

Note that in order to make the procedure work correctly, it is essential that the parameter of `InvertList` and `ShiftLeft` be passed 'by reference'. In both the procedures, the formal parameter `L` contains the base address of the passed array; this implies that each operation involving `L` operates on the variables of the calling environment as needed to invert or shift the original list.

8.3 Execution of recursive subroutines

In Section 8.2, we roughly outlined the execution of the subroutine `RecFact` with a parameter value of 3. We will now examine more closely how recursive routines are executed. This will help to improve our understanding and use of this powerful programming tool.

As is well known, the call of a subroutine `S` from within a subroutine `P` (which can be `main`) essentially consists of two actions:

(1)   passing the actual parameters from `P` to `S`;

(2)   'transferring control' to S, that is, to the start of the execution of S (keeping in mind the 'point of return', that is, the point in P at which execution is resumed, once execution of S is terminated).

During execution, S accesses the data in its own local environment, contained in a data area assigned to it, and possibly data in the global programming environment, according to the scope rules described in Section 7.5.2.

When its execution terminates, S transfers control back to P which resumes its execution at the point immediately following the call of S. If S is a function type subroutine, its call takes place inside an expression, and the evaluation of that expression is resumed, with P acquiring the value of the result produced by the execution of S.

Let us now apply this execution scheme to the call RecFact(3) of the procedure defined in Section 8.2.

First, the value of the actual parameter, 3, is copied into the data area of RecFact that corresponds to the formal parameter, n – parameter passing is carried out, in this case, *by value*. The data area of the subroutine, therefore, contains a cell, n, which contains the value 3 and a cell to contain the result of the computation, that is, a cell whose identifier is the same as that of the function: RecFact. The value of RecFact is undefined at the beginning of the computation.

Now, the execution of RecFact begins. It soon reaches the execution of n*RecFact(2), whose result should be assigned to the cell RecFact, in order to be passed to the calling program later on. At this point, the new call to RecFact takes place: it is recursive, because it occurs *during the execution* of RecFact itself. If we now apply the same scheme to the new call of RecFact, the new value of the actual parameter, 2, is copied into cell n, *overwriting* (that is, deleting) *the previous value* 3! It is obvious that this makes any correct continuation of the whole computation impossible. Indeed, even if we assumed that computation of RecFact(2) ended successfully and produced the value 2 in the result cell (but the reader can easily verify that the same problem would repeat itself, *recursively*, in calculating RecFact(2)), the result of n*RecFact(2) would be 4, not 6, because n now contains 2, not 3.

This simple analysis shows that the normal subroutine execution scheme cannot be applied correctly if subroutines can be called recursively. This is because the data corresponding to the call of a subroutine must not be deleted when its subsequent execution is started: indeed, the execution of the previous call is not terminated yet!

The above remark suggests a natural solution to the problem: because *different executions of the same procedure are going on* simultaneously, it is necessary to *associate a data area not with the procedure, but with each of its executions* – which we also call **activations**. In this way, because the calculation of RecFact(3) requires the activation of the procedure four times, four data areas must exist simultaneously, each of which must contain one cell for the formal parameter n (the identifier of the parameter is the same, but not its contents) and a cell for the result of RecFact (note that if the procedure also contains local variables, each area has also to contain a 'copy' of each local variable). The four cells identified by n in the four data areas contain the values 3, 2, 1 and 0,

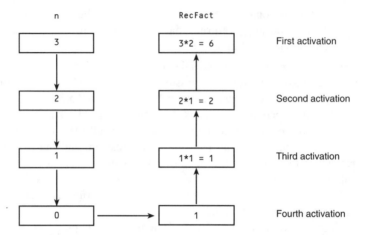

Figure 8.1 The computation of RecFact(3).

respectively. The four result cells identified by RecFact in the four data areas contain, at the end of the respective executions, the values 6, 2, 1 and 1. Figure 8.1 summarizes the computation of RecFact(3). Note that, following a general rule, the first activation to terminate is the last one activated.

A careful analysis of the computation of RecFact(3) should offer an understanding of the general mechanism of recursive subroutine calls. If a parameter is passed by reference instead of by value, the cell associated with it contains, during the execution of the subroutine, the *address* of the actual parameter, not its value. Also in this case, if the subroutine is called recursively, there must be a cell corresponding to the formal parameter for each activation of the subroutine. Therefore, if the call to a procedure P, with a formal parameter x passed by reference, yields four recursive activations of P, then there must be four cells identified by x: one in each data area associated with each individual call of P. Each of these cells will contain the address of another cell.

Consider, for example, the following procedure:

```
void    increment(int  *n, int   m)
{
   if (m != 0)
   {
      *n = *n + 1;
      increment(n, m - 1);
   }
}
```

Now imagine executing the call increment(&x, y), with x = 2, y = 3. Because the first actual parameter of the recursive call to increment coincides with the first formal parameter (it is n itself), the various increments corresponding to the statement *n = *n + 1, executed by the different activations of the procedure, are executed on the same variable x. Figure 8.2 shows the execution of increment(&x, y).

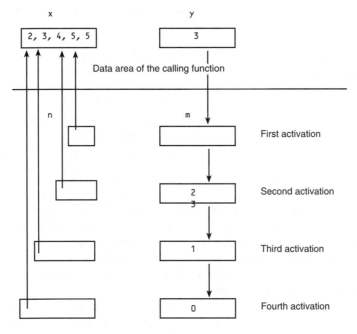

Data area of the 4 activations of procedure increment

Figure 8.2 Execution of `increment(&x, y)`, with x = 2, y = 3. The sequence of the values contained in the cell x denotes the values that this variable assumes through the several activations of the procedure. The arrows leaving the cells marked by the identifier n denote that the contents of these cells are the address of the cell x.

8.3.1 Stack organization for memory management

The execution scheme for recursive procedures just described requires the availability of an amount of memory not predictable a priori. In fact, the number of activations of a procedure changes with each execution of the program. Therefore, the memory needed for the execution of programs containing recursion *must be allocated dynamically during the execution* itself. This violates the principle laid down in Chapter 5, according to which the compiler must know the amount of memory needed for the execution of a program before its execution begins. The problems of implementation efficiency caused by dynamic memory allocation explain why the first programming languages did not allow the use of recursion at all.

However, theoretical studies on compilers have produced memory management techniques which reach a very high level of efficiency, while allowing the use of recursive subroutines. Therefore, nearly all modern programming languages allow recursion.

Although the description given above is sufficient for the correct use of recursion, it may be useful to describe these memory management techniques briefly.

Each subroutine (including the `main` program) is associated with an **activation record**. This contains:

- all the data of the subroutine's local environment;
- the return address (that is, the point in the calling program to which control must be passed when terminating execution);
- other data, some of which will be explained shortly.

As the term suggests, during execution there exists one activation record for each execution of each subroutine actually in progress. Therefore, if recursion is not used, we can associate statically, that is, before beginning the program's execution, one record with each subroutine, but when recursion comes into play, the number of activation records required is unpredictable.

To manage the activation records efficiently, we exploit the fact that in each sequence of subroutine calls (whether recursive or not) *the last subroutine called is the first to terminate execution.*

Suppose, for example, that the main program M calls subroutine P1; P1 calls P2; P2 calls P3; P3 calls P2, thus generating an indirect recursion; the new activation of P2 terminates without further calls: thus control returns to P3, which was the last subroutine activated before P2. When the execution of P3 terminates without further calls, control returns to the first activation of P2. P2 then calls P4; P4 terminates, returning control to the first activation of P2. P2 terminates, returning to P1 which then terminates, returning to M. Finally, M also terminates. Such a sequence of 'calls' and 'returns' is illustrated in Figure 8.3.

Figure 8.3 suggests a natural way of managing the activation records of the various calls: a data structure governed by the principle 'Last In–First Out' (LIFO). Such a structure is widely used in computer science and is called a **stack** or **pushdown store**, analogous to how we handle a pile of dishes: if we want to take a dish, the easiest way is to take the last one put on top of the pile.

In Chapter 11, some hints on implementing a stack via appropriate data structures will be given. Here, we are only interested in the fact that such a structure is very suitable for managing subroutine activation records. The compiler just has to

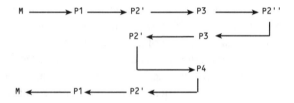

Figure 8.3 An example of a subprogram call chain.

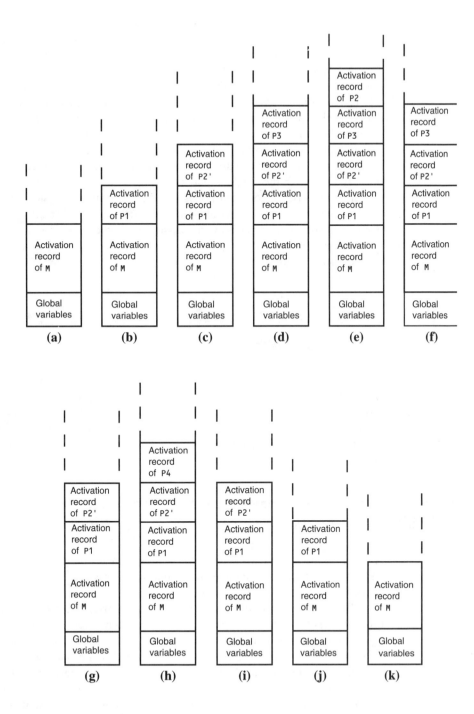

Figure 8.4 Evolution of the activation records stack during program execution.

assign an appropriate area of physical memory to a program. At the beginning of execution, the global variables and the activation record of the main program are put at the bottom of that area. At each subroutine call, the corresponding activation record is placed on the top of the stack (that is, it is allocated the memory cells immediately above those already occupied); at the end of each subroutine execution, the corresponding activation record is on top of the stack and can therefore easily be deallocated. All this is made possible by a datum contained in each activation record: the value of the pointer to the top of the stack (the **stack pointer**) corresponding to the specific activation. In this way, the portion of memory used by the program is always made up of contiguous cells: the 'lower' part of the memory initially allocated; the 'higher' part contains the cells still available for further activation records. Obviously, it is possible for the available physical memory to be filled up before the program terminates: in this case, if a further activation record is required, the machine suspends execution, signalling **stack overflow**.

Figure 8.4 shows the evolution of the stack with reference to the sequence of calls shown in Figure 8.3.

8.4 Further examples of recursive programming

In this section, we consider some more examples of recursive programming. Emphasis will be put on the naturalness of representing an algorithm in recursive form rather than on the efficiency of execution, which will be discussed in Chapter 12. However, it will sometimes be useful to refer back to the execution scheme described in Section 8.3, in order to evaluate better the alternatives available for a particular project.

EXAMPLE 8.3   Recognition of palindromic strings

A string of characters is called a **palindrome** if it reads the same from left to right and from right to left. Examples of palindromic strings are noon, level, madam, abbbcbbba.

The following program, RecPalindr, reads a string and uses a recursive function Palindrome to recognize palindromic strings composed of a sequence, possibly empty, of characters. Palindrome is based on the simple statement that a string of the desired type is either empty, or is composed of a single character, or has the first and the last characters equal and encloses another palindromic string. On the basis of this statement, Palindrome examines the received string. If it is empty or it is composed of only one character it returns a true value. Otherwise it compares the first and the last character of the string: if they are equal it calls itself recursively excluding the first and the last characters, otherwise it returns a false value.

RecPalindr reads the string to be checked (ending with the end-of-string character \0), computing its length. In case of an empty string it declares it to be a palindrome, otherwise it initializes the variable OK to true, calls the function Palindrome and tests the returned value.

```
                                                  /*Program RecPalindr*/
#include   <stdio.h>
#include   <string.h>

typedef enum {false, true} boolean;

main( )
{
   #define MaxStringLength   100

   char        String1[MaxStringLength];
   boolean     OK;
   unsigned    StringLen;

   boolean     Palindrome(char *FC, char *LC);

   scanf("%s", String1);
                           /*the previous statement assumes that the
                           characters composing the string do not
                           contain spaces*/
   StringLen = strlen(String1);
   if (StringLen == 0)
      printf("The string is a palindrome");
   else
   {
                           /*Palindrome is called passing by reference
                           the first and the last character of the
                           string to be analysed*/
     OK = Palindrome(&String1[0], &String1[StringLen-1]);
     if (OK == true)
        printf("The string is a palindrome");
     else
        printf("The string is not a palindrome");
   }
}

boolean Palindrome(char *FC, char *LC)
{
   if (FC >= LC)
                           /*if the string is either empty or consists
                           of a single character*/
        return true;
   else if (*FC != *LC)
                           /*if the first and the last characters are
                           different*/
        return false;
   else
                           /*calls itself recursively excluding the
                           first and the last characters*/
        return Palindrome(FC+1,LC-1);
}
```

EXAMPLE 8.4 *Operations on a list of elements*

Assume that we have a list of *n* integers and that it is stored as a variable of the following type:

```
typedef struct   { int   length;
                    int   cont[MaxLength];
                  } ListOfIntegers;
```

Notice that we adopt here a more abstract definition of the type `ListOfIntegers` than the way we managed sequences of integers in Section 8.2.

Various fundamental operations on such a list can be easily expressed and therefore coded, recursively. Let us look at some examples which make use of the following preliminary operations, (1) and (2), realized as suitable functions:

(1)   Elimination of the first element from a list, transforming it into its tail.

```
ListOfInteger  tail(ListOfInteger  l1)
                        /*l1 is a structured type variable
                        containing a copy of the list. The function
                        transforms l1 into the list consisting of
                        the last n - 1 elements, where n is the
                        length of the list at the time of the call.
                        The transformed list is returned by the
                        function*/
{
   int   i;

   for(i = 1; i < l1.length; i++)
      l1.cont[i-1] = l1.cont[i];
   l1.length = l1.length-1;
                        /*a result with length = -1 indicates to the
                        caller an incorrect operation*/
   return   l1;
}
```

(2)   Insertion of new element at the beginning of a list.

```
ListOfInteger  insertElem(int  el, ListOfInteger  l1)
                        /*the function transforms l1 into the list
                        composed of the new element el followed by
                        the pre-existing elements. The transformed
                        list is returned by the function*/
{
   int    i;

   if (l1.length < MaxLength)
   {
      for (i = l1.length; i > 0; i--)
         l1.cont[i] = l1.cont[i-1];
      l1.cont[0] = el;
      l1.length = l1.length + 1;
   }
```

```
      else
         printf("List full\n");
      return  l1;
}
```

(3)   Deletion of an element from the list (allowing for the possibility that the
       element may occur more than once in the list).

```
ListOfInteger    deleteElem(int  el, ListOfInteger  l1)
                             /*the function deletes from l1 the element
                             el. The transformed list is returned by the
                             function*/
{
   int   temp;

   if (l1.length > 0)
   {
      temp = l1.cont[0];
      if (temp==el)
         return deleteElem(el, tail(l1));
      else
         return insertElem(temp, deleteElem(el, tail(l1)));
   }
   return l1;
}
```

(4)   Searching for an element in the list.

```
boolean          searchElem(int  el, ListOfInteger  l1)
                             /*the function searches for the element el
                             in l1. Returns value true when the element
                             has been found, false otherwise*/
{
   if (l1.length > 0)
      if (l1.cont[0] == el)
         return  true;
      else
         return  searchElem(el,tail(l1));
   else
      return false;
}
```

(5)   Calculating the minimum and maximum elements of the list, realized by the
       following two functions, whose coding is left to the reader as an exercise.

```
int     min(ListOfIntegers   list);
int     max(ListOfIntegers   list);
```

(6)   Ordering the list (in increasing order).

```
ListOfInteger    orderListOfInteger  l1)
                             /*the function transforms l1, ordering its
                             elements. The transformed list is returned
                             by the function*/
```

```
{
    int   temp;
    if (l1.length > 1)
    {
        temp = min(l1);
        return insertElem(temp, order(deleteElem(temp,l1)));
    }
    return   l1;
}
```

The reader is invited to compare the implementation of operations on list elements proposed in this example with the realization proposed in Chapter 10, where new techniques are used to realize data structures.

EXAMPLE 8.5 Calculating the determinant of a square matrix

The determinant of a square matrix A of order n is defined as follows:

If $n = 1$, then $\det(A) = a_{11}$

otherwise

$$\det(A) = \sum_{i=1}^{n} (-1)^{i+1} \cdot a_{1i} \cdot \det(A_{1i})$$

where A_{1i} indicates the matrix obtained from A by eliminating the first row and the ith column.

In general, thanks to well-known properties of linear algebra, we can say that:

$$\det(A) = \sum_{i=1}^{n} (-1)^{i+1} a_{i,1} \det(A_{i1}) = \sum_{j=1}^{n} (-1)^{j+1} a_{1,j} \det(A_{1j}) \qquad (8.1)$$

where A_{ij} indicates the minor of index $<i,j>$ of matrix A, that is, the submatrix obtained from A by deleting the ith row and the jth column.

It is interesting to observe the naturally recursive formulation inherent in (8.1), which suggests a quick transformation into an equally recursive subroutine.

A formulation of the recursive function to calculate the determinant of a square matrix is the following:

```
                                    /*Program determinant of a square matrix*/
#include <math.h>

double   det(SquareMatrix   mat)
{
    double     result;
    int        j;

    if (mat.ord == 1) result = mat.cont[0][0];
    else
```

```
{
    result = 0;
    for (j = 0; j <= mat.ord-1; j=j+1)
        result = result +
            pow ((-1), j)*mat.cont[0][j]*det(SubMatrix(mat, 0, j));
}
return   result;
}
```

In this code, the type of the argument mat is assumed to be declared as:

```
typedef  struct {  int        ord;
                   double     cont[OrdMax][OrdMax];
                } SquareMatrix;
```

which, thanks to a technique already used, allows the logical contents of an array to be separated from its physical dimensions.

The auxiliary function SubMat produces the matrix obtained by deleting from mat the *i*th row (in this case, the first) and the *j*th column. The pow function is a function of the standard library raising the first argument to the power indicated by the second; its prototype can be found in the file math.h. It produces a domain error if its first argument is zero and the second is less than or equal to zero, or if the first argument is less than zero and the second is not an integer.

Given that the language allows us to write functions whose result is of structured type, it is quite straightforward to declare the function SubMatrix which receives as its parameters:

- a value of type SquareMatrix with ord > 1;
- two integers, *h* and *k*, whose values must lie between 0 and ord-1;

and yields as its result a value of type SquareMatrix whose ord field is that of the parameter decreased by 1 and whose cont field is the matrix obtained by deleting the *h*th row and the *k*th column of the cont field of the parameter (see Exercise 8.4).

Before we leave this example, it might be useful to mention that the complete execution of the det procedure, except for very small argument values, is extremely onerous in terms of both the amount of memory and the time needed. The reader will readily agree with this statement on the basis of an intuitive analysis of the procedure's functioning: a more precise analysis is left until Chapter 12. However, it should be said that the above procedure is not intended as a practical tool for calculating the determinant, but is only given to underline the fact that often a recursive algorithm can be obtained directly from the *definition* of a problem. Fortunately, there are algorithms for the solution of this problem which are much more efficient, but they are also much more difficult to construct.

Many of the examples and exercises presented in this chapter could have been as easily solved without using recursive programming. However, they are particularly aimed at facilitating the learning of this powerful and (after a bit of experience) natural programming technique, whose practical use will be highlighted further in the following chapters. The design choice of whether or not to code subroutines recursively will become part of the programmer's personal style.

Exercises

8.1 Reformulate the Weighing algorithm so that it can identify a marble of different weight from the others (not knowing, a priori, whether it is heavier or lighter) among any number of marbles of the same weight.

8.2 Provide recursive definitions of the following concepts:

(a) the product of two natural numbers,

(b) the set of permutations of a list of elements.

8.3 Complete the algorithm for calculating the determinant of a square matrix (presented in Example 8.5) by coding the function `SubMatrix`. Assume that this function yields as its result a structured variable of type `SquareMatrix`.

8.4 Modify the coding of both `det` and `SubMatrix`, realizing `SubMatrix` as a procedure.

8.5 The Tower of Hanoi problem is defined as follows. There are n disks of different diameter on a peg, such that the largest disk is at the lowest point and all the others are on top of it in decreasing diameter order. There are another two pegs which are initially free (see Figure 8.5(a)). We want to transport all the disks to another peg, moving them one at a time from one peg to another and operating in such a way that a larger disk is never put on top of a smaller one (obviously, in order to move a disk from one peg to another it is necessary to have removed the disks on top of it, always respecting the above rules). Figures 8.5(b) and 8.5(c) complete the illustration of the problem.

Provide an algorithm to solve the Tower of Hanoi problem.

Suggestion: Use a recursive formulation of the algorithm making use of the following remarks:

- If the number of disks n is small (for example, 1 or 2), the solution to the problem is immediate.
- If we can solve the problem for n disks, we can solve it for $n + 1$ as follows:
    - Transfer the n upper disks onto the free peg which is not the eventual destination of all the $n + 1$ disks, applying the solution algorithm recursively to the n upper disks (during the execution of this procedure, the $(n + 1)$th disk, being the largest of all, can be quietly ignored: consequently, the peg that contains only that disk is equivalent to an empty peg).

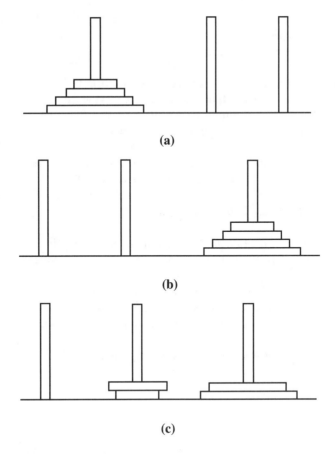

Figure 8.5 The tower of Hanoi problem: (a) the initial state, (b) the goal state, (c) an inadmissible state.

- Transfer the largest disk onto the desired peg.
- Put the remaining disks back on top of the largest disk (which, again, does not inhibit the movement of the other disks).

Try to formulate the algorithm in a nonrecursive way: very probably, you will run into much greater difficulties.

8.6 Give a recursive formulation of Euclid's algorithm for calculating the greatest common divisor of two numbers, which is recalled below in nonrecursive form.

```
int     GCD(int   x, int   y)
{
   while (x != y)
      if (x > y) x = x - y; else y = y - x;
   return   x;
}
```

8.7 If the parameter list of the function searchElem declared in item 4 of Example 8.4 was passed by reference instead of by value, it would be advisable to modify the code of the procedure. Why and how?

8.8 Recode the functions tail, insertElem, deleteElem and order presented in Example 8.4 as functions which receive the list l1 by reference and return a pointer to the list. Comment on the differences to the proposed coding and the consequences of their use in other procedures/functions.

8.9 Recode the functions tail, insertElem, deleteElem searchElem and order presented in Example 8.4 as procedures dealing with a list declared as global variable. Comment on the differences to the proposed coding and the consequences of their use in other procedures/functions.

8.10 Modify the functions for searching for elements in a list and deleting elements from a list, assuming that the list is ordered and does not contain duplicate elements.

8.11 Write a function that inserts a new element in the list, avoiding repetitions: if the element already exists, it must not be inserted again. Then write another function that inserts a new element in an ordered list, keeping it ordered.

8.12 Implement, in C, the Weighing algorithm described in Example 8.1.

File management

This chapter is dedicated to the treatment of files in C. Files require particular attention because they are permanent 'information containers' (held in mass storage) which often transcend the 'life' of a program, that is, they exist before its execution and continue to exist after its termination. Files are therefore part of the system and are managed, as we will see in Chapter 15, by the file system: a specialized functional layer of the operating system. Programs written in different languages must be able to manipulate the information contained in the files, calling on the operating system to create, read, write and delete files.

A file of information may have been created by programs written in different languages. It may contain a program, written using a word processor and subsequently translated into object code by a compiler, or it may contain data processed by programs dedicated to data management. In particular, it may contain data suitable for processing by a C program: these are the files upon which we concentrate in this chapter.

In some languages there are points of controversy in defining the handling of files and the latest trend tends not to define file handling as part of the programming language at all. In C, there is a precise definition of the treatment of files available through the standard library which provides a set of functions for handling files. The implementation of the library functions (made available by the C system) takes into account the operating system under which the C program is executed, allowing the correct invocation of the functions of the operating system itself. This allows the programmer, as we will see in the next section, to handle files quite easily, independently of the file management implemented by the operating system.

We have said that a file is a 'permanent information container', but, in order to understand fully the possibilities offered to the programmer, we must not neglect another fundamental aspect. We will see in Chapter 15 that the operating system shows the programmer the input and output peripherals (terminals, printers) as files, so that the programmer can write to the Standard Output by writing into a particular file that 'represents' the standard output device and read from the Standard Input by reading from a particular file that 'represents' the standard input device.

The programmer can thus implement an input/output operation or an operation on permanent storage in an identical way: by writing to or reading from a file using the functions made available by the standard library. The file under consideration can therefore be an 'information container' held in mass storage or the 'representative' of an input/output device.

9.1 Streams, files and C programs

A C program that wants to use a file for permanent storage or input/output operations must open a **communication stream**, signalling to the operating system its intention to open an existing file or its requirement to create and open a new file. At the end of the set of operations involving this file, the communication stream is closed, thereby also closing the file. The similarities between the two kinds of operations allow us to use, in the following, the term 'input/output operation' both for operations involving an input/output device and for operations on permanent storage.

In order to open a communication stream, a C program must declare a variable of pointer type and request that the stream be opened via a library function (`fopen`) which asks the operating system to create a new file or to open an existing one. The opening of the communication stream causes the assignment of the pointer variable. The value taken by the pointer variable is used by the C program to refer (in subsequent operations) to the file corresponding to the particular communication stream opened. The communication stream is closed by the `fclose` library function.

A C program can open a **binary** or a **text communication** stream. The file corresponding to the communication stream is opened as a binary or text file and is treated in subsequent operations according to how it has been opened. A binary stream is a sequence of bytes. A text stream is a sequence of characters, normally divided into lines which are separated by a newline character. In a text stream, some characters are translated by the environment (for example, the newline character in a text stream may be converted into a carriage return and line feed of the print head on the printer that constitutes the physical output device). In a binary stream, no byte is translated.

We have said that opening a communication stream assigns a value to the pointer variable local to the C program and that this value allows the program to refer to the stream (and the file) in subsequent operations. This variable must point to an object of type `FILE` capable of recording all the information needed to control a stream. `FILE` is therefore a structured type which might contain:

- a field containing the **usage mode** of the file involved (read, write or read and write mode),

- a field containing the **current position** in the file (a field that points to the next byte to be read from or written to the file),

- a field containing an **error indicator** that records whether a read/write error has occurred,

- a field containing an **end-of-file indicator** that records whether the end-of-file has been reached.

Each variable pointing to a file in a C program must be defined as follows:

```
FILE    *fp;
```

In order to understand what this variable points to (and how it succeeds in hooking into the file management of the operating system) we need to say something about variables managed by the operating system itself.

As we will see in Chapter 15, the operating system manages a data structure that keeps track of the files used by programs being executed and holds information on how each file is used. Suppose that the operating system (not the C program!) manages a variable named OpenFileTable declared as follows:

```
FILE    OpenFileTable[MaxNumHandFiles];
```

OpenFileTable is a vector with a maximum number of elements corresponding to the maximum number of files that can be handled simultaneously by the operating system. Information on how the individual files are used is stored in the elements of the vector.

When a program opens a file, by specifying the name of the file to be opened and its usage mode, the operating system creates a new element in the OpenFileTable, assigns to the appropriate fields the usage mode and the position of the next byte to read or write, and assigns to the pointer variable defined as local to the C program the address of the structure of FILE type that describes the file in question. It is important to note that it is the operating system that manipulates the fields of the FILE type structure; the user causes this manipulation indirectly by invoking functions in the standard library.

Thus, a C program can open a communication stream, provided it declares a pointer variable to FILE. The program imports the definition of the FILE type (which depends on the system) and the definition of some constants (used in the library functions that handle files), by importing the contents of the header file stdio.h using the directive #include.

There are three **standard streams** which are automatically opened when program execution starts: stdin, stdout and stderr. Normally, these three streams are associated with files that 'represent' the display screen of the terminal (stdout and stderr) and the keyboard of the terminal (stdin). stdin, stdout and stderr are the pointer variables to the descriptors of these files, and their values are assigned when program execution begins.

The functions for formatted input and output, printf and scanf, described in Chapter 4, use these standard streams: printf writes to the file referred to by the pointer stdout, and scanf reads from the file referred to by stdin.

All of these concepts are illustrated in Figure 9.1.

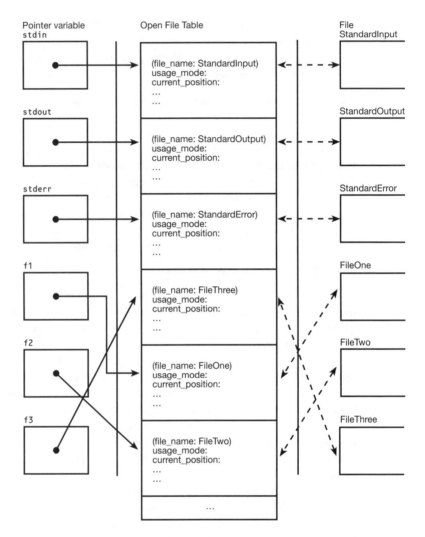

Figure 9.1 Relationship between variables pointing to FILE, the elements of the OpenFileTable and files.

9.2 Operations on files

In this and the following section, we describe the principal functions provided by the standard library for handling files. Nearly all of these functions return a value that indicates whether the operation has been executed correctly. Parameters that are not completely defined here, indicated in italics, are explained in terms of the role they play with respect to the function.

9.2.1   File management operations

In this group, we include the functions for opening, closing, deleting and renaming a file. The examples presented later in this chapter involve the open and close functions and show the link between the name of a file and the pointer to FILE returned by the open function, together with the link between the open mode of a file and the operations that can be executed on it.

- FILE   *fopen(*filename, mode*)

  opens a file, creating it if it does not already exist, and associates it with a stream; it returns the address of the FILE type structure that describes the opened file; its parameters are the name of the file to be opened and the open mode string which determines the operations that can be carried out on the file. The opening modes are "r" (read in text mode, position at the beginning of the file), "w" (write in text mode, position at the beginning of the file), "a" (write in text mode, beginning at the end of the file), "rb", "wb" and "ab" (reading, writing and writing from the end of the file in binary mode), "r+", "w+" and "a+" (reading from and writing to the file in text mode), "rb+", "wb+" and "ab+" (reading from and writing to the file in binary mode).

- int   fclose(FILE *fp)

  closes the file referred to by the pointer fp. The close operation involves assigning fp the value NULL and releasing the descriptor of FILE type. If the close operation is executed correctly, it returns the value 0, otherwise it returns the value EOF (EOF is a constant defined in stdio.h).

- int   remove(*filename*)

  deletes the file identified by *filename*. It returns 0 if the operation has been executed correctly, a nonzero value otherwise. If the user tries to delete an open file, the function's behaviour depends on the implementation.

- int   rename(*oldname, newname*)

  changes the name of a file from *oldname* to *newname*. It returns 0 if the operation has been executed correctly, a nonzero value otherwise. If the user tries to rename an open file or if the new name is the name of an already existing file, the function's behaviour depends on the implementation.

9.2.2   Error handling operations

In the structure that describes the state of an open file (the structure, as we have already said, is managed by the operating system), there are two fields used to record a generic error condition and the condition that 'the end of the file has been reached'. An attempt to read data from beyond the end of the file provokes the end of file condition (normally indicated by eof) and the eof detector field of the structure records this anomalous event. The error field records other types of error that may occur during an operation involving a file. The contents of these fields may be checked by calling the two functions `feof` and `ferror`, provided by the standard library. The programmer can thus check whether the end of the file has been reached (useful, for example, when a file is scanned sequentially) or whether a different kind of error has occurred (if this cannot be inferred from the value returned by the function invoked).

- **int**   `ferror(FILE *fp)`
  checks the structure that describes the status of the file referred to by `fp` to see if an error occurred in the previous read or write operation. It returns 0 if no error occurred, a nonzero value otherwise.

- **int**   `feof(FILE *fp)`
  checks the structure that describes the status of the file referred to by `fp` if the end of the file was reached in the previous read or write operation. It returns 0 if the end of the file was been reached, a nonzero value otherwise.

- **void**   `clearerr(FILE *fp)`
  resets the `eof` detector and `error` detector fields of the structure that describes the status of the file referred to by the pointer `fp` to their default values.

9.2.3 Read and write operations

Read and write operations on files can be carried out in four different modes: defining the data format for input and output, and accessing the data character by character, line by line, or block by block. Generally, line by line access is used in text streams, and character by character or block by block access in binary streams.

Formatted read and write

In Chapter 4 we introduced and described in detail the library functions `scanf` and `printf`. They allow us to implement formatted read and write operations from the Standard Input device and to the Standard Output device, respectively (or, as we could now say, from and to the files pointed to by the variables `stdin` and `stdout`, respectively). The control string, which contains the format descriptors and conversion characters, allows us to specify the format in which data is read or written.

The functions `fscanf` and `fprintf` provide formatted operations similar to those of `scanf` and `printf`, but involve the file identified by the user via the pointer `fp`. They return the number of elements read or written, or a negative number if an error occurs. We just show the headers of the functions:

- **int**   `printf(control string, elements)`
- **int**   `scanf(control string, address of elements)`
- **int**   `fprintf(FILE *fp, control string, elements)`
- **int**   `fscanf(FILE *fp, control string, elements)`

Reading and writing characters

Six functions in the standard library allow us to read and write characters from and to files. getchar reads the next character from Standard Input and returns it as an integer. putchar writes the character it receives as a parameter as the next character output to the Standard Output file, returning the character written. getc and fgetc read the next character of the file specified in the input parameter and return it as an integer. putc and fputc write the character specified in the input parameter as the next character of the file and return it as an integer. All the functions return EOF in case of error: to check whether it is an end of file or another error, feof or ferror have to be used. getc and putc are normally implemented with a view to execution speed, but carry the risk of side-effects. Example 9.1 uses fgetc to read characters from a text type file and putchar to write characters to the Standard Output. The headers of the functions described above are:

- int   getchar(**void**);
- int   putchar(**int** c);
- int   getc(FILE *fp);
- int   putc(**int** c, FILE *fp);
- int   fgetc(FILE *fp);
- int   fputc(**int** c, FILE *fp);

EXAMPLE 9.1

The following program reads and displays on screen the contents of the text type file charfile:

```
#include <stdio.h>
                                /*contains the definition of EOF,
                                the type FILE and the headers of the
                                functions that operate on files*/
#include <stddef.h>
                                /*contains the definition of NULL*/
main()
{
   FILE     *fp;
   char     c;

   if((fp = fopen("charfile","r")) != NULL)
                                /*the file is opened for reading in
                                text mode*/
   {
      while((c = fgetc(fp)) != EOF)
                                /*one character at a time is read
                                and printed, up to the end of the
                                file*/
```

```
        putchar(c);
     fclose(fp);
  }
  else
     printf("The file cannot be opened\n");
}
```

Reading and writing strings (access by line)

Four functions in the standard library allow us to read and write character strings from and to files: gets and puts, respectively, read from Standard Input and write to Standard Output, while fgets and fputs, respectively, read or write lines (character strings terminated by a newline) from or to the file specified as an input parameter.

- **char** *gets(**char** *s);

  reads characters from the Standard Input file until it reaches a newline character or the end of file. s points to the first element of the vector in which the data read is stored. The newline character is not inserted in the vector; the string terminator \0 is inserted instead. The function returns s if the operation executed correctly, NULL otherwise.

- **int** puts(**char** *s)

  writes to the Standard Output the contents of the string pointed to by s, followed by a newline character; the string terminating character \0 is not written. It returns the number of written characters if the operation executed correctly, 0 otherwise.

- **char** *fgets(**char** *s, **int** n, FILE *fp)

  reads characters from the file pointed to by fp until it has read $n-1$ elements, reaches a newline character or encounters the end of the file. s points to the first element of the vector in which data read is stored. The function inserts any newline character read in the vector, plus the string terminator \0 . It returns s if the operation executed correctly, NULL otherwise.

- **int** fputs(**char** *s, FILE *fp)

  writes to the file pointed to by fp the contents of the string pointed to by s; the string terminating character 0 is not written. It returns the number of written characters if the operation executed correctly, 0 otherwise.

Example 9.2 uses fgets to read lines from a text type file and fputs to write lines to another text type file.

EXAMPLE 9.2

The following function receives a reference string as its input parameter, reads the contents of the text file infile line by line and writes, into the text file outfile, only the lines that contain the reference string. The function returns the value 1 if the operation executed correctly, 0 otherwise.

```
#include <stdio.h>
#include <stddef.h>
#include <string.h>
#define OK          1
#define ERROR       0
#define  MAXLINE    100

int     electivecopy(char  refstr[])
{
   char   line[MAXLINE];
   FILE   *fin, *fout;

   if((fin = fopen("infile","r")) == NULL)
                          /*infile is opened for reading in text mode*/
      return  ERROR;
   if((fout = fopen("outfile","w")) == NULL)
                          /*outfile is opened for writing in text mode*/
   {
      fclose(fin);
      return ERROR;
   }
   while(fgets(line,MAXLINE,fin) != NULL)
                          /*fgets reads from infile a maximum of
                          MAXLINE - 1 characters and assigns the
                          characters read to the vector line,
                          including any newline character, and ends
                          the string with the character \0*/
      if(strstr (line,refstr) != NULL)
                          /*the function strstr returns the position
                          of the first occurrence of the string
                          pointed to by refstr in the string pointed
                          to by line; if the second string is not
                          contained in the first one, the value NULL
                          is returned*/
         fputs(line,fout);
   fclose(fin);
   fclose(fout);
   return OK;
}
```

Reading and writing structures (block access)

It is possible to access data in a file by reading or writing an entire block of text or binary data. The two functions `fread` and `fwrite` allow us to specify the address of a vector that either receives the elements that compose the block (`fread`) or contains the elements to be written (`fwrite`), the number of elements to be read or written and the dimensions of a single element. Example 9.3 shows a typical use of `fread` and `fwrite`: reading from and writing to files that contain structured type data.

- **int** `fread(`**void** `*ptr,`*dimelement, numelements,* `FILE *fp);`

  reads a block of binary data from the file referred to by `fp` and stores it in the vector identified by `ptr`. The function terminates correctly if it reads the number of bytes required (`dimelement*numelements`); it also terminates if it encounters the end of the file or if a read error occurs. The function returns the number of bytes effectively read; if this number is less than the number required, `feof` or `ferror` must be used to determine the reasons for the (mal)functioning.

- **int** `fwrite(`**void** `*ptr,`*dimelement, numelements,* `FILE *fp);`

  writes a block of binary data to the file referred to by `fp`, taking it from the vector identified by `ptr`. The function terminates correctly if it writes the number of bytes required (`dimelement*numelements`); it also terminates if a write error occurs. The function returns the number of bytes effectively written; if this number is less than the number required, `feof` or `ferror` must be used to determine the reasons for the (mal)functioning.

EXAMPLE 9.3

Suppose you have constructed a `Personnel` file consisting of records of `Person` type. Each `Person` contains the fields `FirstName`, `LastName` and `Address`. We want to modify the file by adding the field `SocSecNum` to each `Person`.

In order to do this, a file `SocSecNum` has been prepared, whose records contain the tax codes of the persons contained in `Personnel`, *in the same order.*

Let us assume that these files are constructed within the same program, starting from input information read in (the data acquisition operations could be put into appropriate procedures, such as `ReadPerson`, `ReadSocSecNum` and so on: this exercise is left to the reader). We now want to construct a file `NewPersonnel`, drawn from the file `Personnel` and adding to each person the field `SocSecNum`, whose value is read from the file `SocSecNum`. Let us assume that the files `Personnel` and `SocSecNum` are open for reading and writing and that `NewPersonnel` is open for writing. The three files are binary.

This operation is carried out by the following function, which takes the files to be used as parameters. The function is preceded by the necessary type declarations.

```
typedef struct  { char    FirstName[20];
                  char    LastName[20];
                  char    Address[50];
                } Person;
typedef char     SSNum[16];
typedef struct  { char    FirstName[20];
                  char    LastName[20];
                  char    Address[50];
                  SSNum   SocSecNum;
                } NewPerson;
                     /*we suppose that the files Personnel, SocSecNum
                     and NewPersonnel have been opened by main. pp, tc
                     and np refer to the three files in question*/
int    UpdatePerson (FILE  *pp, FILE  *tc, FILE  *np)
{
   Person            CurrentPerson;
   SSNum             CurrentSSNum;
   NewPerson         CurrentNewPerson;

   rewind(pp);
                     /*makes possible the following reading and writing
                     operations on the file identified by pp, starting
                     from the first byte of the file. See Section 9.3*/
   rewind(tc);
   rewind(np);

   while (fread(&CurrentPerson, sizeof(Person),1,pp) != 0)
                               /*until we reach the end of file*/
   {
      fread(&CurrentSSNum, sizeof(SSNum),1,tc);
      strcpy(CurrentNewPerson.FirstName, CurrentPerson.FirstName);
      strcpy(CurrentNewPerson.LastName, CurrentPerson.LastName);
      strcpy(CurrentNewPerson.Address, CurrentPerson.Address);
      strcpy(CurrentNewPerson.SSNum, CurrentSSNum);
      fwrite(&CurrentNewPerson, sizeof(NewPerson),1,np);
   }
}
```

9.3 Direct access

It can be useful, in some cases, to access a particular byte within a file directly. Example 9.4 and Exercise 9.1 illustrate two situations in which direct access to a byte is preferable to sequential access. The function fseek in the standard library allows a file to be positioned at a particular byte and the function ftell returns the number of the byte at which the file is currently positioned. Note that the value of the current position (expressed as a number of bytes, assuming that the first byte of the file is position 0) is the value of a field of the FILE type structure that describes the state of the opened file.

- **int** fseek(FILE *fp, **long** offset, **int** refpoint)

  allows the position indicator to be moved in order to access directly the file referred to by fp. The displacement offset (which can take positive or negative values and is expressed in bytes) refers to the fixed position indicated by refpoint, which can assume three different values defined in stdio.h: SEEK_SET is a constant which indicates an offset from the beginning of the file, SEEK_CUR indicates an offset from the current position and SEEK_END indicates an offset from the end of the file. The function fseek returns 0 if the request is correct, a nonzero value otherwise.

- **long** ftell(FILE *fp)

  returns the current value of the position indicator of the specified file. For binary files, the position is the number of bytes from the beginning of the file, but for text files its value depends on the implementation.

- One further function allows the value of the current position in a file to be altered, assigning it the value of the beginning of the file: rewind.

  ```
  rewind(f)
  ```

  is equivalent to:

  ```
  fseek(f, 0, SEEK_SET);
  ```

  Unlike fseek, rewind does not return any value.

EXAMPLE 9.4

Suppose we want to reverse the contents of a file of integers, numint, exchanging the first element with the last, the second with the second last and so on. This could be achieved via the following code:

```
#include <stdio.h>
#include <stddef.h>
#include <stdlib.h>

main()
{
    FILE          *f;
    long int      start, end;
    int           tempi, tempf;
    unsigned int  size;

    if((f = fopen("numint","rb+")) == NULL)
    {
        puts("impossible to open file numint");
                        /*the function puts is more efficient than
                        printf for the display of a message, because
```

```
                                    it does not require a control string to be
                                    scanned and interpreted*/
        exit(1);

                                    /*the function exit causes the program to
                                    terminate correctly and returns control to
                                    the operating system*/
    }
    start = 0;
    size = sizeof(int);
    fseek(f, -size, SEEK_END);
                                    /*the SEEK_END constant is defined in the
                                    file stdio.h - its value is 2*/
    end = ftell(f);
    while (start < end)
    {
        fseek(f, start, SEEK_SET);
                                    /*the SEEK_SET  constant is defined in the
                                    file stdio.h - its value is 0*/
        fread(&tempi, size, 1, f);
        fseek(f, end, SEEK_SET);
        fread(&tempf, size, 1, f);
                                    /*it is necessary to reposition because the
                                    previous fread statement has moved the
                                    current position to the next element*/
        fseek(f, end, SEEK_SET);
        fwrite(&tempi, size, 1, f);
        fseek(f, start, SEEK_SET);
        fwrite(&tempf, size, 1, f);
        start = start + size;
        end = end - size;
    }
    fclose(f);
}
```

9.4 Some concluding remarks

The next example takes up the various points raised in this and previous chapters, leading to a critical analysis and some conclusions.

EXAMPLE 9.5

Consider the problem of managing a flight booking service.

The customers, or rather, the employees who operate the terminals on their customers' behalf, ask the system to execute simple operations, such as booking a flight, cancelling the booking, being put on the waiting list and displaying various pieces of information: timetables, availability of seats, recommended routes and so on. In response, the system accesses the archive, or archives, executes the required operations and produces the desired answers.

We present a simplified and incomplete version of a system to provide the required service. However, along with the various exercises, this should suggest the different ways in which it could be rendered more complete and realistic.

The main program offers the user a menu of possible operations. When the user selects an operation, the main program delegates it to a suitable function capable of handling the archive. Using the technique of gradually deriving the code from partial formulations of the program written in pseudocode, we write a first version of the main program.

```
                                              /*Program FlightServices*/
main()
{
                              [various declarations to define: variables
                              needed to refer to the files that store the
                              archive, functions to manage the archive with
                              regard to the required operations, variables and
                              types associated with the archive, and variables
                              and types needed to implement the menu]
End = false;
do
{
  [ClearScreen]
  puts("\nThe following operations are available. To select, press
      the key indicated to the right of the operation, followed by
      <enter>.\n");
  puts("Flight booking             B");
                          /*remember that puts inserts a newline after
                            the string*/
  puts("Cancel a booking           C");
  puts("Insertion into waiting list  W");
  puts("End of operations          E");
  getchar(Answer);
  switch (Answer)
  {
    case 'B':  ServBooking();
               break;
    case 'C':  ServCancel();
               break;
    case 'W':  ServWaitList();
               break;
    case 'E':  End = true;
               break;
  }
} while (End == false);
[ClearScreen]
puts("\n\n\nBye\n");
}
```

As you can see, the main program contains a 'master switch', delegating the execution of the operations to the various functions. These, in turn, require a further dialogue with the user, in order to ascertain the information required (flight number and date, passenger's name and so on).

Let us now go into more detail, specifying first the structure of the archive. It will be stored in a file named FlightArchive: each element (record) of the file contains information about one flight. Each flight is described by a flight number, a date, a passenger list and a waiting list.

```
#define  MAXSEATS   350
typedef    struct   { char      LastName[30];
                       char      FirstName[30];
                     } Passenger;
typedef    struct   { int       FlightNum;
                       char      Date[10];
                       Passenger Booking[MAXSEATS];
                       Passenger WaitingList[100];
                     } FlightDescription;
```

To these declarations, we add the variable declarations of the main program and a first informal description of the procedures used to carry out the various operations:

```
boolean  End;
char     Answer;
FILE     *fa;          /*pointer to the file descriptor of FlightArchive*/
void     ServBooking(void);
                       /*executes the required booking, if possible.
                       Otherwise, it asks if the customer wants to be put
                       on the waiting list. If the answer is positive, it
                       calls the function WaitListServ without having to
                       return to the main menu. After WaitListServ has
                       been executed, ServBooking is terminated.
                       Execution of the function includes interaction
                       with the user, via an appropriate menu in which
                       the user is asked to input the number and date of
                       the desired flight and the first and last names of
                       the passenger.
                       After obtaining the required data, the function
                       accesses the archive and proceeds with the
                       necessary interrogation and updating operations.*/
void     ServCancel(void);
                       /*via an appropriate menu, passenger data and
                       identification of the flight whose booking is to
                       be cancelled are requested. The passenger is
                       deleted from the corresponding list.
                       Furthermore, if the flight's waiting list is not
                       empty, its first element is extracted and inserted
                       in the list of bookings. Then, a message is
                       written to the terminal informing the operator
                       that one element of the waiting list now has the
                       passenger's booking confirmed.*/
void     ServWaitList(void);
                       /*the usual information is requested, and the
                       passenger is inserted in the desired waiting
                       list.*/
```

At this point, the project can continue specifying the details of the various functions. For each one, the following have to be defined:

- The menu or menus for interacting with the user.

- The structure of the local data.

- The body of the function. This will have a structure similar to `main`, consisting of a series of calls, selected via a `switch` construct, to further auxiliary functions that execute simple operations to consult the archive and return the required answers. The `ServBooking` function, for example, after acquiring the client's data and the required flight, will look up that flight in the archive and determine whether seats are available.

The main goal of Example 9.5 is to show how even complex projects can be tackled step by step, making only a few choices at a time. Normally, the individual subproblems are not particularly complex (very often they access, interrogate and update archives), if they are suitably isolated from their context.

Without going too deeply into the problem of complex software system development, it is useful to highlight some critical points in the development technique we have used.

(1) It seems natural to store the flight descriptions in a binary file, not in a text file: this certainly allows a higher level of abstraction. Obviously, the file allows the data to be persistent. When the program terminates, the data remains available for future processing.

(2) The way in which the program has been constructed emphasizes the service to be provided: booking flights. Each design choice has therefore been made on the basis of the required operations, the dialogue for interacting with the user and so on. The structure of the archive and its access procedures are a consequence of the previous choices. In practice, very often the opposite happens: there are one or more archives equipped with their own handling mechanisms. On that basis, various applications are constructed (for example, in addition to the booking service, there might be programs to produce statistics about flight usage, to construct timetables and so on). The language has constrained us to concentrate on a single program to which the archive structures are subordinate: it does not lend itself to the opposing scheme which would start with the implementation of a set of archives and then proceed with the different programs that use and share them.

(3) Owing to the syntax of the language, large programs are rather difficult to understand: the reader who has completely developed the program set up in Example 9.5 will have obtained a certain number of pages containing declarations of data structures, the main program and functions. This

certainly does not facilitate the immediate identification and reading of the fundamental parts of the program.

These fairly superficial remarks show that the structure of C could make the development of large software projects rather complex. Although this kind of discussion lies outside the goals of this book, we deal with it briefly in Chapters 22 and 25, referring also to programming languages more suitable for overcoming these difficulties.

Exercises

9.1 Suppose we have a file containing data about 1000 books. The data collected conforms to the following structured type:

```
typedef struct { int     catmark;
                 char    author[40];
                 char    title[50];
                 char    publisher[30];
                 int     year;
               } book;
```

Assuming that the data is randomly placed in the file, we want to obtain a printout of the data in ascending numerical order of the catmark field.

This exercise must be carried out using **indexed ordering**. This ordering strategy requires the file to be scanned once, reading from each structure only the value of the field that determines the order of the printout (this field is called the **key** field) and associating this value with a pointer to the file (called the **index**) which points to the relevant structure within the file. Thus, a data structure that can be ordered on the basis of the key field is constructed (the ordering of this structure, consisting of the elements of only two fields, may be much less onerous than ordering the structures of the file directly). Using the values of the indexes, 1000 direct accesses to the file are carried out and the book data is printed out in key field order.

Outline execution: define an auxiliary structure for the ordering as follows:

```
typedef struct { int     index;
                 int     key;
               } TforOrd;
TforOrd    forordering[1000];
```

- During the first scanning of the file, the value of the catmark field of each record is read and assigned to the key field of the next free element of forordering. The index field is assigned a number corresponding to the number of the record in the file that contains the key value in the key field.

- Order the elements of the vector forordering in key field order.

- Scan the vector forordering and execute the following operations for each element i, using the value of the index field of element i:

– an fseek on the file with offset = forordering[i].index * **sizeof**(book) and mode SEEK_SET;

– a read operation to retrieve the book data contained in the file, starting from the current position given by the fseek operation;

– an operation to print the data.

An alternative version of the program could assign the index field elements of forordering the position of the record in the file, not the record number.

9.2 Extend the menu of the FlightServices program illustrated in Example 9.5 to offer other useful operations for such a service.

9.3 Complete the FlightServices project according to the outline presented in Example 9.5 and the extensions you defined in Exercise 9.2. We suggest using further service functions, such as ResetArchive, ResetFlight, InsertNewFlight, DeleteFlight and so on.

9.4 Modify the FlightServices program described in Example 9.5 so that the customer can specify the required flight not only by its number, but also by its departure time and its journey (place of departure, place of arrival).

9.5 Further modify the FlightServices program so that it can also handle the assignment of a seat at boarding time, taking into account the different classes, smoking and nonsmoking areas and other possible differentiations and/or customer wishes.

9.6 Modify the FlightServices program so that flights are also classified by different airline companies (remember that, normally, flights are identified by the initials of the company and the flight number).

Using a different file for each airline company is recommended.

9.7 Note that in the system described in Example 9.5, the WaitListServ function is sometimes called automatically by the ServBooking function but, once it is called, it asks again for the passenger data and the flight required. Modify the program to avoid this drawback.

9.8 Assume we have a file employees, containing, among other things, the first name, last name and salary of each employee. We do not allow duplicate first and last names. We also have a file UpdateSalaries containing the first name, last name and new salary of some of the employees. Write code that updates the employees file so that the salary field contains the new salary if one is found in the UpdateSalaries file. Otherwise, the salary remains unaltered.

Solve this exercise for the case where both files are ordered alphabetically (by last name and first name), the case where neither of them is ordered and the case where only the `employees` file is ordered.

9.9 Solve Exercise 9.8 assuming that: each record in the `employees` file also contains an `id` field consisting of a number that uniquely identifies the employee; the `employees` file is ordered in ascending order of `id` numbers; and the file `UpdateSalaries` contains structures made up of the pair `id` number, new salary, stored in any order.

Suggestion: We recommend coming back to this exercise after reading Chapter 12 and checking whether improvements can be made.

9.10 Write a function that, given a file `Invoices` containing structures of `InvoiceDescription` type as defined in Section 5.5.2, and an invoice of that same type, inserts the new invoice at the end of the file.

9.11 Write a function that, given a file with the same characteristics as in Exercise 9.10, but with the invoices ordered by date, and an invoice of the same type, inserts the new invoice immediately after those whose date field is the same as that of the invoice to be inserted (if there are none, the invoice is inserted in such a way that the sorting order is maintained).

9.12 A file contains different decks of playing cards of various colours (by colour we mean the back of the cards). The cards are shuffled randomly (the various decks are intermingled) and some decks might even be incomplete.

Write a program that orders the above file by colour, by suit (hearts, diamonds, spades, clubs) and by card value (ace, 2, 3, ..., jack, queen, king).

Then print a list of the missing cards.

Suggestion: In this case, as C already knows the list of elements to be ordered, even with some 'holes' in it, it is easier not to order the existing elements explicitly, but to create a file in which all the elements that 'should be' in a deck of cards are already ordered; then scan the original file sequentially, marking each scanned element in the new file. At the end, print the unmarked elements as missing.

Note that by using direct file access we need a number of access operations proportional to the number of elements to be ordered, a result that could not be obtained if we simply ordered the existing elements.

Note also that this algorithm is exactly the one we use when we execute this procedure manually: we put the various cards in their correct position; we do not order them in the strict sense of the term.

If, however, the number of missing cards is relatively high, strict ordering might turn out to be more convenient.

We suggest coming back and carrying out an efficiency analysis of the program after reading Chapter 12.

9.13 Write a function which reads a text file containing in each line a string with the name of a geometric shape (TRIANGLE, SQUARE or RECTANGLE) and a sequence of real numbers representing the length of sides needed to calculate the perimeter of a figure having that geometric shape. For each line of the input file the function calculates the shape of the figure and its perimeter and writes this information to an output text file.

Dynamic data structures

C, along with most widely used programming languages, requires the physical size of each variable to be known before the program is executed. This requirement has a major benefit: the storage necessary to execute a program can be computed by the compiler *before* the execution of the program, that is, at compile time rather than at run time. A general principle that is adopted by most common programming languages is to try to maximize the number of actions performed at compile time so that run time can be managed more efficiently. Thus, static, that is, compile time, memory allocation is generally pursued. The only exception is the case of recursive programming which, as we saw in Chapter 8, requires the allocation and deallocation of activation records at the time of procedure call and exit, respectively. Fortunately, this policy allows stack management of the run-time memory which is fairly efficient, since it imposes only a little overhead at the time of procedure call and procedure exit.

In many cases, however, there is the problem of managing data whose size varies during the execution of a program. For instance, we have already faced several times the problem of inserting elements in and deleting elements from a table. Implementing such a table using an array requires the array to be sized according to the maximum foreseen size: this often results in considerable wastage of physical memory and still does not exclude the risk of underestimating the necessary size thus causing table overflow. Furthermore, in some cases, managing normal operations can be excessively time-consuming. For instance, suppose we want to delete an element from a given table, implemented as an array. Normally we proceed as follows: first, we find the position where the element to be deleted is located; then we move all succeeding elements backwards by one position in order to keep the array 'compact', that is, to avoid leaving holes consisting of entries with no meaningful information between the meaningful table entries. All this clearly requires a considerable amount of time, which depends on the size of the table (see Chapter 12 for a more thorough analysis of the time needed to perform such an operation). A similar situation occurs if we wish to insert a new element in a sorted table, for example a name in an alphabetically ordered table of names.

To overcome these difficulties, some programming languages allow the definition of **dynamic data types**, that is, data types where the size of their values is not fixed a priori and can vary during program execution: in such languages we could easily define a type TableOfNames to contain any non-negative number of elements of type Name. This choice, however, violates the above-mentioned principle, which is adopted by C and most other languages, of knowing at compile time the amount of memory to allocate for each program variable.

To remedy the dilemma between the efficiency of static memory allocation and the flexibility of dynamic data types, several modern languages, including C and Pascal, introduced a limited way of allocating memory during the execution of the program. Data types are still static in the sense that each element of a given data type has an a priori fixed size; however, some variables of a given data type can be 'created' through an explicit statement by the programmer during program execution.

This chapter describes these mechanisms (Section 10.1) and how they can be used to construct flexible data structures (Sections 10.2–10.5): we will obtain the result of building dynamic data structures (that is, collections of a dynamically variable number of elements) without resorting to dynamic data types (that is, without being compelled to declare data types whose structure and size can change during program execution.)

10.1 Tools for dynamic data management and their use

In this section we present the basic programming tools for dynamic memory allocation, their characteristics, their implications on the structure of the abstract machine of the language and the risks and problems connected with their use.

Dynamic allocation and release of memory is possible in C by using some functions available in the standard library. The two principal functions are malloc and free which, respectively, allocate and release one or more memory cells suitable for a specified type of data. The cells created by these functions can be accessed and manipulated through pointers, described in Section 5.5.3.

10.1.1 Memory allocation and release operations

The function call:

```
malloc(sizeof(DataType));
```

creates in memory a variable of type DataType and returns as its result the address of the variable (more precisely, the returned value is the address of the first byte reserved for the variable).

If P is a pointer to the type DataType, the statement

```
P = malloc(sizeof(DataType));
```

assigns to P the address returned by the malloc function. Consequently, after execution of this statement, P 'points' to the new variable, losing its original value. We should emphasize that memory is allocated for a datum of type DataType, *not for* P, which is an already existing variable.

In C, a variable created dynamically is necessarily 'anonymous', that is, it can only be referred to through a pointer, whereas a variable declared via an identifier can either be referred to by its identifier or be pointed to. A pointer behaves like any identified variable (it can be referred to by its identifier or it can be pointed to by another pointer).

Symmetrically, the function call free(P) releases the space in memory pointed to by P; this means that the corresponding physical memory is made available for other uses. It is important to note that, in order to be effective, the function free must receive, as its input parameter, a pointer whose value is an address returned by a dynamic memory allocation function (malloc, in our case).

The use of the functions malloc and free requires inclusion of the file header <stdlib.h> via the statement

```
#include <stdlib.h>
```

Its inclusion guarantees the presence of the prototypes of the functions for dynamic memory allocation and the definition of the constant NULL used to initialize the pointers.

We saw in Section 8.3.1 that memory can be managed very efficiently by a stack on which, at each function call, an activation record is placed, containing the data area reserved for the function. This record is released after the termination of the function's execution.

Dynamic data is allocated to a second memory zone, called a **heap**. This memory zone, however, does not have the characteristic that the last cell allocated is also the first one released (allocation and release are controlled directly by the programmer). Therefore, its management is less efficient. Figure 10.1 shows some salient aspects of a machine state during execution of a function Proc which has two local variables Point1 and Point2 declared as

```
int     *Point1;
int     **Point2;
```

Point1 is a pointer to an integer variable: it belongs to the stack, but the variable it points to is in the heap and stores the value 5. Point2 is a double pointer, that is, a pointer that points to another pointer. Both the anonymous pointer pointed to by Point2 and the integer variable – storing the value 3 – pointed to by the anonymous pointer are in the heap.

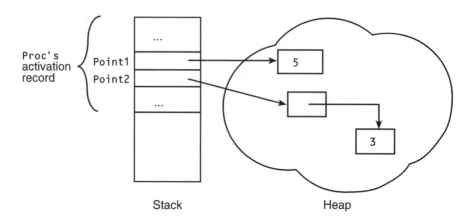

Figure 10.1   Stack and heap in the memory of the C abstract machine.

10.1.2 'Risks' of dynamic memory management

Pointers are a flexible and powerful tool for managing dynamic data. This will be illustrated in detail in the next sections with reference to some widely used classic data structures. However, as early as Section 5.5.3 we had occasion to describe some risks connected with their use (the possibility of creating *side-effects* is not easily or entirely foreseeable during programming). Let us now look at two further problems, typical of programming with pointers and with dynamic memory allocation.

The first problem is the **production of garbage**. This occurs when memory allocated dynamically is logically inaccessible and therefore wasted, because there is no more reference to it. A trivial example of garbage production is the following:

```
P = malloc(sizeof(DataType));
P = Q;
```

The cell originally pointed to by P, immediately after its creation, becomes inaccessible. To avoid this, it would have been necessary to 'save' the value of P (for example, via the statement TempPoint = P) before assigning it a new one. Of course, production of garbage can also occur as a consequence of less trivial operations and therefore is more difficult to identify.

The second problem is the production of **dangling references**. This problem is symmetrical to the previous one: it is caused by creating wrong references to logically non-existent memory zones. Consider, for instance, the following statements:

```
P = Q;
free(Q);
```

The operation free(Q) releases the memory previously allocated for the variable that Q points to, but it does not normally provoke an automatic assignment of the value NULL to the pointer Q. After the execution of free(Q), P and perhaps Q remain unaltered and refer to a memory cell that no longer exists. The worst consequence of this occurs when subsequently, in a way over which the programmer has absolutely no control, the cell pointed to by P receives other values which have nothing to do with the meaning of P . For example, P could be a pointer to **int** and the cell could receive a value of **char** type. At this point, a reference to *P would involve access to the physical address pointed to by P, and the subsequent interpretation of its contents as an integer value with results that are unforeseeable and erroneous.

The production of garbage and the production of dangling references have clearly symmetric disadvantages, but it is quite evident that the latter is more dangerous: the former just involves a waste of memory, but not erroneous results. For this reason, in some languages it has been decided to accept the production of garbage in order to avoid the risk of dangling references: this has led to the elimination of the **free** statement. Consequently, the production of garbage cannot be avoided, but neither can dangling references be created. It is left to the abstract machine of the language to execute **garbage collection**, employing techniques and rules of various kinds which relieve the programmer of the burden and the responsibility of deciding when a memory cell is no longer required, at the expense of a certain loss of efficiency during execution.

This analysis of the characteristics of pointers and dynamic memory allocation, even with the limitations typically imposed by high-level languages, leads us to regard them as a low-level programming technique. Consequently, their use is recommended only for the construction of dynamic high-level data structures (exemplified in the following sections) which cannot be realized efficiently using the traditional constructors (arrays and structures) or in the use of particular programming techniques (such as parameter passing by address).

10.2 Lists and list management

In earlier chapters we more than once used linear structures of homogeneous elements whose cardinality was not fixed a priori (by calling them list, table or sequence); operations were provided to insert elements into and remove elements from the structure, thus providing the full notion of abstract data type. So far we have used arrays to implement such structures, despite the inefficient use of memory. Now, thanks to the dynamic allocation of variables, we can implement lists in such a way that the physical memory used corresponds to the number of elements in the table.

The basic idea for constructing a list using pointers is to connect together elements composed of two parts: the first part contains the information and is therefore a value of a generic type which we indicate by ElementType; the second part is a pointer that points to the next element in the list. The second part of the last element has the value NULL which is used to mean 'end of list'; the beginning of the list is identified by a variable of type pointer. We shall make it a habit to give this variable the name of the list itself, thus identifying the concept of the 'beginning

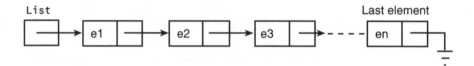

Figure 10.2   The structure of a list realized using pointers. e1, e2, ... indicate
values of the type ElementType.

of the list' (often also called the 'head of the list') with the list itself: this is because,
owing to the use of pointers, access to a list is effectively done through the pointer
to its first element.

Figure 10.2 shows a graphic representation of this list structure.

To realize such a structure by means of the constructs of the language is
extremely easy. Each element of the list is defined as a structure; the object labelled
'List' in Figure 10.2 is given a type consisting of a pointer to the type of the
generic list element being defined. A classic example of this implementation
scheme is the following:

```
struct  EL {
                ElementType    Info;
                struct  EL     *Next;
            };
typedef struct  EL     ElemOfList;

typedef ElemOfList     *ListOfElems;
```

The above declaration uses a different syntax from the one analysed in
Chapter 5. This syntax, offered as an alternative by the language, produces the
desired declaration through the following steps:

(1)   The first declaration of the structured type **struct** EL defines a first field,
Info, of type ElementType and allows the Next field to be declared as a
pointer to the structured type that is being defined.

(2)   The second declaration uses **typedef** to *rename* the type **struct** EL as
ElemOfList. Thus, variables of type ElemOfList also have a Next field that
points to other elements of type ElemOfList, as required for the definition of
a list.

(3)   Finally, the third declaration defines the type ListOfElems as a pointer to the
type ElemOfList.

At this point, different variables of 'list' type can be declared through
declarations such as the following:

```
ListOfElems    List1, List2, List3;
```

As in the case of other type definitions, abbreviated declarations can be used:

```
ElemOfList        *List1;
```

could replace the second **typedef** if there were no special interest in making the type of the list explicitly evident. Or even

```
struct  EL    *List1;
```

could replace both **typedef**s if neither the type of the list nor the type of its elements needs to be explicitly named.

As we have emphasized several times, a *data type* is identified by a set of values and a set of operations that can be applied to them. In order to realize completely the type ListOfElems, we need to specify and implement the operations for its management. In the following, we present some basic ones, leaving some details and additions to the reader as an exercise.

10.2.1 Initialization

The first function illustrated is very simple: it initializes a list by assigning the value NULL to the variable that points to it (the variable 'head of the list'). Some attention, however, should be paid to the necessity to pass the variable 'head of the list' by address: this results in the presence of a double pointer in the header of the function. Assume that the previous declarations realizing the list elements are given in main; then, procedure Initialize can be coded as follows:

```
#include <stdlib.h>

void Initialize(ListOfElems *List)
                         /*List is the local variable that points to
                         the 'head of the list'. The function assigns
                         to the 'head of the list' the value NULL,
                         corresponding to the value of the empty
                         list.*/
{
   *List = NULL;
}
```

Suppose now that Initialize is called with the address of the variable List1 (the head of the list) as its actual parameter:

```
Initialize(&List1);
```

In this way we simulate passing the variable 'head of the list' by address: in fact when the call is executed the value of the formal parameter List becomes the address of the actual parameter List1 as indicated by Figure 10.3. Thus, when Initialize executes the statement

```
*List = NULL;
```

the obtained result is to modify List1 by assigning it the desired NULL value, as depicted in Figure 10.3.

Notice that the same effect could be obtained by declaring the header of the procedure as

```
void Initialize(ElemList  **List)
```

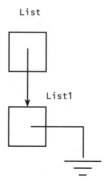

Figure 10.3   The effect of the call `Initialize(&List1)`.

Many C programmers often avoid the intricacies of such a double pointer mechanism and use an alternative solution consisting of declaring the list as a global variable which `Initialize` can access directly:

```
#include <stdlib.h>

ElemOfList *List1;

void Initialize(void)
{
    List1 = NULL;
}
```

This practice, however, is clearly not equivalent to the previous one since, as we emphasized in Chapter 7, it binds the procedure to the single variable `List1` rather than to the abstract data type `List`.

10.2.2 Testing the emptiness of a list

Let us now examine other fundamental abstract operations for managing lists. The second function checks whether the list (whose head is passed by value) is empty.

```
#include <stdlib.h>

boolean EmptyList(ListOfElems  List)
                        /*returns the value true if the list passed
                        as parameter is empty, false otherwise. List
                        is passed the value contained in the
                        variable head of the list. List therefore
                        points to the first element of the list
                        under scrutiny*/
{
    if(List == NULL) return true; else return false;
}
```

Assuming that the declarations presented above are present in `main`, `EmptyList` should be called with the value of the variable `List1` (the head of the list) as its parameter:

```
EmptyList(List1)
```

10.2.3 Testing the existence of an element in a list

The third function checks whether a specified element is in the list (whose head is passed by value).

```
#include <stdlib.h>

boolean     Search(ListOfElems  List, ElementType  SearchedElem)
                /*returns the value true if there is an element in
                the list whose Info field has the value SearchedElem,
                false otherwise. It is based on a natural sequential
                scan of the list, element by element, using a cursor
                that points to the different elements, until the
                element sought is found or the end of the list is
                reached.*/
{
   ElemOfList *Cursor;

   if(List != NULL)                             /*the list is not empty*/
   {
      Cursor = List;
      while (Cursor != NULL)
      {
         if(Cursor->Info == SearchedElem) return true;
         Cursor = Cursor->Next;
                        /*in this way, Cursor is made to point at
                        the next element in the list*/
      }
   }
   return  false;
}
```

The `Search` procedure could have been formulated recursively, just as easily and maybe more naturally, in the following way:

```
#include <stdlib.h>

boolean     Search(ListOfElems  List, ElementType  SearchedElem)
                /*returns the value true if there is an element in
                the list whose Info field has the value SearchedElem,
                false otherwise. It is based on the principle that if
                the list is empty, the answer is false; otherwise, if
                the first element of the list matches SearchedElem,
                the answer is true; otherwise, the answer is the same
                as the one we would get if we applied the procedure
                to the sublist pointed to by the Next field of the
                first sublist-element that is still a list. Note the
```

similarity of this procedure to the homonymous
procedure defined in Example 8.4 for a list realized
with the array constructor.*/

```
{
   if(List == NULL)
      return  false;
   else
      if(List->Info == SearchedElem)
         return  true;
      else
         return Search(List->Next, SearchedElem);
}
```

This recursive formulation of the Search procedure is based on the fact that, if we eliminate the first element of a non-empty list, what remains is a list, possibly empty.

We can now continue the analysis of typical operations on the list type, choosing a recursive or iterative formulation at will.

10.2.4 Extracting the head or the tail from a list

The following operations are only defined. Their implementation is left as an exercise for the reader.

- ElementType   HeadOfList(ListOfElems List)
  /*this can be applied only to non-empty lists. If the
  list is empty, an appropriate error message is
  produced, otherwise the function returns the value of
  the Info field of the first element of the list.*/

- ListOfElems   TailOfList(ListOfElems List)
  /*produces as its result a pointer to the sublist
  obtained from List by deleting its first element. It
  must not modify the original parameter. Figure 10.4
  shows the desired effect of the procedure. This, too,
  assumes that the passed parameter is not an
  empty list.*/

☛ 2

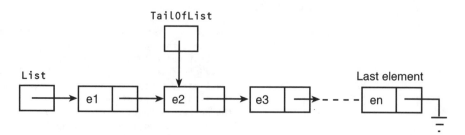

Figure 10.4   Extraction of the tail of a non-empty list.

10.2.5 Inserting a new element in a list

The next operation, `InsertAtHead`, inserts a new element as the first element of the list, that is, at its 'head'. It does not check whether the element already exists in the list. Figure 10.5 shows how the procedure operates when it is called with the actual parameter `List1`.

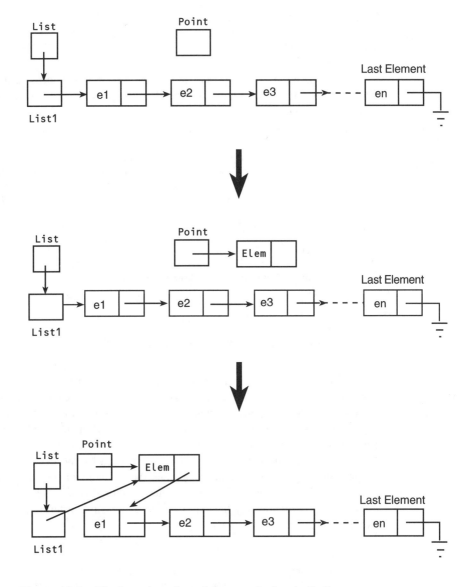

Figure 10.5 The insertion of an element at the head of a list.

```
#include <stdlib.h>

void InsertAtHead(ListOfElems *List, ElementType Elem)
                    /*modifies the list passed 'by address', inserting as
                    its first element the value Elem.*/
{
   ElemOfList *Point;
                    /*allocation of the necessary space to store the new
                    element and initialization of the pointer*/
   Point = malloc(sizeof(ElemOfList));
   Point->Info = Elem;
   Point->Next = *List;
   *List = Point;
}
```

The operation `InsertAtTail` inserts the new element in the last position of the list. Figure 10.6 shows how the procedure operates when it is called with `List1` as actual parameter.

```
#include <stdlib.h>

void InsertAtTail(ListOfElems *List, ElementType Elem)
                    /*modifies the list passed 'by address', inserting as
                    its last element the value Elem. It does not check
                    whether the element already exists in the list.*/
{
   ElemOfList *Point;

   if (EmptyList(*List))
   {
      Point = malloc(sizeof(ElemOfList));
      Point->Next = NULL;
      Point->Info = Elem;
      *List = Point;
   }
   else InsertAtTail(&((*List)->Next), Elem);
}
```

If the list is ordered (this implies the assumption that for the type `ElementType` the relation < is defined) the operation `InsertInOrder` is useful: it inserts the value of the new element in such a position that the list remains ordered. Figure 10.7 shows how the procedure operates when it is called with actual parameter `List1`. For simplicity, we assume that the ordering relation between the `Info` contents of the list's elements can be denoted by the usual < symbol. This happens in simple cases, for instance when the elements of the list are integers. In other cases, for example if the elements are structured types such as `Invoices`, we use an ad hoc function, say `GreaterThan`, to express the ordering relation between list elements.

```
#include <stdlib.h>

void InsertInOrder (ListOfElems *List, ElementType  Elem)
                    /*modifies the list passed 'by address' – which is
                    assumed to be in ascending order – inserting the
```

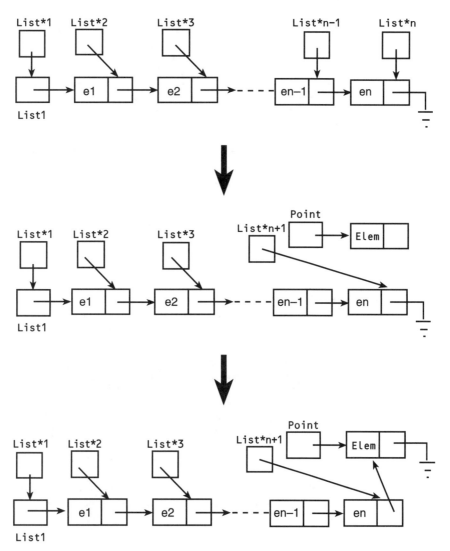

Figure 10.6 Insertion of an element at the tail of a list, corresponding to the last call of the recursive function `InsertAtTail`. `List*i` denotes the value of the formal parameter `List` at the `i`th call.

```
                              value Elem in such a position that the list remains
                              ordered. It does not check whether the element
                              already exists in the list.*/
    {
        ElemOfList *Point, *CurrentPoint, *PreviousPoint;

        PreviousPoint = NULL;
        CurrentPoint = *List;
```

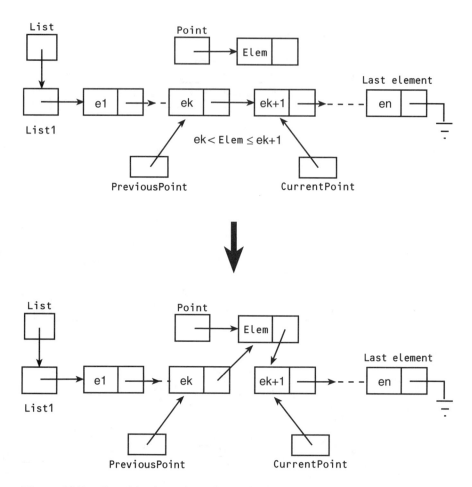

Figure 10.7 Graphical explanation of the functioning of the procedure
`InsertInOrder` in the case where the element does not have to be
inserted at the head.

```
while(CurrentPoint != NULL && Elem > CurrentPoint->Info)
{
    PreviousPoint = CurrentPoint;
    CurrentPoint = CurrentPoint->Next;
}
Point = malloc(sizeof(ElemOfList));
Point->Info = Elem;
Point->Next = CurrentPoint;
if(PreviousPoint) != NULL
    PreviousPoint->Next = Point;                /*insert inside list*/
else
    *List = Point;                              /*insert at head of list*/
}
```

Observe the role played, in the `InsertInOrder` procedure, by the pointer `PreviousPoint`, which allows the element that should point to the new element to be traced easily.

10.2.6 Deleting an element from a list

Finally, operation `DeleteElem` erases from the list the given element, assuming that the list does not contain repeated elements.

```
#include <stdlib.h>

void DeleteElem(ListOfElems *List, ElementType Elem)
                    /*deletes from the list passed 'by address'
                    the element Elem, if it exists, assuming
                    that there are no repetitions in the list.*/
{
   ElemOfList *TempPoint;

   if(EmptyList(*List) == false)
      if((*List)->Info == Elem)
      {
         TempPoint = *List;
         *List = TailOfList(*List);
         free(TempPoint);
      }
      else DeleteElem(&((*List)->Next), Elem);
}
```

To summarize, we have succeeded in building the abstract data type 'list' as a dynamic structure even if the C language does not allow the definition of dynamic data types: the trick is to use pointers as a means of accessing the collection of list elements. Each element of the list, whose type and size are known at compile time, can be allocated and deleted dynamically, but, strictly speaking, the list itself is not a data type.

By this means we have achieved the main goal that we stated at the beginning of this chapter: to use only the memory that is necessary during program execution. Rigorously speaking, we introduced the small overhead required to add to each element the memory necessary to store a pointer. This extra memory requirement, however, is usually negligible compared to the benefit of allocating only the memory that is necessary to store the elements that are effectively used. Consider, for example, the implementation of a table of invoices, where each invoice contains names, addresses, dates and so on. Suppose that storing a single invoice requires 50 memory cells and that we implement a list of invoices as an array of 1000 elements although normally we use only 500 elements of the array. Suppose also that we choose a dynamic implementation: now we need 51 cells to store a single invoice, but we save 500 entries of 50 words each in normal use.

Even considering the amount of time required to implement several operations to manage lists, we have gained in flexibility since, for example, the insertion of elements into and deletion of elements from the list can be performed without shifting the other elements. A more thorough analysis of the effort required to manage lists implemented through pointers will be possible in Chapter 12.

Notice also the benefit that we have obtained from the realization of lists as an *abstract* data type: once we have defined its structure and the operations needed to manipulate it, we can use any list without knowing its internal structure, even without knowing if it is managed dynamically. For instance, suppose we wish to read 10 integers and create a list containing those numbers exactly in the order they have been read. All we need write is the following piece of code:

```
...
ListOfElems List1;int i;int x; ...
...
Initialize(&List1);
for (i = 1; i <= 10; i++)
{
    scanf(%d, &x);
    InsertAtTail(&List1, x);
}
```

Notice that if we had implemented the abstract data type `ListOfElems` by using arrays instead of dynamically allocated elements, the above code would not have been affected. The benefits of such discipline in separating *type definition* from *type use* will be further emphasized in Chapters 22 and 25 when dealing with the modularization of large programs. We strongly recommend keeping the use of pointers and dynamic memory management inside the construction of suitable data types in such a way that the part of a program using those data types can be written without resorting to the direct use of these programming mechanisms.

Lists, however, are just one possible dynamic data structure that can be realized by means of pointers and dynamic allocation mechanisms. They are quite simple but they force the various elements to be accessed in a strictly sequential and ordered way. In general, if we want to access the ith element of a list we must follow the 'chain' of all $i - 1$ preceding elements starting from the head of the list. As a consequence, insertion at the end of the list requires scanning the whole list. This suggests the use of different data structures when the access policy does not match the logical chaining of elements. The following sections provide a few examples of other dynamic data structures. More sophisticated ones are introduced in Chapter 11. Eventually, however, the reader should be able not only to choose the appropriate data structure from those presented here or in more advanced literature, but also to design new structures suitable for each application problem.

10.3 Bidirectional lists

A simple way of generalizing lists is to make them bidirectional. **Bidirectional lists** are still linear data structures in that they contain a linearly ordered sequence of elements. As the term itself suggests, however, bidirectional lists can be traversed

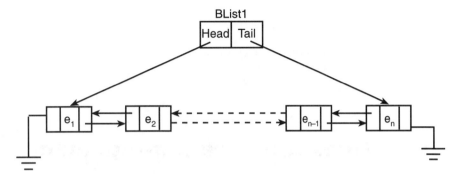

Figure 10.8   A bidirectional list.

in both directions: from the head to the end and from the end to the head. This makes their use more efficient if it is frequently necessary to access elements at both extremes of the structure.

In a bidirectional list each element points to two elements: the one that succeeds it and the one that precedes it. Figure 10.8 and the corresponding type declaration explain how to realize a bidirectional list.

```
struct  EBL  { ElementType  Info;
               struct EBL   *Next, *Prec;
            };

typedef struct   EBL  ElBidList;

typedef struct   { ElBidList  *Head, *Tail;
                 } BidirList;

BidirList        Blist1;
```

Once we have understood the logical structure of a bidirectional list and its implementation through the usual mechanism, the completion of this abstract data type, defining the appropriate operations, can be easily obtained in a similar way to monodirectional lists. For instance, the operation `InsertAtTail` can be easily implemented in a symmetric way to the operation `InsertAtHead`:

```
#include <stdlib.h>

void InsertAtTail (BidirList *List, ElementType  Elem)
                        /*modifies the bidirectional list passed by
                        address, inserting as its last element the
                        value Elem. It does not check whether the
                        element already exists in the list.*/
{
   ElBidList   *Point;

                        /*allocation of the necessary space to store
                        the new element and initialization of the
                        pointer*/
```

```
Point = malloc(sizeof(ElBidList));
Point->Info = Elem;
Point->Next = NULL;
Point->Prec = List->Tail;
List->Tail->Next = Point;
List->Tail = Point;
}
```

10.4 Trees and tree management

A lot of information is structured hierarchically; that is, the principal or top-level information includes chunks of information at a lower level that can, in turn, include further, simpler chunks of information and so on, until a level of elementary pieces of information which have no other levels below them is reached. The following are examples of hierarchic structures:

(1)   The organization chart of an enterprise, an army and various other organizations where, at least in simple cases, there is a 'chief', a certain number of 'subchiefs' on the level immediately below, each of whom may have other 'subchiefs' at the next level down and so on.

(2)   A family tree, which refers to one head of family (that is, ignoring the spouse), who has one or more children, who then give birth to grandchildren and so on.

(3)   The description of a commercial invoice which consists, for example, of the fields 'holder', 'date of issue' and 'amount'. The date of issue has the components 'day', 'month' and 'year'. The holder field contains 'first name', 'last name', 'address', 'social security number' and so on.

To describe structures of this kind, we use a mathematical construct that lends itself to graphical representation, not for nothing called a **tree**. The following is a recursive definition of a tree, which is clearly a generalization of the corresponding definition of a list.

DEFINITION 10.1

Given a set E of elements,

- a tree may be empty, that is, not contain any elements;
- a non-empty tree may consist of one single element $e \in E$, called a **node**, or
- a tree consists of a node $e \in E$, connected by directed arcs to a finite number of other trees.

Figure 10.9 shows some examples of trees, highlighting the recursive aspect of the definition. It also shows that these data structures really look like trees,

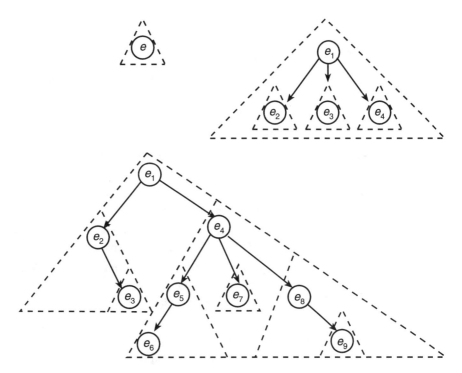

Figure 10.9   Examples of trees.

although 'upside down'. The reason why computer science has developed the habit of representing trees upside down is that the first element of the tree is normally the most important in the hierarchy and therefore deserves to be put at the top.

A good deal of tree-related terminology, whose salient points are summarized by the following definition, is inspired by the original meaning of the term.

DEFINITION 10.2

- The first node of a tree, normally drawn in the top position, is called the **root** of the tree.
- The arrows that connect one node to another are called **arcs** or **branches**.
- The **terminal nodes**, that is, nodes from which no arc comes out, are called **leaves**.
- The nodes that are not leaves are called **internal nodes** or **nonterminal nodes**.
- If in a tree a branch goes from a node n_1 to a node n_2, we say that n_1 is the **parent** of n_2 and that n_2 is a **child** of n_1.

- n_1 is called an **ancestor** of n_2 if n_1 is the parent of n_2 or if n_1 is the parent of an ancestor of n_2.
- n_2 is called a **descendant** of n_1 if n_1 is an ancestor of n_2.
- A **path** from n_1 to n_2 is a sequence of contiguous arcs that goes from n_1 to n_2.
- The **length** of a path is the number of arcs it contains (in other words, the number of nodes − 1).
- The **level** of a node is the length of the path that connects it to the root.
- The **depth** or **height** of a tree is the length of the longest path that connects the root to a leaf.
- A **subtree** of a tree is a subset of nodes of the tree, connected by branches of the tree itself, that is in its turn a tree.
- Let *SA* be a subtree of a tree *A*: if for each node *n* of *SA*, *SA* also contains all the descendants of *n* in *A*. *SA* is called a **complete subtree** of *A*.
- A tree is **balanced** when, given a maximum number *k* of children for each node and **the height of the tree** *h*, each node of level $l < h − 1$ has exactly *k* children. The tree is **perfectly balanced** when each node of level $l < h$ has exactly *k* children.

For example, in the third tree of Figure 10.9, e_1 is the root; e_4 is an internal node; e_9 is a leaf; e_4 is the parent of e_5 and an ancestor of e_5, e_6, e_7, e_8 and e_9; e_4, e_8

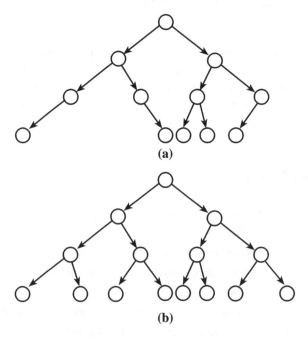

Figure 10.10　(a) A balanced tree and (b) a perfectly balanced tree.

and e_9, together with the arcs that connect them, are a path; e_4, e_5, e_8 and e_9, together with the arcs that connect them, are a subtree of the main tree. The subtrees enclosed in broken triangles are complete. Figure 10.10 shows two examples of balanced trees, the second of which is perfectly balanced.

10.5 Implementing trees via dynamic data structures

Let us now tackle the problem of representing trees through suitable data structures. If the structure of a tree does not change during the execution of a program, it can be adequately represented by the **struct** mechanism: each component of the structure is a child of the corresponding node of the structure itself (see, for example, Exercise 10.8).

In many cases, however, it will be necessary to change the structure of the tree during program execution, by inserting and deleting elements. This will happen, for example, with a tree representing the organizational chart of an enterprise in which employees come and go and restructuring takes place. In such cases, the analogy with the lists treated earlier suggests a natural way to represent trees, that is, with a typically dynamic, recursively defined structure using pointers.

Let us therefore define and construct the abstract type 'tree' in a similar way to that used for the list. For simplicity, we consider initially a particular type of tree, the **binary tree**, in which each node has at most two children. Later, in Section 10.5.2, it will be easy to generalize the rules to cover any type of tree. For the sake of brevity, until Section 10.5.2 the term 'tree' will be used in place of 'binary tree'. Figure 10.11(b) shows how a structure based on pointers can naturally represent a binary tree, with reference to the sample tree given in Figure 10.11(a). The declaration in C of the abstract data type BinaryTree can be expressed as follows:

```
struct EBT { ElementType  Info;
             struct EBT   *LeftChild, *RightChild;
           };

typedef struct EBT        ElemOfBinTree;
typedef ElemOfBinTree     *BinaryTree;
```

Some simple operations on trees such as initialization and checking for emptiness can be easily implemented in a similar way as for lists (see Exercise 10.9). Let us consider now the problem of searching for an element within a tree. In this case too, the extension of the recursive search procedure for lists to trees seems to be perfectly natural: it is based on the fact that, if an element exists in a tree, it is either in the root, or in the left-hand or the right-hand subtree. Coding the procedure is just as natural:

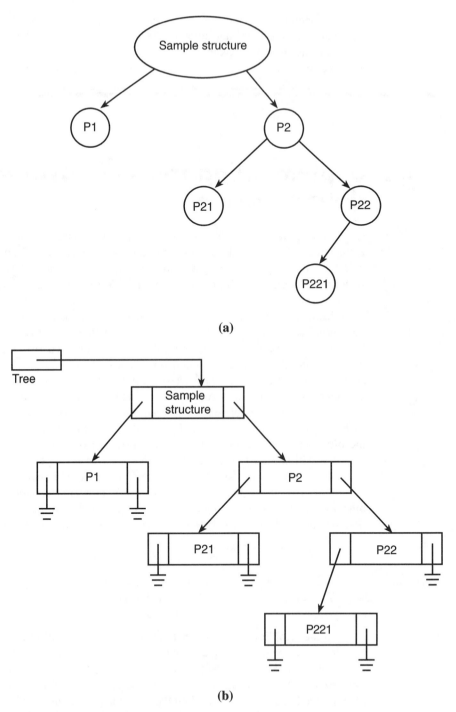

(a)

(b)

Figure 10.11 (a) Sample binary tree. (b) Graphical representation of the pointer-based data structure representing the binary tree of part (a).

```
#include <stdlib.h>

boolean  Search(BinaryTree  Tree, ElementType  SearchedElem)
                /*returns true if there is a node in the tree whose Info
                field has the value SearchedElem, false otherwise.*/
{
   if (Tree == NULL)
     return  false;
   else if (Tree->Info == SearchedElem)
          return true;
        else
          return (Search(Tree->LeftChild, SearchedElem) ||
               Search(Tree->RightChild, SearchedElem));
}
```

Note how much more difficult it would be, this time, to construct a non-recursive search procedure.

10.5.1 Tree visiting

The above search procedure requires, in the worst case, a complete visit of the tree, that is, the analysis of all its elements. Visiting a tree is necessary on many occasions, for example if we want to print the information contained in each node. Therefore, it is important to analyse tree visiting algorithms in some depth. This problem has trivial solutions for linear structures such as arrays, or lists implemented by chains of pointers, but the nonlinearity of the tree structure poses the problem of the order in which to visit the different elements of the structure. Now, there are various ways of visiting a tree. We present some which should be sufficient to enable the reader to understand and possibly invent other methods; not surprisingly, the formulation of the various types of visit will be recursive.

Visit in left preorder

The algorithm visits and prints the root of the tree, then visits the left-hand subtree and finally visits the right-hand subtree.

A simple coding of this algorithm is the following:

```
#include <stdlib.h>

void PrintLeftPreord(BinaryTree   Tree)
                /*prints the tree passed as parameter in left preorder*/
{
   if (Tree != NULL)
   {
     WriteElement(Tree->Info); printf("\n");
     PrintLeftPreord(Tree->LeftChild);
     PrintLeftPreord(Tree->RightChild);
   }
}
```

Figure 10.12(a) shows the result of applying the procedure `PrintLeftPreord` to the tree of Figure 10.11(a).

Visit in right preorder

The algorithm visits and prints the root of the tree, then visits the right-hand subtree and finally visits the left-hand subtree. Figure 10.12(b) shows the result of applying printing in right preorder to the tree of Figure 10.11(a).

Visit in right postorder

The right-hand subtree of the given tree is visited; then the left-hand one; finally the value of the Info field of the root is printed. Figure 10.12(c) shows the result of applying printing in right postorder to the tree of Figure 10.11(a).

(a)	SampleStructure	(b)	SampleStructure	(c)	P221
	P1		P2		P22
	P2		P22		P21
	P21		P221		P2
	P22		P21		P1
	P221		P1		SampleStructure

Figure 10.12 Printout of the tree in Figure 10.11(a): (a) in left preorder; (b) in right preorder; (c) in right postorder.

10.5.2 Nonbinary trees

So far, we have concentrated on binary trees. In some cases, however, the logical organization of data reflects a tree structure that is not necessarily binary. In such cases, if the number of children of each node is limited and does not vary much from node to node (for example, each node has at most four children), we can immediately extend the techniques used for binary trees to ternary trees, quaternary trees and so on. This is left as a simple exercise for the reader. But when the number of children per node is highly variable, for example from 0 to 100, or even unlimited, constructing a node using a structure that contains one field for each child raises the same problems of waste or insufficient memory that led to the construction of dynamic data structures.

In this case too, the solution is to make the number of children of each node dynamically variable. This can be done in various ways. One of the easiest is to associate a **list of children** with each node. In this way, each node points only to the first child in that list (for example, the first left-hand child) and to its own right-hand sibling. Figure 10.13 shows how such a structure can be realized.

The details of the complete construction of the abstract data type 'nonbinary tree' are left as exercises for the reader (Exercises 10.13 and 10.14.)

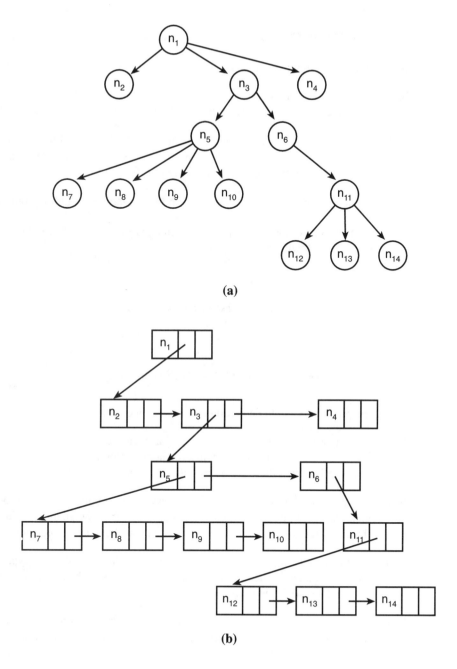

Figure 10.13 (a) A nonbinary tree. (b) Representation of the tree in part (a) by a structure using pointers, in which each node points to the leftmost child and the rightmost sibling. Empty fields contain the NULL value.

Exercises

10.1   Implement functions `HeadOfList` and `TailOfList` defined in Section 10.2.

10.2   Write a procedure `DeleteAll` that eliminates from the list passed as parameter (not necessarily without repetitions) all elements whose `Info` field `== Elem`.

10.3   Complete the construction of the abstract type 'bidirectional list', defining the appropriate operations, including `Initialize`, `Search`, `InsertAtHead`, `InsertAtTail`, `DeleteAtHead`, `DeleteAtTail`, ...

10.4   Implement the operation 'reverse' for both a mono- and a bidirectional list.

10.5   If the executive part of the procedure `InsertAtTail` described in Section 10.2 had been the following:

```
{
    if (EmptyList(*List))
    {
        Point = malloc(sizeof(ElemOfList));
        Point->Next = NULL;
        Point->Info = Elem;
        *List = Point;
    }
    else InsertAtTail(&(TailOfList(*List)), Elem);
}                                              /*InsertAtTail*/
```

the procedure would have turned out to be incorrect. Why?

10.6   Write a procedure which, receiving as parameters a list without repeated elements and one element to be inserted, inserts the new element while maintaining the characteristic that there are no repeated elements.

10.7   Write a procedure which, receiving as parameters an ordered list without repeated elements and one element to be inserted, inserts the new element while maintaining the characteristics that the list is sorted and that there are no repeated elements.

10.8   Supply a complete type declaration for the description of the data type `Invoice` (which includes elements such as name and address of the addressee, amount, issue date and so on). Then represent this structure by means of a tree.

10.9   Along the lines of what has been done for lists, write the procedures `Initialize` and `EmptyTree` which, respectively, initialize a binary tree as 'empty' and check whether a given binary tree is 'empty'.

10.10   Write a sequence of instructions which, assuming that the generic type `ElementType` is appropriate, constructs the tree of Figure 10.11(b).

10.11   Supply the procedures that code visiting binary trees in right preorder, right postorder and left postorder whose definition is also left as an exercise.

10.12   Define other natural orders of visiting binary trees (for example, orders of a 'centralized' type where the root is visited between the visits to the left-hand and right-hand subtrees) and implement them.

10.13   Supply the necessary type declarations for the realization of the type '(nonbinary) tree', following the scheme in Figure 10.13(b).

10.14   Construct procedures for searching, visiting in different orders, and inserting and deleting elements in nonbinary trees.

10.15   In some cases it is necessary to walk back from a child node to its parent node. Define a suitable data structure to facilitate this operation in an analogous way to bidirectional lists.

☛   **1.**   Provide more examples of garbage production.

   2.   Reformulate the recursive version of the `Search` function given in Section 10.2, using the abstract operations `EmptyList`, `HeadOfList` and `TailOfList`.

*More data structures

The ways of logically organizing data to improve management of the information it represents are manifold and depend on the particular application under consideration. In this chapter, we briefly discuss some of the most commonly used data structures, besides those presented so far: graphs (Section 11.1), stacks (Section 11.2) and queues (Section 11.3). We will not go into too many details. The reader is, however, invited to verify how the application of some essential principles allows the construction of data structures suited to the requirements of the particular problems to be solved.

11.1 Graphs: their representation and use

Graphs are a mathematical structure with many uses. They are defined as follows.

DEFINITION 11.1

- A **directed graph** consists of a finite set[1] of **nodes** or **vertices** and a set of **arcs** or **arrows** between them. Here, we assume that arcs are directed from one node to another and that there is at most one arc from any one node to another. Consequently, each arc is often denoted by the pair of nodes that it connects.

- A **nondirected graph** is defined in an analogous way to a directed graph, with the difference that arcs symmetrically connect a pair of nodes. For

---

[1] Graph theory also contemplates infinite graphs, which have been excluded from this text.

this reason, they are graphically represented as lines with no orientation (no arrowheads).

For example, the directed graph G whose set of nodes is $\{n_1,n_2,n_3,n_4,$ $n_5,n_6,n_7\}$ and whose set of arcs is $\{<n_1,n_2>,<n_2,n_3>,<n_3,\ n_2>,<n_3,n_1>,<n_1,n_4>,$ $<n_4,n_1>,<n_5,n_6>\}$ is graphically represented in Figure 11.1(a). Figure 11.1(b) presents the nondirected graph G' whose set of nodes is $\{n_1,n_2,n_3,n_4,n_5,n_6,$ $n_7\}$ and whose set of arcs is $\{[n_1,n_2],[n_2,n_3],[n_3,n_1],[n_1,n_4],[n_5,n_6]\}$, obtained from G by taking the arc orientation off and unifying arcs denoted by the *same pair* of nodes, regardless of their ordering.

Arcs of directed graphs are enclosed in angle brackets, whereas arcs of nondirected graphs are enclosed in square brackets.

It is evident that trees are a particular case of graphs.

Many types of information can be represented by means of directed or nondirected graphs, as shown by the following examples:

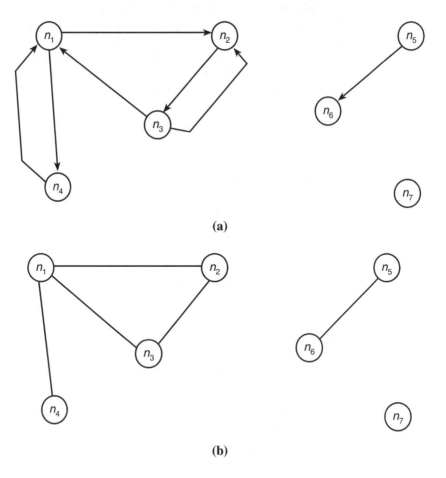

(a)

(b)

Figure 11.1 An example of (a) a directed graph and (b) a nondirected graph.

- The neighbourhood relation between geographic regions: each region is represented by a node. An arc (in this case nondirected) connects two nodes if and only if the two regions are adjacent.

- The precedence relation between university courses: each course is represented by a node. An arrow goes from n_1 to n_2 if and only if n_1 must precede n_2.

- A road network: a node represents a town and a nondirected arc represents a road that connects two towns. In this case, the graph could be enriched by labelling the arcs, as suggested in Figure 11.2, by adding the distances between towns.

- Organizational structures of various types: for example, different offices can be represented by nodes; arcs, suitably labelled, can represent various relations between the offices (communication, coordination and so on).

- Friendly relationships between persons.

For this reason, **graph theory**, that is, the study of the characteristics of these structures, has acquired a strong impetus and is now rich in important theoretical and practical results. In this section, we shall limit ourselves to some basic definitions and a brief discussion of the problem of representing graphs by adequate data structures. When, in the following definitions, it is not specified whether a graph is directed or not, the definition is valid in both cases.

DEFINITION 11.2

- A **path** in a graph is a sequence of contiguous arcs, that is, a sequence in which an arc leaves the node in which the preceding arc arrives. More formally, a path is a sequence of the following type:

$$\{<n_1,n_2>,<n_2,n_3>, ...,<n_{k-2},n_{k-1}>,<n_{k-1},n_k>\}.$$

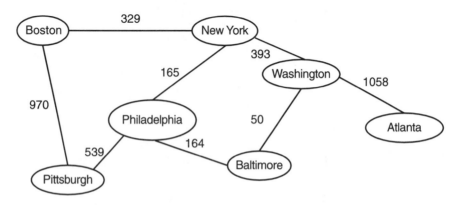

Figure 11.2   Nondirected labelled graph representing a road network.

- The number of arcs that constitute the path is called its **length**.
- A node n_2 is **reachable** from a node n_1 if there is a path that starts from n_1 and arrives at n_2.
- A path is **cyclic** if it arrives at the same node that it started from. A particular case of a cycle is the **self-loop**, that is, an arc that connects a node with itself.
- A graph is **connected** if each of its nodes is reachable from every other node. For example, if a graph that represents a road network is not connected, it means that not every town can be reached from all other towns.
- A graph is **complete** if for each pair of nodes there is an arc that connects them.
- The term DAG is an acronym for **directed acyclic graph**, that is, a directed graph without cycles.

11.1.1 **Representation of graphs using data structures**

In this section, we present two simple ways of realizing graphs using C type constructors: the first uses the array constructor; the second uses pointers. A third alternative is suggested in Exercise 11.2.

Representation of graphs by two-dimensional arrays

A natural way of representing graphs is by an **adjacency matrix**. The adjacency matrix GM of a graph G of n nodes is a square matrix $n \times n$ defined by the relation $GM\,[i,j]$ = true if and only if the vertex v_i is *adjacent* to vertex v_j, that is, there is an arc that connects v_i and v_j; false otherwise.

Figure 11.3(a) shows the adjacency matrix of the directed graph of Figure 11.1(a). For simplicity, we have used 'T' for true and the empty box for false.

Notice that in a nondirected graph the adjacency relation is symmetric, that is, $GM\,[i,j]$ = true if and only if $GM\,[j,i]$ = true. Thus, a **triangular matrix** is sufficient to represent the graph. As the term itself suggests, a triangular matrix consists only of the cells whose indexes i, j are such that $i \leq j$, or conversely. Special techniques can be used to represent and to manage triangular matrices more efficiently. We leave such techniques, however, to more advanced texts. Figure 11.3(b) shows the triangular adjacency matrix of the non-directed graph of Figure 11.1(b).

Representation of graphs by pointers

The representation of a graph by a matrix has the same advantages, but also the same disadvantages, as the representation of tables and various sequences by linear arrays. In particular, if the size of the graph is unpredictable and, furthermore,

variable, there is a risk of overflow or of waste of memory. In such cases it is therefore natural to use structures realized using pointers. One possibility is a bidimensional list, in which the *n* nodes are connected to each other, making one node the
'first node of the graph'. At each node there is a list that contains all the nodes
adjacent to it. Such a list is exemplified in Figure 11.4, again with reference to the
graph of Figure 11.1(a).

A structure of this kind can be realized by the following declarations:

```
struct    A { Element      Info;
                struct  A    *Succ;
            };

typedef struct  A          Adjacent;

struct NG  { Element       Info;
                struct  NG    *SuccNode;
                Adjacent     *ListOfAdjacents;
            };

typedef struct NG          GraphNode;

typedef  GraphNode         *GraphOfElem;

GraphOfELem                Graph;
```

11.1.2 Operations for the management of graphs

Many typical operations for the management of data structures such as insertion,
search and deletion of elements can also be applied to graphs. Their definition and
implementation are the object of Exercise 11.4.

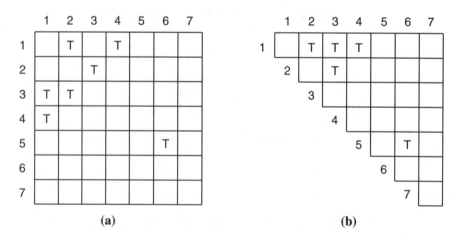

Figure 11.3 (a) Representation of the graph in Figure 11.1(a) by an adjacency
matrix. (b) Representation of the graph in Figure 11.1(b) by a
triangular adjacency matrix.

Another classic problem of graph theory is how to reach a node, starting from another node (for example, how to reach one town from another, possibly choosing the shortest of several routes: recall the extended example of Section 1.2). This problem is formalized and generalized as follows.

DEFINITION 11.3 Reachability of the nodes of a graph

The problem of **node reachability** of a graph consists, given a graph G, of determining for each vertex v of G all and only those vertices of G reachable from v.

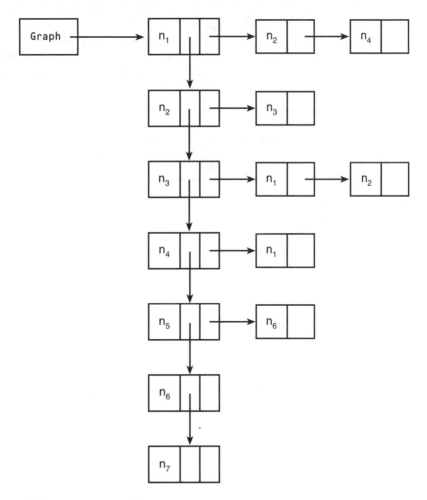

Figure 11.4 Representation of the graph in Figure 11.1(a) by a bidimensional list. The empty boxes contain the NULL value.

Solving the reachability problem on the basis of the adjacency relation is facilitated by the observation that, if there is a path that connects node v_1 to node v_2, there is certainly also a path whose length is $< n$, where n denotes the number of nodes in the graph. Indeed, to go from one node to any other node it is never necessary to pass the same node twice: it would just make the path longer. Obviously, the longest path that never passes a node more than once is of maximum length $n - 1$.

On the basis of this observation it is easy to construct an algorithm that iteratively produces all paths of length k, with $1 \leq k \leq n$ (in this way, we also detect cycles): the set of paths of length 1 is given by the set of arcs of the graph. At the first iteration, the algorithm identifies all sets of three nodes v_1, v_2, v_3, such that the arcs $<v_1,v_2>$, $<v_2,v_3>$ exist: this gives all paths of length 2; then it identifies all sets of three nodes v_1,v_2,v_3, such that there is a path of length 2 between v_1 and v_2 and $<v_2,v_3>$ is an arc of the graph, and so on for $n - 1$ times.

The following function implements such an algorithm, based on the adjacency matrix whose type declaration is included for completeness. For simplicity, the variables `Graph` and `ReachMat` have been declared as global variables instead of parameters of the function.

```
typedef boolean BoolMat[MaxSize][MaxSize];

typedef struct  { int      Card;
                   Element  Nodes[MaxSize];
                   BoolMat  AdMat;
                 } GraphOfElem;

GraphOfElem        Graph;
BoolMat            ReachMat;

void Reachable(void)
                        /*again, a matrix of logical values is used
                        to represent reachability: ReachMat[i,j] =
                        true if and only if the ith node is
                        reachable from the jth.*/
{
   int   i, j, m, k;

   for(i = 0; i < MaxSize; i++)
      for(j = 0; j < MaxSize; j++)
         ReachMat[i][j] = Graph.AdMat[i][j];
                        /*the matrix ReachMat is initialized with
                        the values of the adjacency matrix of the
                        graph.*/
   for(k = 2; k <= GraphCard; k++)
      for(i = 0; i < GraphCard; i++)
         for(j = 0; j < GraphCard; j++)
            for(m = 0; m < GraphCard; m++)
               if(ReachMat[i][m] && Graph.AdMat[m][j])
                  ReachMat[i][j] = true;
}
```

11.2 Stacks: their representation and use

A widely used data structure is the stack. It consists of a variable number of homogeneous elements, that is, elements of the same type, with the characteristic that, every time an element has to be removed from the stack, it is necessarily the last element put onto it. This rule, also called LIFO (Last In–First Out), explains the use of the term 'stack': its management is like that of a stack of plates where every new plate is placed on top and a plate is always taken from the top (if you want to avoid a disaster).

Stacks are a natural data structure for many problems: a major example was presented in Chapter 8 when we introduced recursive programming: the fact that procedure calls and exits follow the LIFO policy made the stack a natural candidate to manage the allocation/deallocation of procedure activation records.

In this section, we briefly discuss how a stack-like data organization can be represented using C type constructors and how the basic operations for its management (allocation and deallocation of data to and from the stack) can be realized. Finally, some hints are given for further possible applications of stacks, besides the major one already mentioned.

11.2.1 Representation of stacks and implementation of operations

The normal C type constructors, already used for the realization of graphs and other structures, can also be applied, in a completely analogous way, to the representation of stacks, with similar relative advantages and disadvantages between the different techniques. In particular, we present a declaration of the generic type `StackOfElem` realized by means of the array constructor, leaving it to the reader to realize the same structure using the dynamic mechanisms of the language (Exercise 11.12).

```
typedef struct  { int     ElemNum;
                  Element Contents[MaxElem];
                } StackOfElem;
```

The principal operations that can be executed on a stack of generic elements are the following, described as subroutines:

- **void** `Initialize(StackOfElem *Stack)`
  the stack of type `StackOfElem` pointed to by `Stack` is initialized with the value 'empty stack', that is, a stack without any elements.

- `boolean EmptyStack(StackOfElem  Stack)`
  establishes whether `Stack`, of type `StackOfElem`, is empty or not.

- **void** `Push(StackOfElem *Stack, Element  Elem)`
  receives one parameter which is a pointer to a stack of type `StackOfElem` and one of type `Element`, and modifies the stack pointed to by adding the element received at the top.

- **void** Pop(StackOfElem *Stack)

  receives a parameter which is a pointer to a stack of type StackOfElem. It deletes the element at the top of the stack pointed to.

- Element Top(StackOfElem Stack)

  receives a parameter Stack of type StackOfElem and produces as its result the value of the element that is at the top of the stack.

Here, we present the code for the procedure Push, leaving the implementation of the other operations as an exercise for the reader (Exercise 11.11).

```
#include <stdio.h>

void Push(StackOfElem *Stack, Element  Elem)
{
   if (Stack->ElemNum == MaxElem)
     printf("Operation cannot be executed because the stack is full\n");
   else
   {
     Stack->ElemNum = Stack->ElemNum + 1;
     Stack->Contents[ElemNum-1] = Elem;
   }
}
```

11.2.2 Use of stacks

As we recalled, the stack structure has various applications in computer science. Our first application of the stack structure was presented in Section 8.3: during the execution of a C program, the activation records associated with subroutine calls are put on a stack at the time of the call and deallocated at the end of execution, following the LIFO discipline.

Another typical example of the use of a stack structure is the recognition of a string of well-balanced brackets. Given a finite set of types of pairs of brackets (for example, round, square and curly), brackets can be opened in any order, but a closing bracket can occur only if it is of the same type as the last opening bracket that has not yet been matched with a closing one. In other words, pairs of brackets cannot cross each other. The following are examples of well-balanced bracket strings:

　({}[[()]{}])
　{[](){{{}}}]}[()]
　(((())))

The following are incorrect strings:

　({}[[()]{}]))
　)(
　[({])}
　({])

The stack is the natural data structure to use for recognizing well-balanced strings, by means of the following algorithm which uses a stack of characters:

(1) Initialize a stack of characters *P* with the value 'empty stack'.

(2) For each character read:

    (a) if it is an opening bracket, copy it to the top of the stack;

    (b) if it is a closing bracket, check that the stack is not empty and that there is an opening bracket of matching type at the top. If so, delete this bracket from the top of the stack; otherwise interrupt execution and signal the error.

(3) The algorithm terminates successfully, accepting the input string, if and only if the stack is empty when the whole string has been scanned.

11.3 Queues

A 'dual' structure with respect to the stack is the queue, which is ruled by the FIFO (First In–First Out) discipline. The main distinction between queues and stacks is that objects are extracted from the end of the queue, whereas in a stack elements are extracted from the top. The basic operations of the abstract data type `QueueOfElem` are the following:

- `Initialize`: analogous to the corresponding operation defined on the stack.

- `EmptyQueue`: analogous to the corresponding operation defined on the stack.

- `InsertInQueue`: receives one parameter of type pointer to queue of type `QueueOfElem` and one of type `Element`, and modifies the queue pointed to by the first parameter, adding the second parameter at its end.

- `Extract`: receives a parameter of type pointer to queue of type `QueueOfElem` and deletes from the queue the element that is at the front (the opposite end from the one where new elements are inserted).

- `Front`: receives a parameter of type `QueueOfElem` and produces as its result the value of the element that is at the front.

Queues can be represented in computer memory in a similar way to stacks. The only further requirement, in the case of representation via arrays, is to manage two indexes, named `front` and `end`, which indicate the front and the end of the queue, respectively. The two indexes are shifted by one position in the same direction for each extraction and insertion operation, respectively. To avoid blocking all operations as soon as one of the two indexes reaches one end of the array allocated to the queue, they are managed in a 'circular' way; that is, their value is calculated up to the remainder operation (%) with respect to the dimensions of the array. Figure 11.5 provides an intuitive explanation of the circular managing of the queue implemented through an array.

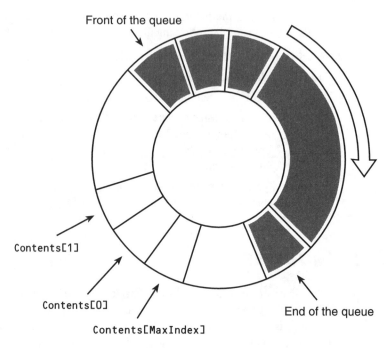

Figure 11.5   A 'circular array' implementing a queue. The grey area denotes the full part of the queue. The large arrow denotes the direction of the movement of the front and of the end of the queue.

The following declarations supply the realization of the type `QueueOfElem` by means of arrays and the code of the operation for inserting an element into the queue. Completing the operations is left, as usual, as an exercise for the reader.

```
typedef struct  { int      ElemNum;
                  Element  Contents[MaxIndex];
                  int      front, end;
                } QueueOfElem;

#include <stdio.h>

void InsertInQueue(QueueOfElem  *Queue, Element  Elem)
{
   if (Queue->ElemNum == MaxIndex)
     printf("Operation cannot be executed because queue is full\n");
   else
   {
     Queue->ElemNum = Queue->ElemNum + 1;
     Queue->Contents[Queue->end] = Elem;
     Queue->end = (Queue->end + 1) % MaxIndex;
         /*remember that the remainders modulo k are 0, 1, ..., k - 1*/
   }
}
```

Exercises

11.1 The construction of the list associated with a graph given in Section 11.1.1 is correct only if we assume that the Info field, which contains the value of the node of the graph, uniquely identifies its node, that is, there are no nodes with repeated names. Why? Modify the construction in such a way that it also represents the graph correctly when this hypothesis is not true.

11.2 The adjacency matrix technique to represent graphs can lead to a considerable waste of memory even when the graph does not have a highly variable number of nodes. Indeed, it requires n^2 cells to represent graphs of n nodes, which corresponds to the maximum number of arcs possible in a graph with n nodes: such a case occurs when the graph is complete. In many cases, however, the effective number of arcs is far lower than those in a complete graph. In such cases, it might be suitable, if we want to adopt a static data structure, to represent the graph by means of a pair of arrays: one containing the list of the nodes of the graph, the other the list of the arcs. Define the details of this representation technique with the help of Figure 11.6 which exemplifies its use for the graph of Figure 11.1(a).

11.3 Extend all data structures discussed so far for the representation of graphs in such a way that they describe graphs whose arcs are labelled with labels of various types (strings, numbers and so on).

11.4 For each of the proposed data structures for the representation of graphs, implement the appropriate procedures for:

- the insertion of a new arc that connects two existing nodes;
- the insertion of a new node and a set of arcs that connect, in both senses, the new node with some of the other nodes;
- the deletion of a node and all the arcs that go into and come out of it;
- the deletion of an arc.

n_1
n_2
n_3
n_4
n_5
n_6
n_7

n_1	n_2
n_2	n_3
n_3	n_2
n_3	n_1
n_1	n_4
n_4	n_1
n_5	n_6

Figure 11.6 A further representation of the graph in Figure 11.1(a).

11.5   Modify the procedure `Reachable` given in Section 11.1 to solve graph reachability in such a way that it deals, possibly more efficiently, with nondirected graphs.

11.6   Implement the algorithm for the construction of the reachability relation given in Section 11.1 using the other data structures discussed for representing graphs. Evaluate and compare their complexity (after reading Chapter 12).

11.7   Modify the algorithm for calculating the reachability relation in the following way: calculate the shortest paths between each pair of nodes of graphs whose arcs are labelled with numeric labels. Assume that each label has a non-negative value (for example, distances between towns). Implement it for various graph representation techniques.

11.8   Construct an algorithm to establish whether a graph is connected or not and implement it by using several graph representation techniques in such a way that comparisons can be made between the different techniques.

11.9   Construct an algorithm to establish whether a graph is complete or not and implement it by using several data representation techniques in such a way that comparisons can be made between the different techniques.

11.10   Construct an algorithm to establish whether a graph is acyclic or not and implement it by using several data representation techniques in such a way that comparisons can be made between the different techniques.

11.11   Write the code for the operations `Initialize`, `EmptyStack`, `Pop` and `Top` on a stack realized as indicated in Section 11.2.1.

11.12   Supply a type declaration that realizes the `Stack` structure using pointers as suggested by Figure 11.7. Then redefine the typical stack operations accordingly. Discuss the advantages and disadvantages of the two ways of realizing the stacks and their respective operations.

11.13   Implement the algorithm for recognizing well-balanced bracket strings as a C program, using the structures proposed in Section 11.2.1 and the corresponding procedures. Discuss the differences between an implementation that uses arrays and one that uses pointers to realize the stack.

11.14   Supply a nonrecursive algorithm that recognizes palindromic strings (see Example 8.3), using a stack structure (suppose that the string is composed of an odd number of characters and that the central character is equal to %).

11.15   Construct a nonrecursive procedure that visits a binary tree in right preorder, using a stack structure.

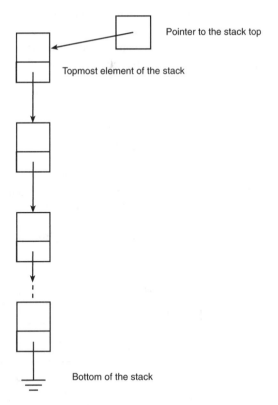

Pointer to the stack top

Topmost element of the stack

Bottom of the stack

Figure 11. 7   A stack implemented through pointers.

11.16   Supply the implementations of the other operations on queues.

11.17   Supply an alternative realization of the queue structure that uses dynamic memory allocation mechanisms. Implement the corresponding operations and compare the two implementation techniques.

11.18   Supply some examples of uses of the queue structure.

11.19   The pointer construct and the operations for the allocation (and deallocation) of memory during execution are, nowadays, available in the vast majority of languages. There are, however, important exceptions, especially among older languages still in widespread use. In such cases, it can be important to make up for the lack of such mechanisms by constructing one or more abstract data types that simulate dynamic memory management through an appropriate data area allocated statically.

   To illustrate the method, let us consider the construction of linear lists of elements. The idea is to create a 'pool' of elements of that list realized by an array. This pool will be called `FreeList`, insofar as it contains elements available for allocation to various lists of elements of the element type under consideration. Initially, this variable (which simulates the memory heap not supplied by the language) contains its various elements connected together in a single list. The various pointers are simulated by integers that denote the indexes of the array, following the scheme suggested by Figure 11.8.

Now suppose that you want to create a new list of elements, List1, initially empty: analogously to the creation of a list based on pointers, a variable List1 which functions as a pointer to the head of the list is used; the type of List1 is the type of the index of the array; its initial value is 0, that is, the representation of NULL.

At this point, all that remains to be done is to construct the operations malloc and free. malloc receives as a parameter, passed by address, a variable that functions as a pointer. It must 'draw out' an element from FreeList and make it accessible via the parameter, following the scheme suggested by Figure 11.9.

Obviously, the free operation is completely symmetric.

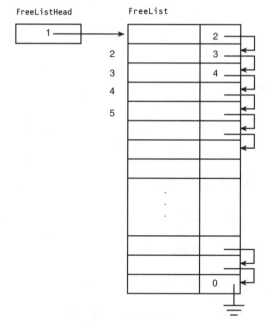

Figure 11.8 Initial state of a free list. Each pointer, realized as the second field of a structure that constitutes the generic element of the list, points to the next element of the array. The variable FreeListHead, which functions as a pointer to the first element of the list, therefore has the value 1. The value 0 simulates the value NULL. Obviously, the first field of the structure is of type Element and does not contain a meaningful value as long as the structure belongs to the free list.

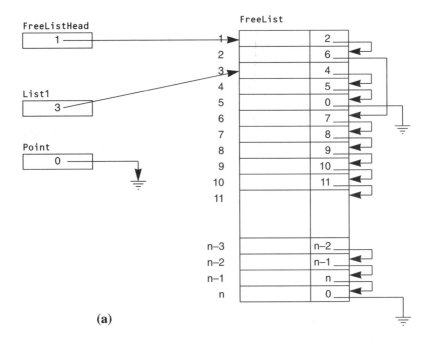

(a)

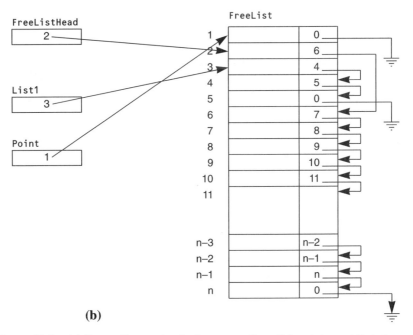

(b)

Figure 11.9 (a) State of FreeList before execution of the statement Point = malloc(**sizeof**(...)). (b) State of FreeList after execution of the statement Point = malloc(**sizeof**(...)).

Thus, implement the abstract data type `FreeList`, together with the operations `malloc` and `free`. Verify whether, on its basis, the previous abstract data type `ListOfElem` can be used without modifications with respect to the case in which pointers and their corresponding operations are built into the language.

11.20   In an analogous way to Exercise 11.19 for linear lists, construct a `FreeList` of elements suitable for building binary trees. Note that, although the elements are to be used to build a tree, in the `FreeList` they are grouped in a linear way (this implies that one of the pointers is not used).

Complexity analysis of algorithms $\boxed{12}$

Each industrial product generates *costs* that have to be evaluated and related to the *benefits* produced. Different types of cost factors are associated with each industrial product, often competing with each other. For example, the product 'car' has a running cost (fuel, maintenance, road tax, ...) and a building cost. The building cost can in turn be subdivided into design cost and physical construction cost (material, labour, energy, ...). Much the same applies to the product 'software': the only difference from other types of manufactured goods is the lack of a serial reproduction phase and its associated cost: once a software product has been completed, any number of copies of that product can be produced without any particular difficulties and with little associated cost.

The evaluation of industrial software costs must therefore take several factors into account, from the resources employed for its execution (hardware) to the staff time necessary for its realization. In this chapter, we restrict our attention to the analysis of software efficiency, that is, to examining how costly its use is. Following the analogy with the 'car' product, we could say that here our interest is restricted to understanding how much fuel, oil and tyres the car uses, without analysing how much it costs to build. In the case of software the major resources necessary to use it are the amount of time and memory required to execute it. There are several reasons for this choice:

- First, in our case, the 'user point of view' predominates over the 'producer point of view'.

- Second, the use-cost analysis is simpler, more intuitive and less subjective than the evaluation of industrial development costs. For instance, stating that 'four megabytes of core memory are necessary to run a given software product' is much less controversial than stating that '10 person-years are needed to develop the product': in such a case one could argue, for example, that the measure 'person-year' (the work performed by one person during a year of normal work) is highly questionable and subjective. It is hard to accept that if we change the designer the measure does not change, or that the work performed by two people in six months equals the work performed by one person in one year.

Thus, issues concerning the evaluation of industrial software development costs are left to the more specialized realm of software engineering. The reader should remember, however, that an appropriate cost evaluation should always be performed in the right context, managing the trade-offs among different goals. For instance, consider two different programs P1 and P2 that solve the same problem, P. P1 runs 10% faster than P2 but its development requires two person-months whereas P2 can be developed in one person-month. If the program is only executed very rarely because P is a very specialized and unusual problem, it would be unwise to invest human time in producing P1 instead of P2. On the other hand, if P is a common problem and the program solving it has to run many times and may be stored in a widely used library, then it is certainly worth the effort to develop a more efficient program.

The chapter is organized as follows. Section 12.1 introduces the problem of quantitative analysis of computing complexity with reference to a simple example; Section 12.2 introduces a notation suitable for the measurement of complexity; Section 12.3 shows the complexity analysis for some basic algorithms; Section 12.4 goes back to dynamic data structures and evaluates the complexity of their management, thus aiding the choice of a suitable data structure from the point of view of the required resources; finally, Section 12.5 briefly introduces the problem of evaluating minimum complexity for the solution of problems and shows how, for some of them, it is impossible to find reasonably efficient solutions.

12.1 Quantitative analysis of complexity of program execution: a first example

Consider the following procedure, which searches for an element in a sequence of integers. This problem was introduced informally in Section 1.2 with reference to finding a book in a library catalogue (Example 1.3). We take it up now in a more rigorous way as a first example of the comparative evaluation of the efficiency of different algorithms.

Following a commonly used scheme, the sequence of integers is realized by a structure whose first component indicates the number of elements effectively present in the sequence and whose second component is an array that stores its contents. The search procedure receives as parameters a sequence and an integer to search for in that sequence, and produces as its results a logical value that indicates whether the integer is present in the sequence and its position within the sequence (this value is negative if the integer is not in the sequence). The procedure has been coded in an intentionally redundant way to permit an extremely simplified analysis.

```
typedef struct  {  int      NumElem;
                   int      Contents[MaxElem];
                }  SeqOfIntegers;

void    Search (SeqOfIntegers  Sequence, int  Elem,
                boolean  *PointToFound, int  *PointToPosition)
{
  int   Count;

  *PointToFound = false; *PointToPosition = -1;
  for (Count = 0; Count < Sequence.NumElem; Count++)
    if (Sequence.Contents[Count] == Elem)
    {
      *PointToFound = true;
      *PointToPosition = Count;
    }
    else
    {
      *PointToFound = *PointToFound;
      *PointToPosition= *PointToPosition;
    }
}
```

Let us analyse the `Search` procedure from the point of view of the memory and time required for its execution.

(1)   The number of memory cells required to execute the procedure is the sum of:

(a)   the number of cells required to contain the object code of the procedure;

(b)   the number of cells required for the procedure's activation record to store the return address and other information needed to execute the call to the procedure and the return from it correctly (see Section 8.3.1);

(c)   the number of cells needed to contain the data of the local environment (local variables and parameters): `MaxElem` + 5 (assuming that a parameter passed by address requires one memory cell).

In general, the sum of the first two values depends on the compiler of the language, since different compilers can translate source code in different ways. It is, however, a constant quantity with respect to the data of the problem. We can therefore say that the memory m necessary for the execution of `Search` is given by the following equation:

$$m = c + \texttt{MaxElem}$$

Both c and `MaxElem` are constant values, but `MaxElem` is directly related to the data of the problem because different values could be used for different executions.

(2)   The time necessary to execute `Search` depends on:

(a)   The execution speed of the machine. The term 'machine' is to be understood in an abstract sense as the processor of the programming language. The efficiency of an 'abstract processor' of languages normally depends on both the hardware and the software employed for its realization, whether as a compiler or as an interpreter.

(b)   The characteristics of the data to be processed, in particular the value of the actual parameter. Just compare executing the procedure on a sequence of 5 elements with executing it on 10 000 elements. In this case, however, the number of elements referred to is the number of elements that are actually significant, indicated by the variable NumElem, not the value of the constant MaxElem. Thus, there is a true variability in execution time, as a function of the actual parameter passed at each call.

This type of dependency could make an absolute evaluation of procedure efficiency rather difficult in terms of execution time. Let us suppose that we want to do some experiments to compare Search with another procedure OtherSearch and decide which is the better one. How could we be sure that, if Search is faster on a PC, it is also faster on any other computer? Furthermore, Search could require less time with input parameters Sequence1 and Elem1, whereas the opposite could happen with parameters Sequence2 and Elem2: in this case, which of the two procedures should be considered more efficient?

In effect, the absolute execution time of any procedure or program is a function, sometimes rather complex, of all the above factors and more besides. However, some simple considerations can help to make the problem much easier to deal with. Let us start by considering the dependency that arises from the characteristics of the machine that executes the computation.

Notwithstanding considerable differences in performance between various existing computers, their 'structure' often has a common base, as described in Chapter 2. Consequently, the instruction sets of the different machines may vary in many details (addressing modes, number and types of registers, execution times and so on), but not in their essence, which is their ability to retrieve and store data in memory and transform it by applying simple operations.

Similarly, compilers of varying degrees of sophistication can generate different object code for the same procedure, depending on how intensively they exploit the characteristics of the physical machine. However, the gain achieved by employing one compiling technique rather than another is, at most, the translation of a certain source code instruction into, for example, a sequence of 4 machine instructions rather than 7. Consequently, if the source code instruction is repeated 100 times, its execution requires 400 machine cycles in the first case and 700 in the second (assuming that each object code instruction is executed in one machine cycle): the gain achieved by using the first compiler is 3/7 of the time consumed by the code generated by the second compiler, independently of the number of times the source code instruction is executed.

Generally speaking, it can be said that *the efficiency of the computing device used affects the overall execution time of any given program at most by a constant factor*. In other words, if the execution of a program P operating on input data d takes a time $f(d)$ on a given machine, the same program, executed on another machine, will take a time $c \cdot f(d)$. Obviously, the value of c can be quite considerable (otherwise there would be no explanation for why computer prices can vary from a couple of hundred dollars to several millions), but we will shortly see that important efficiency analyses can be carried out *without taking constant factors into account*. In other words, significant conclusions regarding the time needed to execute an algorithm can be obtained without taking the performance of the computing device into account.

Let us now consider the dependency between execution time and the data of the problem. We have already stated that it seems natural to expect the time to search a sequence to increase when the size of the sequence (the value of NumElem) increases. This fact evidently has general validity: think, for example, of the problems of inverting a series of numbers, calculating the determinant of a matrix and so on. Generally speaking, we say that the execution time, as well as other efficiency factors, depends on the 'size' of the problem. A sufficiently rigorous definition of this term is the following.

DEFINITION 12.1

The **size** of a problem is understood as a measure of the quantity of memory needed to represent the input data of the problem.

Obviously, such a measure can be expressed in different ways according to the occasion: for example, the size of a problem does not always have to be expressed in physical terms (number of bits or memory words needed); it can be expressed as the number of rows and columns of a matrix, the number of elements in a table, the number of characters or words in a text and so on, as long as in each case a precise relation can be established between the parameter adopted for the size of the problem and the physical memory needed. In the example under consideration, it therefore seems natural to take NumElem as the size of the problem.

A deeper analysis of the procedure allows us to draw further conclusions regarding its efficiency. In particular, it is easy to see that each execution of Search requires a certain time (let us denote it by c_1 without worrying too much about its absolute value) to execute the part of the code that precedes the **for** cycle. Clearly, c_1 does not depend on the sequence and the element sought. Subsequently, the **for** cycle is executed: it is immediately clear that a single execution of the cycle requires a time (let us denote it by c_2) that does not depend on the data. What depends on the data, in fact on the number of elements in the sequence, is the number of repetitions of the cycle: consequently, the total time required for the execution of the cycle is $c_2 \cdot$ NumElem. Thus, the execution time of the procedure is:

$$t = c_1 + c_2 \cdot \text{NumElem} \tag{12.1}$$

Formula (12.1) contains much useful information, even though it does not specify the actual time it takes to execute the Search procedure.

Firstly, it separates dependency on the data from dependency on the machine that executes the algorithm. It is quite clear that changing the language compiler and/or the hardware can change the values of the constants c_1 and c_2, but not the structure of (12.1). This structure is *linear with respect to the length* of the sequence that we have adopted as the size of the problem. This means, for example, that execution of the procedure for a sequence of 2000 elements requires 'a bit less than double' the time required for a sequence of 1000 elements. The rather vague term 'a bit less than double' is due to the component c_1 which does not depend on the size of the problem; it is clear, though, that with increasing problem size its influence tends to disappear.

It is easy to see that, at least for sufficiently large sizes, the linear dependency on the data influences the total execution speed of the procedure much more than the dependency on the execution device which is expressed by the values of the constants c_1 and c_2. Therefore, (12.1) gives us very important information regarding the complexity of the execution of Search without going into the details necessary to calculate the real values of the proportionality constants.

Finally, it should be noted that the Search procedure could be modified to operate on tables of names instead of integers (the reader is invited to construct such a procedure as an exercise) without changing the algorithm on which it is based. The code would be a bit more complex. However, the above analysis which led to the construction of (12.1) could be repeated in an almost identical way, on the assumption that a comparison between names certainly requires more time than a comparison between integers, but is still independent of the length of the sequence. We can therefore come to the conclusion that (12.1) is also a valid formula for the execution time of the new procedure, but with different values for the constants c_1 and c_2. This statement, too, will be discussed in more depth later on.

Now, consider the following procedure OtherSearch, a slight modification of the preceding one.

```
void    OtherSearch (SeqOfIntegers  Sequence, int  Elem,
                     boolean  *PointToFound, int  *PointToPosition)
{
  int   Count;

  *PointToFound = false;
  Count = 0;
  while (*PointToFound == false && Count < Sequence.NumElem)
  {
    if (Sequence.Contents[Count] == Elem)
    {
      *PointToFound = true;
      *PointToPosition = Count;
    }
    Count = Count + 1;
  }
}                                                    /*OtherSearch*/
```

Although they have a rather similar 'structure', it is easy to see that the two search procedures differ in terms of performance time.

Unlike Search, the execution time of OtherSearch depends not only on the length of the sequence, but also on the position in which the element sought is found. Search scans the whole sequence, whereas OtherSearch interrupts scanning as soon as it finds the element sought, if it exists. This simple analysis leads us to the following formulation of the execution time of OtherSearch:

$$t = k_1 + k_2 \cdot n \tag{12.2}$$

where

```
n == if (Elem ∈ Sequence) NumElem else *PointToPosition+1
```

*PointToPosition is the index of the first element of the array that stores Elem, that is:

☛ 1, 2, 3, 4
```
Sequence.Contents[*PointToPosition] == Elem &&
Sequence.Contents[h] != Elem for each h, 0 <= h < *PointToPosition
```

(12.2) differs from (12.1) in the value of the constants, although not by much. On the one hand, the execution of the **while** cycle requires a slightly more complex test than the execution of the corresponding **for** cycle. On the other hand, the branch that is executed inside the cycle, if the condition of the **if** statement is true, is executed at most once, that is, in the last iteration of the cycle (for simplicity, we could attribute its execution time to the constant k_1). It is therefore highly probable that k_2 is very close to c_2. (Remember, however, that in order to obtain precise evaluations of the value of the constants, one has also to take into account how the compiler translates the source language instructions.) The fundamental difference, however, lies in the parameter n, which in (12.1) is always equal to NumElem, whereas in (12.2) it can assume much smaller values (in the luckiest case, it would be 1, even for a sequence of 10 000 elements).

This first remark is of general validity: we cannot say that in all cases the complexity of the solution of a problem only depends on its size, in the sense of the 'volume' of data on which the algorithm operates. For example, a program to calculate the determinant of a matrix could terminate earlier than usual if the matrix has a particular structure (such as being triangular, having its principal diagonal constituted entirely by zeros, ...); a procedure for sorting a list could be faster if the list were already ordered; a compiler could take considerably different times to compile programs of equal length.

Taking this observation to the extreme would imply the construction of extremely complex formulas to express the execution time, and sometimes also the space, required for various algorithms. Often they would turn out to be very difficult to construct and also barely usable. Therefore, in most cases we try to obtain complexity formulas that depend exclusively on the *size* of the data, disregarding other characteristics, such as their distribution, ordering and so on.

The most natural and useful way to achieve this aim is to consider the **worst case** among all those of equal size: this means that we want to obtain a formula in which the execution time of the program, procedure, or algorithm is a function $f(n)$

only of the size of the problem, in such a way that it is guaranteed that in no case of size n is the execution time higher than $f(n)$ and in some cases it is exactly $f(n)$. This type of analysis, called **worst-case analysis**, is very useful in practice because it allows us to obtain an assured upper bound with respect to the behaviour of a program. For example, if the program is part of the control system of a highly critical plant whose functioning depends on certain data being processed within a certain time, one clearly wants a *guarantee* that the execution of the program terminates within the established time *in every case*.

Applying the worst-case criterion to the two procedures Search and OtherSearch, we obtain nearly identical formulas, apart from the values of the constants – we have already observed that k_2 is likely to be slightly higher than c_2. We therefore have to conclude that, *in the worst case*, OtherSearch is not better, and may even be worse, than Search. And yet, many of us would underwrite the statement that '*normally* OtherSearch would be preferable to Search'. This statement can be justified in a common-sense way as follows:

- The difference between the constants k_2 and c_2, disregarding the others whose weight is negligible, is likely to be very small.
- There is a non-negligible number of cases in which the element sought can be found in Sequence. In these cases the number of iterations of the cycle co-incides with the position of the element sought; often this will be considerably less than Sequence's size; thus, *on average*, the improvement obtained by the reduced number of iterations largely compensates for the difference between the constants k_2 and c_2.

The above reasoning is not without foundation, but like all reasonings based on common sense, it could hide pitfalls. In fact, when the search procedure is applied in a context where the element sought is normally not found in the sequence and the search is only occasionally successful, Search turns out to be preferable to OtherSearch.

This shows how the above 'common sense' statement is based on – often implicit – **probabilistic hypotheses** about the distribution of data and tends towards a case different from a worst-case analysis: the **average case**. The conclusion of the reasoning could, indeed, have been worded more precisely by making explicit the underlying assumptions as follows: '*assuming a uniform distribution of data*, on average, OtherSearch is more efficient than Search'.

Efficiency analysis of this kind can be as useful in evaluating an algorithm as worst-case analysis, or can complement it. Nevertheless, its rigorous application requires solid bases of statistics and probability calculus and goes beyond the scope of this book. Therefore, we concentrate on worst-case analysis and otherwise restrict ourselves to passing remarks.

In conclusion, the worst-case analysis leads us to conclude that Search and OtherSearch are 'essentially equivalent' with respect to efficiency of execution. This statement may seem vaguely disappointing, because it does not seem to support the intuitive feeling that led us to prefer OtherSearch. However, it provides relevant information for evaluating efficiency, as synthesized in (12.1) and (12.2) in which, in the worst case, n is equal to NumElem; the next example shows us that these are the first, fundamental items of information about the complexity of the execution of algorithms.

EXAMPLE 12.1

Suppose that the sequence of integers in which we must search for a certain element is ordered, for example in ascending order: that is, for each i such that

```
0 <= i < NumElem - 1, Sequence.Contents[i] <= Sequence.Contents[i+1]
```

Obviously, the problem of searching for a certain element within the sequence can be resolved by applying one of the previously analysed procedures Search and OtherSearch. However, the fact that the set of input data is now restricted with respect to the original problem can be exploited to construct a search algorithm which is (much) more efficient than the previous ones, as was intuitively stated in Section 1.2. This algorithm is based on a cycle that, during each iteration, divides the portion of the sequence to be searched into two and is therefore called the **binary search algorithm**.

Informally, the binary search algorithm can be explained as follows:

(1) A first comparison is made between the element sought and the median element of the sequence.

(2) If the median element matches the element sought, the search terminates successfully, otherwise the following two cases are treated separately:

(a) the median element is greater than the element sought;

(b) the median element is less than the element sought.

Case 2(a) implies that, if the element sought exists in the sequence, it must necessarily be in its first half because, given that the sequence is ordered, all elements with an index higher than the median are of a greater value. Case 2(b) is symmetrical to case 2(a). Consequently, the search is resumed, but restricted to the half that can still potentially contain the element sought. This is carried out by repeating the procedure from point 1, that is, comparing the element sought with the median element of the chosen half of the sequence.

The above algorithm naturally lends itself to being coded recursively (just consider the fact that the chosen half of the sequence is still a sequence and that the search must terminate when the length of sequence that remains to be examined is zero). This is the object of Exercise 12.8.

Next, we present a procedure that implements the binary search algorithm in an iterative way, which allows a simple complexity analysis.

```
void  BinarySearch (SeqOfIntegers  Sequence, int  Elem,
                    boolean  *PointToFound, int  *PointToPosition)
{
   int bottom, top, median;

   bottom = 0; top = NumElem - 1; median = (bottom + top)/2;
                                  /*remember that the integer division
                                  operator truncates the result of the
                                  division if it is not an integer*/
   *PointToFound = false;
   while (bottom <= top && *PointToFound == false)
   {
      if (Elem == Sequence.Contents[median])
      {
         *PointToFound = true;
         *PointToPosition = median;
      }
      else
      {
         if (Elem < Sequence.Contents[median])
            top = median - 1;
         else
            bottom = median + 1;
         median = (bottom + top)/2;
      }
   }
}
```

☛ 5, 6

Let us now analyse the temporal complexity of `BinarySearch`. Like the other procedures, `BinarySearch` will require a constant time, that is, a time independent of the data, to execute the portion of code outside the cycle. Let us call this time c_1. The time needed to execute the cycle depends on the data. If the element sought matches the median element of the sequence, the first sequence of statements of the first conditional statement is executed: this is certainly shorter than the corresponding **else** branch. If we carry out a worst-case analysis, however, we will certainly find a value c_2 such that the execution of the cycle never requires a time longer than c_2. Consequently, the total time necessary to execute `BinarySearch` is, once again, given by the formula:

$$t = c_1 + c_2 \cdot n$$

where n indicates the number of times that the cycle is executed. Let us now analyse in more detail the value of n as a function of the input data, in particular as a function of the size of the problem, which again is the value of `NumElem`.

In the most fortunate case, the element sought would be found in the first iteration of the cycle: hence n would be 1. We are, however, only interested in the worst case. This occurs when the element sought is not in the sequence. In fact, in this case, condition `*PointToFound == false` is always true and the exit from the cycle is eventually determined by the condition `top < bottom`.

Let us now consider the 'distance' d between the two extremes of the zone of the sequence within which we search for `Elem`. This is given by the value d = top −

`bottom + 1`. Initially, therefore, d is equal to `NumElem`. At each iteration of the cycle, the new value of d, which we call d', is:

$$d' = ((\texttt{bottom} + \texttt{top}) / 2 - 1) - \texttt{bottom} + 1$$

in case 2(a) and

$$d' = \texttt{top} - ((\texttt{bottom} + \texttt{top}) / 2 + 1) + 1$$

in case 2(b).

In both cases we have $d' \leq d/2$. Therefore, using d_k to indicate the value d at the kth iteration of the cycle, we have:

$d_{k+1} \leq d_k/2$, that is, $d_k \geq 2d_{k+1}$

$d_1 = \texttt{NumElem}$

$d_n = 1$ (in the worst case)

From this, we can deduce $d_{n-k} \geq 2^k$; $d_1 = \texttt{NumElem} \geq 2^{n-1}$; $n \leq \log_2(\texttt{NumElem}) + 1$.

In conclusion, including the value 1 within the constant c_1, the execution time of `BinarySearch` is, in the worst case,

$$t = c_1 + c_2 \cdot \log_2(\texttt{NumElem}) \tag{12.3}$$

It is important to dwell a bit more on the quantitative difference between (12.3) and the preceding (12.1) and (12.2). Independently of the values of the constants involved, for tables of a reasonable size the execution time of `BinarySearch` is very much shorter than that of the other two procedures, whose relative difference now appears irrelevant with respect to the behaviour of `BinarySearch`. This analysis states more rigorously in mathematical terms the intuitive considerations concerning the efficiency of algorithms expressed in Example 1.3.

Let us now recapitulate what we have learnt from the examples analysed in this section:

- The complexity of an algorithm, understood as the amount of memory and time needed for its execution, depends on both the machine used to execute it and the data of the problem.
- The dependency on the characteristics of the machine has an influence of at most a proportionality constant and can be – at least in first approximation analysis – disregarded in evaluating the efficiency of the algorithm.
- The dependency on the data of the problem can be synthesized as a function of the size of the problem, referring to:
  - the worst case,
  - the average case.

We concentrate exclusively on worst-case analysis.

- Even if we leave the exact values of the proportionality constants in the formulas out of the calculation, there are cases where the complexity formulas show a considerable difference in efficiency between one algorithm and another, which, quite often, makes more detailed comparison analyses superfluous.

Thus, these observations seem to suggest that we should analyse the efficiency of algorithms by trying, first, to highlight 'macroscopic' differences such as those that distinguish `Search` and `OtherSearch` from `BinarySearch`, and then to refine the analysis further, if this is necessary and useful. It is likely, however, that such a refinement has to take into account factors that are more difficult to measure, such as the elementary operations of the machine or the distribution of data.

In this text, therefore, we limit ourselves to an evaluation of macroscopic characteristics of algorithms. The following section provides us with a mathematical framework, in order to lead us to a systematic evaluation.

*12.2 The 'big-theta' notation

In Section 12.1, we found formulas that express the execution time of certain programs as a function of the size of the data, applying the worst-case method of analysis and thus ensuring that in no case, by supplying the program with data of a certain size (numbers of elements in a sequence, length of an array or a list), would execution time exceed the value found.

Although we constructed the complexity formulas without the constants, that is, without taking into consideration the multitude of details that would have been necessary to determine them, we were able to evaluate and compare the efficiency of various algorithms in quite a meaningful way. Indeed, we were able to conclude that a binary search, where applicable, is enormously more efficient than a sequential search. Even if we executed the procedure `Search` on a supercomputer and `BinarySearch` on a simple PC, with a significant number of values in the sequence, the execution time of the latter would still be much less than that of the former. In such a case we say that the second algorithm is faster than the first by an **order of magnitude**.

Our examples suggest that we should analyse the complexity of algorithms first with respect to their order of magnitude and then, within the same order of magnitude, go on to analyse further details. This practice is suitable for a vast majority of cases, but there are also a considerable number of exceptions which common sense and experience would not permit the project designer to neglect. Some hints on this will be given later.

The concept of order of magnitude of a function has a natural and simple mathematical formalization that allows the fundamental aspects of the complexity of execution of a program to be highlighted.

DEFINITION 12.2

Let $f(n)$ and $g(n)$ be two functions of the integer variable n, strictly greater than 0 and **monotonic** (recall that a function f is monotonic if and only if for every n, $f(n) \leq f(n+1)$. Notice that this hypothesis is certainly verified by most algorithm complexity functions: increasing the size of a problem will increase the resources needed to solve it.

We say that $f(n)$ is $\Theta(g(n))$ (in other words, that f and g are of the same order of magnitude) if

$$\lim_{n \to \infty} \frac{f(n)}{g(n)} = c, \text{ with } c \neq 0 \text{ and } c \neq \infty$$

Θ thus establishes a relation between the two functions f and g. This is also indicated by the notation $f \Theta g$ (often read as 'f is big-theta of g'). A simple knowledge of mathematical analysis allows us to state that Θ is an **equivalence relation** between functions, which means that it has reflexive, symmetric and transitive properties.

Once a relation of Θ-equivalence between functions has been established, it is equally easy to define a Θ-order. This is done as follows.

DEFINITION 12.3

f is called Θ-minor than g ($f <_{\Theta} g$) if

$$\lim_{n \to \infty} \frac{f(n)}{g(n)} = 0$$

f is called Θ-greater than g ($f >_{\Theta} g$) if

$$\lim_{n \to \infty} \frac{f(n)}{g(n)} = \infty$$

Again, $<_{\Theta}$ is actually a **strict ordering relation**, in other words, it has irreflexive, antisymmetric and transitive properties. Furthermore, $f <_{\Theta} g$ implies $g >_{\Theta} f$.

Some examples of relations established by the big-theta notation are the following.

(1) n^2 is $\Theta(5 \cdot n + 0.000\,01 \cdot n^2 - \log_3(n))$

(2) $\log_{10}(n)$ is $\Theta\,(\log_2(n^3))$

It is well known that, once an equivalence relation R has been defined on a set S, the **classes of equivalence modulo R** on S are automatically defined. They are constituted by sets of elements which are R-equivalent among each other. These equivalence classes are **partitions of** S, that is, their union produces the entire S and they are mutually disjoint.

Normally, a class of equivalence modulo R (R-class) is indicated by any one of its elements enclosed in square brackets. In the case of the Θ-equivalence relation we would thus have $[n] = [13 \cdot n] = [n - \log(n) + \sqrt{n}]$ and so on. The ordering relation $<_\Theta$ (and its symmetric $>_\Theta$) is also defined in a natural way on the classes of equivalence modulo Θ. Indeed, it suffices to put $[f] <_\Theta [g]$ if and only if $f <_\Theta g$.

12.2.1 The use of Θ to evaluate the order of magnitude of algorithm complexity

Let us apply the Θ-notation to the complexity formulas of the search algorithms analysed in Section 12.1:

- The complexity of `Search` and `OtherSearch` is $\Theta(n)$

☞ 7

- The complexity of `BinarySearch` is $\Theta(\log(n))$

The difference between the two orders of magnitude is such that we can conclude with certainty that, every time it is applicable, `BinarySearch` is preferable to the other two, independently of the results of further complexity analysis.

In general, if we can conclude that an algorithm A has complexity $\Theta(f)$ and an algorithm B has complexity $\Theta(g)$, with $[f] <_\Theta [g]$, we can prefer A to B. The only elements of caution in the application of this rule depend on the following facts.

- $[f] <_\Theta [g]$ implies that $f(n) < g(n)$ *for sufficiently high values of n*, not for all values of n. In some cases, therefore, the algorithms could operate with values of problem size, n, that do not guarantee the above inequality. For this reason, the Θ-notation is often called the **asymptotic complexity** notation. In experiments, complexity relations deriving from the normal conditions of use of algorithms seldom fail to coincide with the relations of asymptotic complexity.

- Let f^a and f^w be the complexity functions in the average case and in the worst case, respectively. $[f^w] <_\Theta [g^w]$ does not necessarily imply $[f^a] <_\Theta [g^a]$.

  In the next section, we discuss a classic example of an algorithm that is considered highly efficient thanks to a good average-case complexity, in spite of a poor complexity rating in the worst case.

Thanks to the notion of asymptotic complexity and to the big-theta notation, we are now equipped to perform a fairly simple algorithm analysis that goes straight to the essential aspects of their complexity.

12.2.2 The 'big-oh' notation

In the literature the big-oh notation is used more than big-theta as a measure of the order of magnitude of algorithm complexity. Big-oh is defined as follows.

DEFINITION 12. 4

A function $f(n)$ is said to be $O(g(n))$ if there exists a positive constant c and a positive integer $\bar{n}$ such that for every $n \geq \bar{n}, f(n) \leq c \cdot g(n)$.

It is clear that $f \Theta g$ implies that f is also $O(g)$ but the converse does not hold in general. Thus, while big-theta is symmetric, the big-oh relation is not: it provides only an *upper bound* to the order of magnitude of algorithm complexity. Once we have stated that an algorithm has an $O(n^2)$ time complexity, we cannot exclude the possibility that it can run in linear time in all cases. Instead, if we prove that it has a $\Theta(n^2)$ complexity, there are certainly cases where execution time grows with the square of the problem's size.

We adopted the rather unusual choice of big-theta as a complexity measure, as opposed to the more traditional big-oh notation, because big-oh provides a less accurate measure; big-oh is sometimes easier to compute for sophisticated algorithms, but this is not the case in our relatively simple examples.

*12.3 Complexity analysis of some basic algorithms

In this section, we calculate the asymptotic complexity of some widely used, classic algorithms.

EXAMPLE 12.2

Consider the basic operations `tail` and `insertElem` described in Example 8.4. If n is the length of the list to which both are applied, and given the fact that, in both cases, it is essentially a **for** cycle that scans the entire list, it becomes immediately clear that their execution time is a function $\Theta(n)$.

EXAMPLE 12.3

Now consider the procedure deleteElem also described in Example 8.4. It is coded recursively. In this case, it is convenient to define its complexity function $f(n)$ via appropriate equations, in such a way that the $f(n)$ we look for is their solution. For this reason, we also say that $f(n)$ is *defined implicitly*. We assume the size of the problem, denoted by the parameter n, to be the length of the list: by this we mean the value of the length field, not the physical length, that is, the number of memory cells occupied, which is always equal to MaxLength. It is evident that the execution time depends on the former, not on the latter.

Let us now examine the code of deleteElem, in order to construct the equations that the corresponding complexity function $f(n)$ must satisfy.

The body of the function is a single conditional statement whose condition (l1.length > 0) allows us to conclude immediately that, if the list has zero length, the execution time of the procedure has the constant value c_0. This is formalized by the equation

$$f(0) = c_0 \tag{12.4}$$

For $n > 0$, we have to execute, in a constant time c_1, the test temp == elem. If its result is positive, the tail operation has to be executed, which, as we have seen, requires a time $\Theta(n)$, followed by the same deleteElem operation, applied this time to a list whose length has become $n - 1$. Consequently, the time needed to execute the first sequence of statements of the internal conditional statement is

$$c_2 \cdot n + f(n - 1)$$

In the case where the test result is negative, the tail operation that modifies TempList has to be executed (this evidently requires a time $\Theta(n)$); subsequently deleteElem has to be applied to tail(l1), of length $n - 1$, and the element el must be inserted in the tail of l1 (modified by the preceding deleteElem). All this requires a time

$$c_3 \cdot n + f(n - 1) + c_4 \cdot n$$

Applying a worst-case analysis, we can easily establish that, independently of the values of c_2, c_3 and c_4 and of the test result, for $n > 0$ the execution time of deleteElem is given by the equation

$$f(n) = c_1 + c_5 \cdot n + f(n - 1) \tag{12.5}$$

(12.5) is a finite difference equation that, together with the terminal condition constituted by (12.4), implicitly defines the function f as that function which satisfies both (12.4) and (12.5).

Without going into mathematical theories that allow us to prove the existence and uniqueness of the solution of such systems and to calculate their numerical value, it is easy to realize that, in this case, $f(n)$ is $\Theta(n^2)$. Indeed, because the value of the constants has no influence with respect to the order of magnitude, we can assume, without losing generality, that $c_1 = 0$ and $c_5 = 1$. In this case it is evident that

$$f(n) = \sum_{k=0}^{n} k$$

whose value is notoriously $n \cdot (n + 1)/2$, that is, $\Theta(n^2)$.

Note that it is easy to construct nonrecursive searchElem and deleteElem functions that have a $\Theta(n)$ complexity. This has been verified in Section 12.1 for the first case, and it is a simple exercise for the second case. However, this should not lead us to the erroneous conclusion that recursive programming is generally less efficient than nonrecursive programming. It would not be difficult to modify the two recursive procedures in such a way as to obtain a complexity of $\Theta(n)$. There are no general guidelines to compare a priori recursive programming with traditional programming from the point of view of efficiency.

Let us now examine some classic sorting algorithms.

EXAMPLE 12.4 *Sorting by linear insertion*

Consider the following sorting algorithm for an array of n elements. For simplicity, we omit the coding of its declarative part, whether coded as a procedure or as part of a program. a indicates the array to be sorted. It is stored in the elements 1 ... n, while the 0th element is used to store temporary values. i and j are counters and x is a temporary variable. The algorithm is based on the following idea.

The array is divided into two parts. The first part, a[1 ... i − 1], always has to be sorted (this is initially true in a trivial way, when it consists of a single element, that is, when the i counter equals 2). The second part, a[i ... n], contains the elements still to be sorted. Thus, the algorithm executes, $n - 1$ times, a cycle whose task is to move the element a[i] into a position in the first part such that the first part is still sorted, but increased by one element (i is incremented by 1 unit). Figure 12.1 shows a graphical explanation of the procedure.

In order to identify the 'right position' into which to insert the element a[i], we proceed as follows.

We save the value of a[i] in two different temporary cells, x and a[0] (the use of a[0] is a little trick that allows us to consider the temporary cell as an 'appendix' of the array, called a **sentinel**, and to access it via the index of the array

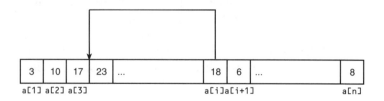

Figure 12.1   Illustration of sorting by linear insertion.

itself: the usefulness of this expedient will become clear shortly). Then we compare, via an internal cycle, the value of a[i] stored in x with all the superior elements of the already sorted part of the array, until it is greater than or equal to one of them: when this occurs, we have found the position where it has to be inserted. During this series of comparisons, steps are taken to move all elements greater than x one position to the right (with respect to the placing in Figure 12.1). This explains the necessity of using the temporary cell: indeed, it is likely (if a[i] < a[i − 1]) that the value of a[i] gets deleted. In this way, when we have identified the correct position for a[i] (currently in cell x) its value will be immediately available to be written without deleting the value that was previously found in this position. The following fragment of code implements the above algorithm:

```
for (i = 2; i <= n; i++)
{
    x = a[i];
    a[0] = x;
    j = i - 1;
    while (x < a[j])
    {
        a[j + 1] = a[j];
        j = j - 1;
    }
    a[j + 1] = x;
}
```

Note that, in the particular case in which, at a certain iteration of the cycle, the element a[i] is less than all the elements in the first part of the array, the termination of the internal cycle is guaranteed by the 'sentinel' a[0] where we find the value of a[i].

Let us now evaluate the complexity of the algorithm of sorting by linear insertion. The external cycle is executed $n − 1$ times. However, its execution time is not constant, because it contains another cycle which, in its turn, has a constant execution time. Thus, if we call c_1 the execution time of the external cycle, excluding the internal cycle, and c_2 the execution time of the internal cycle, we have

$$f(n) = (n-1) \cdot c_1 + \sum_{i=1}^{n-1} c_2 \cdot m_i$$

where m_i is the number of times the internal cycle is repeated during the ith iteration of the external cycle. Thus, we have to calculate the value of m_i as a function of i.

The worst case occurs when, at each iteration, $a[i]$ is less than all the elements of the array $a[1 \ldots i - 1]$ (that is, the array is sorted in the reverse direction to the one desired). In this case, the internal cycle is repeated i times (the last time, to be exact, only the test $x < a[0]$ is executed, which results in false, but the error of taking c_2 as the execution time in this case too is certainly not going to change the order of magnitude of the complexity function). Consequently, we have

$$f(n) = (n-1) \cdot c_1 + \sum_{i=1}^{n-1} c_2 \cdot i = (n-1) \cdot c_1 + \frac{(c_2 \cdot (n-1) \cdot n)}{2}$$

that is, $f(n)$ is $\Theta(n^2)$.

Many simple and 'natural' sorting algorithms turn out to be of square complexity (see also Exercise 12.5). There are, however, more sophisticated algorithms with decidedly better performance. One of the best known and simplest is the algorithm described in Example 12.5.

As a preliminary background for the next example, let us introduce the following procedure – which will be used by the sorting algorithm – whose task is to 'merge' two sorted sequences (whose structure is supplied by an appropriate declaration) into a single sorted sequence that contains all the elements of the two given sequences:

```
typedef struct { int       length;
                 int       contents[MaxLength];
               } sequence;
void Merge (sequence  a, sequence  b, sequence  *c)
{
   int   i,j,k;

   i = 0; j = 0; k = 0;
   while (i < a.length && j < b.length)
   {
      if (a.contents[i] < b.contents[j])
      {
         c->contents[k] = a.contents[i];
         i = i + 1;
      }
      else
      {
         c->contents[k] = b.contents[j];
         j = j + 1;
      }
      k = k + 1;
   }
```

```
while (i < a.length)
{
    c->contents[k] = a.contents[i];
    i = i + 1; k = k + 1;
}
while (j < b.length)
{
    c->contents[k] = b.contents[j];
    j = j + 1; k = k + 1;
}
c->length = k;
}
```

It is an easy exercise (Exercise 12.6) to show that the complexity of the above procedure Merge is $\Theta(n)$, where n denotes the length of the sequences. We can now go back to the sorting problem.

EXAMPLE 12.5 Merge–sort

We realized above that the problem of 'merging' together two already sorted lists, of length n, is substantially simpler than sorting one not yet sorted, of the same length, at least on the basis of what we have learnt so far. This observation suggests that we should exploit the solution of the merging problem as a tool to arrive at the solution of the sorting problem.

Imagine dividing the sequence to be sorted into two equal parts (if it is of odd length, we arbitrarily select a first part of length $\lfloor n/2 \rfloor$ and another of length $\lfloor n/2 \rfloor$ + 1, where the symbol $\lfloor n/2 \rfloor$ denotes the greatest integer not greater than $n/2$). If we had succeeded in sorting the two parts separately, we could now sort the original sequence by merging the results of the partial sorting operations. We also observe that a sequence of length 1 is already automatically sorted. These observations can be easily synthesized in a recursively formulated sorting algorithm which we summarize below.

(1)   If the sequence to be sorted, seq, is of length 1, it is already sorted and the algorithm terminates immediately leaving it unaltered; otherwise

(2)   (a)   the sequence to be sorted is divided into two consecutive subsequences, seq1 and seq2, each half the length of seq (if the length of seq is odd, the first is of length $\lfloor n/2 \rfloor$ and the second $\lfloor n/2 \rfloor$ + 1);

(b)   seq1 and seq2 are sorted separately;

(c)   seq1 and seq2 are merged into a single sequence that replaces seq.

The coding of the above algorithm into the following procedure should not require further explanation (we assume that pseq is a pointer type variable to a structure of sequence type and we use the Merge procedure defined above).

```
void   MergeSort (sequence   *pseq);
{
   sequence   seq1, seq2;
   int        i;

   if (pseq->length != 1)
   {
      seq1.length = pseq->length/2;
      if ((pseq->length%2) == 0)
         seq2.length = pseq->length/2;
      else
         seq2.length = pseq->length/2 + 1;
      for (i = 0; i < seq1.length; i++)
         seq1.contents[i] = pseq->contents[i];
      for (i = 0; i < seq2.length; i++)
         seq2.contents[i] = pseq->contents[i + seq1.length];
      MergeSort (&seq1); MergeSort (&seq2); Merge (seq1, seq2, pseq);
   }
}
```

At first sight, the new sorting algorithm may seem more complicated than the previous one: it contains some 'preparatory work' to construct the two subsequences which itself requires the execution of two cycles; then there are two recursive calls to the MergeSort procedure, and finally a call to an auxiliary procedure Merge. Let us apply, however, a more thorough analysis, constructing a set of formulas to define the complexity $f(n)$ of execution of MergeSort, where n denotes the value of pseq->length.

Obviously

$$f(1) = c_1 \tag{12.6}$$

(it is assumed that the parameter of the procedure is never an empty sequence; the reader can easily modify the procedure to include this case, too) because in this case a single statement is executed once.

For values of $n > 1$ the following are executed:

(1)   The assignments to the variables seqi->length which require a constant time c_2 (obviously, we consider the maximum value among the various possible cases).

(2)   The assignments to the variables seqi->contents which require one execution cycle each. The overall duration of these cycles is clearly $c_3 \cdot n$.

(3)   The calls MergeSort (&seq1); MergeSort (&seq2). Their execution requires a time of $2 f(n/2)$. In the first instance, we assume that n is a power of 2, so that $n/2$ is an integer value at each call of the procedure. This hypothesis is easily removed later.

(4)   The Merge operation on the results produced by the two recursive calls. We know that this operation requires a time of $c_4 \cdot n$.

In conclusion, we can write

$$f(n) = c_2 + c \cdot n + 2 \cdot f(n/2) \quad \text{(with } c = c_3 + c_4) \tag{12.7}$$

The system (12.6), (12.7) can be easily solved in the following way. We *hypothesize* that $f(n)$ is of the type $k_1 \cdot n \cdot \log_2(n) + k_2 \cdot n + k_3$ and we *verify* that it is effectively a solution of the system for appropriate values of k_1, k_2 and k_3. (Strictly speaking, we verify that the hypothesized function f is *one* solution of the system. Only a more in-depth mathematical analysis, which we omit here, could guarantee that it is also the *only* solution.)

The condition $f(1) = c_1$ imposes

$$k_2 + k_3 = c_1 \tag{12.8}$$

(12.7) imposes

$$
\begin{aligned}
&k_1 \cdot n \cdot \log_2(n) + k_2 \cdot n + k_3 = \\
&c_2 + c \cdot n + 2 \cdot [k_1 \cdot n/2 \cdot (\log_2(n) - 1) + k_2 \cdot n/2 + k_3] = \\
&c_2 + c \cdot n + k_1 \cdot n \cdot \log_2(n) - k_1 \cdot n + k_2 \cdot n + 2 \cdot k_3
\end{aligned} \tag{12.9}
$$

In order that (12.9) be *identically satisfied*, that is, for each value of n, the following must hold:

$$k_2 = c - k_1 + k_2$$

and

$$k_3 = c_2 + 2 \cdot k_3$$

which, together with (12.8), impose

$$k_1 = c, \quad k_2 = c_1 + c_2, \quad k_3 = -c_2$$

In conclusion, independently of the value of the constants, $f(n)$ is $\Theta(n \cdot \log(n))$. This fact also remains true for values of n which are not a power of 2. Indeed, it is easy to see that $f(n)$ is a monotonic function, that is, $f(n + 1) \geq f(n)$. Therefore, for $2^h \leq n < 2^{h+1}$, $f(n) < c \cdot 2^{h+1} \cdot (h + 1) + r(n) = 2 \cdot c \cdot 2^h \cdot h + r'(n)$, where $r(n)$ and $r'(n)$ have an order of magnitude less than $n \cdot \log(n)$. Therefore, $f(n)$ is bounded by a function $\Theta(n \cdot \log(n))$.

This result is of fundamental importance because it allows the complexity of the sorting problem to be reduced substantially. For example, for $n = 10\,000$ (still a small number with respect to the quantities of data involved in various applications), $n^2 = 100$ million, whereas $n \cdot \log_2(n) = 10\,000 \cdot 4 \cdot \log_2(10)$, that is, a bit more than $100\,000$!

The merge–sort algorithm can also be formulated in a nonrecursive way. In this case it seems better to analyse the problem in reverse order with respect to the recursive formulation, observing that a sequence of n elements can first be trivially split into n subsequences of one element which are therefore a priori sorted. We can then merge the first subsequence with the second, the third with the fourth and so on, obtaining $n/2$ new sorted subsequences of two elements each (as before, we start by assuming that n is a power of 2 and then remove this hypothesis after having grasped the essential aspects of the algorithm). At this point, we can repeat the procedure with the new subsequences, obtaining $n/4$ sorted subsequences of 4 elements each and so on, until we get a single sequence of n elements which is thus the sorted permutation of the initial sequence.

The order of magnitude of the complexity of this new merge–sort algorithm (which we call 'bottom-up merge–sort') can be easily found even without going into all the details of the coding (the reader is invited to solve Exercise 12.9 and see how the code obtained is considerably more complicated than both the recursive version of merge–sort and the other sorting algorithms which are less efficient).

Each 'pass' consists of merging $n/2^h$ sequences of 2^h elements into $n/2^{h+1}$ sequences of 2^{h+1} elements. Consequently, it always requires a time of $\Theta(n)$, independently of the value of h. Because the algorithm terminates when $2^h = n$, the number of passes is $\log_2(n)$ and therefore the complexity of the algorithm is $\Theta(n \cdot \log(n))$, as in the recursive case.

Given the importance of the sorting problem, there are a large number of algorithms for its solution. In general, we can state that the simple and natural algorithms are of complexity $\Theta(n^2)$, whereas the more sophisticated ones have a complexity of $\Theta(n \cdot \log(n))$. A particularly interesting case is that of the famous Quicksort algorithm, due to C. A. Hoare, which is considered to be one of the most efficient sorting methods. We do not include it here, because it is too sophisticated for the introductory purposes of this text. It is, however, worth stressing that it has a complexity of $\Theta(n^2)$ in the worst case, whereas on average its complexity is $\Theta(n \cdot \log(n))$. It is therefore surprising that this algorithm is preferred to others with a complexity of $\Theta(n \cdot \log(n))$ even in the worst case. However, this is one of those typical cases in which it is preferable to have better performance (even though within the same class of Θ-equivalence) in the average case, even at the cost of worsening the behaviour in the worst case.

Let us now derive some remarks and suggestions from the examples examined in this section.

12.3.1 Use of the 'divide and conquer' technique to design algorithms

The examples examined so far have emphasized a general approach to the (possibly recursive) solution of problems involving data structures of a certain complexity (sequences, matrices and so on): the structure to be operated on is divided into simpler components for which the solution to the problem under scrutiny is less complex. The solution to the original problem is then constructed on the basis of the solutions of the individual components. For this reason, such an approach is often called **divide and conquer** from the famous saying of the ancient Romans *'divide et impera'*. When the approach is formulated recursively, it is easy to express the complexity function of the procedure by difference equations in which the complexity variable is the size of the instance of the particular problem (length of a sequence, order of a matrix and so on).

It is particularly interesting to observe that there are various ways of dividing a problem into subproblems referring to different instances of the same problem: for example, sorting a sequence of length n can be decomposed into sorting one sequence of length $n - 1$ and one of length 1, whose case is trivial, or it can be decomposed into sorting two sequences of length $n/2$. Not all of these ways are equivalent to each other in terms of computational complexity: in general, we have observed that dividing a problem into 'equal parts' (for example, into two subsequences of equal length) is advantageous with respect to more 'unbalanced' solutions. We will not deal with this observation in more depth in mathematical terms, but limit ourselves to the intuitive evidence of the examples discussed.

12.3.2 Algorithms to process data in mass storage

The algorithms analysed so far referred to data structures implemented via the array constructor. However, in many cases, the data to be processed is stored in mass storage, that is, in files. Sometimes it is easy to rewrite algorithms designed for processing in main memory in such a way that (some of) their data can be in files, instead. There are important differences, however, both quantitative and qualitative, between main memory and mass storage.

First, it is well known that each access to a datum in mass storage (for both reading and writing) requires, at best, a time a thousandfold longer than the access time to main memory. In principle, this fact does not alter the order of magnitude of the performance of an algorithm, only the multiplying constants in the various complexity formulas. In practice, however, there are many cases where it cannot be neglected. Suppose, for example, that an algorithm contains two nested **for** cycles and that only the external one contains I/O operations. It will very probably have a complexity of type $f(n) = c_1 \cdot n + c_2 \cdot n^2$, but c_1 will be a thousandfold higher than c_2. Therefore, even though asymptotically the complexity of the algorithm will be 'dominated' by the constant c_2, in many real cases the main addendum of $f(n)$ could be the first one.

This observation suggests that, in some cases, a complexity analysis should be carried out with respect to some dominating operations. More precisely, we establish a priori that the execution time of an algorithm is by and large proportional to the number of executions of certain operations, called **dominating operations** (typically input/output operations) and, consequently, we calculate the complexity function $f(n)$ as the number of these executions, ignoring all others. For example, this practice is widely adopted in the analysis of database management software where algorithmic processing is generally negligible compared to the use of mass storage.

*12.4 The complexity of managing dynamic data structures

In Chapter 10 we motivated the use of dynamic data structures by the need to make more efficient use of computing resources, in particular, of core memory. The treatment given there should have provided evidence that, indeed, the use of dynamic data structures often results in better use of the computer memory resource, so that we have to pay only for the effectively used memory. We are now in a position to analyse in more depth and with more rigour the benefits and the costs of using dynamic data structures as compared with more traditional implementation techniques, such as arrays. In this section we will perform this comparative analysis: this should also help readers to arrange suitable evaluations of their own data structure designs.

We shall first compare the use of arrays versus linear lists to implement generic tables (Section 12.4.1); then we shall consider the case of tree managing in some depth. At that point analysing the complexity of other classic data structures will be a fairly simple exercise.

12.4.1 The complexity of managing linear structures

Let us first examine the complexity of managing linear tables realized via arrays versus those realized via pointers.

(1) The spatial complexity is of order $\Theta(\texttt{MaxSize})$, where `MaxSize` is the maximum size of the table, in the case of array implementation, and of order $\Theta(n)$, where n is the number of elements actually present in the table, in the case of dynamic list implementation. This is a fairly obvious mathematical confirmation of our initial statement that dynamic memory allocation helps to ensure that we pay only for the memory actually used.

Remember, however, that within the class $\Theta(n)$, the storage for each element of the list requires an additional field for the pointer. This may be negligible if the type of element requires a high number of bytes, but, for a list of integers, it involves doubling the memory needed for each element.

Let us now consider time performance with respect to several operations.

(2) The emptiness test and the initialization of the table to an empty value each require a time of $\Theta(1)$, that is, they are independent of the cardinality of the list, for both types of implementation.

(3) Insertion at the head (first position of the table) requires a time $\Theta(1)$ for dynamic lists whereas it requires a time $\Theta(n)$ for array implementation. Just the opposite occurs for insertion at the tail (last position of the table).

(4) Most other operations (insertion in an ordered table, search – in unordered tables – deletion, ...) require a time of $\Theta(n)$ in both cases. There are minor differences that we pointed out owing to the fact that in pointer-based

structures we do not need to shift elements to avoid holes, but such differences do not affect worst-case analysis from the point of view of the order of magnitude and we do not worry about them here.

As a first summary the above analysis shows a substantial improvement of dynamic lists over static handling in terms of memory occupation and a practically unchanged performance in terms of time.

There is, however, a case in which the performance of dynamic list management is considerably worse than that of static management: searching sorted tables. In that case, we exploited the possibility of *direct access* to the individual elements of an array, which produced a logarithmic complexity. In lists implemented via pointers, however, it is not possible, for example, to access the median element of the list directly: a sequential scan is always necessary, which makes the binary search mechanism ineffectual.

☛ 8   At first glance, therefore, dynamic structures seem to lose the efficiency of direct access provided by array-based structures. This limitation, however, is only due to the strictly linear and sequential structure of lists. If we store our tables in richer structures such as trees, we will be able to implement more efficient managing algorithms, in terms of both search and other fundamental operations.

To achieve such a goal, however, we need some preliminaries. In fact, we already noticed that, if we store the elements of a table within a tree (for the time being we consider only binary trees), the search for an element will generally be exhaustive; that is, it will involve, in the worst case, the analysis of all elements. Therefore, it has a complexity of $\Theta(n)$, n being the number of nodes of the tree, just like a sequential search in linear tables. Unlike lists, however, in the case of trees it is possible to exploit the property of being ordered to improve the efficiency of the search, by applying the essential features of binary search in much the same way as we have done with arrays. In the next subsection we show how **ordered trees** can be managed and we evaluate the complexity of such management.

12.4.2 Managing ordered trees

First of all, since a tree is not a linear structure, we have to state precisely what we mean by an ordered tree.

DEFINITION 12.5

Let an ordering relation – denoted by the usual symbol $<$ – be defined on a given set ElemType. A tree whose elements have an Info field belonging to ElemType is ordered if and only if, for each of its nodes n, the values of the Info fields of all its left-hand descendants are $<$ than the value of the Info field of n and those of all its right-hand descendants are $>$ than the value of n.

An example of an ordered tree storing integer values is shown later in Figure 12.3(a). Now, if a tree is ordered, it is easy to apply to it the same binary search principle that proved to be so efficient for tables realized using arrays. The element sought is compared with the root of the tree: if the two match, the search terminates successfully; if the element sought is less than the value of the root, the search proceeds exclusively in the left-hand subtree, otherwise in the right-hand subtree. This algorithm is easily implemented by the following function:

```
#include <stdlib.h>

boolean OrderedSearch (BinaryTree  Tree, ElementType  Elem)
                       /*searches for the value of Elem in the
                       nodes of the tree, taking into account that
                       it is ordered*/
{
    if (Tree == NULL) return false;
    else if (Tree->Info == Elem) return true;
    else if (Tree->Info < Elem)
        return  OrderedSearch (Tree->RightChild, Elem);
    else return  OrderedSearch (Tree->LeftChild, Elem);
}
```

Let us now evaluate the complexity of ordered searching in trees. It is clear that the temporal complexity is proportional to the number of nodes examined during the search. These, in turn, constitute a path which, in the worst case, goes from the root to a leaf. Therefore, the temporal complexity of the ordered search algorithm is proportional to the height of the tree.

Unfortunately the height of a generic tree is, in the worst case, $\Theta(n)$, if n is the number of nodes of the tree; Figure 12.2 shows this case.

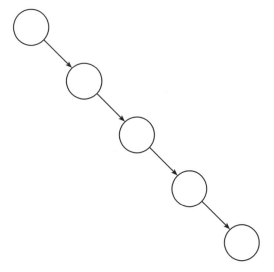

Figure 12.2 A tree whose depth is $\Theta(n)$.

The situation changes radically, however, when the algorithm is applied to balanced trees or perfectly balanced trees. Indeed, if a tree is perfectly balanced, it can be easily shown that the number of nodes of the tree is $n = 2^{h-1} - 1$ for positive values of h and that the depth of the tree is h (see, for example, Figure 10.10).

In general, then, if a tree is balanced and h is its height, the following relation holds:

$$2^h - 1 < n \le 2^{h+1} - 1$$

In conclusion, *the height of a balanced tree, and therefore the complexity of search for an element in it, is* $\Theta(\log(n))$.

Therefore, if a tree is constructed in a balanced way, we can search it with the same order of complexity as the binary search applied to ordered arrays. Obviously, it is always possible to construct a tree of n nodes as a balanced tree. It has still to be verified, though, whether this pleasant characteristic can be maintained while various elements are inserted and deleted. Let us therefore examine further operations on the data type 'tree' for inserting and deleting elements.

Insertion and deletion in ordered trees

The following procedure inserts an element in an ordered tree, maintaining the tree's characteristic of being ordered:

```
#include <stdlib.h>

void InsertInOrder (BinaryTree  *Tree, ElementType  Elem)
{
   if (*Tree == NULL)
   {
      *Tree = malloc(sizeof(BinTreeElem));
      (*Tree)->Info = Elem;
      (*Tree)->LeftChild = NULL;
      (*Tree)->RightChild = NULL;
   }
   else if ((*Tree)->Info > Elem)
           InsertInOrder (&((*Tree)->LeftChild), Elem);
   else if ((*Tree)->Info < Elem)
           InsertInOrder (&((*Tree)->RightChild), Elem);
}
```

The following procedure deletes an element from an ordered tree assuming that there are no repeated elements. It is based on the following observation: once the element to be deleted has been identified, if it is not a leaf, the problem arises of which element to choose to replace it (supposing that we do not want to leave a node empty, which would cause more than a few problems for future comparisons). If the node has only one child, the solution is easy: the node to be deleted is replaced by its child, as illustrated in Figure 12.3(a).

If, however, the node has two children, the algorithm produces a correct result by replacing the node to be deleted with either the descendant of minimum value – that is, the leftmost descendant (not necessarily the leftmost *leaf*!) – of its right-hand child *or* with the rightmost descendant of its left-hand child. In the absence of further selection criteria, we choose the first alternative (Exercise 12.15 and further analyses that follow show, however, that this choice is not without consequences). Figure 12.3(b) shows the effect of this operation.

```
#include <stdlib.h>

void  OrdDelete (BinaryTree  *Tree, ElementType  Elem)
{
    BinTreeElem  *NodeToDelete, *Parent, *Child, *TempNode;

    if (*Tree != NULL)
        if ((*Tree)->Info > Elem)
            OrdDelete (&((*Tree)->LeftChild), Elem);
        else if ((*Tree)->Info < Elem)
                OrdDelete (&((*Tree)->RightChild), Elem);
        else                        /*the node contains the element sought*/
        {
            NodeToDelete = *Tree;
                        /*the pointer to the node to be deleted is stored*/
            if (NodeToDelete->LeftChild == NULL)
            {
                *Tree = NodeToDelete->RightChild; free(NodeToDelete);
            }
            else if (NodeToDelete->RightChild == NULL)
            {
                *Tree = NodeToDelete->LeftChild; free(NodeToDelete);
            }
            else            /*the node to be deleted has both children*/
                if (NodeToDelete->RightChild->LeftChild == NULL)
                            /*if the right-hand child of the node to be
                            deleted does not have a left-hand child, then
                            it is this child that has to replace the node
                            to be deleted, as shown in Figure 12.3(c).*/
                {
                    TempNode = NodeToDelete->RightChild;
                    NodeToDelete->Info = TempNode->Info;
                    NodeToDelete->RightChild = TempNode->RightChild;
                    free(TempNode);
                }
                else
                            /*otherwise we look for the leftmost node of
                            the right-hand subtree of the node to be
                            deleted: it replaces the node to be deleted and
                            is then destroyed.*/
                {
                    Parent = NodeToDelete; Child = NodeToDelete->RightChild;
                    while (Child->LeftChild != NULL)
                    {
                        Parent = Child; Child = Child->LeftChild;
                    }
                            /*at this point of the execution, the state of
                            the procedure applied to the tree in Figure
                            12.3(a) is that described in Figure 12.3(d).*/
```

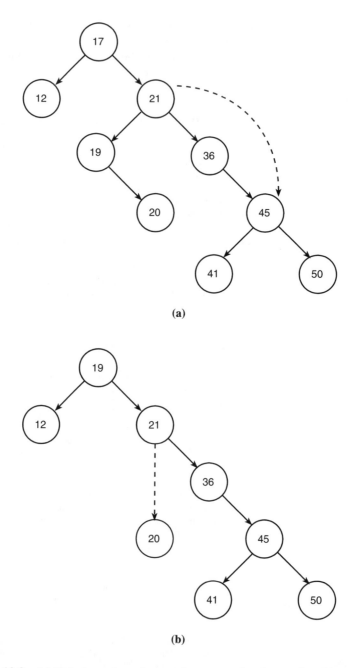

Figure 12.3 (a) Deletion of an element from an ordered tree: the element '36' is deleted by simply changing the value of the right-hand pointer of its parent, as indicated by the dotted arc. (b) Deletion of the element '17' from the tree in part (a): it is replaced by the value '19', while the node that contained '19' is deleted.

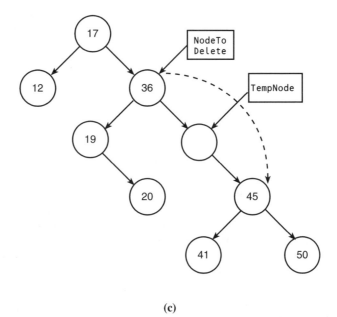

(c)

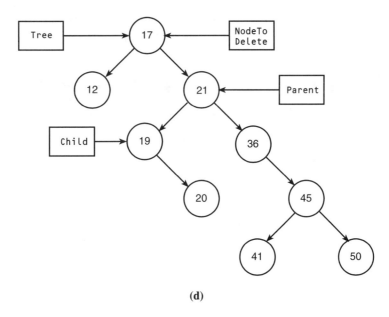

(d)

Figure 12.3 (c) Deletion of the element '21' of the tree in part (a): it is replaced by the value '36', while the node that contained '36' is deleted. (d) State of execution of the procedure `DeleteOrd` just before the deletion of the node '17'. The end result will be the state described in part (b).

```
NodeToDelete->Info = Child->Info;
                /*the information of the node to be deleted is
                replaced with the contents of the node that is
                going to replace it.*/
        Parent->LeftChild = Child->RightChild;
        free(Child);
    }
  }
}
```

Let us now return to the complexity analysis of tree management. Using reasoning completely analogous to that used for searching, it can easily be demonstrated that insertion and deletion also require a time of the order of the depth of the tree, thus $\Theta(\log(n))$ if the tree is balanced, $\Theta(n)$ otherwise.

Suppose that we want to implement an archive using a tree. Initially, we would be able to construct it so that it was balanced (see also Exercise 12.17). This would allow both insertion and deletion to be executed in logarithmic times, with a big advantage over storage in an ordered array, in which only searching can be logarithmic. However, repeated insert and delete operations tend progressively to unbalance the tree, which worsens performance up to a point where it becomes linear. Consequently, one way of operating which, in practice, turns out to be very useful, is to manage the tree using the above procedures until performance degrades. When that happens, a procedure that rebalances the tree is carried out (see again Exercise 12.17); in many cases performance similar to that of balanced trees is obtained, with a minimum overhead for periodically rebalancing the tree.

*12.5 Lower bounds of complexity and intractable problems

In the previous sections we have learnt to evaluate the complexity of algorithms. Thus, we can compare different ways of solving a problem and identify the most efficient. For example, we have stated that the MergeSort algorithm is undoubtedly a better sorting method than the linear insertion method. Now, a new question arises: which is the most efficient algorithm to solve a certain problem? It is clear that, after solving, for example, the problem of sorting a sequence with an algorithm whose complexity is $\Theta(n \cdot \log(n))$, one could hope to solve it in a still more brilliant way, with a complexity of $\Theta(n)$ or $\Theta(n \cdot \log(\log(n)))$. In other words, after achieving a certain improvement for a fairly trivial solution, one could always hope to improve further, but how much further? It is intuitively evident that there has to be some limit to improving the efficiency of algorithms, otherwise each problem could be solved in an infinitesimal time. It is therefore natural to try to determine the intrinsic complexity of a problem, meaning the complexity of the best algorithm that solves the problem. Such a goal is extremely hard to reach and the problem is, in a certain sense, ill-defined. In this section, we briefly try to describe the argument, providing some important preliminary results, but without attempting any kind of complete or in-depth treatment which would lie outside the aims of this text.

First, we observe that the algorithm of minimum complexity for the solution of a problem does not exist in absolute terms. Indeed, the so-called **linear speed-up theorem** holds, which, leaving out some of the mathematical details, can be formulated as follows:

THEOREM Linear speed-up theorem

Given any algorithm A, whose temporal and/or spatial complexity is given by the function $f(n)$, for each constant $c > 0$ it is possible to find an algorithm A' whose complexity is $c \cdot f(n)$.

The demonstration technique of the linear speed-up theorem is based on the principle that, if only the available computing resources are sufficiently increased, the speed of execution can be increased at will, but still remains in the region of linear type improvements: the execution of a sorting algorithm by linear insertion will be a lot faster on a supercomputer than on a PC, but always of a quadratic order of magnitude with respect to the length of the sequence to be sorted. This further supports our previous decision to concentrate complexity analysis mainly on the order of magnitude Θ.

Once we have stated that no best algorithm can be found within a Θ-equivalence class, we would at least want to determine the minimum order of magnitude to solve certain problems. This is unfortunately extremely difficult. Indeed, very few results exist in this respect. Sometimes, it is easier to determine a **lower bound of complexity** of the solution of a problem, that is, a function $g(n)$ such that each algorithm for the solution of the problem is itself of a complexity $\geq_\Theta g(n)$.

Some lower bounds can effectively be determined in a rather trivial way. For example, it is evident that it is not possible to sort a sequence of n elements if we do not at least examine all elements of the sequence: therefore, the problem requires a complexity of at least $\Theta(n)$. Analogously, it is not possible to multiply two matrices of order n without examining each element of the two matrices and without writing into some memory cell each of the n^2 elements of the result: therefore the problem is at least of complexity $\Theta(n^2)$. But the complexity of the best algorithms currently known is about $\Theta(n^{2.7})$. Thus, there is a discrepancy with the lower bound $\Theta(n^2)$ that leaves the minimum necessary complexity to multiply two matrices as an open question.

Unfortunately, our knowledge about the lower bounds of complexity of problems is still very sketchy. It is quite difficult to identify nontrivial limits and, even when intuitively it does not seem possible to solve a certain problem with a complexity lower than a certain order of magnitude, proving such an assumption mathematically often remains an insurmountable problem. In the following we present some of the more important facts about this argument.

12.5.1 Lower limit of complexity of sorting

The first important fact concerns the sorting of sequences. It is possible to prove that, in order to sort a sequence of n elements via successive comparisons between them, a number of comparisons of $\Theta(n \cdot \log(n))$ are required in the worst case.

This is extremely important because it shows that the complexity of algorithms such as `MergeSort` is optimal with respect to the order of magnitude of the worst case, even though, as we have been able to observe, there are algorithms which for various reasons are preferable to it.

12.5.2 Intractable problems and NP-complete problems

Conventionally, **tractable problems**, that is, problems whose solution can be calculated by means of an automatic tool at an acceptable price, are considered to be those problems for which there is an algorithm whose complexity is of an *order of magnitude of polynomial type*. Problems for which there is no algorithm of this type of complexity are called **intractable problems**: for example, a problem for which an algorithm of complexity n^{50} is known is considered tractable, whereas one for which there exist no algorithms with a complexity lower than 2^n is considered intractable. The reluctance to accept the fact that a complexity of the order n^k, with an arbitrary k, is considered tractable can be overcome by keeping in mind the following considerations:

- The distinction between tractable problems with polynomial complexity and intractable problems with higher than polynomial complexity is only a theoretical convention.

- In any case, n^k is always a complexity much lower than an exponential complexity.

- Practical experience has shown that for nearly all application problems (this statement does not hold in absolute terms from a theoretical point of view!), once the existence of polynomial algorithms of any order of complexity has been demonstrated, it has been possible to find algorithms whose complexity has the order of a polynomial of only a few units.

- There are important theoretical results that confirm the validity of the convention.

There is a vast category of problems, called **NP-complete** for reasons that we cannot explain here, for which there is a strong suspicion, but not yet a mathematical certainty, that it is not possible to solve them in polynomial time. If this became a certainty, they would have to be considered intractable.

An important example of an NP-complete problem is the following.

Problem of satisfiability of propositional formulas

Assume as given a formula constructed with identifiers of logical variables and logical connectives (&&, ||, !, ...). An example of such a formula is

(A && !B) || (C && A)

Is there a way to assign logical values to the variables of the formula in such a way that the formula result is true?

A trivial algorithm for the solution of this problem is the following:

Enumerate all possible assignments of logical values to the various identifiers and establish for each of them whether the formula result is true.

Now, once we have assigned a logical value to each identifier, the evaluation of the formula can clearly be carried out in a linear time with respect to its length (see Exercise 12.25). This operation must, however, be repeated for each possible assignment to the various identifiers. If these are of number m, there are 2^m different ways of assigning them logical values. As the correlation between the length n of a formula containing m identifiers and the number m is at least of the order of $\log(m)$ (indeed, to code m identifiers using an alphabet of cardinality k, strings of a length of at least $\log_k(m)$ are needed), the total complexity of the algorithm is clearly exponential with respect to the length of the formula and the number m.

Unfortunately, there is no known algorithm for this problem that succeeds in overcoming the 'barrier' that separates the exponential complexity from the polynomial complexity.

The class of NP-complete problems, of which the problem of satisfiability of propositional formulas is one of the most illustrious representatives, is incredibly rich in problems of great theoretical and practical interest. One fact that makes it even more important is that either all its members are tractable (that is, solvable in polynomial time) or they are all intractable: in other words, finding one single algorithm with polynomial complexity to solve one single NP-complete problem would be sufficient to be able to solve them all in polynomial time; vice versa, proving the intractability of one of them would be sufficient to conclude that this characteristic is owned by all of them. As already stated, the problem is still open on the theoretical level, notwithstanding that all intuitive analyses make one tend to vote for the intractability of NP-complete problems. The reader is invited to do some further reading on the theoretical level for a complete treatment of this fascinating and important argument.

12.5.3 Unsolvable problems

Before we close this section, we would like to remind you of another important result of theoretical computer science, which goes beyond the complexity of computing in the strict sense, but has a great practical impact.

Not only is it the case that many problems are of an intractable complexity for quite small sizes, but some problems are simply algorithmically unsolvable, meaning that there are no algorithms to solve them. Therefore, there is no hope of an automatic solution for these problems: they can be tackled only by human intuition, possibly still using some 'help from the computer', even though it can never guarantee that a solution will be identified.

Important examples of algorithmically unsolvable problems are:

- The problem of **termination** of programs: given a generic program, is it possible to establish that its execution terminates for each possible value of its input data?

- The problem of **equivalence** between programs: given two generic programs, do they solve the same problem? (For example, do they calculate the same function?)

- The problem of **correctness** of a program: given the **specification** of a program, that is, a precise and rigorous definition of the problem that the program has to solve, and given a program, does it solve the problem defined by the specification?

- The proof of **arithmetic theorems**: given a formula that expresses a property of arithmetic type (for example: 'there is an infinite number of prime numbers'), is it a theorem, that is, always true, or not?

An in-depth treatment of the argument belongs to the domain of theoretical computer science and falls outside the scope of this book.

Exercises

12.1 Which Θ relations hold between the following pairs of functions?

(a) $\log_2(\log_e(n^n))$ and n

(b) e^{n^2} and 1000^{e^n}

(c) $n \cdot \sin(n)$ and n

12.2 Verify that the complexity of the searchElem function of Example 8.4 is $\Theta(n^2)$.

12.3 The big-omega relation between functions is defined as the symmetric relation of big-oh; that is, f is $\Omega(g)$ if and only if g is $O(f)$. Prove that f is $\Theta(g)$ if and only if it is both $O(g)$ and $\Omega(g)$.

12.4 Change the algorithm of Example 12.4 in such a way that it orders an array of structures containing a field FirstName and a field LastName in alphabetical order (first with respect to the last name and, in the case of identical last names, with respect to the first names). Show that the order of complexity of the modified algorithm has not changed.

12.5   In an analogous way to Example 12.4, show that the complexity of the following sorting algorithm is also $\Theta(n^2)$:

```
                                                        /*Bubblesort*/
        for (i = 2; i <= n; i++)
          for (j = n; j >= i; j--)
            if (a[j-1] > a[j]) { x = a[j-1]; a[j-1] = a[j]; a[j] = x; }
```

12.6   Show that the complexity of the `Merge` procedure given in Section 12.3 is $\Theta(n)$.

12.7   What is the asymptotic complexity of the recursive sorting algorithm `order` formulated in Example 8.4?

12.8   Formulate the binary search algorithm described in Section 12.1 in a recursive way and prove that the complexity of execution for this coding is also $\Theta(\log(n))$.

12.9   Write a procedure that codes the nonrecursive merge–sort algorithm described in Example 12.5. The procedure must be able to operate on sequences whose length is not necessarily a power of 2.

Then show that the complexity of the bottom-up merge–sort algorithm is $\Theta(n \cdot \log(n))$ for arbitrary values of n.

*12.10   Prove that the complexity of `MergeSort` is also $\Theta(n \cdot \log(n))$ in the best case and therefore in the average case.

*12.11   Modify the procedure `MergeSort` of Example 12.5 in such a way that it does not receive as parameter, at each recursive call, a new sequence passed by value, but only a subsequence of the original one, specified by its indexes. Show that the new version of the procedure does not improve the order of magnitude of the temporal complexity of execution, but that it is very reasonable to expect considerable improvements in the multiplying constants of the function $f(n)$. Also, show that the order of magnitude of the spatial complexity changes. Why and how does it change?

12.12   Write a procedure that, given a tree, establishes whether it is ordered or not. Evaluate its complexity.

12.13   Supply a nonrecursive version of the search algorithm for ordered binary trees. Verify that it has the same order of complexity as the recursive version.

12.14   Show that the procedure `InsertInOrder` defined in Section 12.4.2 does not create duplication of elements in the tree. Modify it in such a way that the element is inserted in the tree in any case, even at the risk of creating duplications.

*12.15   Modify the procedure `OrdDelete` described in Section 12.4.2 in such a way that, when the node to be deleted has both children, both possible alternatives are examined and the one that leads to the removal of the node most distant from the node to be deleted is chosen. In this way, there is a good probability of producing less loss of balance in the tree. Discuss the advantages and disadvantages with respect to the previous version from different points of view (efficiency of the procedure, but also efficiency of subsequent operations of various types).

12.16 Construct procedures for insertion and deletion of elements in non-ordered binary trees, both with and without repetitions. Evaluate their complexity.

12.17 Construct a procedure that balances an ordered binary tree. Evaluate its complexity.

12.18 Construct a procedure that, given a binary tree, transforms it into an ordered and balanced tree without repetitions. Evaluate its complexity.

12.19 Go back to the procedures you coded in Exercise 10.14 for searching, visiting in different orders and inserting and deleting elements in nonbinary trees, and discuss their complexity.

*12.20 It is possible to give various definitions of nonbinary ordered trees. For example, it could be established that each node has two lists of children: a left-hand one, containing elements all less than the parent; and a right-hand one, containing elements all greater than the parent. Each node must then be of value < (or ≤ depending on whether repetition is allowed) of its own right-hand sibling. Supply different possible definitions of nonbinary ordered trees. Then implement the appropriate procedures for their management (search, insertion, deletion) and discuss their complexity.

12.21 Give one or more reasonable definitions of nonbinary ordered and balanced trees. Discuss the complexity of their management, including the operation for balancing them, like the one used for binary trees.

12.22 Write a procedure to calculate the product of matrices and calculate its asymptotic complexity.

12.23 Calculate the order of complexity of the procedure for calculating the determinant of a matrix described in Example 8.5.

12.24 Evaluate and compare the complexity of the operations to manage graphs that you realized in Exercise 11.4.

*12.25 Prove that the truth or falsity of a logical formula can be evaluated in linear time with respect to the length of the formula.

Hint: Exploit the similarity with the evaluation of arithmetic expressions; use a stack to store the elements and partial results of the evaluation as suggested by the following sample evaluation:

Expression to be evaluated: `((T&&(T&&F)) || (!T))`

Sequence of stack contents during the evaluation:

```
(,
((,
((T,
((T&&,
...
((T&&(T&&F,
((T&&(T&&F),
((T&&F),
(F,
...
(F || (!T),
(F || F,
(F || F),
F
```

12.26   Write a program to colour a geographical map. The map contains a certain number of regions and a certain set of colours is supplied: each region must be coloured with a different colour; if that is not possible, this fact must be appropriately signalled. Evaluate the complexity of the program you wrote.

*12.27   Solve the problem of Exercise 12.26 with the following modification: two regions may have the same colour, provided that they are not adjacent. Evaluate its complexity.

Suggestion: The reader can make use of the fact that, if the number of colours is greater than 3, a colouration of the required kind can always be found (with a bit of patience). This property is known as the 'four colour theorem'.

☞ **1.**   `OtherSearch` and `Search` also differ slightly in their functional behaviour, that is, in the results produced. Specify their difference.

2.   Are there differences in memory occupation between the two procedures? What are they?

3.   Formula (12.2) concerning the complexity of the procedure `OtherSearch` described in Section 12.1 contains a small flaw: the branch of the conditional statement that should be executed when the condition is verified might never be executed. Correct (12.2) to remove the flaw.

4.   How do time and space complexity formulas for both `OtherSearch` and `Search` change if the parameter `Sequence` is passed 'by address' rather than 'by value'?

5. Verify that the functional behaviour of `BinarySearch`, that is, its result as a function of the input data, differs slightly both from `Search` and from `OtherSearch`. Specify the differences.

6. Determine the quantity of memory necessary to execute `BinarySearch`.

7. Notice that we used the notation $\Theta(\log(n))$ without specifying the base of the logarithm. Why?

8. Show that the implementation of the binary search algorithm applied to pointer-based lists is even less efficient than a sequential search.

PART II
Hardware and software architecture

This part of the book describes the hardware and software architecture of computer systems. Our ultimate goal is to give an overall picture of modern architectures involving networks of interconnected computers, but we move slowly, bottom-up: within a single computer, we move from the internal hardware organization up to its basic software organization and to database management; then we break the frontier of a single system and describe the ways in which computers can be interconnected to serve the needs of advanced distributed applications. The ultimate result of this part is to show user-friendly interfaces of modern computers and describe the functionalities of the Internet, a worldwide distributed system which is becoming increasingly popular.

The teaching objective for this part of the book is to show that the architecture of complex computer systems is the outcome of a successful interaction between hardware and software, and the result of progressive layers offered by abstract machines, that is, machines defined in terms of their functionalities. Of course, a thorough description of the internal mechanisms supported by each machine and layer is not possible in the context of an introductory course, but we aim to give the reader a good idea of the functionalities offered at each level and the ways in which functionalities interact to produce the expected behaviour. Note that abstract machines, besides being simpler, are generally more stable than real machines; thus, there is a good likelihood that the principles learned by studying abstract machines will last, while real computer architectures evolve at an impressively fast rate.

Let us analyse the content of each chapter in more detail. Chapter 13 goes back to the problem of coding information in binary format, which was briefly mentioned in Chapter 2, and also describes the way in which information is managed by physical devices, such as ports and registers. We also give some information about the electronic components that make up the circuits within a machine. Chapter 13 concludes with an extended example, dedicated to VLSI circuit design (a typical hardware design technique).

Chapter 14 returns to the computer architecture that was also introduced in Chapter 2, and describes the machine language as well as the assembly language. The machine language includes all the instructions which are actually executed within a computer; the assembly language is a low-level, symbolic language that can be used for programming critical parts of the system. This chapter concludes by looking at advanced computer architectures.

Chapter 15 is dedicated to the operating system; this is the software which hides the low-level features of the hardware, providing users with high-level functionality to simplify programming and computer usage. We shall first describe a layered operating system architecture and then the functionalities of each layer in detail, analysing the processor and memory management in particular. This chapter concludes with an extended example dedicated to UNIX, a widely used operating system.

Chapter 16 deals with file and database management. It includes a description of mass storage media (tapes, hard disks, floppy disk drives) and provides details of archive organization techniques (sequential, direct, indexed). Finally, we describe database management systems, by introducing the models and languages used for data organization and management. An extended example is dedicated to the relational data model and language, the most popular type of database system on the market.

Chapter 17 deals with the construction of distributed systems and computer networks. After describing the main data transfer techniques, we introduce WANs (wide area networks, linking computers over a wide geographical area) and LANs (local area networks, linking computers and peripherals in the same office or within a short distance). An extended example is dedicated to transaction systems; we briefly discuss the properties of transactions (including reliability, concurrency, security, privacy) and illustrate a classic banking application.

Chapter 18 focuses on the Internet, the best-known and most popular distributed computing system. We give some information about the history, structure and organization of the Internet, and then we focus on Internet services, describing the Internet as an abstract machine which provides some functionalities, including electronic mail and the World Wide Web (WWW).

Finally, Chapter 19 closes this part by focusing on user interfaces, which give the end user a view of the computer system. We describe input/output devices and logical interfaces, based on windows, menus, icons and dialogue boxes; an extended example is devoted to Windows. We also describe productivity tools. The chapter concludes with extended examples devoted to word processors (with the popular Word) and spreadsheets (such as Excel and Lotus 1-2-3).

Encoding and managing binary data

13

In this chapter we discuss how a computer can represent, store, transfer and transform various kinds of data (text, integers, real numbers, images and so on) through proper coding techniques and electronic circuits.

In Chapter 2 we anticipated that all data, no matter how complicated, has to be coded into binary form in order to be understood by a computer. A *bit* denotes the most basic unit of data in a computer and corresponds to the state of a physical device which is interpreted as either 0 or 1. The values 0 and 1 are represented differently by different devices: for instance, high or low electrical voltage for main memory, positive or negative magnetic polarity for mass memory, or light and dark for data transmission. In all cases, the code corresponds to a physical phenomenon which can be observed in two distinct states; observing more than two states is excluded, because this would give rise to the risk of errors. From the computer architecture described in Chapter 2, we further recall that bits are structured in *bytes* (a sequence of 8 bits) and *words* (sequences of bytes which fit into each main memory cell, typically consisting of 16, 32 or 64 bits); and we have already observed that data types, such as integers or characters, can be adequately translated into appropriate bytes and words.

This chapter goes into a bit more depth on this translation, also called the *encoding of information into a binary code*. We address the various types of data (numbers, characters, images) and show how they can be represented in a binary format, without too many technical details. Fortunately, the computer can also perform the reverse operation, converting binary code into more intelligible forms. Therefore, when operating the computer, there is no need to use all the coding techniques which are discussed in this chapter; indeed, Part I has shown how the computer can be programmed in C without knowing anything at all about how data is encoded in the computer.

An overview of encoding techniques is required before turning to the second main argument of this chapter, namely the *management of binary data which occurs within the computer*. Binary data management is based on the use of electronic circuits, such as gates and registers, which can store, transfer and transform binary coded data; in particular, we exemplify some arithmetic and logical operations which are available within the CPU, performed by dedicated electronic circuits.

The chapter ends with an extended example related to hardware project techniques and especially the design of Very Large Scale Integrated (VLSI) circuits and the use of CAD tools for design automation.

13.1 Encoding numbers

In this section, we describe the coding of natural numbers, (signed) integers, fractions (between zero and one) and real numbers.

13.1.1 Natural numbers

Let us start with natural numbers. The number system that we normally use is called Arabic, since it was introduced into Europe by the Arabs in the Middle Ages. It represents the natural numbers by a sequence of digits. Normally, digits are ten (0, 1, ..., 9) and thus the system is called **base 10**. It is also called a **positional system** because the value of each digit is a function of its position in the sequence.

Not all number systems are positional. The main alternative is an **additive system** where the value of any symbol is independent of its position. An example of an additive system is one in which each unit is represented by a unique symbol (for example, shells or twigs) and each number is represented as a sequence of units. A more complex system is the Roman one in which different symbols (I, V, X, L, C, D, M) indicate different numbers (1, 5, 10, 50, 100, 500, 1000). The system is additive because, for example, the number 3000 is represented by a string of three symbols MMM. The Roman number system, however, also follows other rules not discussed here. Positional number systems have a marked advantage because they allow numbers to be represented in a far more compact way and calculations to be carried out more efficiently.

We shall now consider a positional number system with a generic base p. Digits of this number system range between 0 and $p - 1$. A generic number N in base p is represented by a sequence of digits:

$$a_n, a_{n-1}, ..., a_0$$

a_n is the **most significant digit**, while a_0 is the **least significant**. The value of number N coded in base p is given by the following formula:

$$N_p = a_n \times p^n + a_{n-1} \times p^{n-1} + ... + a_1 \times p^1 + a_0 \times p^0 = \sum_{i=0}^{n} a_i \times p^i \qquad (13.1)$$

Formula (13.1) allows us to express the meaning of any number in base p and to convert a number in a base q that is distinct from p. To do this, it is enough to express the coefficients a_i and the powers p^i in base q and to carry out the additions and multiplications expressed in the formula with an arithmetic in base q. Since we are in the habit of using base 10, we shall use this formula to interpret numbers in different bases as numbers in base 10. Formula (13.1) also shows us that by means of m digits in base p, it is possible to represent p^m natural numbers, from 0 to $p^m - 1$.

Let us first apply (13.1) to decimal numbers. If we assume $p = 10$, we interpret the string 587 as:

$$587 = (5 \times 10^2 + 8 \times 10^1 + 7 \times 10^0)$$

Bases 2, 8 and 16, called binary, octal and hexadecimal, respectively, are particularly important for use in computers, for reasons we shall show shortly.

- The **binary system** has base **$p = 2$**; the alphabet consists of the digits 0 and 1. For instance, the binary number 101001011 corresponds to the following number in base 10:

$$101001011_2 = (1 \times 2^8 + 0 \times 2^7 + 1 \times 2^6 + 0 \times 2^5 + 0 \times 2^4$$
$$+ 1 \times 2^3 + 0 \times 2^2 + 1 \times 2^1 + 1 \times 2^0)_{10}$$
$$= (256 + 64 + 8 + 2 + 1)_{10} = 331_{10}$$

- The **octal system** has base $p = 8$; the alphabet consists of the digits 0, 1, ..., 7. The octal number 534 corresponds to the following number in base 10:

$$534_8 = (5 \times 8^2 + 3 \times 8^1 + 4 \times 8^0)_{10} = (320 + 24 + 4)_{10} = 348_{10}$$

- The **hexadecimal system** has base **$p = 16$**; the alphabet consists of the digits 0, 1, ..., 9, A, B, C, D, E, F. The hexadecimal number B7F corresponds to the following number in base 10:

$$B7F_{16} = (11 \times 16^2 + 7 \times 16^1 + 15 \times 16^0)_{10} = (2816 + 112 + 15)_{10} = 2943_{10}$$

Table 13.1 shows the numbers from 0 to 15 expressed in decimal, binary, octal and hexadecimal.

The above examples also show how to *convert* a number in base p to base 10. Now we show the simplest way of converting a number in base 10 into binary form. We just keep dividing the decimal number by two; the result is the sequence of zeros and ones obtained by taking the remainder of each division in order from the lowest-order to the highest-order digit. For example:

$$331 \div 2 = 165 \text{ with remainder } 1$$
$$165 \div 2 = 82 \text{ with remainder } 1$$
$$82 \div 2 = 41 \text{ with remainder } 0$$
$$41 \div 2 = 20 \text{ with remainder } 1$$
$$20 \div 2 = 10 \text{ with remainder } 0$$
$$10 \div 2 = 5 \text{ with remainder } 0$$
$$5 \div 2 = 2 \text{ with remainder } 1$$
$$2 \div 2 = 1 \text{ with remainder } 0$$
$$1 \div 2 = 0 \text{ with remainder } 1$$

Thus, the conversion of 331 from base 10 to base 2 generates the number: 101001011.

Table 13.1 The first 16 numbers in base 10, 2, 8 and 16.

	Number system		
Decimal	**Binary**	**Octal**	**Hexadecimal**
0	0000	0	0
1	0001	1	1
2	0010	2	2
3	0011	3	3
4	0100	4	4
5	0101	5	5
6	0110	6	6
7	0111	7	7
8	1000	10	8
9	1001	11	9
10	1010	12	A
11	1011	13	B
12	1100	14	C
13	1101	15	D
14	1110	16	E
15	1111	17	F

Why are bases 2, 8 and 16 of such major interest in computing? We have already seen that there are technological reasons for using the binary representation. Octal and hexadecimal representations are of interest because of the ease of conversion from base 2 to base 8 or 16. This conversion can be done in chunks, taking a group of (three or four) binary digits each time. Let us illustrate this method with an example. The number 001010110111_2 is the same as 1267_8 and $2B7_{16}$. Indeed:

- We can divide the number into triples, 001 010 110 111, and translate each triple into the corresponding octal digit; 001 corresponds to 1, 010 to 2 and so on.

- Or we can divide the number into quadruples, 0010 1011 0111, and translate each quadruple into the corresponding hexadecimal number; 0010 corresponds to 2, 1011 to B and so on.

This easy conversion allows binary numbers stored in the computer to be expressed in the more concise octal or hexadecimal form.

13.1.2 Integers

The difference between natural numbers and integers is that integers include negative numbers as well as zero and positive numbers. Therefore, the *sign* of the number must be represented, as well as its modulus. Let us analyse two different ways of coding integers. The first, called **sign and modulus representation**, is more intuitive; the second, called representation in **two's complement**, is widely used to simplify arithmetic operations on integers as we will see in Section 13.4.1.

If m bits are available to represent an integer, the sign and modulus representation uses the first bit (the leftmost position) as the sign bit; by convention, 0 indicates a positive number, 1 a negative number. With this convention, when m binary digits are available as a fixed length data holder, integers from $-(2^{m-1} - 1)$ to $+(2^{m-1} - 1)$ can be represented. In fact, given that one bit is used to represent the sign, only $m - 1$ bits are available to represent the modulus of the number. In Table 13.2 the sign and modulus representation is given in three bits for integers from -3 to $+3$. Note that in the table, when the sign and modulus representation is used, there are two representations of the number 0: a 'positive zero' and a 'negative zero'.

The representation of the negative number $-N$ in two's complement in m binary digits is obtained by subtracting N from 2^m. With this convention, when m binary digits are available as a fixed length data holder, integers from -2^{m-1} to $+(2^{m-1} - 1)$ can be represented.

For example, the two's complement representation of the number -3 in three bits can be obtained by subtracting 3 from 2^3 and converting the result to binary (5 = 101). The representation of the integers from -4 to $+3$ in two's complement form is shown in Table 13.2. Note that in two's complement there is only one representation of the number 0 and that also with this representation the leftmost bit is 1 in the case of negative numbers and 0 in the case of positive ones.

In practice, the two's complement of a negative integer $-N$ is calculated as follows:

- Complementing each bit of the m-bits binary form of its modulus N (that is, changing each zero into one and vice versa).

- Adding a 1 to the result.

For example, taking the number -3, the binary representation of its modulus (3) in three bits is 011; complementing it we obtain 100; and adding 1 we have the two's complement representation 101.

Table 13.2 Representation in sign and modulus and in two's complement in three binary digits.

Integer	Integer binary representation	
	Sign/modulus	Two's complement
-4	$-$	100
-3	111	101
-2	110	110
-1	101	111
-0	100	$-$
$+0$	000	000
$+1$	001	001
$+2$	010	010
$+3$	011	011

13.1.3 Fractional numbers

Fractional numbers are real numbers between zero and one; they are represented by a zero, a point and a sequence of digits that represents a fraction of unity: $N = 0.a_{-1}a_{-2}...a_{-n}$. The weight of the digits a_i normally depends on the base of the chosen number system. The meaning of a fractional number in base p can be expressed by the following formula:

$$N_p = a_{-1} \times p^{-1} + a_{-2} \times p^{-2} + ... + a_{-n} \times p^{-n} = \sum_{i=-n}^{-1} a_i \times p^i \qquad (13.2)$$

First of all, let us look at our usual decimal numbering. Assuming base $p = 10$, we can interpret, for example, the number 0.587 as:

$$0.587_{10} = (5 \times 10^{-1} + 8 \times 10^{-2} + 7 \times 10^{-3})$$

As in the previous sections, we can use (13.2) to convert a fractional binary number into decimal, for example:

$$0.1011_2 = (1 \times 2^{-1} + 0 \times 2^{-2} + 1 \times 2^{-3} + 1 \times 2^{-4})_{10} = 0.6875_{10}$$

Fractional numbers can introduce approximations, because of the presence of a limited number of digits after the decimal point; the error in the approximation is less than p^{-n}, where n is the number of digits used. The simplest way of converting a fractional number in base 10 into binary form consists in multiplying the fractional number by two; the result is the sequence of ones and zeros obtained by taking the integer part of each multiplication in order from the highest-order to the lowest-order digit.

Let us consider the binary representation of the fractional number 0.587_{10}:

$0.587 \times 2 = 1.174$: fractional part 0.174 and integer part 1
$0.174 \times 2 = 0.348$: fractional part 0.348 and integer part 0
$0.348 \times 2 = 0.696$: fractional part 0.696 and integer part 0
$0.696 \times 2 = 1.392$: fractional part 0.392 and integer part 1
$0.392 \times 2 = 0.784$: fractional part 0.784 and integer part 0
$0.784 \times 2 = 1.568$: fractional part 0.568 and integer part 1
$0.568 \times 2 = ...$

Thus, the conversion of 0.587 from base 10 to base 2 generates the number 0.1001 (with 4 binary digits after the decimal point) or the number 0.100101 (with 6 binary digits after the decimal point). In the first case, the approximation is accurate to within 2^{-4} whereas in the second case it is within 2^{-6}.

13.1.4 Real numbers

The real numbers that can be represented in a computer are, in reality, rational numbers, containing an integer part and a fractional part; as always in mathematics, rational numbers approximate real numbers with arbitrary precision. Conceptually, in order to represent real numbers, it is sufficient to combine two numbers (one integer and one fractional), represented as described in the previous sections. For example, the number 00101001011.10110, where the integer part consists of 11 bits and the fractional part of 5 bits, corresponds to the real number 331.6875 in base 10. We saw in Chapter 2 that this representation is called *fixed point*, because a fixed number of digits is dedicated to the integer and the fractional parts, respectively.

A second representation, called *floating point*, uses exponential notation to code real numbers. For this representation, no unique standard exists; let us therefore consider one of the many possible conventions. With each real number, we associate two numbers; the first number, m, is called the **mantissa** and is interpreted as a fractional number, that is, a number in the interval between -1 and $+1$; in addition, a separate bit allows the sign of the mantissa to be represented. The second number, n, interpreted as a signed integer, is called the **characteristic** and is used as an exponent. The formula that expresses r as a function of m and n is the following:

$$r = m \times b^n$$

where b is an integer number indicating the base used in the exponential notation. Note that b may be different from p, the base chosen for the number system.

As an example, let us assume $b = p = 10$. The number -331.6875 is represented in floating point with $m = -0.3316875$ and $n = 3$. The advantage of floating point notation lies in its ability to represent very large numbers with few digits and to represent very small numbers with high precision. You may verify this by transforming into a fixed point representation the two numbers that have mantissa $m = -0.3316875$ and exponents 10 and -10, respectively.

Floating point notation also applies to binary numbering. For example, setting $b = p = 2$, the binary number with sign bit 0, mantissa 1011 and characteristic 01010 is interpreted in base 10 as: $0.6875 \times 2^{10} = 0.6875 \times 1024 = 704.01$. Note that the set of numbers that can be generated using this notation is not uniformly distributed; more precisely, there are values extremely close to each other around the number zero, and values extremely far away from each other in the region of the highest expressible positive or negative number. If l_1 and l_2 denote the length of the two numbers m and n (including their sign), respectively, the biggest number that can be expressed in this notation has the absolute value $(1 - 2^{-l_1}) \cdot 2^{(2^{(l_2-1)}-1)}$.

It is also possible that b and p are different. For example, we can set $p = 2$ and $b = 10$ (the choice of $p = 2$ is for technological reasons, that of $b = 10$ comes from our old habit of calculating in base 10). In this case, a number with mantissa 1011 and exponent 11 is interpreted as $0.6875 \times 10^3 = 687.5$.

A number in floating point is said to be **normalized** if the highest-order position of the mantissa is different from zero. For example, the number $+0.45676 \times 10^2$ is normalized, whereas $+0.00456 \times 10^4$ is not. Obviously, non-normalized numbers have a smaller number of significant digits; if we want to represent the real number 45.67682 by using a code that allows five decimal digits for the mantissa, the number is better approximated using the normalized representation.

However, whatever the chosen coding, the representation of real numbers in a computer is subject to approximations; these approximations, as we will see, propagate in the course of the execution of operations and can cause significant numerical errors. **Numerical calculus** is the discipline that studies the properties of the execution of operations in a computer, allowing the extent of the numerical errors introduced by these operations to be evaluated and controlled.

13.2 Encoding characters

The characters that make up a text are coded as bit sequences, using a translation code. The most widely used code is ASCII (American Standard Code for Information Interchange); it uses seven bits and thus allows a maximum of 128 characters to be represented (there are other versions of the standard that use one more bit and thus allow another 128 characters to be represented). Characters are classified into three categories: command characters, alphanumeric characters and symbols. The **command characters** describe transmission and printer control codes; the **alphanumeric characters** describe letters (upper case from A to Z, lower case from a to z) and digits (from 0 to 9); the **symbols** include the separators used for punctuation and the arithmetic operators. Note that the code does not contain all possible characters; accented and Greek letters, for example, are missing.

Each character is stored in one byte in the computer. When the seven-bit ASCII code is used, the eighth bit is ignored; as we said, some versions of ASCII use the eighth bit to represent another 128 characters. In data storage the eighth bit (or an extra ninth bit) can be used as a **parity bit**, set to 0 or 1 in such a way that the total number of bits set to 1 is always even. In this way, it is possible to detect malfunctions and errors; this topic is discussed further in Chapter 16.

Other less frequently used codes are: the EBCDIC 8-bit code, used on IBM computers; the BCD 4-bit codes (for representation of decimal numbers); and the 6-bit FIELDDATA. The ASCII code is listed in Appendix A.

A new standard for data representation, called **Unicode,** will provide two bytes for representing symbols. With two bytes, a Unicode character could be any one of more than 65000 different characters or symbols – enough for every character and symbol in the world, including the vast Chinese, Korean and Japanese character sets. If a single character set were available to cover all languages in the entire world, the interchange of computer programs and data would be easier.

13.3 Encoding of images

Images, too, are coded as sequences of zeros and ones. The step from an image to a binary sequence is called **digitization**: the image is divided into points, or **pixels**, and each point is coded with a number that corresponds to a particular colour (or, in black and white images, to a particular shade of grey). Normally, the number of colours or greyshades used is a power of 2, so that the information associated with one pixel can be coded in an appropriate number of bits.

Images are often stored as very long bit sequences; to interpret these sequences we have to know the dimensions of the image (base and height of the rectangle in which the image is contained), the **resolution** (measured in **dpi**, that is, dots per inch) and the number of colours or greyshades available for each pixel. If an image is coded with a given resolution, it can generally be reproduced on a device with lower resolution, by transforming or ignoring some of the bits that represent each pixel.

As for characters, several coding standards for images have been defined to ensure compatibility between different systems with regard to image transmission and visualization. One of the most common standards is TIFF (Tagged Image File Format), which adopts a technique that reduces the space needed to represent the points of an image, compressing the sequences of points that have the same colour. Data compression is also necessary to reduce the amount of memory needed to store images and the time taken to transmit images between various devices. For the latter purpose, standard compression methods have been defined by the bodies involved in transmission standardization, such as the CCITT (International Consultative Committee for Telephones and Telegraphs).

13.4 Arithmetic and logical operations

In this section we discuss very briefly some arithmetic and logical operations; in Section 13.5 we will see some simple electronic circuits that realize them.

13.4.1 Sum and difference of integers

The sum of two positive numbers of length k in base p is carried out by aligning the numbers columnwise and calculating the sum of pairs of digits in the same position; when the sum of two numbers in position i exceeds the value $p - 1$, a unitary **carry-over** is added to position $i + 1$. This mechanism is illustrated in Figure 13.1 which shows one sum in base 10 and one in base 2. Note that, generally speaking, we need $k + 1$ positions for the result, as the kth sum may generate a carry-over; if this occurs and only k digits are available, the sum operation will produce an erroneous result, called **overflow**.

The sum of signed numbers utilizes the two's complement representation. The rule for summing two numbers in two's complement is very simple: the operands must be summed column by column. Figure 13.2 illustrates the sum of

Carry-over	111		11	1
	8731		10001000011011	
	5698		01011001000010	
	14429		11100001011101	

Figure 13.1   Sum operations in base 10 and base 2.

```
+ 5    0000101          + 5      0000101
+ 8    0001000          - 8      1111000
─────────────          ──────────────────
+13    0001101          - 3      1111101


- 5    1111011          -64      1000000
+ 8    0001000          - 8      1111000
─────────────          ──────────────────
+ 3 (1)0000011          -72 [1](1) 0111000
```

Figure 13.2 Sum operations using two's complement representation. The carry is enclosed in parentheses and the overflow is enclosed in square brackets.

two integers; each number has seven bits. With this coding we can represent the numbers between −64 and +63; any operation that would yield a value outside this interval causes an overflow. Figure 13.2 shows all possible combinations of signs; in two cases a carry-over on the sign bit is generated and represented between parentheses, in one case an overflow is generated and represented between square brackets. The overflow condition occurs only if both operands have the same sign; it is detected when the sign of the result is different from the sign of the operands.

We have seen that two's complement representation allows negative numbers to be added algebraically. Therefore, the difference operation also utilizes the complement representation: in order to subtract two numbers, the two's complement of the second operand (subtrahend) is calculated and added algebraically to the first operand (minuend).

Arithmetic operations on floating point numbers are more complex than on integer or fixed point numbers. For example, let us suppose that we want to add the two normalized numbers:

$0.767\,55 \times 10^2$
$0.171\,34 \times 10^{-1}$

Obviously, before we can proceed with the addition, it is necessary to *align* the two numbers; we can add the mantissas only if they have the same exponent. In this case, aligning is carried out by introducing zeros in the highest-order positions of the number with the smaller exponent:

$0.767\,55 \times 10^2$
$0.000\,17 \times 10^2$

The result of the sum is the normalized value: $0.767\,72 \times 10^2$. You can see the error introduced during the execution of this procedure.

As illustrated in this example, operations on floating point numbers have higher execution times than those in fixed point; on the other hand, they are essential for scientific applications.

We will not discuss more complex operations here, such as multiplication, division and exponentiation.

13.4.2 **Logical operators and Boolean algebra**

Let us consider now the logical operators, defined in a formalism called **Boolean algebra**. This algebra is based on logical operations OR, AND and NOT introduced in Chapter 3 (also called **Boolean operations**). They are applied to operands that can take only two values: *true* or *false*. Conventionally, we represent the value true by the digit 1 and the value false by the digit 0; therefore, one bit can adequately represent an operand in a Boolean expression.

Boolean expressions of any complexity can be constructed by applying suitable combinations of the three operations OR, AND and NOT to various operands, in the same way as arithmetic expressions are obtained by combining the basic arithmetic operations; the evaluation of an expression consists of evaluating the truth value (true or false) of the expression as a function of the truth values of its operands. On the basis of the truth tables of OR, AND and NOT, which were presented in Chapter 3, it is possible to calculate the truth tables of any Boolean expression; Table 13.3(a) shows the truth tables for two Boolean functions operating on three Boolean variables A, B and C. Note that the evaluation of a logical expression must respect the different priorities of the three operations: NOT must be evaluated first, AND secondly and OR finally. As for arithmetic expressions, brackets can alter the order of evaluation.

Boolean expressions are equivalent when they have the same truth tables. In particular, the following two famous equivalent expressions are **De Morgan's laws**:

A AND B = NOT ((NOT A) OR (NOT B))
A OR B = NOT ((NOT A) AND (NOT B))

Table 13.3   Truth tables of given Boolean expressions.

A B C	A AND NOT(B OR C)	A OR (B AND (NOT C))
0 0 0	0	0
0 0 1	0	0
0 1 0	0	1
0 1 1	0	0
1 0 0	1	1
1 0 1	0	1
1 1 0	0	1
1 1 1	0	1

(a)

A B	NOT ((NOT A) OR (NOT B))	NOT ((NOT A) AND (NOT B))
0 0	0	0
0 1	0	1
1 0	0	1
1 1	1	1

(b)

The truth table of the expressions on the right-hand side of the above equivalences are indicated in Table 13.3(b). De Morgan's laws are demonstrated by comparing their truth tables with the truth tables of the AND and OR operations, given in Table 3.1.

*13.5 Binary data management through electronic circuits

We said in Chapter 2 that binary coded data can be stored, transferred and transformed through arithmetic and logical operations inside the CPU. This data management is realized through dedicated electronic circuits: the **hardware structure** of the CPU. To be realized, the global architecture and the logical functionalities of the CPU need **hardware design**:

- Proper *physical devices* must be chosen to implement the desired elements of the CPU (logic gates, registers and the ALU itself).

- Proper *connections* (wires) must be designed and implemented to obtain the correct ways of transferring data between functional elements.

- The correct use of a *system clock line* and of *control signals* must be included to obtain a correct synchronization between the CPU and the control unit.

We have said that all data, no matter how complicated, has to be transformed into a sequence of bits in order to be used by a computer and that a bit corresponds to the state of a physical device which is interpreted as either 1 or 0. With more precision, we can now say that:

- A computer is a **digital system**: the information managed by it can assume only *discrete values* (instead of continuously varying values as in the case of **analogue systems**).

- Further, a computer is a **binary digital system**: the information can assume only *two* discrete values (zero or one).

- Finally, a computer is a **synchronous binary digital system**: its functioning is ruled by a system clock. Data transfers or transformations can happen only at particular moments, ruled by the clock.

The basic elements from which all digital systems are constructed are amazingly simple: elementary switches are used as primitive elements and combined in innumerable ways to make powerful systems and to represent their binary states. Figure 13.3 shows how a binary digit could be represented by mechanical switches (open or closed) or lamps (light or dark). Within digital systems, binary digits can be represented by **transistors** as shown in Figure 13.3; transistors are electronic circuit elements having three connections to the outside world: the **collector**, the **base** and the **emitter**. High or low voltage at the collector can be interpreted as zero or one. The reason why transistors are very effective is that they can operate as very fast binary switches, passing from high to low voltage and vice versa in a few nanoseconds.

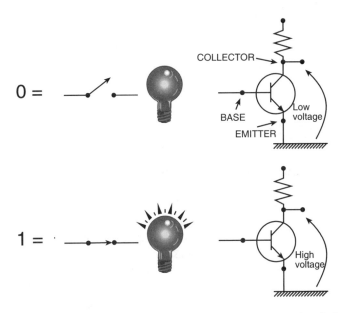

Figure 13.3 Binary representation of information by means of switches, lamp and transistors.

13.5.1 Logic gates

Circuit elements that correspond to logical operators are called **logic gates**; they have electrical connections which are interpreted as input and output, and an electronic circuit which produces the voltage at the output connection as the effect of the voltage at the input connections. All gates have one output connection, interpreted as the gate result. OR and AND gates have two input connections (corresponding to the two logical operands of OR and AND Boolean operations), while the NOT gate has only one input connection (corresponding to the logical operand of the NOT Boolean operation). In addition to OR, AND and NOT gates, other commonly used gates are the NAND and NOR gates:

- The NAND gate produces the same effect as an AND gate followed by a NOT gate, that is, the Boolean expression NOT(A AND B), where A and B represent the inputs.

- The NOR gate produces the same effect as an OR gate followed by a NOT gate, that is, the Boolean expression NOT(A OR B), where A and B represent the inputs.

OR, AND, NOT, NAND and NOR gates are shown in Figure 13.4. De Morgan's laws, described in the previous section, have an immediate application to electronic circuits, as they enable logical operators to be expressed by means of other logical operators; thus, it is possible to use a small number of different gates

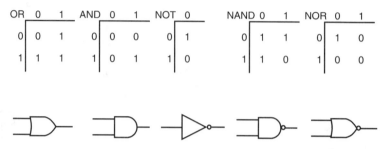

Figure 13.4 Representation of OR, AND, NOT, NAND and NOR logic gates.

to generate any Boolean expression. Although we do not give a demonstration, it turns out that both NAND and NOR gates can express any Boolean operation.

To exemplify the use of logic gates, consider the two binary digital systems shown in Figure 13.5. The system in part (a) uses an AND gate; it lights a lamp when the window of the monitored room is closed and the stove present in the room is on. The system in part (b) uses an OR gate; it lights a lamp when towns A and B are connected by at least one open road.

Although describing the gates goes beyond the scope of this book, we briefly take a look at how NOT, NAND and NOR gates are realized by means of transistors; the next paragraphs require some basic knowledge of electric and electronic circuits to be fully understood, but readers without this background knowledge will get some idea about the process that takes place within a gate.

Figure 13.6(a) shows a single transistor (enclosed in the circle) embedded in a simple circuit. This circuit operates as a NOT gate, converting a logical 0 to a logical 1 and a logical 1 to a logical 0. When the input voltage, V_{in}, is below a critical value (by convention, 0), the transistor turns off and acts like an infinite resistance (= the switch is open), causing the output of the circuit V_{out} to take on a value close to V_{cc} (by convention, 1). When V_{in} exceeds the critical value (by convention, 1), the transistor turns on and acts like a perfect conductor (= the switch is closed), causing V_{out} to be pulled down to ground (by convention, 0). The important thing to notice is that when V_{in} is low, V_{out} is high and vice versa. The time required to switch from one state to the other is typically a few nanoseconds.

Figure 13.6(b) shows two transistors cascaded (technically, they are in 'series'). This circuit operates as a NAND gate. If both V_1 and V_2 are high, both transistors will conduct and V_{out} will be pulled low. If either input is low, the corresponding transistor will turn off and the output will be high. In other words, V_{out} will be low if and only if both V_1 and V_2 are high.

Figure 13.6(c) shows two transistors wired in parallel instead of in series; this circuit operates as a NOR gate. In this configuration, if either input is high, the corresponding transistor will turn on and pull the output down to the conventional 0 value. If both inputs are low, the output will remain high.

Logic gates find many applications in computers; they are used to synthesize **logical networks**, that is, circuits which realize any logical function. Furthermore,

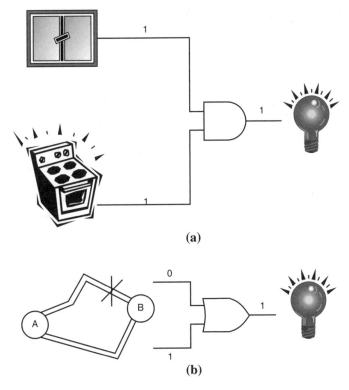

Figure 13.5 Examples of the use of (a) AND and (b) OR gates.

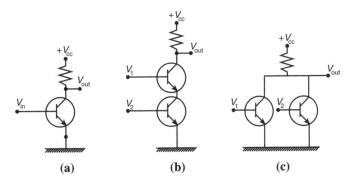

Figure 13.6 (a) NOT gate, (b) NAND gate and (c) NOR gate.

logic gates can be used selectively to modify some bits in a sequence of binary digits, forcing them to zero or one; or to copy a sequence of binary digits into another sequence of equal length (for example, to load a register with the contents of another register; see also Section 13.5.3 and Chapter 14).

13.5.2 Latches and flip-flops

Latches and **flip-flops** are the simplest circuit elements which can store a zero or one. To create a 1-bit memory, we need a circuit that somehow 'remembers' previous input values. Such a circuit can be constructed, for example, using a NOT gate, two NAND gates and two NOR gates as shown in Figure 13.7(b). This circuit, called a **clocked D latch**, has one input line (D), a clock line (T) and an output line (Q), as schematically shown in Figure 13.7(a). We shall not discuss the internals of this circuit, but just describe its behaviour at the three connections D, T and Q. The value on the input line, either a zero or a one, can be 'stored' in the circuit from the input line only if the clock line is set to one (that is, only when a positive pulse arrives on the clock line); the 'stored' value is always present on the output line.

The behaviour of a clocked D latch is as follows. When a one arrives on the clock line, the latch captures the value present on its input line and sets its output line at the same value. The captured value is stored in the latch (that is, it is present on the output line) until a new one arrives at the clock line. Figure 13.7(c) exemplifies the behaviour of a latch in different time instants:

- At instant t_1 the latch has a zero on lines T, D and Q.

- At instant t_2 a one arrives on line D but nothing happens on line Q because at line T a zero is still present; the latch will store the previous zero value until a one arrives on line T.

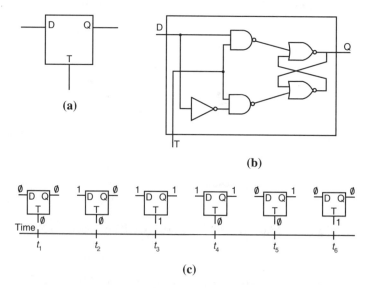

Figure 13.7 Clocked D latch: (a) symbolic description, (b) circuit implementation and (c) behaviour in time.

- At instant t_3 a one arrives on line T; the latch looks on line D and captures a one which is propagated to line Q (more precisely, this happens after a small delay, but we do not consider timing problems here).

- At instant t_4 a zero on line T does not cause any change to the output line of the latch.

- At instant t_5 a zero arrives on line D but, as at time t_2, nothing happens on line Q .

- At instant t_6 a one arrives on line T: the latch looks on line D and captures a zero, presenting it on its output line Q, after a small delay.

The previous considerations allow us to say that a clocked D latch is a **1-bit memory** (one bit can be stored) and a synchronous circuit element (its behaviour is ruled by the signal on its clock line).

13.5.3 **Registers and data transfers between registers**

An n-bit register can be realized with n latches or flip-flops, each one storing one bit of information. Figure 13.8 shows an 8-bit register with its 8 input lines, 8 output lines and 8 clock lines (the 8 clock lines are grouped to make the figure more readable and concise). The register stores the binary value 00001110 (corresponding to value 14 in base 10).

We consider next data transfers between registers. Assume two 8-bit registers R1 and R2 and consider the loading of R2 with the contents of R1. As shown in Figure 13.9, in order to support the transfer between registers, the output of each latch composing register R1 is connected to the first input operand of an AND gate whose outputs are connected to the input lines of register R2; the second input operand of each AND gate is connected to an input, called the **control signal,** which is produced by the system's control unit to activate the transfer operation (see also Chapter 14). Another signal, called the **system clock**, is produced by the clock to synchronize all operations occurring in the computer. The control signal and the system clock are the input operands of another AND gate, whose output is

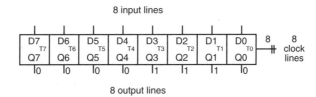

Figure 13.8   Eight-bit register.

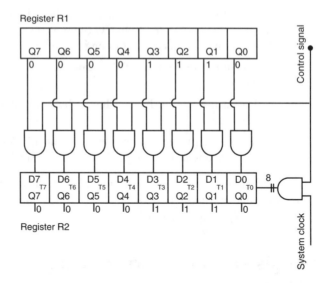

Figure 13.9 Use of AND logic gates to load the contents of register R1 into register R2.

connected to the clock line of each latch composing register R2. Transfer between registers occurs in the following way:

- *When both the control signal and the system clock are set to one,* the contents of register R1 are loaded into register R2. In fact, when the control signal is set to one, the input lines of register R2 are set to the same value as the output line of register R1. In addition, when the control signal and the system clock are set to one, a one arrives (through the AND gate) on the clock line of each latch composing R2; as a consequence, each latch composing R2 samples the value present on its input line and sets its output line to the same value.

- *When either the control signal or the clock signal is set to zero,* a zero arrives (through the AND gate) on the clock line of each latch composing R2. Thus, they are unaffected by the value of their input lines and register R2 keeps its current value.

Registers are the main components of the CPU and the control unit is the functional element responsible for the control signal. Transfers between registers (and more generally all the operations inside the CPU involving latches) happen only when a specific control signal is set by the control unit. Transfers between registers (and all the operations involving latches) happen synchronously when the system clock line is high. Timing aspects, which are not discussed here, are concerned with the time required to propagate signals along lines, logic gates and registers.

13.5.4 Adder circuits

Logic gates can be combined into electronic circuits for carrying out various arithmetic and logical functions. We consider next some simple circuits for adding two numbers represented in binary format. The sum operation on two bits can be realized by an electronic circuit, called a **half-adder**, which accepts two bits as input and generates two bits as output: the result and the carry-over. When the addition is applied to two binary numbers with h digits, this circuit is used to realize the sum of the two bits in position zero. To add two bits in a generic position i, we need a more complex circuit, called an **adder**, which also accepts as input the carry-over of position $i-1$. These two circuits are illustrated in Figure 13.10; they are called ADD and ADDC, respectively, to indicate the presence of the carry-over, C, in the second one.

Half-adder and adder circuits can be realized using logic gates. Let us take the simpler half-adder circuit, in which two logical functions are evaluated (carry-over C and result R) as a function of two inputs (B1 and B2); the logical functions are:

C = B1 AND B2
R = (NOT(B1) AND B2) OR (B1 AND NOT(B2))

Figure 13.11 shows the realization of the half-adder circuit via AND, OR and NOT gates.

A circuit capable of carrying out the sum of two binary numbers of four digits is illustrated in Figure 13.12. It consists of one half-adder circuit and three adder circuits, connected in such a way that the carry-over of the first circuit is an input to the second one and so on. The circuit outputs four result bits and one carry-over bit. To obtain a circuit for eight digits, it is sufficient to connect two circuits of four digits, but in this case, the first element of the second circuit has to be an adder whose carry-over input is connected to the carry-over output of the first circuit. This example illustrates a general characteristic of electronic circuits: they can be put together from quite simple elementary circuits.

One essential feature of electronic circuits is their speed in executing operations; this speed is an obvious prerequisite of computers, which have to be capable of

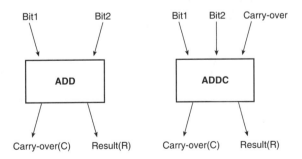

Figure 13.10 Adder and half-adder circuits.

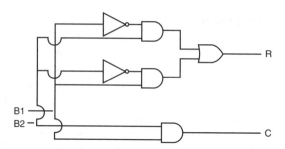

Figure 13.11   Realization of the half-adder circuit via logic gates.

executing millions of elementary operations per second. In particular, the speed of executing a sum via a circuit of the type illustrated in Figure 13.12 is affected by the computation of the carry-over: before the value of the highest-order digit can be calculated, one must know the carry-over of the preceding one and so on; the carry-over thus propagates in sequence from one circuit to another. Some circuits allow the carry-over operation to be accelerated; they are known as **carry look-ahead**. With these more sophisticated circuits, the execution of sums is carried out in nanoseconds.

Arithmetic operations on floating point numbers are more complex than on integer or fixed point numbers and need more complex hardware than those in fixed point; specific, dedicated circuits can realize more complex operations such as multiplication, division and exponentiation. Their discussion is beyond the scope of this book.

Other typical operations on sequences of bits allow the contents of registers to be manipulated in an elementary way (bit by bit); among these, two operations are used most frequently: **rotate** (which is applied to a sequence of k bits, placing the first bit in the last position and letting the remaining bits advance one place) and **shift** (which is applied to a sequence of k bits, advancing them all by one place; the first bit is lost).

Figure 13.13(a) shows the effects of a rotate operation on a sequence of 8 bits and Figure 13.13(b) shows a circuit which rotates the contents of an 8-bit register. The design of a simple circuit which shifts the contents of a register is left to the reader (see Exercise 13.11).

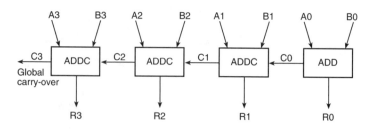

Figure 13.12   Adder circuit for numbers of four binary digits.

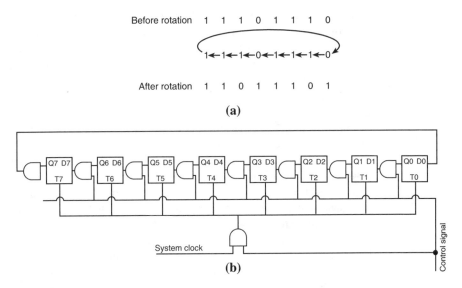

Figure 13.13   (a) The effects of a rotate operation on a sequence of 8 bits. (b) A circuit which rotates the contents of an 8-bit register.

*13.6 Extended example: design of VLSI circuits

The advances made by microelectronics during the past 30 years have enabled the development of hardware components which are characterized not only by enhanced performance, but also by increasingly smaller dimensions and reduced costs. **Integrated circuits** combine on very small surfaces a huge number of elements (transistors, resistors and so on), which perform sophisticated and complex functions; in particular, **VLSI** (Very Large Scale Integrated) **circuits** contain millions of components within minuscule surfaces.

VLSI technology is characterized by a particular approach to design, realization and testing. The building of VLSI circuits requires the use of modular design and optimization strategies and the employment of consolidated models and techniques that allow designers to start from an implementation-independent **functional design** of the circuit (which indicates the logical elements of the circuit itself) and arrive at an **implementation specification,** capable of guiding the proper physical realization, which specifies the position of each component element and the connections between them.

Several sophisticated design, optimization and validation methodologies and a large number of tools allow the designer to manage complex design problems and increase the probability of an early elimination of design errors. The use of methodologies and tools shortens the realization times and permits the optimization of space, cost, reliability and performance. These factors combine to improve the level of competitiveness of products, in a market which is characterized by the rapid obsolescence of circuits.

Figure 13.14 shows the main phases of **design** and **manufacturing** of a VLSI circuit. We focus on the design phase, as the description of manufacturing of integrated circuits requires a knowledge of microelectronics which would largely exceed the scope of this book. We consider the design of synchronous digital circuits, given that in this sector the design methodologies are consolidated and that there are a lot of tools available dedicated to design automation.

The design of a VLSI circuit begins with the **specification of the requirements** associated with each circuit. This specification is independent of the technology with which the circuit will be realized (for example, the type of transistors to be used and the particular technologies used to fabricate them) and often uses formally defined languages (HDLs: **Hardware Description Languages**) to specify the *functions* to be realized by the circuit (and the modules of which it is composed) and the overall *structure* (architecture) of the system. VHDL is one of the standardized languages commonly used for specifications at this level. Via VHDL it is possible to define a circuit as being composed of *design entities*. Each entity is defined through an *interface* (connections to external entities) and one or more *implementations*; each implementation is described in terms of its *structure* (that is, in terms of interconnected hardware), in terms of its *behaviour* (the output signals are described as a function of the input signals), or in terms of its *information flow* (that is, in terms of information transfer between basic elements of the circuit itself, for example, between registers). During this phase, the designer can be supported by graphical tools which avoid direct use of the complex VHDL syntax.

Next comes the process of **synthesis and optimization,** which is further sub-structured into three processes: architectural, logical and physical design (see Figure 13.14).

The first step is called **architectural design**. This step starts from the system's requirements specifications (expressed, for example, in VHDL) in order to define in greater detail the architecture which is capable of supporting the functionalities of the circuit previously defined. Architectural design produces, in successive steps, an architectural specification and a behavioural specification which include details of operation *scheduling* that guarantees the overall behaviour, *shared resources* during information transfer and transformation, and *control signals* that have to be 'administered' to the circuit to ensure the desired scheduling. For this specification, the architectural design phase can make use of predefined functional modules.

At this level, as well as in subsequent design phases, the designer can choose to proceed autonomously (in **custom mode**) or with the aid of existing synthesizing and optimizing tools (in **semi-custom mode**). The first mode is more expensive in terms of time and money and sometimes unsuitable because of project size problems, but it generally leads to higher performance for particular application needs. The second mode (which is most widely applied) allows lower costs and shorter time scales and the evaluation of a number of design alternatives, which otherwise could hardly be undertaken by a single designer.

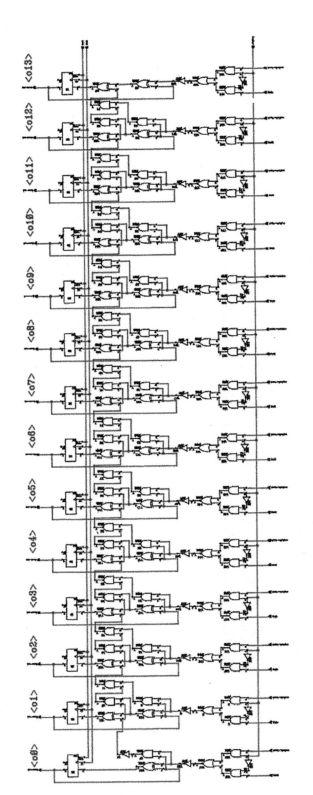

Figure 13.15 *Logical design*: a logical network that realizes, among other components, an adder.

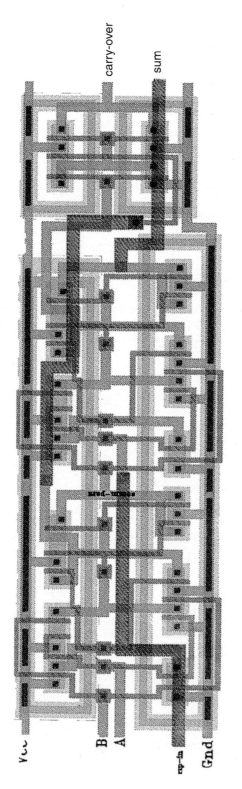

Figure 13.16 *Physical design:* the layout of one of the full adders that make up a 14-bit adder.

Figure 13.17 *Physical design*: the layout of an integrated circuit that realizes the neuron of a neural network.

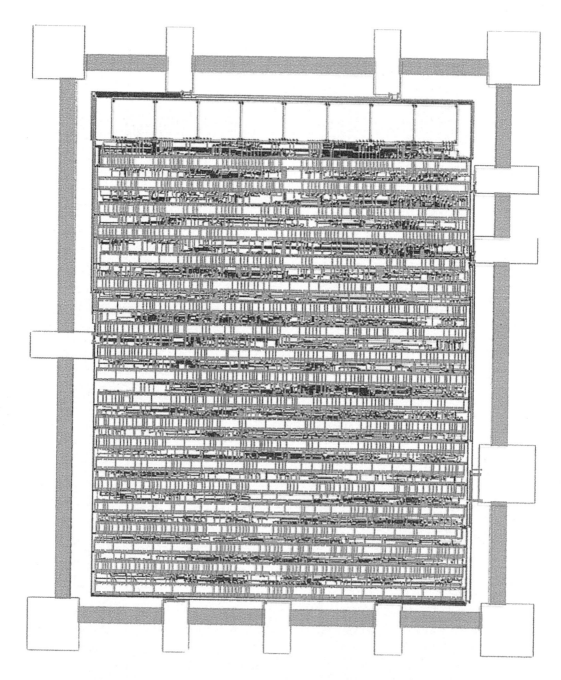

Figure 13.18 *Physical design*: the layout of an entire neural network.

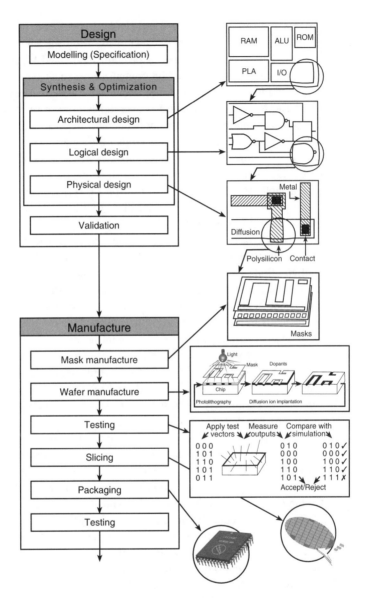

Figure 13.14 Phases in the design, manufacture and testing of a VLSI circuit.

The subsequent phase of **logical design** (see Figure 13.14) defines, for each functional module in the overall architecture, a set of constituent elements (logic gates or memory elements) and the connections between them. It defines, therefore, the logical network that realizes the previously proposed functional modules. During the logical design phase, special tools enable the designer to proceed by progressive refinements, by focusing on logical networks of different levels of abstraction and fixing at each design iteration the elements that constitute the circuits. The designer can use, if desired, predefined blocks (thus doing a *library binding,* where some of the components are taken from large libraries of components). Figure 13.15 shows part of a logical network that realizes a 14-bit adder.

The logical design phase is accompanied by a series of operations to verify the correct functioning of the network and to optimize it. *Simulation of logical behaviour* and *timing analysis* establish the delays with which output signals are produced with respect to input signals and detect the critical paths with respect to this delay. This phase allows the verification of the behaviour of the proposed logical network, leads to the definition or verification of the frequency of the synchronization signal at which the circuit will function, and permits the definition of an optimized logical network.

Optimization of a network normally involves the following parameters: size, performance and testability. *Size* depends on the complexity of the network and the configurations chosen to realize single modules or parts of them. *Performance* is tightly linked to the signal propagation delay in the network, the synchronization signal applicable to the network (the highest frequency that allows all of its components to behave correctly), the speed of the circuit (expressed as the number of impulses of the synchronization signal necessary to realize one operation) and the number of operations that the circuit can carry out in a given unit of time (*throughput*). *Testability* refers to the possibility of completely verifying the functioning of each part of the network and of automatically generating test patterns suitable for completely verifying the desired functioning at the end of manufacturing, in order to detect any faulty circuits.

The **physical design** phase (see Figure 13.16) is tightly linked to the type of components that will be used in manufacturing the previously defined logical network. This phase defines the circuit that realizes the logical network and the layout that guides the production of masks used during the manufacturing phase. On the *layout*, the positions of the individual component elements and the positions of the necessary connections are indicated, together with the type of treatment that the substrate material has to undergo to realize the circuit elements (in an integrated way). Fundamental operations in this phase, therefore, are the *placement* and *wiring* (often called *routing*) of the circuit components.

Figures 13.16, 13.17 and 13.18 describe the layouts of a full adder, a neuron of a neural network and an entire neural network. We neither discuss the features of neural networks nor give a detailed description of these figures; note, in passing, that Figure 13.17 describes the result of a full-custom design, leading to a component placement that optimizes the length and position of connections, while Figure 13.18 illustrates a semi-custom design which incorporates several standard cells, highlighting the cells and the connections.

There are different semi-custom methodologies of physical design that can be used. With a **cell-based design** approach, it is possible to proceed by progressively refining the positioning and wiring of circuit cells available in a library (standard-cells approach). The cell-based approach allows components obtained via custom design to be combined easily with elements coming from semi-custom design.

Another design approach, called the **array-based approach**, uses a matrix of places (sites) which are not a priori finalized to realize a particular component. These sites are programmed and connected according to the function of the circuit to be realized. The use of the matrix for the specification of placement and routing allows *prediffused* or *prewired* layers to be used during the manufacturing phase.

The optimization parameters considered during logical design are reconsidered during physical design, with particular regard to the proposed realization. Only at this level are the size and performance of the circuit finally fixed, since these aspects are closely connected to the particular technology adopted to realize the components.

During the physical design phase, test operations which were previously determined are made more precise so as to be fully applicable at the end of the manufacturing process. Note that a good logical design strongly influences the testability of the final product and the possibility of generating the test patterns automatically.

Different **verification** techniques are applied to test the correctness of the whole design process: the layout obtained at the end of the physical design phase must be correct with respect to the results of the architectural and logical design phases. For this purpose, for example, the logical network obtained from the final layout could be compared with the logical network defined at the logical design level.

The designer's task can be assisted by various tools for automating the design; they are called **CAD** (Computer-Automated Design) **tools**. Some CAD products support optimization and verification of the various design phases, while others support the application of different design methodologies or facilitate the use of functional modules, predefined at the architectural, logical or physical level.

Among the existing families of CAD products, we should mention those products dedicated to synthesis and optimization and those dedicated to verification. The first group supports performance optimization by proposing solutions for circuit design and minimization, test generation, placement and routing at the electrical level. The second group supports the verification of design rules or electrical rules, together with simulation and verification at different levels of abstraction.

The first CAD tools handled physical verification and design; later, tools to support logical and architectural synthesis were developed and became widely used; recent packages support the different phases of VLSI design in an integrated way. Today, designers have at their disposal very powerful and diversified tools and they can work in flexible design environments, with predefined modules and available methodologies. All this has been made possible by the existence of accepted specification standards: for instance, the VHDL language mentioned earlier supports high-level specifications that can be handled by various CAD tools.

Exercises

13.1 Carry out base conversions for the following natural numbers:

(a)   from base 2 to base 8: 10011100101, 10010101111, 1010111010

(b)   from base 2 to base 10: 10011100101, 10010101111, 1010111010

(c)   from base 2 to base 16: 10011100101, 10010101111, 1010111010

(d)   from base 8 to base 2: 64752, 34251, 536777

(e)   from base 8 to base 10: 64752, 34251, 536777

(f)   from base 8 to base 16: 64752, 34251, 536777

(g)   from base 10 to base 2: 45, 56789, 2453, 500012

(h)   from base 10 to base 8: 45, 56789, 2453, 500012

(i)   from base 10 to base 16: 45, 56789, 2453, 500012

(j)   from base 16 to base 2: 1E59, AB45, C5E7

(k)   from base 16 to base 8: 1E59, AB45, C5E7

(l)   from base 16 to base 10: 1E59, AB45, C5E7

13.2 Represent the following integers in two's complement (using a format with ten binary digits):

456, −321, 7, −90, 42, −78, −468

13.3 Carry out base conversions for the following fractional numbers:

(a)   from base 2 to base 10: 0.100111001, 0.100101011, 0.1010111

(b)   from base 10 to base 2: 0.45, 0.56789, 0.2453, 0.500012

13.4 Given the following real numbers (in base 10 and fixed point): 67.56, 0.00787, 2.78, 564000.56, represent them:

(a)   in floating point, with $p = b = 10$

(b)   in base 2 and fixed point

(c)   in floating point, with $p = b = 2$

(d)   in floating point, with $p = 10$, $b = 2$

13.5 Represent in two's complement the following pairs of integers and calculate their algebraic sums (using a format with seven binary digits):

(+54, +3), (−54, −3), (−54, −32), (+32, −6), (−32, +6)

13.6 In real number arithmetic, is it possible that $(2.00000 \times 2)/2 = 1.999999$? What is the reason?

13.7   Construct the truth tables of the following logical expressions:

(a)   (A OR B) OR NOT(A AND B)

(b)   NOT((A OR C) OR B) OR (A AND C)

13.8   A **tautology** is a logical expression that is always true, a **contradiction** is a logical expression that is always false. Write down one tautology and one contradiction.

13.9   Construct, using the logical gates AND, OR and NOT, the networks that realize the functions denoted by the logical expressions described in Table 13.3 and those described in Exercise 13.7.

13.10   Construct, using the logical gates AND, OR and NOT, the networks that realize an adder circuit (ADDC).

13.11   Construct, using the logical gates AND, OR and NOT, a logical circuit that realizes a shift register, which contains a sequence of binary digits.

13.12   Using the ADD and ADDC circuits, presented in this chapter, as components, draft a project for an electronic circuit that calculates the product of two binary natural numbers of length 4 digits.

Suggestions: You may consider the execution of a multiplication as a sequence of sums, or you may use the fact that the multiplication of a binary number by 2 can be obtained by shifting all bits one position to the left and adding a zero on the right.

☛   1.   Demonstrate that gates NAND and NOR can be used for defining any AND, OR and NOT gate. (*Hint*: It is sufficient to write Boolean expressions which use only NAND and NOR operations having truth tables equivalent to those of AND, OR and NOT).

Machine language and architecture $\boxed{14}$

In Chapter 13, we discussed coding techniques for data representation and described the mechanisms that enable the computing of simple logical and arithmetic expressions, data storage in registers and data transfers between registers. In Chapter 2, we described the von Neumann machine as a highly simplified model of a computer; we can now reconsider that model and illustrate its behaviour in more detail, by taking into account the material covered in Chapter 13 and also the programming experience acquired in Part I.

We start by recalling the architecture of the von Neumann machine, and then we present an operational language which allows us to program this machine. The language belongs to the category of so-called **machine languages**, that is, languages that can be directly executed by a computer. The description of the language is qualitative, with drastic simplifications with respect to real machine languages. However, it allows the reader to understand how the high-level programs analysed in Part I can be executed even by a machine with a simple architecture. It is not our aim, however, to teach the reader how to program in machine language.

The knowledge we acquire about the von Neumann architecture allows us to discuss, at the end of this chapter, the difference between this 'reference framework' and the architecture of real computers. In particular, we describe and compare different architectures and computers currently available on the market: **CISC**s (Complex Instruction Set Computers), **RISC**s (Reduced Instruction Set Computers) and **parallel computers**.

14.1 The architecture of the von Neumann machine

We start by recalling the architecture of the von Neumann machine, which was introduced in Chapter 2 as a premise in order to understand programming. Analysing

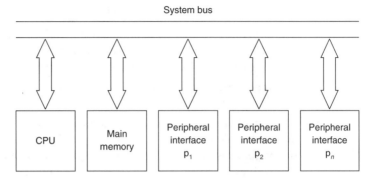

Figure 14.1 Architecture of the von Neumann machine.

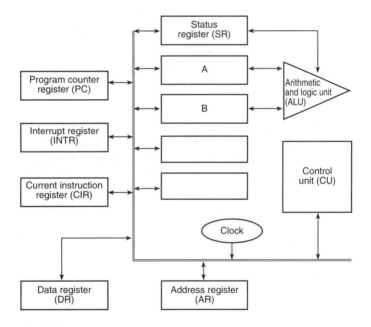

Figure 14.2 Components of the processor.

this architecture a second time is instructive, as the reader now has an opportunity to understand better the behaviour of each functional element of the architecture and the interaction between them. The organization of the von Neumann machine is illustrated in Figure 14.1 (a copy of Figure 2.1), which shows the four basic functional elements of a von Neumann machine (processor, main memory, peripherals and system bus) and Figure 14.2 (a copy of Figure 2.4), which shows the components of the processor.

We now review the main components of the von Neumann machine.

- The **processor** (the CPU) coordinates the various activities within the von Neumann machine. It contains the electronic devices capable of *fetching*, *decoding* and *executing* the program's instructions.

- The **main memory** contains the information needed to execute a program: *instructions* and *data*.

- The **peripherals** allow the exchange of information between the computer and the outside world, via *input* and *output* operations. Only the *interfaces* to the peripherals are considered to be part of the computer, the peripherals themselves being considered as separate devices. In the von Neumann architecture, the peripherals also include the *mass storage devices.*

- The **system bus** connects these functional elements, allowing the transfer of: data (*data bus*), control signals (*control bus*) and addresses (*address bus*) between different functional elements.

We next look inside the processor, responsible for loading and executing instructions, stored in memory. The processor is composed of several components:

- The **system clock** synchronizes the processing phases in the von Neumann machine by issuing a *clock signal* (a value which is periodically set to one and then reset to zero at a given frequency).

- The **control unit** is part of the processor and coordinates the timely execution of the functions to be carried out in the processor itself and in the other functional elements. It interprets the instructions of the program being executed and ensures that execution is carried out in the right sequence. In particular, it coordinates the behaviour of data transfers between registers, the processing of information by the ALU (described next), the loading and storing of data from and into the main memory, and the exchange of data with peripherals. The control unit operates by issuing *control signals* that, in coordination with the clock signal, enable the various operations.

- The **arithmetic and logic unit** (ALU) realizes the manipulation of data needed for the execution of arithmetic and logical instructions. Thus, the ALU is capable of executing the arithmetic and Boolean operations and the shift and rotate operations that were reviewed in Chapter 13.

The functioning of the computer is enabled by special registers, each performing a given function. We review the most important of them:

- The **data register** (DR) is h bits long, equal to the length of a word. It contains the data to be stored in memory or loaded from main memory during the execution of the specific get or put instruction.

- The **address register** (AR) is k bits long; so that it can address 2^k memory words. During the execution of a get or put instruction, it contains the address of the main memory word to be accessed.

- The **current instruction register** (CIR) is h bits long and contains the instruction that is being executed by the computer.

- The **program counter** (PC) is k bits long and stores the address of the next instruction of the program being executed.

- The **interrupt register** (INTR) contains information about the functional state of the peripherals.

- **Registers A** and **B** contain the operands and the result of the operations carried out by the ALU.

- The **status register** (SR) contains information about the result of the operations carried out by the ALU. These include:

  - the **carry bit**, which indicates the presence of a carry-over;

  - the **zero bit**, which indicates that the A register contains the value 'zero';

  - the **sign bit**, which indicates the sign of the result of an arithmetic operation;

  - the **overflow bit**, which allows an overflow condition to be detected when the result of the last arithmetic operation executed by the ALU exceeds the maximum value that can be represented in the h bits of the A register. When an overflow condition occurs, the overflow bit indicates that register A contains a wrong result with respect to the last arithmetic operation executed by the ALU.

  These bits also allow comparison operations between two operands to be carried out. These can be done by subtracting the second operand from the first and testing the result.

- A large number of **working registers** can be read and written very quickly and contain frequently used data or instructions or the intermediate results of processing.

An **input/output interface** contains registers to send commands to a peripheral, exchange data and control the functioning of the peripheral. An elementary standard interface generally contains the following elements:

- A **peripheral data register** (PDR) to exchange data with the peripheral.

- A **peripheral command register** (PCR) which contains the command being executed by the peripheral.

- **Status information** about the peripheral (for a printer, for example, the status could be: 'ready to receive new data', 'busy printing data', or an error condition, such as 'no paper' or 'no ink').

The data register is connected to the data bus and the command register to the control bus; the status information can be transferred into a special **peripheral status register** (PSR) and read 'on command' by the processor (using the bus), or connected via special electronic circuits to the processor (in which case the information is transferred to the interrupt register, INTR).

This architecture gives us an idea of how a computer works, but we are still missing a fundamental ingredient, which in Chapter 2 we could only sketch but here we can describe in more detail: the language of the computer. Describing the machine language is the main objective of this chapter.

14.2 The format of instructions

A program written in machine language, similarly to a program written in C, is a sequence of instructions. The instructions of the machine language, however, have a very rigid structure. They have two parts, an **operational code** and one or more **operands**; the operational code is always present, whereas the operands are optional. The operational code specifies the operation to be executed; the operands specify in various modes the location of the memory words to be operated on. In most machine languages, operations have several operands (perhaps two or three), but in this chapter we describe a simple language in which each instruction has at most one operand.

Given that the machine language instructions have to be stored in memory words on physical devices, they are coded in binary; thus, an instruction is simply a sequence of zeros and ones – much less readable than an instruction in C! Furthermore, we impose the restriction that the operational codes and operands have a fixed length, so that each instruction is regularly divided into these two parts.

We denote the length of an instruction by s; the number of bits dedicated to the operational code by m; and the number of bits of the operand by n; thus, $s = m + n$. The **instruction set** of the language is the set of executable instructions, each of which corresponds to an operational code; given the above dimension in bits of the operational code, the cardinality of the instruction set is therefore less than 2^m. Similarly, the number of words that can be addressed by the operand is 2^n. The value n is linked to the number of memory words, 2^k; indeed, to ensure that all memory words can be addressed, $n \geq k$ must hold. We will see in the course of this chapter, however, that memory addresses can also be represented in synthetic form, requiring a smaller number of bits.

The length of the instructions, s, is related to the length of the words, h. In many cases, s and h are the same: each instruction is contained exactly in one memory word. It is also possible that s is a multiple or submultiple of h; in this case, each instruction occupies several memory words or one memory word hosts more than one instruction. Finally, the length of an instruction may depend on the operational code; for example, assuming that most instructions occupy one memory word, the operational code in specific instructions could be used to indicate that the instruction occupies two consecutive memory words. In this chapter, we assume, for the sake of simplicity, that each instruction occupies exactly one memory word.

Summarizing the hypotheses formulated so far, the format of our machine language instructions is an operational code field of m bits, optionally followed by a single address of n bits; each instruction is contained in one memory word.

14.3 The execution of instructions

We saw in Chapter 2 that a computer's normal functioning consists of reading and executing the instructions of a program, repeating a sequence of operations in the CPU. Each instruction is *fetched* from main memory, *decoded* and *executed.* Let us recall the four steps needed to execute the *fetch phase* of each instruction:

(1)   The contents of the program counter register (PC) are transferred into the address register (AR).

(2)   The contents of the memory word that corresponds to the address contained in AR are transferred into the data register (DR) via the system bus.

(3)   The contents of the data register are transferred into the current instruction register (CIR).

(4)   The value of register PC is incremented by 1, so that PC contains the address of the instruction immediately after the instruction currently loaded in CIR. Thus, the execution of the next fetch phase is prepared. Remember that it is possible to store, during the execution of the current instruction, a different address in the PC register, thus changing the 'sequential' execution of the program.

Each step is a **micro-instruction,** that is, a data transfer between CPU registers or between the functional units of the machine connected by the bus. Adopting a synthetic notation to express micro-instruction, we can express the fetch phase as being composed of the following four micro-instructions:

$$PC \rightarrow AR$$
$$MEM[AR] \rightarrow DR$$
$$DR \rightarrow CIR$$
$$PC + 1 \rightarrow PC$$

Each micro-instruction corresponds to a data transfer between registers or specific memory locations. Our notation indicates a data transfer from the element to the left of the arrow to the element to the right of the arrow. The notation MEM[AR] indicates the memory location addressed by the AR register.

The next phase, *interpreting* the instruction, involves analysing the contents of the CIR register to find out which operation is to be executed. In this phase, only the operational code of the current instruction is analysed. Finally, the *execution phase,* which is different for each operation, consists in executing the operation itself. If the instruction involves an operand, it will be fetched during the execution phase. The next section describes the execution phase of the main instructions.

14.4 Main instructions

In the following, we describe the main instructions of the machine language.

(1)   The **load** instruction reads from memory. It loads the contents of a memory word into a register. Our language includes two instructions, loada and loadb, referring to the registers A and B, respectively. In real systems, other load instructions refer to the other working registers. The execution of the instruction loada ind1, where ind1 represents an address present in the operand part of the instruction, is carried out as follows:

(a)   The contents of the operand field of the current instruction register (OP(CIR)) are copied into the address register (AR).

(b)   A get operation is executed. The memory word corresponding to the address in AR is copied into the data register (DR).

(c)   The contents of the register DR are copied into the A register.

The loada instruction thus involves the following micro-instructions (where OP(CIR) indicates the last n bits of the CIR register which correspond to the operand field of the current instruction):

$$OP(CIR) \rightarrow AR$$
$$MEM[AR] \rightarrow DR$$
$$DR \rightarrow A$$

(2)   The **store** (save) instruction writes to memory. It assigns the contents of a register to a memory word. In our simple language, we consider the two instructions, storea and storeb, referring to the registers of the ALU. The execution of the instruction storea ind1, where ind1 represents an address contained in the operand part of the instruction, is carried out as follows:

(a)   The contents of register A are copied into the data register (DR).

(b)   The contents of the operand field of the current instruction register (OP(CIR)) are copied into the address register (AR).

(c)   A put operation is executed. The contents of DR are copied into the memory word corresponding to the address contained in AR.

The instruction storea thus involves the following micro-instructions:

$$A \rightarrow DR$$
$$OP(CIR) \rightarrow AR$$
$$DR \rightarrow MEM[AR]$$

(3)   The instruction to **read from a peripheral**, read ind1, where the operand ind1 represents an address in main memory, obtains a value from a peripheral (for example, from the keyboard of a terminal or a personal computer) and stores it in the addressed memory word. The execution of this instruction is carried out as follows:

(a)   The contents of the data register PDR, in the peripheral interface, are transferred into the data register DR, using the bus from the peripheral to the processing unit. This micro-instruction assumes that the PDR contains a datum originating from the peripheral; this can be verified by checking the contents of the status register PSR of the peripheral interface or the (interrupt) register INTR of the CPU; input/output from peripherals is further described in Chapter 15.

(b)   The contents of the operand field of the current instruction register (OP(CIR)) are transferred into the address register (AR).

(c)   A put operation is carried out in main memory, thus bringing into memory the datum that was initially in the PDR register.

To summarize, the `read` instruction involves the following micro-instructions:

> PDR → DR
> OP(CIR) → AR
> DR → MEM[AR]

(4)   The instruction to **write to a peripheral**, `write ind1`, where the operand `ind1` represents an address in main memory, obtains a value from the addressed memory word and outputs it to a peripheral (for example, the screen of a terminal). The execution of this instruction is carried out as follows:

(a)   The contents of the address field of the current instruction register (OP(CIR)) are transferred into the address register (AR).

(b)   A get operation is carried out. The contents of the memory word corresponding to the address contained in AR are transferred into the data register DR.

(c)   The contents of the DR register are transferred, via the bus, into the PDR data register in the peripheral interface.

Furthermore, by using an appropriate command, the processing unit activates the visualization of the character on the peripheral. To summarize, the execution of the `write` instruction involves the following micro-instructions:

> OP(CIR) → AR
> MEM[AR] → DR
> DR → PDR

(5)   Instructions concerning **operations on integers** are carried out by the ALU. The numerical instructions are: `add` (sum), `dif` (difference), `mul` (multiplication) and `div` (division). The effect of each of these instructions is to transfer into the A register the result of the operation executed on the contents of registers A and B; in the case of integer division, the result is stored in register A and the remainder in register B.

(6)   The **branch instructions** allow control to be transferred to any instruction in the program. Branches modify the normal execution of a program in which the instructions are executed one after the other. There are two types of branches:

(a)   The **unconditional branch**, jump ind1, causes the execution of the program to continue with the instruction that corresponds to the address ind1. The instruction is executed by transferring the contents of the operand field of the current instruction register (which has the value ind1) into the program counter register (PC). Thus, the next fetch phase gets the instruction contained in word ind1 instead of the instruction immediately following the last instruction executed.

(b)   The **conditional branch**, jumpz ind1, causes the execution of the program to continue with the instruction ind1 only if the contents of the A register are equal to zero. The instruction is executed using the status register (SR): the branch to the address ind1 only takes place if the zero bit of the SR register is set to 1.

(7)   The **pause instruction**, nop (no operation), is used to allow an instruction cycle to elapse without executing any instruction; this allows the processing unit to wait for some external event to occur.

(8)   The **stop instruction**, halt, terminates the execution of the program.

We have omitted several important instruction types from our simple language, such as the instructions for handling subprograms and the stack. Furthermore, we have omitted all operations on specific bits of the registers.

Table 14.1 summarizes the machine language instructions presented in this section. Give that the language contains 14 different types of instruction, 4 bits

Table 14.1   Machine language instructions.

Binary operational code	Symbolic operational code
0000	LOADA
0001	LOADB
0010	STOREA
0011	STOREB
0100	READ
0101	WRITE
0110	ADD
0111	DIF
1000	MUL
1001	DIV
1010	JUMP
1011	JUMPZ
1100	NOP
1101	HALT

$(14 \leq 2^4)$ suffice for the operational code field of our executor; the binary codes are also given in Table 14.1. Generally, computers have a much higher number of instructions (the DEC VAX, for example, had 304 different instructions).

14.5 Data representation in main memory

We saw in Part I of the book that the execution of a program generally manipulates data stored in memory. In fact, each program defines a transformation of an initial set of data, called *input data*, to a final set of data, called *output data*. Input and output data normally have a life span corresponding to the duration of the program. During program execution, the set of data handled in main memory is called the *program data*.

Input data is obtained through read operations (from peripherals or from mass storage); output data is calculated by the computer and normally also sent to peripheral units so that the user can see the result of the calculation. At the end of the calculation, the program data ceases to exist, but the output data can be written to mass storage in order to make it available for further use after the termination of the program itself.

Program data, too, has its own format: in main memory, the computer represents an integer, a real number and a character in different forms. We saw in Chapter 13 the binary coding of integers, real numbers and characters. In the simplified machine language described in this chapter we can only handle the integer data type; in real machines, a large number of data types are supported, so that the various data types of high-level programming languages, such as C, can be handled.

In order to manipulate data in our machine language, we just have to arrange for some memory cells to contain data of integer type. These cells, which obviously have their own addresses in main memory, can be in any position with respect to the program. In the load, store, read and write instructions which refer to data contained in memory, the operand field must contain the memory addresses of cells ready to accept program data. In the jump and jumpz instructions, the operand field must contain the addresses of memory locations that contain program instructions.

14.6 Examples of programs

We are finally ready to describe a simple program using the machine language introduced above. It consists of two parts, the instructions and the data. Generally speaking, machine language programs are loaded into memory by a system device, starting at some appropriate memory cell (not necessarily the first one) and can be moved around in memory, occupying different positions in different instants of time during program execution (this aspect is discussed in Chapter 15). In this chapter, for simplicity, we suppose the first instruction to be loaded in the first memory cell and the program to be written such that the instructions are situated before the data. Memory is thus partitioned into two zones: the first contains the program instructions, the second the data on which the program operates. The two parts are separated by the last instruction of the program, which must be the halt instruction.

The executor that we have constructed so far is very limited; indeed, it can only execute elementary numerical programs. It is, however, possible at this point to follow the execution of such programs step by step and to determine the micro-instructions needed to execute each instruction, the registers involved and the flow of data between registers and along the system bus. The examples in this chapter give us the opportunity to show what happens in the machine during the execution of very simple programs.

Our first example of a complete program – which will be thoroughly discussed – is given in Table 14.2. This simple program obtains two integers from the terminal and prints the result of their multiplication on the screen. The program instructions occupy the first eight memory cells (cells 0–7); cells 8 and 9 are defined to contain data of integer type. In order to make the program more readable, we use the symbolic names of the instructions and decimal numbers to refer to the operational codes and the program addresses, respectively. Furthermore, we indicate to the left of each instruction the address of the memory cell in which it is contained. Finally, in order to remember that cells 8 and 9 must contain an integer number, we put the word INT in lines 8 and 9 of the program.

We can now simulate the execution of the program. Initially, it carries out two read operations which put into memory, at locations 8 and 9, two numbers read from the keyboard of the terminal. Let us suppose that the numbers typed in by the user are 5 and 4 (we ignore the problems of recognizing numbers composed of

Table 14.2 Multiplication program.

Main memory cell's number	Operational code	Operand field
0	READ	8
1	READ	9
2	LOADA	8
3	LOADB	9
4	MUL	
5	STOREA	8
6	WRITE	8
7	HALT	
8	INT	
9	INT	

more than one digit and of converting numerical data, which is normally read in as character strings and subsequently interpreted as numbers). The following two load instructions load the two numbers into registers A and B of the processing unit. The next command, mul, executes the multiplication; thus, the value 20 is loaded into the A register. Then the store instruction transfers the value 20 from the A register into memory cell 8; finally, the write instruction prints the value contained in memory cell 8 onto the screen of the terminal, thus obtaining the desired result. The reader will have noticed that this program requires a high number of apparently superfluous transfers; for example, the multiplication result has to be written into memory before it can be transferred to the peripheral. However, the execution described here is necessary, owing to the intrinsic limitations of the instruction set of our machine.

In Table 14.3 we represent the machine code in binary. We can do this quite easily: it is sufficient to convert the addresses and the operational codes into binary. Let us assume that we have a memory of 4 kbytes with memory cells of 16 bits. In this case, $h = s = 16$, $m = 4$, $n = 12$. The length of the memory cells is enough to contain natural numbers between 0 and $2^{16} - 1$, or (signed) integer numbers between -2^{15} and $2^{15} - 1$. Obviously, the computer must know the type of variable stored in memory cells 8 and 9; that is, it must know whether they contain natural numbers or signed integers, in order to interpret the meaning of the variables correctly.

We can also follow the program's execution at the micro-instruction level; the list of micro-instructions corresponding to each instruction of the program is given in Figure 14.3. Note that each instruction corresponds to four fixed micro-instructions in the fetch phase and a variable number of micro-instructions in the execution phase. Before starting program execution, we assume that the program counter register is set to 0, corresponding to the first instruction of the program. We do not translate the execution part of instruction 7 which halts the machine.

Table 14.3 Coded multiplication program.

Main memory cell's number	Operational code	Operand field
0	0100	000000001000
1	0100	000000001001
2	0000	000000001000
3	0001	000000001001
4	1000	000000000000
5	0010	000000001000
6	0101	000000001000
7	1101	000000000000
8	0000	000000000000
9	0000	000000000000

0	fetch	PC → AR
		MEM[AR] → DR
		DR → CIR
		PC + 1 → PC
	execution	PDR → DR
		OP(CIR) → AR
		DR → MEM[AR]
1	fetch	PC → AR
		MEM[AR] → DR
		DR → CIR
		PC + 1 → PC
	execution	PDR → DR
		OP(CIR) → AR
		DR → MEM[AR]
2	fetch	PC → AR
		MEM[AR] → DR
		DR → CIR
		PC + 1 → PC
	execution	OP(CIR) → AR
		MEM[AR] → DR
		DR → A
3	fetch	PC → AR
		MEM[AR] → DR
		DR → CIR
		PC + 1 → PC
	execution	OP(CIR) → AR
		MEM[AR] → DR
		DR → B
4	fetch	PC → AR
		MEM[AR] → DR
		DR → CIR
		PC + 1 → PC
	execution	MUL
5	fetch	PC → AR
		MEM[AR] → DR
		DR → CIR
		PC + 1 → PC
	execution	A → DR
		OP(CIR) → AR
		DR → MEM[AR]
6	fetch	PC → AR
		MEM[AR] → DR
		DR → CIR
		PC + 1 → PC
	execution	OP(CIR) → AR
		MEM[AR] → DR
		DR → PDR
7	fetch	PC → AR
		MEM[AR] → DR
		DR → CIR
		PC + 1 → PC

Figure 14.3   Micro-instructions corresponding to the instructions of the multiplication program.

14.7 Address modes

So far, we have assumed that the operand field of an instruction contains the exact address of the memory location of the operand, called the **absolute address**. This mode of addressing is called **direct addressing** and has two drawbacks: first, the presence of an absolute address makes the allocation of programs in memory rather awkward, because all addresses have to be recalculated whenever the program is moved; as we shall see in Chapter 15, the allocation of a program to a different portion of the memory, or *relocation*, is a rather frequent operation. Second, if the memory is very big, the address fields become very long (remember that the length of the operand field must enable the addressing of all memory locations). There are other address modes for operands, three of which we present in this section: indirect, via an index register and immediate.

(1) In the case of **indirect addressing** (also called deferred addressing) the effective address of the operand is contained in the memory location addressed by the operand field of the instruction. The effective address of the operand can thus be represented in all h bits and not only in n bits as in the case of direct addressing. The retrieval of an operand in indirect addressing requires, though, one more memory access than is required in direct addressing. Indeed, in indirect addressing, once we obtain the address from the operand field of the instruction that is being executed, we access memory again to retrieve the address of the operand, and then again to retrieve the

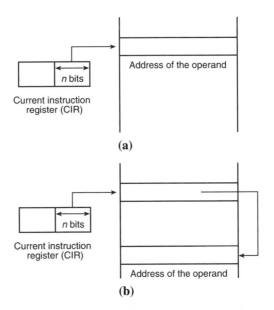

Figure 14.4   (a) Direct addressing. (b) Indirect addressing.

operand itself. Finally, the memory cell that contains the address of the operand contains its absolute address. Figures 14.4(a) and 14.4(b), respectively, show the direct and indirect address modes.

This address mode allows the implementation of pointer variables in high-level programming languages, as will be discussed in Example 14.3. Pointer variables were introduced in Chapter 5 with reference to the C programming language.

(2) In the case of **addressing via an index register**, the effective address of the operand is calculated by the machine. With this method, the address is obtained by algebraically adding the contents of a particular register, called the **index register** (I), to the operand field of the instruction. The I register is one of the high-speed-access registers in a CPU. This address mode, which requires a single memory access to retrieve the operand, is particularly useful for accessing the n words that follow a particular memory location (which we call the base word). To obtain this effect, it is sufficient to repeat n times an instruction that has the address of the base word in its operand field, incrementing the I register by one before each subsequent execution of the instruction. Figure 14.5 shows the index address mode. This mode, too, allows a higher number of memory cells to be addressed than direct addressing does, as the absolute address of the operand is obtained by adding the contents of the index register (which could consist of up to h bits) to the contents of the operand field of the instruction (n bits).

This address mode allows a natural treatment of arrays and index variables of high-level programming languages as will be discussed in

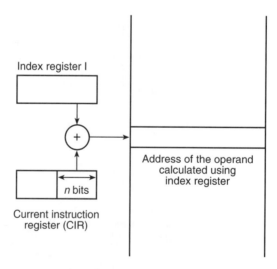

Figure 14.5 Addressing via an index register.

Example 14.2. Arrays and index variables were introduced in Chapter 3 with reference to the C programming language.

(3) **Immediate addressing** assumes that the value of the operand is already present in the operand field of the instruction. Therefore, no further memory access to retrieve the operand is necessary during the execution phase. The value of the operand, in this case, is limited to the n bits assigned to the operand field.

These four address modes must be recognized by the control unit, which accesses the memory in a different way according to the various methods. One possibility would be to define operations with different names (and therefore different operational codes) in the machine language, corresponding to the different address modes. At machine-language level, we could, for example, have the following instructions:

loada	ind1	for direct addressing
loaddefa	ind1	for deferred (indirect) addressing
loadinda	ind1	for index register addressing
loadimma	ind1	for immediate addressing

However, this would lead to a vast increase in the number of machine language instructions (analogous definitions would be required for the loadb, storea, storeb, read and write instructions).

Considering the format of the instructions again, it is possible to adopt a better solution, which allows the processing unit both to recognize the current address mode and to retrieve the operand correctly. This can be done by introducing, into the instruction itself, a part that indicates the address mode of the operand. For this purpose, we divide the machine language instructions into three parts: the operational code, the address mode of the operand and the operand. If s is the length of the instruction, m the number of bits for the operational code, i the number of bits for the address mode of the operand and n the number of bits for the operand (where $s = m + i + n$), the number of address modes that the machine can recognize is less than or equal to 2^i. Having introduced four address modes, they are well represented by two bits:

00	direct addressing
01	indirect addressing
10	addressing via the index register
11	immediate addressing

If, for example, the first instruction of the multiplication program shown in Table 14.3 involved addressing via the index register, it would be represented as follows (the value referring to the address mode is in bold):

Main memory cell's number	Operational code	Mode field	Operand field
0	0100	**10**	0000001000

14.8 Assembler language

Programs in machine language use operational codes and addresses in binary format, as illustrated in Table 14.3. It is obvious that reading a program and understanding its meaning is rather difficult.

In order to solve this kind of problem, as we underlined in Chapter 3, *high-level* programming languages were invented. Not by chance, this term indicates the need to put a vast distance between the machine code (which operates directly on the machine), and programming languages, which do not depend on the architecture of the machine and, therefore, on the presence of registers. By using high-level languages, the programmer *abstracts* from a series of details and concentrates on the production of readable and correct programs.

However, whatever level of abstraction the user chooses, the executable code is always written in machine language. The higher the level of abstraction, the more complex the programs that translate from **source code**, written by the user in a high-level language, to **object code**, written in machine language. The programs that perform the translation (compilers and interpreters) are part of the programming environment, briefly discussed in Section 1.4.5.

However, sometimes it is appropriate to program in a language as close as possible to machine language. In fact, programs produced by translating high-level languages can be relatively inefficient compared to programs written in machine language. The need for a low-level programming language is satisfied by the so-called **assembler languages**.

The instructions of an assembler language correspond directly to the instructions of a machine language; therefore, the expressive capacities of the languages are exactly the same. Assembler languages differ from machine languages in a few important features:

(1) The instruction codes are expressed symbolically; therefore, in assembler language it is legitimate to write the instructions `LOADA` or `WRITE` without having to remember their binary encoding.

(2) References to program instructions or memory cells containing data are made by labels, that is, again symbolically. In this way, it is not necessary to indicate the specific addresses of memory cells in the programs; it is sufficient to refer to labels placed in the program in certain corresponding positions.

(3) The address modes that the program uses are also expressed symbolically.

In a program written in assembler language we therefore find explicit instructions `LOAD`, `STORE`, `READ`, `WRITE`, `ADD`, `JUMP` and so on, as illustrated in Table 14.1. The address mode is also indicated in the assembler language by means of suitable indications on the `LOAD`, `STORE`, `READ`, `WRITE`, `JUMP` and `JUMPZ` instructions (the ones which are followed by an operand). For instance, for the `LOAD` instruction, we have the following alternatives, where `NUM` is a label associated with a memory cell:

- `LOADA NUM`
  which loads into the A register the value contained in the cell labelled `NUM` (direct addressing).

- LOADA @NUM

  which loads into the A register the value contained in the memory cell whose address is contained in the cell labelled NUM (indirect addressing).

- LOADA NUM(I)

  which loads into the A register the value contained in the cell whose address is obtained by adding to NUM the value contained in the I register (addressing via the index register).

- LOADA #NUM

  which loads into the A register the value of the label NUM (immediate addressing).

The translation of the above instructions into machine language is as follows (assuming that the label NUM corresponds to address 9):

	Operational code	*Mode field*	*Operand field*
LOADA NUM:	0000	00	0000001001
LOADA @NUM:	0000	01	0000001001
LOADA NUM(I):	0000	10	0000001001
LOADA #NUM:	0000	11	0000001001

The translation of the instructions into machine language shows the binary code of address 9 in the 10 lowest-order bits, the binary code of the address mode in the next two bits, and the binary code of the LOADA operation (0000) in the four highest-order bits.

Table 14.4 shows the multiplication program written in assembler language. Note the use of the words READ, LOADA, LOADB, MUL, STOREA, WRITE and HALT to represent the various instructions; we used these same keywords for describing the program in the machine-language example (shown in Table 14.2), but there the use of symbolic names was inappropriate: we should have used their binary encoding. However, at this point Table 14.2 can be 'read' as an example of use of assembler language. Table 14.4 rewrites the program of Table 14.2 in assembler language.

A program written in assembler language has to be translated into machine language before it can be executed. This function is carried out by a specific translator, called an **assembler**, which translates the keywords into operational codes and the labels into addresses.

Note that the use of symbolic names as labels, instead of absolute or relative addresses of memory cells, facilitates the loading of the program into any position in memory, not necessarily a fixed position. This kind of loading operation is called **relocation** and is carried out by the operating system (see Chapter 15).

The labels assigned to memory cells must obviously all be distinct; when we use a label to refer to a memory cell in the data area, we give a variable of the program a symbolic name.

We saw in Part I that generally speaking, in any programming language, a program's data is classified into *constants* (which do not change during processing)

Table 14.4 The multiplication program in assembler language.

Main memory cell's number	Operational code	Operand field
	READ	X
	READ	Y
	LOADA	X
	LOADB	Y
	MUL	
	STOREA	X
	WRITE	X
	HALT	
X	INT	
Y	INT	

and *variables* (which can change value). Each constant or variable has its own *type* (for example, integer or real) and its own *symbolic name*.

In the example in Table 14.4, the symbolic names X and Y correspond to two variables of integer type. They also correspond to two memory cells defined to contain integers. In this example, there is a one-to-one correspondence between variables and memory cells (each variable corresponds to a memory cell and vice versa); in general, this correspondence may be more complex (for example, more than one memory cell is used to store a C double or float variable). Later on, we will also see memory cells reserved for constants, that is, values which do not change during processing.

14.9 Examples of programs in assembler language

Let us now look at three examples of small programs written in our assembler language: the calculation of multiplications as sequences of sums (Example 14.1), the inversion of a sequence of numbers (Example 14.2) and the update of data concerning an employee (Example 14.3). To emphasize the relationship between high-level programming features and our assembler language, a C version of each program is given before the assembler version.

EXAMPLE 14.1 Multiplication as a sequence of sums

This program is a variation of the program discussed in Section 14.8. Here, we again calculate the product of two numbers (assumed to be positive), but for teaching purposes we assume that the computer cannot execute a multiplication instruction; therefore, multiplication has to be carried out as an appropriate sequence of sums.

```
#include <stdio.h>
main()
{
  int        x,y,z;

  scanf("%d", &x);
  scanf("%d", &y);
  z = 0;
  while (x > 0)
  {
    x = x - 1;
    z = z + y;
  }
  printf("%d\n", z);
}
```

Figure 14.6 C program for multiplication using a sequence of sums.

The program uses three variables: X, Y and Z. X and Y, as before, contain the input values. At the end of the program, Z contains the output value produced by the program: Z = X * Y. In order to obtain the result, it is necessary to increment Z by Y at each iteration of a loop executed exactly X times. For this reason, X is decremented by one in each iteration; the end of loop condition is that X is equal to zero. The C program corresponding to this algorithm is shown in Figure 14.6.

To express the same algorithm with our assembler language, we must transform the assignments into appropriate numerical operations, preceded by load instructions and followed by store instructions; also, the tests of the conditions have

```
              READ      X
              READ      Y
              LOADA     #0
              STOREA    Z
TEST          LOADA     X
              JUMPZ     END
              LOADB     #1
              DIF
              STOREA    X
              LOADA     Z
              LOADB     Y
              ADD
              STOREA    Z
              JUMP      TEST
END           WRITE     Z
              HALT
X             INT
Y             INT
Z             INT
```

Figure 14.7 Assembler program for multiplication using a sequence of sums.

to be transformed in such a way that they can be executed via the conditional branch instruction JUMPZ.

To make the program execute correctly, the assembler program reserves three memory cells to store variables, labelling them X, Y and Z. Note that the immediate address mode is used to initialize the variable Z with value 0 and the contents of register B with the value 1, in order to decrement the variable X.

The resulting program is shown in Figure 14.7. We invite the reader to follow the execution of the program step by step, using specific input values (for example, 3 and 5) to see the effect of each instruction and the program as a whole. To follow the execution of the program, it is useful to follow the evolution of the contents of the memory cells corresponding to the variables X, Y and Z. We also suggest translating the program, or some of its instructions, into a sequence of micro-instructions.

EXAMPLE 14.2 Inversion of a sequence of numbers

We want to write a program that reads a sequence of numbers, terminated by a zero, and prints the numbers in the opposite order to that in which they were read. This example is introduced to show the relationship between index variables for arrays in high-level programming languages and the index register address mode in an assembler language.

The C program is listed in Figure 14.8 and its assembler version in Figure 14.9. The assembler program starts by reading a number from the terminal: if the first number read equals zero, the program execution immediately stops, otherwise, two loops follow:

```c
#include <stdio.h>
main()
{
    int      Count, Num;
    int      Memo[100];

    Count = 0;
    scanf("%d", &Num);
    while(Num != 0)
    {
        Memo[Count] = Num;
        Count = Count + 1;
        scanf("%d", &Num);
    }
    Count = Count - 1;
    while(Count >= 0)
    {
        printf("%d\n", Memo[Count]);
        Count = Count - 1;
    }
}
```

Figure 14.8   The C version of the program to invert a sequence of *n* numbers.

- In the first loop, the numbers are read and stored in memory in order of arrival. Cell MEMO and the following $n - 1$ cells are used to store the values read.

- In the second loop, the n numbers are written starting with the last cell and going back to the first.

- Cell MEMO and the following cells (MEMO+1), (MEMO+2), ..., (MEMO+99) are available to contain the array elements.

- Cell NUM contains the number which was last read.

```
                    LOADA        #0
                    STOREA       COUNT
                    READ         NUM
                    LOADA        NUM
                    JUMPZ        END

LOOP1               LOADI        COUNT
                    STOREA       MEMO(I)
                    LOADA        COUNT
                    LOADB        #1
                    ADD
                    STOREA       COUNT
                    READ         NUM
                    LOADA        NUM
                    JUMPZ        CONTINUE
                    JUMP         LOOP1

CONTINUE            LOADA        COUNT
                    LOADB        #1
                    DIF
                    STOREA       COUNT

LOOP2               LOADI        COUNT
                    WRITE        MEMO(I)
                    LOADA        COUNT
                    JUMPZ        END
                    LOADB        #1
                    DIF
                    STOREA       COUNT
                    JUMP         LOOP2

END                 HALT

COUNT               INT
NUM                 INT
MEMO                INT
MEMO+1              INT
...
MEMO+99             INT
```

Figure 14.9 The assembler version of the program to invert a sequence of n numbers.

- Cell CONT contains the value of the counter which is incremented during the read loop and decremented during the write loop (the index variable of the C program).

In the program, we find the instructions STOREA MEMO(I) and WRITE MEMO(I) which use the index register address mode. They operate on the memory cell p whose address is obtained by algebraically adding the value of the label MEMO (corresponding to an address) to the value contained in the index register I. STOREA MEMO(I) copies the contents of the A register into cell p; WRITE MEMO(I) prints the contents of cell p. We also find the instruction LOADI COUNT which assigns to the I register the value contained in the memory cell with address COUNT. LOADI extends the set of instructions allowed in our assembler language; its binary code (and therefore, its representation in machine language) is 1111.

The program is designed in such a way that cell MEMO and the following 99 cells are ready to store integers; therefore, the program works correctly only if the number of integers read in is less than 100 (as happens with the fixed length of the array in the C program). In the first loop (read loop) the data is read into cell NUM and transferred into cell MEMO or into the cells immediately following MEMO if its value is not 0; the loop is terminated when a zero is read. In the second loop (write loop), the data is printed starting with the last element of the array and 'going back' towards the first element, thus producing the inverted sequence.

EXAMPLE 14.3 Update the salary of an employee

In our third example, we write a program which updates the salary of two employees, named Bob and Lucy. The example illustrates the relationship between pointer variables in high-level programming languages and the indirect address mode in an assembler language.

Suppose that each employee is associated with a structure containing information about the employee, and that each structure can be referenced, in the C version of the program, through a pointer variable named after the employee (Bob, Lucy and so on). The C program also defines two constants (named FirstInc and SecondInc) used for updating the salaries of the two employees. Figure 14.10 shows the relevant part of the C code.

The assembler program, shown in Figure 14.11, is a rather 'liberal' translation of the C program. The program initializes the two pointer variables BOB and LUCY with the address of the cell containing, respectively, Bob's salary and Lucy's salary. This effect can be obtained by the following two pairs of instructions below (note that an immediate address mode is used to guarantee that the address of the proper cell is assigned as the value):

```
LOADA     #BOBSAL
STOREA    BOB
LOADA     #LUCYSAL
STOREA    LUCY
```

The program continues with the update of salaries. Bob's old salary is contained in the cell pointed to by the variable BOB: its value is loaded into register A through the instruction LOADA @BOB (which means: load register A with the contents of the cell whose address is contained in cell BOB); register B is loaded with the contents of cell FIRSTINC which is initialized with the value 1000 as required by the C program; the result of the addition is copied into the cell pointed to by BOB

```
#include <stdio.h>
main()
{
    typedef  struct  {  int   years;
                        int   salary;
                     }  EMP;
    const    FirstInc = 1000;
    const    SecondInc = 2000;
    EMP      *Bob, *Lucy;
    EMP      BobInfo, LucyInfo;

    Bob = &BobInfo;
    Lucy = &LucyInfo;
    Bob->salary = Bob->salary + FirstInc;
    Lucy->salary = Lucy->salary + SecondInc;
}
```

Figure 14.10 The C version of the program updating employees' salaries.

```
              LOADA       #BOBSAL
              STOREA      BOB
              LOADA       #LUCYSAL
              STOREA      LUCY
              LOADA       @BOB
              LOADB       FIRSTINC
              ADD
              STOREA      @BOB
              LOADA       @LUCY
              LOADB       SECONDINC
              ADD
              STOREA      @LUCY

BOB           INT
LUCY          INT
BOBYEAR       INT
BOBSAL        INT
LUCYYEAR      INT
LUCYSAL       INT
FIRSTINC      1000
SECONDINC     2000
```

Figure 14.11 The assembler version of the program updating employees' salaries.

and this produces the desired update. Lucy's salary is incremented in the same way with the value contained in the constant SECONDINC. Note that the assembler program handles constants by reserving a cell for them and assigning them a value at the beginning of the execution of the program; this does not guarantee that the value remains constant during the execution, as a STORE instruction could change its value.

14.10 Extensions of the von Neumann architecture

The von Neumann architecture which has been used throughout this textbook is just a reference architecture; real computers differ from this simple, 'ideal' structure in several important ways. Indeed, the von Neumann machine architecture illustrated in this book presents several problems, due to the strict sequentiality imposed on all operations:

- programs are executed sequentially, one instruction after the other, even though the programs lend themselves to parallel execution, and
- the CPU sequentially transfers data on the bus to main memory or to other functional components and waits for a sequential answer from slower components (this problem is often called the 'von Neumann bus bottleneck').

Various modifications of the von Neumann architecture have been proposed in the past decades to introduce various forms of parallelism; many of them rely on the existence of several processors within the same computer architecture.

- The first and simplest extension uses **dedicated processors** (or **coprocessors**) capable of executing specific tasks, such as numerical calculus or the presentation of graphics on the screen, very efficiently and in parallel with the CPU.
- A second extension modifies the structure of the processors in such a way that various phases of an instruction can be carried out separately and in parallel. As we saw, each instruction has to be fetched, decoded and executed. Each phase can be assigned to a specific part of the processor: thus while one part of the processor is executing an instruction, the following instruction can be fetched and interpreted by other parts of the processor (this technique is called **pipelining**).
- A third extension uses **hierarchies of memories**, characterized by increasing performance and price. In particular, many computers use **cache memories**, which temporarily store the information most commonly or most recently used by the CPU. With this extension, the memory hierarchy has three levels: mass storage, main memory and cache memory.
- A fourth extension uses dedicated processors (or **input/output channels**) capable of transferring large quantities of data from mass storage to main

memory and vice versa without interfering with the normal functioning of the processing unit.

- Finally, it is possible to construct architectures with multiple independent processors, or **multiprocessor architectures**. In this case, there are many functional units (including processors and memories), connected in various ways. Multiprocessor architectures are described further in Section 14.12.

Several other architectural factors affect the processing speed and capabilities of computers.

- The **size of the registers** determines the amount of data the computer can work on at a given instant. The bigger the register, the faster the computer can process a set of data. The registers in the first personal computers could hold two bytes – 16 bits – each. Most CPUs sold today for personal computers have 32-bit registers.

- The **amount of main memory** (RAM) in a computer can have a significant effect on the computer's processing power. More RAM means that the computer can use bigger, more powerful programs, and that those programs can access bigger data files. More RAM also can make the computer run faster; and indeed the memory available in today's computers is becoming larger and at the same time less expensive. The computer does not need to load an entire program into memory to run it; in Chapter 15, we discuss a technology for memory access, called *virtual memory*, which enables the computer to behave as if the available memory were larger than the real memory. Thus, a computer can execute programs whose size exceeds the physical size of the memory of the computer; however, the more the program can fit into memory, the faster the program will run.

- The computer **system clock** sets the pace for the CPU. Like modern wristwatches, the system clock is driven by a piece of quartz crystal. The molecules in the quartz crystal vibrate millions of times per second, at a rate that never changes. The CPU uses the vibrations of the quartz in the system clock to time its processing operations. Over the years, clock speeds have increased steadily to make computers run faster. The first personal computers operated at 4.77 MHz (*hertz* is a measure of clock pulses per second; *megahertz* – MHz – means 'millions of pulses per second'). Nowadays, speeds of 100 MHz and more are common.

- The width of the **data bus** determines how many bits at a time can be transmitted between the CPU and other devices. The number of lines in the data bus affects the speed at which data can travel between hardware components, just as the number of lanes on the motorway affects how long it takes people to get to their destination. Nowadays 32-bit or 64-bit data buses are used.

- The width of the **address bus** determines the number of bytes of memory the CPU can access. Most of the early personal computers had 20-bit address buses, so that the CPU could address 2^{20} bytes (or 1 Mb). Today, most CPUs have 32-bit address buses that can address 4 Gb (over 4 billion bytes) of memory.

*14.11 CISC and RISC architectures

Many computers are available on the market and different terms are used to distinguish their different sizes and capabilities. Each individual computer can be said to be a microcomputer (or a personal computer), a workstation, a minicomputer, a mainframe or a supercomputer, but the interpretation of these terms is continuously changing, especially concerning their average size and performance. The reason is clear: technological leaps have made computers increasingly powerful, and have enabled this power to be crammed into ever-smaller packages. The shapes, sizes and capabilities of computers described using the above terms have altered radically in the past decade, and their characteristics continue to change.

In this section we describe the main characteristics of the architectural 'design philosophy' of some of the computers available on the market. We note that the evolution of computers has followed a manufacturing strategy called **upward compatibility**. The big computer manufacturers, such as IBM, Digital, Sun and HP, have realized very many computer models during the past three or four decades; however, as they evolved, manufacturers made sure that new models were compatible with previous ones, so that users could buy new computers without having to rewrite their application programs. Compatibility is obtained by gathering various models into computer families, characterized by the same basic architecture. Computers subsequently realized within the same family become more and more powerful with regard to processing speed, addressable memory and grade of parallelism.

Computers can be classified according to the number and complexity of their instruction set, respectively as **CISCs** (Complex Instruction Set Computers) and **RISCs** (Reduced Instruction Set Computers).

14.11.1 CISC architectures

Most microcomputers (personal computers) actually on the market have a CISC architecture, characterized by the following aspects:

- The **instruction set** of the machine language contains a large number of instructions.

- Instructions are syntactically heterogeneous; they can involve zero, one or more operands and different address modes (direct, indirect, via an index register, ...). Operands can be fetched from memory or from registers. These aspects make the processing of each instruction quite complex for the CPU.

- Each instruction can be functionally complex, requiring many micro-instructions and a complex CPU hardware structure for its execution. An increase in the complexity of the CPU generally results in slower execution of each individual instruction by the CPU.

Most of the CISC-architecture CPUs in personal computers are made by two companies: Intel and Motorola. The Intel group of processors is known as the

Table 14.5 The evolution of the Intel 80*x*86 and the Motorola 680*x*0 families.

		Intel processors			
Model	Year introduced	Data-bus width (bits)	Registers size (bits)	Addressable memory	Maximum clock (MHz)
8086	1978	16	16	1 Mb	8
80286	1982	16	16	16 Mb	20
80386	1985	32	32	4 Gb	33
80486	1989	32	32	4 Gb	100
Pentium	1993	64	32	4 Gb	150
Pentium MMX	1997	64	32	4 Gb	266

		Motorola processors			
Model	Year introduced	Data-bus width (bits)	Registers size (bits)	Addressable memory	Maximum clock (MHz)
68000	1979	16	32	16 Mb	8
68020	1984	32	32	4 Gb	16
68030	1987	32	32	4 Gb	32
68040	1989	32	32	4 Gb	40
68060	1993	32	32	4 Gb	66

80*x*86 family' and the Motorola group as the '680*x*0 family'. Table 14.5 shows the evolution of the two processor families.

To underline the technological gap, note that the 486 has approximately 1.2 million transistors; the Pentium has over 3 million transistors, and can process more than 100 million instructions per second. The Pentium instruction set is compatible with those of earlier Intel chips, allowing Pentium-based computers to run all the software written for Intel's other chips, but the Pentium runs application programs approximately five times faster than a 486 processor. Note finally that further improvement in performance has been obtained, in the most recent CISC processors, by extending the traditional von Neumann architecture with cache memory and with a maths coprocessor, specially designed to handle efficiently floating point arithmetic operations (for example, a maths coprocessor and a cache memory controller are combined on a single Intel 486 chip).

Intel processors are used in Intel based personal computers, produced since the 1980s by IBM and many other manufacturers, whereas Motorola processors have been widely used in Apple Macintosh personal computers.

Looking ahead to the operating system which can be used in each computer family, Intel based PCs mainly use the operating systems MS-DOS (Disk Operating System, implemented by Microsoft) or Windows 95. They can also support the OS/2, LINUX and SCO UNIX operating systems; LINUX and SCO UNIX are evolutions of UNIX, which is described in the next chapter together with MS-DOS. Windows 95 is described in Section 19.2.

Apple Macintosh personal computers use the MacOS 8 operating system. The Motorola chips are used by companies that build larger, UNIX-based computers (for example, NCR's Tower series and AT&T's 3B series). Finally, we mention the IBM

AS/400, one of the most widespread computer families, which has a CISC processor and is mainly used for data management applications.

14.11.2 RISC architectures

Recently, a new philosophy has been adopted by computer architecture designers. RISCs (Reduced Instruction Set Computers) are characterized by a reduced set of simple instructions all in the same format and by a small number of address modes.

These instructions are the most frequently used ones, and they are carefully optimized at the design stage, using a large number of working registers and reducing access to main memory to a minimum. Furthermore, the instructions generated by a compiler for a RISC machine are directly executed and need not be interpreted via microcode. These characteristics combine, according to supporters of this approach, to make RISC architectures faster than traditional CISC architectures with many instructions, most of them hardly ever used.

In the design of a RISC the time required to load the operands from their registers, process them in the ALU and store the result in a register (called the **data cycle time**) is optimized. During the design phase of a RISC, only those operations that can be executed in one data cycle are included in its instruction set. The exceptions to this rule are the memory access instructions (reduced to the minimum owing to the large number of registers) and the branch instructions. Through the introduction of pipeline techniques and the use of particular techniques during the compilation of high-level programming languages into machine code, it is possible to reduce the instructions that require more than one cycle to a minimum. By eliminating microcode and optimizing the fetch time it is possible to reach the high processing speeds typical of RISCs.

SPARC (developed by Sun), ALPHA (developed by Digital), PowerPC (developed by Motorola) and MIPS are widespread RISC CPUs, used in many workstations: many IBM workstations use the Motorola PowerPC or the IBM RISC processor Power2, Sun uses the SPARC processor, and Digital uses the ALPHA processor.

The influence of this new philosophy on performance has been so great that the term 'workstation' is actually often used to identify computers that have a RISC architecture and support the UNIX operating system (see Chapter 15). But a RISC CPU is also found in some personal computers, such as the Apple Macintosh PowerPC which uses a Motorola PowerPC processor.

14.11.3 Comparison between CISC and RISC architectures

The debate between the CISC and RISC philosophies is still open: it is difficult to evaluate the speed and importance of such different architectures correctly, because of the number of factors that come into play in the comparison (including efficiency

Table 14.6 A comparison between the von Neumann architecture used for teaching purposes (MvN), CISC and RISC architectures.

	MvN	Intel 80386	Motorola 68030	MIPS	SPARC
Classification	–	CISC	CISC	RISC	RISC
Number of registers	3	8	16	32	32
Length of words	16	32	32	32	32
Instruction formats	1	many	many	3	4
Address modes	4	8	18	3	4
Maximum number of operands per instruction	1	2	2	3	3
Logical address space (bytes)	2^{16}	2^{46}	2^{32}	2^{31}	2^{32}
Presence of a cache memory on chip	no	no	yes	controller	no
Presence of a coprocessor for floating point operations	no	yes	yes	yes	yes
Other coprocessors	0	0	1	2	1
Pipeline steps	0	3	3	5	4

with respect to the different programming languages available, the possibility of constructing families of computers with different performances and costs suitable for heterogeneous applications, the ease of compiler construction with respect to the resources provided by the architecture and so on). The comparison is also complicated by the fact that today's CISCs have to respect the limitations imposed by the need to remain 'compatible' with earlier machines.

Reconsidering the arguments presented in this chapter, we can now compare the architecture of the von Neumann machine presented here for teaching purposes with some real architectures, as shown in Table 14.6. For this comparison, we take two CISC processors (Intel 80386 and Motorola 68030) and two RISC processors (SPARC, MIPS). In the table the von Neumann machine used for teaching purposes is named MvN.

*14.12 Parallel architectures

Parallel machines have a **multiprocessor architecture**: they have multiple independent functional units, including processors and memories, connected in various ways.

In order to describe a **parallel architecture**, it is necessary to analyse the nature, dimensions and number of processing elements and memory modules, and the strategy used for connecting processors and memories. The processing elements can be simple ALUs or complete CPUs. Some parallel architectures are designed to carry out independent tasks simultaneously; they include complete CPUs working in parallel and executing different programs, possibly sharing portions of memory. Some architectures execute a single task that consists of parallel processes; some are characterized by a high degree of pipelining and the presence of many ALUs which allow parallel processing of data (think, for example, of the parallel processing of vector data).

A widely used scheme for the classification of architectures was defined by Flynn[1] in 1972. A machine may have one or more instruction streams and one or more data streams. The von Neumann machine belongs to the **SISD (Single Instruction Single Data)** category. It has one CPU and thus one program counter register and a single stream of instructions. Furthermore, it has only one ALU and, therefore, a single data stream.

Machines belonging to the **SIMD (Single Instruction Multiple Data)** category also have just one control unit which executes one instruction at a time, but they have several ALUs to execute that instruction simultaneously on different sets of data. The following are examples of SIMD machines:

- the ILLIAC IV: the world's most powerful computer in the 1970s, used by NASA for problems of intensive calculus;

- the Connection Machine: the computer with the largest number of processors ever built, designed by W. Daniel Hills in 1985 for symbolic processing in artificial intelligence;

- the Cray-1: the first supercomputer designed to execute fast floating point calculations.

The ALUs which operate in parallel may be simple, as in the case of the Connection Machine which is designed to process only symbolic data in parallel, or very complex, as in the case of the Cray. The processing speed that characterizes supercomputers is also obtained by using pipeline techniques.

MIMD (Multiple Instruction Multiple Data) machines are composed of many independent CPUs which operate as parts of a bigger system. Within this category, a distinction is sometimes made between **multicomputers** (machines each with their own memory) and **multiprocessors** (machines which access the same, shared main memory).

Two CPUs with **disjoint memory** communicate by sending each other messages (see Chapter 17). Two CPUs with **shared memory** can have either a physical or a logical sharing. When two CPUs share the same *physical* memory, one can read memory words written by the other one. Figure 14.12 shows four different configurations of MIMD architectures with memory physically shared via a bus; three of them also use cache memory.

Logical memory sharing can be realized in the following way: at a hardware level, the CPUs exchange messages, but this exchange is hidden by the higher levels, so that the programmer sees and addresses one logical memory shared by the various processors.

[1] Flynn M.J. (1972). Some computer organizations and their effectiveness. *IEEE Trans. on Computers*, **C-21**, 948–60

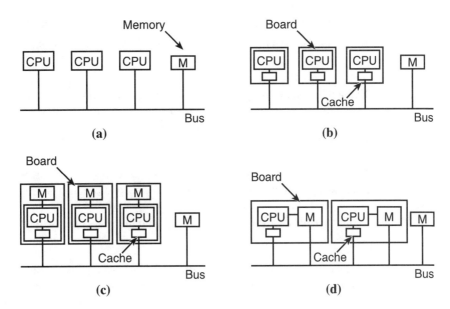

Figure 14.12 Four different configurations of MIMD architectures with memory shared via a bus.

Hypercubes and many transputers are examples of MIMD machines with disjoint memory, whereas the IMB RP3 prototype (designed in 1989 to connect 512 nodes) and the NYU Ultracomputer (designed in 1989 to connect 4096 CPUs to a large number of memory modules) are examples of MIMD machines with shared memory.

There are also alternative models to the von Neumann architecture, all characterized by highly parallel processing; that is, the instruction execution model is not sequential. Among these, let us mention **dataflow machines**, in which the execution of operations is dictated by the flow of data produced as a result of the computations, and **systolic machines**, in which the execution of operations is carried out by synchronizing the activities of many processors whose behaviour in processing input data and producing output data is similar to the circulation of blood around the body.

Exercises

14.1 Based on the register structure of the processing unit described in Section 14.1, describe the execution of the following instructions:

(a) `jumpgtz ind1`, jump to address `ind1` if register A contains a positive number;

(b) `jumpgez ind1`, jump to address `ind1` if register A contains a positive number or zero;

(c) `jumpltz ind1`, jump to address `ind1` if register A contains a negative number;

(d) `jumplez ind1`, jump to address `ind1` if register A contains a negative number or zero.

14.2 Explain how a machine supporting a language that contains instructions with three operands can execute the instruction `jumpgt ind1 ind2 ind3` which causes a jump to address `ind3` if the number contained in address `ind1` is greater than the number contained in address `ind2`.

14.3 Write an assembler program that performs the division of two integers; the program stops without calculating the division if the second operand is zero.

14.4 Write an assembler program that obtains ten integers from the terminal and prints their sum.

14.5 Write an assembler program that obtains a variable number of integers from the terminal and prints their sum. Data input terminates when the user enters zero.

14.6 Modify the assembler program that inverts n numbers assuming that the instruction `jumpltz`, described in Exercise 14.1, is available. Note that the new version of the program can be more concise, more efficient and similar to the C program presented in Example 14.2.

14.7 Modify the assembler program that inverts n numbers so that the execution is halted when 100 numbers have been read (remember that 100 cells – from MEM0 to MEM0+99 – have been reserved by the assembler program of Example 14.2 to store the data read). Assume that the instructions described in Exercise 14.1 are available.

14.8 Write an assembler program that obtains a variable number of integers from the terminal and prints the sum of only the even numbers. In order to determine whether a number is even or not, use the remainder of a division by 2. Data input terminates when the user enters zero. Assume that the instructions described in Exercise 14.1 are available.

14.9 Write an assembler program that executes a multiplication as a sequence of sums, assuming that the input may contain negative integers. Assume that the instructions described in Exercise 14.1 are available.

14.10 Write an assembler program that finds the greatest of ten numbers read from the terminal. Assume that the instructions described in Exercise 14.1 are available.

14.11 Design an assembler language in which the instructions have three addresses (for example, `sum ind1 ind2 ind3`, which executes the sum of the numbers stored in cells ind1 and ind2 and stores the result in cell ind3). Show the micro-instructions that correspond to each instruction of the language and reprogram some of the above exercises using this more powerful language.

*14.12 Develop a program that realizes an interpreter of the assembler language illustrated. The interpreter reads the program to be executed from one file (each statement is made up of an operational code and address fields) and the data on which the program is to operate from another file. The results are written to the Standard Output.

The operating system

15

The operating system is a software layer that operates directly on the hardware, isolating the users from the details of the hardware architecture and providing them with high-level functionalities. By means of the operating system, the user can perform functionalities such as running a program or copying a file; the operating system performs the required actions in order to load programs into main memory, execute them, read data from and write data to mass memory, perform input/output operations with peripherals and so on. Thus, the operating systems make the computer architectures, as described in Chapter 14, fully available to users.

An operating system can be **single-user**, when the entire system (typically a personal computer) is dedicated to a single user, or **multi-user**, when several users share the same system; in a multi-user system, the operating system hides the presence of other users, giving each user the impression that the whole system (CPU, memory and peripherals) is dedicated.

The operating system is rather complex, especially in a multi-user context. In order to make its organization easier and at the same time isolate the various components of the system from each other, the operating system is typically functionally layered, with an 'onion skin' architecture; each functional layer realizes a **virtual machine**, that is, a machine which hides the features of the hardware and offers its users a well-defined set of functions. Such an organization guarantees a modular structure for the operating system, in which each module exports some functionalities to the outside and keeps its own implementation mechanisms within. Usually, each virtual machine appears to be more powerful than the corresponding physical machine, because it offers the illusion of being dedicated, whereas, in fact, the physical machine is shared by the users.

This chapter illustrates the features of multi-user operating systems, starting with a description of their overall organization and the functionalities offered by the various layers: process management, memory management, input/output with peripherals and file management. These layers are then illustrated separately, and special attention is given to a description of the first two, which involve mechanisms that are very general and also interesting from a teaching perspective. When describing the file system, we refer to user-level commands available for MS-DOS and UNIX, two of the most popular operating systems.

The chapter concludes with an extended example on UNIX, a widely used operating system; we focus on process management and on the UNIX file system, to exemplify the internal structures of these two important components of an operating system in a concrete case. UNIX makes available to its users a small number of well-defined, standardized, basic functions, available on a variety of different machines. Indeed, the wide availability of UNIX is the primary reason for its success.

15.1 Operating system functions

In this section, we summarize the main functions performed by the operating system; these are described in more detail throughout this chapter. Figure 15.1 shows the layered organization of the operating system. Starting from the bottom, it includes five layers.

(1) The **process manager** (or **nucleus**) is responsible for managing the CPU and deciding how programs are executed. With several users, each one interested in the execution of a specific program, the process manager must enable their almost simultaneous execution; thus the process manager decides which process should use the CPU. Further, the process manager is responsible for reacting to events outside the CPU (signals from the peripherals), which indicate how the computer communicates with the external world.

This layer offers to higher layers a virtual machine in which each program operates as if it had a fully dedicated CPU. Note that even when a system has multiple CPUs, as in the parallel architectures discussed in Section 14.12, these are normally shared between many more users, and therefore all CPUs must be managed by this operating system component.

(2) The **memory manager** is responsible for allocating memory and partitioning it among the various programs that need it. In fact, in a multi-user system, it is necessary for many programs to be present in memory at the same time, so that their pseudo-simultaneous execution can take place. This layer offers to higher layers a virtual machine in which each program operates as if it had a dedicated memory.

(3) The **drivers** are responsible for the input/output operations involving peripherals; drivers are programs which perform input/output operations for a specific device. This layer offers its users an abstract picture which hides the hardware features of the peripherals; the user has available a set of standard, high-level procedures which read input data from and write output data to the peripherals. In this case, too, each program operates as if it had fully dedicated peripherals.

User programs
Command interpreter activation of user or system programs
File system control and management of file access
Peripherals management management of input/output from/to peripherals
Memory management allocation and management of memory
Process management (nucleus) process and interrupt management
Physical machine

Figure 15.1 'Onion skin' architecture of the operating system; each layer corresponds to a virtual machine.

(4)   The **file system** is responsible for managing files in mass storage; it structures data into files, organizes them into **directories** (collections of files) and provides the user with a set of high-level functions to operate on both files and directories, hiding the operations which are actually performed in order to allocate mass storage and to access it in read or write mode. Through the file system, users can organize their own area of mass storage and be sure that their files are adequately protected from external access; the file system may allow some files to be shared by several users.

(5)   Finally, the **command interpreter** allows the user to activate programs (for example, to run an editor); in order to run a program, the command interpreter performs a set of operations which are transparent to the user, such as:

(a)   access the program, typically resident in mass storage, via the file system;

(b)   allocate memory and load the program, via the memory manager;

(c)   activate a process, via the process manager.

Note that the command interpreter uses the layered structure of the operating system: it can request the execution of all the functions on lower layers. In some cases, the command interpreter is not included in the operating system, but rather in the application's lowest level, called the application manager. We do not describe this layer further.

The first three layers of the operating system, dedicated to process management, memory management and device drivers, constitute the **kernel** of the operating system.

The operating system attempts to make choices that better satisfy the users; when many users are terminal operators requesting services (for example, in the account management system of a bank), this objective is often to reduce waiting time at the terminals. The operating system tries to optimize the performance of the computer system, defining the best management strategies for each kind of resource. A user is affected by the presence of other users proportionally to the **load** of the system, that is, with the growth of the demands made by all the users; the system slows down and the response time becomes longer. In particular, a computer system can become **overloaded**; that is, it can be subjected to an excessive number of demands.

15.2 Process management

The term 'process' refers to the execution of a program on a processor; therefore, a process is a *dynamic* object which evolves with time, as opposed to a program, which is a *static* object which does not vary with time. More appropriately, a process P is a set of two elements (E,S), comprising the **executable code** E of the program and the **state** S of the process, that is, the collection of all values in main memory and in the registers of the CPU; the program counter (PC) register indicates the next instruction to be executed. Within the operating system context, the CPU that executes the processes is called a **processor**. The standard von Neumann architecture includes only one processor, but in practice, as illustrated in Sections 14.10 and 14.12, many computers use an evolution of the von Neumann architecture characterized by the presence of several processors. In what follows, we assume for simplicity that the processor is unique, but most of the considerations of this section apply equally in the context of multiprocessor machines when each process can be assigned at random to any processor.

The correspondence between programs and processes is not necessarily one to one. The same program could be associated with several processes, each process performing one task required by the program. For example, a program can be broken up into three parts, one each for data acquisition, processing and printing of results; each one of these parts can be associated with a different process. More commonly, the same executable program could be associated with several processes, when different copies of the same process are executed by different users.

There are also special programming languages, called **concurrent languages**, in which each program involves executing several processes, each of which executes a specific task; the processes belonging to the same program must cooperate with each other, synchronizing their execution. In the rest of this section, we make the additional simplifying hypothesis that each program is associated with exactly one process; the mechanisms described do, however, have general validity.

In summary, we assume that a program being executed by a given user is associated with a process and that the system has a single processor. Processes can be in three distinct **states**: executing, ready and waiting. Given our assumptions, only one of the processes can be **executing** at a given moment, that is, can be executed by the processor. When a given process is executing, we say that the processor is assigned to that process. All other processes are either **ready** or **waiting**: the former can immediately proceed to execution if the process manager so decides, while the latter are waiting for an external event (for example, data from an I/O device) before they can move to the ready state. The three states of a process are shown in Figure 15.2. In the next two subsections, we show the mechanisms that allow a process to change its state, and in this way we describe the various connections between states illustrated in Figure 15.2.

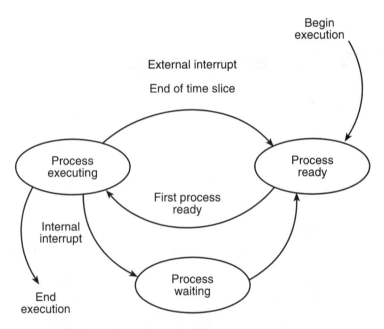

Figure 15.2   Description of process evolution via a state/transition diagram.

15.2.1 Internal interrupts

In the course of its evolution, the process in execution may need the execution of input/output operations, involving a peripheral; in such a case, the execution of the process is interrupted and the kernel becomes active. This is called an **internal interrupt** (that is, it is generated within the process, in a synchronous way) to differentiate it from a second type of interrupt, called an *external interrupt*, which we consider later. The process subject to an internal interrupt goes from 'in execution' status to 'waiting' status. The internal interrupt corresponds to the execution of a specific instruction, called a **Supervisor Call** (SVC), which shifts the processor from the execution of a user process to the execution of an operating system process.

The need to suspend the process in execution when it requires an input/output operation follows the logic of efficient resource management. There is, in fact, a significant difference between the execution time of the instructions in main memory (which take only microseconds) and the execution time of input/output operations involving peripherals, which may take several milliseconds (when mass storage is involved) or even several seconds (when waiting for input from a terminal). It is therefore not useful to keep the processor assigned to a process which will in any case have to wait for the end of an input/output operation before being able to continue.

The suspension must take place so as to allow the process to restart its activity from exactly the same point and with the same data. For this reason, it is necessary to save its **context**, that is, the contents of the processor registers, including the program counter, into an appropriate memory area, called a **process descriptor**. Before the execution of this process can continue, the opposite operation is required, called **context restore**, which consists in copying the process descriptor into the processor registers. In this way, the process continues its execution from exactly the point where it was suspended.

After the context saving of the process that was running is completed, the process manager chooses one of the processes in the ready state and puts it into the executing state; note that several processes can be ready at the same time, and each of them can be assigned to the processor. The context of the selected process is restored, so that its execution can continue from the instruction stored in the memory address pointed to by the program counter register. The overall operation of suspending a process, saving its status, selecting another ready process, restoring its status and activating it is called **context switching**.

15.2.2 External interrupts

We must now analyse the circumstances that allow a waiting process to return to ready status, after it has been suspended by an input/output operation. Such circumstances apply when a peripheral has finished executing the operation; for example, if the operation is getting some input from a terminal, the operation is finished when the data register of the peripheral's interface contains a character that needs to be transferred into memory. When this happens, the normal execution of processes must be interrupted, to allow the input/output operation to be completed and to create the conditions for the waiting process to start up again. This mechanism is called an **external interrupt**. These interrupts are asynchronous events, that is, events which are not coordinated with the other events occurring within the processor. In this way, the computer coordinates with the external world by means of its peripheral devices.

In order to notify the processing unit that these external events are taking place, the processor has a register, called the **interrupt register** (INTR, described in Section 2.3). The INTR has several positions, each one corresponding to a different source of interrupt signal. By convention, the value 1 indicates the presence of the event, while the value 0 indicates its absence; thus, peripherals must simply change the value of their respective bits from 0 to 1, to indicate that an external event has occurred. The presence of an interrupt condition is checked by the CPU via electronic circuits which calculate the logical OR of all the bits of the register. In this way, the test for the presence of an interrupt is conceptually reduced to the checking of one bit; this checking is done during the normal functioning of the computer, by inserting it in the fetch phase (described in Section 2.4).

When an external interrupt condition occurs, the kernel is called into action. It saves the context of the active program (which switches from executing status to ready status) and calls up one of its subroutines, the **interrupt manager**. This subroutine executes the operations required to handle the particular interrupt; for example, if the interrupt signals the presence of input data in the data register PDR of the interface of a peripheral corresponding to a read operation requested by a process P1, the interrupt manager program transfers the data in the PDR into memory and modifies the status of the process P1, which is switched from waiting to ready status. When the interrupt manager has finished, the kernel selects one of the ready processes (not necessarily the program that was active before the interruption) and executes it.

Figure 15.2 sums up the evolution of a process as described in this section. An executing process can be suspended by an internal interrupt, generated by the process itself (in which case it switches to the waiting state), or by an external interrupt (in which case it switches to the ready state). A process can also be suspended (**pre-empted**) by the kernel after a given amount of time so as to guarantee all processes equal use of the CPU. The supervisor program selects the process to be executed, which goes into the executing state. Finally, when the external event expected by a process takes place, the process switches from the waiting to the ready state. Figure 15.2 is a typical state/transition diagram, in which the nodes represent the possible states of a process and the arcs represent the possible transitions between states.

15.2.3 CPU management strategies

We said that, beyond being suspended because of interrupts, the executing process may be suspended by the kernel itself. The objective is that each user program should be executed within a time approximately proportional to the complexity of the program, without creating injustices.

The simplest strategy is to ensure a rotation of processes, called a **round robin**. The nucleus assigns the processor to a process for a given time interval; when the time interval expires, the executing process is interrupted and rejoins the ready processes. To alternate processes, the nucleus manages a **queue** of ready processes. The queue is managed by assigning the processor to the first process in the queue; when an active process is interrupted because its time interval is exhausted, it moves to the end of the queue of ready processes. Those processes which switch from waiting to ready status are also inserted at the end of the queue.

A queue which works in this way is called FIFO (First In–First Out). Figure 15.2 shows a transition from execution to ready status, corresponding to the end of the allotted time interval.

It should be noted that the time interval allotted to each process must obviously be much longer than the time required for a context switch; otherwise, most of the execution time would be wasted in executing the context switching. However, this time must also be significantly shorter than the program execution time and the average execution time between two input/output requests, otherwise the effect of the round robin strategy is lost.

Thus, the waiting time for the execution of a program becomes more or less proportional to the length of the program itself and to the number of input/output operations requested; the computer system users are therefore handled fairly. Furthermore, breaking up program execution favours the completion of short programs; usually, this strategy maximizes the number of programs completed in a unit of time (called the system **throughput**).

The supervisor may adopt more complex strategies, aimed at maximizing users' satisfaction. For example, if processes have different priorities, it is possible to associate a different queue of ready processes with each priority and take up the first process from the highest priority queue every time. In a safety-critical system, some external signals (for example, engine problems in an aircraft) are much more important than others (for example, failure of the entertainment system). In most data processing applications, low priorities are associated with the so-called **batch jobs**; these are long processes that transform input data into output data without interacting with the user (for example, programs for number crunching or statistical programs or the production of reports).

Such a model assigns priority statically, based on the type of processing executed. Static allocation of priority may cause long delays for low priority processes. There are therefore other more complex methods which dynamically assign priorities to processes, thus ensuring that all processes are eventually executed.

15.2.4 Process synchronization

Processes must be synchronized; this means that they need to coordinate their activity. The simplest way of coordinating them is sequential: when a process terminates, it calls for the activation of another process. More complex synchronizations occur when processes need either to *compete* for some resources, or to *cooperate*.

- One example of competition is provided when two processes simultaneously want to access the same resource, called a **critical resource**, which can only be granted to one process at a time; when two concurrent requests occur, only one of the two requesting processes gains access to the critical resource, and the other must wait for the first to finish using it before being able to access it in turn.

- An example of cooperation is when the nature of two processes is such that each one needs the other in order to evolve. A typical example is the pair of processes *producer/consumer*, where the first produces data (for example, collecting it from a peripheral) while the second consumes it (for example, processing it).

Process synchronization is necessary for both competition and cooperation. It is done through two main mechanisms: the use of specific mechanisms for accessing critical parts of the programs (called **semaphores**) and the use of explicit interprocess communication (by means of **messages**). A description of these mechanisms goes beyond the scope of this book.

15.3 Main memory management

The presence of many programs in main memory is paramount for the concurrent management of many processes. In fact, the programs that are executed by ready processes must, at least partially, reside in main memory. Main memory therefore takes a role very similar to that of the processor: it is a unique resource, usually scarce, which must be shared among the various programs.

Main memory management has to solve a number of problems. First, to allocate programs into memory it is necessary to relocate them. A **relocation** is the transformation of the logical addresses, which are specified within the programs, into physical addresses, corresponding to the memory locations where the programs are loaded. Note that the use of logical addresses within a program is essential to enable the loading of the program in different portions of the memory; as we will see, this property yields efficient memory management. Relocation will be described in Section 15.3.1.

An important mechanism for partitioning main memory and programs is called **pagination**. Main memory is considered by memory management to be partitioned into pages; each page is a contiguous memory area, of a fixed size. Programs are also partitioned into pages and allocated an integer number of pages, not necessarily contiguous. Pagination will be described in Section 15.3.2.

Another mechanism widely used for partitioning main memory and programs is called **segmentation**. During compilation, a program can be segmented into parts which perform different functions (for example, by separating the instructions from data). This logical partition of a program allows memory management to independently load the segments composing a program. Segmentation will be described in Section 15.3.3.

Note that while pages have a fixed length, segments, being semantically meaningful, have variable length. Therefore memory and programs are considered by the memory manager as being partitioned into blocks having either fixed or variable length. Segmentation and pagination are not alternative techniques: in many operating systems they are applied together, as described in Section 15.3.3.

With both pagination and segmentation, the memory manager can give the impression of a **virtual memory**, which can be bigger than the physical one; it is sufficient to allocate more pages or segments than can fit into memory at the same time. The pages or segments which are not currently loaded in memory remain available in mass storage, where the program and related data are stored within suitable files. Thus, a computer system may have a virtual memory of v megabytes and a physical memory of p megabytes, with $v > p$. Virtual memory allows the efficient sharing of memory among multiple programs and enables the execution of those programs whose size s exceeds the size p of the physical memory. Of course, the size s of the program cannot exceed the size v of virtual memory. Further, the address contained in the program must refer to the virtual memory, rather than the physical memory; therefore, physical registers must be suitable for addressing the entire virtual memory. It is the responsibility of the memory manager to convert virtual addresses into physical addresses, as explained below.

Finally, note that memory management must be coordinated with process management. When a process is executed by the kernel, the corresponding program must at least partially reside in memory; more precisely, the pages or segments which are currently being executed or which contain the data currently being addressed must be loaded into memory. If a page or segment is needed by the program and is not present, then the process must be suspended while the page or partition of the program is loaded by the memory manager. Thus, the corresponding process goes from an executing state to a waiting state; it will become ready again when the input/output operations required for bringing the page or the segment into memory have been completed.

15.3.1 Relocation

In order to understand the problems posed by relocation, one must refer to the **programming chain**, that is, the sequence of transformations a source program undergoes before being executed.

(1) The first transformation is performed by the **compiler**, the computer program which transforms a source program module into an object program module. We refer here to **separate compilation**: a program can be broken down into parts, called **modules**, each of which can be compiled separately. In the object program, the names of the variables local to the program module (that is, of the variables defined within it) are translated into **relocatable addresses**, that is, addresses which are expressed logically and independently of the allocation of the program in memory. To make manipulation of the addresses easier, these are computed as though the program had been loaded starting from cell zero. However, references to the variables external to the module, that is, variables which are defined in other program modules, are left in a symbolic format.

(2) The second transformation is produced by the **linker**, which transforms various object modules (obtained by compiling the various modules of the user program separately) into a single executable program; the linker can also connect the user program to utility program libraries, available in the programming

environment of each language. The linker solves references to variables defined externally to each module, changing the residual symbolic addresses into relocatable addresses. The addresses in an executable program can present themselves in two different ways:

(a) in **relocatable format**, that is, computed as though the program is to be loaded into memory starting from cell zero – this is the most common occurrence;

(b) in **absolute format**, that is, computed starting from a specific memory cell – this is a less common case and only happens when memory is statically partitioned and programs are allocated to memory without flexibility.

Other useful information is then associated with each executable program; for example, its size and the position of its first executable instruction (called the **entry point** of the program). If the addresses are in absolute format, the address from which the program must be loaded is also provided.

The system program whose task is to load programs into memory is called the **loader**. If the object program contains absolute addresses, the loader has little room for manoeuvre: it must load the program into a specific memory area. When the object program contains instructions in relocatable format, the loader is responsible for their relocation.

Relocation may take place while the program is loaded into memory, by modifying, instruction by instruction, the addresses which appear in the program; such a process is called **static relocation** and involves a heavy transformation operation being executed on the programs at load time. However, once it has been loaded into memory, the program will have absolute addresses which do not require further processing.

Alternatively, the **dynamic relocation** process does not involve a code conversion (the code is loaded into memory in relocatable format), but it requires the use of a special CPU register (called the **base register**), which stores the address of the first memory cell at which the program was loaded. During program execution, every time memory is accessed, the access address is computed by adding the contents of the base register to the relocatable address, as shown in Figure 15.3.

A second register, called the **dimension register** and containing the size of the program, allows a check to be made that the address generated by the program lies within the space addressable by the program. If the generated address exceeds the value obtained by adding the size of the program to the contents of the base register, an error condition occurs; in this case the operating system aborts the program. Manipulation of the contents of the base register takes place through software or hardware mechanisms (through a device called the **MMU**, **Memory Management Unit**).

Let us now look at the two main techniques for partitioning main memory: segmentation and pagination. These parts are fairly technical and can be skipped; however, they give a good example of fruitful hardware–software interaction.

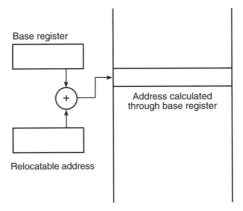

Figure 15.3 The dynamic relocation mechanism.

*15.3.2 Pagination

Partitioning memory by pages is shown in Figure 15.4. A page is a contiguous memory area, of a fixed size equal to 2^p memory cells; given k as the length of the address register and $q = k - p$, memory contains 2^q pages. Programs are also partitioned into pages and allocated an integer number of pages, not necessarily contiguous. This is shown in Figure 15.4(a) where memory is shown partitioned into 16 physical pages, from physical page M_0 (physical page number = 0000) to physical page M_{15} (physical page number = 1111). This situation is described by the **page table** (*see* Figure 15.4(b)) that indicates, for each logical page, whether it is allocated in memory (and if so at which physical page) and where it is stored in mass memory; addresses I_{10} to I_{14} point to mass memory and will be explained in Chapter 16.

Then, each page is dynamically allocated to a program. Let us consider program P_1 which is partitioned into five (logical) pages, from P_{10} to P_{14} (the first index denotes the program, the second index denotes the logical page number). In the particular situation depicted in Figure 15.4(a), pages P_{10}, P_{11}, P_{12} and P_{14} are allocated in memory, while page P_{13} is not. Thus, the program is only partially allocated in memory; in particular, instructions in pages P_{10}, P_{11}, P_{12} and P_{14} can be executed immediately, while the execution of instructions in page P_{13} requires that this page first be loaded into memory.

Relocation occurs as follows. Given an address in relocatable format, we take its most significant q bits; these allow us to identify the logical page number to which the address refers. We then use the table of pages in memory, checking whether the logical page thus selected is resident in memory; let us assume that it is. At this point, a physical page has been selected; the physical page number (q bits) is combined with the relevant address, p bits long, thus obtaining an absolute address

Physical page number   *Main memory*

Physical page number	Main memory
0000	M_0 contains P_{20}
0001	M_1 contains P_{12}
0010	M_2 contains P_{40}
0011	M_3 contains P_{11}
0100	M_4 contains P_{30}
0101	M_5 contains P_{42}
0110	M_6 contains P_{33}
0111	M_7 contains P_{21}
1000	M_8 contains P_{22}
1001	M_9 contains P_{14}
1010	M_{10} contains P_{32}
1011	M_{11} contains P_{23}
1100	M_{12} contains P_{10}
1101	M_{13} contains P_{43}
1110	M_{14} contains P_{31}
1111	M_{15} contains P_{34}

(a)

Logical page number	Allocated in main memory	Physical page number	Mass storage address
0000 (P_{10})	Yes	1100 (M_{12})	I_{10}
0001 (P_{11})	Yes	0011 (M_3)	I_{11}
0010 (P_{12})	Yes	0001 (M_1)	I_{12}
0011 (P_{13})	No	–	I_{13}
0100 (P_{14})	Yes	1001 (M_9)	I_{14}

(b)

Figure 15.4   (a) Partitioning of main memory into pages. (b) Page table for program P_1.

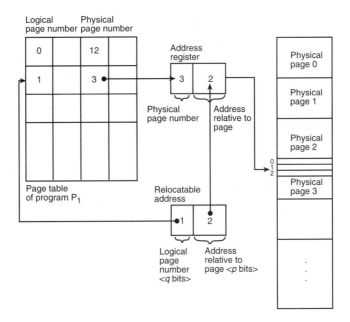

Figure 15.5   Relocation when using pages.

(k bits long). This mechanism is shown in Figure 15.5 with an example that refers to program P_1 and its page table as shown in Figure 15.4(b).

When a program makes a reference to a memory location that is in a page which is not currently loaded into the physical memory, we have a situation called a **page fault**. After a page fault, the process that executes the program must be suspended and set to the waiting state, while it waits for the page to be loaded from mass storage into main memory. The location of the 'missing page' in mass memory is given in the page table.

The main criterion for optimizing memory management consists in reducing the probability of page faults as much as possible. To achieve this, the following strategies are employed:

(1)   The system attempts to load an appropriate number of pages for each program, called the program **working set**. This number of pages should be neither too many (in order not to waste memory) nor too few (in order to avoid frequent page faults).

(2)   After a page fault, one page currently loaded into memory must be downloaded to mass memory to make room for the page which is needed. The system selects a page which has not been recently used and downloads it. This strategy is pragmatically motivated by the principle of **program locality**, which states that a program has a higher probability of accessing in future the pages that have recently been used; thus the least recently used page is the one which is least likely to be accessed in the future, so downloading it will probably not cause another page fault.

*15.3.3 Segmentation

Segmentation can be used as the primary memory management technique, or in addition to pagination. When segmentation is used as the primary technique, the programs are subdivided into segments of arbitrary lengths and each segment is contiguously allocated to memory. Partitioning memory into segments is shown in Figure 15.6(a). Segment M_0 is taken up by the code segment of program P_1, named P_{1C}, segment M_1 is free (not allocated to any program's segment), segment M_2 is taken up by the code segment of program P_2 (P_{2C}), M_3 is taken up by the data segment of program P_1 (P_{1D}), and M_4 is taken up by the data segment of program P_2 (P_{2D}).

Relocation is done by consulting the **segment table**, handled by the memory manager. This table contains, for each segment of a particular program: its dimension, the logical address, the residence in main memory, the physical address and the address in mass storage. Thus, the memory manager can check whether a given portion of the program is loaded into memory, and reacts to the situation when that segment is not resident in memory, called a **segment fault**. Figure 15.6 illustrates that the table of segments contains sufficient information to produce absolute addresses for each instruction.

☛ 1

Segmentation and pagination are not alternative techniques: in many operating systems they are applied together. Programs are first partitioned into segments which perform different functions, and then segments are further subdivided into pages by the memory manager. For instance, the executable code and the data of a program could constitute two different segments, each of which is further divided into pages. This option enables an important optimization when the same program may be executed by multiple users (for instance, the program corresponding to an editor); in this case, the code containing the executable segment could be *shared* by the users, whereas the data must remain distinct (users have their own data). Sharing the code, in process terms, means that each user executes the program with a different state (different register contents, including of course the program counter pointing to the current instruction) and different data; however, many processes may execute the same code.

15.3.4 S mode and U mode memory

Memory must also be assigned to the programs that realize the operating system functions and to their data structures. However, programs belonging to the operating system are special: they may use the entire set of instructions of the computer (while some instructions are not available to other programs), they can be optimally allocated to memory and they must be protected from faults caused by other programs.

For this reason, memory is divided into **S mode memory** (supervisor) and **U mode memory** (user). Operating system programs are loaded into the S mode part and the data structures it uses are created there; user programs are loaded into U mode memory.

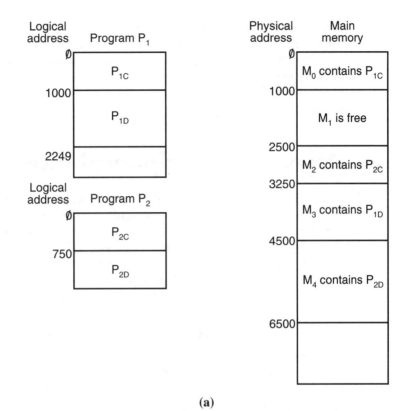

(a)

Segment	Dimension (in words)	Logical address	Allocated in main memory	Physical address	Mass storage address
(P_{1C})	1000	$\emptyset$	Yes	$\emptyset$	I_{1C}
(P_{1D})	1250	1000	Yes	3250	I_{1D}

(b)

Figure 15.6 (a) Partitioning of memory into segments and (b) the segment table of logical images of programs P_1 and P_2 and partitioning program P_1.

If the processor is executing a user process, it is defined as active in **user mode** (U mode); if it is executing a kernel process, it is defined as active in **supervisor mode** (S mode). If the processor is active in S mode, it can access both S and U mode memory areas and has at its disposal a wider set of instructions (it can execute 'privileged' instructions, such as the HALT instruction, made available by the underlying machine). The processor active in U mode, on the other hand, can only access U mode memory areas (and specifically those U mode memory areas where the program associated with the active process was loaded).

This partitioning of memory protects the code and the data structures of the operating system to ensure the correct and efficient sharing of resources. In fact, the instructions of a user program cannot access S mode memory areas, unless they use operating system functions.

15.4 Drivers for peripheral management

Drivers are software mechanisms that are responsible for communicating data to and from the peripherals. Drivers guarantee programs that use them a high-level view, because they normally provide read or write primitives which are independent of the peripherals' hardware structure. For example, in the UNIX system, peripherals are seen as special files, which can be read and written using normal read and write instructions. Obviously, these high-level functions are implemented within the operating system by low-level operations. In particular, we distinguish between:

- **physical drivers** (hardware), which are activated directly by the interrupt manager in order to execute data transfer and manipulation operations;
- **logical drivers** (software), which are part of the operating system and supply a hierarchy of operations, with a layered organization.

Drivers are specifically written for each device, thus we do not describe them further; a description of devices is postponed to Chapters 16 (mass storage) and 19 (user interfaces).

15.5 File management

The portion of the operating system which performs file management, called the **file system**, allows users to create a file, name it, place it in an appropriate area in mass storage and access it for reading or writing. The file system provides transparent file management with respect to the physical features of mass storage components, thus enabling simple users' commands. This section describes file system properties from the user's point of view, disregarding for the moment the mechanisms that guarantee such properties.

Files are placed within structures called **directories** (or **catalogues**), which typically have a hierarchical structure, as shown in Figure 15.7. Thus, each directory contains several files and possibly also several subdirectories; a hierarchical organization is implemented by *trees*, introduced in Chapter 10. This is a simplification of the general case; for instance, UNIX files (or even directories) can belong to multiple directories, thus yielding more general *graph* structures, introduced in Chapter 11.

The whole file system has several directories containing system programs, that is, programs that may be executed by the operating system itself or by several users, and directories containing users' files. Each user is normally associated with a particular directory, called the **home** directory; the user places files either in the home directory or in the directories below it. The name of a user's home directory matches the user's name. In Figure 15.7, the directories *bin* and *dev* contain executable codes of programs or parts of the operating system. The directory *usr*, dedicated to users, contains three directories, each belonging to a different user: the directory *martin* contains two files (*f1* and *f2*) and one directory (*d1*), which in turn contains two files (*f3* and *f4*).

When a file is created, the user specifies the **protections** that apply to the file; that is, it indicates which operations can be performed by each user on the file. Each file has a **pathname** which covers the whole path from the root of the tree to the file. For example, the pathname for *f3* is */usr/martin/d1/f3* (this pathname follows UNIX conventions). Each file or directory within a single directory must have a different name; thus, each complete pathname is unique. A user interacting with the file system has a given **context**, a specific position in the file system (node in the tree). Given that the file system is shaped as a tree, the context can be changed by going up, reaching the node which is immediately above the current context, or down, reaching one of the subdirectories of the current directory.

For instance, in UNIX and MS-DOS, the symbol '.' refers to the current context and the symbol '..' refers to the directory immediately above the current context. When writing a file or directory name, the string relating to the current context may be omitted; for example, the file */usr/martin/d1/f3* may be called *d1/f1*, or *./d1/f1*, within the */usr/martin* context.

The classic functions which are available to file system users include:

- Commands for *creating files*: normally, these are performed by applications or by productivity tools, such as editors and word processors, which immediately put the user in the position of manipulating files.

- Commands for *creating directories*. This command is most often performed directly by the user, who creates a suitable directory structure.

- Commands for *listing* all files contained in a directory. By means of this command, typically a user can read the file's name, its length in bytes, the date and time when it was last written and the current setting of protection controls.

- Commands for *changing context*, by moving up and down in the tree representing the file system. For example, let us consider the command *cd*, which is very similar in MS-DOS and UNIX, with reference to Figure 15.7. When the user *martin* logs on to the system, the context is the directory */usr/martin*; a command *cd d1* changes context, which becomes directory */usr/martin/d1*. The command *cd..* brings the context back to the directory */usr/martin*; the commands *cd..* and *cd hugo* bring the user *martin* into the home directory of the user *hugo*.

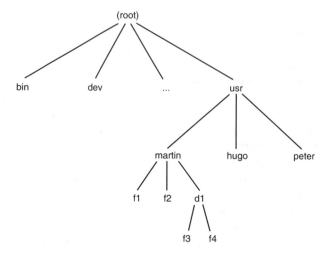

Figure 15.7   Organization of files within directories.

- Commands for *copying* one file into another, or for *appending* a sequence of files in order to create a bigger file that contains all of them.
- Commands for *typing* a file on the screen, possibly by means of subcommands which control the way in which the file is displayed on the screen.
- Commands for *renaming* files; changing file names may be useful to avoid name conflicts.
- Commands for *deleting* files or for *removing* directories. This last operation requires, in general, that the directory is first emptied by deleting all the files in it.

The file system is immediately available to users and therefore quite well known to students; thus, we further exemplify the file system commands of the two most popular operating systems, MS-DOS and UNIX. In both systems, file creation is performed from within applications and productivity tools. In UNIX, the file system commands are as follows:

- **mkdir** creates a directory within the current context,
- **ls** lists files or directories within a directory,
- **cd** switches context,
- **cp** copies one file into another,
- **more** prints a file on the terminal,
- **rm** deletes a file,
- **rmdir** removes a directory.

The organization of files in directories within the MS-DOS operating system follows the tree structure discussed above. There is a slightly different pathname notation, as the separating element between names is a backslash. For example:

$\usr\martin\d1\f3$

The following are typical file system user commands in MS-DOS:

- MD creates a directory within the current context,
- DIR lists files or directories within a directory,
- CD switches context,
- COPY copies one file into another,
- TYPE prints a file on a terminal,
- DEL deletes a file,
- RD removes a directory.

*15.6 Extended example: a look inside UNIX

In this extended example, we look inside UNIX, a popular operating system that was originally developed at AT&T Bell Laboratories in the early 1970s and is now widespread on most hardware platforms. We concentrate on process management and file management; for these two subsystems we present, with many simplifications, the functions made available to high-level programs as well as the main data structures. This extended example, which is rather technical, exemplifies some of the mechanisms which were previously introduced for a generic operating system.

15.6.1 Process management in UNIX

In Section 15.2 we described a process as a pair of elements (E,S), where E denotes the executable code and S denotes the state, that is, the set of values contained in memory and in the CPU registers. We now illustrate functions which are offered by UNIX to higher-level programs, such as programs written in C, for generating processes and for controlling them. The functions enable a process to:

- generate one or more child processes that 'have an independent life' (that is, that can execute a program different from the one associated with the parent process);
- synchronize with them, waiting for completion of their task (and therefore, their termination);
- exchange information with them, sharing appropriate 'data structures'.

In what follows, arguments of functions have the following types: *file_name* of type string; *proc_id* and *status* of type integer; *arg_list* denotes a generic (untyped) list of arguments. The following UNIX functions are provided:

- **Process fork**: `proc_id = fork()`
  Using this function a (parent) process causes the creation of a (child) process. The child process initially possesses the same program E and the same set of values S as the parent. The function `fork` returns to the parent process the value that identifies the child process, while the process identifier of the child is set to 0.

- **Program execution by processes**: `exec(file_name, arg_list)`
  This function replaces, in the process that executes it, the program E with the executable code contained in the file `file_name`. The process then continues, executing a different program. The data of S is only partially replaced.

- **Process termination**: `exit(status)`
  This function terminates execution of a process and provides the parent process with a numerical value that indicates how the child process terminated.

- **Process wait**: `proc_id = wait(status)`
  This function places a parent process in waiting mode, awaiting termination of one of the child processes. When one of the child processes executes an `exit`, the parent process is awakened and the function `wait` returns the identifier of the child process that has been completed, together with the numerical value of the variable `status` which indicates how the child process terminated.

The program associated with a parent process might call these functions as shown in Example 15.1. This code could be embedded within an application proposing a game with two players; the parent process sets up the rules for the game and spawns two processes, each associated with a user, which contain the code for playing the game. Then, the parent process waits until the game has been completed: the child process ending first is the process associated with the winner; this is illustrated in Figure 15.8.

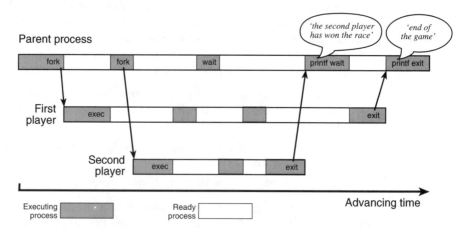

Figure 15.8 Concurrent process execution within a game.

EXAMPLE 15.1

```
                                                      /*Program E*/
    ...
p_id1 = fork();                          /*a new process is created*/
  if (p_id1 == 0)            /*if the active process is the first child*/
  {
     exec("prog-game",...);
                  /*program E is replaced by the executable of the game*/
  }

p_id2 = fork();                       /*a second child process is created*/
  if (p_id2 == 0)           /*if the active process is the second child*/
  {
     exec("prog-game",...);
                  /*program E is replaced by the executable of the game*/
  }
                              /*the program of the parent process now
                              executes operations that precede the
                              termination of the two child processes, then
                              waits for their termination. After the first
                              termination, it outputs a message to say
                              which of the two child processes terminated
                              first winning the game*/
    ...
                              /*the parent waits for one of the child
                              processes to terminate*/
proc_id = wait(status);
if(proc_id == p_id1)
   printf("the first player has won the race!!!");
else
   printf("the second player has won the race!!!");
/*endif*/
                              /*the parent waits for the other child
                              process to terminate*/
proc_id = wait(status);
printf("end of the game");
                              /*the program of the parent process executes
                              operations that can be executed only after
                              termination of the two child processes*/
    ...
```

In order to manage several processes at the same time, UNIX uses a vector type data structure: the **process table**. Each element of the vector describes one process. Each process descriptor includes:

- the process identifier,
- the identifier of the parent process,

- the state (execution, waiting, ready),
- the address of the memory cell where the executable E was loaded,
- the size of the executable E,
- the execution time,
- the execution priority,
- the list of open file descriptors (see Section 15.6.2 and the description of the *process open file table*),
- the terminal associated with it,
- the value of the PC saved when the process was interrupted, either synchronously or asynchronously,
- the value of the CPU registers (including the value of the status register) saved when the process was interrupted, either synchronously or asynchronously,
- the event the process may be waiting for (for example, data from an I/O device).

Whenever a new process is created, its descriptor is entered in the process table. Whenever a process is interrupted, changes state, opens a file, or changes its current position in one of its files, the relevant descriptor fields are modified.

15.6.2 The UNIX file system

A file in UNIX is a sequence of bytes with the associated concept of current position (byte). Files are classified as ordinary files, catalogue files or special files. **Ordinary files** contain data or programs; **catalogue files** allow implementation of the tree structure shown in Section 15.5 (each catalogue file contains the information concerning which files and other directories are included in the tree structure and which directory includes it); **special files** contain input/output drivers.

Each authorized UNIX system user has a **user-id**; each user belongs to a specific group and has a **group-id**. Whenever a file is created, the file's owner can protect it by indicating the modes of access available to the user, to the members of the user's group and to all other users; possible modes include read-only access, write-only access and read-and-write access. A special user, called the **system manager**, can access any file and perform any operation, even if the file was created as protected for read and/or write for users other than the 'owner'.

We analyse the low-level functions which are offered in UNIX as building blocks for building the above file management functions; they are also used by the C language compiler to implement the file management functions in C that were presented in Chapter 9. These functions enable creating a file, opening it, moving the current position pointed to from within the file system, and reading or writing bytes from the file into a buffer and vice versa; they provide an example of an 'internal' interface, that is, an interface which is not made available to end users. In what follows, arguments of functions have the following types: *file_name* of type string, *mode, file_id, base, offset, location, count* and *n* of type integer, *buffer* of type pointer. Low-level file management functions in UNIX are:

- **Open:** file_id = open(file_name, mode)
  This function opens the file whose (path)name, of type string, is given as the first argument and whose mode, of type integer, can be read-only (mode=0), write-only (mode=1), or read and write (mode=2). It returns an integer file_id which must be used to request further operations on that file. The return value is –1 if the operation is not executed correctly.

- **Close:** i = close(file_id)
  This function closes the file identified by file_id, releasing the identifier.

- **Create:** file_id = create(file_name, mode)
  This function creates a file called file_name, specifying the protections associated with it (parameter mode). The created file is also opened. The function returns the identifier to the file; the current position points to the first byte in the file.

- **Change Location:** location = lseek(file_id, offset, base)
  Within each open file, the file manager keeps a *current position*. This function moves the current position identifier to the following position:

  ```
  StartFile + offset          if base is 0
  EndFile + offset            if base is 1
  CurrentPosition + offset    if base is 2
  ```

  offset can have a positive or negative value.
  The function returns the new current position computed as the offset from the start of the file and –1 if there is an error.

- **Read:** n = read(file_id, buffer, count)
  This function reads count bytes from the file identified by file_id, starting from the current position, puts the data read into the buffer vector and returns the number n of bytes actually read. If the operation is correctly executed, n must be the same as count.

- **Write:** n = write(file_id, buffer, count)
  This function writes count bytes to the file identified by file_id, starting from the current position; it takes data to be written from the buffer vector and returns the number n of bytes actually written. If the operation is correctly executed, n must be the same as count.

The library functions for input/output which are available in the C standard library (see Chapter 7) use these simple functions, made available by the file system, to realize the more sophisticated functions available to C programmers.

The main data structures used by the UNIX file system to support file management are shown in Figure 15.9, with some simplifications:

- The **i-node table** describes all the files existing in the system (in mass storage) at a certain time. The contents of each table element (called an **i-node**) depend on the file's type (remember that files are classified as ordinary files, catalogue files and special files). Ordinary files are stored in one or more blocks in mass storage, each block containing a certain number of bytes. These blocks contain the file's information. The **i-node of an ordinary file** therefore contains, among other things, the following information:

–   the file type (= ordinary)

–   the file dimension

–   a list of the addresses in mass storage of the blocks that contain the file's information.

The **i-node of a catalogue file** contains:

–   the file type (= catalogue)

–   a list of pairs containing the name of a file included in the catalogue and a reference to the i-node which describes the particular child file.

We postpone the description of the contents of the i-node of a special file.

●   The **global open file table** describes all the open files existing in the system at a certain point, possibly opened by different processes. Each element of the table includes the following information:

–   the current position of the file

–   the opening mode

–   a reference to the i-node describing the specific file in the i-node table.

●   The **process open file table** contains the file descriptors of the files opened by a specific process at a certain point. Each descriptor contains, among other information, a pointer to the element of the global open file table describing it.

Figure 15.9 shows the relationships between variables pointing to file descriptors in the program environment, the elements of the process open file table, the elements of the global open file table, the elements of the i-node table and blocks in mass storage. When the user requires the operating system to perform an open operation, the file manager acts as follows:

(1)   It reserves an element for the file in the global open file table, setting its current position to 0 and specifying its opening mode.

(2)   It reserves an element for the file in the process open file table, writing into it a reference to the element of the global open file table created at step 1.

(3)   It returns to the user the pointer to the file descriptor, set equal to the reference to the element of the process open file table created at step 2.

(4)   It searches the i-node of the file which has the symbolic pathname specified in the open request.

(5)   Finally, it writes into the element of the global open file table created at step 1, the address of the i-node found at step 4.

Note that step 4 requires an access to the i-node of the catalogue which contains the file name and the reference to the i-node of the specific file. When a

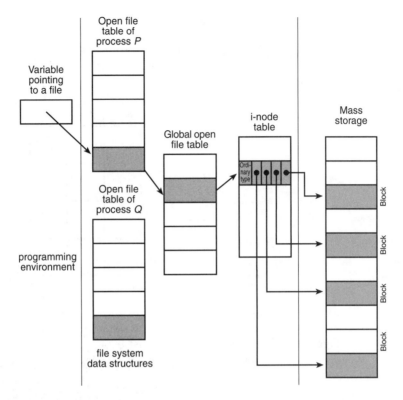

Figure 15.9 Relationships between the variables used by different processes, the file system data structures and mass storage.

pathname is involved, for example /cat1/f2, the system accesses the i-node associated with the root catalogue (/), determines the address of the i-node of the file named cat1 (which is a catalogue), and accesses this i-node where it can finally find the reference to the i-node of the file named f2.

The operations required by the user on an ordinary open file use the variable pointing to the file descriptor (returned by the system as a result of the open operation); this allows the system to retrieve (through the data structures we have just analysed) the addresses of the blocks containing the file in mass storage.

Let us now consider peripheral devices: in UNIX they are represented by special files. Each peripheral device is identified by a pair of numbers <device_type, unit>. Identical peripherals have the same device_type number.

The **i-node of a special file** contains, among other things:

- the file type (= special)
- the device_type number
- the unit number of the particular device

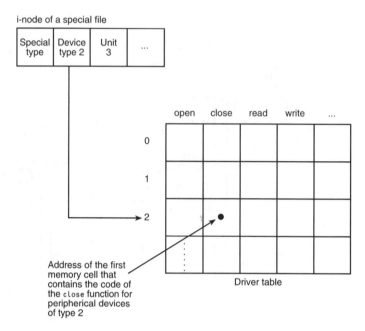

i-node of a special file

Figure 15.10 Relationships that exist between an i-node of a special file and some elements of the driver table.

If a device of a new type is added to the system, the operating system has to be extended to include a set of functions (read, write, open, close, ...) for this particular device type. The **driver table** contains, for each type of device, the load addresses of the functions associated with this device type. Figure 15.10 shows the contents of the driver table and the links that exist between an i-node of a special file and some elements of the driver table.

When a program requires an operation on a special file (which represents a peripheral), the file system uses its data structures to invoke the implementation of the appropriate function for the required device:

(1) Via the pointer to the file, the file system retrieves the process's open file descriptor, the specific element of the global open file table and the specific i-node.

(2) Via the device type, it selects the row of the driver table that corresponds to that device type.

(3) By looking in the column of the table that corresponds to the requested operation, the file system finds the memory address of the function to be invoked.

(4) Finally, it uses the retrieved address to invoke the function, by passing the number of the desired unit as an input parameter.

Exercises

15.1 Describe the possible functioning of a system with four active processes for a period of 10 seconds. Assume that a time interval is 0.5 s long and that each program executes some SVCs. The exercise consists in listing the status of the CPU and the status of each active process as a consequence of the internal and external events, which should be invented by the reader.

15.2 Describe a priority mechanism that favours short programs and one that favours long programs. Supposing that we do not know a priori whether a program is short or long, discuss a mechanism in which, in order to obtain the desired result, the priority of a program is modified during its execution.

15.3 The following situation, very frequently considered in the construction of operating systems, is called **deadlock**. Two processes have to use two different resources, for example, two peripherals to transfer data from one to the other. The first process accesses the first peripheral and blocks it, reserving it for its own use. Then the second process accesses the second peripheral and blocks it, also reserving it for its own use. At this point, the processes make a cross-request: the first process requests use of the second resource, and the second process requests use of the first resource. Both are destined to wait forever, because both resources are blocked. Discuss methods to avoid such a situation.

15.4 Assuming a partitioning of memory into pages, describe a memory management system that implements the following strategies for loading and unloading memory pages:

- when a **page fault** occurs, load only one page of the program at a time (that is, load the page whose request has caused the page fault to occur);
- the page to unload is the least recently used one, chosen independently of the program it belongs to.

Discuss a modification of the page table that allows this strategy to be implemented.

15.5 Discuss a modification of the strategy illustrated in Exercise 15.10 such that a fixed number of pages is kept assigned to each program.

15.6 In a page-based system, it is sometimes not necessary to unload a page, that is, copy it from main memory back to mass storage. This is the case when the page in memory has not been modified (for example, because it contains instructions and not data). The copy of the program page stored in mass storage is the same as the one in main memory; therefore it is unnecessary to copy the page in main memory back to mass storage.

(a) Describe a modification of the page table to indicate whether a page has been modified.

(b) Describe a memory management strategy that takes advantage of such a situation.

*15.7 Describe a fetch phase (modified with respect to Section 2.4) that includes interrupt handling. Assume that the interrupt management program starts at memory cell 100 (in S mode memory) and that interrupts are disabled by the micro-instruction DIS. The modified fetch phase must:

- Check for the presence of an interrupt. If an interrupt is present the fetch cycle must:
  - disable the interrupt;
  - save the contents of the SR and PC registers (assume cells 50 and 51 are available for the save operation);
  - invoke the interrupt management program.

*15.8 After solving Exercise 15.5, write, in assembler language, two parts of the interrupt management program:

- The first part must save the context of the process previously in execution, in the process descriptor contained in the process table (assume that the process table element for this process starts at cell 1000), and save as the state of the processor the contents of the registers listed at the beginning of Chapter 14.
- The second part must restore the context of a ready program; for simplicity, we assume that the ready program is the one that was active at the moment the interrupt occurred. Assume that the ENABLE instruction (in assembler language) has the effect of re-enabling interrupts.

Assume the availability of appropriate load and store operations to copy the CPU register contents into memory and vice versa, as illustrated by Example 14.2 for register I in Section 14.9.

15.9 Consider the process management functions available to users in UNIX and analyse the effect of each function on the process table.

15.10 Consider the management of internal interrupts as described in Section 15.2.1 and describe the modifications that need to be made to the contents of the process table to allow a correct context switch.

15.11 Consider the management of external interrupts as described in Section 15.2.2 and describe the modifications that need to be made to the process table to allow the interrupts to be managed correctly.

*15.12 Consider some file access functions available in the C standard library. Describe how the UNIX system handles these requests (which system functions are involved, which data structures are used and how they are modified). Distinguish between the functions that operate on mass storage files and functions that operate on files representing (standard or nonstandard) peripherals.

☞ 1. With reference to Figure 15.6, given an address in relocatable format, describe how the memory manager can produce the absolute address by consulting the segment table and say what happens if the needed segment is not resident in memory (if a **segment fault** occurs).

File and database systems

16

Data storage and management is a fundamental application of computers. Using computers, it is possible to insert, modify, delete, organize and retrieve data; we say that data is **persistent**, as it remains safely stored when the computers are turned off or fail. We normally rely on data storage and management when we perform any banking operation: nowadays very few applications involve cash exchange; most of them involve data exchange. Thus, data within the banks' computer systems have replaced the function that was once performed by cash – and they must be equally or more reliable. Although data management was originally focused on financial applications, it has now turned to a variety of application fields, involving new kinds of media; for instance, the Bible or an entire encyclo-paedia can be stored on CD-ROM disks.

In this chapter, we turn our attention to the mass storage of a computer system, describing the organization of files and analysing ways of storing large quantities of data and retrieving it efficiently. When designing data organization in mass storage, two objectives have to be met: storing large quantities of data in a compact manner on devices of limited capacity, and guaranteeing the efficient retrieval of information, accessing mass storage selectively. In order to satisfy these requirements, we have to define appropriate data structures and appropriate mecha-nisms for inserting, deleting, modifying and searching for data in these structures.

The **file organization** described in this chapter is used by data management systems and by several programming languages (for example, Cobol) to construct data management applications, where the need to handle large quantities of data (relating, for example, to the management of a business) is paramount. File organizations are used by special software systems, called **Database Management Systems** (DBMSs), which provide high-level languages dedicated to data manage-ment. These systems have a number of properties different from those of traditional programming languages, including greater efficiency, robustness (which, as we will see, is the ability to recover from system failures) and a language which is independent of the specific organization of data in mass storage, although they use file organization techniques internally.

The chapter is organized as follows. First, we describe the physical devices used to store data (disks and tapes). Then we introduce the basic methods of file organization: sequential, random access and indexed. Finally, we look at database management systems, illustrating differences with respect to the handling of traditional file systems. A long extended example is dedicated to **relational databases**, which are the most widely used database systems on the market.

16.1 Mass storage

The term 'mass storage' makes one think of large quantities of stored data and it would be interesting to find out what quantities of data are typically involved in computer applications. In reality, the capacities of mass storage vary greatly, from a few hundred megabytes on PC hard disks to the giga- or terabytes of bigger systems. One example of large mass storage is the system that collects incoming satellite images at NASA; data has to be collected and stored at a rate of several gigabytes per minute. The measurement units used (from mega- to terabytes) give a good indication of the typical capacities of mass storage.

Even though there are several very different types of mass storage devices, they can be reduced to two fundamental classes. The first, known as **tape**, enables only *sequential access*: to read specific information from a tape, it must be rewound and then advanced to the desired point. The second, known as **disk**, allows *direct access* to the data: it is possible to read from any disk position, selecting it appropriately, without having to do a sequential search.

Information is represented by positive or negative states on small particles of disks or tapes. With **magnetic technology**, nowadays the most widely used, disk and tape surfaces have a magnetic film, with several iron particles scattered on them; the positive and negative states correspond to magnetization of iron molecules in the disk coating, which is induced by an electrical field. Although each magnetic state (corresponding to a bit) requires very little space, this space can be reduced by means of **laser technology**, which is becoming increasingly popular and widespread; more precision yields much greater device capacity.

Given the limitations on data access, tapes are now normally used only for **disk backup**, that is, for creating a tape-resident copy of data which is stored on disk; copies can be used in case of data management failures, by executing a **disk restore** which recovers the data on disk. During backup operations, data is serially written from disks to tape; during restore operations, data is serially written back from tapes to disks.

16.1.1 Tapes

Magnetic tapes typically come rolled up on circular supports; when the tape is unrolled, it looks like a ribbon of magnetizable material and can be hundreds of metres in length. Parallel horizontal **tracks** are recorded on the tape (Figure 16.1); data is serially recorded on each track. The main parameter of a tape is its density, measured in bits per inch (bpi); this parameter enables the tape's capacity, measured in bits, to be evaluated.

In order to be read or written, a tape is inserted into a tape unit that contains various supports and guides. The tape winds on a circular support so that a specific portion of the tape passes below a device called the **read/write head**; this device creates suitable magnetic fields in order to write on the tape, or detects the magnetic field on the tape to read from it. Tapes can start off on one circular support and then be wound to another empty support while they are read or written, as happens with projectors in cinemas (movie theaters).

More frequently, they are included within a cartridge with only one circular support; when the tape reaches one of its ends, its movement is reversed. In this case, each tape contains several parallel tracks, which are read or written in spiral fashion: at each change of direction, the head goes over the next track, until all the tracks have been used.

When information is copied to tape, some additional **control bits** are added to enable erroneous data to be detected; erroneous data may occur because the copying is incorrect or the tape is physically damaged. Control bits introduce redundancy and this may be used to detect errors. For instance, a **parity bit** may be added to each byte so that the sum of all the ones in the byte, including the parity bit, is even; this simple additional bit can be used to reveal a one-bit error whenever the result of the sum is odd. More complex redundant information is added at

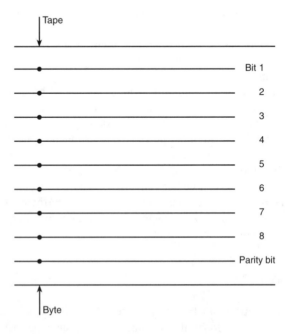

Figure 16.1 Coding information on magnetic tapes.

specific places; complex control bits may enable not only the detection of errors, but also, in certain cases, their correction.

In order to be read or written, tapes must pass the head at a given speed; therefore at the beginning of the tape there is an information-free zone that allows the tape to accelerate from a state of inertia to the required speed. Data is stored on the tape in contiguous zones called **records**, which are separated by information-free zones (called **inter-record gaps**). The only way to access a specific record is to rewind the tape, start reading it and count the records as they pass the read/write head, until the desired record is reached; at this point, it can be read.

Given the slow speed of this operation, which can require times of up to several minutes, accessing specific records is rarely used; generally, a tape is read or written in sequence, starting with the first record. Operations on tapes are therefore carried out in strict serial order. Magnetic tape was the standard mass storage device before disks were invented, and therefore they were used by application programs; today, they are used for backups only, as already discussed. In particular, they store **transaction logs,** recording all the activities performed by the computer system; these will be described in Chapter 17.

16.1.2 Disks

Disks are the most widely used mass-memory devices; their capacities range from a few hundred kilobytes to several gigabytes. Disk technology is in constant evolution and produces devices which have larger capacities, are faster and are becoming cheaper all the time.

The organization of a typical disk unit is shown in Figure 16.2. A disk consists of a number of **platters**, which are covered by a magnetic coating; platters rotate around a central axle. Each platter has two **surfaces** on which data is stored; each surface has a series of concentric circles, or **tracks.** Tracks are further subdivided into segments of equal size, called **sectors**. Disks are **formatted** by writing on them a pattern of zeros and ones that marks where sectors begin and end; the number of sectors and tracks accommodated on a disk determines the disk's capacity (a typical average capacity is one gigabyte).

A typical **disk-pack** device may have 18 surfaces (corresponding to 10 disks, because the top and bottom surfaces are not used), 400 tracks and 32 sectors. A sealed metal housing protects disk components from dust, which could prevent the correct functioning of the disk unit.

Data is written in consecutive positions along the tracks; it is represented by (negative or positive) polarization of the magnetic material. An **input/output block** is a group of contiguous data items that are read or written with a single input/output operation; each block corresponds to a specific sector of a specific track of a specific surface and can therefore be selected via a triple, interpreted as the number of the surface, track and sector, respectively.

Reading or writing a block is carried out by one **read/write head** per surface; the heads, all joined together, move lengthways across the tracks, back and forth,

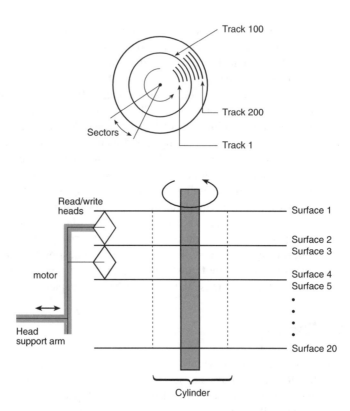

Figure 16.2   Disk organization.

with a movement regulated by an electric step motor. Thus, the heads are always on tracks that are equidistant from the rotation axis.

An input/output operation involves a movement of the heads and a data transfer; an entire block is copied into main memory in a single read operation, or is written from main memory in a single write operation. A specific main memory space, called a **buffer**, contains an entire block prior to being written to disk or after being read from disk. The movement of the heads towards the required track is called a **seek** and the amount of time required to accomplish this movement is called the **seek time**. It is then necessary to wait for the required sector to pass beneath the read/write head; on average, this **latency time** equals half the **rotation time** of the device. Finally, some amount of time is required to transfer data from disk to memory or vice versa. The time needed to carry out an input/output operation is therefore given by the sum of three components:

$$t_{i/o} = t_{seek} + t_{latency} + t_{transfer}$$

The first of these terms is the most important insofar as it includes the time needed for the mechanical movement of the arm that supports the heads. There are more expensive devices, called fixed-head disks, which have one head for each track of each surface; in this case, the input/output time does not include the first component and is therefore very much shorter.

The term **cylinder** indicates a set of tracks equidistant from the centre on all surfaces. Consecutive data, forming a file, is placed in sequence along the tracks belonging to a cylinder; in this way, if the program reads the various blocks of a file in sequence, most input/output operations involve blocks of the same cylinder and do not require head moves.

16.1.3 Floppy disks

Floppy disk units are widely used in personal computers. A **floppy disk** is a removable unit that can be inserted in and extracted from a **floppy disk unit**; each user of a personal computer typically owns a large number of floppy disks, storing programs and files. Each floppy disk has a single platter and only two surfaces; thus, in the floppy disk unit there are only two read/write heads. Typical floppy disks are 3.5 inches in diameter.

Each floppy disk is individually formatted by a special program; this operation divides disks into sectors. During formatting, the bit density on the disks is specified and consequently their capacity is determined. The typical capacity of a floppy disk for personal computers is about one megabyte.

16.2 File organization

This section describes typical data organizations that can be provided to speed up the operations on data; these are not normally provided by the operating system and must be superimposed on the basic file system provided by the operating system. Data is organized in memory as **logical records**; a typical case is illustrated in Figure 16.3. Each logical record contains a sequence of bytes and is subdivided into fields; each field contains a specific piece of information. In Figure 16.3, the record corresponds to a phone book entry; the first field contains last and first name, the second field the address, the third the phone number. A file contains a large number of logical records; in the remainder of this chapter we assume that the records of a file have the same format (that is, that they are fixed-length records).

A number of logical records can be stored in one input/output block; there may also be logical records of such a length that they occupy several input/output blocks. When accessing data, programs are generally interested in reading or writing logical records; therefore, they have to select the appropriate logical records within one or more blocks. The file access structures provide appropriate functionalities for extracting logical records from blocks. However, from the previous section we know that blocks are the unit of input/output from disks; therefore, large amounts of raw data are read within blocks in order to extract logical records. We define the **usage factor** of a file as the ratio of the number of bytes allocated to logical records in the file and the number of bytes of the physical blocks allocated

Record	Name	Address	Telephone
1	Smith John	341 Harper St.	415-338-5031

Figure 16.3 Sequential file organization.

to the file. In the following, we make the simplifying assumption that each logical records fits exactly within a block; this assumption is clearly unrealistic, but it allows us to concentrate on the various file organization types and their features.

16.2.1 Sequential file organization

In a sequentially organized file, all records are stored in the file in order, according to the value of one of its fields, called the **key** field. An example of a sequentially organized file is the phone book, where all names are given in alphabetic order; phone book records have a structure similar to that described in Figure 16.3.

A sequentially organized file lends itself to efficient search algorithms. Think of the way we look for a name in a phone book, let us say George Robinson. Given that the surname starts with R, we take the volume or section that contains the names, say, from M to Z; we hypothesize that the letter R is more or less in the middle of the list, so we open it somewhere in the middle. Depending on the names we read, we move backward and forward in the list, until we have located the page, column and zone within the column where we will find the required name. Only at that point do we start to scan the names in the list sequentially (although even at this point it is possible to proceed by jumping through the list).

More formally, to access a record in a sequential file efficiently on the basis of a key value, we use the **binary search** method. This method was first informally illustrated in the extended example of Chapter 1, and was then discussed more precisely in Chapter 12, with reference to array and tree data structures. It clearly applies to mass storage searching as well: it consists in accessing the middle element (called the barycentric element) of the file and comparing its key with the value of the search key. If the two values are the same, the search terminates; if the barycentric value is lower than the search value, the search continues in the upper half of the file; otherwise, the search continues in the lower half of the file. Applying this method recursively, the search terminates after at most $\log_2 n$ accesses (see Example 12.1 for a more detailed analysis), where n is the number of records in the file.

The main problem with a sequential file is the insertion of new elements; think of the cost of rewriting the phone book each time a new user is inserted. There are various solutions to the problem.

(1) Collect all the changes to the file in a **differential file** and store all changes accumulated over a period of time (that is, all record additions, updates and deletions); this file is periodically merged with the main file. The disadvantage of this solution is that the main file is not updated immediately; therefore either both the main file and the update file must be searched, or only the

main file is searched, disregarding the more recent data. This occurs with telephone directories being updated anually.

(2) Place the records so as to leave **free blocks** between them. In this case, the file has a low usage factor and storage space is wasted. On the other hand, new records can be inserted in the free blocks, although normally some local file reorganization is required.

(3) Use an additional storage zone, called the **overflow zone**, to insert the new data; connections between the main file and the overflow zone are maintained by pointers. A pointer contains the address of an input/output block (and therefore allows the surface, track and sector of a specific disk to be identified) and forms a link between one record and another. If, for example, record *R3* has to be inserted between records *R2* and *R4* and there is no space available between them, *R3* is inserted in the overflow zone; a pointer connects record *R2* to record *R3*. By following the pointers, it is possible to retrieve data from the overflow zone, although this reduces the efficiency of the search.

16.2.2 Hash-based file organization

In hash-based file organization, the allocation of records in mass storage is defined by an algorithm (called a **hash algorithm**) which generates an address on the basis of the value of one field in the record, called the key field. The search for a logical record in storage is simply carried out by applying the algorithm to the requested key value; the address thus obtained is also the address of the record in storage. This address is normally produced in logical form; it is then transformed into a triple (surface–track–sector), typically calculated starting from the first physical block allocated to the file.

For example, suppose that the file has 13 input/output blocks available which, for simplicity, we indicate with the numbers 0 to 12; recall that we also assume each logical record is exactly contained in one input/output block. Let us assume that we want to store 7 records and that the key is numeric. In particular, we consider the following 7 key values: 68, 2, 34, 57, 91, 22, 43. The algorithm consists in dividing the key values by 13 and assuming that the address is the remainder of the division (that is, a number between 0 and 12); for example, the record with numeric key 68 is allocated to the position that has the address 3, since 68/13 gives remainder 3. Figure 16.4 shows the correspondence between addresses and key values obtained by applying the above algorithm. Note that the figure shows only the value of the key field corresponding to each address, whereas in reality the whole logical record is stored together with the key field.

Address	0	1	2	3	4	5	6	7	8	9	10	11	12
Key	91		2	68	43	57			34	22			

Figure 16.4   Hash-based file organization.

The main problem posed by hash-based organizations is the **conflict** that occurs when two key values correspond to the same address. In the example described in Figure 16.4, the key values 11 and 24 would correspond to the same address (since 11/13 and 24/13 both have remainder 11). The second record to be inserted finds the place allocated to it by the algorithm already occupied; this generates a conflict. Conflicts can be resolved in two ways.

(1) It is possible to put the second record in the **first available free place** immediately after the address generated by the algorithm. This method assumes that no deletion is done on the file and requires the usage factor of the file to be sufficiently low to give a large number of free places. Note, however, that this method complicates the search for a record: when the address generated by the algorithm is occupied by a record different from the one required, it is necessary to access the subsequent records, up to the first empty place, before the presence or absence of the search record in the file can be determined.

(2) It is possible to use overflow zones, in exactly the same way as discussed in the previous section.

The advantage of hash-based structures is the search speed: when there are no conflicts, each search requires just one input/output operation. The number of operations required grows as the number of conflicts grows. A particular case occurs when the key values are in a complete interval of integers that starts with 1 (for example, the first 100 integer numbers); in this case, the hashing algorithm degenerates into a simple identity function and access to mass storage occurs in direct mode.

16.2.3 Index-based file organization

As in hash-based files, an index-based file organization is used to access the records of a file on the basis of a key field. However, in an index-based file structure, the position of the records in mass memory is not determined by an algorithm: records can be stored in any order in the **base file.** The correspondence between key values and records in the base file is maintained explicitly, by separate files called **index files,** whose blocks point to each other, forming a tree structure. In each index file, the tree must be traversed from the root to the leaves, thereby implementing a binary search while traversing the tree; the leaves of the tree contain pointers to the blocks of the base file. Thus, by using the index, fast access to the records of the base file which store given values of the key field is possible; several index files can be associated with the same base file. Each index can be of two types:

- If the index is of type **unique,** only one record can correspond to each key value; the insertion of two records with the same key is impossible.

- If the index is of type **multiple,** several records can correspond to the same key value.

Given that each index file uses a considerable amount of space, the usage factor decreases with the addition of index files; this and other considerations concerning the effort of maintaining the index file when data is modified suggest that the number of index files for each base file should be small. Further description of index files would go beyond the scope of this text.

16.3 Databases

The function of memorizing information is 'normally' carried out by the human mind, which is capable of memorizing information and organizing it in such a way that it can be remembered later; how this process occurs in the mind is quite extraordinary and, to a large extent, still a mystery. In comparison, a computer is subject to great limitations; to make it possible to extract information, data has to be collected according to precise rules and organized in rather rigid structures, called **databases**.

Consulting a database is a common everyday activity. For example, when we consult *Yellow Pages* or the phone book, or when we look up the departure and arrival times of a train in the timetable, what we are really doing is consulting a database. When data is put into a computer, however, searching is generally facilitated by appropriate programs which process information at high speed, consulting large archives. Furthermore, computer systems allow a large number of users in different places to access the same collection of data; think, for example, of systems for managing bank accounts or booking flights.

A database is a collection of data organized and managed by a specific software system, the **Database Management System** (DBMS). This software system operates on top of the operating system; it offers specific languages for data organization and management, and internally supports efficient and robust methods for data organization, including several file management structures described in the previous section.

DBMSs are an essential ingredient for building information systems. They can be very complex and handle databases of gigabyte dimensions on big (mainframe) computers, or very simple, storing small, personal databases on personal computers. Most DBMSs are relatively simple to use, as they are dedicated to nonspecialists; in particular, a DBMS is typically associated with a collection of tools that facilitate its programming. Thus, any student can acquire a first experience of data management by using DBMSs on personal computers; in particular, the long extended example in the next section provides sufficient information about relational databases to enable the acquisition of such experience.

16.3.1 Differences between file and database management

Databases offer unified and organized software for data management. Their effect can be best appreciated by comparing them with conventional data access from a programming language, without a database; the comparison is illustrated in Figure

16.5. When application programs, possibly written in C, use files as provided by the operating system, the main problems are caused by file sharing; for instance, files storing the accounts of bank customers are typically accessed by several programs, each doing a different operation (depositing, transferring money, checking the balance and so on). When the same files are shared by several programs, many problems can arise:

- **Redundancy and inconsistency**. When each programmer autonomously defines the required files, a potential source of redundancy (because the same information belongs to several files) and inconsistency (because the contents of the various files can be different) is immediately created. Consider again the banking application. Suppose that the address of an account holder is stored in both the accounts file and the deposits file. This duplication is a potential source of inconsistency when, for example, a change of address is registered in one of the files, but not in the other. In any case, the duplication of the information is a waste of storage space.

- **Privacy.** Consider again a banking system. It is clear that only appropriately authorized programs can operate on the value of accounts. Among the situations to avoid is the possibility that a client, using an automated teller machine, activates a program that draws money from a bank account other than the client's own. Of course, there are file access control mechanisms in the file system of an operating system, but these are generally not very robust

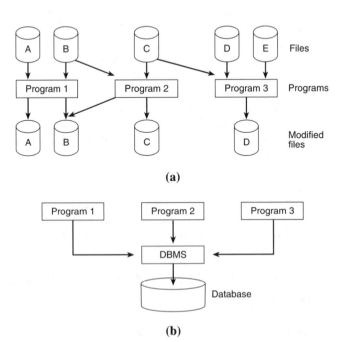

Figure 16.5 Comparison between the management of separate files and a database.

or sophisticated; they consider the whole file as a single object, whereas, in an application, it is often necessary to protect each field or record in a different way.

- **Data integrity**. The integrity of a set of data can be specified by an appropriate set of rules, called consistency constraints. For example, a cheque cannot be paid if cashing it would cause the value of the account to become negative. In a system with separate files, data consistency is managed by the application programs, and this can be very dangerous because each of them is subject to errors.

- **Concurrency.** Let us consider once more the account file. At the same moment, several programs that operate on it and access its data may be active. In particular, it is possible that two programs try to operate on the same account; in such a case, programs must be protected from each other. File systems offer very basic protection mechanisms, which allocate the entire file to a program for reading or writing, but these mechanisms may impose too heavy a performance penalty.

DBMSs, if properly used, can remedy the above difficulties, insofar as:

- Data has a unique representation, even when it is used by many users; thus the danger of data redundancy and the potential data inconsistency deriving from it is reduced.

- Access to the database is controlled by the DBMS, in which it is possible to define the usage modes of each datum for each user, thus protecting data privacy.

- Some consistency constraints that define the correctness of the database can be defined inside the DBMS and automatically verified by the system. The DBMS prevents programs that violate integrity constraints being executed.

- Concurrent data access is controlled by the DBMS through operations that allow mutual exclusion of programs, without slowing down execution excessively.

16.3.2 Models and languages for data management

Databases are organized and structured on the basis of a **data model**, that is, a specific collection of type constructors that can be used by a DBMS; the principal DBMS data models include the *hierarchical*, *network*, *relational* and *object-oriented* models, in chronological order of development.

- The **hierarchical model** characterized the first DBMSs developed in the mid-1960s and is still used today in various database installations. The hierarchical model is based on trees – in other words, hierarchical data structures.

- The **network model**, also called the Codasyl model, was conceived in 1973 and improved in 1978. It was designed as an extension to the Cobol programming language to handle complex data structures. The network model is based on graphs – in other words, on network data structures.

- The **relational model**, invented by Codd in 1970, entered the world of commercial DBMSs only at the beginning of the 1980s; however, since then it has enjoyed ever-growing success. The relational model is based on the concept of set and the structuring of data in tables.

- The **object-oriented model**, developed since 1985, characterizes the new generation of DBMSs. They extend to databases some of the characteristics of object-oriented programming languages (see Chapter 25).

The **schema** of a database is a description of the data of a specific application context conforming to the data model present in the DBMS; it is defined via a process, called **database design**, that precedes the use of the database. The **instance** or **occurrence** of a database is the value taken by the database in a particular instant of time; the instance is modified by executing the programs of the DBMS during the lifetime of the information system.

The languages made available by a DBMS reflect this difference between schema and instance and therefore carry out two different functions.

- The **Data Definition Language** (DDL) is used to define the schema of the database; it has statements similar to those that allow type definitions in programming languages. The definitions of the schema are stored in a special database, called the **data dictionary**.

- The **Data Manipulation Language** (DML) is used to manipulate the database, that is, to carry out the following functions:

  - **Formulate queries** about the database: with the query language, it is possible to extract information from the database, connecting data to each other in a complex way.

  - **Modify** the contents of the database, that is, carry out operations such as inserting new data, deleting existing data and modifying specific values of existing data.

In the extended example, we illustrate the characteristics of the relational data model and the language SQL, a language for defining, querying and modifying relational databases.

16.3.3 Levels of abstraction in a database

A DBMS provides its users with an abstract vision of the database. We distinguish three levels of abstraction, shown in Figure 16.6.

(1) **Physical level.** This is the lowest level of abstraction. It describes the database as a set of records in mass storage. At this level, the data distribution on the various supports that constitute the mass storage is decided together with the modes of storing the data in the files, using the mechanisms already described (that is, sequential, hash-based, or indexed access structures).

(2) **Logical level.** This level shows the organization of data from the point of view of its information content, describing the structure of each datum and

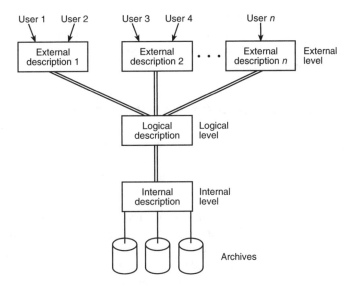

Figure 16.6 Abstraction levels of a database.

the connections between different items of data. For example, the logical description of account data indicates that this data contains the account number and the personal data of the account holder, the value of the account, the date of the last operation and its amount; the database can also store other characteristics of account holders, for example their bond trading and other financial activities.

(3) **External level.** This is the highest level of abstraction, it presents the data as seen by a particular user or class of users. Thus, there can be many external representations of the same database, each associated with a particular user. Still referring to the accounts database, users of accounting procedures could, for example, have a view of the database that excludes the personal data of the account holders.

The three levels of representation allow the concepts of logical and physical independence of data to be introduced. A DBMS should always guarantee both properties.

- **Physical independence** allows the physical level to be redefined without modifying the logical level and, therefore, without modifying the users' programs. Such redefinitions might be due to changes in mass storage configuration, or to the necessity of improving the performance of the database. In this case, all modifications are contained inside the physical level.

- **Logical independence** allows new external schemas to be defined or the logical schema to be extended in order to satisfy the requirements of a set of users who want to see the existing database from another point of view without having to alter the existing external schemas.

The concepts of levels of abstraction and logical and physical independence recall the concept of abstract data type in programming languages; they allow implementation details to be hidden so that users can concentrate on the structural characteristics of the data.

16.3.4 Databases and transactions

An important characteristic of databases is the support of **transactions,** that is, robust program executions that never leave the database in an inconsistent state. In particular, they must have four fundamental characteristics: atomicity, consistency, isolation and durability. Let us look at their definitions.

(1) **Atomicity** requires that a transaction behaves in one of only two possible ways. Either it terminates correctly and modifies the data it accesses, or it terminates unsuccessfully, but without modifying any data at all. Correct termination is called **commit**, unsuccessful termination is called **rollback**. It is important to note that intermediate situations, in which only part of the modification of the data is actually carried out, are excluded. To understand the importance of this requirement, consider a money transfer operation from one account to another: it is acceptable for the operation to be successful, transferring the money, or unsuccessful, without carrying out any transfer (and advising the client of the negative outcome); but it is unacceptable for the transaction to terminate with money having been taken out of one account but not put into the other.

(2) Transactions are also units of **consistency**, in the sense that their execution must not violate data integrity. When a transaction causes the violation of some integrity constraints, its actions are nullified by a rollback, which is imposed by the DBMS software. In some cases, it is possible to nullify the actions of the operations that are causing the integrity violation but not the entire transaction; this situation is called a **partial rollback**.

(3) Another important property of transactions is **isolation**, which is required because of concurrent executions on the database; for instance, because of concurrent execution some data updates could be lost, or some invalid data could be read (for example, invalid data is written by a transaction which later executes a rollback). With isolation, transactions are protected from each other: each one has the impression of acting alone in the database.

(4) Finally, transactions must be **durable**; once completed, their effects should never be lost. In practice, after a credit operation, one wants the current account to reflect the presence of the paid-in sum and to ensure that the effects of this operation will not be forgotten in the future.

These four properties (Atomicity, Consistency, Isolation, Durability) are also referred to as the ACID properties of transactions. Transactions are essential to guarantee the correctness of a database, especially in the context of multiple users and distributed data.

16.3.5 **Programming and use of a database**

A database is a complex software system that serves various users with different, sometimes conflicting, needs. For this reason, the definition of a database is a complex task, entrusted to a computer science expert called a **Database Administrator** (DBA).

The main problem for the DBA is to determine the organization of data that best represents the data of a specific application. Among DBA tasks, we find the definition of the external, logical and physical schemas and the definition of the integrity constraints and privacy requirements. For these tasks, the DBA uses the DDL, which is generally not available to the users of the database. The DBA also has to make sure that the application programs that operate on the database can be executed sufficiently fast. Obviously, a system that takes several seconds or even minutes to calculate the balance of a customer's account is unacceptable, whereas a waiting time of minutes or even hours is acceptable for the procedure that produces all the monthly statements; the DBA must ensure that all interactive users are serviced in acceptable times.

Database users are very different from one another. For example, consider account management systems in which account holders can access the database by using automated teller machines to withdraw cash. The user can read the balance and indicate a sum of money to be drawn in cash; the system then decrements the balance value, stores the money transfer and finally controls the paying out of the sum by the machine. Obviously, in this case we are dealing with an ordinary person, a non-programmer who interacts with the database in the most intuitive way possible.

Another classic database user is the **terminal operator**; consider, for example, clerks at a customer service desk in a bank. In this case, too, the clerks do not interact with the database via a programming language, but via a set of operations designed for them. However, given the higher number of operations under their control and the more critical nature of these operations, the clerks must have a more precise idea of the consequences of what they are doing. Generally, terminal operators have a large number of operational codes available to select and execute the different operations.

Another type of database user is the **application programmer**, that is, the person who writes the procedures and makes them available to the users, but without changing the structure of the data (only the database administrator can do that). The programs must, as always, be designed, coded, installed and tested before they can be used; furthermore, a rather large percentage of the application programmer's time is dedicated to program maintenance.

Finally, there are **casual users** who access the database directly, using the DML. These users query the database in unanticipated ways, formulating their queries directly in the query language.

16.4 Extended example: relational databases

The remainder of this chapter is dedicated to a particular type of database, called a **relational database**, which has become very successful because of its simplicity and generality. We deal particularly with the concepts that are necessary to construct simple relational databases managed by a personal computer; however, many of the notions described in this chapter also apply to large systems. First, we look at the relational data model, then we describe the SQL query language (DDL and DML), the most widely used query language for commercial relational systems, and finally we briefly discuss some of the issues in database design and programming.

16.4.1 Relational model

The relational model has an extremely compact and elegant definition: a relational database is a collection of relations. Each **relation** is a **table** which has a fixed number of columns (called **attributes**) and a variable number of rows (called **tuples**); each column takes values belonging to one **domain,** that is, a predefined set of possible values. For simplicity, it is a good idea to think of domains as being something like the types of a programming language: for example, integers, reals, character strings. Domains normally offer more possibilities for data definition than the types of programming languages, although each DBMS allows only a limited number of domains to be used. We define the number of columns of a relation to be its **grade** and the number of rows its **cardinality.**

From a more rigorous and formal point of view, a relation is defined as a set of tuples; therefore, each tuple must be different from the others. Commercial DBMS, however, do not verify the uniqueness of tuples automatically.

Each relation has a unique name; furthermore, each attribute of the relation has a name and the names of the attributes of one relation must all be different from one another. The description of the structure of a relation is called the **schema of a relation**. It consists of the name of the relation, followed by the names of its attributes; each attribute has its domain associated with it. The schema of a relational database is given simply by the list of the schemas of relations present in the database.

The **instance of a relation** is the set of tuples of the relation present in the database at a given moment. The schema of a relation is fixed, once and for all, when the database is created; subsequently, it is possible to insert, delete or modify tuples and therefore modify the instance of the relation. Thus, the schema is a static characteristic which does not change over time, whereas the instance is a dynamic characteristic that is modified according to the actions that are carried out on the database. The instance of a relational database is simply the collection of all instances of relations present in the database.

Figure 16.7 illustrates the schema of a database containing two relations: BANK-ACCOUNT (with account number, name and address of the account holder

Relation BANK-ACCOUNT
(ACC-NUMBER: integer,
NAME: char(20),
ADDRESS: char(20),
BALANCE integer).

Relation TRANSACTION
(ACC-NUMBER: integer,
TRANS-DATE: date,
TRANS-NUMBER: integer,
AMOUNT: integer,
TYPE: char(1)).

(a)

BANK-ACCOUNT

ACC-NUMBER	NAME	ADDRESS	BALANCE
1	Jones	5675 High St	3,678.00
2	Richards	341 Harper St	664.00
3	Quinton	11 Hanna Pl.	6,777.50
4	Murdock	3131 Emerson St	3,400.00

TRANSACTION

ACC-NUMBER	TRANS-DATE	TRANS-NUMBER	AMOUNT	TYPE
1	14-1-96	1	+200.00	D
1	14-1-96	2	−500.00	W
1	27-1-96	1	+2,700.00	S
4	27-1-96	1	+1,850.40	S
3	25-1-96	1	−650.00	C

(b)

Figure 16.7 Example of (a) a schema and (b) an instance of a relational database.

and the balance) and TRANSACTION (with account number, date, transaction number, amount and type).

The two tables contain data required for the management of a bank account, although in a simplified way. In the schema, *char(n)* indicates a string of *n* characters; *date* is a domain used for attributes that are calendar dates, which we assume is available in the DBMS (other domains generally available are *time* and *money*).

The first table has a tuple for each account holder; it contains, in addition to the name and address of the customer, the account number and the balance of the account. The second table contains the transactions made on the account: deposits, withdrawals, payment of cheques, salary credits. The attribute TYPE, defined as a string of length 1, is actually a coded field; for example: D = deposit, W = withdrawal, C = payment of cheques, S = salary credit and so on. Each tuple corresponds to a transaction carried out on a bank account; transactions on the same date are numbered progressively. For example, on 14 January 1996, two transactions were carried out on account 1, one deposit and one withdrawal.

This simple example illustrates that the relational model constrains us to provide information that satisfies a particular structure. For example, with the schema illustrated in Figure 16.7, it is not possible to give information about the customer's Social Security number: if it became necessary to hold this information, we would have to change the schema of the database. Similarly, it is not possible to insert information about joint account holders. For this reason, the construction of a database schema is a particularly critical operation, in which the designer must be capable of applying a good deal of far-sightedness in intuiting the data structure that best suits the requirements of the applications of the present *and of the future*.

On the other hand, the example shows that it is possible to construct other information from the information stored in the tables. For example, it is possible to obtain the value of Jones's balance on 26 January 1996, or find out the names of customers who have withdrawn more than 200.00 in 1996. The construction of useful information from the data is performed by means of the SQL query language, illustrated in the next subsection.

As we can see, the relational model is very easy and basic. Its Spartan simplicity must not, however, deceive us: a rather rich and complex theory has developed around a very simple model. This theory makes the relational model a good vehicle for reasoning about databases.

A useful concept for describing the characteristics of relations is a key; as a preliminary, we define the restriction operation. The **restriction** of a tuple t on the attributes A of R, indicated as $t[A]$, is given by the list of values assumed by t on the attributes A of R. For example, if $t = (100, x, y)$ is a tuple of relation R with attributes A, B, C, then $t[A, B] = (100, x)$, $t[C, B] = (y, x)$.

A **key**[1] of a relation R is a subset K of its attributes which guarantees the following two characteristics:

- *uniqueness*: in any instance of R, there cannot exist two distinct tuples of R whose restriction on K is the same;
- *minimality*: it is not possible to remove an attribute from K without making the uniqueness condition invalid.

On the basis of the definition of a key and assuming that a relation does not contain identical tuples (as required by the formal definition of the relational model), it must necessarily have at least one key, which may be the set of all its attributes; in general, a relation may have more than one key.

In the above example, the relation BANK-ACCOUNT has ACC-NUMBER as its key; we assume that all bank accounts have a different number. Generally,

---

[1] Do not let the terminology confuse you: in the context of physical data structures, illustrated in Section 16.2, the attributes used for accessing files by means of special data structures are called keys (for instance, the 'key of the index'); in the context of the relational model, the term 'key' indicates attributes that uniquely identify the tuples of a relation.

however, an attribute such as NAME is not a key of the relation (there may be two account holders with the same name); for a similar reason, ADDRESS is not a key. Finally and most certainly, BALANCE is not a key (there may be two accounts with the same balance). Improbable though it may be, we cannot discount the possibility that there may be accounts held by different persons with the same name, living at the same address and having the same balance; therefore the list of attributes (NAME, ADDRESS, BALANCE) is not a key. Finally, the pair (ACC-NUMBER, NAME) is not a key, because it violates the minimality condition: the attribute NAME is superfluous.

In the second relation, defining the key is more problematic. Certainly, we exclude AMOUNT and TYPE. Many tuples have the same value for ACC-NUMBER, so this attribute is not sufficient to guarantee the characteristic of uniqueness. If we add TRANS-DATE to it, there is still the possibility that there are several transactions on the same day on the same account (see the example in Figure 16.7); thus, (ACC-NUMBER, TRANS-DATE) is not a key. Finally, we consider (ACC-NUMBER, TRANS-DATE, TRANS-NUMBER); this is the key we need. We may be certain that for a given bank account, on a certain day and for a certain transaction number, there is exactly one tuple in the relation; the reader is invited to verify that none of the attributes is superfluous.

In our example each relation has a single key. When there are several keys, it is possible to select one of them as the **primary key**; in general, the primary key corresponds to the set of attributes that is used most often to access the data. A concise form of description of a relational schema, in which the domain of the attributes does not appear, simply gives the name of the relation and the names of the attributes, identifying primary key attributes by underlining them, as follows:

BANK-ACCOUNT (ACC-NUMBER, NAME, ADDRESS, BALANCE)
TRANSACTION (ACC-NUMBER, TRANS-DATE, TRANS-NUMBER, AMOUNT, TYPE)

16.4.2 SQL (Structured Query Language)

SQL is supported on all relational databases; it was named 'intergalactic dataspeak' owing to its wide use in products of all kinds. Its success is in part due to standardization: the most recent definition of SQL, called SQL92, was produced by ANSI (American National Standards Institute) and ISO (International Organization for Standardization), two international standards bodies, in 1992, and while this book was being written a new version of the standard was being produced, with planned publication in 1998.

SQL operates on all DBMSs that use the relational data model; it allows relations to be defined and queries and modifications to a database to be expressed. The syntax of SQL is rather complex and its formal description would go beyond the aims of this book; also, the language is quite rich and 'redundant', so that the same query can be expressed in different ways. The following examples should, however, allow the reader to understand the principal elements of the language.

Relations are created in SQL via the command **CREATE TABLE**, which is followed by the name of the relation and the list of names and domains of the attributes; each relation is created individually. The set of relations created in this way constitutes the *logical level* of the database schema (see Section 16.3.3).

Each attribute of a relation may be defined together with some integrity constraints; for instance, it is possible to define primary keys, as illustrated in Figure 16.8. When the primary key is constituted by a single attribute, the specification directly follows that attribute; when the primary key is constituted by several attributes, its definition is given at the end of the relation definition. Another popular constraint is the indication **NOT NULL**, which indicates that a given attribute must always possess a legal value of its domain. When this constraint is not specified, any attribute instance can take a **NULL** value, a special symbol which indicates that the corresponding attribute value is not known.

In addition to the relations, it is possible to create **indexes**, that is, particular data structures that guarantee efficient access, by means of pointers in mass storage, to the tuples of a relation on the basis of the values of some of its attributes. An index is declared by giving it a name and specifying on which table and, within a table, on which attributes it operates. In particular, if indexes are declared 'unique', the attributes of the relation do not admit repeated values. Generally, a unique index is created for the primary key of the relation. Indexes are part of the so-called *physical level* of the database (see Section 16.3.3).

The definition of the schema at the logical and physical level for the database described in Figure 16.7 is illustrated in Figure 16.8.

```
CREATE TABLE  BANK-ACCOUNT
(ACC-NUMBER integer, PRIMARY KEY, NOT NULL,
NAME: char(20), NOT NULL,
ADDRESS: char(20),
BALANCE integer, NOT NULL).


CREATE UNIQUE INDEX BANK-ACCOUNT-KEY
ON BANK-ACCOUNT(ACC-NUMBER)


CREATE TABLE TRANSACTION
(ACC-NUMBER: integer, NOT NULL,
TRANS-DATE: date, NOT NULL,
TRANS-NUMBER: integer, NOT NULL,
AMOUNT: integer,
TYPE: char(1),
PRIMARY KEY(ACC-NUMBER, TRANS-DATE, TRANS-NUMBER).


CREATE UNIQUE INDEX TRANSACTION-KEY
ON TRANSACTION(ACC-NUMBER, TRANS-DATE, TRANS-NUMBER)
```

Figure 16.8   Definition of a relational schema in SQL.

The instructions **CREATE TABLE** and **CREATE INDEX** are part of the data definition language (DDL) in SQL; dual instructions such as **DROP TABLE** and **DROP INDEX** allow tables and indexes to be deleted. Data definition is not a very frequent operation and, being a highly critical operation, it is typically entrusted to the database administrator.

In the remainder of this section, we describe the data manipulation language (DML) of SQL. It is used by interactive users who sit at their terminals and send their SQL queries to the system; after each query, the system visualizes the result (typically in relational form). The language enables a user to manipulate relations by means of special operations, such as *selection, projection, join, union* and *difference*; they constitute a formal language (called **relational algebra**) which is capable of expressing most of the data manipulation operations required for querying a database. They are progressively introduced together with the SQL constructs that enable their expression.

The principal function of SQL is to describe computations involving databases in the context of application programs written in a conventional programming language; but we do not consider the construction of such programs because the interaction between SQL and conventional languages, through the so-called **Application Program Interfaces** (API) to databases, is rather complex.

Instructions in SQL are grouped into blocks; each block contains three types of clauses, **SELECT, FROM** and **WHERE**:

> **SELECT** names of attributes
> **FROM** names of relations
> **WHERE** search conditions on the data

The three clauses identify, respectively:

- The attributes to be included in the result.
- The relations from which to extract the data.
- The search condition. This condition may be very complex and may include other SQL blocks inside itself; it can also be omitted.

It has to be noted, however, that in commercial DBMSs relations may contain duplicates; if their elimination is required, it is necessary to add the DISTINCT clause in SQL:

> **SELECT DISTINCT** names of attributes
> **FROM** names of relations
> **WHERE** search conditions on the data

However, the elimination of duplicates is rather onerous and sometimes even undesirable, so SQL queries very often do not have the DISTINCT clause.

The following series of examples progressively introduce the various features of SQL; they are all based on the database schema and instance described in Figure 16.7 and they give a good idea of how, by means of a query language, it is possible to extract information from a database.

EXAMPLE 16.1

The simplest SQL queries involve just a single relation. For example, the query 'extract the names and addresses of all account holders' is simply expressed as:

> **SELECT** NAME, ADDRESS
> **FROM** BANK-ACCOUNT

The above expression performs a **projection** of the relation on two of its attributes; a projection is a relational operation which includes in the result only some of the columns of the relation, thereby reducing its grade. This query yields the result:

NAME	ADDRESS
Jones	5675 High St
Richards	341 Harper St
Quinton	11 Hanna Pl.
Murdock	3131 Emerson St

EXAMPLE 16.2

The query: 'extract the balance of account 2' is expressed as:

> **SELECT** BALANCE
> **FROM** BANK-ACCOUNT
> **WHERE** ACC-NUMBER = 2

The above expression performs a **selection** of the relation, by extracting all the tuples which satisfy a selection predicate, expressed in the **WHERE** clause; a selection reduces the cardinality of the relation. In this example, the condition extracts those tuples which satisfy the condition: ACC-NUMBER = 2. Then, the result is projected on the column BALANCE of the relation. The result is:

BALANCE
664.00

These two examples have introduced selections and projections, the two operations that are used for extracting information from a single relation. Let us now look at examples that involve several relations.

EXAMPLE 16.3

Consider the query: 'extract the names and addresses of account holders who had a transaction on 27 January 1996'. The corresponding SQL query is:

> **SELECT** NAME, ADDRESS
> **FROM** BANK-ACCOUNT, TRANSACTION
> **WHERE** TRANS-DATE = 27-1-96
> **AND** BANK-ACCOUNT.ACC-NUMBER = TRANSACTION.ACC-NUMBER

This SQL expression introduces a **join** operation; joins combine two relations into a single one, by concatenating the tuples from the two relations that satisfy a condition, called the join predicate, expressed within the **WHERE** clause. In this example:

> BANK-ACCOUNT.ACC-NUMBER = TRANSACTION.ACC-NUMBER

Thus, tuples of the BANK-ACCOUNT and TRANSACTION relations are concatenated when they have the same ACC-NUMBER. Joins produce a relation whose grade is the sum of the grades of the operand relations; its maximum possible cardinality is given by the product of the cardinalities of the operands, but its actual cardinality is normally much lower because few tuples satisfy the join predicate.

In addition to a join, the above query selects the tuples satisfying the condition: TRANS-DATE = 27-1-96, and then projects the result on attributes NAME, ADDRESS. Thus, the above query is an example of the so-called **select–project–join** queries, mixing these three relational operations into one SQL block. The result of the SQL query evaluation is:

NAME	ADDRESS
Jones	5675 High St
Murdock	3131 Emerson St

An alternative syntax, available in the most recent versions of SQL, allows this query to be expressed as follows, separating the two predicates:

> **SELECT** NAME, ADDRESS
> **FROM** BANK-ACCOUNT **JOIN** TRANSACTION
> **ON** BANK-ACCOUNT.ACC-NUMBER = TRANSACTION.ACC-NUMBER
> **WHERE** TRANS-DATE = 27-1-96

This syntax makes the join condition (JOIN) between the two tables more explicit.

Binary queries allow the **union** (UNION), **difference** (MINUS) and **intersection** (INTERSECT) of two tables to be calculated, where the tables are produced as a result of evaluating SQL blocks. The syntax of binary queries is simply obtained by placing a binary operation between two SQL blocks.

EXAMPLE 16.4

Consider the query: 'extract the accounts with a balance above 2,000 or those accounts for which some transactions for an amount higher than 1,000 have been performed'. The query in SQL is:

SELECT ACC-NUMBER
FROM BANK-ACCOUNT
WHERE BALANCE > 2,000
   UNION
SELECT ACC-NUMBER
FROM TRANSACTION
WHERE AMOUNT > 1,000

This query introduces a union operation between two relations; **union** operations can be performed only between relations with a **compatible schema**, that is, relations with the same grade and with attributes whose values are ordinately on the same domains. In the above case, the union is performed between relations having a single attribute ACC-NUMBER, which is compatible, and produces as its result the union between tuples in the first operand and tuples in the second operand. The first operand of the union is the relation:

ACC-NUMBER
1
3
4

The second operand is the relation:

ACC-NUMBER
1
4

The relation that results from the evaluation of the entire expression is:

ACC-NUMBER
1
3
4

EXAMPLE 16.5

Consider the query: 'extract the accounts with a balance above 2,000 for which no transaction for an amount higher than 1,000 has been effected'. The query in SQL is:

SELECT ACC-NUMBER
FROM BANK-ACCOUNT
WHERE BALANCE > 2,000
   MINUS
SELECT ACC-NUMBER
FROM TRANSACTION
WHERE AMOUNT > 1,000

This query introduces a difference operation between two relations; **difference** operations can be performed only between relations with a compatible schema, and produce as their result the difference between tuples in the first operand and tuples in the second operand. The relation that results from the evaluation of the entire expression is:

ACC-NUMBER
3

With this example, we have completed the analysis of the five relational operations (selection, projection, join, union and difference); they are the main ingredients for learning how to manipulate databases. We consider a few other examples of select–project–join queries, then further extend their expressive power.

EXAMPLE 16.6

Consider the query: 'extract the date, number, amount and type of Mr Jones's transactions'. The corresponding query in SQL is:

SELECT TRANS-DATE, TRANS-NUMBER, AMOUNT, TYPE
FROM TRANSACTION, BANK-ACCOUNT
WHERE NAME = Jones
AND BANK-ACCOUNT.ACC-NUMBER = TRANSACTION.ACC-NUMBER

The answer to this query is:

TRANS-DATE	TRANS-NUMBER	AMOUNT	TYPE
14-1-96	1	+200.00	D
14-1-96	2	−500.00	W
27-1-96	1	+2,700.00	S

EXAMPLE 16.7

Consider the query: 'extract the name of the account holder, the amount and transaction type of all account holders with a balance higher than 2,000 and a deposit or salary credit transaction type'. The corresponding query in SQL is:

SELECT NAME, AMOUNT, TYPE
FROM TRANSACTION, BANK-ACCOUNT
WHERE BALANCE > 2,000
AND (TYPE = D **OR** TYPE = S)
AND BANK-ACCOUNT.ACC-NUMBER = TRANSACTION.ACC-NUMBER

The answer to this query is:

NAME	AMOUNT	TYPE
Jones	+ 200.00	D
Jones	+2,700.00	S
Murdock	+1,850.40	S

SQL allows us to evaluate new attributes, obtained by simple numeric operations (sums, differences and so on) on each tuple of the resulting relation; numeric operations can also be used in the **WHERE** clause.

EXAMPLE 16.8

Consider the query: 'extract the account number and date, transaction number and 10% of salary credit amounts'. The corresponding query in SQL is:

SELECT ACC-NUMBER, TRANS-DATE, TRANS-NUMBER, AMOUNT * 0.1
FROM TRANSACTION
WHERE TYPE = S

The result is:

ACC-NUMBER	TRANS-DATE	TRANS-NUMBER	AMOUNT * 0.1
1	27-1-96	1	+270.00
4	27-1-96	1	+185.04

EXAMPLE 16.9

Consider the query 'extract the name of the account holder, balance and transaction amounts, for all transactions corresponding to payment of cheques whose amount exceeds the balance of 50,000':

SELECT NAME, BALANCE, AMOUNT, TYPE
FROM TRANSACTION, BANK-ACCOUNT
WHERE BALANCE + 50,000 < AMOUNT
AND TYPE = C
AND BANK-ACCOUNT.ACC-NUMBER = TRANSACTION.ACC-NUMBER

The result of this query is empty, as no tuple satisfies the join and selection conditions.

Other important characteristics of SQL include the ordering and grouping of tuples and the use of nested subqueries. At the end of an SQL block, it is possible to insert a clause, called **ORDER BY**, to order the resulting relation on the basis of the values of some of its attributes.

EXAMPLE 16.10

Consider the query: 'extract the entire relation BANK-ACCOUNT, ordering the accounts in ascending balance order'. The corresponding query in SQL is:

SELECT *
FROM BANK-ACCOUNT
ORDER BY BALANCE

Note the use of the 'asterisk' to indicate all attributes of a relation. The result is:

ACC-NUMBER	NAME	ADDRESS	BALANCE
2	Richards	341 Harper St	664.00
4	Murdock	3131 Emerson St	3,400.00
1	Jones	5675 High St	3,678.00
3	Quinton	11 Hanna Pl.	6,777.50

The order is ascending; the ASC clause is implied. Descending order is obtained by postfixing fields with the DESC clause, as follows:

SELECT *
FROM BANK-ACCOUNT
ORDER BY BALANCE **DESC**

The ordering of transactions in ascending order of accounts, descending order of dates and ascending order of transaction numbers is obtained by:

SELECT *
FROM TRANSACTION
ORDER BY ACC-NUMBER **ASC**, TRANS-DATE **DESC**,
    TRANS-NUMBER **ASC**

The resulting relation is:

ACC-NUMBER	TRANS-DATE	TRANS-NUMBER	AMOUNT	TYPE
1	27-1-96	1	+2,700.00	S
1	14-1-96	1	+200.00	D
1	14-1-96	2	−500.00	W
3	25-1-96	1	−650.00	C
4	27-1-96	1	+1,850.40	S

Inside an SQL block, it is possible to place a clause, called **GROUP BY**, to group together all the tuples that have the same value for certain attributes, called **grouping attributes**. More formally, the clause **GROUP BY** referring to attributes $A1, ..., An$ of a relation R induces a partition on R, such that each equivalence class of the partition contains tuples that assume the same value on the restriction $t[A1,..., An]$. For example, the clause **GROUP BY** ACC-NUMBER applied to the TRANSACTION relation of Figure 16.7 induces a partition into three classes:

ACC-NUMBER	TRANS-DATE	TRANS-NUMBER	AMOUNT	TYPE
1	27-1-96	1	+2,700.00	S
1	14-1-96	1	+200.00	D
1	14-1-96	2	−500.00	W
3	25-1-96	1	−650.00	C
4	27-1-96	1	+1,850.40	S

Once the partition is built, it is possible to evaluate functions aggregated on the numeric attributes of the tuples of each equivalence class: **MIN** (minimum), **MAX** (maximum), **SUM** (sum), **AVG** (average); furthermore, it is possible to count the number of elements using the function **COUNT**. It is also possible to express, by means of the **HAVING** clause, predicates that apply to the equivalence classes. The **GROUP BY** and **ORDER BY** clauses are optional; the **HAVING** clause is optional and can be used only when the **GROUP BY** clause is used. Therefore, a more precise (but still incomplete) syntax of the SQL block is the following, where square brackets include optional parts:

SELECT names of attributes
FROM names of relations
[**WHERE** search conditions on data]
[**GROUP BY** names of attributes creating equivalence classes]
[**HAVING** conditions on equivalence classes]
[**ORDER BY** names of attributes]

EXAMPLE 16.11

Consider the query: 'extract bank account numbers, sum of amounts and number of transactions for all accounts whose total transactions in January 1996 exceeded 1,000'. The corresponding query in SQL is:

SELECT ACC-NUMBER, SUM(AMOUNT), COUNT(*)
FROM TRANSACTION
WHERE TRANS-DATE > 1-1-96 **AND** TRANS-DATE < 31-1-96
GROUP BY ACC-NUMBER
HAVING SUM(AMOUNT) > 1,000

The result of this query is:

ACC-NUMBER	SUM(AMOUNT)	COUNT(*)
1	+2,400.00	3
4	+1,850.40	1

In SQL it is possible to construct predicates that contain other, lower-level SQL blocks inside them; thus, nested blocks are created. The simplest case of nesting is a join condition, as illustrated by the following example.

EXAMPLE 16.12

Consider again the query: 'extract the names and addresses of account holders who had a transaction on 27 January 1996', already expressed in SQL in Example 16.3. It can also be expressed, using nested blocks, as follows:

SELECT NAME, ADDRESS
FROM BANK-ACCOUNT
WHERE ACC-NUMBER **IN**
    SELECT ACC-NUMBER
    FROM TRANSACTION
    WHERE TRANS-DATE = 27-1-96

The above query has two blocks, denoted as upper- and lower-level blocks, connected by a special keyword, called a **connector** (in the above example, **IN** is the connector). The meaning of this query is as follows:

- Initially the lower-level block is evaluated, producing as a result a collection of account numbers; in general, the result produced by the lower-level block is an arbitrary, unnamed relation.

- Subsequently, the upper-level block is evaluated: for each tuple *t* at the higher level a predicate is evaluated that involves *t* and the result of the lower-level block. In the above case *t* is selected if its account number appears among the numbers extracted by the lower-level block.

IN is one of the possible connectors; other connectors include **NOT IN**, **ANY** and **ALL** (preceded by a comparator), **EXISTS** and **DOES NOT EXIST**. A complete treatment of connectors goes beyond the scope of this book.

EXAMPLE 16.13

Consider again the query: 'extract the date, number, amount and type of Mr Jones's transactions', already formulated in Example 16.6. With nested blocks, it becomes:

SELECT TRANS-DATE, TRANS-NUMBER, AMOUNT, TYPE
FROM TRANSACTION
WHERE ACC-NUMBER **IN**
    SELECT ACC-NUMBER
    FROM BANK-ACCOUNT
    WHERE NAME = Jones

Note that the connection between two blocks in Examples 16.12 and 16.13, which are equivalent, respectively, to Examples 16.3 and 16.6, is particularly simple, because the attributes projected in the result belong to a single relation. Constructing a query with nested blocks whose **SELECT** clause includes attributes of several relations (see Example 16.7) requires the use of relational variables which will not be introduced in this text.

SQL allows the contents of the database to be modified, by means of the instructions *insert*, *delete* and *update*. Each of these instructions refers to a single relation, even though the blocks and predicates used inside the instructions can involve other relations.

An **INSERT** instruction allows tuples or the result of a query (provided it has a schema compatible with that of the relation) to be inserted into a relation, according to the following syntax:

> **INSERT INTO** Relation **VALUES** (<tuple>,<tuple>,...)
> **INSERT INTO** VALUES ([SQL-Block])

A **DELETE** instruction deletes from a relation the tuples that satisfy a selection predicate:

> **DELETE FROM** Relation **WHERE** Predicate

An **UPDATE** instruction modifies the contents of a relation's attributes, for all tuples that satisfy a selection predicate:

> **UPDATE** Relation
> **SET** Attribute = Expression
> [, Attribute = Expression]
> **WHERE** Predicate

The expression indicated in the syntax of **UPDATE** can be a simple numeric value or a numeric expression that involves the modified attribute; in this case, the expression refers to the value of the relation before the operation is carried out.

EXAMPLE 16.14

A new account holder is inserted via the SQL instruction:

> **INSERT INTO** BANK-ACCOUNT VALUES
> (<5, Richardson, 1102 Ramona St, 100.00>)

EXAMPLE 16.15

Transactions of type S (payment of salary) are deleted via the SQL instruction:

> **DELETE FROM** TRANSACTION
> **WHERE** TYPE = S

EXAMPLE 16.16

An increase of 0.1% in the balance of account holder Richards is obtained via the following SQL instruction:

UPDATE BANK-ACCOUNT
SET BALANCE = BALANCE * 1.001
WHERE NAME = Richards

After the queries contained in Examples 16.14–16.16 have been executed, the instance of the database of Figure 16.7 is modified as illustrated in Figure 16.9.

BANK-ACCOUNT

ACC-NUMBER	NAME	ADDRESS	BALANCE
1	Jones	5675 High St	3,678.00
2	Richards	341 Harper St	664.66
3	Quinton	11 Hanna Pl.	6,777.50
4	Murdock	3131 Emerson St	3,400.00
5	Richardson	1102 Ramona St	100.10

TRANSACTION

ACC-NUMBER	TRANS-DATE	TRANS-NUMBER	AMOUNT	TYPE
1	14-1-96	1	+200.00	D
1	14-1-96	2	–500.00	W
3	25-1-96	1	–650.00	C

Figure 16.9   Instance of the database after some modifications.

In SQL, all commands are normally executed within a transaction, which is started automatically when the interactive user connects to an SQL interface, or when an application program executes the first SQL command. Thus, the system guarantees that the execution of a given sequence of SQL queries, issued by a given user, possesses the ACID properties (discussed in Section 16.3.4) with respect to all other transactions that are concurrently being executed. At the end of a transaction, a user executes one of two commands to terminate a transaction:

- **COMMIT WORK** causes correct termination of the transaction: after its execution, the instance of the database reflects all modifications performed by the SQL instructions executed since the start of the session (or since the execution of a previous **COMMIT WORK** command).

- **ROLLBACK WORK** causes the transaction to be nullified: after its execution, the instance of the database returns to its value before the start of the transaction. This command allows the effects of the execution of some operations on data to be nullified when it is not possible to guarantee a correct and complete execution of the transaction.

A transaction cannot terminate without executing one of the two above commands (**COMMIT WORK** or **ROLLBACK WORK**); if they are not specified by the programmer, they are forced by the system. The DBMS makes sure that committed transactions have the ACID properties mentioned above, while transactions which are rolled back leave the database unchanged. These outcomes occur in any case, even if there is a failure in the computer system, owing to the robustness of DBMS software.

EXAMPLE 16.17

Suppose the following SQL instructions are executed in sequence:

UPDATE BANK-ACCOUNT
SET BALANCE = BALANCE + 500.00
WHERE NAME = Richards;
UPDATE BANK-ACCOUNT
SET BALANCE = BALANCE – 500.00
WHERE NAME = Jones;

These instructions allow money to be transferred from Richards' account to Jones's account. If, at this point, the user gives the system the command:

COMMIT WORK

execution terminates correctly and the money is transferred; if, instead, the user gives the command:

ROLLBACK WORK

execution is terminated, leaving the database unchanged.

*16.4.3 Elements of database design

Designing a database is a demanding and critical task. To make good use of a database, it is essential to design its schema properly, so that it gives a faithful representation of the data that exists in the application being designed. Schema design can be approached using different design methodologies. One widely used technique uses special data models, called **conceptual models**, which are very expressive and therefore the most suitable for describing reality; conceptual schemas are then transformed into relational schemas. This design methodology is certainly commendable, especially if the schema to be designed is rather complex, but it requires a different data model and a certain number of design steps. In this book, a different approach is preferred, the so-called **normalization of relations**, which uses the relational model for the design.

Normalization is a design methodology that transforms an initial database schema into a schema that contains **normalized relations**; these relations enjoy particular characteristics. When relations are normalized, each 'fact' of the real world corresponds to one tuple, so that its insertion, deletion or modification in a single operation is possible. During the normalization process, relations which do not satisfy the above property are identified and their schema is modified, while maintaining their original information content.

The starting point of normalization is the so-called **first normal form** (1NF); any relation which satisfies the definition given in this text is already in first normal form. The normalization process produces relations in higher normal forms (**second normal form** (2NF), **third normal form** (3NF) and so on; in this book, we go up to third normal form, but higher-order normal forms have been defined). Before we go deeper into the process of normalization, we illustrate some examples of anomalies that can occur when relations are not normalized.

Relation SUPPLIER			
SUP-ID	SUP-TOWN	PROD-ID	QUANT
1	MILAN	1	100
1	MILAN	2	10
1	MILAN	3	500
2	LONDON	1	50
2	LONDON	2	20
3	FRANKFURT	2	12
4	BOSTON	1	200
4	BOSTON	4	25

Figure 16.10   Example of a non-normalized relation.

Consider the schema illustrated in Figure 16.10, which describes data relating to suppliers, products and orders. The attributes of the SUPPLIER relation are: SUP-ID (identifier of supplier), SUP-TOWN (town of supplier), PROD-ID (product identifier) and QUANT (quantity ordered). The key of the relation is the pair of attributes (SUP-ID, PROD-ID): we assume that there is at most one tuple for each supplier/product pair containing the total quantity of product ordered from a supplier.

The relation SUPPLIER presents some 'anomalies':

- In *insert*: it is not possible to introduce information about the town of a supplier until the first purchase order has been issued.

- In *delete*: when a supplier has just one order in the database and that order is deleted, the information about the supplier's address also disappears.

- In *modification*: if a supplier's town changes, it is necessary to modify all the tuples of the relation.

These anomalies arise because the relation SUPPLIER contains two distinct kinds of facts: the description of suppliers and the description of orders.

Normalization is a technique that helps to identify and eliminate these anomalies, by transforming the schema. There are several types of anomalies, which correspond to certain formal properties of relations. At each normalization step, we get rid of one kind of anomaly, by changing the database schema; thus each normalization step corresponds to a given schema transformation. We make sure that the information content of the database is left unchanged by each transformation; that is, the original database can be reconstructed by means of suitable operations.

Normalization of relations is based on **functional dependences**. Given two sets of attributes A and B of a relation R, there is a functional dependence $A \rightarrow B$ if, for any instance of R, each distinct value of the restriction $t[A]$ is associated by R with only one value of the restriction $t[B]$. As a consequence of the above definition, whenever two tuples t_1 and t_2 have the same value of attributes A, they must also have the same value of attributes B. We also say that A *determines* B or that B *functionally depends on* A. In the above example, we say that A is the *left side* of the dependence, B is the *right side*.

For example, in the relation SUPPLIER illustrated in Figure 16.10, we can define the functional dependences:

- SUP-ID → SUP-TOWN
- SUP-ID, PROD-ID → QUANT

We have assumed that there is only one town for each supplier and only one quantity on order for each *<supplier, product>* pair.

From the definition of a key we can deduce that, for any given key, *each non-key attribute functionally depends on the key*; therefore we have the functional dependence:

- SUP-ID, PROD-ID → SUP-TOWN, QUANT

The above functional dependence is equivalently written as two distinct dependences:

- SUP-ID, PROD-ID → SUP-TOWN
- SUP-ID, PROD-ID → QUANT

Note that some functional dependences are **redundant**, because they contain superfluous attributes. For example, the next example is redundant in the left side, because the attribute SUP-ID can be eliminated and the functional dependence is still valid:

- SUP-ID, SUP-TOWN, PROD-ID → QUANT

In the next example, PROD-ID on the right side is clearly superfluous, because it appears on the left side.

- SUP-ID, PROD-ID → PROD-ID, QUANT

In the following, we consider only nonredundant functional dependences.

Finally, let us turn to normalization. The definition of second normal form first requires a class of functional dependences, called **full dependences**, to be identified. A dependence $A \rightarrow B$ is full when there is no attribute of the right side that functionally depends on a subset of the attributes of the left side. From this definition, we deduce that the functional dependence:

- SUP-ID, PROD-ID → SUP-TOWN, QUANT

is not full, as the attribute SUP-TOWN depends only on the attribute SUP-ID.

We are now ready to define second normal form. *A relation is in* **second normal form** (2NF) *if, for all keys, non-key attributes fully depend on the key.* From this definition and from the example illustrated earlier, we deduce that the relation SUPPLIER is *not* in 2NF. (SUP-ID, PROD-ID) is the key of the relation and SUP-TOWN does not fully depend on the key. Relations that are not in 2NF undergo the following **normalization process**. Let us assume a prototype relation $R(K1, K2, A, B)$. Assume that R has the key $(K1, K2)$ and that, in addition to the dependence $K1, K2 \rightarrow A, B$, the dependence $K1 \rightarrow A$ holds, too. Therefore, R is not in 2NF. The relation R is decomposed into two relations $R1$ and $R2$, defined as follows:

- $R1$ contains the attributes $K1$, A and has the key $K1$; it contains the *projection of R on the dependences $K1 \rightarrow A$.*

- $R2$ contains all other attributes of R except A and has the key $(K1, K2)$.

This process produces two relations with an information content identical to the original table, which can be obtained from $R1$ and $R2$ by means of a join on the key $K1$. Applying normalization to the relation SUPPLIER of Figure 16.10, we obtain the two relations illustrated in Figure 16.11. Note that the two relations contain the same information as the original relation, but each fact is represented by only one tuple.

Relation ORDERS		
SUP-ID	PROD-ID	QUANT
1	1	100
1	2	10
1	3	500
2	1	50
2	2	2
3	2	12
4	1	200
4	4	25

Relation SUPPLIER	
SUP-ID	SUP-TOWN
1	MILAN
2	LONDON
3	FRANKFURT
4	BOSTON

Figure 16.11 Example of relations in second normal form.

Relation EMPLOYEE		
EMP-ID	DEP	DIV
1	K55	Sales
2	K55	Sales
3	J12	Sales
4	T32	R&D
5	T32	R&D
6	K55	Sales
7	J12	Sales
8	T32	R&D
9	T33	R&D

Figure 16.12   Example of a non-normalized relation.

We continue our description of normalization by looking at another cause of anomalies. Consider the example of Figure 16.12. The relation EMPLOYEE has three attributes: the key (EMP-ID) and the department (DEP) and division (DIV) the employee belongs to; in the firm, divisions are subdivided into departments. Thus, the following functional dependences hold:

- EMP-ID $\rightarrow$ DIV
- EMP-ID $\rightarrow$ DEP
- DEP $\rightarrow$ DIV

This relation EMPLOYEE presents some 'anomalies':

- In *insert*: it is not possible to introduce a department into a division if that department has no employees.

- In *delete*: when a department has only one employee and this employee is deleted, the information about which division this department belongs to also disappears.

- In *modification*: if a department changes division, it is necessary to modify many of the tuples in the relation.

The definition of third normal form first requires the identification of another class of functional dependences, called **transitive dependences**. A dependence $A \rightarrow B$ is transitive if there is a set of attributes C for which the dependences $A \rightarrow C$ and $C \rightarrow B$ are valid. In this case, we say that B *transitively depends* on A via C. From the above definitions, we deduce that the dependence EMP-ID $\rightarrow$ DIV is transitive, as DIV transitively depends on EMP-ID via DEV.

We are now ready to define the third normal form. *A relation is in* **third normal form** *(3NF) if it is in second normal form and, for all keys, none of the non-key attributes transitively depends on the key*. Relations that are not in 3NF undergo the following normalization process. Let us assume that the relation $R(K1, A, B)$ has the key $K1$ and that, in addition to the dependence $K1 \rightarrow A, B$, the dependence $A \rightarrow B$ holds, too. Therefore, R is not in 3NF. The relation R is decomposed into two relations $R1$ and $R2$, defined as follows:

Relation EMP-DEP	
EMP-ID	DEP
1	K55
2	K55
4	T32
5	T32
6	K55
7	J12
8	T32
9	T33

Relation DEP-DIV	
DEP	DIV
K55	Sales
J12	Sales
T32	R&D
T33	R&D

Figure 16.13 Example of relations in third normal form.

- $R1$ contains the attributes $K1$, A and the key $K1$; it contains the *projection of R on the dependence $K1 \rightarrow A$*.
- $R2$ contains the attributes A and B and has A as a key; it contains the *projection of R on the dependence $A \rightarrow B$*.

This process produces two relations with an information content identical to the original table, which can be obtained from $R1$ and $R2$ via a join on the attribute A.

By applying the definition, we deduce that EMPLOYEE, although in 2NF, is not in 3NF; thus we apply the normalization process, obtaining the two relations shown in Figure 16.13. Note that, as in the relations of Figure 16.11, each fact is represented by only one tuple in the database.

Thus, we have seen two consecutive transformations that produce normalized relations. The theory of normalization includes further normalizations, but these are less useful and therefore omitted from this text. Normalization can be applied individually to all relations in a database; when all relations are in at least second (or third) normal form, we say that the schema is in second (or third) normal form.

EXAMPLE 16.18

Consider the following problem. A shipping agency handles its orders using a small relational database. Its data describes the quantity of merchandise contained on each shelf of the warehouse, the quantity of merchandise ordered by each distributor and the deliveries to be made to the customers, together with the type of payment for the order. The corresponding relational tables are:

WAREHOUSE(<u>PART, SHELF</u>, Q-AV, COST, PACK)
ORDER(<u>CODE-ORD, PART</u>, Q-ORD, DISTRIBUTOR, DATE)
DELIVERY(<u>CODE-ORD</u>, FIRM, DELIV-DATE, BANK-COD, PAY-MODE)

The relations are not normalized and this causes severe anomalies; for example, the data common to each order (date and distributor) are repeated for each ordered part, and the data for each firm to which deliveries are made (bank code and payment mode) is repeated for each delivery.

An analysis of the data identifies the following functional dependences:

PART, SHELF → Q-DISP
PART → COST, PACK
CODE-ORD, PART → Q-ORD
CODE-ORD → DISTRIBUTOR, DATE
CODE-ORD → DELIV-DATE, FIRM
FIRM → BANK-COD, PAY-MODE

On the basis of these functional dependences, we recognize that the relations WAREHOUSE and ORDER are only in first normal form, while the relation DELIVERY is only in second normal form. In particular: attributes COST and PACK do not fully depend on the key (PART, SHELF) of relation WAREHOUSE; attributes DISTRIBUTOR and DATE do not fully depend on the key (CODE-ORD, PART) of relation ORDER; and attributes BANK-COD and PAY-MODE transitively depend on the key CODE-ORD of relation DELIVERY via attribute FIRM. Each of the above relations is therefore transformed into third normal form, decomposing it into two relations as illustrated above. Thus, we obtain the following schema (in third normal form):

PART(<u>PART</u>, COST, PACK)
WAREHOUSE(<u>PART, SHELF</u>, Q-DISP)
ORDER(<u>CODE-ORD</u>, DISTRIBUTOR, DATE)
ORDER-LINE(<u>CODE-ORD, PART</u>, Q-ORD)
DELIVERY(<u>CODE-ORD</u>, FIRM, DELIV-DATE)
CLIENT(<u>FIRM</u>, BANK-COD, PAY-MODE)

Note that this schema allows each part, each order line and each client to be described, separating this information from the original table. Each functional dependence corresponds exactly to one table and each table has only one key, constituted by the left side of the corresponding functional dependence.

16.4.4 Tools for the programming of applications

What we have seen so far allows us to design an appropriate schema in which each relation is in an acceptable normal form. Let us now see how to construct applications, that is, user programs to query and manipulate a database. The SQL language presented in Section 16.4.2 allows all these operations to be carried out, but SQL is not suitable for the end users of a database, who normally perform repetitive and predefined tasks. For these users, applications that allow simple and schematic interaction are built. To understand the nature of these applications more clearly, consider again the bank accounts database illustrated in Figure 16.7; before it can be used, it is necessary to prepare programs that allow users to:

- open a new account
- withdraw cash from the account
- deposit cheques in the account
- transfer money to and from other accounts
- obtain a statement of the balance and recent operations
- close the account

Each of these applications involves the execution of operations on the database and is designed to satisfy the requirements of the bank's employees; in some cases, the applications can also interact directly with customers, who may use automated teller machines and cash dispensers. A typical interaction involves the acquisition of some initial data: choice of application, account number, amount to withdraw. After execution of the application, its outcome and the resulting data are shown on the terminal: for example, the balance after a withdrawal operation.

Information exchanged with the user during the execution of an application is shown on the terminal in a particular kind of format, called **forms**. A form contains fixed information (text and/or diagrams) which illustrates its structure, and some **fields** designed to contain the data exchanged between the application and its user; this data is typed in by the user (input data) or written by the application (output data). The design of the structure of forms is essential to the success of an application; there are standard tools for **form management** and for 'attaching' to each form the operations to be carried out on the database.

Figure 16.14 illustrates the definition of a form to be used by a bank employee to perform the normal credit and debit operations seen earlier in this chapter. The form is divided into parts concerned with the initial identification of the account, the submission of an operation and the description of its effect. Some fields on the form are associated with attributes of the relations in the database, indicating, for example, the name of the attribute inside each field; other fields are used to describe the interaction with the user. Obviously, in addition to this description, the programmer must supply further specifications that allow the various fields on the screen to be connected to appropriate queries on the database.

Let us analyse the form in Figure 16.14 in more detail. In the first part of the form we find two fields, concerning the account number and the name of the account holder. Normally, the terminal operator uses the account number, but if the account holder cannot remember the number, the operator can use an appropriate substring of the last and first names, provided that homonyms are checked (for example, by orally asking the customer for his/her address and comparing it with the one displayed on the screen). Subsequently, the terminal operator enters the

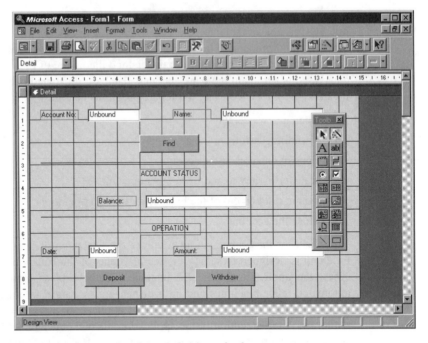

Figure 16.14   Example of the definition of a form.

operations, one after the other, and the system reacts by showing the outcome and the balance after each operation. Interaction is normally simplified to a minimum, avoiding asking the user for superfluous information; for example, the current date can be inserted automatically by the application, while the transaction number (necessary for the database) is automatically generated by increasing a counter. Therefore, the execution of this application involves:

- a query on the BANK-ACCOUNT relation (to connect the number, name and address of the account holder and to extract the balance);

- a query on the TRANSACTION relation (to extract the highest transaction number and latest date for this account);

- an insertion into the TRANSACTION relation for each execution of an operation;

- a modification of the BALANCE of the BANK-ACCOUNT relation after each operation.

Figure 16.15 illustrates the use of the form to enter a new transaction; the fields contain the data after a deposit operation accepted by the system.

Another way of extracting information from databases is to generate **reports**. In general, reports contain large amounts of information extracted from databases, constructed by means of aggregations; the generation of reports is requested periodically and does not involve interaction with the users. As in the case of forms, there

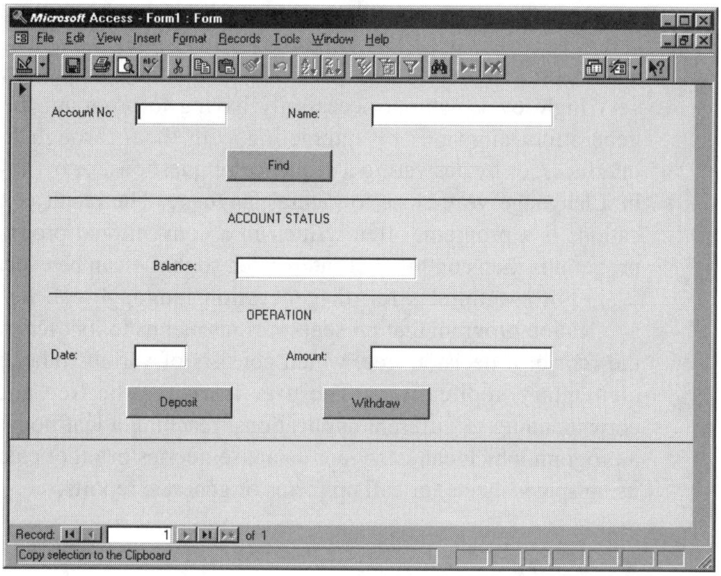

Figure 16.15 Example of the use of a form.

are standard instruments for producing reports, known as **report generators**, which contain commands to generate the format of the reports in an appropriate manner, combining textual and graphic information with the information extracted from the database.

An example of a report is the monthly balance statement sent to all account holders, which summarizes all transactions carried out during the month and the balance of the account. The report shown in Figure 16.16 contains a label (used as the postal address) and the balance statement (indicating the current month, list of transactions and final balance).

to: G. Jones
     5675 High St
     94301 Palo Alto (CA)

Statement of balance no. 1 January 1996

DATE	TRANSACTION NO	AMOUNT	TYPE
14-1-96	1	+200.00	D
14-1-96	2	−500.00	W
27-1-96	1	+2,700.00	S
28-1-96	1	+500.00	D

Balance on 31-12-95:   4,178.00

Figure 16.16 Example of a simple report.

Finally, there are other software tools for generating applications, the so-called **fourth-generation languages** which integrate other tools (including form and report generators) and allow applications to be built by specifying them at a very high level, without necessarily having to program; the designer uses fourth-generation languages by interacting with them through forms and menu-based interfaces, or by answering a sequence of questions, or by describing the application in a language very close to natural language. The result of processing the specifications is a program, often written in a conventional programming language; this program is then compiled or interpreted so that it can be executed.

For example, a fourth-generation language can be used for building an application program that presents various menus to its users; the first menu contains the root of a decision tree, which consists of various other menus and other more elementary applications. The user traverses the tree and reaches the leaves, corresponding to different applications; reaching a leaf node corresponds to calling a program which can carry out database queries or other calculations (for example, using spreadsheets) or call up forms or generate reports.

Exercises

16.1   Construct a sequential file containing 20 records and with a usage factor of 0.75.

    (a)   Describe the binary search procedure. How long does the search take in the worst case? And in the average case?

    (b)   Add another 4 records to the file and handle conflicts by moving records to nearby empty blocks. How many move operations are necessary to maintain the ordering?

16.2   Describe, in detail, the search procedure in an ordered sequential file with overflow. Assume that the records in the overflow zone can be connected to each other, forming chains of arbitrary length.

16.3   Construct a file with hash-based access, containing 10 records distributed over 15 blocks. Choose the algorithm and the 10 key values such that there are no conflicts.

    (a)   Add another 4 records to the file and handle conflicts by placing records in the first free blocks available.

    (b)   Consider the key-based search procedure on the file thus obtained. How many accesses are necessary in the worst case?

16.4   Suppose that at a certain point a disk unit in a computer system is changed and the data is reorganized. Which database properties guarantee that the application programs will not need to be rewritten?

16.5   Consider a typical information system (for example, a flight booking system). Describe its users in terms of the classification proposed in Section 16.3.5 and describe some of the operations they carry out on the data.

The next exercises refer to the following relational database:

> **RELATION** STUDENT
> (REG-NUMBER: char(5), **PRIMARY KEY, NOT NULL**,
> NAME: char(20), **NOT NULL**,
> DATE-N: date,
> COURSE-YEAR: integer,
> COURSE-TYPE: char(1)).
>
> **RELATION** COURSE
> (COURSE-CODE: char(6), **PRIMARY KEY, NOT NULL**,
> TITLE: char(20),
> LECTURER: char (20)).
>
> **RELATION** EXAM
> (COURSE-CODE: char(6), **NOT NULL**,
> REG-NUMBER: char(5), **NOT NULL**,
> DATE-E: date, **NOT NULL**,
> MARK: integer, **NOT NULL**,
> **PRIMARY KEY**(COURSE-CODE,REG-NUMBER)).

16.6 Discuss the choices of the keys of the relations. Explain what assumptions are implied by these choices.

16.7 Populate each of the relations with at least 5 tuples.

16.8 Write the definition of some indexes in SQL.

16.9 Express in SQL the following queries:

(a) Extract course codes and lecturers of 'Foundations of Computer Science' and 'Analysis'.

(b) Extract the names of third- and fourth-year students enrolled in the 'Elements of Aeronautics' course.

(c) Extract the names and registration numbers of students who sat exams in 'Analysis' on 10 January 1996 and obtained a mark higher than 28.

(d) Extract the registration numbers, names and marks of students who have passed the exam of a course taught by Jones or Richards.

(e) Extract the registration numbers of students who have passed 'Analysis' but not 'Foundations of Computer Science'.

(f) Extract the lecturers of courses whose exams have been passed by 'G. Jones' with marks higher than 25.

16.10 Express, if possible, the queries of Exercise 16.9 using nested SQL queries.

16.11 Express the queries (c) – (e) of Exercise 16.9 ordering the result in ascending registration number order.

16.12 Express in SQL the following modifications to the database:

(a) Add some students and exams.

(b) Delete student A67578 and all of his/her exams from the database.

(c) Modify the database, renaming the courses 'Computer Programming' and 'Elements of Computer Science' as 'Foundations of Computer Science'.

(d) Add one extra point to the marks of all students who passed the exam AG0010 on 6 June 1992.

*16.13 Given the following relations and functional dependences:

$$R1(A, B, C, D)$$
$$R2(C, D, E, F, G)$$
$$R3(F, H, I)$$
$$R4(I, L, M)$$
$$A, B \rightarrow C, D$$
$$B \rightarrow D$$
$$D \rightarrow E, F$$
$$C, D \rightarrow G$$
$$F \rightarrow G$$
$$F \rightarrow H$$
$$H \rightarrow I$$
$$I \rightarrow L, M$$

(a) Determine the keys of the relations.

(b) Indicate which normal form each relation is in.

(c) Produce a schema in:

(i) second normal form,

(ii) third normal form.

16.14 Construct a set of relations in 3NF for the following problem. 'In a hospital, data relating to patients and their admission is stored: name, address and National Health Service code. Each admitted patient is assigned a hospital number, and the admission date and hospital department are recorded; later, the date of discharge (or decease) is added. Each department deals with one pathology and has a consultant and several other doctors and nurses. Furthermore, a department has a certain number of beds whose status (free or occupied) is known at any time. Patients who remain hospitalized for more than one day are assigned a bed.'

16.15 Construct a set of relations in 3NF for the following problem. 'A car rental company keeps data on available cars, customers and rental contracts. For each car, the following are known: registration plate, model, category, gearbox (automatic or manual) and luggage volume. For each customer the following are known: name, address, nationality, number of driving licence and number of the credit card used for payment; if a customer does not have a credit card, a deposit of 2,000 has to be paid. For each rental: customer, car, duration of rental contract, conditions (monthly, weekly, daily and hourly cost of rental) and additional insurance. When the customer terminates the rental, the following is registered: actual duration and overall cost of rental, plus the form of payment used.'

16.16 Construct a set of relations in 3NF for the following problem. 'A school registers data concerning their teachers, pupils and courses. For each pupil, the following is known: name, address, phone number of a relative to contact in case of emergency, year of enrolment and current class. Each class is characterized by its course year, section and the foreign language taught (French, German or Spanish). Each teacher teaches a particular subject in a class; in addition, each teacher adopts one or more textbooks for each subject. Every four months, each pupil obtains marks in the various subjects; some subjects have written and oral examinations, others only a global mark. At the end of the school year, some pupils have to resit exams in one or more subjects; at the end of the year, a pupil is promoted (in this case, the pupil is automatically enrolled in the next higher class, if the current year is not the last one), or not (in this case, the current course year does not change).'

16.17 Describe some forms and reports for the databases constructed for Exercises 16.14, 16.15 and 16.16.

16.18 Assuming the university database, describe the report containing the exams taken, which is issued by the university at a student's request. In addition, describe a form that the student could use autonomously to request the issue of the certificate.

16.19 Write the SQL programs to execute, on the database illustrated in Figure 16.7, all computations corresponding to the form in Figure 16.15.

16.20 Write the SQL programs necessary to extract from the database in Figure 16.7 all the data needed to generate the report illustrated in Figure 16.16.

Distributed systems and computer networks

Distributed systems are made up of many interconnected computers which interact with each other; such systems adapt very naturally to the distributed structure of the companies and organizations in which they are used. The move towards distributed systems began at the beginning of the 1980s as a reaction to the prevailing centralized organization of computer systems, based on one big data processing centre; a solution that had the advantage of centralizing computational functions, but the serious drawback of rarely being able to adapt rapidly enough to changing application requirements. A constant, strong trend towards distributed systems has characterized the past decade and brought in its wake the development of computer networks, both within and across organizations; the most well-known example of a computer network spanning multiple organizations is the **Internet,** a worldwide network of interacting computers.

This chapter is dedicated to the technology of distributed systems, while the next chapter is dedicated to the Internet. The subject of this chapter is part of a discipline called **telematics**, situated between computer science and telecommunications, which studies data transmission techniques and protocols, that is, the methods computers use to talk to each other. Given the complexity of the issues, the treatment is necessarily rather broad and superficial; however, we believe that distributed computing systems have become so popular and important that they cannot be omitted from the material covered by a first course in computer science.

The essential prerequisite for the realization of distributed systems is the capability of performing **data transmissions** through several media and channels; Section 17.1 deals with this subject. Note that data transmission along telephone lines is often necessary to connect users' homes to computer systems, by means of modems.

Then we describe **computer networks**, which introduce us to really distributed systems. We first describe how the information exchanged is structured by means of messages, and how computers communicate with each other by adopting certain communication protocols. Then, we analyse two types of computer network:

Wide Area Networks (WANs) which connect computers situated at great distances from one another, and **Local Area Networks (LANs)** which connect computers situated fairly close together (for example, in the same building); in particular, we describe **Ethernet**, a widely used LAN.

We then dedicate Section 17.4 to **client–server computing**, an emerging paradigm in the development of distributed systems. Finally, Section 17.5 deals with **transaction processing systems**, which support the most important commercial applications of distributed systems within large organizations; in particular, an example describes the Bancomat system, used for interconnecting the automated teller machines of several Italian banks.

17.1 Data transmission techniques

Data transmission allows two computers to be connected to one another or a computer to be connected to its remote terminals.

17.1.1 Transmission media

The most important parameter in data transmission is transmission speed, measured in bps (bits per second). The principal media used for data transmission can be divided into four categories:

- **Twisted pair wire**: a pair of copper wires used for telephone communications through which data can also be transmitted. Typical transmission speeds vary from 2400 to 33 600 bps; twisted pairs can be used at 10^7 bps and higher, but not with the same type of wires as used for telephony.

- **Coaxial cable** (often abbreviated to **coax**): a cable used for telephone communication or to carry a television signal, made up of a central carrying wire covered with plastic insulating material, surrounded by a mesh of copper wires covered with an external coating. Coax cables can carry many telephone calls. When used for data transmission, coax cables guarantee speeds up to 10^7 bps over short distances; this transmission speed is considerably reduced in longer connections and varies between 10^4 and 10^5 bps.

- **Optical fibre**: a transmission medium specifically designed for rapid data transmission which can reach transmission speeds of up to 10^9 bps. The signal is transmitted by light-emitting diodes; this allows binary digits to be coded in terms of the presence or absence of light. The light is transmitted without leaking out of the fibre which is coated with an opaque material.

- **Electromagnetic waves in space**: for transmission over short distances (via radio waves) or across long distances (by means of satellites). For instance, portable computers can be connected by using simple radio waves as the communication medium. In the case of satellite communications, information travels at the speed of light, occupying specific transmission frequencies. The delay in satellite communications, which is practically independent of the position on Earth of the transmitting and receiving stations, is about 200 ms.

17.1.2 **Modulation and demodulation**

Telephone lines (or cellular connections used by mobile telephones) are often used for data transmission; these enable anyone to connect to a computer system from home, send messages to friends, go shopping on the Internet and so on. There is one problem, though: telephone lines are designed to transmit speech (voice), that is, a continuous or *analogue* signal, and not a sequence of binary digits, that is, a *digital* signal. Therefore, a digital signal has to be converted into an appropriate analogue signal before it can be transmitted through a telephone line, and then, at the receiving end, it has to be reconverted into a digital signal. This process is named **modulation** (from a digital to an analogue signal) and **demodulation** (from an analogue to a digital signal); the device that carries out this transformation is called a **modem** (*mo*dulator–*dem*odulator). Figure 17.1 shows modems used to connect a computer to one of its terminals; the signal, output in digital form from the computer and input in digital form to the terminal, is transported through the phone line in analogue form. Two modems, one attached to the computer, the other to the terminal, carry out the digital–analogue and analogue–digital conversion.

The main types of signal modulation are frequency modulation, phase modulation and amplitude modulation; in all three cases, the phone line transports a signal, called a **carrier signal**, which is altered in two different ways to convey a zero or a one, respectively. Figure 17.2 shows **frequency modulation**. In this case, the carrier signal is a single frequency which, in the absence of a signal, is normally 1700 Hz (cycles per second). The waveform corresponding to the carrier frequency is sinusoidal. Frequency modulation transforms the carrier frequency into a higher (2100 Hz) or lower (1300 Hz) frequency, that is, a narrower or wider sinusoidal wave; conventionally, the lower frequency is interpreted as zero, the higher frequency as one.

Figure 17.2 shows the carrier frequency and the frequency modulation necessary to convey the signal 01011. Given a transmission speed, the modulator alters the carrier frequency in relation to the signal received; the demodulator, given the frequency of the arriving signal, carries out the demodulation. Frequency modulation is only one of the possible ways of altering the carrier signal, but it serves the purpose of illustrating how modulation and demodulation work.

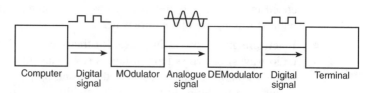

| Computer | Digital signal | MOdulator | Analogue signal | DEModulator | Digital signal | Terminal |

Figure 17.1   Data transmission via telephone lines.

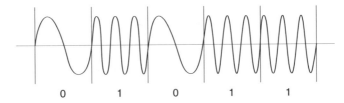

Figure 17.2 Frequency modulation.

Transmission via phone lines has the following important characteristics:

- Lines can be **dedicated**, when they permanently connect two points. In this case, the switches present along a phone line take a fixed position (in order to keep the transmission channel permanently open); this improves the quality of the transmitted signal. A dedicated line is leased, with the lessee paying a monthly fee. Alternatively, phone lines are **switched**, that is, connection is established by dialling a phone number. As with any phone call, the switches along the phone lines are opened and closed as a result of dialling in order to create the communication channel.

- Data may flow through a line in only one direction (**simplex**), or alternating in one of the two directions (**half-duplex**), or in both directions at the same time (**full-duplex**).

17.1.3 **Remote terminal connection**

Before turning to distributed computing, we overview a problem that characterizes centralized computing as well: the remote connection of terminals to computers. Computers have **input/output ports** that enable them to send data to and receive data from terminals, seen as remote peripherals (in the von Neumann architecture of Chapter 2 a port was abstracted as a *peripheral interface*). Remote terminals are normally connected to the computer via phone lines, either dedicated or switched. Figure 17.3 shows the possible connections.

- A **single-point** line connects one of the computer's ports to a single terminal. In this case, the transmission line is fully dedicated to the terminal.

- A **multi-point** line connects one of the computer's ports to several terminals. In this case, only one of the terminals situated along the line may transmit or receive information; the computer is responsible for selecting one of the terminals and communicating with it for a certain time span, then cyclically communicating with all the others. In this scheme, the transmission line is shared by several terminals; this can lead to a slow-down in the interaction between computer and terminals, but it is more economical.

- Finally, it is possible to use a special device, called a **concentrator**, to which the various terminals are connected. This method reduces the number of

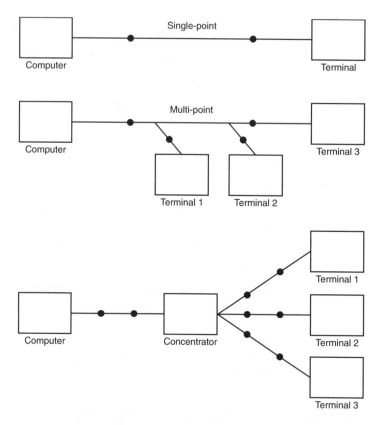

Figure 17.3   Terminal connection modes.

devices directly connected to the computer. The concentrator collects all the data to be transmitted to the computer and sends it through a single line. It also sorts the data coming in from the computer and sends it to the relevant terminals. Figure 17.3 shows a concentrator connected to a computer through a single-point line.

17.2 Elements of computer networks

Computer networks connect computers situated at some distance from one another, called the network **nodes**, by providing each of them with some **network service,** that is, some functionality that is available to all computers in the network (an example of such functionality is the ability to transfer files between computers, called a **file transfer**; but much more powerful functionalities than this are provided).

Communication between network nodes takes place via messages, that is, packages of information which are sent from any computer to any other. The emphasis is on **peer-to-peer** communication, that is, on communication techniques where each computer, in its turn, manages the communication. In the communication between a computer and its terminals, the computer always plays a coordinating role.

17.2.1 Network topology

A wide area or local area network may have a regular **topology**, that is, a given regular structure of computer interconnections. The classical network topologies are illustrated in Figure 17.4.

- A **star network** has a central node connected to a set of peripheral nodes. In a star network, the role of the central computer is fundamental, and the efficiency of the system significantly depends on the efficiency of its central node; for this reason, the central node is generally more powerful than the others. A star network is normally used in a distributed data processing system involving a main office and various decentralized offices. Consider, for example, a bank with a head office and various branches, or a large city with a central registry office and local branch offices. In a star network, many functions are simplified; for example, sending a message between two peripheral nodes is done by sending the message to the central node of the star which then routes it to the destination node. This example also shows that a star network critically depends on the reliability of its central node: the whole network fails if the central node fails.

- In a **ring network**, the computers are situated on a closed circuit, one after the other; all nodes have the same importance. Messages circle around the ring; more precisely, a train of messages circles around the ring. Each node receives the train of messages from the node that precedes it, takes the messages addressed to it off the train, adds its own messages to other nodes to the train and, finally, sends the train to the next node on the ring. In this model, the waiting time for a message is proportional to the number of nodes. To make waiting times shorter, it is possible to run several trains of messages

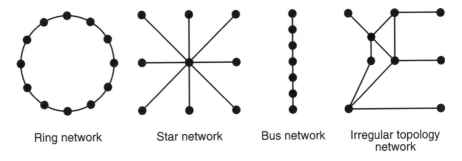

| Ring network | Star network | Bus network | Irregular topology network |

Figure 17.4 Principal topologies of computer networks.

simultaneously, but with slightly more complicated protocols. In a ring network, the failure of one node may be tolerated by some protocols which reverse the train direction before hitting the failed node.

- Finally, in a **bus network**, all nodes are situated on a single bus. The bus is used to connect any two nodes and to allow messages to be passed between them; the connection lasts only for the amount of time it takes to exchange information between the two nodes. A bus connection is used in the von Neumann architecture, described in Chapter 2; an example of a LAN that uses a bus topology is *Ethernet*, described in Section 17.3.1.

While the above regular topologies are dominant in LANs, **irregular topologies** are most used in wide area computer networks. Figure 17.4 also shows an example of irregular topology.

17.2.2 Message structure

Information is exchanged between nodes after being structured into messages; a given flow of information to be transmitted between two nodes is packaged into messages, and each message is individually transmitted. A **message** is a sequence of bytes, generally of fixed length. The typical structure of a message is shown in Figure 17.5; the message contains useful information enclosed within **control bytes** at the start and end of the message. The control bytes indicate: start and end of message; sender and receiver (computer users or programs at the sender and receiver nodes); and various characters that allow the correct transmission of the message to be verified (via parity and more sophisticated checks similar to those already mentioned in Section 16.1.1). In particular, control characters enable incorrect transmissions to be detected; that is, transmissions where some of the bits constituting the message were changed due to some fault in the communication channels. Incorrect transmissions are quite frequent and may slow down the communication, as messages have to be retransmitted along the channels.

In a network with an irregular topology, each message travels from a sending node to a receiving node through other nodes. When an intermediate node receives a message, it identifies the addressee and retransmits it immediately, either to the addressee, if it is directly connected, or to another node that is nearer the addressee. This process is called **routing**. Note that routing can be either fixed or variable: routing is *fixed* when any message between two nodes is sent through a specific sequence of nodes; it is *variable* when the nodes in the network can dynamically and autonomously decide the route of a message to its destination.

The use of variable routing leaves the responsibility of choosing the best route to the intermediate nodes. This choice can be based upon the current **load** on the network connections, that is, the number of messages that have to be sent through a connection; as with traffic management within a city, the routing algorithms try to send messages along the connections that are least loaded. Variable routing may avoid nodes and connections that are not available, and therefore generally leads to a higher probability of success for a transmission. In some wide area networks, the

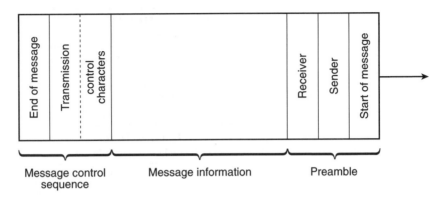

Figure 17.5 Message structure.

sender must specify the route the message should take; in this case, an error or the unavailability of one of the connections is sufficient to make the transmission fail.

17.2.3 **Communication protocols**

A protocol establishes the rules of communication that have to be followed by two interlocutors. To understand what a protocol is, consider the start of a phone conversation between two people; the first sentences that are exchanged (*Hi! Hi, it's John! Hi, John, it's Paul – how are you?*) are an example of a protocol in which the two interlocutors declare their identity.

Communication protocols used by computers are far more complex. Since the protocols have to be used by all computers, they are defined in the context of international standards. The most famous of these, called the OSI (Open System Interconnection) standard of the ISO (International Organization for Standardization), describes an architecture for computer communications which serves as a reference model for communication protocols. The ISO-OSI model contains several layers, as illustrated in Figure 17.6. Like the operating system, each layer represents an abstract machine. In particular:

(1) The **physical layer** deals with protocols masking the physical aspects of the connection mechanisms; these protocols provide the higher layers with functionality that is independent of the transmission media used.

(2) The **logical connection layer** includes data transfer protocols.

(3) The **network layer** deals with protocols which control the physical flow of messages and, in particular, manages and controls routing.

(4) The **transport layer** includes protocols which segment the transmission units into physical messages of equal length; for example, if the transmission of a file is requested, this layer is responsible for segmenting the file into several numbered messages.

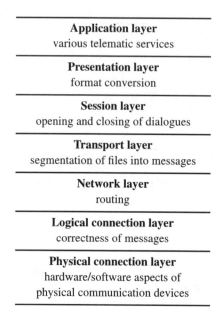

Figure 17.6 Layered architecture of the ISO-OSI standard.

(5)   The **session layer** deals with protocols which are responsible for opening and closing the dialogue between the computers and for detecting closure of this connection due to failures or malfunctioning.

(6)   The **presentation layer** includes protocols which are responsible for the conversion of codes and formats between the sender and receiver of the message.

(7)   The **application layer** is responsible for providing general telematic services, including *electronic mail* (discussed in Chapter 18) and *file transfer* (discussed below).

It is important to note that the ISO-OSI standard is a reference model for protocols; existing protocols map loosely onto it and normally cover several layers at one time. The protocols associated with layers used at the source and destination nodes are called **end-to-end protocols**; these include the transport layer and all layers above it. The protocols used to connect contiguous nodes in a connection sequence are called **network access protocols**, and include the network layer and all layers below it. End-to-end protocols establish a communication between processes (or applications) at the source and destination nodes, whereas at lower levels protocols are independent of these processes.

Figure 17.7 shows the various ISO-OSI functions required by a **file transfer operation**. File transfer is a service, available as a layer 7 protocol. Layer 6 protocols are responsible for data format and code conversions; we assume they are not necessary. Layer 5 protocols are responsible for opening the dialogue (session)

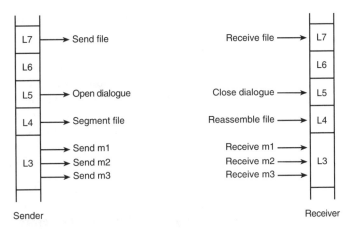

Figure 17.7 File transfer by means of protocols in the ISO-OSI standard.

between the sending and the receiving computer. Layer 4 protocols segment the file into messages; in this particular example, we assume that the file is subdivided into three messages. Layer 3 protocols are concerned with controlling the physical flow of messages between computers. Layer 2 protocols are responsible for routing and, in particular, identify a receiving node to which the three messages can be sent. Intermediate nodes which are only involved in the routing process interact with other nodes by means of network access protocols which are at layer 3 and below, since they are concerned only with controlling the physical flow of messages and their rerouting. We omit the description of the functions called on the lower layers of the architecture to transmit and receive each message. At the receiving node, layer 3 protocols are responsible for receiving the various messages, layer 4 protocols compose the messages back into a file in their original sequence, layer 5 protocols close the session, and layer 7 protocols correspond to the high-level function of receiving the file; in particular, they enable the user at the sending site to be informed that the file transfer has been completed.

17.3 Wide and local area networks

Wide area networks (WANs) connect computers situated at great distances from one another. The computers connected by a WAN perform specific application tasks; for example, they manage large databases or execute sophisticated scientific programs. In a network, programs that run on one node can involve other nodes, thus constructing distributed data processing; for example, a program running in a travel agency can look up airline databases to verify availability of flights and book seats. A WAN may contain dedicated computers, called **Intermediate Message Processors** (IMPs), which essentially carry out the function of receiving and retransmitting messages; in other words, they guarantee the connection between the various WAN nodes. We will show an example of a system based on a WAN in Section 17.5.3: the Bancomat system.

Local area networks (LANs) were developed around the beginning of the 1980s as an advanced technology solution to exploit the power of personal computers and high-powered workstations to the highest degree. Such systems generally have a high-performance processor and a high-resolution graphics screen to satisfy most of their users' requirements, but they also need external services, such as high-resolution printers or a large mass storage. The LAN allows each user to be connected to these services; it can also allow the workstation to be connected to a medium to large computer and thus to the WAN of which this computer may be a part.

17.3.1 An example of a LAN: Ethernet

The most widely used LAN is Ethernet, developed in the Xerox Palo Alto Research Labs (PARC) and adopted as a common standard by Xerox, Intel and Digital, three important producers of computer systems. The original form of the network uses a coax cable whose length must not exceed 500 metres, with a transmission speed of 10 Mbits/s. Recent developments of Ethernet include 10BaseT unshielded twisted pair cabling which permits transmission speeds of up to 100 Mbits/s.

The nodes of the network are situated along the cable; there must be fewer than a maximum number of nodes on each cable. A node connects to the network via a device called a **transceiver**, which is responsible for transmitting data onto the network. Behind the transceiver, there is an **interface** which is responsible for performing data conversion, transforming the bytes coming from a node into a series of bits to transmit on the network. This is followed by a **controller** which decides when to activate communication between two nodes on the basis of a protocol called CSMA/CD, which is described below. Two Ethernet cables can be connected to each other by a device called a **repeater,** which receives information from one cable and transmits it on the other; however, a transmission can involve at most two repeaters. The characteristics of the Ethernet network are illustrated in Figure 17.8.

The method of transmitting messages in an Ethernet network is called **CSMA/CD (Carrier Sense Multiple Access/Collision Detection)**, briefly described in the following. The protocol differs considerably from the means of communicating on a computer's system bus, as described in Section 3.2: in the von Neumann architecture the CPU plays the role of a master and decides how to utilize the bus; in the case of an Ethernet LAN, each node can decide asynchronously to communicate with another node, that is, this protocol does not assign any node an a priori master role.

The CSMA/CD communication protocol consists of the following phases:

- A node that wants to communicate listens to see if there is a communication in progress on the network (*carrier sense*).

- When no communication is in progress, any node may activate a communication (*multiple access*).

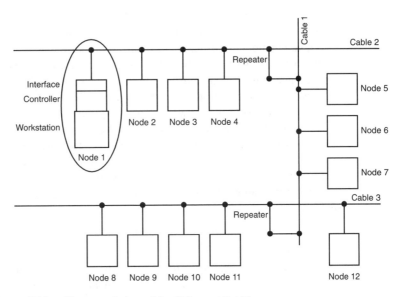

Figure 17.8 Characteristics of the Ethernet LAN.

- If two nodes transmit simultaneously, a collision occurs; the messages arrive garbled and incomprehensible at both receiving nodes and therefore the transmission has to be repeated. The transmitting nodes know, however, that there is a collision (*collision detection*) and each retransmits its message. In order to avoid another collision, each node waits a randomly generated amount of time before it retries its transmission.

17.4 Client–server architecture

Local area networks were the technological precondition for the advent of client–server architecture, a new approach to the construction of computer applications. Client–server architecture is based on a functional subdivision of computer applications into two subsystems: the **client** contains that part of the application code that deals with the interaction with the user, whereas the **server** provides computer services, for example printing documents, image processing, or data management. The LAN constitutes a communication system between the processes that guarantees the interaction between client and server in such a way that the two processes interact to perform distributed processing, although of a rather simple nature.

Both client and server are autonomous, that is, they are associated with a process that operates in the context of the operating system of an individual computer. Generally, the client is a machine with a good user interface (for example, a window-based interface with dialog boxes and menus, see Chapter 19), whereas the server is a specialized machine for the service provided; thus, if the service is image processing, fast computing speed is needed; if the service is data storage, we need a large amount of efficiently organized mass storage. A server has to meet the requirements of a vast number of clients that share a common resource, and its performance must be commensurate with that task.

Normally, the server has a simple **procedural interface**, that is, it can be activated to execute a limited number of procedures (for example, printing a document or processing an SQL query). The interaction therefore consists of the client's request for the execution of a service, to which the server responds by carrying out the processing and presenting the result to the client; interaction takes place through a simple communication (for example, an exchange of messages or the remote activation of a procedure). The interaction protocols between client and server are quite simple:

- The client **requests a service** and, if the service involves an answer, goes into a wait state.

- The server handles a **queue of requests**, that is, a sequence of requests which are processed, one by one, in the order of receipt. If the service involves an answer, the server communicates with the client as soon as it has completed the service.

- The client receives the answer and processes it, resuming interaction with the user.

This type of interaction can take place several times during the execution of an application; furthermore, the server can communicate with another server to request services in its turn (for example, in the case of processing that involves access to data distributed on several servers); in this case, the first server acts as a client and follows the protocol just described.

The main reason for the vast success of this architecture, which is being adopted ever more widely in the 1990s, is that it is far more economical than using big computers (also called **mainframes**): the market actually offers computers suitable for hosting the client or server parts at quite low prices but with a processing power nowadays comparable to that of mainframes. Also, the client–server architecture guarantees a vast increase in performance and functionality over individually run personal computers. It is clear that personal computers cannot handle 'structurally' shared applications (such as data management), and also that they request other types of service only sporadically (for example, providing every personal computer with a high-resolution printer would be a waste of resources); therefore, the client–server approach fits in very well with the ever-growing use of personal computers and workstations connected to a LAN.

All this has led to a phenomenon called **downsizing**, in which a growing number of applications traditionally handled by mainframes are ported to client–server architectures. This tendency is particularly striking in the context of data management systems and has therefore been adopted by the new generation of database management systems (relational and object-oriented systems).

*17.5 Extended example: transaction systems

Transaction systems constitute one of the main applications developed on top of distributed systems (both LANs and WANs). To exemplify transaction systems, let us consider a typical computer system which operates in a bank. Each bank clerk in the various branch offices is constantly interacting with a terminal, to consult the balance of a client's current account (checking account), cash a cheque, look up the exchange rates of various currencies and so on. In this context, we denote as an **application transaction** every unit of interaction with the system in which an elementary operation is carried out. The bank clerk has a set of codes with which to call up a transaction; when a specific transaction is activated, the operator has to supply some input parameters (for example, the account number, the type of operation, its amount and so on). When the transaction has been completed, the clerk sees the outcome of the transaction on the screen and can then call up another transaction or discuss what to do with the client at the counter.

This example shows a typical characteristic of application transactions: they are short execution units, characterized by an initial message from the operator to the system and a final message from the system to the operator. This is actually the most common type of transaction, but there are also more complicated ones. Inside the computer system, each transaction is associated with the execution of a program and with some access to a file or a database. Very often, a transaction also requires transmission of data, for example when the terminal is situated in a decentralized branch office. However complex these operations may be, they have to be carried out in a short time, typically one or two seconds, after which operators begin to show signs of irritability (it is quite common to see the operators of a transaction system becoming dissatisfied when response times rise to 10 or 15 seconds). Therefore, transaction systems must be sufficiently efficient to guarantee the rapid execution of the majority of the transactions.

Another characteristic is evident from this description, namely the extremely critical nature of the transactions. With financial applications, each computer transaction corresponds to an economic transaction in which amounts of money may pass from one account to another. It is obvious that a transaction system has to function properly and that it must not suffer malfunctions or failures that could jeopardize the correctness of the data, or permit fraudulent actions by nonauthorized users. Banks replaced the flow of money by a flow of documents which, in turn, have been replaced by records in the computer's mass storage. Jeopardizing this information means jeopardizing the functioning of the entire bank.

Other very large, widely used and important transaction systems are flight booking and credit card systems. With booking systems, consider how many booking terminals exist in the various airports, travel agencies and airline branch offices. With credit card systems, consider the fact that many shops, restaurants and hotels are equipped with a device that enables them to verify the availability of clients' funds necessary for payment. In this case, there are several million terminals, even though of a rather rudimentary kind; the international validity of credit cards allows, for example, an Australian shopkeeper to charge an amount to a British customer's account.

Transaction systems generally access one or more large databases, responsible for managing efficiently and reliably the data stored in large mass storage systems; thus, each application transaction corresponds to a **database transaction** which must satisfy the ACID transactional properties discussed in Section 16.3.4. For example, the VISA credit card organization operates a WAN with three big computer centres situated in different geographical regions (North America, Europe, Asia), each of which has a database storing a copy of all the data for all card holders. Debit and credit operations on a credit card are carried out on the database of one node and subsequently copied to the databases of the other nodes. The combination of transactional access on top of interconnected, distributed databases generates a lot of technological problems, the most important of which is reliability, which we discuss next.

17.5.1 Reliability of transaction systems

A transaction system is reliable when it is capable of suffering failures and malfunctioning without jeopardizing the atomicity and persistence of transactions and therefore without making data inconsistent. Reliability is entrusted to two components:

- the presence of a failsafe mass memory, called stable storage;
- the use of robust protocols (that is, protocols in which the possibility of errors is anticipated and prevented) in dealing with modification operations on data.

Mass memory is a physical device and as such is subject to failures and malfunctioning. For example, a tape can become unreadable or a head might scratch over the surface of a disk, damaging some tracks. **Stable storage** is an abstraction in which it is assumed that the storage does not suffer any damage. In reality, this abstraction is not achievable because it is impossible to make a mass storage absolutely free of failures; it is, though, possible to make the probability of data loss from mass storage extremely low.

In order to obtain this result, some implementers have introduced **device mirroring**: the same information is written on two disks, or on one disk and one tape, with different failure characteristics. In this way, the **mean time between failures** (MTBF), estimated to be some years for a normal disk unit, is increased to about 700 years for mirrored disk pairs.

In the following, we assume that each node executing a transaction has a stable storage; depending on the level of acceptable cost, sometimes this will be a pair of mirrored disks, or a disk coupled with a tape, or just a simple disk. The protocols we describe assume that data is never lost from stable storage; the likelihood of losing data can be arbitrarily reduced through data replication, provided that the increasing levels of cost are acceptable.

The transaction **log** (also called a **journal**) is a file containing a sequence of records, written to stable storage; each record describes actions carried out on data (read, modify, insert, delete) or actions carried out in the context of transaction control (including commit and rollback). The actions carried out on data are described by storing the initial state of the datum (preceding the operation) and the final state of the datum (following the operation); these two items are called the **before-image** and **after-image**, respectively. Periodically, a complete copy of the database, called a **database dump**, is written to stable storage.

During normal transaction execution, the log records are written in the chronological sequence of the actions carried out on the data; each transaction first writes a begin-transaction record, followed by a number of records describing the various actions on the data, followed by a commit (or rollback) record, followed by an end-transaction record. In coordinating actions on the log and on the data, a protocol is used that involves writing to the log *before* carrying out the corresponding operations on the data.

The moment in time when the transaction comes to a satisfactory conclusion coincides with the moment in time when the commit record is written to the log. If a failure occurs after this moment, all data written by the transactions active at the moment of failure are rewritten using their after-image; this process is normally called **redoing the transaction**. If a failure occurs before the writing of the commit record, then the state prior to the start of the transaction has to be reconstructed. Data of active transactions that had not yet written their commit record into the log are rewritten using their before-image, nullifying the effects of the transaction; this process is normally called **undoing the transaction**.

The moment when the transaction terminates coincides with the writing of the end-transaction record. This log entry can be made only if all data-modifying operations have been completed successfully.

After any kind of failure, the transaction system executes a **restart procedure** and then resumes normal functioning.

- The **warm restart** procedure is used when a malfunctioning has not jeopardized the correctness of data in mass storage, for example when the system stops because of a power supply failure. In this case, the actions of the active transactions at the moment of failure have to be undone or redone in order to guarantee atomicity. The warm restart uses the log, but not the dump.

- The **cold restart** procedure is used when a malfunctioning entails a deterioration of data, for example when part of a disk has become unreadable. The cold restart uses both the log and the dump.

The warm restart uses the log to determine which of the active transactions have to be undone and which have to be redone:

- The set of transactions to be undone includes those that have executed a begin-transaction but have not yet executed a commit, and those that have executed a rollback but have not yet executed an end-transaction.

- The set of transactions to be redone includes those that have executed a commit but have not yet executed an end-transaction.

The warm restart works as follows:

- First, the two sets of transactions to be undone and redone, respectively, are determined, by looking at the contents of the log.

- Actions are undone by replacing the data affected by the transaction with its before-image; actions are redone by replacing the data affected by the transaction with its after-image.

A cold restart takes place when part of the database is damaged. The cold restart algorithm works as follows:

- The dump is copied into the database (this copy can be limited so that only the damaged portions of mass storage are replaced).

- The log is processed: each action carried out by a transaction and recorded in the log is repeated; in this way, the situation immediately preceding the failure is recreated.

- A warm restart is executed.

The cold and warm restart procedures can be made more efficient; the various possible optimizations are not discussed here.

Committing a transaction in a distributed system is more complex than in a centralized system; the problem is that a commit or rollback must be performed on all the databases used by the transaction, while the transaction cannot be committed on some nodes and rolled back on other nodes. In other words, the main problem is achieving atomicity in a distributed system, in the presence of a large number of possible failures.

In order to achieve this property, transactions must perform the so-called **two-phase commit protocol**, which involves a coordinator process (called the **transaction manager**) and as many participants as there are databases involved in the distributed transaction; the transaction manager is a process which is resident on one node of the network.

The protocol has a **first phase** where the coordinator checks that each participant can safely commit the transaction by sending each participant a message and receiving an explicit response. If all responses are positive, the coordinator commits the distributed transaction by writing a **global commit record** in its own log; if any participant is unavailable (for instance, because it does not respond to the coordinator's request), the coordinator decides that a rollback is necessary and writes a **global rollback record** in its log. Then, during the **second phase**, the coordinator communicates the decision (commit or rollback) to all participants, and these in turn complete the transaction at their nodes.

This protocol is similar to a wedding ceremony, performed by an officiant who plays the role of coordinator, and by the prospective husband and wife who play the role of participants. The first phase corresponds to the questions, 'Harry, do you want to marry Sally?' and 'Sally, do you want to marry Harry?' and the officiant can decide to perform the marriage only after getting a positive reply from both participants. Occasionally, a participant changes his/her mind. Similarly, the two-phase commit is normally successful; however, when a failure occurs, complicated recovery procedures are required, which are outside of the scope of this textbook.

17.5.2 Security and privacy of transaction systems

Security is the capability to prevent fraudulent actions by nonauthorized users, and is an essential aspect of transaction systems. Unfortunately, because transaction systems are often used to manipulate information of high economic value, criminal activities have developed to defraud organizations or individuals using these systems. It is also necessary to defend the system against **sabotage**, understood as the explicit desire to destroy a computer system in a way that causes the organization that uses it the greatest possible damage, on the grounds of terrorism or unlawful competition. In other cases, an attack on a computer system takes the form of a **virus**, that is, a program deliberately introduced into the computer system to cause damage when it is executed (for example, it makes mass storage unusable, thus destroying the data stored in it). Finally, the security of a transaction system can be jeopardized by **natural events** (fire, earthquakes, other natural disasters). Whereas the security of a transaction system involves all of these aspects, **privacy** only involves access control, that is, ensuring that data access operations are carried out exclusively by authorized users.

The principal defence mechanism of a transaction system is the **authentication system**; this allows users to be identified. Each user, provided with a name known to the system, can access the transaction system only after entering a **password**. Critical operations can be further protected by passwords that users have to key in before they can proceed with the operations; generally, the more critical the operations, the more complex the identification operations, which put up a barrier against malevolent users.

Other, more sophisticated mechanisms can be used, as well as passwords; for example, **magnetic cards** to activate computers and terminals, or methods that control physical access to the rooms in which access to the computer system is possible.

The privacy of a transaction system is defended by differentiating the permitted actions according to the functions of each user. For example, an obvious privacy condition is that only the holder of an account can read the balance or withdraw cash from a self-service cash point; in this case, each datum referring to bank accounts has to be protected by associating it with a specific password (the Personal Identification Number (PIN)).

This example highlights the main problem of privacy control systems: defending access to the password (and, more generally, defending access to all software systems that can access the password). It is quite obvious that if intruders could manipulate the passwords, they would find it very easy to commit a fraud.

Protection from fraud is also guaranteed by the transaction log which records all operations carried out on the data; in fact, the log can be used a posteriori to reveal the presence of fraud. An **audit** is carried out periodically on transaction systems that manage financial aspects of large organizations, for the purpose of certifying the correctness of the financial management of the enterprise; analysing the log of a transaction system is completely analogous to inspecting the account books.

The security of a transaction system against natural disasters or fraud generally requires the protection of the computer centres and the provision of some **redundancy** which can go as far as creating complete copies of computer centres. For example, in California (a seismic region par excellence), many transaction systems for managing banks and other financial activities have twin systems that completely emulate their activity, but are situated in geographically safer areas. A twin system executes exactly the same transactions as the original system and can take over in a very short time when required.

A distributed system is naturally vulnerable during data transmission; indeed, the security of phone lines is not very high, and it is therefore fairly easy for a potential intruder to read data transmitted on these lines. To protect against this threat, transmission of confidential data is normally protected by **encryption**, that is, by applying a code that transforms the data, making it incomprehensible. Only a knowledge of the code used for this transformation allows the machine at the receiving end to carry out the inverse transformation, making the data comprehensible again.

17.5.3 Example: the Italian Bancomat system

We conclude this section with an example of a typical transaction system; we have chosen a system that enables cooperation between separate Italian banks. Similar systems exist in most countries of the world, including the USA which is by far the most advanced country in the use of computers; but for once we would like to describe a system developed in Europe and particularly in the authors' country. Banks operating in Italy offer their clients a service called Bancomat, through which they can withdraw cash, debiting the drawn amounts to their own bank account. The principal characteristic of the system is to allow any person who has a Bancomat card to use a cash machine in any national bank; the service is managed by the banks' regional computer centres coordinated by SIA, *Società Interbancaria per l'Automazione*, located in Milan.

Access to the service takes place using a card equipped with a magnetic strip; the user goes to an Automated Teller Machine (ATM) which functions as a cash dispenser. The user must insert the magnetic card into a reader and key in a secret personal code; the system identifies the user by checking that the secret code keyed in matches the one stored in the system's tables, which are protected by an *encrypting device* (SSM – see below). If the identification is positive, the user can proceed by indicating the amount to be withdrawn, selecting this information on a display; at this point the computer system activates the cash dispenser. Thus it is possible to get cash from a machine situated in one bank – the paying bank – while having one's bank account in a different bank – the issuing bank.

From the computer science point of view, this transaction involves coordination between the computer centres of the two banks participating in the transaction. However, it is not possible to guarantee at the single transaction level the ACID properties discussed in Section 16.3.4, because the system involves different data handling systems, characterized by the use of different and continuously evolving computers, networks and database management systems.

Coordination between the banks takes place as follows. The SIA manages the computer centres of various banks; there is a certain number of computer centres distributed throughout the country. The computer centres of the paying banks separate internal payments from those of the issuing banks; information about amounts of money transfers are sent to the issuing banks, which make the corresponding amounts available at the central node of the SIA system; the central node thus manages the so-called **compensation** between banks. All these dispatches in the SIA system happen in deferred mode, and therefore the modification of the amount in each account takes place in non-atomic mode. The guarantee that cash is dispensed only to well-identified users requires a guarantee of a high degree of reliability and security of the user identification procedures implemented by SIA.

The most feared fraud in a system of this kind involves the use of a duplicated Bancomat card. For this reason, it is essential to check the validity of the cards used in the cash dispenser, but this requires access to data available in the issuing bank. Initially, these controls were not available, but the growing use of the system and repeated frauds made it necessary to realize an online validity check procedure. This procedure requires the banks to distinguish three classes of cash dispensing requests.

(1) Requests involving cards issued by the paying bank are verified locally, without involving interbank exchanges.

(2) Requests involving cards issued by a paying bank managed by the same computer centre require online authorization of the request by that centre.

(3) Requests involving cards issued by a paying bank managed by a different computer centre require an online connection of the two centres such that the validity check is executed by the centre of the issuing bank.

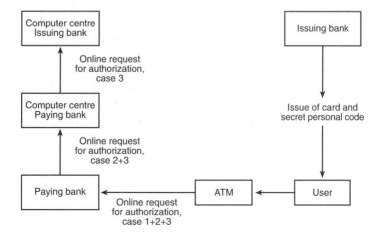

Figure 17.9 Authorization of a Bancomat cash withdrawal.

Figure 17.9 illustrates the three different cases which obviously involve an increasing amount of complexity; in each case, the validation is carried out online, that is, before dispensing the cash, and is an ACID transaction in the classic sense.

The most critical information from a security point of view is the table that associates each user with a secret code; the SIA protects this information via various techniques, trying to reduce the number of copies existing in the system, and using a special-purpose hardware system called the SIA Security Machine (SSM) for the manipulation of data and the generation of new codes.

Exercises

17.1   Design a wide area network with eight nodes:

(a)   Establish its topology such that each node is connected to all other nodes by at least two different routes.

(b)   Outline a routing algorithm carried out at a node that has at least three connections to other nodes; the program must accept incoming messages, read their addressees and retransmit them to the most appropriate node.

(c)   Describe the operations involved when transmitting a message from node 2 to node 5.

(d)   Describe the operations involved when transmitting a file from node 2 to node 5.

17.2   Illustrate the principal differences between the protocol that manages the bus in the von Neumann architecture and the CSMA/CD protocol.

17.3   Answer the following questions:

(a)   If a transaction ends with an abort, are its effects persistent?

(b)   Which of the transaction characteristics ensures that two separately correct transactions cannot mutually damage each other?

17.4   Consider the following log where each line corresponds to a different record: B(T1) indicates the begin-transaction of transaction T1; A(T1) indicates its abort; C(T1) indicates its commit; E(T1) indicates its end-transaction; and U(T1, D1, B1, A1) indicates that transaction T1 modifies datum D1 with before-image B1 and after-image A1.

```
B(T1)
B(T2)
B(T3)
U(T1, D1, A1, B1)
U(T2, D2, A2, B2)
B(T4)
```

A(T2)
U(T3, D3, A3, B3)
C(T3)
C(T1)
E(T1)
U(T4, D4, A4, B4)

Suppose that a failure occurs immediately after writing the record U(T4, D4, A4, B4). At system restart:

(a)   Under which hypotheses is only a warm restart carried out?

(b)   During a warm restart, which transactions have to be undone? And which have to be redone?

(c)   What is the value of D1, D2, D3 and D4 after carrying out a warm restart?

*17.5   Design an algorithm to encrypt a text and the corresponding algorithm to decipher it. With reference to the file transmission described in Figure 17.7, at which level should these algorithms be executed?

Internet services

18

The Internet is the name given to a large number of interconnected resources (computers, networks, users, resources and applications) spread all over the world. At the beginning of 1994, the Internet consisted of more than 2 million computers, structured into 31 000 networks, growing at a rate of about one new network connected every 10 minutes, and used in 150 different countries. Estimates indicate that by the year 2000 about 20 million computers will be connected through the Internet. But it would be a mistake to think of the Internet as a physical link between computers, insofar as the network is only the technological support on which an impressive collection of services is based, all geared up for the dissemination, management and exchange of information.

In this chapter, we present the principal services offered by the Internet. After a brief historical introduction, we describe the family of TCP/IP protocols used for the transmission of data on the Internet, with a more in-depth discussion of the addressing modes used for nodes and users, and the connection protocols for remote systems and file exchange. Then we concentrate on electronic mail, which is perhaps the most important service offered by the Internet. Finally, we describe the World Wide Web (WWW), which provides hypertext documents on the Internet.

18.1 A brief history of the Internet

The Internet originated in ARPA, the Advanced Research Projects Agency of the American Department of Defense, which at the beginning of the 1970s set up **ARPANET**, a national network with a couple of dozen nodes dedicated to research projects; still within the ARPANET environment, TCP/IP was developed, which was initially used for the transmission of messages and later became the technological standard on which all the Internet services are based.

At the beginning of the 1980s, ARPANET expanded and diversified, distinguishing, in particular, the subnets **MILNET**, dedicated to military applications, and **CSNET**, dedicated to research in computer science, financed by the NSF (National Science Foundation). Since the mid-1980s, CSNET has connected all the computer science faculties in the United States. Other networks have emerged to support research in other sectors, for example **HEPNET** (network for high-energy physics), **ESNET** (network for energy science) and **NSI** (Science Internet of NASA, the United States space agency).

Towards the end of the 1980s, CSNET expanded into the Internet and opened its doors to commercial applications, starting with non-academic research laboratories. At the same time, other private networks were developed, such as **CompuServe** and **MCI**; they became easily accessible from the Internet through special connection nodes, called **gateways**.

Currently, the Internet is managed by the **Internet Society**, an association of professionals which is funded by public and private contributions. The management of the Internet is becoming more and more difficult and challenging, with ethical problems concerning access control and with economic problems concerning how to charge for the commercial services that are becoming widespread; thus, we expect that the Internet management will soon further evolve in some unpredictable direction. The Internet, originally developed in North America, is embracing more and more countries; in fact, more than half of the Internet nodes are located in about 150 different countries outside North America.

To conclude this brief history section, it might be useful to clarify the relationship between the Internet and the UNIX operating system. Originally the vast majority of systems connected via the Internet use the UNIX operating system. Indeed, the services we describe further on are UNIX programs, or Internet programs that integrate perfectly into UNIX; the programs and statements we illustrate are therefore always available on UNIX systems that belong to the Internet network. However, it is also possible to use the Internet from non-UNIX environments, the classical example being the Internet access offered by IBM and compatible PCs and by the Macintosh.

18.2 The connection protocol

TCP/IP is the name of a protocol used to connect computers and networks; in particular, this term indicates a combination of two protocols, the **Transmission Control Protocol** (TCP) and the **Internet Protocol** (IP).

The first protocol, TCP, is responsible for controlling data transmission: each communication that is exchanged between two computers is split up into small parts of identical size, called **packets**, each of which is sent separately through the network; the communication is then reconstructed from the various packets by the addressee's computer. Thus, TCP maps more or less onto the ISO-OSI transport layer, described in Section 17.2.3. The second protocol, IP, is responsible for transmitting each individual packet from one computer to another; it maps quite well onto the ISO-OSI network layer. Note that packets in the Internet terminology are equivalent to messages as introduced in Section 17.2.2, while messages in the Internet terminology are exchanged between users, as we will see in the next section.

Each packet can use a different (variable) routing; the protocol that determines the routing can choose the most favourable connections on the basis of the network load situation, and can modify a route if, for example, a connection is interrupted. In this way, the Internet guarantees high reliability (measured in terms of messages that arrive at their destination, it largely exceeds 99%) and very good performance (most messages reach their destination within just a few minutes).

18.2.1 Network addresses

Each node of the Internet has an **IP address**, that is, an identity code. The Internet addresses are four bytes long and consist of four parts, separated by a dot; the first two parts identify a 'network', the third a 'subnetwork' and the fourth a specific computer within the subnetwork. Network addresses are assigned on the basis of recent conventions (established by Standard RCF1366 developed in 1992) that take into account the geographical distribution of nodes. For example, the address 131.175.21.1 corresponds to the computer 'morgana', situated at the Politecnico di Milano in Italy.

Internet users are not forced to remember their numeric address: each node is also assigned a **symbolic name**. More precisely, each user address consists of the symbolic name of the user and the name of the user's **domain**, that is, the node on which the user resides; the two symbolic names are separated by the symbol '@'. Consider, for example, the following five user addresses:

```
widom@cs.stanford.edu
ceri@elet.polimi.it
apers@cs.utwente.nl
alex@ecrc.de
manthey@uran.informatik.uni-bonn.de
```

In all the addresses, the domain is made up of a number of parts; the last, most general one refers to the subnet ('edu' for 'education', 'it' for Italy, 'nl' for the Netherlands, 'de' for Germany). Moving left from the last part, we find increasingly specific references; for example, 'stanford', 'polimi', 'utwente' and 'uni-bonn' refer to universities, while 'cs', 'elet' and 'informatik' refer to specific departments (and, therefore, to machines that are used as Internet nodes in these departments).

Most domains have three parts, but two parts are possible (see the fourth example where 'ecrc' indicates a German research centre), as are four (see the fifth example, where 'uran' is the name of a specific computer within the department of computer science of Bonn University). Finally, each user has a code based on the user's first and/or second name, according to the conventions or rules valid in the context of the user's organization.

In North America, where the Internet was first introduced, the nodes are subdivided into five principal domains: 'edu' (universities), 'gov' (government), 'mil' (military), 'com' (commercial organizations) and 'org' (other organizations).

The transformation of symbolic domains into numeric addresses and vice versa is managed by a TCP/IP protocol called Domain Name Server (DNS); in particular, it is possible to invoke DNS commands to find out the network address of a specific computer. For example, by executing the command:

```
nslookup morgana.elet.polimi.it
```

one obtains, among other things, the corresponding Internet address:

```
Name:    morgana.elet.polimi.it
Address: 131.175.21.1
```

Generally, the symbolic addresses are equivalent to the numeric ones, insofar as they are stored in special **domain tables**. Sometimes, however, domain tables are incomplete or inexact, and it might be better to use the numeric addresses.

Internet users can interact with users of other networks, even though interaction is often limited to the exchange of electronic mail. In effect, special nodes, called gateways, are responsible for the physical connection between networks and execute address conversion protocols. Internet users can thus see users of other networks via symbolic names, such as:

```
lewen@forsythe.bitnet
trash@myhost.uucp
```

where 'bitnet' and 'uucp' are symbolic names of other networks connected to the Internet.

18.2.2 Other protocols

Other protocols, built on top of TCP/IP, are universally supported by Internet nodes; for example telnet, finger and ftp.

telnet is a protocol for connecting to a generic node of the network. By means of telnet, it is possible to become a user of a generic system, specified by its Internet address. After executing this command, the system produces one of two responses: if the requested node is reachable, its **login prompt** is shown and the user can start a session on the remote system, as if connected by a local terminal (the only difference is that commands, being transmitted along the network, take a longer time to be executed); if it cannot be reached, an error message is displayed (typically something like: 'host is unreachable'). Once connected to a remote node, it is possible to execute any function; the local node simply emulates the behaviour of a terminal of the remote node.

finger is a protocol for acquiring information about a generic user. After executing the command, which is followed by the name of a user, the system provides the corresponding information: for example, the user's first and last name, the location and phone number of the user's office (in UNIX systems, this information is stored in special files called .plan and kept up to date by each user), or whether the user is logged in to the system or has recently read their electronic mail.

ftp (File Transfer Protocol) is a protocol for the transfer of files between one Internet node and another. ftp uses the client–server approach described in Chapter 17: each time the ftp command, which is followed by the address of a remote node, is executed, the protocol activates an **ftp client** process on the local node and sets up a connection to a remote **ftp server** capable of answering further requests from the ftp client. These commands allow the user to enter the remote system (login), move around its directory tree (cd) and transmit (put) or receive (get) files.

In particular, it is possible to connect to some remote nodes via **anonymous ftp** to transfer files from these nodes without having to be registered on them. In practice, nodes that support anonymous ftp connections allow free distribution of files to Internet users (and in particular, of programs and documents: most of the TCP/IP protocols can be obtained by anonymous ftp).

18.3 Electronic mail

Electronic mail is the most important service on the Internet. Each day, billions of messages are exchanged by users of the Internet and the other networks connected to it. This new means of communication, initially used mainly by researchers (for example, to facilitate scientific cooperation and manage common projects), is now spreading rapidly in commercial environments, as an alternative to communication via phone or fax or regular mail; it is increasingly used to exchange personal communications (for example, to agree on the sales price of second-hand items, to give advice on how to connect via a modem, or even to report about the holidays just finished).

The main advantage of electronic mail is its inexpensiveness, insofar as sending a message even to remote locations incurs no cost for the sender (except possibly the cost of connecting to an Internet computer from home). Furthermore, the receipt of a message does not require the presence of the addressee, nor does it oblige the addressee to read it immediately; for these reasons, communication via electronic mail is sometimes more flexible and less exacting or tiresome than telephone communication.

A **message** is a character string of arbitrary length and contents (some networks impose maximum limits on the length of messages, in the order of hundreds of kbytes); each message is transmitted from a sender (from) to a certain number of direct addressees (to); in addition, the message may be copied (cc, that is, 'carbon copy') to another set of addressees. The sender and addressees are identified by their symbolic names. Each message has a title (subject) which succinctly describes its contents.

Instead of the names of individual users, it is possible to use **mailing lists** that contain a vast number of users; in this way, only one symbolic name is specified for an arbitrary number of users. Mailing lists can be public (available to any user) or private (defined by a specific user on the basis of the user's personal requirements).

18.3.1 A sample message

The message shown in Figure 18.1 illustrates a sophisticated use of the facilities offered by the Internet. The message announces to a mailing list called dbworld, which connects researchers in the database sector, the availability of public domain software for the design of relational databases. The message has been sent by Victor Markowitz, of the Lawrence Berkeley Laboratory, to the mailing list, at the managing node; it is then automatically sent on by the management program to all users that form part of the list dbworld, and in this way it is received by Stefano Ceri. Note that the message is short, but it refers, for further information, to a hypermedia WWW document (see Section 18.4). The message terminates with a standard ending, automatically inserted by the manager of the dbworld list, in which users are notified that answers to the message are sent only to the original sender, a short description of the goals and limits of using the dbworld list is given, and the instructions for registering with and leaving the list are summarized.

18.3.2 Transfer of electronic mail

Electronic mail is managed by the **SMTP** (Simple Mail Transfer Protocol), supported by TCP/IP, which coordinates the behaviour of special processes, called **transport agents**. Each of these processes has the task of handling transmission and reception of messages, storing them in appropriate memory areas.

Figure 18.2 shows what happens when a user sends a message by means of the standard command **mail**, available on UNIX, with an option **-v**, which indicates a verbose option. Normally, the option is not used and the message is sent out without any further information; but with the verbose option, the various steps of the SMTP are shown (echoed) on the screen. The mail command requires the sender of the message to indicate the address of the receiver, the subject of the message and the text of the message itself, completed by a period character in the first column of a new line.

Then, a protocol is executed; a connection is made to the transport mailer of the receiving node (HELO), and the transport mailer of the sending node communicates the identity of the sender (MAIL) and of the receiver (RCPT). In the specific example of Figure 18.1, the sender is ceri@elet.polimi.it and the receiver is ceri@cs.stanford.edu; then, the message is entered (DATA) and its text is ended with '.' on a line by itself, as indicated by the protocol. At that point, the message is accepted by the transport mailer at the receiving node and delivered to the recipient. Finally, the message is received at the destination node and can be read by the recipient; in the situation considered here, the communication required a few seconds.

Once received on the node of the addressee, the electronic mail is managed by a software system, called a **mailer**, which operates on the messages which have arrived for a specific user. When logging in to the computer, the user is informed of the presence of messages not yet read (for example, those that arrived while the

```
Date: Tue, 28 Jun 94 13:16:43 -0500
Received: from localhost by fyvie.cs.wisc.edu; Tue, 28 Jun 94 13:16:43 -0500
Message-Id: <199406281725.KAA02207@victor.lbl.gov>
Reply-To: victor@csr.lbl.gov
Originator: dbworld@fyvie.cs.wisc.edu
Sender: dbworld@cs.wisc.edu
Precedence: bulk
From: Victor Markowitz <victor@csr.lbl.gov>
To: ceri@DB.Stanford.EDU
Subject: [DBWORLD:303] Data Management Tools available on WWW
X-Listprocessor-Version: 6.0a   ListProcessor by Anastasios Kotsikonas
X-Comment: Messages of interest to the research db community
Status: OR
Two suites of data management tools that facilitate developing database with
commercial relational database management systems are available via World Wide
Web using URL:
               ftp://gizmo.lbl.gov/pub/DM_TOOLS/DMTools.html
Victor M. Markowitz

Mail Stop 50B-3238
Data Management Research & Development Group
Information and Computing Sciences Division
Lawrence Berkeley Laboratory
1 Cyclotron Road, Berkeley CA 94720
Email: VMMarkowitz@lbl.gov
REPLIES TO THIS MESSAGE WILL GO ONLY TO THE SENDER

The dbworld alias reaches many people and should only be used for messages of
general interest to the database community.

Requests to get on or off dbworld should go to listproc@cs.wisc.edu.
  to subscribe send
    subscribe dbworld <Your Full Name>
  to unsubscribe send
    unsubscribe dbworld
  if your address is going to change
    send an unsubscribe request from the old address (before the change)
    send a subscribe request from the new address (after the change)
  to find out more options send
    help
```

Figure 18.1 An example message.

user was not logged in). At this point, the user can decide to analyse the messages; to do this, the user activates the mailer, which provides a number of functions:

- Read new messages; store them on file or print them out.

- Send answers to the senders of the messages.

- Send new messages to other users or groups of users, sometimes using mailing lists.

- Collect some of the new messages in appropriate containers (or **folders**), so that they can be reread on future occasions.

```
mail -v ceri@cs.stanford.edu
Subject: A test for the CS Book
This is a dummy message

.

ceri@cs.stanford.edu... Connecting to Sunburn.Stanford.EDU (tcp)...
220 Sunburn.Stanford.EDU ESMTP Sendmail 8.7.1/8.7.1 ready at Sun, 18 Feb 1996
09:14:05 -0800
>>> HELO ipmel2.elet.polimi.it
250 Sunburn.Stanford.EDU Hello ceri@ipmel2.elet.polimi.it [131.175.21.1], pleased
to meet you
>>> MAIL From:<ceri@elet.polimi.it>
250 <ceri@elet.polimi.it>... Sender ok
>>> RCPT To:<ceri@cs.stanford.edu>
250 Recipient ok
>>> DATA
354 Enter mail, end with '.' on a line by itself
>>> .
250 JAA12543 Message accepted for delivery
>>> QUIT
221 Sunburn.Stanford.EDU closing connection
ceri@cs.stanford.edu... Sent

Posted-Date: Sun, 18 Feb 1996 09:14:06 -0800 (PST)
Date: Sun, 18 Feb 1996 18:14:02 +0100
To: ceri@CS.Stanford.EDU
Subject: A test for the CS Book

This is a dummy message
```

Figure 18.2 An example of message transmission.

- Manage **aliases**, that is, simplified names instead of complete user names – for example, one could give the alias 'rainer' to the user:

  `manthey@uran.informatik.uni-bonn.de`

- Manage personal mailing lists, including adding and deleting users to and from the lists.

Other programs permit the management of mailing lists, allowing automatic registration and deletion of users (who send appropriate messages to the management program); reading the names of the individuals registered in the mailing list (in some lists, however, users may choose to remain anonymous); collecting, handling and searching all messages exchanged in a certain interval of time. There are also programs for managing **bulletin boards** in which news and comments about specific subjects may be published (for example, a list of examination subjects, or advertisements for buying and selling second-hand items).

An example of a mailer is the program **ELM**, available on most Unix systems; it extends the functionalities of the basic *mail* program and simplifies the management of messages. With ELM, messages can be grouped into folders;

```
Folder is '=db' with 5 messages [ELM 2.4 PL23]

1  Feb 8   Mengchi Liu          (88)   (DBWORLD) ROL DOOD System Release
2  Feb 5   sharma@cis.ufl.edu   (88)   (DBWORLD) VLDB'96 INFORMATION
3  Jan 31  Peter Scheuermann    (135)  (DBWORLD) ACM-SIGMOD'96 awards
4  Jan 31  Phokion G. Kolaiti   (300)  (DBWORLD) CFP - Conference on Datab
5  Jan 29  'gorrieri@cs.unibo   (523)  coordination'96 Call for participants

You can use any of the following commands by pressing the first character;
d)elete or u)ndelete mail, m)ail a message, r)eply or f)orward mail, q)uit
  To read a message, press <return>. j = move down, k = move up, ? = help

Command:
```

Figure 18.3   Example of the use of the ELM mailer.

simple instructions are available for deleting or undeleting received messages, for mailing new messages to other users, for replying to or forwarding received messages. Messages are listed within folders in date order; each message is described by the date of its arrival, the sender, the length (number of lines) and the message title. This information is shortened (cut) in order to show each message on one line of the display.

Figure 18.3 shows a folder containing five messages, managed by ELM, and the commands that can be issued by a user. When a message arrives, it is included in the input folder; each user can then distribute the incoming messages to other folders, so as to store them in an organized manner. Each folder is physically managed by the file system as a file of characters.

ELM enables a user to define aliases so as to simplify the network addresses of the people and thus improve the sending or forwarding of messages. Figure 18.4 shows a small collection of aliases of persons, which are sorted by name; each alias is shown on a screen row including its name and the nickname used as its alias (such

```
Alias mode: 5 aliases [ELM 2.4 PL23]

1  Alain Pirotte          Person     alain
2  Alexandre Lefebvre     Person     alex
3  Alfonso Cardenas       Person     cardenas
4  Arie Shoshani          Person     shoshani
5  Arnie Solvberg         Person     solvberg

You can use any of the following commands by pressing the first character;
a)lias current message, n)ew alias, d)elete or u)ndelete an alias,
m)ail to alias, or r)eturn to main menu. To view an alias, press <return>.
j = move down, k = move up, ? = help

Alias:
```

Figure 18.4   Example of the use of aliases with the ELM mailer.

as alain or alex). As well as individuals, it is possible to store the aliases of groups of people. The available commands allow the user to inspect the list of aliases (by moving up and down the list), view an alias (that is, the corresponding full electronic mail address), define new aliases and delete or undelete them; in particular, it is possible to give an alias to the sender of the message that was last received.

18.4 Hypermedia documents: the World Wide Web

The **World Wide Web** (**WWW**) is a system for the management of documents on the Internet. WWW was conceived at CERN (Conseil Européen pour la Recherche Nucléaire) in Geneva, Switzerland; the project was conceived to document the development of projects distributed across several international laboratories, but shortly after its introduction it was quickly adopted as an Internet standard.

The WWW is an evolution of **hypertexts**. In a generic hypertext, which presents a user-reader with documents composed of texts and images, some words or phrases are used as references to other texts and can be used for 'navigation' within the hypertext document, by following a path which corresponds to the user's interests; underlined words or phrases denote references from one text to another. The principal characteristic of the WWW is that the documents are located on different nodes: indeed, each connection may refer to texts located on a different Internet node. References (also called **anchors**) are provided in a variety of forms, such as underlined text, buttons or places on drawn maps. The user can request access to remote texts by simply 'clicking' on a reference; with a click, the user moves to a hypertext that may physically reside on a remote node (for instance, the user jumps from London to Tokyo to Melbourne).

When the WWW system is activated to read a document, the **WWW client** program installed on the requesting user's node displays the corresponding hypertext. Whenever the user selects a remote reference, by means of a mouse click, the client program requests the **WWW server** of the remote node to send the hypertext corresponding to the reference. As soon as the selected hypertext arrives at the user's node, normally after a short delay, it is displayed, thus allowing the user to continue navigation. Thus, in quite a short time, the user can navigate through documents, located on remote nodes, that refer to one another, constituting an enormous web – the World Wide Web. From a technical point of view, the WWW is based on several standards:

- A system of addresses, called **Uniform Resource Locators** (URLs), that identify an Internet location where the document itself is stored; each URL indicates a document on a node and a suitable transfer mode for retrieving the document when the URL is accessed (opened) from a remote computer.

- A communication protocol between the WWW client and server, called **HyperText Transfer Protocol** (HTTP), which allows hypertexts to be exchanged efficiently, taking into account the type of information transmitted (texts, hypertexts, images and so on).

● A standard 'mark-up' language for hypertexts, called **HyperText Markup Language** (HTML), which contains the commands for the presentation of documents on screen and for the definition of anchors.

WWW clients require the use of software tools, called **browsers**, to navigate around the hypertexts. Although very simple browsers can be used, the two most widespread and powerful browsers for WWW documents are **Netscape** and **Explorer**. Both of them make a sophisticated use of icons, menus and colours. By means of icons or colours, for example, it is possible to recognize documents already read, or trace back the navigation path taken through the hypertext.

Generally, each hypertext document has a hierarchical structure, with a **home page** that summarizes the document and presents the main references; pages which are directly or indirectly linked to the home page and constitute a unitary collection of information are denoted as a **web site**. Figure 18.5 shows the home page of the web site of the Department of Electronics and Information (DEI) of the Politecnico di Milano.

We illustrate next an example of navigation which starts from the home page of the DEI, illustrated in Figure 18.5; this page is simply accessed by opening, with a browser, the URL called http://www.elet.polimi.it[1]. The page has a typical structure which characterizes all the access pages of a web site: it is substructured into an informative part, introducing DEI, and a list of references (anchors) for further navigation; clicking on each reference causes other pages of the web site to be loaded.

For instance, clicking on the icon relating to the 'main menu' causes the loading of another WWW page, shown in Figure 18.6, containing references to the various disciplines hosted in the department (automatica, computer engineering, electronics, telecommunications), to the personnel of the department, to course offerings, to other information (such as seminars) and instructions about how to reach the department's building. By clicking on the last item, a map appears giving the exact location and details of access by means of public transportation (omitted here for brevity); by clicking on 'Computer Engineering', we access another WWW page, shown in Figure 18.7, listing the research activities and laboratories. Finally, from the DEI home page, clicking on the icon corresponding to the WWW of the Politecnico di Milano causes the loading of the home page of another web site, relating to the entire Engineering Faculty.

At all times, the user can issue browser commands for going backwards along the sequence of previously accessed pages, go back to the home page, open new URL locations or files, print the displayed information or save it to a local file. On Netscape, a facility called a 'bookmark' enables the names of URL locations to be stored for subsequent easy access.

---

[1] We are aware that most of the readers of this book will be already familiar with navigation on the Internet and that there are many web sites which are much more exciting than the one being described here. But, if you have a browser available and you want to try this URL address, you are more than welcome: you will find among others the (familiar?) names of this book's authors and find out what we do.

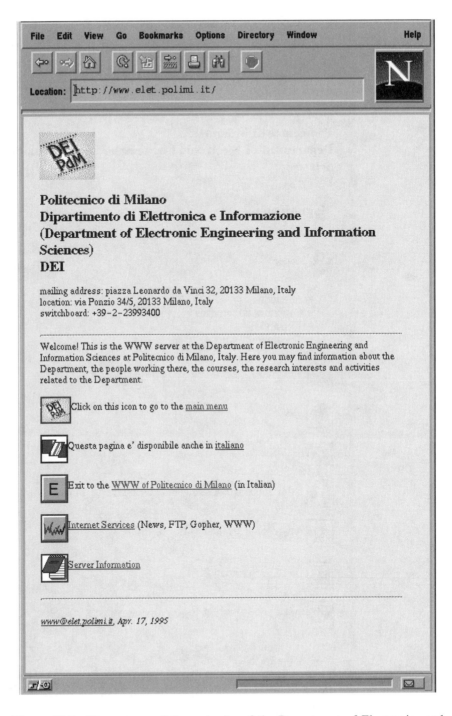

Figure 18.5 Home page of the web site of the Department of Electronics and Information of the Politecnico di Milano.

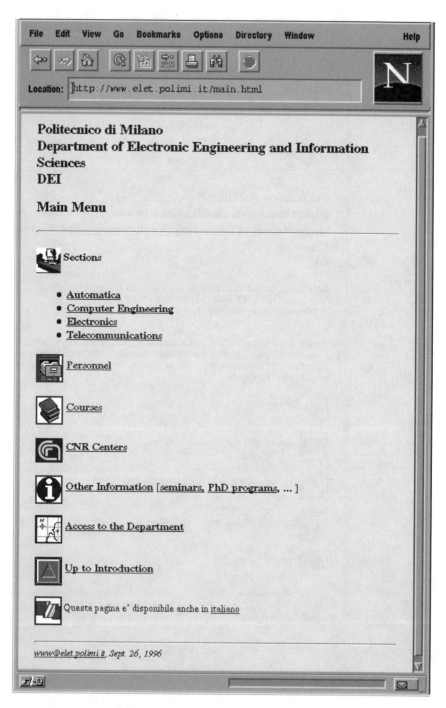

Figure 18.6 The WWW page containing references to the various disciplines hosted in the department.

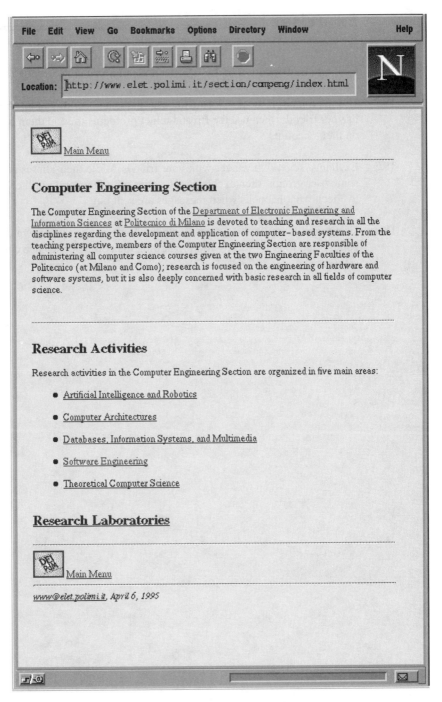

Figure 18.7 The WWW page listing the research activities and the laboratories in the computer engineering section of the department.

Exercises

for students who have access to the Internet

18.1   Find out the IP address of the Internet node that you are currently using.

18.2   Use the finger protocol to locate the user name and additional information of some of your friends, then use the ftp and telnet protocols to send them files and to login on their accounts.

18.3   Exchange several messages with your friends. Write their aliases and organize some user groups, then exchange messages with them and use the verbose option to check what happens when messages are sent out.

18.4   Using your favourite browsers, locate the home page of your own university or college and look for information regarding the computer science courses which are offered.

The end-user view of computer systems $\boxed{19}$

In our journey from the inside of the computer architecture to the outside, we have reached the last level, the end-user interface. By **end user** we mean the immediate user of a computer application: an engineer using a computer-aided design tool, a citizen using an automated teller machine, a writer using a word-processing system or a professional using a computer for managing an archive are all examples of end users. An **end-user interface** is the physical and logical means through which human–machine interaction occurs, facilitating the user in interaction with the computer. The ideal interface strongly depends on the characteristics of the application: for instance, a flight simulator could be used for training a pilot even with a screen-and-keyboard interface, but obviously the simulator is much more effective if virtual reality is used for rendering the aeroplane motion and the actual commands and devices existing in the pilot cabin are available to drive the simulator. In general, the use of a computer by someone who is not a computer expert should always take place by means of a high-level user interface, which masks the underlying hardware and software system, as shown in Figure 19.1.

In earlier times, the end users of computer applications were specialists and human–machine interaction took place in an extremely rigid and unfriendly way, but today the panorama of computer applications is so wide that practically everybody can be the end user of a computer system, and the means of interacting with the system can assume very different features according to the application being used: the outermost sphere of Figure 19.1 can look very different in different contexts.

It is not always possible (or economically feasible) to construct applications suited to the individual requirements of each user. For example, keeping track of a small family budget, with incomes and expenditures of various kinds, has some common aspects for all families, but also some specific aspects for each family: income may include salaries, profits from commercial activity, returns on investments; expenses may include a child's enrolment in a school or the membership fee of a gym. Furthermore, both incomes and expenditures might vary over time, by

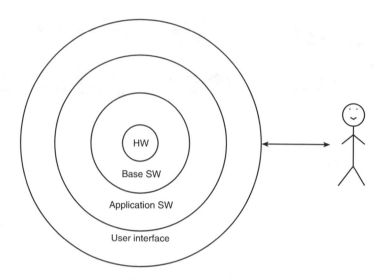

Figure 19.1 From the hardware to the user.

amount or by category; the birth of a child might require the insertion of a new item in the budget. In summary, constructing individual 'turnkey' applications suiting the requirements of each individual family is inconceivable.

However, several classes of applications are sufficiently similar that they can be managed by means of general-purpose software, called **personal productivity tools**. A few simple operations are required to create these applications from general software packages, without forcing the user to face the typical difficulties of complete program design. Thus, productivity tools are the simplest and most usable tools for the development and management of applications; they are made available to end users who normally are not computer experts but nevertheless can develop and use small applications. Of course, productivity tools themselves need to be associated with simple, user-friendly user interfaces.

This chapter presents a brief overview of the way in which computers are used. Section 19.1 is dedicated to user interfaces; in particular, the extended example in Section 19.2 describes the *Windows95* interface, which is now becoming a standard. Section 19.3 deals with productivity tools, and introduces two extended examples devoted to *word processors* (Section 19.4) and *spreadsheets* (Section 19.5), the most widely used tools in this category.

19.1 User interfaces

Today, there exists a wide variety of devices to realize human–machine interaction; some of them are described below.

19.1.1 Input and output devices

The traditional ways of interacting with computers include **keyboards**, which accept letters, numbers and commands from the user, and the **mouse**, an analogue-type tool suitable for pointing to a position on the screen. Besides these, we mention the following, less widely used input devices:

- The **trackball** (illustrated in Figure 19.2) and the **trackpad** (illustrated in Figure 19.3) are used as an alternative to the mouse in portable computers.
- The **electronic pen** (illustrated in Figure 19.4) enables the continuous tracing of trajectories of any kind directly on the screen.
- The **joystick** (illustrated in Figure 19.5) is commonly used in games for controlling positions and for sending commands (typically interpreted as the firing of guns in war games).
- The **touch screen** (illustrated in Figure 19.6) identifies a position on a video screen by simply touching it with a finger. It is suitable only for limited applications, because of its lack of precision and the tendency to soil the screen.
- The **dataglove** (illustrated in Figure 19.7) is a sophisticated instrument capable of revealing the position and movement of a hand, including even quite complex movements. It is used in virtual reality applications.

Figure 19.2   A trackball.

Figure 19.3   A trackpad.

Figure 19.4   A lightpen.

Figure 19.5   A joystick.

Figure 19.6 A touch screen.

Figure 19.7 A dataglove.

- **Three-dimensional tracers**. These instruments, already a lot more sophisticated, employ various types of technology (ultrasound, electromagnetic waves, laser) to identify the position and orientation of a body in space. They are often used as components of very high-level interfaces.

- **Sonic sensors**. These are sensors of various types capable of receiving and sending various sound signals. They are used, for example, in voice-based database query systems.

- Special **sensors for disabled people**. These obviously depend on the type of handicap. Sensors to detect movement of the head or of the eyes and mouth are typical cases. An example is illustrated in Figure 19.8.

- Finally, the most widely used input devices, besides the classical keyboard and mouse, are **bar-code readers**. These are found in department stores and supermarkets for reading information (including the price) encoded in the form of bars printed directly on the products.

We turn next to output devices. Besides the traditional **character screens** of video terminals (less and less used these days) and **printers** of various types, we would like to mention the following mechanisms:

- **Graphical colour screens** (and printers) supporting the high-resolution visualization of images in very rich ranges of colours, making it possible to handle extremely complex images (for example, high-resolution reproductions of famous paintings). They are also available in large sizes, to accommodate several logical interfaces at the same time.

- **Sound generators**, used both for the generation of artificial sound (sounds of cars and aeroplanes) and for the synthesis of the human voice; sound is then reproduced by means of headphones or speakers.

- **Mechanical actuators**, which move mechanical devices. For example, they can be used in robotics and in virtual reality applications to simulate the acceleration of a vehicle.

Finally, **multimedia interfaces** combine more than one medium for output, for instance intertwined textual and graphical outputs displayed by high-resolution

Figure 19.8 Sensors for the detection of movement of the head (HeadMouse™).

colour screens and associated with sounds; multimedia interfaces are becoming more and more important, with applications in a variety of fields (including virtual reality, database interfaces and instruction systems). An essential technological element in the construction of multimedia outputs is the capacity for coordinating different information channels, in the same way as in movies it is necessary for the soundtrack to be synchronized with the video.

19.1.2 Logical interfaces

The devices introduced in the previous section enable the flow of information between the user and the computer, thereby enabling the physical communication between them; we now turn to the (more difficult) issue of discussing the rationale behind the human–machine interaction. Input/output devices enable the development of various forms of **dialogues**, structured to a greater or lesser degree. The most trivial form of dialogue is the traditional one, in which the user supplies commands to the machine through sequences of characters communicated via the keyboard, and receives similar responses through the video or the printer. Other forms of dialogue enable a different, potentially much more effective communication with the user; these are supported by a new user interface technology, which is based on a few logical methods for organizing and presenting information on the screen. Let us recall the most widely used ones.

- **Window-based interfaces**. The screen is partitioned into different virtual portions called windows. Each window represents a kind of virtual screen with a certain autonomy of its own, following the metaphor of the desktop on which we find several sheets of paper. Each window can be moved around the screen and resized. Various windows can (partially) overlap. Figure 19.9 shows a screen organized as a set of windows.

- **Menus**. The menu is a means of presenting the available commands to the user in such a way that the user can select the desired command without

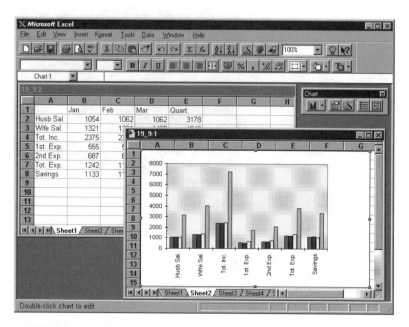

Figure 19.9   A screen organized as a set of windows.

having to remember particular syntax issues, just by clicking with the mouse on a predefined set of alternatives. In many cases (see, for example, Figure 19.9), the menu appears in the top part of a window.

- **Icons**. These are instantly recognizable graphics symbols that denote a set of functionalities associated with them: for example, an icon can be used to represent a word processor, a document, or the operations available in a tool. Figure 19.10, for example, shows a window, containing several icons. The icon labelled 'Calc' represents a simple calculator application.

- **Dialog boxes**. A dialog box (see Figure 19.11) is a graphical structure through which the user can supply and receive structured information, such as database records (recall also Chapter 16) or commands with the choice of several options.

Interaction with computers is increasingly based on **Graphical User Interfaces** (GUIs); this general term denotes interfaces which are based on the use of windows and on the presentation of commands by means of menus, icons and dialog boxes. In most GUIs, programs get executed on rectangular windows on the screen, enclosed within border areas. Some other buttons placed on the border of the window typically control the display of the window itself, by enabling its enlargement (to occupy the entire screen) or restriction (possibly to a simple icon on the screen). In this way, windows can be reduced to icons (closed) or return to their normal size (open); several windows may be present on the same screen, either opened or closed.

Logical interfaces are heavily used in Windows 95, a GUI for the Intel-based personal computer described in the next section.

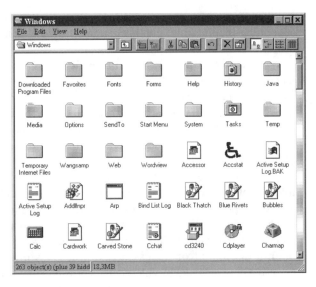

Figure 19.10   A window containing icons.

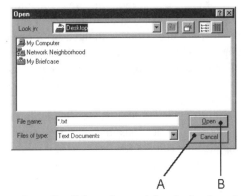

A   Selecting this button closes the dialogue box and deactivates the selected command.
B   Selecting this button executes the selected command.

Figure 19.11   A dialog box.

19.2 Extended example: Windows 95

The big success of the Macintosh graphical interface in the 1980s and the simplicity of use of the functions offered by its operating system to non-expert users was the premise to the dissemination of graphical interfaces for personal computers in the nineties. If Windows 3.1 has been for years the most widely used graphical interface on Intel based personal computers using the MS-DOS operating system, Windows 95 is nowadays a complete operating system with a friendly graphical interface supporting multitasking, multimedia data handling, and powerful functions for the access to local and network resources.

Windows 95 provides the user with an easy-to-use **environment** for simultaneous execution of different application programs. Icons and windows help the user to interact homogeneously with, and to interchange data among, different applications. Input from screen is facilitated by buttons, scroll bars, menus, and dialog boxes showing commands that can be clicked on by using the mouse.

The screen can be seen by the Windows 95 user as a **desktop** containing **objects** (folders, programs, documents, local or external resources). Each object is represented on the desktop as an **icon** (if closed) or as a **window** (if opened). A folder contains a collection of objects. Each folder can be created, deleted, moved, closed or opened using the mouse (for example, opening requires a double clicking on the icon and closing a single clicking on the botton located on the right-top corner of the window). During a working session, the user can launch a program, open a document or access a resource by simply double clicking on the corresponding icon and by entering the corresponding window. If the user interacts in sequence with a word processor, a spreadsheet and a drawing program, Windows 95 permits passing from one application to the other, either by producing independent documents or by exchanging information between the different applications in order to produce one or more integrated documents.

All applications written to be run in the Windows 95 environment use very similar ways of interacting with the user; for example, they are launched by double-clicking on the icon that represents them in the environment, and can be aborted by selecting the close option in a menu that exists in all applications.

The pattern of interaction with suites of applications (such as Microsoft Office) and with the operating systems (including the opening and closing of files or printing of documents) is almost identical. This aspect reduces the learning phase for new applications: the user need only learn the interactions specific to the new application (until a few years ago, it used to be said that the most difficult part to grasp of a new application was how to get out of it).

Figures 19.9 to 19.14 illustrate some characteristic aspects of the interaction with Windows 95. The first three figures were described already as classical examples of GUI features; Figure 19.9 shows a single application that processes two different visual descriptions of the same document, each represented within a window. Figure 19.10 shows some icons corresponding to folders, documents and programs that can be opened or launched by double clicking with the mouse. Figure 19.11 shows a classical dialog box which is used in Windows 95 to choose and open a file. Figure 19.12 shows the control options which are offered on every window for controlling its 'look'.

Figure 19.13 shows some of the elements that the user can use to communicate with the programs: menus, dialog boxes, command buttons, text boxes, list boxes, radio buttons (buttons that represent mutually exclusive options).

Windows 95 provides the application programmer with a set of predefined (built-in) functions, linkable at run-time, for the realization of menus, dialog boxes,

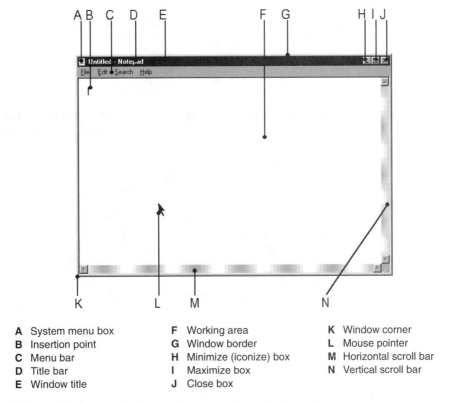

A System menu box	**F** Working area	**K** Window corner
B Insertion point	**G** Window border	**L** Mouse pointer
C Menu bar	**H** Minimize (iconize) box	**M** Horizontal scroll bar
D Title bar	**I** Maximize box	**N** Vertical scroll bar
E Window title	**J** Close box	

Figure 19.12   Standard control commands enclosing a window.

scroll bars, and so on. The programmer can thus realize uniform interfaces by taking advantage of predefined libraries. Programming under Windows is, however, not a trivial exercise: the Windows programmer must possess non-elementary knowledge of object-oriented and asynchronous programming.

We have said that Windows 95 is a **multitasking** operating system (it supports the simultaneous execution of different application programs). For each application launched by the user, Windows 95 opens a window on the screen. On the desktop, there are as many open windows as there are running applications: each window interacts with the user according to the requirements of its associated application, and contains the result of the interaction with the user. By passing from one window to another (via mouse or keyboard), the user selects one program for a direct interaction. At any given moment, only one window can receive input data from the user, but all information regarding the state of the other current applications and of the special Windows 95 application itself is kept up-to-date. On the Windows 95 desktop, the **taskbar** (see Figure 19.14) enables the user to switch between running applications, thus avoiding problems related to overlapping of open windows. Running applications appear as buttons on the taskbar. To switch to

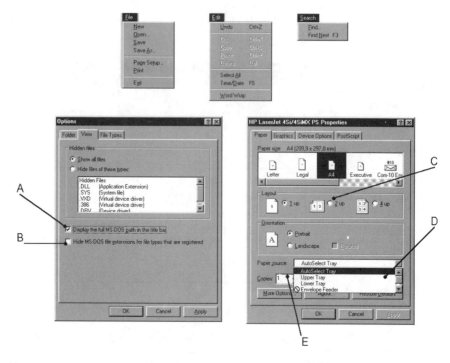

A, B Control boxes represent options which are not mutually exclusive
A This is the selected option
C Buttons represent options that are mutually exclusive
D Pull-down list box open to visualize available settings
E Edit text box

Figure 19.13 Menus and dialog boxes with command buttons and control boxes.

a particular program, the user can just click on the corresponding button, and the application then moves to the foreground, putting the previous application in the background.

Being a **preemptive multitasking** operating system, Windows 95 retains full control of the processor and is able to preempt an application's access to the processor. When another application requires the use of the processor, Windows 95 takes control from the running application and shifts access to the second application in agreement with specific policies. Preemptive multitasking, therefore, enables applications to work more smoothly together and eliminates the problem of an ill-behaved application taking full control of the system.

The taskbar also includes a **start button** (see Figure 19.14) that gives the user access to a hierarchical menu, which in turn enables the start-up of applications, opening documents, modifying the system's configuration, invoking the operating system or accessing other standard objects by clicking on different items; this

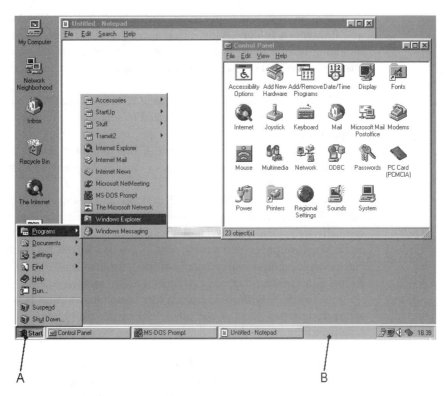

A The Start button and its hierarchical menu
B The task bar with the running applications

Figure 19.14 The icons *My Computer*, *Network Neighborhood*, *Inbox*, *Recycle Bin*, *The Internet*, the Start button and the task bar.

interface can be customized by each user, but it contains, among others, the standard buttons 'Programs', 'Documents', 'Settings', 'Find', and 'Shut Down'.

Programs displays a hierarchical menu of program groups to be enriched and personalized by the user. Among others: Accessories (programs for doing simple word processing, sending and receiving faxes using a fax-modem, playing a variety of games or working with multimedia devices), and Windows Explorer (which provides a consistent mechanism for viewing files, folders and all objects to which the PC has access, including network printers and directories).

Documents gives to the user a quick access to documents with which he/she has recently been working on, automatically accessed by invoking the suitable application (for example, a file created using the application Word, is opened automatically invoking that application).

Settings allows the user to modify the system's configuration through the items Control Panel (a folder containing, as shown in Figure 19.14, a variety of tools available to control the way the PC, its components and Windows 95 operate, as well as to control the appearance and behaviour of the Windows 95 interface) and Printers (a folder giving quick access to all printers available to the PC, including remote network printers; an icon represents each printer and double-clicking on the icon opens a queue window usable to set printer options and monitor printer jobs).

Find enables searching for files and folders on the PC or on the network, to search for computers on the network, and to search the Microsoft Network online service for topics.

Shut Down enables shut down of the computer, restart of the computer, restart the computer in MS-DOS mode or close all programs of a given user and log on as a different user.

A last look at the Windows 95 desktop, and to Figure 19.14, shows, among others, five icons related to the configuration of the system and to networking, that normally are present when Windows 95 is initially installed.

My Computer is a folder containg icons for all disks connected to PC (including local disks and remote networks), for the Control Panel, for Printers and for the Fonts folder (displaying all fonts installed on the system)

Network Neighborhood is a folder containing, when a PC is connected to a network, icons of each of the other PCs in the workgroup, as well as an icon labelled Entire Network that enables to browse for network resources outside of the workgroup.

Inbox (Microsoft Exchange) is a folder containing icons for communications tools (electronic mail, faxing, and access to online services).

Recycle Bin is a special folder where all the objects to be deleted are temporary placed before a recovery or a definitive deletion. The delete operation can be accomplished by simply dragging the object's icon into the Recycle Bin.

The Internet allows accessing the Internet Explorer application, to navigate on the World Wide Web and to exchange ideas, information, and opinions, by accessing different usenet newsgroups.

Finally, note that Windows 95 provides a Device Independent Graphic Interface to all applications written for its environment. Programs do not access the screen or the graphical output devices directly and therefore do not need to know which kind of device is connected to the system at I/O time. A program written for the Windows environment is capable of interacting correctly with each peripheral device 'known' to Windows, which in turn must contain the appropriate device drivers. This has the following advantages:

(a) the software of each individual application does not have to include the specific software for all peripheral devices that could be connected to the system;

(b) the user selects the configuration of peripherals once and for all, and this selection is used by all the different applications in the same working session;

(c) the Windows application programmer can think of the various peripheral devices in a more abstract way, thus disregarding characteristic aspects of the individual interfaces.

19.3 Productivity tools

Productivity tools are general-purpose software systems that can be used by nonspecialists to develop very simple, standard applications. They can be classified as follows (as discussed in Section 1.4.6):

- Tools for **document processing**. These include the traditional word processors and the graphical applications for drawing various types of figure. Word processors are described in Section 19.4.

- Tools for **personal communication**. In this category we include mechanisms and services for handling information traffic through various kinds of network. The electronic mail service supported by the Internet is the most relevant example in this family of tools: it is described in Chapter 18.

- Tools for **data management**. These are the database management systems suitable for use by nonspecialists; their organization and programming and the end user's view of them were discussed in Chapter 16.

- Tools for numerical and semi-numerical data processing. These tools, often called **spreadsheets**, are particularly suitable for simple calculations applied to simple matrix-type data structures. Spreadsheets are described in Section 19.5.

- Tools for the **definition and implementation of interfaces**. These tools are used to construct, in a systematic and automated way, logical interfaces based on menus, dialog boxes, icons and so on. They allow these generic interfaces to be adapted to the requirements of particular applications. They are reserved for experts, and therefore go beyond the limits of simple personal productivity tools.

*19.4 Extended example: word processors

Word processors are certainly the most widely used computer-based tools: in fact anyone can produce and manage textual documents. Text-processing tools have been available for a long time: a few 'pioneering' books dealing with computer systems were produced entirely on the computer even in the 1960s. The quality of those books, however, was definitely inferior to books produced using traditional printing techniques.

In the past decades, word processing tools have evolved dramatically, bringing increased ease of use and documents of better quality. This evolution is essentially due to two facts:

- From the document quality standpoint, the availability of graphics terminals and high-resolution printers enables the production of sophisticated page layouts and the inclusion of special characters (such as Greek and mathematical symbols) and variable-size elements and figures integrated in the text.

- From the ease of use standpoint, a major breakthrough was obtained by the 'What you see is what you get' (WYSIWYG) paradigm; that is, the possibility of seeing the effect of a formatting command immediately on the screen. For instance, in the older tools, special command characters were required in order to emphasize a portion of text by making it 'italic', as indicated below:

  ... plain text ^I italic portion of text I^ plain text ...

  The text was shown on the screen as above and the desired effect was only obtained when it was printed:

  ... plain text *italic portion of text* plain text ...

  The inconvenience of lacking a precise view of the text while editing becomes even more striking during the composition of complex texts, such as mathematical formulas. In contrast, with the WYSIWYG paradigm, the text appears on the screen exactly as it will appear in print.

Today, most word processors conform to the WYSIWYG paradigm and offer sophisticated commands which enable the production of high quality books and documents ready for printing (camera-ready format). In the following we summarize the main features of such tools, referring to one of the most widely known word processors: Word 7, a Microsoft program available on PC-compatible and Macintosh computers.

19.4.1 **Word processing with Word 7**

Word 7 is a window-based menu-driven word processor. During an editing session, each open document appears in a window which can be managed in the usual way. The frame of the screen consists of the menu (at the top) and the **toolbars** (at the top and the bottom, in the normal configuration). The menu contains the commands and the toolbars contain icons that represent (approximately) the same set of commands in graphical form. For instance, under the Edit menu we find the traditional Cut command which drops a portion of text from the document and keeps it in a suitable memory space, called the **clipboard**. The same command is represented by the ✂ icon in the toolbar. The dual Paste command can be used to move text from the clipboard back into the document, usually from a different starting location. Figure 19.15 presents a snapshot of the screen while editing a document in Word 7.

Word includes a fairly standard set of commands that allow a text to be edited, such as:

- selecting (with the mouse) a portion of text which appears suitably emphasized on the screen;

- cutting, pasting and moving portions of text from one position to another;

- searching and changing portions of text or text formatting (for example, from italic to boldface or from one font to another).

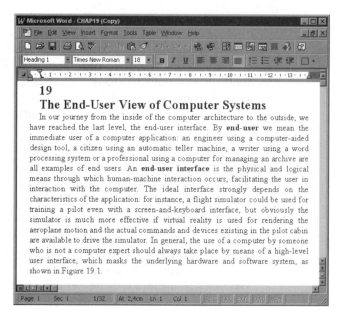

Figure 19.15   An example of a Word screen while editing a document.

In addition, it includes more powerful features that are aimed at supporting not only the simple editing of a document, but also its 'design' from its conception to the production of the camera-ready layout. The most significant features are:

- The possibility of 'viewing' the documents in different ways, according to different needs. For instance, the **Page Layout** and **Print Preview** modes (with minor differences in the way they are used) present the text, page by page, as it will appear in print; the **Outline** displays the 'skeleton' of the document which consists of the titles of chapters, sections, subsections and so on. The outline view is particularly useful when conceiving the document and designing its structure, especially when dealing with complex documents such as a thesis. The page layout and print preview are useful when we are close to the final production and are concerned with 'cosmetics', such as the position of figures and titles.

- The possibility of defining several styles. A **style** is a collection of formatting commands that is packaged under a unique identifier and can be applied to a given portion of text. For instance, we may define a Program style to be applied to portions of texts which consist of C programs: this style may specify that programs have to be written in a special font, different from the normal one, that their lines should be indented with respect to the margins of the page of normal text, and so on. Other styles could be applied to chapter and section titles and could include specifications such as emphasizing characters in bold or using larger character sizes. The advantage of using styles, instead of directly formatting single portions of text, is uniformity and ease of use. Furthermore, if at a later stage we decide to change some formatting rules (for example, moving titles from italic to boldface, or changing their font) we have only to change the style definition rather than going through the text and changing the formatting of all portions of text that have to be changed: style application to the text is performed automatically by the word processor.

- The availability of a set of services (tools in Word's terminology) that provide support for several time-consuming and error-prone activities. For example:

  - **Spell checking**, which automatically checks the spelling of words against the dictionary, is provided in all major languages. There is also a grammar checking utility which should help to detect syntax errors, but at its present stage it does not seem very useful.

  - Facilities to build an **index** in a book, enabling collections of index terms to be listed. The user marks the terms in the text and the word processor automatically builds an index of these terms, including the page numbers where they occur.

  - Automatic **numbering** of list items, references, figures, etc and cross-referencing to them.

  - Automatic displaying and numbering of **footnotes**.

- The possibility of including and integrating within a single document the items built by means of other tools, such as tables (using a spreadsheet), figures and equations. Word also supplies limited facilities to build objects of this type by using Word itself, as it includes tools for drawing figures, tables and equations. This redundancy, in principle, is quite useful, since it relieves the nonsophisticated user of the need to buy special tools for such purposes. There may be compatibility problems, however, if, for instance, we initially draw a figure directly with Word and later decide to improve it by using a special-purpose drawing tool, or conversely.

*19.5 Extended example: spreadsheets

Spreadsheets are systems designed to carry out simple, very commonly used processing of tabular information. The best-known spreadsheet products on the market are Excel (by Microsoft) and Lotus 1-2-3 (by Lotus). This section contains general concepts that apply to any spreadsheet product and the examples are inspired by Lotus 1-2-3.

Data in a spreadsheet is arranged in a three-dimensional space made up of **rows**, **columns** and **pages**; the maximum size of a spreadsheet depends on the product under consideration. Spreadsheet elements are called **cells** and they are addressed using a triple: page, column, row. Pages and columns are indicated by

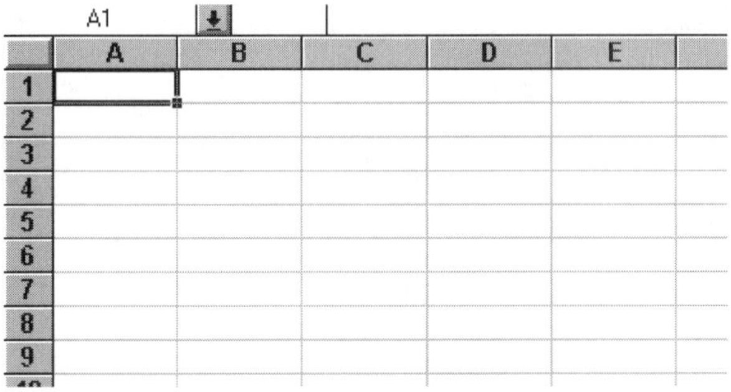

Figure 19.16 Current position within a spreadsheet.

letters of the alphabet, starting with A, whereas rows are numbered from 1 onwards; for example, the top left cell on the first page is indicated by A:A1, where the first symbol refers to the page. In general, pages are only needed for sophisticated uses of spreadsheets; in this chapter, we assume that we are always operating on the first page (A) and therefore we omit the page indicator from cell addresses.

Information within a spreadsheet is organized into rectangular matrices, called **ranges.** Each range is identified by a pair of addresses: the top left cell and the bottom right cell. For example, the range B7..G11 contains six rows (B, C, D, E, F, G) and five columns (7, 8, 9, 10, 11) and therefore has 30 cells.

At the beginning of a working session, the spreadsheet can be loaded from a file in mass storage; during the working session, the spreadsheet is normally present in main memory. During a working session, the entire spreadsheet or selected ranges can be copied to a file; in this way, the work carried out is saved, so that it can be reused in future working sessions.

Part of the spreadsheet is displayed on screen, constituting the **visible window** of the sheet. The cells are displayed in a default size, which can be modified by the user. A particular cell inside the visible window constitutes the **current position** in the spreadsheet; it is highlighted as shown in Figure 19.16. The user can move around the spreadsheet by moving the current position or by selecting (by means of appropriate commands) a nonvisible cell; the visible window moves in tandem with the current position, thus keeping the current position always in view.

19.5.1 Cell types: values, labels and expressions

Spreadsheet cells can contain three types of information: values, labels and expressions. In addition, cells may be empty, that is they may contain no information at all.

- **Values** are integers or real numbers. Spreadsheets allow numbers to be input in many different formats and do not distinguish between integers and reals. Special conventions are used for the input of date and time values.

A1					
A	**B**	**C**	**D**	**E**	**F**
1	Jan	Feb	Mar	Quart.	
2 Husb Sal.	1054	1062	1062	3178	
3 Wife Sal.	1321	1321	1400	4042	
4 Tot. Inc.	2375	2383	2462	7220	
5 1st Exp.	555	532	643	1730	
6 2nd Exp.	687	666	754	2107	
7 Tot. Exp.	1242	1198	1397	3837	
8 Savings	1133	1185	1065	3383	
9					

Figure 19.17   Spreadsheet for a family budget.

- **Labels** are texts, consisting of character strings of arbitrary length. Text that exceeds the size of the cell is displayed only if the adjacent cell is empty.
- **Expressions** are formulas whose evaluation produces a result (a value or a label). As we will see, expressions can refer to the contents of other cells. Formulas are normally invisible, insofar as the spreadsheet displays the *result* of the evaluation of a formula and not the formula itself. However, it is possible to have the formula displayed by making the cell that contains it the current position; in this case, the formula is displayed in an appropriate part of the screen.

When inputting data, users must specify whether the contents of a cell are a number, a label, or a formula, by taking into account the default type associated with the data in each specific product. For example, 56 is interpreted as a number by default; in order to use it as a string, it has to be quoted as '56'.

Figure 19.17 illustrates a spreadsheet for a family budget. Ranges A2..A8 and B1..E1 contain labels which illustrate, respectively, the contents of the rows and columns of the spreadsheet. The range B2..E8 contains a combination of values and expressions; more precisely:

- the range B2..D3 contains the values of the monthly salaries of husband and wife;
- the range B5..D6 contains the values of the monthly expenses;
- ranges B4..D4 and B7..D7 contain expressions that combine, respectively, the income (salaries) and the expenses;
- the range B8..D8 contains an expression that calculates the monthly savings, subtracting the expenses from the income;
- the range E2..E8 contains expressions that combine the monthly data into quarterly data.

The main characteristic of a spreadsheet is its ability to adapt automatically to modifications of its values. Thus, expressions that contain references to cells are automatically re-evaluated each time a cell's contents change. If, for example, the value of the husband's March salary, in cell D2, is changed, the system automatically modifies cells E2, D4, E4, D8 and E8, whose expressions refer to cell D2; in the following section, we will see the various ways of propagating modifications.

Note that the entire range A1..E8 is presented as a matrix, even though it contains cells of different types. In fact, there is nothing to prevent us selecting a range containing heterogeneous cells; the range A1..E8 can, for example, be saved in a file or moved, in the context of a spreadsheet, by a single operation. Furthermore, it is possible to give a range a symbolic name and use this in the spreadsheet, instead of the positional reference; for example, the range illustrated in Figure 19.17 could be called 'income-expenses'. All the cells of the matrix are presented in the same way, and it is therefore impossible to know which cells contain values and which expressions; to inspect the contents of a specific cell, it is necessary to make it the current position.

19.5.2 The construction of formulas

A user tells the system that a formula is being input using an initial symbol; for instance, Lotus 1-2-3 uses the sign (+ or –) of the first operand of the formula. Formulas can be of three types, text, numeric or logical.

- **Text formulas** operate on strings; the most frequently used operator for text formulas is concatenation (&), which produces a string $s = s_1 \ \& \ s_2$ by appending s_2 to s_1. The following are valid text formulas:

    + 'income' & 'expenses'
    + A2 & A3

- **Numeric formulas** operate on numeric values. They can be constructed using the classic numeric operations (sum, difference, product, division, power) and take as their operands numeric values or references to cells; other formulas are obtained by applying predefined functions to a set of arguments. Predefined functions can be of mathematical type (including the aggregate functions AVG, MIN, MAX, SUM, COUNT already seen in SQL) or statistical-financial (for example, interest calculations). Other functions express search conditions on a database (as we will see) or treat items such as date, time and strings in a special way. Aggregate and statistical functions which apply to a range of values are preceded by the symbol @. Valid numerical formulas in Lotus 1-2-3 are:

    + B2 + B3 + B4
    + @SUM(B2 ..B3)
    + @AVG(B4 ..D4) – @AVG(B7 ..D7)

- **Logical formulas** include Boolean expressions, constructed by using the logical operators AND, OR, NOT on simple predicates, which are constructed with the usual comparators (=, ≠, >, ≥, <, ≤). The result of the evaluation is given by the values 1 (true) and 0 (false). Valid logical formulas are:

> + B2 > 2000 OR B3 > 2000
> + B1 = 'total-income'

19.5.3 Spreadsheet evaluation

Spreadsheets are recalculated to produce correct values, according to the various operations carried out on the cells. Normally, a spreadsheet performs all modifications automatically, as soon as a formula or a value is changed.

- **Automatic recalculation**: this is performed immediately after any change to the spreadsheet. The user can carry on modifying the spreadsheet while recalculation is being carried out.

- **Manual recalculation**: this is carried out at the request of the user. With this option, the spreadsheet may become inconsistent, that is, show values that should have been recalculated. This option is useful for very complex spreadsheets where recalculation involves a large number of operations.

Furthermore, the order of calculating a formula can be:

- **natural**, when a formula is recalculated after all the formulas of the cells on which it depends have been recalculated;

- **columnwise**, when formulas are recalculated in column order;

- **rowwise**, when formulas are recalculated in row order.

Note that, when recalculation does not follow the natural order, cells that depend on other cells that come later in the order do not reach their correct value in a single recalculation.

One problem that can arise when spreadsheets become very complex is the definition of **circular references** in formulas; in general, circular references are caused by programming errors in the formulas. For example, consider inserting the formula +@SUM(A1..A6) in cell A6, instead of the formula +@SUM(A1..A5), which would correctly express the intentions of the user. Assuming that cell A6 is initially empty, after the first evaluation of the formula A6 correctly contains the sum of the values of cells A1..A5; however, when the formula is recalculated, it will include the previous value of A6 in producing the final value.

Circular references can be much more complex and involve quite long sequences of formulas. However, the products available today are generally capable of signalling the presence of circular references and helping users to eliminate them. Sometimes, circular references are inserted on purpose and allow the spreadsheet to be recalculated by successive iterations, especially when used together with the manual recalculation mode discussed above.

19.5.4 Reorganization of a spreadsheet

Spreadsheets can be easily reorganized; for example, it is possible to move or duplicate ranges, insert new rows or columns, widen or narrow the cells and so on. Furthermore, it is possible to open several windows into the spreadsheet and display them on screen, simultaneously displaying noncontiguous parts of the spreadsheet.

When a range containing formulas is moved or duplicated, taking a different position in the spreadsheet, references to cells in the range are automatically changed so that the formulas continue to be valid in the range's new position. For example, suppose that cell A5 of the range A1..A5 contains the formula @SUM(A1..A4): if the range is now copied or moved to positions F5..F9, the formula in position F9 is automatically changed into @SUM(F5..F8).

The transformation described above treats cells within a range as **relative addresses**; however, it is possible to specify that addresses used in formulas are **absolute addresses** by using a different notation, and in this case the automatic transformation does not take place.

19.5.5 Data presentation

One of the most successful characteristics of spreadsheets is their ability to present data graphically. For example, the data corresponding to the spreadsheet illustrated in Figure 19.17 can be visualized by means of the following diagrams.

- A **bar chart**, in which each datum to be represented corresponds to a bar; the height of the bar is proportional to the value to be shown. Bars can be grouped and each bar can be visualized in a different colour (or shade of grey) to make the diagram more readable. See Figure 19.18.

- A **pie chart**, in which each datum is represented by a segment of pie proportional to the value to be shown. This type of diagram efficiently displays the percentages represented by the various values; each segment can be annota-

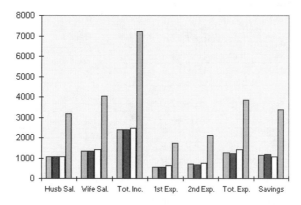

Figure 19.18 Example of bar chart.

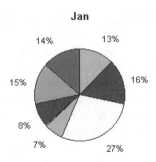

Figure 19.19 Example of pie chart.

ted, for example to indicate the percentage of 'pie' corresponding to it. See Figure 19.19.

- A **linear graph**, in which data is represented on a Cartesian plane; each datum is associated with a point. A line connects all data belonging to the same observation, for example all data corresponding to the quarterly sum. See Figure 19.20.

- A **surface graph**, in which data is again represented on a Cartesian plane. Each datum corresponds to a point, arranged vertically on top of other points for comparison; points corresponding to the same observation are joined by a line. The area between two lines, highlighted by a different colour (or shade of grey), is thus proportional to the data represented. See Figure 19.21.

Graphics are specified using simple menus that allow graphics elements to be associated with the various ranges of the spreadsheet. It is possible to display the graphs on screen, in order to correct them and add information that makes them more readable (for example, labels to explain the meaning of axes and points).

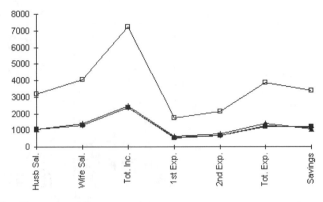

Figure 19.20 Example of linear graph.

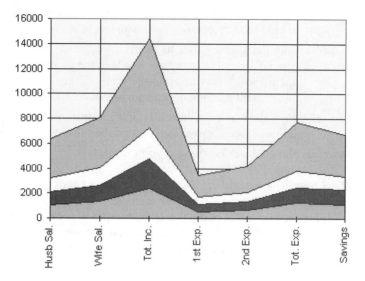

Figure 19.21   Example of surface graph.

When the result is satisfactory, the graphs can be printed or displayed in appropriate windows on the spreadsheet.

Spreadsheets can be used in a much more sophisticated way than illustrated in this chapter. It is possible to program macro-instructions (corresponding to procedures in a programming language) or manipulate matrices (for example, for the solution of linear equations), or calculate correlations between data (for example, using regression analysis). These and other applications are not described further.

Exercises

This exercise should be carried out on a word processor.

19.1   Copy a small fraction of this text into a document of your own. You should not include too much text, but you should concentrate on including nontextual features, such as titles, programs, figures and tables. Use style definitions whenever you feel they are appropriate and try to make them look as close as possible to the present layout. Then:

(a)   Change program font to `Courier` or a similar one (Courier is the traditional font of typing machines and is still often used in textbooks for programs).

(b)   Change the font of all titles to Helvetica or other similar font (Helvetica is the font used in this text for programs).

(c)　Change the numbering convention of footnotes (to stress this feature you should have at least one page with more than one footnote).

(d)　Run the spell-checker to verify if you made typing errors. Pay attention to special symbols that are not words in the English dictionary. Possibly find in the manual a way to avoid the spell-checker continually warning you about possible misspelling of program identifiers such as 'TableOfElements'.

(e)　Print the whole document, avoiding a situation where the last line of a page is a title or where a page starts with a short line or with the last line of a program.

The next exercises should be done using a spreadsheet.

19.2　Construct a spreadsheet to calculate the cost of your car repairs. Suppose you know the cost of the various parts (for example, cylinder head, pistons, carburettor, spark plugs and so on). Suppose that labour costs $30 per hour. The spreadsheet should be used as follows: the mechanic enters the various parts used and the time necessary for the repair, and the system then calculates the costs and adds a sales tax (or VAT) percentage where appropriate.

19.3　Construct a spreadsheet for garbage collection. For each month and for each collection point, describe the quantity collected. Calculate the total yearly quantities per collection point and the total monthly quantities. Describe some graphs that compare the quantities of garbage collected at three different points.

19.4　Construct a spreadsheet that generalizes the one illustrated in Figure 19.17, adding further expense categories and extending it to 12 months. In addition, insert subtotals for each expense category and per quarter.

19.5　Consider a tax return form. Realize some of its tables as a spreadsheet.

19.6　Write formulas that contain circular references into a spreadsheet and observe their behaviour.

PART III
Software development

So far our attention has been focused on the construction of small computer applications: we dealt with well-defined and small-sized problems, although they sometimes required some nontrivial insight. For instance, the description and analysis of the merge–sort algorithm given in Chapter 12 was not trivial but started from a well-known problem and ended up with fairly short code and a compact formula for its complexity.

Real-life computer applications rarely exhibit the above features; more often, they consist of a large number of imprecisely defined functionalities that could require a lot of design effort and huge investments in both time and money. Consider, for instance, the problem of 'automating banking services': the meaning of this phrase is far from clear and has changed fundamentally over time. In the 1950s such a phrase indicated the keeping of an electronic record of all customer accounts and of their transactions; later it also included the managing of interactive services at the bank branch; now it involves sophisticated services that may be distributed over different banks in different countries and even be supplied at customers' homes through telephone interaction. The development of all these services as a complete and integrated application requires a lot of effort and the careful design of a huge amount of code, even if, eventually, such code is a collection of well-defined library routines for searching and updating files, sending messages and guaranteeing secure access to private data. Although none of the routines requires the invention of 'smart algorithms', the construction of the whole application is a tremendous job.

Thus, the development of industrial computer-based applications cannot be reduced to the programming activity examined so far. This part introduces a more general and complete view of software development: this is often called **programming-in-the-large** as opposed to the term **programming-in-the-small** which usually refers to the construction of single small programs. Attention is mainly devoted to software construction since, in general, developing a computer application means designing suitable application software to run on top of standard hardware, basic software and networks. The purpose of this part is to give readers some understanding of the process of building industrial software, not to give them the professional ability to develop and manage large software applications, a skill that is typical of the specialized **software engineering** field. As a result, readers should be able to develop their own, modest-sized, real-life applications and to interact properly with specialists in the case of large projects.

This part is structured as follows. Chapter 20 presents the general goals (qualities) of a software production process and the models through which it can be described and managed. Chapters 21 through 23 are devoted to the main phases of the process: requirements analysis and specification, design-in-the-large, verification. Finally, Chapter 24 presents the tools that help software designers in their job.

Two more chapters are included in this part for convenience, although they are not (exclusively) devoted to the issue of software design. Chapter 25 presents object-oriented design, a modern approach which applies not only to software design and programming, but also to the development of a whole computer application: in fact, it can be applied to hardware and database design as well. Chapter 26 briefly introduces nonconventional approaches to programming which are based on a different way of dealing with computer organization and computation theory; we give the reader a basic understanding of these approaches, even if this text follows a more traditional way of describing and teaching computer science.

The software life cycle

20

Software construction in an industrial context is, like other production activities, a complex process of considerable economic and social impact. Furthermore, computer applications are very often part of a product of a completely different type, for example in automated industrial plants, or in embedded applications, such as electrical household appliances, cars and so on. This means that, at least in some phases of product development, its computer components cannot be completely distinguished from other elements, which further complicates their industrial development.

For many years, people have been speaking of the **software crisis**, indicating that industrial production in this sector does not meet the ever-growing demands of the market. In general, there are complaints about the poor quality of software, especially in terms of reliability for highly critical applications (such as avionics systems), about the fact that software is often delivered late, and about the unpredictability of the cost of the development itself. The folklore of software literature reports many anecdotes of disastrous failures (whether in terms of human life, as in the case of the THERAC 25 system which controlled radiation therapies, or in economic terms, as in the case of millions of dollars 'electronically stolen' by exploiting a hole in a banking security system) due to software errors.

Certainly, the software production process has improved over the years as much as any other design activity; however, the term 'software crisis' is still widely mentioned. The reason is probably because software production is a *human-intensive* activity, whereas hardware production is a *technology-intensive* activity; thus, software does not succeed in keeping pace with the evolution of hardware technology which, in turn, generates increasing expectations. (Empirical studies report that in the early 1960s the relative costs of hardware and software development were 80% versus 20%; in the 1980s this ratio was totally reversed and kept going in the same direction.)

For instance, to give a less safety-critical software anecdote, the authors of this text found the most recent version of a widely used word processor painful to

511

use, although some of them had happily used previous versions of the same product. The availability of more powerful hardware led to more ambitious software, but the new version turned out to be far slower, less reliable and less user-friendly.

In summary, quoting a folk assertion, 'the market wants it Better, Faster, Cheaper, and forget the Better, if necessary'. Following this 'rule' seldom results in increased user satisfaction and never in greater industrial success.

This chapter sheds some light on the various problems of the industrial software production process. First, we identify the most important qualities of software (Section 20.1). Subsequently (Section 20.2), we present some of the best-known models for representing the process of software production and management; these models reflect the title of this chapter: the 'software' product has a 'life' which, as we will see, is often anything but short. Finally (Section 20.3), we briefly discuss some organizational aspects of the software production process.

20.1 Quality in software design

Each activity has the aim of satisfying quality requirements. Only a precise formulation of the quality characteristics one intends to pursue allows a comparison of the costs involved to achieve them and thus a final judgement of the success or failure of the enterprise.

Quality requirements may differ quite a lot, not only as a function of the activity considered (for example, the production of crockery rather than electrical household appliances), but also as a function of the environment in which the product will be used (for example, an artisan or industrial environment).

In this section we deal with the quality objectives of industrial software production. Of course, software production in non-industrial contexts (such as personal software or software developed in scientific institutions) is also important, but many of our considerations would be of a rather different character in a non-industrial framework.

In general, a software product shares many quality objectives with nearly all other industrial goods; however, it has some particular characteristics caused by the fact of being 'soft', that is, almost completely disconnected from physical matter. Whereas in the production of cars, dams and other traditional manufactured goods the construction material plays a fundamental role in determining the quality and cost of the product, in the case of software the support on which it is distributed is immaterial. In fact, it is not by chance that software is often associated with other typical 'products of the mind', such as books, music and so on.

In order to analyse software quality issues somewhat better, it may be useful to resort to the following two classifications, which are independent of one another.

(1) **Quality of the product and quality of the production process**
    As in any other industrial activity, in order to obtain high-quality products, much attention must be paid to the process that leads to the final manufacture of the product. Consider, for example, the organization of the production of

an economy car and that of a Ferrari. It is clear that the final objective is to obtain a car that is of high value compared to its cost; but it is also evident that the way the assembly line is organized heavily influences the quality of the product and its production cost.

In the case of software production, many problems connected with the quality of the product are caused by a lack of quality in the production process.

(2) **External and internal qualities**

Those features of a product that can be directly perceived by the user are classified as **external qualities**, whereas the **internal qualities** can be measured only by the producer. For example, efficiency is a typically external quality, whereas understandability of the design documentation is normally internal. Note that some qualities can be considered external or internal depending on the particular production and application context. For example, if a customer requested the delivery not only of the software but also of the corresponding design documentation (as typically happens with military orders), the clarity of the latter would become an external quality.

The attribute of internal or external quality applies not only to the product, but also to the production process. For example, 'robotization' of car manufacturers' assembly lines is an internal quality, although it is widely cited by various industries to show potential customers the efficiency of the production process.

We now present a short list of important software quality features, from the different points of view discussed above.

- **Correctness**. It seems natural to consider this quality feature as the most important of each product and of software in particular: if a product does not satisfy the requirements, it is virtually useless and may even be harmful. Unfortunately, in many cases, software products have proved to be incorrect, sometimes with catastrophic consequences.

  The **reliability** of software, in other words, the level of trust that its user can place on it, is strongly dependent on its correctness. A considered analysis would show that correctness and reliability, although closely related, are not exactly the same. However, for simplicity, in this text they are considered to be synonyms.

  Correctness is obviously an external quality of the software product. It can also be attributed to the production process: in fact, once the rules for organizing this process are established (for example, complete phase 1 before starting phase 2), they can be complied with to varying degrees during its execution.

- **Efficiency**. This term indicates the possibility of obtaining the desired goal with a limited use of resources (such as time or hardware). It is evident that efficiency is an external quality, attributed both to the product and to the production process.

  Very often its importance has been overestimated, and in order to obtain improvements in efficiency other quality features have been sacrificed, including even correctness on occasion: very complex programs have been written to obtain just a small improvement, which then produced errors. This observation shows that, in general, different quality features can conflict with one another.

- **Modifiability**. This term indicates the possibility of adapting the software to different environments (for example, to changes in laws that govern the reality of an enterprise into which a computer system is integrated). Modifications can also be due to changes in the hardware on which the software is running, or to the desire to obtain better efficiency. In practice, modifications also have to be made to correct the errors not detected during software development.

  This quality feature has become ever more important with growing production costs, which makes it more desirable to modify existing software than to develop new software from scratch. Experience has shown that this feature is highly critical and very difficult to obtain: on many occasions, a modification applied to remove one error introduces others.

  Normally, modifiability is an internal quality. It can be relevant for both the product and the production process.

- **Reusability**. By this term we mean the possibility of using the same product in different applications. This feature therefore refers particularly to general-purpose software components that can be adapted for reuse in different systems. As in the case of modifiability, the objective of this feature is to avoid repetition of costly development to obtain (parts of) software products that differ only slightly from products already available.

  A typical example of easily reusable software is the libraries of numerical calculus subroutines, which can be used in many different applications. In other sectors, this feature is much harder to obtain.

20.2 Models of the software production process

As we have mentioned before, software construction is split into different phases. The precise definition of these phases and their organization constitutes a **software development model**. It is also often called a **software life cycle model**, to underline the fact that a complex system such as an industrial software product has a life that often continues for decades and that covers the period from the first inception of the product to its eventual withdrawal from the market or until it ceases to be operational. The long life of software is a clear indication of its economic relevance.

It is clear enough that a good software life cycle model is at the root of all the quality features of the production process. Much attention has therefore been paid to this subject since the dawn of software engineering, and various models have been proposed. In this section, we briefly present two of the best-known and most significant ones, which have somewhat opposing characteristics.

20.2.1 The waterfall model

The term 'waterfall model' suggests successive phases of software construction in which, after completing one phase, one moves on to the following phase with no possibility of going back (a waterfall never moves upwards). Figure 20.1 presents the waterfall model in a classic and intuitive way.

The phases shown in Figure 20.1 are given as examples: actually, there are numerous variations of the model in which the number and type of phases vary considerably, as well as the required level of detail.

- **Feasibility study.** This is the preliminary analysis phase in which the likely costs and benefits of the proposed product are evaluated in order to make a final decision on whether to proceed with the project.

- **Requirements analysis and specification.** In this phase a detailed analysis of the required characteristics of the system is carried out. These characteristics are described in a document called the **system requirements specification**.

- **System architecture design.** In this phase the system is designed as a collection of various components, or **modules**, each integrated with and interacting with the others.

- **Implementation and verification of individual modules.** In this phase the individual modules are implemented. Each module is verified autonomously, in order to guarantee that it can be integrated with the rest of the system.

- **System integration and verification.** In this phase the individual modules are integrated with each other to make up the system, which then undergoes an overall verification.

- **Installation.** In this phase the system is made ready for use, passing from the production environment to the environment in which it is to be used.

- **Maintenance.** This term includes the whole evolution of the system from delivery onwards. It therefore includes modifications and various other developments.

To judge the waterfall model correctly, one has to take into account that it was proposed at the dawning of software engineering as a first reaction to the original vision of software construction as a purely creative process, and therefore not subject to particular rules or restrictions (in those days, one talked about the 'art of programming'). As a reaction to this state of affairs, the model is extremely rigid and prescriptive: for example, no executable code may be written until the architectural design phase has been completed.

In practice, this model rapidly showed its flaws. For example, in many cases, and especially in nontraditional application areas, it is extremely difficult to describe all the system requirements without making mistakes and without needing to introduce changes in subsequent phases. In general, therefore, the rigidly sequential approach highlighted by the name 'waterfall' has proved to be impracticable.

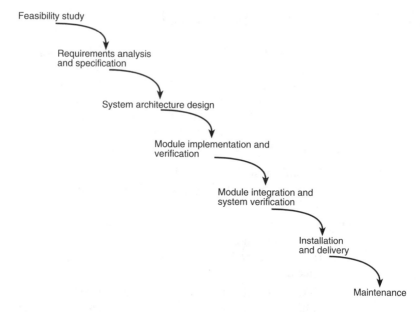

Figure 20.1 The waterfall model of the software life cycle.

The waterfall model showed further deficiencies with the increasing importance of the maintenance phase in the software life cycle. This term includes every activity that follows the delivery of the product. Over the course of time these activities became more and more predominant, until they represented, in many cases, more than half of the overall cost of the entire life cycle. This is due to constantly prolonging the 'life' of the software. In particular, as we have already mentioned, during the product's lifetime changes may become necessary due to a change in requirements (for example, changes in the law or in the operational environment). This makes it necessary to repeat, at least partially, all the development phases and cannot be confined to a generic maintenance phase.

As a consequence of these inadequacies, the waterfall model was subject to criticisms that led to the identification of alternative models. These models try to make the entire software production and management process more flexible. In the next section we present the *spiral model*, because of its fame and generality. The waterfall model, however, though seldom used in a rigorous way, remains an important reference model, in the sense that many more modern models can be explained and understood by referring to the original one. Furthermore, it is still an important model for design documentation. Even if the real development process does not rigidly follow the waterfall model, many experts advocate that *process documentation should be built and managed as if it were derived according to this model*. In other words, there should be a first document reporting on the results of the feasibility study, a second document reporting requirements specifications and so on. Most important, the documents should always be *aligned and consistent*, in such a way that a reader should be able to verify that a document related to a given phase is derived from a document related to the previous phase. Experience has shown evidence of major problems caused by changes introduced in the source code (sometimes even in the object code without recompilation!) without changing the higher-level documentation to keep it consistent.

20.2.2 The spiral model

In the spiral model, the various phases of the life cycle are iterated a nonspecified number of times. There is no maintenance phase as such, because it is nothing more than the continuous repetition of new and more in-depth analyses, based on the experience acquired in previous developments, followed by new and richer realizations. Figure 20.2 represents, in an intuitive way, the evolution of software development in this model and also shows the reason for its name.

The different quadrants of the figure indicate the different phases of development (analysis and specification, design, implementation and verification). The spiral indicates the evolution of the activity over time, underlining the fact that a priori no final point is envisaged and that each evolution must be the 'fruit' of the experience acquired in previous realizations.

The model also shows that, in general, the first realization will not be an official delivery of the product, but will be a prototype. Note, however, that in some extreme cases, one could stop after only one cycle through the quadrants: in this case, the model would be the same as the waterfall model.

20.3 Organizational aspects of the software production process

We conclude this chapter by touching on an issue that, although not technical, has a great impact on the overall success of a technical project involving industrial software development.

In each industrial activity, technical aspects intertwine with organizational and economic aspects. For example, in car production there would be no sense in 'robotizing' the assembly line to produce a larger number of cars at lower cost, if those cars remained unsold. In the case of software development, this kind of problem is made even more critical by the high rate of creativity involved in the entire process. In comparison, consider the process of building a physical structure, such as a dam or a bridge. These projects certainly need much creativity, but the costs deriving from design activities are only a very small part of the total costs. The software production process is different, because the physical construction of the product is practically non-existent and all costs typically derive from design activities. This is the reason why the evaluation of software development costs is generally more error-prone than in other cases.

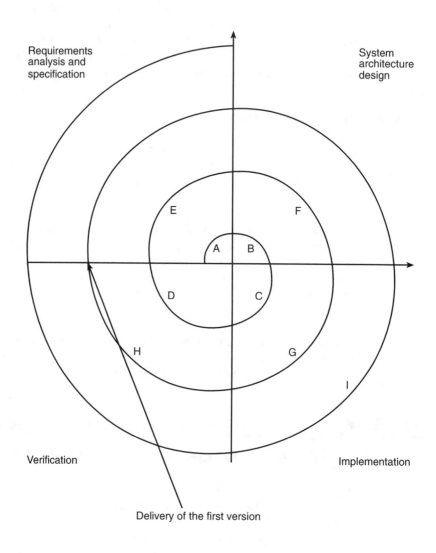

Requirements
analysis and
specification

System
architecture
design

Verification

Implementation

Delivery of the first version

A Initial analysis	**E** New draft of	**G** First version of
B Initial design	specifications based	the system
C First prototype	on the analysis of the	**H** Verification of the
D Verification of the	first prototype	first version
first prototype	**F** Complete system	**I** New version of
	design	the system

Figure 20.2 The spiral model of the software life cycle.

Until recently, these economic–organizational problems were approached in an entirely empirical way, on the basis of the intuition and experience of designers and managers. This was certainly a factor in the already mentioned software crisis. Therefore, in more recent times, software engineering has tried not only to find new methods and tools for producing a better design from the technical point of view, but also to identify models and suggestions for a more efficient and rigorous management of the entire process from the organizational point of view.

These models help to forecast development costs, optimize allocation of resources to the production process, control and estimate the progress of work and so on. However, they are still in an experimental phase and have many controversial characteristics; thus, their validity remains to be verified, though many expectations are based on them. With the advent of better planning and internal organization, software factories would become more competitive and capable of mastering the production process. We therefore simply emphasize the relevance of the problem and report that research is actively trying to propose satisfactory solutions.

Exercises

20.1 Discuss the classification of reusability as an internal or external quality of both the product and the production process.

20.2 Indicate other software quality features and discuss their various attributes and their importance in different application sectors.

Requirements analysis and specification

21

Requirements analysis and specification is an extremely critical phase within the software life cycle. Errors committed in this phase, for example misunderstanding the exact needs of the user or poor formulation of the requirements, nearly always have extremely serious and costly consequences, often leading to the necessity to redo a good deal of the project. This is amply confirmed by experience and it is the main reason that, in the spiral model, the requirements analysis is periodically checked and improved.

In spite of its importance, specification has been, and often still is, carried out in a nonrigorous way, without applying any method or tool which would make it more reliable; this fact contributes to the majority of today's specification documents being particularly unsatisfactory. There are, however, some models, languages and tools which are specially designed to help in the specification phase, and these are becoming more widely used and developed, albeit slowly.

In this chapter we focus on specification: first, we analyse its goals and quality requirements (Section 21.1); then we provide a classification of the various types of software specification (Section 21.2); finally, we present two of the best-known and most widely used specification models, applied to simple examples (Sections 21.2.2 and 21.3).

21.1 Goals and qualities of the specification

In many environments, different types of specification are rather subtly distinguished: there are **user requirements specifications** to define the fundamental characteristics that the system must possess to satisfy user needs, **functional specifications** to indicate the functions or operations that the system must provide, **design or architectural specifications** to indicate the overall structure of the system and so on.

The finer the distinction between different types of specification, the more the borders between them dissolve. Here we prefer to take a more general view, in which the term 'specification' is synonymous with a *definition* of some *aim* to be attained. Thus, the sentence 'the automated teller machine system must also be capable of being used by persons with limited movement and eyesight' is a specification as well as the definition of tasks that a procedure has to carry out within a program. The entire process of software construction can be seen as continuous alternation between the activities of 'specification and realization', possibly including 'verification' of the adequacy of the second with respect to the first. The realization of the ith level of this process constitutes the specification of the $(i + 1)$th level, until the coding stage is reached; the output of this stage (the code) is the specification for the compiler that has to produce the executable code.

Therefore, rather than discuss the wealth of possible types of specification, we prefer to comment briefly on the different aims that the specification must have at different stages and in different contexts of the development process. Also, various requirements (quality objectives) derive from the diversity of these aims and sometimes from the contrast between them, and the specification must meet these requirements at best, possibly managing trade-offs.

- The specification must be a *definition of the user requirements* that the product has to satisfy. Consequently, this definition often is (or should be) part of the *contract* between the producer and the user of the product. Notice that the terms 'user', 'producer' and even 'contract' should be interpreted in a fairly general sense: the accent here is on the end user of the application who may not even know that there is some software in the product being purchased (for example, the car driver who only 'sees' the ABS from the effects it produces when the brakes are applied). In other cases, however, the user could be the system architect (high-level designer) who delivers specifications to lower-level implementers. In yet another extreme case the user and the producer could be the same person, who, nevertheless, should distinguish the definition of what he or she is designing from true design decisions: in a fairly extreme view he or she is giving a 'contract' to him/herself.

- The specification must be a *guide for the implementation* of the product. As the implementation team may be large (from high-level software designers to programmers charged with coding simple modules) and have many different tasks, there may be numerous specification documents with this aim, at different levels of process development.

- The specification must be a point of *reference for verification*. Once the realization is complete, it is necessary to check that it satisfies the requirements imposed by the specification. Note that verification must be carried out for each *<definition, realization>* pass, not just when the product is finished and ready to be delivered. For example, when a particular function has been defined and then implemented as a subroutine, the correctness of this subroutine with respect to the corresponding functional specification must be verified.

- The specification must be a point of *reference during each evolution* of the system, even after its delivery (the maintenance phase in the waterfall model). If a new version is produced to correct errors, it must be verified that the new version satisfies the specification where the previous version turned out to be incorrect. If a new version involves changing some hardware or software components, for example to improve efficiency, it must be verified that the specified functionalities are not jeopardized. If the new version is intended to satisfy new or different needs, the first thing to do is to modify the old specifications to describe the new requirements.

As we can see, the activity of specification and the corresponding documents that reflect its results must aim at different goals[1]. Consequently, they must satisfy different requirements, sometimes in partial contrast to each other. The main requirements are the following:

- The specification must be *precise and non-ambiguous*. Experience has shown that many of the problems of unsatisfactory software quality are due to lack of precision in the initial drafting of the specifications. This lack of precision is the cause of serious misunderstandings between producer and user, with consequent mutual dissatisfaction and heavy additional costs, independently of which party finally has to bear them.

  For instance, consider the following fragment taken from the manual of a widely used word processor: it specifies the **select** command in the following way:

  > Selecting is the process for designating areas of your document that you want to work on. Most editing and formatting actions require two steps: first you select what you want to work on, such as text or graphics; then you initiate the appropriate action.

  Such a definition does not specify exactly what the term 'area' means. It turns out that in most products this is intended as a '*contiguous* sequence of characters'. This can sometimes be inferred by reading the manuals carefully or, more likely, by direct experimentation. One might, however, interpret the term 'area' as the union of *scattered* sequences of characters, so that one could go through a text, selecting different – not necessarily contiguous – words and then, say, italicize all of them by a single command. This is not possible in standard word processors. The main point, however, is that the original specification does not make clear whether it is possible or not.

- The specification must be *clear and easily understandable*. The importance of this requirement seems obvious, so that it does not require justification. Let us rather note that what is clear to a designer is not always clear to a user who has no technical background. This requirement therefore assumes different

[1] Very often, the term 'specification' is used both for the *activity of specification* and for the *result* of this activity, that is, the *specification documents*; as this ambiguity generally does not create confusion, it is also adopted in this text.

characteristics according to the users of the specification documents. Think, for example, of a system for the automation of solicitors' offices and a system for the control of an electric power plant.

- The specification must be *complete*. Everything that is relevant to the successful use of the product must be specified. A typical source of incompleteness in specifications is system behaviour under abnormal circumstances. For instance, we could specify a suitable user–machine dialogue, but often we omit to state clearly how the machine should react if the user makes a mistake during operations (for example, pushes the wrong button): in such cases the machine could react in an unforeseen and even disastrous way.

- The specification must be *noncontradictory*. For instance, consider the following specification, inspired, again, by the use of a word processor:

  > The whole text should be kept in lines of equal length, with the length specified by the user.
  > Unless the user gives an explicit hyphenation command, a carriage return should occur only at the end of a word.

  This definition, however, does not cover the case where a particular word is longer than the length specified for lines. In such a case, the specification is self-contradictory, or *inconsistent*. Therefore no implementation can satisfy it. Notice that the risk of inadvertently including some inconsistency in a specification increases as the specification documents become longer and more complex, which is often the case in real-life projects.

- The specification must be *nonredundant*. It is useless and harmful to repeat the same requirement in different ways: it increases the risk of contradictions. Another way of introducing redundancy into specifications is to indicate not just *what* the system is supposed to do, but also *how* it is to do it. This means trespassing into the area of system design, thus limiting the freedom of the designer. Notice, however, that there is a trade-off between the freedom left to the designer and the help which can be provided by the knowledgeable specifier who gives suitable suggestions. Thus, in practice, the generic suggestion to 'separate strictly the "what" from the "how"' should be followed with some common sense.

It is clear that writing good specifications that conform to the above requirements is rather a difficult activity, especially for complex systems. With rare exceptions, it is impossible for systems of vast size and cost to be defined easily: nearly always, there is a strong link between the difficulty of definition and the difficulty of realization.

Consequently, analysis and the production of specifications should be guided by sound principles and, possibly, by the use of tools that make the task easier and help to identify possible errors. Without going deeper into this important aspect, we remind the reader that, in general, the best way to approach complex problems is to decompose them into simpler problems. This is particularly true for the implementation of software, but it must also be true for its definition. Therefore, it is a good idea for the specification of a complex system to be **modularized**; in other words, structured into parts that can be easily understood individually and, when combined, allow the reader to grasp the overall sense of the specification.

Furthermore, it is often useful to develop the specifications in an **incremental** way, that is, to start from incomplete and perhaps even incorrect preliminary versions, and take them through a process of continuous analysis and refinement until a version that satisfies all stated requirements is reached. Note how an incremental approach to drafting specifications adapts itself much more to the spiral model of the software life cycle than to the waterfall model.

21.2 Classification of the various types of specification

There are different ways to write specifications, depending on their aims, the style and experience of those who write them and the attitudes of those who read them. The language used has great influence: this can be a **natural language**, such as English or Italian, or an **artificial language**, developed for the purpose.

The types of specification can be classified in various ways. The most important are the following.

21.2.1 Formal versus informal specifications

Technical or scientific work often uses formal notations normally inspired by mathematics. In the case of software, the use of a formal language (the programming language) is indispensable in the coding phase, because execution by a machine imposes a syntax and semantics defined with absolute rigour.

This is not as necessary in other phases of software development, because their product is documentation intended to be understood by human readers. Therefore, in many cases, a natural language is used for writing such documents. This is certainly convenient from the point of view of comprehensibility of the specifications, at least at first sight, except for problems caused by the use of foreign languages.

However, experience has amply shown that the use of a natural language considerably increases the risk of inaccuracy and ambiguity. Formally defined languages, such as mathematical formulas, equations, or abstract models, are considerably more precise, even though often less comfortable and less immediately accessible than a natural language.

On the other hand, rigorously formalized languages are not yet widely used in practice, although several pilot projects (for example, the specifications of aircraft control systems, or hydroelectric or nuclear power systems), mainly developed in cooperation with scientific environments, confirmed that the use of formal specification languages does help to discover subtle errors that otherwise would remain hidden until very late, with disastrous consequences.

It is often argued that a major obstacle to the widespread adoption of formal specification languages is the high level of mathematical skill required. As a compromise, their use is sometimes recommended as a partial alternative to natural languages (for example, in the specification of particularly difficult and highly critical aspects of the system).

Instead, there is an increasing use of **semi-formal languages**, in which some syntactic aspects are precisely defined, but other aspects, mostly related to the meaning of the notation used, are left to the intuition of the writers and readers of the documents. As the term suggests, semi-formal languages have advantages and disadvantages somewhere between those of natural and completely formalized languages.

In Section 21.3 we will present an example of one of the most widely used languages of this kind.

21.2.2 Operational versus descriptive specifications

There are two basic ways of defining a product:

(1) Construct a model that includes the aspects of the system that are considered to be most relevant. The system must be as similar as possible to the model: thus, its correctness will be measured on the basis of its correspondence to the model.

This practice is widely adopted in nearly all sectors of engineering. The model can be physical (for example, a scaled model of a dam, a bridge or a car) or abstract or mathematical (for example, a set of mathematical equations that represents the dynamics of the system under construction).

A specification provided by means of such a model, also called an **abstract machine**, is often called an **operational specification**, because the model indicates how the system is to operate.

(2) Define explicitly the desired, or undesired, behaviour of the system without resorting to an explicit description of the actions (operations) the system should carry out to reach such a goal. This specification method is also called **descriptive**, because the emphasis is on the description of system properties.

For example, the specification of an automated teller machine (ATM) could contain the following requirements:

(a) The machine must never be out of use for more than 24 hours (if only the machines currently in service satisfied this requirement!).

(b) Each operation requested by a user must be terminated within half a minute.

(c) Each user must have access only to the current account(s) for which the user has authorization.

In this case we do not provide a model of the ATM, but simply list all the properties the user may wish (or not wish) to have.

Let us now introduce a very simple example of an abstract machine, also used widely outside the context of software engineering: the finite state automaton model. The easiest way to define this model is the following (there are several variations of the definition proposed here).

DEFINITION 21.1

A **finite state automaton** consists of:

- a *finite set of states*, Q, that represents the different configurations in which the described system can be found;

- a *finite set of inputs*, I, that represents the different stimuli to which the described system can be subjected;

- a function δ, called the transition function, which, given a state q and an input i, results in a new state q'. It represents the way the machine behaves: if it is in state q and it receives the stimulus i, it moves into state q'.

A finite state automaton can be represented very simply and efficiently in graphical form, by representing the states by appropriate symbols enclosed in a circle and drawing an arrow with a label i that goes from state q to state q' if and only if $\delta(q, i) = q'$.

Figure 21.1 shows a two-state automaton that models an electric lamp. It can be in either of the two states {on, off}, and it can receive a single stimulus caused by pressing the switch button.

If you press the switch button when the lamp is off, it goes on and vice versa.

The careful reader will have noticed that a finite state automaton was used in Chapter 15 to show the functioning of processes in an operating system.

Note that the finite state automaton model is a formal model, whereas the requirements for the automated teller machine were written in natural language, that is, in an informal way. Obviously, it is possible to provide operational specifications in an informal way and to use a formalized language to provide descriptive specifications.

These two methods of producing specifications naturally have complementary characteristics. For example, the operational method is well suited to simulating the behaviour of the system long before it is realized, in order to verify that the specifications are formulated correctly; on the other hand, the descriptive method is sometimes considered to be more abstract, because it tends to focus attention on the characteristics of the system without influencing the designer in any particular direction. Consequently, in many practical cases, both methods can be used to improve the overall quality of the specifications.

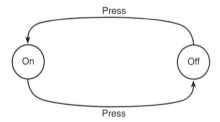

Figure 21.1   A simple finite state automaton.

21.2.3   Textual versus graphical specifications

Technical documentation has nearly always been printed (we are using the term to include any form of writing). Consequently, the main means of expression have been text and figures.

The automation of document management and archiving encouraged a purely textual type of documentation. Recent progress in graphical information processing and management, however, has ensured that nowadays graphical and textual representation of information can be used with equal efficiency, in specification as well as in many other activities of document construction and management. This has brought considerable benefits, particularly in the naturalness and understandability of specifications: a figure, whether a formally defined model or a more informal figure appealing to the intuition of its author and reader, can often replace or complement the information contained in a text.

Other recent methods of handling documents, such as *hypertext* (see Section 1.4.6), can be used to provide high-level specifications. However, other multimedia mechanisms, such as sound, do not currently seem to be of particular interest for this purpose.

21.3   The specification of data processing systems using data flow diagrams

We conclude this chapter with the presentation of one of the most widely used models for specifying data processing systems, particularly for management applications: the so-called **data flow diagram** (DFD).

DFDs are a semi-formal model that uses a simple graphical representation, a fact that has certainly contributed to its success. They constituted the kernel of many software development methods that were proposed and adopted in the 1970s, but, with minor adaptations and complements, they are still used by several more modern methodologies. Among the many definitions of this model to be found in the literature, we quote here one of the simplest.

DEFINITION 21.2

A DFD consists of a composition of elements of the following types:

- **Function** symbols, graphically indicated by circles, also called **bubbles**. A function symbol indicates an operation that is applied to data supplied as input and that produces data as output.

- **Data flow** symbols, graphically indicated by arrows. These represent data that flows inside the system, for example from one function to another.

- **Input** symbols, indicated by rectangular boxes. These represent a source of information for the system, such as a terminal through which the user supplies data.

- **Output** symbols, indicated by rectangular boxes with one S-bend side. These represent a mechanism by means of which the system supplies information to the outside world, such as a printer.

- **Archive** symbols, indicated by two segments of parallel straight lines. These represent a mechanism by means of which the system stores information in a nonvolatile way, for example files.

Functions, archives, input and output mechanisms are connected to one another by various data flows.

Figure 21.2 shows the graphical representations of the different elements that compose a DFD. Figure 21.3 shows a DFD that describes the calculation of the arithmetic expression $(a + b) * (a * d + c)$: the input device, for example a video terminal operated by a human being, produces four values, named a, b, c and d; a is input to both a '+' function and a '*' function; b is input to the same '+' function as a; d is input to the same '*' function as a; the result of the '*' function is given as input to the second '+' function together with c; then, the results of the two '+' operations are multiplied by the second '*'; and, finally, the result of this last operation is output by the output device, for example a printer.

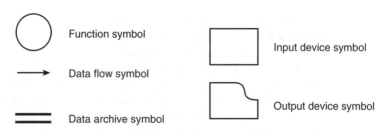

Figure 21.2 Elements constituting a DFD.

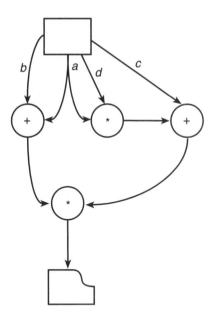

Figure 21.3   A DFD that describes the calculation of the arithmetic expression $(a + b) * (a * d + c)$.

The following example briefly illustrates the use of DFDs.

EXAMPLE 21.1

Figure 21.4 is a DFD that roughly outlines the organization of the computer system of a library. Attention is centred on two typical library activities: borrowing books and searching data about existing books, for example all books related to a certain subject. The library has several archives: the list of book authors, with a reference to the books written by each author; the list of book titles, each one referring to other important information such as authors, date of publication, position of the book in the shelves; the list of subjects, each referring to the books related to a certain subject and so on.

The DFD highlights the data dependencies for the execution of the actions considered. For instance, the `Search by subject` function requires the user to supply one or more subjects of interest; then the archive storing the list of subjects is accessed and a set of related titles is extracted; this set is used to access the list of titles and to obtain all requested data and visualize it for the user (either on a screen or by printing data).

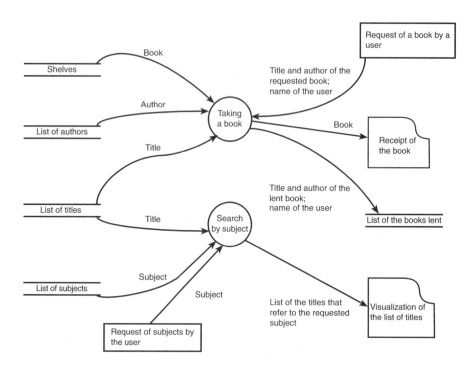

Figure 21.4 Rough outline of a library using a DFD.

Note that part of the above description is clearly formulated by the DFD of Figure 21.4, that is, the necessary information for completing the operation. Other elements of the description can be understood on the basis of our knowledge of the organization of a library but are not explicitly stated in the DFD. For instance, there is no evidence from the figure that the titles that are searched in the archive 'List of titles' are exactly those titles that have been extracted from the 'List of subjects', where, in turn, the subjects indicated by the user have been searched for. This accounts for the attribute 'semi-formal' we have given to DFDs. (In the scientific literature there are also fully formalized versions of DFDs. These, however, have not gained wide use in the industrial world.)

Note also that the model describes each element of the system without specifying whether it is a physical object (such as a book or a shelf) or a collection of information (such as the list of authors). Each set of information, in turn, is seen as an archive without stating whether it is realized by means of computer memories (files or databases) or more traditional methods (cards). Indeed, many aspects of information organization and management in a library can be described with sufficient precision without taking into account the physical means used to store the various types of information (in some cases, the physical action of taking books from the shelves could be automated by using mechanical arms capable of accessing precise locations on the shelves). This feature of the model helps its users to

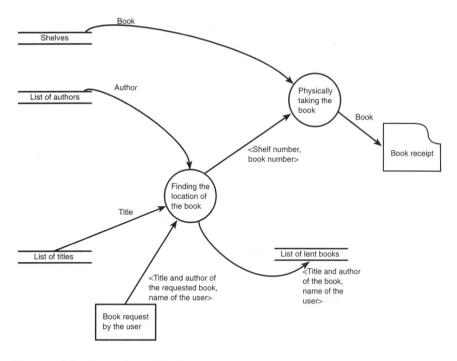

Figure 21.5   Explosion of the bubble Taking a book in the DFD of Figure 21.4.

concentrate, in the initial phases of application development, on the logical aspects of the problem without worrying about implementation aspects that are more subject to change.

Another important feature of DFDs is that they naturally support the construction of complex specifications by **successive refinements**, according to the requirements of **structured analysis**, a specification methodology widely used in the 1970s and 1980s. This methodology suggests writing a first draft of a specification document in rough outline, highlighting the main actions carried out by the system. The use of DFDs naturally combines the choice of actions with the bubbles that represent them. Subsequently, this draft is refined by going through various iterations, adding more and more detail. The most natural method of refining a DFD is the so-called **bubble explosion**; in other words, replacing one bubble with new portion of diagram containing more bubbles, flows and other elements: the result is a more precise description of the whole system.

For example, the diagram of Figure 21.4 could be refined by specifying in more detail the meaning of the function Taking a book, via the subdiagram shown in Figure 21.5. The new diagram explains that the action of Taking a book actually consists of two subactions: first the location of the book is searched; then the book is taken from the shelves.

Exercises

21.1   Find other requirements for an automated teller machine in addition to those already mentioned in Section 21.2.2.

21.2   Refine the `Search by subject` function by 'exploding' the corresponding bubble in a similar way as for the `Taking a book` function.

21.3   Enrich the diagrams of Figures 21.4 and 21.5 with new functions that are useful both to the user and to the administrator of the library. Refine some that you consider to be particularly important.

21.4   Represent the specification of the requirements of an automated teller machine outlined in Section 21.2.2 (and completed in Exercise 21.1) using DFDs. Critically discuss the correspondence between the original requirement formulation and the meaning of the diagrams produced. If any of the original requirements are not adequately formulated by the DFD explore how they could be expressed, possibly exploiting notations other than DFDs.

Design techniques

22

We saw, at the beginning of Part III, that the activity of constructing software cannot be reduced to the simple activity of programming. Programming in the strict sense, also called 'programming-in-the-small', must be supported by 'programming-in-the-large', whose aim is to construct complex software systems by putting together simpler modules. Some of these modules will be constructed specially for the application under development. Other, more general-purpose modules might already exist, archived in appropriate libraries.

In Chapter 20, we looked at the realization of software as the set of phases in its life cycle, from the definition or specification of the system up to its verification.

This chapter offers a panoramic view of software construction, with reference to programming-in-the-large, as programming-in-the-small has already been dealt with in Part I. Since we must limit ourselves to the essential aspects, attention is focused on the basic principle of **modularization**, that is, decomposition into simpler parts that cooperate and are integrated with one another. Modularization is an essential aspect of the construction of complex systems in general – not just software.

First, in Section 22.1, we give the main definitions and concepts of modular software system construction and we describe some general criteria for good modularization. We also give a few hints on the two main approaches to deriving the construction of a **modular architecture**, that is, designing the structure of a complex system as a collection of modules, namely **top-down** refinement and **bottom-up** aggregation of modules.

Subsequently, in Section 22.2, we face the problem of applying such general principles of good modularization to the practice of writing C programs. Unfortunately, C lacks good constructs for programming-in-the-large (such constructs are only available in a few modern programming languages). Therefore, we circumvent this problem by first introducing a formal, though ideal, description of modularization mechanisms, which is presented in a pseudocode style; then, we briefly show how these mechanisms can be at least 'approximated' in the context of the C programming language.

Whereas the first part of this chapter maintains the fairly descriptive and generic style of the whole of Part III, the second part goes back to the 'programming style' which was typical of Part I. The reason is that a general understanding of software engineering principles should be enough for the reader of this text who is not (yet) a professional software designer; writing programs in a modular way, however, is a fundamental skill even for nonsophisticated computer users.

22.1 Modularization: a basic tool for the design of complex systems

The most natural way to design systems of a certain complexity has always been to modularize them, that is, to decompose them into separate elements, called **modules**, each of which is considerably less complex than the whole system. In this way, the whole project is broken down into separate projects dealing with the individual elements and their coordination. The structure represented by the coordinated modules is often called the **system architecture**.

If necessary, the process of modularization can be iterated: if some modules are still too complex to be implemented as a single unit, they can be decomposed into further submodules and so on, until the complexity of each module is sufficiently limited for it to be implemented as a single task.

The principle of modularization is so general that it can be applied to any kind of design activity. Therefore, we need some more precise definitions before we can enjoy its benefits in practical work. It should be clear that the decomposition of a system into components does not in itself guarantee the success of the project: we have to apply some criteria to establish what a module must and must not contain, what has to be attributed to one module and what to another, and so on.

In this section we analyse some modular design criteria that are often useful in the construction of software, without claiming either generality or a particularly in-depth investigation. First, we introduce some terminology.

- A software system consists of a set of modules and of **relations** between the modules. Each module consists of an interface and a body.

- The **interface** of a module is the set of all and only those of its elements that must be made available to its users so that they can use it appropriately. Such elements are also called module's **exported resources**.

- The **body** of a module, also called the **implementation** of the module, is the set of mechanisms that realize the functionalities, that is, the tasks, that the module must guarantee to the rest of the system.

Various relations can be defined between the different modules. Among these, the following two are of particular importance.

- The **import/export** relation. We say that a module M imports a resource from a module M' if it uses it. A module M can import from another module M' only resources belonging to the M' interface. When we do not specify the entity(ies) imported by M from M', we simply say that M **uses** M' [1].

- The relation is_composed_of. We say that a module M is_composed_of a set of modules {M$_1$, M$_2$, ..., M$_k$} if that set realizes all the functionalities of M. Consequently, we also say that M$_1$, M$_2$, ..., M$_k$ are **components** of M.

It is often convenient to represent the modular architecture of a software system in graphical form. One such notation is illustrated with the help of Figure 22.1:

- A module is represented by a rectangular box.

- The import/export relation is represented by an arrow that goes from the exporting module to the importing one. The arrow is labelled with the name of the exported/imported resource. When there is no such label – that is, the exchanged resource(s) are not explicitly defined – the arrow denotes the generic use relation.

- The relation is_composed_of is represented by drawing the boxes M$_1$, M$_2$, ..., M$_k$ inside the box M, if M is_composed_of {M$_1$, M$_2$, ..., M$_k$}.

Figure 22.1 is a (partial) example of modular architecture. It consists of four high-level modules X, Y, W and Z. Here attention is focused on module X. X uses Z and is used by W and Y. In particular X's interface consists of elements A, B and C. A

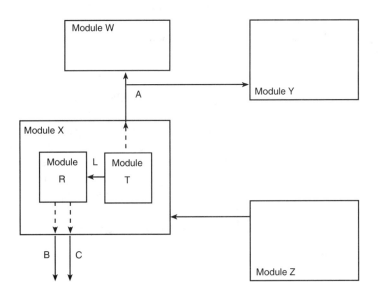

Figure 22.1 Example of (partial) modular architecture of a software system.

---

[1] In the specialized literature the use relation is sometimes used with a slightly different meaning than importing/exporting resources.

is exported to both W and Y (this fact is denoted by a fork in the arrow labelled A). X imports *some* resource from Z but the figure does not specify *which* resource(s). B and C, though belonging to X's interface, are not imported by any module in the figure.

Figure 22.1 also shows that X `is_composed_of` R and T. The interface of T includes the element L which is imported by R and the element A which is 're-exported' by X: the dashed continuation of arrow A inside X denotes that resource A exported by X actually comes from T. The same holds for B and C which are exported by R and re-exported by X.

The concept of a module has precise definitions in the context of particular languages (we will see an example in Section 22.2), but it can also be left to the intuition and experience of the designer who could adapt its definition to particular needs deriving from the project's characteristics. For instance, a module could be a whole program that interacts with other modules via the operating system, or a subroutine, or even a set of portions of code that does not correspond to any syntactically well-defined component, but that includes some well-defined logical relations that prompted the designer to put them together within a common frame.

Analogously, the elements of a module's interface can be quite disparate objects, such as variables, functions, data types, memory areas and so on. Consequently, a typical, but certainly not unique, way of one module using another is calling a function that is part of its interface.

Thus we have seen, in rough outline, *what* has to be specified in order to define a modular software system architecture. Let us now approach the problem of *how* to construct such an architecture, that is, how to divide a system up into modules, what to include in their interfaces, which relations to establish between them and so on.

22.1.1 Criteria of good modularization

There are various criteria for modularizing systems. Although, in the end, each choice in the design process must be determined by the specific characteristics of the application to be realized and by the intuition and experience of the designer, it may be worth while recalling the following recommendations extracted from the many recipes that different software methodologies have proposed in the past two decades.

Principle of information hiding

The interface of a module must be very carefully separated from its body. Very often, the interface contains too little or too much information, with respect to the use that will be made of the module.

For example, let us suppose that the service offered by a module is to sort tables of various elements. Its interface should include:

- the sorting procedure that must be called in order to obtain the desired service;

- the type of parameter that must be passed to the procedure (the type of the elements of the table, the format of the table itself, ...);
- limitations in the use of the procedure (for example, the procedure cannot handle tables of a cardinality greater than a certain number of elements);
- information on the performance of the procedure, if this can be significant in deciding whether or not to use the service offered by the module: for example, the procedure sorts a table of n elements in a time not greater than $k \cdot n \cdot \log (n)$.

On the other hand, information about the sorting algorithm used in the module must not be part of its interface. This kind of information is not relevant to the usage of the module.

In general, the less information given to the user of a module, the less constrained its implementer is and the greater the security achieved in its use. This is why this principle is called the 'principle of information hiding', meaning, obviously, irrelevant information. Of course, one must not forget to define all relevant information in the interface, so that the user of the module is not forced to analyse its implementation.

Principle of low coupling and high cohesion

In deciding into which modules to put certain elements (data, functions, types, according to the methods and programming languages used), one should always keep in mind that, in general, **intermodule relations** (that is, relations between different modules) are more critical than **intramodule relations** (that is, relations between elements of the same module). An error in the interface of one module involves the designer of the module plus the designers of all the modules that use it, whereas an error in the body of the module concerns only the person responsible for its design, although the other designers might signal the existence of the error when it causes their own modules to malfunction.

Consequently, it is good practice to group together into the same module those variables, functions and other programming elements that are often used together, thus giving to each module a **high internal cohesion**, while elements that rarely interact can be put into the interfaces of different modules, thus organizing modules so that they exhibit a **low coupling**. For example, it would not be very advisable to put a table of elements into one module and the procedure to insert new elements into it into a different module.

Principle of design-for-change

The problem of software evolution, in other words, its modification because of changes in its requirements and/or environment, is assuming an ever greater importance in determining the overall cost of software products. Intuition and experience confirm that it is much more difficult and expensive to modify software designed solely on the basis of the initial specifications, than software designed from the beginning with possible future changes in mind.

Obviously, it is well-nigh impossible to construct a software product that will adapt well to all possible changes that might occur in the future. However, it is useful to make a preliminary analysis of the most likely future changes and to 'encapsulate' the elements subject to such changes into appropriate 'frames', so that it will be possible to modify the contents of a frame without altering its context.

A very simple and efficient example of design-for-change has already been given in the context of programming-in-the-small: the use of constants. The declaration of a constant `TaxRate`, for example, constitutes the frame in which its value can be changed when changes in fiscal regulations occur.

More generally, in the context of programming-in-the-large, a typical example of foreseeable change is the hardware used for the execution of certain software. It is useful, for example, to construct a module `PeripheralDriver` that offers users the standard mechanisms for using a peripheral and includes everything that is likely to change if and when the peripheral is changed (for example, when a disk is replaced by a bigger and faster one).

22.1.2 Top-down and bottom-up design

We have seen how design involves transforming a system into a modular structure. We have also seen some useful criteria for deciding the contents and the interfaces of the various modules that make up the system. Now, there remains the problem of how to construct a software architecture made up of modules.

Design is a creative process and building a modular architecture of a system is somewhat like building the skeleton of the whole project. Certainly, there may be many ways to decompose a system into several, well-integrated modules. Thus, giving precise modularization rules such as 'module size should not exceed 30 lines of code', 'a module should not be composed of more than four smaller modules' is quite difficult and may be even counter-productive.

In this section, however, we briefly analyse the two fundamental techniques to which we can refer in order to manage the difficult process of designing a system. As always, the reader should be aware that, in practice, many other techniques can be applied, by integrating the fundamental ones or by enriching them with the intuition and personal experience of the designer.

The design techniques presented here refer to the relation `is_composed_of`: this relation reflects the fundamental concept of the realization of a system, or a part of it, as a collection of other subparts.

Top-down design

Designing a system top-down means decomposing it into various modules, each one with a precise task (and, therefore, interface). This decomposition can be iterated until modules are obtained that are sufficiently small to consider their realization as a programming-in-the-small task.

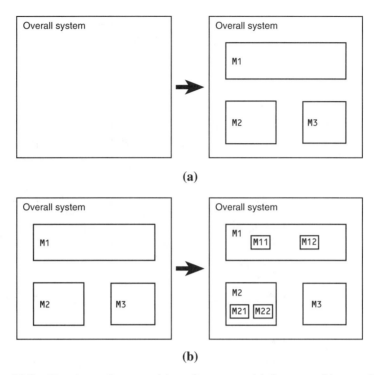

Figure 22.2 Top-down decomposition of a system: (a) first step, (b) second step.

Adopting the graphical notation introduced in Figure 22.1, a typical process of top-down decomposition of a system into modules is exemplified in Figure 22.2.

Obviously, this process, which highlights only the relation `is_composed_of`, must be completed by defining the interfaces of the various modules and the `use` relations between them.

Bottom-up design

In a symmetrical way to top-down design, designing a system bottom-up means aggregating already constructed modules in order to obtain a more complex and functionally richer one. In this case also, the process can be iterated as often as you like. Figure 22.3 exemplifies the process of bottom-up construction of a system.

Not surprisingly, the advantages and disadvantages of the two approaches are symmetrical. In particular, the top-down approach, widely used in the 1970s and early 1980s, favours the construction of systems whose components are well coordinated, but it sometimes tends to duplicate effort (for example, groups charged with the realization of different modules could independently produce submodules very similar to each other).

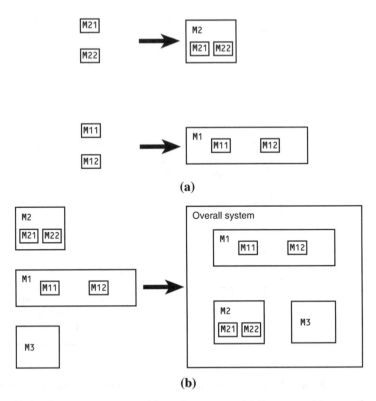

Figure 22.3   Bottom-up composition of a system: (a) first step, (b) second step.

On the other hand, the bottom-up approach favours the reuse of software already available and the construction of general-purpose software, but it might force designers to use components that are not perfectly adapted to the application that is being realized. The fact that software reusability and generality are qualities that are becoming ever more important is one of the main reasons for the growing preference for bottom-up techniques. In particular, one of the most promising techniques, the so-called **object-oriented design**, is typically bottom-up. Chapter 25 gives a detailed introduction to object-oriented programming.

22.2 Building modular programs

Let us now go a little further into the mechanisms of defining and implementing modules. As we anticipated, such mechanisms cannot be explained precisely without referring to a particular language. C, however, is rather limited from this point of view; thus, we will use an incremental approach based on pseudocoding as we did in Chapter 3 to derive nontrivial programs: first, we will build a modular structure by using mechanisms that do not belong to C but which help define precisely all relevant elements of the structure, such as separation between interface and body, import/export of items between modules and so on[2]. As we did in Chapter 3, pseudocode elements are enclosed with square brackets.

Later we will give hints on how to obtain at least part of the benefits of modular design using C (Section 22.2.3). We will also go back to this issue in Chapter 25 when we deal with object-oriented design – which can be seen as a further improvement of modular design – and we will make use of C++ as a supporting language.

We will illustrate the proposed techniques through a few basic examples which will be worked out in the different languages (pseudocode, C and, later, C++). This should help the reader in understanding the impact of the programming language on modular design.

First, a program consists of a group of modules: a **master** module (also called the **program module**, or **main module**) and some other modules, called **slave modules**. The master module uses other modules, which themselves can use still others. Figure 22.4 shows a modular architecture of a program where the arrows indicate the use relation.

As we saw, a module can export services or resources to several other modules, not just to the master module: for example, input/output operations may be necessary within different modules. Import/export can also occur between modules at different levels (in Figure 22.4, M4 serves M2, M3 and the program module). For reasons that we do not intend to go into, *'circularities' in the* use *relation are forbidden*. For example, M4 could not import services from M2.

Each module must neatly separate its two parts:

- the **interface**, also called the **definition part of the module**; and
- the **body**, also called the **implementation part of the module**.

22.2.1 Module interface

A module interface consists of the following items:

- The module identifier. To emphasize its meaning, we preface it with the 'pseudo-keyword' **module interface**.
- The **import** clause, which lists all entities imported from other modules and their source modules; for instance, with reference to Figure 22.4, the master module could contain the clauses:

```
import   A, B, ...          from M1;
import   X, Y ...           from M2;
import   Alpha, Beta, ...   from M3;
import   Zed, W,...         from M4;
```

where **import** and **from** are pseudo-keywords and A, B, X, ... are the various elements of the interfaces of M1, M2, ... that are used by the program module.

---

[2] The proposed mechanisms are inspired by several modern languages such as Ada and Modula-2 which pay much attention to the modularization issue.

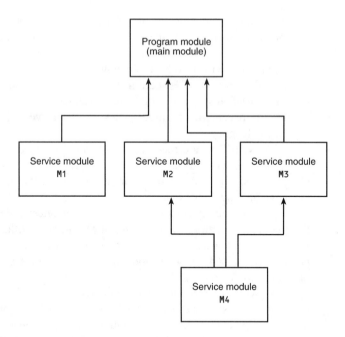

Figure 22.4   Modular structure of a program.

● The **export** clause, which lists all entities that are exported from the module. These are declared similarly to declarations in C programs: they are declarations of types, constants, variables and function prototypes.

Indeed, a module can export types, constants, variables and functions: this means that if a definition part of a module MD declares a type T and another module M1 imports T from MD, then M1 can declare variables of type T as if T had been declared in M1 itself.

In the overall structure of a program the master module plays a special role: in fact it is the only one that imports items from other modules but does not export any.

It should also be noted that comments play quite an important role in the definition of module interfaces. The comment associated with a function prototype, for example, must indicate, as precisely as possible, the effect of the function. The presence of comments safeguards the principle that the interface of a module must contain all and only the information that is needed for its correct use by other modules.

A similar principle should be applied to types: in an interface, the declaration of a type may not necessarily define the structure of the type itself. A type defined in such a way is called **opaque** and its structure is hidden. To emphasize this property in the declaration of an opaque type we use the pseudo-keyword **hidden** in place of the type structure definition, as follows:

```
typedef [hidden] Type1;
```

The aim of opaque types is to hide from the user of the entities exported from a module the details of how the objects of such types are constructed. This pays homage to the principle of information hiding and makes them fully abstract. The following example illustrates its usefulness.

EXAMPLE 22.1 (first part)

The following definition module defines the interface that is needed to handle complex numbers. It can be seen as the definition of an abstract type `ComplexNumbers`, where the attribute 'abstract' is particularly appropriate since it indicates a data type consisting of a set of values and corresponding operations defined on it, whose implementation is completely hidden from the user. The importance of this characteristic will be appreciated when, in the next section, we approach the problem of implementing the following module interface.

```
[module interface] ComplexNumbers
[import scanf, printf from stdio[3]]
                                    /*next, exported items are listed*/
{
   typedef [hidden] Complex;
                         /*this is the set of complex numbers, well
                         known in mathematics. Note the fact that
                         this type is opaque: you will shortly see
                         the importance of this.*/

   typedef enum {RPIP, MODARG} Representation;
                         /*indicates how to represent a complex
                         number externally: RPIP stands for
                         representation by means of the components
                         "real part, imaginary part"; MODARG stands
                         for representation by means of the
                         components "modulus, argument". This allows
                         the user to choose a preferred form for
                         writing a datum of complex type, without
                         influencing the internal representation of
                         the data, as will become clear in the next
                         section.*/

   Complex  SumCompl(Complex  Add1, Complex  Add2);
                         /*returns the sum of two complex parameters
                         Add1 and Add2. It has no side-effects.*/

   Complex  MultCompl(Complex  Mult1, Complex  Mult2);
                         /*returns the product between two complex
                         parameters Mult1 and Mult2. It has no side-
                         effects.*/
```

---

[3] The input/output operations are defined in the interface of a special library module (`stdio`) from which they have to be explicitly imported.

```
...                              /*other arithmetic operations on complex
                                 numbers are not explicitly listed for the
                                 sake of brevity.*/

void  WriteCompl(Complex  Par1, Representation  Rep);
                                 /*prints on the file stdout the complex
                                 value passed as the first parameter. The
                                 printing format varies according to the
                                 second parameter.*/

void  ReadCompl(Complex  *Par, Representation  Rep);
                                 /*reads from the file stdin a complex value,
                                 storing it in the variable indicated as the
                                 first parameter – necessarily passed by
                                 address. The procedure interacts with the
                                 user, asking the user to input data in the
                                 form required by the second parameter.*/
}
```

Observe that this module interface provides all the information required to construct algorithms dealing with data of `ComplexNumbers` type without in any way dictating how the operations described by it are realized in practice.

Also note that this module exports only a type and the operations that can be executed on this type; there are no variables, either of the exported type or of other types. For this reason we say that it is a *module without memory* or that it is a *'pure' abstract type*. We will see in Example 22.2 that modules that have different characteristics can also be constructed.

There must be *at least one* implementation module for each definition module, constructed according to the rules illustrated in the next section. The fact that there may be more than one implementation module further underlines the principle that *externally* it is only the definition module that counts and that, as long as this does not alter its behaviour from the point of view of the modules that use it, it does not matter how it is realized: different implementations can be chosen on the basis of various criteria. In some languages (such as Modula-2) it is the user who has to specify each time which implementation of a module to choose; the choice is necessarily static and has therefore to be made before the execution of the complete program. Other languages (such as C++) support dynamic implementation choices that occur during execution of the program itself (see Example 25.4).

22.2.2 Module bodies

The implementation part of a module must contain all the details that are necessary to realize the resources exported by the module. We mark its identifier – obviously the same as the corresponding definition part – by the pseudo-keyword **module implementation**.

All the elements declared in the export clause of the definition part must be redeclared completely and consistently in the corresponding implementation part. Thus, each function must have the same header as the prototype present in the definition module, but it must contain the appropriate executable part. Obviously, in a module implementation, other elements (variables, types and so on) may be declared that have not been previously declared in the corresponding definition part: in this case, they are part of the module, but not part of its interface. They may also vary in different implementations of the same module.

An import clause exists in the implementation part of a module as well as in the definition part. They do not necessarily coincide, however. In general, we suggest that every imported item that is necessary to guarantee the correct use of the module for any chosen implementation is explicitly listed in the definition part. Elements that are used by the implementation but do not contribute to the logical behaviour of the module could be hidden in the implementation: typically, different implementation parts of the same module could import different items according to specific needs. For instance, in the case of ComplexNumbers, it seems reasonable that I/O operations will be used and will always be imported from the standard I/O: thus, their import should be made known outside the module. However, in *some* implementations we could decide to exploit mathematical libraries, but in others we could decide to implement our own mathematical functions independently, for example to achieve a better degree of precision.

The master module is treated differently: since it only uses other modules but is not itself used (does not export any resource), we do not separate its interface from its body. We attach the import clause to its body and these two items together constitute the whole module.

Example 22.1 (cont.) provides two alternative implementations for the definition module ComplexNumbers: they correspond to two traditional ways of representing complex numbers in mathematics:

- the first implementation represents complex numbers by means of real and imaginary parts;
- the second implementation represents complex numbers by means of modulus and argument.

For the sake of brevity, some parts of the implementations are omitted: their completion is left as an exercise for the reader. We fully describe, however, the implementation of sum and multiplication: note that sum is easier with the first implementation whereas multiplication is easier with the second implementation.

EXAMPLE 22.1 (continued)

First implementation (real and imaginary parts)

```
[module implementation] ComplexNumbers

[import  scanf, printf                       from  stdio
import   sin, cos, asin, acos, pow, sqrt     from  math]
{
   typedef  struct  {  float  RealPart;
                       float  ImaginaryPart;
                    }  Complex;

   Complex  SumCompl(Complex  Add1, Complex  Add2)
   {
      Complex  Result;
      Result.RealPart = Add1.RealPart + Add2.RealPart;
      Result.ImaginaryPart = Add1.ImaginaryPart + Add2.ImaginaryPart;
      return  Result;
   }

   Complex  MultCompl(Complex  Mult1, Complex  Mult2)
   {
      Complex  Result;
      Result.RealPart =
         Mult1.RealPart * Mult2.RealPart -
            Mult1.ImaginaryPart * Mult2.ImaginaryPart;
      Result.ImaginaryPart =
         Mult1.ImaginaryPart * Mult2.RealPart +
            Mult2.ImaginaryPart * Mult1.RealPart;
      return  Result;
   }
   ...                                /*implementation of other arithmetic
                                      operations on complex numbers*/

   void  WriteCompl(Complex  Par, Representation  Rep)
   {
      float  Mod, Arg;
      if (Rep == RPIP)
         printf("Real part: %f, Imaginary part: %f\n",
            Par.RealPart, Par.ImaginaryPart);
      else
      {
         Mod = sqrt(pow(Par.RealPart, 2) + pow(Par.ImaginaryPart, 2));
         Arg = acos(Par.ImaginaryPart/Mod);
         printf("Modulus: %f, Argument: %f\n", Mod, Arg);
      }
   }

   void  ReadCompl(Complex  *Par, Representation  Rep)
                                                         /*Exercise*/
}
```

Second implementation (modulus and argument)

```
[module implementation]  ComplexNumbers

[import  scanf, printf              from  stdio
import   sin, cos, asin, acos, sqrt  from  math]
```

```
{
   typedef struct { float Modulus;
                    float Argument;
                  } Complex;
   Complex SumCompl(Complex Add1, Complex Add2)
   {
      Complex Result;
      float RealPar1, RealPar2, ImPar1, ImPar2, RealParRes, ImParRes;

      RealPar1 = Add1.Modulus * cos(Add1.Argument);
      RealPar2 = Add2.Modulus * cos(Add2.Argument);
      ImPar1 = Add1.Modulus * sin(Add1.Argument);
      ImPar2 = Add2.Modulus * sin(Add2.Argument);
      RealParRes = RealPar1 + RealPar2;
      ImParRes = ImPar1 + ImPar2;
      Result.Modulus = sqrt(RealParRes * RealParRes + ImParRes * ImParRes);
      Result.Argument = acos(RealParRes/Result.Modulus);
      return Result;
   }

   Complex MultCompl(Complex Mult1, Complex Mult2)
   {
      Complex Result;
      Result.Modulus = Mult1.Modulus * Mult2.Modulus;
      Result.Argument = Mult1.Argument + Mult2.Argument;
      return Result;
   }

   ...                                 /*implementation of other arithmetic
                                         operations on complex numbers*/

   void WriteCompl(Complex Par, Representation Rep)
                                                      /*Exercise*/

   void ReadCompl(Complex *Par, Representation Rep)
                                                      /*Exercise*/
}
```

It is now possible to appreciate fully the importance of the protection obtained by hiding the information about how a complex number is represented internally through the use of opaque types. Owing to the fact that Complex is an opaque type, none of the modules that import elements of the module ComplexNumbers could run the risk of using a variable of Complex type in a way that would be incorrect with either implementation. For example, let us assume that the variable x has been declared of Complex type. The instruction:

```
if (x.RealPart > 0) ...
```

is incorrect for both implementations of the module ComplexNumbers, because the fact that x is a structure with a component RealPart (true in one of the implementation modules) is not known to the interface of the module. Consequently, the two implementation modules can be interchanged (for example, to take into account the different efficiency of the sum and multiplication operations) without affecting any module that uses them.

On the other hand, during input and output, it is possible to choose one of the two typical representations of complex numbers without influencing the internal representation in any way. Notice the similarity to the case of real numbers where the user can choose whether to input data in fixed point or in floating point format, independently of how these are represented internally in the computer memory.

EXAMPLE 22.2 (first part)

The following module is a table manager. Unlike the previous example (which exported a type together with its operations), it 'owns' a table and allows other modules to use it by exporting all operations that are necessary to manage it (inserting and deleting elements, printing its contents, ...).

```
[module interface]  NameTableManagement
[import  printf    from  stdio
import   strcmp    from  string]

{
    #define  MaxLen    20
    #define  MaxElem  1000

    typedef  char  Name[MaxLen];

    void  Insert(Name  NewElem);
                        /*inserts the parameter into the first free
                        position of NameTable, which is a global
                        variable on which the various operations are
                        executed and which is exported. The elements
                        to be inserted are passed to the function by
                        other modules from which it is called. If
                        the table is full or the element to be
                        inserted is already present in the table, an
                        appropriate message is printed on the file
                        stdout.*/

    boolean  Exist(Nam  Elem);
                        /*the function accesses the global variable
                        NameTable and returns true if the parameter
                        passed exists in the table, false
                        otherwise.*/

    Name  DeleteReturnLast(void);
                        /*deletes the last value from the table and
                        returns it as the result.*/

    void  Print(void);
                        /*prints the contents of the table, one name
                        per line.*/
```

```
    ...                         /*other functions may be added by the reader
                                as an exercise*/
}

[module implementation]  NameTableManagement

[import  printf    from  stdio
import   strcmp    from  string]
{
   #define  MaxLen    20
   #define  MaxElem  1000

   typedef  char     Name[MaxLen];
   typedef  Name      ContentType[MaxElem];
   typedef  struct  {  int        NumElem = 0⁴;
                       ContentType  Contents;
                    } TableType;

   TableType  NameTable;

   void  Insert(Name  NewElem)
   {
      int      Count;
      boolean  Found;
      if (NameTable.NumElem == MaxElem)
        printf("The table is already full");
      else                      /*check whether the element to be inserted
                                exists already*/
      {
         Found = false;
         for (Count = 0; Count < NumElem; Count++)
           if (strcmp(NameTable.Contents[Count], NewElem) == 0)
              Found = true;
         if (Found == true)
           printf("The element to be inserted is already in the table");
         else
         {
            strcpy(NameTable.Contents[NameTable.NumElem], NewElem);
            NameTable.NumElem = NameTable.NumElem + 1;
         }
      }
   }

   boolean  Exist(Name  Elem)
                                                    /*Exercise*/

   Name  DeleteReturnLast (void)
                                                    /*Exercise*/

   void  Print (void)
                                                    /*Exercise*/
}
```

---

⁴ At the declaration of the field NumElem of the structure it is given the initialization value 0.

Note that, unlike the previous example, the module possesses a *state*, constituted by the variable `NameTable`. This receives a value at the beginning of the execution of the complete program (it is initialized to the empty value), in order to be subsequently handled exclusively via operations requested by other modules. Once we have the module `NameTableManagement` and the corresponding implementation available, it is possible to handle the table within each module that imports it from `NameTableManagement` together with the necessary operations, by means of instructions such as the following:

```
for (i = 0; i < MaxElem; i++)
{
    ReadName(NewName);
    Insert(NewName);
}


if (!EmptyTable && !FullTable)
    printf("The table is in a normal condition");
```

22.2.3 Modularization and information hiding in C

The C language does not provide explicit constructs for building module interfaces and bodies clearly and separately. However, it is possible to adopt a programming style that allows us to write modular programs and to use a form of information hiding, following the criteria analysed in the previous sections.

As a basic guideline we suggest associating the concept of the module with that of the file. This offers more possibilities for module independence and information hiding than associating a module with a subprogram. Thus, *a C program can be distributed over several files*. We therefore advise creating C programs composed of a master module, contained in a file having the name of the program and extension `.c`, and several slave modules, each contained in one or more separate files. The slave modules can be further subdivided into a definition part and an implementation part. The definition part should be contained in a file that has the same name as the module and the extension `.h`, whereas the implementation part should be contained in a file with the same name as the module and the extension `.c`.

Definition parts normally contain declarations of constants, types and prototypes of functions visible to, and usable by, other modules. Less often they contain declarations of variables. In addition, each module declares which other definition modules it uses, using the `#include` directive. The `#include` directive is proposed as a *surrogate for the import clause* although it does not have exactly the same effect: it does not allow the programmer to specify which elements of the interface of another module are used; it simply states which definition modules are used, indicating which .h files have to be included. Usually the (implementation) `.c` part of a module also includes the (definition) .h part of the same module. Redundant #include directives should be excluded: thus, if a module is already included in a .h extension it must not be included again in the .c extension.

Typical examples of slave modules that can be used by a program module or by other slave modules are the following:

- The stdio module realizes the functions of input/output. The file stdio.h contains the prototypes of the functions. The implementations of the functions are contained in other files with extension .c. A master module or another slave module that needs to call input/output functions must include (import) the contents of the file stdio.h.

- The stack module (see Section 11.2) contains the declaration of the stack type and the operations defined on it. The file stack.h contains the declaration of the stack type and the prototypes of the functions. The implementations of the functions are contained in other files with extension .c. A program module or another slave module that needs to operate on variables of stack type must include (import) the contents of the file stack.h.

To support information hiding, in C it is possible to restrict the visibility of a global element (a variable or a function) to the file in which it is declared, by declaring it as **static**. If a global variable is visible only within the file in which it is declared, only the functions declared in that file can see and manipulate it. This possibility allows us to *realize a form of information hiding*. If a module is contained in one file and if this module contains global variables declared as **static**, then these variables are protected from direct manipulation by functions contained in other files (including the file that contains the program module). If others want to manipulate these variables, they must use the functions made available by the interface of the module responsible for manipulating the protected variables.

It is difficult to realize opaque types in C, but C++, as we will see in Chapter 25, offers a wide range of possibilities in this respect.

Let us now exemplify the above suggestions on the use of C to build modular programs by presenting a C version of the first part of Example 22.2.

EXAMPLE 22.2 *(continued)*

A C program that implements and uses the name table defined in the first part of this example could be composed of four modules: the master module (gtmain), an input/output module (stdio), a character string handling module (string) and a module for managing the table of names (gtab). Figure 22.5 displays the structure of these modules through the use relation. Each slave module is composed of a definition part contained in a file with the same name as the module and the extension .h, and an implementation module contained in a file with the same name as the module and the extension .c. The master module consists only of the .c extension.

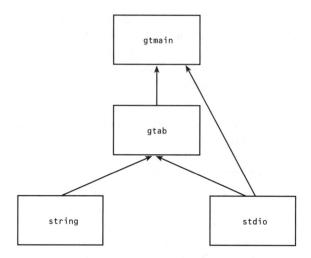

Figure 22.5 The modular architecture of a program that manages a table. Arrows denote the use relation.

The following C program declares the variable NameTable internally in the implementation module of gtab and associates the keyword **static** with the declaration. This solution provides maximum protection for the variable NameTable. main manipulates this variable by always calling the functions declared in the definition module gtab.h. It is important to note that main in this case does not declare variables of type table and does not pass these variables as parameters to the functions responsible for treating tables of names. The functions are called and act on the variable declared and equipped with a state in the implementation of the gtab module.

```
**************************************************************************
                Relevant parts of file gtab.h
**************************************************************************

#include <stdio.h>
#include <string.h>
#define  MaxLen    20
#define  MaxElem  1000

typedef  char  Name[MaxLen];

void     Insert(Name  NewElem);

boolean  Exist(Name  Elem);

void     Print(void);
...
```

```
**********************************************************************
                 Relevant parts of file gtab.c
**********************************************************************


#include <gtab.h>

typedef  Name       ContentType[MaxElem];
typedef  struct  {  int          NumElem;
                    ContentType  Contents;
                 } TableType;
static  TableType  NameTable;

void  Insert(Name  NewElem)
{
   int      Count;
   boolean  Found;
   if (NameTable.NumElem == MaxElem)
      printf("The table is already full");
   else                    /*check whether the element to be inserted
                             already exists*/
   {
      Found = false;
      for (Count = 0; Count < NameTable.NumElem; Count++)
         if (strcmp(NameTable.Contents[Count], NewElem) == 0)
            Found = true;
      if (Found == true)
         printf("The element to be inserted is already in the table")
      else
      {
         strcpy(NameTable.Contents[NameTable.NumElem], NewElem);
         NameTable.NumElem = NameTable.NumElem + 1;
      }
   }
}
...              /*for brevity, we omit the code of the other functions*/

**********************************************************************
                 Relevant parts of file gtmain.c
**********************************************************************


#include <gtab.h>

Name  NewName;

main()
{
   ...
   Insert(NewName);
   ...
   printf("The contents of the table are the following:");
   Print();
}
```

Exercises

22.1 Provide definition modules and one or more corresponding implementation modules to define and realize the following 'abstract data types'.

(a) Sets of words, each word being a string of characters.

(b) Geometrical figures. Define some typical geometrical figures (circles, rectangles, squares) as data types and associate appropriate operations with them, such as calculating their surface, perimeter and so on.

22.2 Realize the abstract type `Stack`, defined in Section 11.2, associating two implementation modules with one definition module. The two implementation modules must realize, respectively, the two implementation techniques suggested in Section 11.2.1 and Exercise 11.12. The definition module must be such that it can be used with both implementations.

22.3 Define a definition module `PackOfCards` and the corresponding implementation module. `PackOfCards` must simulate a real pack of cards in every respect. It must therefore provide operations such as `Shuffle`, `PutInOrder`, `DrawACard` and so on. Then construct various program modules that use `PackOfCards` to simulate different card games from the point of view of different players. For example, a `Bridge` program must first deal the pack of cards to four players (in order to avoid an incorrect flow of information, suppose that each player plays on a different terminal and that the program can redirect information by specifying to and from which terminal the information is sent). Subsequently, the program must use interactive functions to ask the various players, in the right order, how they intend to play, up to the end of the game, and eventually calculate the final score for each player and determine the winner.

22.4 Consider variable `NameTable` in the C version of Example 22.2. If it were declared within the definition module (in the file `gtab.h`), how would the contents of the three files have to be modified? What would change with respect to the protection of the variable `NameTable`?

22.5 Build a C version of the pure abstract data type `ComplexNumbers` defined in Example 22.1.

Verification techniques

23

Like any other production process, software production, too, must aim at quality. Some of the main qualities of software were discussed in Section 20.1. As in any other production process, one can hardly expect that some particular method or technique guarantees a priori the achievement of the predetermined quality objectives. It is therefore necessary to tackle the problem of verifying the product with respect to the pre-established requirements; such verification is often called **quality control**. This chapter deals with this subject and is organized as follows.

First (Section 23.1), we focus on the objectives and requirements of software verification processes. Then (Section 23.2), we provide a classification of the main software verification techniques, by taking into account the types of errors that they can identify. A few particular verification techniques are presented in Section 23.3. Finally (Section 23.4), we briefly outline error correction, which is naturally connected to verification.

23.1 Objectives and requirements of software verification

Software verification is often carried out in a fairly unsystematic way. Indeed, it is often left entirely to the intuition and goodwill of the designers and carried out with no documentation. This causes loss of reliability and efficiency in the subsequent activities of error correction and program polishing. Instead, this activity should be carried out by following rigorous principles and precise techniques, as usually occurs in more 'mature' engineering fields.

In general, the following principles should be kept in mind as a guide to software verification.

(1) *Every feature that could be relevant to the success of the project must be verified.*

Very often, verification simply consists in checking that the system executes the tasks assigned to it (functional verification). In fact, every quality, of both the product and the process, should be adequately controlled, and the effort invested in this activity should be proportional to the importance of the quality itself. It will therefore be useful to verify the *performance* of the product (verification of efficiency), the quality of the *production process* (the production of specifications and design documentation, the ability to meet deadlines), the *reusability* of both the process and the product (if it is envisaged that components of the system and the design techniques will be used in different contexts) and so on.

(2) *Verification can be both subjective and objective.*

Estimating a quality cannot always be carried out in a purely objective way (for example, the comprehensibility of documentation is by definition judged by humans, who may come to radically different conclusions depending on their personal experience and intuition). The subjectivity of the result does not make this type of verification less relevant, but careful attention must be paid to avoid drawing erroneous conclusions based on subjective judgement. Much research activity is devoted to finding mechanisms that will assist subjective judgement.

(3) *Quality parameters are either binary or scaled.*

Some requirements are either met in full or not at all. In other cases, how far an objective has been met can be measured, for example, in percentage terms. Typically, we can say that 'a system is correct or incorrect with respect to the pre-established requirements', whereas 'the new version improves performance by 20% over the previous one'. Sometimes, however, correctness can be measured across a spectrum, for example by measuring the number of errors in relation to their criticality (we have seen that in many cases absolute correctness is practically unachievable and perhaps even useless).

(4) *Errors are more or less critical.*

Verification must aim at the identification and removal of errors. These, however, can be of various types and more or less critical, thus needing different treatment.

For example, an error might be a spelling mistake in a variable identifier; another might be caused by poor understanding of the problem to be solved (the user wanted a banking system capable of performing operations on all the bank's branches, and the system that has been constructed can only serve the customers of a single branch). It is clear that the latter type of error is much more serious than the former, which can be easily identified by the compiler, or even by the editor, and as easily corrected. The second error could, in extreme cases, be signalled only after the delivery of the product.

(5)   *Errors occur at different times.*

It is often useful to classify the various types of error according to when they occur[1]. There is often a correlation between the time an error occurs and its criticality: the earlier it is identified, the less critical its effect. From this point of view, there is an important distinction between compile-time errors and run-time errors. In general, compile-time errors are signalled by the compiler; therefore, once compilation has been successfully achieved, one can be sure of their absence. Run-time errors are harder to identify, because the execution of a program without the occurrence of errors is no guarantee of their absence. Furthermore, building in run-time checks, where this is possible, often penalizes efficiency, and is often omitted for this reason.

For example, a typical run-time error is caused by the index of an array exceeding its limits. In order to verify this, it is necessary to test the value of the index during execution. This test consumes time; furthermore, having executed the program once and found that the index of the array has a correct value does not guarantee that it will not assume a value outside the limits in a subsequent execution. If this occurs without being signalled, the effect of the error may be very serious, because execution will continue and produce completely unforeseeable and unreliable results: if the index i has to be such that $0 \leq i \leq 10$ and the operation x = a[i] (where x is an integer) is carried out with i == 20, the value assigned to x is the value obtained by interpreting as an integer the sequence of bits contained in the 21st cell, starting from the first cell of the array a. In some cases, this cell might not even belong to any of the program's variables, but to another program altogether: in such cases, if the operating system does not stop execution, the result is absolutely unpredictable.

The critical impact of run-time errors explains why many programming languages try to provide programming rules (for example, rules about data types) to ensure that the maximum number of errors are detected at compile time.

23.2 A classification of software verification techniques

In any engineering activity two main approaches are pursued to verify the quality of the artefact produced: experimental verification and design analysis. These approaches are also useful in software design. Their essential features are examined in this section.

---

[1] It would be more precise to talk about the time an error *appears* than the time an error *occurs*. The distinction between the two terms will be clarified in Section 23.4.

23.2.1 Software testing

The most natural way to check any product is to test its behaviour in certain cases, and then try to deduce its general behaviour. For example, bridges, dams, houses, cars and power plants are tested in different conditions and, if the test has a positive outcome, they are authorized for normal use. In principle, the same applies to software; shortly hereafter, however, we will show that the peculiarities of software make its testing more critical.

In any experimental activity, a fundamental requirement is **experiment repeatability**: in order to gain confidence in the results of any experiment, repeating it under the same circumstances should always produce the same results. For instance, we are all confident that, if we heat a pot of pure water up to 100 °C (212 °F) at atmospheric pressure, the water will boil. In the case of software, or, in general, of any computer application, the situation is seemingly identical but it is somewhat complicated by the fact that we can rarely 'freeze' the context of our experiments.

Typically, if we are testing a piece of software, we normally run it under some operating system which manages several concurrent processes including the program under test. As a consequence, it might happen that in running the same program twice with the same input data we get different results, due to different interactions with concurrent programs. It is unfortunately a fairly common experience that, while using, say, a word processor on our personal computer, something suddenly goes wrong even though we are performing an operation that worked properly on previous occasions; this could be due to the fact that while the operation was being executed by the word processor another application was launched by the operating system (for example, checking electronic mail) and a conflict arose in accessing some memory cell. Repeating the same circumstances could be quite difficult and consequently even understanding where the error is located (In the word processor? In the mail program? In the operating system?) could be very hard.

Testing techniques can be divided into two main categories: white-box or structural testing, and black-box or functional testing.

(1) In **white-box** testing, **test cases**, that is, selected input data supplied to the product for verification, are selected on the basis of program structure. For this reason this category is called **structural** or white-box: the choice of test case depends on the implementation contained in the ideal 'box' representing the program to be verified (more rigorously we should talk of 'glass-box' rather than 'white-box').

(2) In **black-box** testing, test cases are selected on the basis of the definition (**functional specification**) of what the program is intended to do rather than on how it is implemented to achieve such a goal. This explains the terms used for its definition.

In the next section we will see examples of both categories.

23.2.2 Analysis techniques

During the design and implementation of a system, all project activities are analysed to detect and remove errors as soon as possible. In the case of software, this analysis has different forms and objectives, according to when it is carried out and the attitude of the person who does it.

For example, some analysis techniques take the form of meetings between designers and colleagues who discuss the project. Experience has shown that explaining their ideas to others forces designers to carry out a more in-depth analysis; designers discover major errors while they are describing the project to colleagues.

Other techniques are more formalized, going so far as attempting **mathematical proofs of correctness**.

Much has been said and is still being said about the strengths and weaknesses of the various verification techniques.

For example, the supporters of formal methods maintain that *testing can only show the presence, not the absence, of errors* in the software. To support this thesis (irrefutable from a theoretical point of view), it is observed that, whereas in traditional engineering products it is relatively easy to extrapolate the behaviour of a system on the basis of a certain number of experiments, owing to the systems' fundamental characteristic of continuity (if I can load a bridge with 1000 tons, there are no doubts about its capability to support a weight of 999 tons), in the case of software, typically a noncontinuous product, it may well be that a program that produces a correct result for the input value 1000, produces erroneous results when the input is 999.

On the other hand, others observe that formal methods are too conditioned by mathematical knowledge to be usable in practice and observe that so far they have nearly always been theoretical exercises and that their application has not eliminated the risk of errors.

Instead of entering into a dispute often influenced by prejudice, we prefer to emphasize that nearly every verification technique can produce considerable benefits if it is well known and well applied. First, therefore, one must develop a thorough knowledge of the various techniques to be able to choose the ones that are most appropriate in the given circumstances. In general, it seems best to exploit the natural complementarities between the various techniques instead of getting involved in boring and often sterile confrontations between them.

A very good corollary to the conscious and rigorous use of any technique is the availability of automatic tools that make applying it easier and more efficient. For example, testing carried out haphazardly (this term is not synonymous with *random testing* which, on the contrary, may be very rigorous and efficient) is of next to no use whatsoever, whereas the determination of a significant number of test cases on the basis of rigorous criteria (as we will see in the next section) can lead to an acceptable certification of software. The effective construction of such test cases can be facilitated by the availability of a tool that produces them automatically, for example on the basis of the code to be verified.

23.3 Analysis of a few verification techniques

In this section we briefly examine a few well-known and widely applied verification techniques. There are many techniques and their relative merits are still under debate, but it is worth emphasizing that they are all rooted in a general principle that we could call the **completeness principle**: however a design or artefact is articulated into several parts, each part should be exposed to verification. Thus, if we are testing a complete program consisting of several modules, it is necessary that we apply experiments in such a way that every single module is executed at least once. Similarly, if we are testing a module that manages a table, it is reasonable to define a few typical table configurations (for example, full table, empty table, neither empty nor full table) and to test the behaviour of the module with test cases that belong to the different situations. It is intuitively clear that, under normal circumstances, testing the module three times in the three cases listed above is more meaningful than, say, testing it 100 times but always with a full table.

We will consider both testing and analysis techniques. In particular, we will present a white-box (Section 23.3.1) and a black-box (Section 23.3.2) testing technique and one analysis technique (Section 23.3.3).

23.3.1 A white-box testing technique: the instruction coverage criterion

A simple and widely used technique for testing a program is the *coverage of all the instructions of the program*. As the term suggests, it consists of verifying the program by supplying it with sets of different input values such that, during the various test executions, each instruction of the program is executed at least once. Thus, this criterion applies the completeness principle to the case of program statements. It is based on the simple fact that, if there is an error in some part of the program, it is impossible to detect it if the program part that contains it is not executed.

For example, consider the following program fragment which codes the well-known Euclid's algorithm (see Example 3.7):

```
{
    scanf("%d", &x); scanf("%d", &y);
    while (x != y)
        if (x > y) x = x - y; else y = y - x;
    gcd = x;
}
```

The simplest way to satisfy the instruction coverage criterion is to execute the program once with input <1,2> and once with input <2,1>. This set of input data ensures that each instruction of the program is executed at least once (in this case, in two different executions). If, for example, the instruction y = y − x; had been erroneously written as y = y + x; the error would have been shown by the fact that execution would not have terminated when the input data <1,2> was used.

☞ 1

Obviously, the criterion of 'covering' each instruction of the program is a necessary but not sufficient condition for detecting errors: reaffirming our previous statement, verifying that the program behaves correctly in some cases does not guarantee its correctness in all other cases.

Consider, for example, the following program fragment:

```
{
    scanf("%d", &x);
    z = x * x;
    printf("%d", z);
}
```

Because the code contains neither conditional nor cyclic instructions, it is enough to execute it once with a random input value, to satisfy the criterion of covering each instruction. But if we had written z = x + x instead of z = x * x, then a test involving the input value 2, although satisfying the above criterion, would not reveal the error.

23.3.2 A black-box testing technique: decision table testing

If we apply the completeness principle to a program's functional specifications we conclude that we should execute the program under test at least once for every condition found in the specifications. For instance, in the Macintosh computer the meaning of the mouse 'double-click' is – roughly – defined as follows: 'If two consecutive clicks occur within a predefined time interval, Δ, then the effect is to select the item the mouse is pointing to and to open it (here the term 'open' must be intended in a fairly general sense depending on the type of the selected item); otherwise, the effect is simply to select the item the mouse is pointing to.' Given this specification, it is fairly natural to test the behaviour of the mouse at least once by giving two clicks within Δ and at least once by giving two clicks separated by a time interval larger than Δ.

Clearly, the more well-structured the specifications the easier it will be to derive test cases from them in a systematic way. In particular, without going deeply into the issue of formal specifications and techniques to derive test cases from them, let us simply observe that in many cases functional specifications consist of a case-by-case definition of what the system should do under several circumstances. In this case it is fairly easy to translate the specifications into a tabular form – called a **decision table** – from which it is quite simple to extract test cases in a systematic way. Let us illustrate the method through a simple example.

EXAMPLE 23.1

Consider the following partial specification for a word processor:

> The word processor may present portions of text in three different formats: plain text (p), boldface (b) and italics (i). The following commands may be applied to each portion of text: make text plain (P), make boldface (B), make italics (I), emphasize (E), superemphasize (SE). Commands are available to dynamically set E to mean either B or I. (We denote such commands as E = B and E = I, respectively.) Similarly, SE can be dynamically set to mean either B (command SE = B), or I (command SE = I), or B and I (command SE = B+I).

The above wordy specification can be expressed in a more compact way in a tabular form as shown in Figure 23.1, which is in fact called a decision table. The table describes the conditions in the rows (here, the commands given to the word processor); columns represent rules, that is, the actions that result when the conditions are true. As an example, the rule represented by the leftmost column of the table shows that condition P generates output p. (To avoid cluttering the table with too many entries, we show only true conditions, marked with an asterisk, '*'.)

One can generate test cases naturally on the basis of the decision table, trying to apply the completeness principle so that each column of the table is exercised by at least one test. This 'blind' application of the principle, however, may be too expensive in terms of the number of experiments to be carried out, due to the exponential growth of the number of test cases with respect to the number of conditions. In fact, in general, if we have *n* conditions that can be arbitrarily combined, the number of possible cases, that is, the number of columns in the

P	*								
B		*							*
I			*						*
E				*	*				
SE						*	*	*	
E = B				*					
E = I					*				
SE = B						*			
SE = I							*		
SE = B + I								*	
Action	p	b	i	b	i	b	i	b,i	b,i

Figure 23.1 Decision table specifying the word processor of Example 23.1.

decision table, can go up to 2^n. Thus, we may need some technique to select a significant subset of all possible input cases. We refer the reader to more specialized literature for such techniques.

23.3.3 An informal analysis technique: code inspection

The term 'analysis' is general enough to cover actions that go from a quick code inspection to well-organized and documented design reviews and to the application of formal techniques to derive design properties as mathematical theorems. In this section we present one particular informal but effective analysis technique: **code inspection**. In its usual meaning this term is characterized by two main factors: the search for a well-defined set of possible errors and the organization as a social, coordinated, activity.

The first factor is based on the assumption that it is easier to detect some kind of error, for example accessing an uninitialized variable, if we explicitly look for that kind of error rather than generically reading through a code to check its correctness. Thus, a list of possible errors is set up and then the people involved in the verification activity inspect the code looking explicitly and type by type for those types of errors. A sample list of typical errors against which code inspection may be directed is the following:

- use of uninitialized variables,
- jumps into loops,
- incompatible assignments,
- nonterminating loops,
- array indexes out of bounds,
- improper storage allocation/deallocation (dangling references or garbage production),
- actual/formal parameter mismatches in procedure calls,
- comparisons of equality for floating point values.

Notice that many of the above errors – as well as others not listed here – have different symptoms and impacts depending on the programming language. For instance, improper storage allocation/deallocation is not even possible with static languages such as Fortran. In C, many mismatches between actual and formal parameters can be caught at compile time, but there might be an exception for pointer parameters and so on. We might also use a language-specific list based on the error-prone features of the language.

Furthermore, we will see in Chapter 24 that many analytical tools exist to help in detecting such errors. In general, the human inspectors should concentrate on what cannot be inspected automatically.

The second factor is based on the belief, widely confirmed by experience, that errors are more easily discovered if the design is discussed among several people; if the designers themselves go through their design several times, there is a high risk that during the analysis they will repeat the same errors as during design.

Several guidelines have been developed over the years for organizing this naive but useful verification technique to make it more systematic and reliable. Of course, these guidelines are based on personal experience, common sense and many subjective factors. Thus, they should be considered more as examples than as rules to be applied dogmatically.

In general, the following prescriptions are recommended:

- The number of people involved in the review should be small (three to five). There is one designer and several reviewers; the designer presents and explains the rationale of the work. A secretary is responsible for writing a report to be given to the designer at the end of the meeting.

- The reviewers should receive written documentation from the designer a few days before the meeting.

- The meeting should last a predefined amount of time (a few hours).

- Discussion should be focused on the discovery of errors, not on fixing them.

- In order to foster cooperation and avoid the feeling that the designer is being evaluated, managers should not participate in the meeting. The success of social verification techniques hinges on running them in a cooperative manner as a team effort: they must avoid making the designer feel threatened.

Notice that code inspection is a fairly low-level verification technique as it aims at searching for typical programming errors. Thus, it will probably be preceded by other types of verification aimed at checking the logical design (algorithm correctness, modular organization and so on). For these types of verification too, social review techniques could be applied.

23.4 Detection and correction of errors (debugging)

Verification leads either to the identification of errors or to a certain level of confidence (almost never the certainty) of their absence.

Once the presence of errors has been ascertained, they must be located and corrected. This activity is called **debugging** in the jargon, and it is often quite difficult. When planning to use debugging, one has to keep the following fact in mind. Experimental verification by testing signals the presence of an error via a **failure** (for example, a program should produce the value 3, but prints 4 instead). A failure is therefore a positive symptom of the presence of an error, but the presence of an error does not necessarily cause a failure.

We must therefore first try to maximize the probability that, if the program contains an error, this results in a failure; secondly, the failure should produce signals that can be used to locate the error. For example, the fact that the output variable y has an incorrect value could be caused by an erroneous assignment to the variable x on which y depends: thus, we must trace back from the *failure* that appears in y to the *error* that is located in x. This job could be helped by keeping (possibly automatically) a list of all variables y depends on.

A traditional, but primitive and wasteful debugging technique is the so-called **memory dump** (a printout of the contents of the entire memory). This allows the values of all variables to be examined, at predetermined points in the program execution, to find out which are correct and which are not. In this method, the whole of the program execution state is output at some given point, which increases the likelihood that an error will result in a failure. However, an enormous quantity of useless information must be handled using this method, with a high risk of confusion.

It is often more useful to make a selective analysis of the values of some critical variables. For example, the program could print the value of the index of an array before each access of the array itself, in order to allow the tester to determine whether the index is within the established limits.

Several techniques and tools for analysing memory state during program execution can help to locate and remove errors. These **spy** mechanisms for checking program states can be removed once the testing and debugging phase is complete, because they needlessly slow down program execution (for example, by printing a large number of values which are useful for analysing the program but not for its operational use).

Exercises

*23.1 Consider the following program fragment:

```
...
if (x == 0)
   printf("abnormal");
else
   printf("normal");
...
```

Assume that the preceding part of the program contains an error such that x is not initialized before the above statement is executed. Discuss the repeatability of testing the program including the fragment above: in other words, state whether, and under which circumstances, two different executions of the same program supplied with the same data are guaranteed to produce the same results.

23.2 Find a set of test cases that satisfy the instruction coverage criterion for the programs of Examples 3.4, 3.5 and 3.9. How many times do you need to run the program to complete the test in each case?

23.3 Design a set of reasonable test cases for a program intended to compute the gcd of two numbers. Verify its effectiveness by applying it to several programs aimed at computing the gcd, including the two presented in this text (Example 3.7), and by introducing a few errors in the programs (for example, replacing an operator symbol with another one).

23.4 The following incorrect program fragment is intended to merge two sorted arrays of n elements each:

```
...
i = 0; j = 0;
for (k = 0; k < 2 * n; k++)
{
    if (a[i] < b[j])
    {
        c[k] = a[i];
        i = i + 1;
    }
    else
    {
        c[k] = b[j];
        j = j + 1;
    }
}
```

First, write a sufficiently detailed specification for its purpose; then, derive a set of test cases from your specification, run the program and check if the error is detected. If not, find the error by means of an intuitive analysis; once you have found it, find a set of test cases that would discover the error.

☛ **1.** Consider Euclid's algorithm given in Section 23.3.1. The set of test cases proposed there satisfies the instruction coverage criterion but requires two executions of the program. Is it possible to satisfy the criterion by 'spending less', that is, with a lower number of executions?

In general, notice that, when we set up a test plan for any piece of software, we should keep in mind not only **test thoroughness**, that is, the ability to catch errors, if any, but also **test effort**, which often can be measured as the number of executions required.

Software production tools 24

Design activities are primarily work of the human mind, but they can draw considerable benefits from the use of appropriate support tools. Thus, until fairly recently, technical drawings were more successful when assisted by a universal or curvilinear drafting device.

It should not therefore be surprising that nowadays many support tools for every kind of design are based on the computer, which not only executes the necessary calculations to solve numerical problems, but also plots extremely precise drawings, handles complex documentation and so on.

Thus, **Computer Aided Design** (CAD), which traditionally covers engineering sectors such as the design of printed circuits, building structures, cars and so on, has been joined by **Computer Aided Software Engineering** (CASE), which systematically covers the areas of software design and production. For a long time, typical software engineering tools were used only in the 'low-level phases' of design. The most important of these was the compiler, an indispensable tool for programming in high-level languages. The 'high-level phases' of the life cycle, not being tied to any rigorously defined language, were aided by at most tools for editing and managing documents, but not, for example, by tools to check the coherence or completeness of specifications.

CASE tools are dedicated to the various phases of the life cycle and to their integration into a single design activity; they have recently become widely accepted in industry. As often happens, however, a rapidly evolving sector may have difficulty in expressing results in such a way that they can be well understood and widely adopted. Thus, faced with such a rich variety of tools, users generally do not fully understand the advantages and disadvantages of the various products, nor do they know which product to adopt. It is therefore likely that the state of the art in this sector must evolve further before it reaches an acceptable level of maturity.

In this chapter, rather than presenting a list of tools and their characteristics (which would quickly become obsolete and meaningless), we prefer to approach the problem from various points of view to allow readers to make their own evaluations of the rich and varied set of present and future tools.

First (Section 24.1), we provide some classification schemes; then (Section 24.2), we present an overview of the various categories of tools. Section 24.3 briefly describes the Turbo C environment, a widely used environment which is dedicated to the C language and applies to the lower phases of the software life cycle. Finally, Section 24.4 presents an ideal scenario of tools integrated into a complete software design environment.

24.1 Classification of software engineering tools

CASE tools can be classified from different points of view, such as the level of formalization they allow or impose, the life cycle phase they refer to, the type of interaction with the user and so on. In this section, we present various criteria for their classification and evaluation.

24.1.1 Type of interaction with the user

For a long time, interaction between user and computer was almost exclusively textual (via the keyboard and character-screen terminal). Recently, however, the advent of interactive graphics (via the mouse and graphical terminals) and multimedia and hypertext mechanisms (which allow the user to manage and query heterogeneous documents, such as texts, figures, archives or numerical data) has dramatically enhanced the quality, richness and ease of use of human–machine interaction.

The impact of these improvements on CASE tools is considerable. For example, the ability to draw various types of figures in an easy and natural way has made it possible to provide tools for drafting specifications based on graphical notations, such as data flow diagrams, which in the past could be produced only on paper.

Analogously, interaction using menus and windows of various types has made looking up and accessing libraries of modules much easier; in addition, this type of interface requires much shorter learning times.

Thus, independently of the objective and functional specification of a tool, the way in which it interacts with the user is particularly relevant to its ease of use, its ease of learning and, therefore, its acceptance.

24.1.2 Level of formalization

The development of software includes the production of various documents, each written in a language whose syntax and semantics can be defined in a more or less formal way.

For example, a programming language or a finite state automaton is completely formal; natural languages are completely informal; and we have also seen examples of partially formal or semi-formal languages and notations such as DFDs which have rigorously defined syntax but whose meaning is left to human interpretation.

The level of formalization of a language heavily influences the tools that can be associated with it. For example, interpreters and compilers can be constructed for programming languages, owing to their formal definition. On the other hand, the various attempts at automatic translation of natural languages have always yielded largely unsatisfactory results; consequently, the only tools that can assist with writing documents in natural languages are word processors, supported by orthographic analysis tools (spell-checkers), word lists (thesaurus) and maybe some simple grammar checking tools, plus document management tools. For semi-formal notations, such as DFDs, the state of the art offers good editors that assist with drawing the diagrams and with syntactic analysis (checking, for example, that all identifiers are used correctly). More powerful analysis tools, such as simulators or demonstrators of characteristics, are not possible, owing to the lack of a rigorous definition of the semantics of the model.

24.1.3 Dependence on the life-cycle phase

The majority of CASE tools support a specific phase of the software life cycle. Thus, we find editors for drafting system requirements, editors and compilers for the construction of programs, various tools for the verification of correctness (for example, automatic test case generators) and so on. Other tools support the integration of the various phases and the corresponding tools, creating a complete environment for the software construction process.

Imagine, for example, that an error is detected during the verification phase: to correct it, it is necessary to re-enter the program editing phase, temporarily abandoning the verification phase, which is resumed after the error has been corrected and the program recompiled and, eventually, relinked. If these activities are supported by tools which are not integrated with each other, this sequence of operations can be very long and burdensome. What is needed is a tool that manages two windows on the same screen, one for program execution, the other for editing, compiling and so on, such that the user can easily pass from one to the other.

Tools that support such integration are often called **software engineering platforms** and are considered the basis of so-called **IPSEs (Integrated Project Support Environments)**. However, they are still far from a satisfactory level of maturity and, at present, are considered a goal to be attained rather than an existing reality.

24.1.4 Dependence on application sector and design method

Many design methods and languages are especially constructed for particular applications. For example, DFDs were invented for management applications, although subsequently versions adapted to the construction of real-time control systems appeared. It is only natural that the characteristics of the various tools are influenced by the methods they are intended to favour, or rather, some 'methodologies' are created together with and at the same rate as the specialized tools to support them. A well-known case of this kind is the Jackson methodology in the information management sector.

24.1.5 Dependence on language or notation

Some tools are associated with a particular language or notation, while others are independent: we call the first **monolanguage**, the second **polylanguage**. For example, a traditional editor or word processor is polylanguage: it can be used to construct documents of various types, such as specifications or programs in different languages. However, there are also specialized editors, *driven by the syntax* of a particular language, such as C, Pascal and so on. These editors allow the characteristics of a language to be exploited while writing programs (for example, immediately correcting syntax errors), but they can be used for only one language.

Compilers are another example of monolanguage tools, while an operating system such as UNIX provides a collection of polylanguage software development tools.

24.1.6 Static and dynamic tools

Some tools do not execute, nor do they require execution of the object on which they operate, be it a program or a specification document. They are applied to the object in order to create it, modify it, or analyse it with respect to various criteria. This kind of tool is called **static**. An example of a static tool is the syntax analyser of a language which determines whether a given program violates the syntax of the language in which it is written.

Other tools, called **dynamic** tools, require execution of the object to which they are applied. Among these, we find programming language interpreters; the simulator of a finite state automaton is another example of a simple dynamic tool.

24.2 Some basic software development support tools

In this section, we provide a brief overview of the principal support tools for software development. Some of them have already been mentioned, whereas others are mentioned here for the first time. In some cases, they are classified according to the criteria presented in the previous section; in the other cases, the reader can complete this classification as an exercise, with the warning that it does not always make sense to classify a tool with respect to all the criteria cited earlier.

24.2.1 Editors

As software is, all in all, a collection of documents (specifications, modular architectures, code and so on) of varying complexity, editors are a fundamental tool for software development. With respect to the various points of view shown in the previous section, they can be classified as follows:

- They can be both text- and graphics-oriented.
- They can be associated with informal, semi-formal and completely formalized languages. This does not prevent an informal editor, such as a word processor, being used for a completely formalized language, such as a programming language.
- They can be monolanguage or polylanguage. Typical examples of monolanguage editors are the so-called syntax-driven editors in which the syntax of the language is used as a guide for interactive program development. For example, at a certain point, the user might want to insert a conditional expression in the program being written. The editor first asks for the condition; next, it asks for the instruction to be executed if the condition is true, and so on.

24.2.2 Linkers

Linkers are tools that combine fragments of object code into complete programs. Thus, they can be either monolanguage (capable only of linking modules obtained by compiling source code of one particular language) or polylanguage. A polylanguage linker is usually limited to establishing the correspondence between elements shared by various modules (for example, variables of one module that can be accessed by another module). A monolanguage linker can also carry out cross-checks (for example, it could check that if a module M1 exports a variable V of integer type, this variable is not used as a character by a module M2 that imports it).

The concept of a linker can also find application outside the traditional context of linking object code modules. For example, modules constituting the specification of parts of a system via DFDs could be linked, in order to obtain the complete specification.

24.2.3 Interpreters

We have already seen that interpreters are typical dynamic tools. Traditional interpreters are the executors of programming languages that do not go through a compilation process. Tools of this kind are particularly suitable for certain programming languages (which will be briefly discussed in Chapter 26), but they can also be useful for traditional languages, such as C: in this case, they usually offer less efficient execution, but excellent facilities for analysis.

Interpreters can also be constructed for other types of languages. For example, it is not difficult to construct an interpreter for a finite state automaton (introduced in Section 21.2.2), with the aim of simulating the specifications defined by means of such a model. Such simulators are often called **prototypers**, because they realize a first prototype of the system under construction.

24.2.4 Code generators

In many cases, people try to describe the scheme for the solution of a problem using a notation as abstract as possible (high-level notation), leaving it to the machine to translate this notation into executable code. The most obvious example is writing a program in a high-level language and having it translated by a compiler which can therefore be considered to be an **automatic code generator**.

Compilers, however, are not the only example of code generators. More generally, any tool that supports translation from a high-level notation into a notation 'nearer' to executable code is called a code generator. This translation need not necessarily be complete, since it uses only that part of the source notation that is sufficiently formalized. Typical examples of code generators of this kind are tools that, starting from a semi-formal specification of a system, provided by DFDs for example, automatically produce part of the code necessary for implementing the specification in a programming language. Usually, this code is declarative, because the part of DFDs that is formalized best is their structure, whereas their semantics, that is, the meaning of the various functions, is left to the intuition of the reader and cannot therefore be 'understood' by the translator.

24.2.5 Verification support tools

As we saw in Chapter 23, software verification can be carried out in various ways which we classified into analysis and testing techniques. For each technique, we have, at least in principle, adequate tools to support it.

Testing support tools are divided into various categories: some are simple tools that assist in documenting the testing activity, recording the type of experiment carried out, its result, the date, the conditions under which it was carried out and so on. However, these tools leave it to the inventiveness of the designer to identify the test cases most appropriate for the verification of the system. Other tools, more ambitious but not yet fully developed and therefore not widely used, provide true (and nearly) automatic generation of test cases. For example, take the following problem: given a generic program, automatically identify a set of test cases that 'cover' all its instructions, according to the criterion stated in Section 23.3.1. Such an objective cannot be completely automated for theoretical reasons that we cannot go into here. Suffice it to say that these tools assist the user in inventing test cases, but they are not completely autonomous and always require some interaction with the user. Therefore they are called 'semi-automatic'.

In addition to being a code generator, the compiler is also an analysis tool, because it detects certain types of errors (compile-time errors) while translating the source code and provides suggestions for their correction.

Other, more sophisticated, analysis tools can help to detect more subtle errors, such as uninitialized variables. Some theoretical approaches, which have not yet received much attention in industrial applications, try to *prove* the correctness of a program as a mathematical theorem. The tools that support such an activity naturally belong to the domain of (semi)automatic theorem proving.

24.2.6 Error correction support tools (debuggers)

As we have seen, error correction follows verification. The corresponding tools should help particularly with inspecting the state of execution at certain critical points. Consequently, their help principally consists in automatically and systematically adding code to the program so that more information is provided than can be obtained through execution of the program. For example, a debugger can display the value of the index of an array before letting the program access the desired element.

24.2.7 User interface construction tools

As we have already emphasized several times, human–machine interaction today is achieved by particular mechanisms (user interfaces) that can be easily learned and make communication between user and computer much more comfortable than in earlier times. Because of this, the computer is now a tool that can be used by anyone.

User interfaces are often made up of elements (windows, menus, icons) that are sufficiently well established to be systematically used in different applications. Naturally, there are tools to make the definition of user interfaces for applications quick and easy, saving programmers considerable energy that would otherwise be spent on highly repetitive tasks (the menus of a word processor are not that different from the menus of a spreadsheet).

24.2.8 Production process management tools

Like any other production process, the process of constructing software does not consist exclusively of technical choices, but requires a lot of attention to organizational aspects (planning, estimating costs, monitoring progress and so on). Various tools are available to assist the user in this type of activity. Sometimes, a single tool can be used to manage production processes of various types (for example, if the requirement is to check that certain tasks have been completed within the established deadlines, it does not really matter whether the tasks involve the production of a software module or the construction of part of a building). In other cases, the tool is geared to the fact that the production process to which it is applied is software development. For example, estimating the cost of a project is a problem common to every production activity, but to estimate the cost of the development of a software system, one has to take into account factors which are typical of and exclusive to this kind of activity.

24.3 A specific case: the Turbo C environment

In this section, we briefly describe a widely used programming environment that is also available on low-cost machines: the Turbo C environment. The description we provide is general and does not take into account details that may differ between existing versions. As the name suggests, this environment is based on the C language and is therefore monolanguage. It supports only the lower phases of the software life cycle (development and analysis of the software), but it is integrated and thus allows the user to pass from one phase to another without leaving the environment.

The Turbo C environment consists of the following elements, organized and integrated according to Figure 24.1:

- The *editor*. This is a normal interactive editing tool equipped with the typical functionalities of a word processor. Although not a syntax-driven editor, it has some characteristics determined by the syntax structure of C (for example, it facilitates 'indenting' so that the user can write programs whose layout reflects the syntax structure, following the style adopted in this and many other books, and it checks that the number of curly brackets opened by the programmer to delimit blocks matches the number of closing curly brackets).

- The *compiler–linker*. This can compile programs edited in different files and link subroutines (functions) that have been compiled separately, including the functions in the standard library and other libraries made available by the integrated environment.

    The compiler offers various code generation options (such as representation of floating point numbers or characters) and analysis options (it signals and locates syntax errors of different types, classifying them as common errors, rare errors, portability errors or errors with respect to the standards imposed by ANSI C). Its integration with the editor allows easy correction, by leaving the compilation phase, entering the editing phase to input the correction and relaunching the compilation. In addition, it is possible to supply the compiler with directives to check for some typical run-time errors (for example, indexes of vectors out of bounds). These directives are transmitted by the compiler to the language's run-time support system which then takes care of flagging errors and their location to the programmer. Typically, these directives should be used during the development and testing

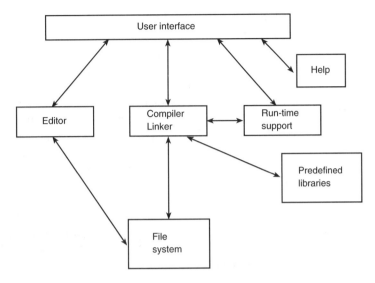

Figure 24.1   The Turbo C environment.

of the program and removed during normal operation, because run-time error checking reduces efficiency (the appropriate control code must be inserted in the object program).

- The *run-time support*. This is the set of procedures that allows the abstract machine of the language to be realized on the hardware available (for example, it provides stack management if this is not directly supported by the hardware).

    As we have seen in the previous point, Turbo C's run-time support is equipped with structures suitable for detecting and signalling errors. The support the debugger gives the programmer is of strategic importance. It allows one or more expressions to be evaluated at run-time and execution to be interrupted so that the value of one or more variables can be displayed, at places in the code previously 'marked' by the programmer (**break points**).

- *Standard library and other predefined libraries*. The standard library is present in the form of object files (extension `.c`) and header files (extension `.h`). The same holds for other library functions supplied by Turbo C (the most widely used are screen handling and graphics functions). When a file includes the contents of a header file, it includes the prototypes of some functions that will actually be used and some functions that will not. At link time, the linker links in only the object code of the functions that are actually used.

- The *file system* and the *shell*. These are, obviously, those of the host machine (of MS-DOS, for example). The file system can be 'masked' by the input/ output library functions or it can be used directly by calls to its procedures. The Turbo C environment allows a temporary exit into the shell (to allow for work that directly uses the functions of the operating system shell) and re-entry from the shell.

- The *online help*. At any time it is possible to call the Help program which explains how to interpret the machine's reactions and suggests the appropriate commands. The online help of Turbo C is 'context-sensitive', that is, it normally shows information relevant to what is being executed. However, the user can also manually select the topic on which information is required.

- The *user interface*. This is organized into hierarchical menus: at any time, the current menu offers a series of options to choose from. The choice made may involve access to a second-level menu and so on, up to the execution of the selected command.

24.4 From CASE tools to integrated environments

As we have seen, the majority of CASE tools available today tend to apply to one or only a few phases of the software life cycle. It would be desirable to integrate different tools into a single integrated software development environment (IPSE), capable of supporting all phases of the life cycle. Several project platforms are under development, especially designed to constitute the basis and the integration tool of an IPSE.

A **project platform** essentially consists of databases that possess rather atypical characteristics when compared to traditional databases. This is due to the considerable diversity of information to be managed in a software project. Think, for example, of source and object code of various modules, specification documentation, testing documentation and so forth, and compare this information with the typical information handled by a traditional database (management information, scientific data, and so on). The mechanisms for managing a **software project database** are therefore peculiar to this type of activity.

On the basis of such platforms, complete environments should be constructed to allow the user, for example, to write project specifications using DFDs, design an appropriate modular architecture that implements the desired system, code the modules in some programming language, verify their correctness and that of the entire system, document the results of the various tests and corrections made, and so on.

An environment of this kind would obviously be conditioned by the application sector in which the software development takes place and by the methods of specification, design and verification adopted, following a formulation intuitively sketched in Figure 24.2.

A software design environment can be closed or open. In the first case, it consists of a fixed and rigid set of tools, often specialized for a particular application sector. In the second case, it can be modified at any time by adding new tools or replacing existing ones.

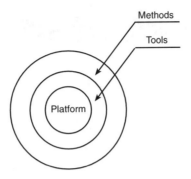

Figure 24.2   Structure of a CASE environment.

A closed environment is usually easier to manage and to learn, but it does not adapt very well to the continuous evolution of tools. Therefore, the current tendency is towards the construction of open environments based on a powerful platform capable of 'taking on board' tools of various types.

*Object-oriented design

25

We saw in Chapter 22 how some of the problems linked to 'programming-in-the-large' can be tackled by adopting suitable modularization techniques. These techniques have been joined, during the past 10 years, by a new software design philosophy: the so-called **object-oriented (OO) design**. This technique, in addition to allowing well-modularized programs to be written, supports two important software qualities described in Chapter 20, *modifiability* and *reusability*, and provides the designer with conceptual and operational tools useful in the different phases of software development. This design philosophy is supported by specially designed languages; in addition to their ancestors Simula 67 and Smalltalk, we mention Eiffel and C++ (an extension of C).

In this chapter we present the essential features of object-oriented design. Section 25.1 stresses the novel aspect of OO design as opposed to the traditional function-oriented approach. Section 25.2 presents OO design as a major tool supporting abstraction and modularization; Section 25.3 introduces inheritance, a specialization mechanism; Section 25.4 deals with genericity, a powerful form of parametrization; Section 25.5 introduces late binding, a mechanism that adds flexibility by allowing the postponement of implementation choices at runtime. Finally, Section 25.6 presents an extended example comparing a traditional design approach with the OO approach. Since these approaches are mainly motivated by 'programming-in-the-large', a comparative case study must necessarily refer to a nontrivial programming problem and results in fairly long pieces of code.

To illustrate the practical application of general OO principles we use C++, an extension of the basic programming language C. The reader should be warned, however, that general OO principles have often rather different instantiations in different programming languages. For this reason we have tried, in our presentation, to distinguish general – but often vague – OO principles from C++ specific technicalities.

25.1 Procedure-oriented versus object-oriented design

Basically, the term 'object-oriented design' is opposed to the term 'function (or procedure)-oriented design' to emphasize the main issues that drive the design process. In general, supporters of OO design claim that focusing attention on objects (that is, data) rather than on operations leads to better programs, mainly in terms of reusability and modifiability. Let us therefore examine more precisely the meaning of this fundamental difference and how it may impact on such qualities.

From the very first chapters on programming, we have stated that, in order to develop software systems, it is necessary to identify a set of *operations* (one or more algorithms) to be applied to a set of *data*. In the initial development phases the designer can be guided either by operations or by data. The chosen approach will heavily influence the architecture of the software system to be implemented.

A designer who adopts a traditional (procedure-oriented) design style concentrates on the operations that the program has to carry out. This traditional design style often uses top-down decomposition, in which each operation is broken down into a sequence of simpler operations which can, in their turn, be further decomposed. The structure of a system designed in this way shows the effects of this initial formulation: modules contain functional subsystems of the overall system.

There are many problems with this approach, which become evident when the system has to be modified to reflect new application requirements. First, the functions initially identified, when putting together the system's specifications, are the most volatile part of the system. A good software system survives over time if it can cope with new operations on the available data. Furthermore, functions designed using a procedure-oriented approach are often mutually related. Think of a dialogue interface whose options become more and more specific according to the user's choices: the functions that satisfy the requirements of the user are invoked in a very precise temporal sequence. The implementation of the individual functions often reflects the temporal sequence of the very first interface designed, and this can severely limit the ability to extend the functionality of the system in the future.

If we wish to construct software systems whose structure is not radically upset by changes in the requirements, we must give more importance to the data because data is the most stable element of the overall system.

Object-oriented design therefore concentrates, in the higher design phases, on the identification and definition of **classes of objects** needed to realize the application. The design is initially abstract: the properties (structural characteristics) of the objects belonging to the application domain and the operations associated with them are defined independently of their implementation aspects.

The concept of **class** catalogues the objects identified as relevant to the application: all objects belonging to the same class can be described using the same set of properties and can therefore be manipulated through the same set of operations. The code that realizes operations is 'packaged' with the defined objects. The defined data thus constitutes small blocks that can be combined and reused in different application contexts.

To gain an initial impression of how these principles affect the writing of code, let us consider Figure 25.1. It displays two different ways of writing code to drive vehicles: in Figure 25.1(a) the code is partitioned (modularized) on the basis of driving actions (for example, GoStraight, TurnRight); in Figure 25.1(b), it is partitioned on the basis of vehicle classes (Car, Bicycle, …). In functional – action-oriented – programming, objects are 'passed' to the function invoked, whereas in OO programming a particular object is asked to realize one of the operations permitted by the definition of the class to which the object belongs.

We have said that OO design supports the modularization principles discussed in Chapter 22. In fact, a class constitutes a module equipped with an interface and one or more implementations. Its interface consists of the properties that can be accessed and manipulated by other modules, and of the declaration of the operations that can be invoked by other modules (other classes). An implementation includes the code that implements the operations of the class and some properties or operations which cannot be seen by other modules (and therefore cannot be manipulated or invoked).

Object-oriented design offers the following advantages:

```
void  GoStraight(obj  Object)              void  TurnRight(obj  Object)
{                                          {
   switch (Object)                            switch (Object)
   {                                          {
      case Car:     ...                          case Car:     ...
      case Bicycle: ...                          case Bicycle: ...
      case Truck:   ...                          case Truck:   ...
      case Bus:     ...                          case Bus:     ...
   }   ...                                    }   ...
}                                          }
```

(a)

```
Car ::          Bicycle ::      Truck ::        Bus ::
GoStraight()    GoStraight()    GoStraight()    GoStraight()
{               {               {               {

  ...             ...             ...             ...
}               }               }               }
Car ::          Bicycle ::      Truck ::        Bus ::
TurnRight()     TurnRight ()    TurnRight ()    TurnRight ()
{               {               {               {

  ...             ...             ...             ...
}               }               }               }
```

(b)

Figure 25.1   (a) Traditional view: code is grouped by functionality. (b) Object-oriented view: code is partitioned through objects.

- It *allows wide reuse of code*: existing classes can be used for the definition of new classes; operations already implemented for one class can be reused and made available to objects belonging to new classes.

- It *allows extensive and correct modifications*: the properties and the operations associated with each class can be augmented and modified at any time; side-effects related to changing some properties or operations can be easily controlled, thanks to the grouping imposed by the concept of class.

- It *efficiently supports the different phases of the software life cycle*: in the requirements analysis, system architecture design and implementation phases, the designer can rely on a powerful abstraction. The designer can also use previously defined and implemented classes from libraries, either created by the designer or made available by the programming environment used. Top-down modularization and design techniques can therefore be easily adapted to OO programming, and bottom-up design techniques can be encouraged by the existence of an already implemented library of classes.

Even though the term 'object-oriented design' is somewhat vague and can be interpreted subjectively in many ways, some typical characteristics are essential. The following sections analyse these characteristics in greater detail, treating the basic concepts (classes, objects and methods) and some peculiar features (encapsulation, inheritance, genericity and polymorphism), not existing in traditional programming, which make OO design a programming technique aimed at reusability and extensibility of code.

However, the reader should bear in mind that a rigorous definition of the concepts presented here is still the object of lively scientific debate and that we are still miles away from an acceptable standardization of the principal requisites of object-oriented languages.

25.2 Classes, objects and methods

A class realizes, in the typical terminology of OO design, the concept of an abstract data type. Indeed, a class groups together **objects** that can be described by the same set of **attributes** and manipulated by the same set of **methods** (operations).

The above concepts are offered by the C++ language in a fairly natural way. In C++ a class definition is similar to the definition of a structured type in C; unlike traditional programming languages, however, the definition includes (in agreement with the concept of abstract data type) the definition of the methods to operate on objects of the class.

Furthermore, the definition of a C++ class allows the definition of **private** and **public** elements. Types, constants, variables (C++ attributes) and functions (C++ methods) can all be public or private. Only public elements are visible and modifiable (if they are variables) outside the class. Private elements can be manipulated by other classes only through public functions made available by the class itself; thus, only the designer of the method – not the user! – needs to know the implementation details of private elements. Private elements are visible and modifiable, together with the public elements, by all public or private functions of the class itself. This ensures that the principle of information hiding can be applied. The protection provided by this mechanism is often called **encapsulation** in OO terminology.

Thus, a C++ class can be seen as a module. Its public elements (types, constants, variables/attributes and function/method prototypes) constitute the interface of the module. The code of the functions can be included in the class definition, but it is generally expressed separately (see Example 25.4 and the extended example of Section 25.6). The use of only the prototypes in the class declaration and the extrapolation of the code that implements the individual functions has to be considered the better programming style, given that it separates more clearly the interface of a module from its implementation.

As in C, in C++ too it is possible to emphasize the modularization of a program by using .h and .c files (see Example 25.4 and the extended example of Section 25.6). However, it is important to note the fundamental difference between the two languages: unlike C, C++ fully realizes abstract data types, information hiding and modularization through special language constructs (the class and its parts declared public or private).

EXAMPLE 25.1

Consider the wheel of any vehicle. It consists of several elements, for example radius, thickness, weight and material. On the basis of these elements it is possible to compute other values of interest for its use, for example the maximum pressure or the maximum speed. In an OO framework we say that a wheel is an object; that all such objects that share the above features constitute the class wheel; that radius, thickness, weight, material, ... are the attributes of the class; and that maximum pressure, maximum speed, ... are the methods of the class.

This information is formalized by the following portion of C++ code:

```
class  wheel
{
   private:                              /*there are no private elements*/
   public:
                                                        /*attributes*/
      double   radius;
      double   thickness;
      double   weight;
      ...
                                                          /*methods*/
      float   CalculateMaxPressure(...);
      ...
};
```

Notice that C++ syntax does not distinguish between attributes and methods: when necessary we emphasize their difference through appropriate comments.

Objects belonging to the class wheel can then be used to build more complex objects such as bicycles. Thus, a new class bicycle can be defined which is linked to the wheel class by the relation is_composed_of described in Section 22.1.

```
class bicycle
{
    private:                            /*there are no private elements*/
    public:
                                                          /*attributes*/
        ...    manufacturer;
        wheel  wheels[2];
        ...    handlebar;
        ...    frame;
        ...    saddle;
        ...    gears;
                                                             /*methods*/
        int    CalculateCost(...);
        ...
};
```

Note that the attribute wheels of each object of class bicycle is a collection of objects of class wheel; similarly manufacturer could be an object belonging to another class firm previously defined and so on.

Other classes (for example, car, truck) could then be defined that also include elements of the class wheel as their components.

25.2.1 Object instantiation

Once a class is defined, its **instances**, that is, the objects that belong to it, can be created in two different ways:

- Statically, via declarations that use the name of the class as if it were the name of a type. For instance, with reference to Example 25.1, the declaration

    wheel   x, y, z, w;

    creates four objects, named x, y, z, w, belonging to the class wheel.
- Dynamically, by an appropriate operation (new in C++).

The different objects created (instantiated) have different values for the attributes but the same methods, which are defined in terms of their interface and implementation (code that realizes the desired operation).

25.2.2 Object reference

Each instantiated object can be referred to in the code either by its name or by the name of an appropriately initialized pointer, and its attributes can be referred to using a notation analogous to the one used for the fields of a structure:

```
x.manufacturer
```

The same notation is adopted to invoke, that is, to execute, one of the methods associated with its class. This syntactic style emphasizes that methods are 'part' of the object. For instance the statement:

```
x.CalculateMaxPressure()
```

would produce the execution of the method `CalculateMaxPressure` using the attribute values of the object x.

In general, if `m()` is a function of a class C, the invocation of `m()` can be obtained by selecting an object of class C either through its name, say x, or through a pointer, say p. Invocation occurs via the dot notation: `x.m()` or `(*p).m()`. As in C, `p->m()` is a short notation equivalent to `(*p).m()`. Function m may receive other objects passed as parameters. For instance, if a class `vehicle` is provided with a method `ChangeDirection` whose parameter is an angle, we could use the notation:

```
x.ChangeDirection(Pi/2)
```

to denote a command to turn right 90 degrees given to vehicle x.

In most OO languages, including C++, there is also another way to denote the object to which a given method must be applied, known as the **current object**. When we are managing a given object through a series of several operations, we might wish to make that object *current* to denote that, at present, we are managing *this* object. In C++ **this** is a predefined pointer to the current object which is available to the instructions belonging to the body of a method. The notation ***this** thus refers to the current object and **this->m()** calls method `m()`, still using the same current object. The use of **this** is compulsory only in ambiguous cases but is recommended whenever it simplifies the readability of the program.

Example 25.4 makes extensive use of this construct, whereas the extended example of Section 25.6 does not use it at all.

25.3 Inheritance

Inheritance is one of the most typical aspects of OO design; it allows hierarchies of classes and subclasses to be defined in such a way that each member of a subclass (also called a **descendant class**) has all the attributes and methods of the principal class (**ancestor class** or **superclass**) plus its own specific attributes and methods.

We illustrate the concept of inheritance through a simple example.

EXAMPLE 25.2

Imagine that a company's personnel is organized as follows.

The personnel includes everybody who works for the company. Each person has a name, a surname, an address, a date of birth and a social security number. Some personnel are employees, whereas others have an occasional working relationship and are called consultants. Each employee has a hiring date, gross yearly salary and pays income tax and national insurance contributions, whereas consultants have a sales tax registration number, a daily rate and a number of working days per year.

Employees are subdivided into managers, clerks and secretaries, each with their specific descriptive characteristics. Some operations are applicable to all personnel, such as hiring a new employee or consultant, ending the working relationship and paying them. Others are specific to certain categories of personnel; for example, overtime is paid only to employees who are not managers. Others again, although common to all or some of the various categories, require different definitions for different categories. For example, different payment procedures are needed for employees and consultants, and there are also different procedures for the various employees; for example, managers are paid differently from other categories of personnel.

Traditional programming languages are not very suitable for dealing with situations of this kind. Object-oriented languages introduce subclasses understood as a subset of the objects with given common attributes and methods. Each subclass is also a class in its own right and can have further subclasses, thus allowing the construction of hierarchies of any depth. In our case, we have a principal class `Personnel`, with `Employee` and `Consultant` as subclasses; `Employee` is further subdivided into the classes `Manager`, `Clerk` and `Secretary`. Thus we arrive eventually at the hierarchy shown in Figure 25.2.

A subclass automatically *inherits* all the attributes and operations defined for its ancestor class. Thus, it is not necessary to specify that the company's consultants have a name, surname and so on, nor that they can be taken on by the company: it is enough to define the attributes (for example, their sales tax registration number) and the operations (for example, calculating their fee) that are typical of the `Consultant` subclass.

Furthermore, it is possible to redefine some operations for the subclasses: thus, the insertion of a new member of `Personnel` can be carried out following a

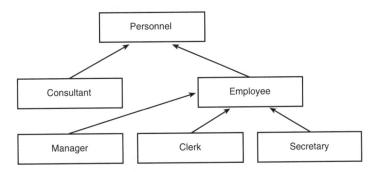

Figure 25.2 A hierarchy of classes and subclasses.

procedure common to all members of staff, whereas payment is carried out differently for consultants and employees, the payment of overtime is defined only for clerks and secretaries and so on.

Let us now see how the above hierarchy of classes can be defined in C++. In C++ inheritance is specified by the keyword **public** followed by the name of the ancestor class. In fact, the subclasses in a hierarchy inherit the public elements of the ancestor class; they can also define additional public or private elements and can redefine some elements (attributes and methods).

Thus, the hierarchy of Figure 25.2 consists of a class definition for each element of the hierarchy. It is partially given below.

```
class  Personnel
{
    private:                                /*there are no private elements*/
    public:
        char    Name[20];
        char    Surname[30];
        char    Address[100];
        void    hire(...);
        void    fire(...);
        int     pay(...);
};

class  Employee:    public  Personnel
                        /*the class Employee is a subclass of the
                        Personnel class; the objects in this class
                        possess all public elements of the personnel
                        class - attributes and functions*/

{
private:
    date    HiringDate;
    int     YearlyGrossSalary;
...
};

class  Consultant:  public  Personnel
                        /*the Consultant class is also a subclass of
                        the Personnel class*/
{
private:
    int     VATNumber;
public:
    int     pay(...);                       /*the pay function is redefined*/
...
};

int  Personnel :: pay(...)
{
                        /*implementation of the pay function for the
                        Personnel class. Subclass Employee does not
                        redefine function pay; thus, this
```

```
                                         implementation is used by objects of
                                         subclass Employee too*/
       };

       int   Consultant :: pay(...)
       {
                                         /* implementation of the pay function for
                                         the Consultant subclass. The pay function is
                                         redefined by the Consultant subclass,
                                         therefore all objects of the Consultant
                                         subclass use this implementation*/
       };
```

Inheritance is a powerful design tool for specializing already defined concepts to meet the requirements of particular applications. Practically all OO languages allow previously defined classes to be reused:

- by increasing the number of attributes and methods;
- by modifying the code of some methods, yet leaving their interface unaltered.

Other languages also allow the deletion or complete modification of attributes and methods of the ancestor class.

Objects belonging to a descendant class thus have a specific structure (deriving from an enrichment of their attributes) or a specialized behaviour (deriving from modifications in the code of the methods or from an increased number of methods). In each case, inheritance allows the wide use of already designed elements and code: many classes can be designed and implemented without having to start from scratch. This not only saves on implementation, but also enables aspects shared by several objects to be detected in the design phase, to the great advantage of the feasibility and correctness of future modifications and extensions.

In some languages a class can inherit only from a single ancestor class, whereas other languages (such as Eiffel and C++) allow **multiple inheritance**. Where multiple inheritance is allowed, a ModelTrain could be seen as an object instance of a descendant class of a class toy and a class vehicle. Multiple inheritance increases the power of the basic mechanism but also makes it more difficult to use and to implement. Being an advanced topic, we will not further pursue multiple inheritance in this text.

25.4 Genericity and polymorphism

The term **genericity** in OO terminology denotes an extension of parametrization: whereas in traditional languages parameters are usually only variables (at most some languages allow procedure parameters), most OO languages allow a much more general type of parametrization. Let us illustrate the meaning and the usefulness of genericity through the following example.

EXAMPLE 25.3

Consider the cases of handling a *table of invoices* and a *table of employees*. It is clear that there is a whole series of operations (insertion, sorting, searching and so on) that are applicable to both types of table – actually, to all types of table (just think of the relational algebra operations introduced in Section 16.4.2). Furthermore, the 'algorithmic structure' for implementing these operations has at least one common part, independently of the type of table considered: to sort a table, it is sufficient to be able to compare elements and to move them in the table, independently of the structure of the individual elements. However, it is also clear that a comparison of two integers cannot be executed in the same way as a comparison of two invoices. Thus, we can state that the handling of tables is **parametric** with respect to the elements that constitute them.

This parametricity with respect to the type is called genericity and is a powerful tool for flexibility which is supported by object-oriented languages. In C++ we can realize such a parametric class `table` using **templates**.

```
template <class elementType>
class Table
{
private:
    elementType  buffer[MAX_NUM_ELEM];
    int          numElem;
public:
    void  insert(elementType el);
    void  sort( );
                                    /*the operator <= is assumed to be
                                    defined for the class elementType*/
    boolean  search(elementType el);
    ...
};


class  Invoices
{
...
};


class  Employee
{
...
};

                                    /*now it is possible to declare the
                                    following variables*/

Table<Invoices>  TableOfInvoices;
Table<Employee>  TableOfEmployee;
```

Closely related to genericity is **polymorphism**, which allows an operation to be defined on different domains. For example, the sum operation is often polymorphic in traditional languages, where the summing of integers, reals, or even arrays is available. Genericity requires polymorphism for various operations: as we have already seen, C++ allows polymorphism as it allows the redefinition (also called **overloading**) of functions that have different implementations in the subclasses of a hierarchy.

25.5 **Early and late binding**

In a hierarchy of classes, a method can be defined with a particular interface in an ancestor class. A descendant class can provide the same method with the same interface and a different implementation which reflects the characteristic properties of the particular descendant class.

Consider, for example, as suggested in Exercise 25.1, a hierarchy of geometrical figures: the subclasses are triangle, square and pentagon, and each of them provides a method that calculates the perimeter or the area of the figure. This same method could be associated with the ancestor class, and the interface of the methods could be the same, but very likely the implementation of the methods of the subclasses would be particular to them. For instance, the perimeter and area of regular polygons can be calculated through more efficient algorithms than in the general case.

Let us now suppose that we want to write a program to handle geometrical figures, using an OO language that provides inheritance and polymorphism. Our program could easily be in a position to invoke the method that calculates the area of a figure, without knowing beforehand whether the figure under consideration is a regular triangle, a square, or another nonregular polygon.

In such a case, it is possible to invoke this method without considering to which class the object in question belongs (the method is invoked using the interface already known at the ancestor class level). At execution time, when we are given an object belonging to a specific subclass, the implementation of the method associated with that subclass is invoked.

This connection between the object involved and the implementation of a method at execution time is often called **late binding**, whereas the same connection made at compile time is called **early binding**. Early binding is generally more efficient and less costly in terms of memory occupation, but it makes programs less flexible. When a language offers both kinds of bindings, the choice of binding technique is left to the programmer and is closely linked to what the program has to do. Very often, a combination of both techniques is used.

C++ and other object-oriented programming languages are particularly flexible because they allow a choice between early binding or late binding; early binding can be used whenever all the information needed to decide which implementation of the function should be invoked is known at compile time.

In C++ early binding is obtained through the redefinition mechanism already examined (for example, the `pay` function of Example 25.2). However, if the declaration of a function prototype in the ancestor class is preceded by the keyword **virtual**, then redefinition of the function in subclasses is allowed, and late binding is used (as in all the public functions of the following example).

A class can indicate the functions by declaring them as **virtual** and omit their implementation; in this case the descendant classes provide the appropriate implementation of the functions whose definitions are inherited from the ancestor class. Different subclasses can have different implementations of the same function.

Example 25.4 illustrates the use of late binding by revisiting Example 22.1.

EXAMPLE 25.4

Let us go back to Example 22.1: it showed how an appropriate modularization could allow the use of different implementation techniques (modulus/argument, real part/imaginary part) for the abstract data type `ComplexNumber` without committing the code that uses that abstract data type to a particular implementation. Thus we were able to pick up the more suitable implementation when building the whole system (that is, linking the component modules) without affecting the code of the master modules that use `ComplexNumber`.

Now we want even more: we want to decide at run-time which implementation to choose. To achieve this goal we proceed as follows. First, we define a superclass `ComplexNumber` where all relevant features of the abstract data type are defined but no commitment is yet made regarding the implementation choice. In this definition functions are classified as **virtual**. Then, we define two heir subclasses, `ComplNumRPIP` and `ComplNumMARG`, where the same operations are redefined without the keyword **virtual**. This means that their implementation is given in the descendant class and not in the ancestor class. Finally, the two different implementations for the descendant classes are provided.

Thus, during the execution of the main program the user may select the preferred implementation; of course, in this case, it is necessary that the *existence* of the two implementation techniques – not their internal structure! – is made apparent in the class's interfaces.

The above design is realized by the following C++ code. (Given the introductory nature of this chapter, we have not introduced the read and write instructions of C++. Instead, we use the `scanf` and `printf` functions (already known to the reader) of the C library which are accepted by C++ programming environments.) As we did in C, we use `.h` and `.c` extensions to separate the interface definition from the implementation.

```
*************************************************************************
              Definition of the superclass ComplexNumber
                    Relevant parts of file CNum.h
*************************************************************************

#include <stdio.h>
#include <math.h>
```

```
class ComplexNumber
{
private:

public:
    virtual  void    ComplexSum(ComplexNumber Add)=0;
                     /*the assignment to 0 indicates that the method is
                     not implemented for this class, only the prototype is
                     present*/
    virtual  void    WriteCompl()=0;
    virtual  void    ReadCompl()=0;

    virtual  double  GetRealPart()=0;
    virtual  double  GetImaginaryPart()=0;
    virtual  double  GetModulus()=0;
    virtual  double  GetArgument()=0;
};
```

```
*********************************************************************
            Definition of the subclass ComplNumRPIP
               Relevant parts of file CN_RPIP.h
*********************************************************************
```

```
#include <ComplexNumber.h>

class ComplNumRPIP : public ComplexNumber
                    /*ComplNumRPIP is a descendant of ComplexNumber*/
{
private:
    double  RealPart;
    double  ImaginaryPart;
public:
    void    ComplexSum(ComplexNumber Add);
    void    WriteCompl();
    void    ReadCompl();
    double  GetRealPart();
    double  GetImaginaryPart();
    double  GetModulus();
    double  GetArgument();
};
```

```
*********************************************************************
            Definition of the subclass ComplNumMARG
               Relevant parts of file CN_MARG.h
*********************************************************************
```

```
#include <ComplexNumber.h>

class ComplNumMARG : public ComplexNumber
                    /*ComplNumMARG is another descendant of ComplexNumber*/
{
private:
    double  Modulus;
    double  Argument;
```

```
public:
   void    ComplexSum(ComplexNumber  Add);
   void    WriteCompl();
   void    ReadCompl();
   double  GetRealPart();
   double  GetImaginaryPart();
   double  GetModulus();
   double  GetArgument();
};
```

Once we have defined the interfaces of class `ComplexNumber` and its descendants, we proceed to their implementation: since functions were labelled as virtual, their implementation belongs to the implementation of descendant classes, not of the ancestor class.

```
**************************************************************************
              Implementation of the methods of ComplNumRPIP
                     Relevant parts of file CN_RPIP.c
**************************************************************************

#include <ComplNumRPIP.h>

void    ComplNumRPIP::ComplexSum(ComplexNumber Add)
{
   this->RealPart = this->RealPart + Add.GetRealPart();
   this->ImaginaryPart = this->ImaginaryPart + Add.GetImaginaryPart();
};


...                                       /*other methods implementation*/


**************************************************************************
              Implementation of the methods of ComplNumMARG
                     Relevant parts of file CN_MARG.c
**************************************************************************

#include <ComplNumMARG.h>
void    ComplNumMARG::ComplexSum(ComplexNumber  Add)
{
   double  TempRealPart, TempImagPart;

   TempRealPart = this->GetRealPart() + Add.GetRealPart();
   TempImagPart = this->GetImaginaryPart() + Add.GetImaginaryPart();
   this->Modulus =
      sqrt(TempRealPart * TempRealPart + TempImagPart * TempImagPart);
   this->Argument = acos(TempRealPart/this->Modulus);
};


...                                       /*other methods implementation*/
```

Finally we are ready to *use* our classes: the following main program asks the user to select the preferred representation for complex numbers, then inputs two complex values and outputs their sum. The choice of the appropriate implementations of the operations involved exploits the following facts:

- The main program declares variables belonging to the ancestor class and to the two descendant classes: cn1 and cn2 are pointers to ComplexNumber; rpip1 and rpip2 are ComplNumRPIP; marg1 and marg2 are ComplNumMARG.

- cn1 and cn2 are bound to (receive the address of) rpip1 and rpip2 or marg1 and marg2 based on user's choice.

- At this point the methods corresponding to the selected variables are available for cn1 and cn2.

```
************************************************************************
                    Main program 'ComplexNumber'
                    Relevant parts of file CN_MAIN.c
************************************************************************

#include <ComplNumRPIP.h>
#include <ComplNumMARG.h>

main()
{
   typedef  enum  { RPIP, MARG } RepType;
   RepType         Representation;
   ComplexNumber  *cn1, *cn2;
   ComplNumRPIP   rpip1, rpip2;
   ComplNumMARG   marg1, marg2;

   printf("Select the desired representation for complex numbers\n
           0=RealPart and ImaginaryPart\n
           1=Modulus and Argument\n");
   scanf("%d", &Representation);

   if (Representation == 0)
   {
      cn1 = &rpip1;
      cn2 = &rpip2;
   }
   else
   {
      cn1 = &marg1;
      cn2 = &marg2;
   }
                          /*cn1 and cn2 both point to a datum of type
                          ComplNumRPIP or of type ComplNumMARG; this
                          information is only known at execution
                          time.*/

   cn1->ReadCompl();
                          /*if cn1 points to a variable of type
                          ComplNumRPIP the implementation of the
                          function ReadCompl belonging to the class
                          ComplNumRPIP is called; if cn1 points to a
                          variable of type ComplNumMARG the implemen-
                          tation of the function ReadCompl belonging
                          to the class ComplNumMARG is called.*/
```

```
        cn2->ReadCompl();

        cn1->ComplexSum(*cn2);
                            /*the function adds the two numbers pointed
                            to by cn1 and cn2; at the end of the
                            operation, cn1 points to the result.*/

        cn1->WriteCompl();

                            /*the function prints the result pointed to
                            by cn1.*/
    }
```

25.6 Extended example: a comparative case study

To conclude this chapter we develop in some detail a program to calculate the yearly income tax of a number of employees and analyse different versions of it. First, we follow a functional programming style, using the C language, and later we apply an OO approach using C++. The various versions of the program will allow us to compare more readily the two programming approaches.

Let us suppose that we want to collect, for *N* employees, the data relevant for calculating their yearly income tax and that we want to compute the yearly income tax for each employee. Let us suppose that the income tax calculation requires:

- the sum of yearly income from work, from real estate and from unearned income, and
- the sum of deductible allowances, namely family allowances and medical and insurance expenses.

The example is (rather freely) inspired by the Italian tax system which is quite similar to that of other western countries.

25.6.1 Procedural version of yearly tax computation

Let us first develop a procedural version of the program using C. Following a fairly well-consolidated practice, we build a program that consists of the following items:

- the declaration of the data type `Employee` and of a list of employees implemented as an array;
- the declaration of several functions implementing the various operations needed: the computation of the total gross income, the computation of allowed deductions, the computation of several tax components, ...;
- a main program which inputs data relative to each employee and for each one computes and outputs the taxes to be paid by using the previous functions.

```
/* Program CalculateYearlyTax - 1st version: functional approach */

#include <stdio.h>
#include <string.h>

typedef struct  { String   Surname, Name, SocSecNumber, Address;
                  int      FamilyAllowances;
                  int      YearlyIncome, RealEstIncome, UnearnedIncome;
                  int      MedicalExpenses, InsuranceExpenses;
                } Employee;

int        I, N;
Employee   EmplList[100];

int   CalculateTaxable(Employee Empl)
                                /*calculate the yearly taxable income*/
{
...
   Taxable = Empl.YearlyIncome + Empl.RealEstIncome
             + Empl.UnearnedIncome;
   return Taxable;
}

int     ForWork(Employee Empl)
                            /*calculate the tax due for the yearly
                            income from work*/
{
                            /*determines on the basis of the Taxable
                            calculated by the function
                            CalculateTaxable the tax bracket and the
                            constant k1 used further down.*/
...
   TaxWork = k1 * Empl.YearlyIncome;
   return  TaxWork;
}

int     ForRealEst(Employee Empl)
                            /*calculates the tax due for possession of
                            real estate*/
{
...
   TaxRealEst = k2 * Empl.RealEstIncome;
   return TaxRealEst;
}

int     ForUnearned(Employee Empl)
                            /*calculates the tax due for unearned
                            income*/
{
...
   TaxUnearnedInc = k3 * Empl.UnearnedIncome;
   return  TaxUnearnedInc;
}
```

```
int     Allowances(Employee Empl)
                          /*calculates the allowances to which the
                          employee is entitled*/
{
...
   TotAllowances = k4 * Empl.FamilyAllowances + k5 * Empl.MedicalExpenses
                   + k6 * Empl.InsuranceExpenses;
   return TotAllowances;
}

void    CalculateYearlyTax(Employee    Empl)
                                       /*calculates the yearly tax*/
{
...
   YearlyTax = ForWork(Empl) + ForRealEst(Empl) + ForUnearned(Empl)
               - Allowances(Empl);
   printf("Mr/Ms %s %s owes the taxman $ %d\n", Empl.Surname,
           Empl.Name, YearlyTax);
}

***************************************************************************

main()
{
   printf("How many employees are to be considered?");
   scanf("%d", &N);
   for (I = 0; I < N; I++)
   {
                              /*acquisition of the data for the number of
                              employees to be considered*/
      printf("Enter employee's surname");
      scanf("%s", EmplList[I].Surname);
      ...
   }
   for (I = 0; I < N; I++) CalculateYearlyTax(EmplList[I]);
}
```

25.6.2 Object-oriented version of yearly tax computation

Let us now build a C++ program to solve the same problem. It is fairly natural to derive it from the C version along the following lines:

(1) From the structured type used in the C version of the program we derive the definition of the C++ class Employee. All attributes are private and only those methods that extract the information that the external user is interested in are declared as **public**.

(2) In the definition of the class Employee only the prototypes of its methods are given. Their code will appear outside of the class. The function headers

include the name of the class to which the function refers, for example:

```
Employee::CalculateTaxable( )
```

(3) The instructions which in the `main` of the C version allowed the tax information to be acquired are grouped together to form the method `AcquireTaxData`.

(4) The code of each function refers to the attributes of the object it is dealing with, without the need for parameters to be passed to it. This shows the tight link between the attributes of an object and the methods that can manipulate it.

(5) The declaration

```
Employee  EmplList[100]
```

given before `main`, produces 100 instances of objects of the class `Employee` and allows the invocation of the method `CalculateTaxable` using the notation already encountered:

```
EmplList[I].CalculateTaxable( )
```

```
/* Program CalculateYearlyTax - 2nd version: object-oriented approach */

#include <stdio.h>
#include <string.h>

class Employee
{
private:
    String      Surname, Name, SocSecNumber, Address;
    int         FamilyAllowances;
    int         YearlyIncome, RealEstIncome, UnearnedIncome;
    int         MedicalExpenses, InsuranceExpenses;
public:
    void        AcquireTaxData(void);
    int         CalculateTaxable(void);
    int         ForWork(void);
    int         ForRealEst(void);
    int         ForUnearned(void);
    int         Allowances(void);
    void        CalculateYearlyTax(void);
}

void  Employee::AcquireTaxData(void)
{
    printf ("Enter employee's surname");
    scanf ("%s", Surname);
    printf ("Enter employee's name");
    scanf ("%s", Name);
    ...
}

int   Employee::CalculateTaxable(void)
{
    ...
    Taxable = YearlyIncome + RealEstIncome + UnearnedIncome;
    return Taxable;
}
```

```
int   Employee::ForWork(void)
{
                    /*determines on the basis of the Taxable calculated
                    by the function CalculateTaxable the tax bracket and
                    the constant k1 used further down.*/
   ...
   TaxWork = k1 * YearlyIncome;
   return  TaxWork;
}

int   Employee::ForRealEst(void)
{
   ...
   TaxRealEst = k2 * RealEstIncome;
   return TaxRealEst;
}

int   Employee::ForUnearned(void)
{
   ...
   TaxUnearnedInc = k3 * UnearnedIncome;
   return TaxUnearnedInc;
}

int   Employee::Allowances(void)
{
   ...
   TotAllowances = k4 * FamilyAllowances + k5 * MedicalExpenses +
                   k6 * InsuranceExpenses;
   return TotAllowances;
}

void  Employee :: CalculateYearlyTax(void)
{
   ...
   YearlyTax = ForWork( ) + ForRealEst( ) + ForUnearned( ) - Allowances( );
   printf("Mr/Ms %s %s owes the taxman $ %d\n", Surname,
          Name, YearlyTax);
}

**************************************************************************

Employee  EmplList[100];

main()
{
   int      I, N;

   printf("How many employees are to be considered?");
   scanf("%d", &N);
   for (I = 0; I < N; I++) EmplList[I].AcquireTaxData( );
   for (I = 0; I < N; I++) EmplList[I].CalculateYearlyTax( );
}
```

At first glance, a comparison between the two programs could appear at most a matter of 'cosmetics': in the OO version an immediate picture of relevant information is gained by the class definition; it also shows some syntactic conveniences (for example, it is not necessary to pass the main object which is being dealt with as a parameter to the functions). This first comparison, however, does not yet fully show the advantages offered by OO design. These will be better appreciated when we have to adapt our program to new needs.

25.6.3 Modifying the original design

Let us now imagine a tax system liable to frequent changes. Certainly, a well-structured functional program could absorb some conceptual changes caused by changes in the tax rules: for instance, a good modular structure would allow simple and limited modifications of the program in case of variations in the overall formula for calculating the tax to be paid, variations in the constants used, or variations in the criteria which determine the taxable income and the tax bracket.

But let us suppose that the tax system now considers self-employed people as a special category. Suppose that self-employed people pay, during the year, a tax advance which has to be subtracted from the end-of-year tax payment and that they have to pay an additional sum of money for their health cover (assume that employees do not have to pay this contribution themselves, because it is paid by their employer).

The OO program can be easily modified: it is sufficient to define a class SelfEmpl which is a subclass of the previously defined class Employee:

```
class  SelfEmpl: public Employee
{
private:
   int     TaxPaid;                              /*new attribute*/
   int     ForHealth(void);                      /*nNew method*/
public:
   void  CalculateYearlyTax(void);
                            /*the function CalculateYearlyTax is
                            redefined*/
   void  AcquireTaxData(void);
                            /*the function AcquireTaxData is
                            redefined to allow acquisition of the
                            attribute TaxPaid*/
}

int  SelfEmpl::ForHealth(void)
{
   ...
   TaxHealth = k7 *CalculateTaxable( );
   return TaxHealth;
}
```

```
void  SelfEmpl ::CalculateYearlyTax(void)
{
   ...
   YearlyTax = ForWork( ) + ForRealEst( ) + ForUnearned( ) + ForHealth( ) -
             TaxPaid - Allowances( );
   printf("Mr/Ms %s %s owes the taxman $ %d\n", Surname,
          Name, YearlyTax);
}
```

Even more radical changes to the tax system could lead to the definition of one class `Employee` and two subclasses `DependentEmpl` and `SelfEmpl`. The two categories of 'employees' (associated with the two subclasses) might require different calculations for allowances and the end-of-year tax payment, but be identical with regard to defining the overall taxable income, including income from the possession of real estate and unearned income.

The OO program considered above can easily be modified by:

- suitably redefining the classes and their hierarchy (note the choice of attributes and methods);

- allowing subclasses to share their parent class's implementation of methods or to define their own implementation;

- taking advantage wherever possible of previously written code (the shared implementation of the function `CalculateTaxable` is used by both subclasses, the implementation of the function `Allowances` is valid for the subclass `DependentEmpl`, the implementation of the method `AcquireTaxData` in the subclass `SelfEmpl` exploits the implementation of the same method for the superclass `Employee` and enriches it);

- exploiting the late binding allowed by OO programming.

The final result is the following complete program.

```
/* Program CalculateYearlyTax - 3rd version: object-oriented approach */

#include <stdio.h>
#include <string.h>

/*-----Definition of superclass Employee-----*/

class Employee
{
private:
   String          Surname, Name, SocSecNumber, Address;
   int             FamilyAllowances;
   int             YearlyIncome, RealEstIncome, UnearnedIncome;
   int             MedicalExpenses, InsuranceExpenses;
public:
   virtual void    AcquireTaxData(void);
                                /*can be redefined - late binding*/
   int             CalculateTaxable(void);
   int             ForWork(void);
```

```
   int           ForRealEst(void);
   int           ForUnearned(void);
   virtual int   Allowances(void);
                              /*can be redefined - late binding*/
   virtual void  CalculateYearlyTax(void);
                              /*can be redefined - late binding*/
}


/*-----Definition of subclass DependentEmpl-----*/

class DependentEmpl: public Employee
{
public:
   int    Allowances(void);
                         /*the function Allowances is redefined*/
   void   CalculateYearlyTax(void);
                      /*the function CalculateYearlyTax is redefined*/
}


/*-----Definition of subclass SelfEmpl-----*/

class SelfEmpl: public Employee
{
private:
   int        TaxPaid;                       /*added attribute*/
   int        ForHealth(void);               /*added method*/
public:
   void       AcquireTaxData(void);
                      /*the function AcquireTaxData is redefined to allow
                        for the acquisition of the attribute TaxPaid*/
   int        Allowances(void);
                         /*the function Allowances is redefined*/
   void       CalculateYearlyTax(void);
                      /*the function CalculateYearlyTax is redefined*/
}


/*-----Implementation of the functions of Employee-----*/

void Employee::AcquireTaxData(void)
{
   printf("Enter employee's surname");
   scanf("%s", Surname);
   printf("Enter employee's name");
   scanf("%s", Name);
   ...
}


int    Employee::CalculateTaxable(void)
{
   ...
   Taxable = YearlyIncome + RealEstIncome + UnearnedIncome;
   return Taxable;
}
```

```
int     Employee::ForWork(void)
{
                        /*determines on the basis of the Taxable
                        calculated by the function CalculateTaxable
                        the tax bracket and the constant k1 used
                        further down. An appropriate function could
                        perform these actions.*/
   ...
   TaxWork = k1 * YearlyIncome;
   return  TaxWork;
}


int     Employee::ForRealEst(void)
{
   ...
   TaxRealEst = k2 * RealEstIncome;
   return TaxRealEst;
}


int     Employee::ForUnearned(void)
{
   ...
   TaxUnearnedInc = k3 * UnearnedIncome;
   return TaxUnearnedInc;
}


/*-----Implementation of the functions of DependentEmpl------*/

int     DependentEmpl::Allowances(void)
{
   ...
   TotAllowances = k4 * FamilyAllowances + k5 * MedicalExpenses
                   + k6 * InsuranceExpenses;
   return TotAllowances;
}

void    DependentEmpl::CalculateYearlyTax(void)
{
   ...
   YearlyTax = ForWork( ) + ForRealEst( ) + ForUnearned( ) - Allowances( );
   printf("Mr/Ms %s %s owes the taxman $ %d\n", Surname,
          Name, YearlyTax);
}


/*-----Implementation of the functions of SelfEmpl-----*/

int     SelfEmpl::ForHealth(void)
{
   ...
   TaxHealth = k7 * CalculateTaxable( );
   return TaxHealth;
}
```

```
void      SelfEmpl::AcquireTaxData(void)
{
   Employee::AcquireTaxData();
                           /*invokes the inherited implementation then
                           acquires the new attribute*/
   printf("Enter amount of tax already paid");
   scanf("%d", TaxPaid);
}

int       SelfEmpl::Allowances(void)
{
   ...
   TotAllowances = k4 * FamilyAllowances + k5 * MedicalExpenses
                           /*let us suppose that the self-employed
                           cannot subtract insurance payments, unlike
                           employees*/
   return TotAllowances;
}

void      SelfEmpl::CalculateYearlyTax(void)
{
   ...
   YearlyTax = ForWork( ) + ForRealEst( ) + ForUnearned( ) + ForHealth( )
                 - TaxPaid - Allowances( );
   printf("Mr/Ms %s %s owes the taxman $ %d\n", Surname,
           Name, YearlyTax);
}

/*-----main program-----*/

Employee    *EmplList[100];
                           /*vector of pointers to objects of class
                           Employee needed to exploit late binding*/
main()
{
   int        I, N;
   int        Emp;          /* 0 = Self-Employed, 1 = Dependent */

   printf("How many employees are to be considered?");
   scanf("%d", &N);
   for (I = 0; I < N; I++)
   {
      printf("Data to be acquired 0=Self-Employed, 1=Dependent");
      scanf("%d", &Empl);
      if (Empl)
        EmplList[I] = new DependentEmpl;
      else
        EmplList[I] = new SelfEmpl
                     /*the following invocation produces late binding*/
      EmplList[I]->AcquireTaxData();
   }
                   /*the following invocation also produces late binding*/
   for (I = 0; I < N; I++) EmplList[I]->CalculateYearlyTax();
}
```

To summarize, classes, hierarchies, inheritance and late binding play a fundamental role in the modifiability of the OO version of the program. It is not difficult to imagine how to absorb, in the OO version of the program, further changes in the tax model. On the other hand, implementing the same changes in the original functional version of the program would have required us to re-examine the whole project from scratch at every change.

Exercises

25.1 Define in C++ a hierarchy of geometrical figures. They could, for example, be classified into open and closed figures. Both subclasses could be associated with a length attribute which, in the case of closed figures, could be called its perimeter. Among the closed figures we could identify polygons, such as quadrilaterals, pentagons and so on. Among the various attributes and operations associated with the figures we should find surface, intersection, union and so on. The classification could also include figures of different dimensions.

25.2 Define a generic queue of elements in which the class of objects that constitute the queue is parametrized. The operations available for such a generic class must include insertion of an element into the queue, withdrawal of an element (following the FIFO – first in, first out – policy of the queue), inspection of the queue to determine if it is empty or not, and the determination of whether a certain object exists in the queue or not.

25.3 With reference to the hierarchy defined in Exercise 25.1, exemplify the mechanism of late binding supported by the C++ language.

25.4 Complete the definition of the hierarchy of Example 25.2 following the informal definition given therein.

25.5 Modify the hierarchy of Example 25.2 by using late binding to the change payment procedure instead of the redefinition mechanism.

25.6 Modify the last version of the extended example of Section 25.6 so that:

(a) For both `employees` and the `self-employed` the taxable amount is calculated as follows:

```
Taxable = YearlyIncome + IncomeRealEst + UnearnedIncome - Allowances()
```

(b) The calculation of allowances remains unaltered with respect to the last version of the program (employees and self-employed have different allowances).

(c) For employees the yearly tax is calculated as follows:

```
YearlyTax = K1 * CalculateTaxable( )
```

where K1 is a known constant.

(d)   For the self-employed the yearly tax is calculated as follows:

```
YearlyTax = K2 * CalculateTaxable( ) + ForHealth( ) - TaxPaid
```

where K2 is a known constant different from K1.

25.7   Modify the solution of Exercise 25.6 supposing that taxes on income from work are progressive instead of proportional. Reconsider the example in Section 25.6.2, using the same rates and limits as the example and appropriately recoding the `CalculateYearlyTax` function of both subclasses.

*Nonconventional software construction paradigms

26

The architecture of the von Neumann machine has heavily influenced the development of computers for decades. Even today, many machines, from simple PCs to expensive supercomputers, have a structure that is strongly inspired by the one we described in Part II of this book.

With rare exceptions, high-level programming languages, although intended to allow the programmer to describe algorithms independently of the machine on which they are executed, are usually conditioned by the fact that they have to be executed by a computer based on the von Neumann architecture. Indeed, a common characteristic of the algorithms discussed in this book is that they are described as a sequence of elementary processing steps, consisting fundamentally of the transfer of information from and to various memory supports (whether input/output devices, cells of the von Neumann machine, or C language variables).

Memory and its transformations are therefore at the centre of automatic information processing, as a direct consequence of the organization of the von Neumann architecture. However, in the short history of computer science, many criticisms have been levelled at this kind of formulation which, from now on, we will call the *von Neumann style*.

At the root of the criticism is the huge number of errors that have been found in data processing applications of various types (often with disastrous consequences) and the observation that before the advent of the computer, problems were formalized in a very different way from the algorithmic style typical of computer applications. In particular, mathematics has always described a problem as the search for the solution of a system of equations. The critics of the von Neumann style therefore assert that it has shifted attention from the formulation of the problem to the solution mechanism, lowering the level of abstraction and therefore increasing the risk of errors. According to these critics, the potential of electronic data processing is so great that it is possible for the software system designer to express, in classical mathematical style, only the definition of the problem to be solved, leaving the entire task of finding its solution to the machine.

To understand the fundamental difference between the von Neumann style and the style of classical mathematics in formalizing problems, consider the different meanings that the term 'variable' has in the two styles: in traditional mathematics, this term indicates a set of possible values attributable to the variable itself, whereas in most programming languages (both low- and high-level) it indicates a container of information, that is, a memory cell.

The critics of the von Neumann style have therefore advocated programming techniques which, in some way or other, constitute a 'return to the origins' of traditional mathematics. Their proposals led, first, to programming languages radically different from those presented in this text. Consequently, computer architectures, programming environments and, in short, entire computer systems have been subjected to a critical revision that has yielded important innovations in many data processing application sectors.

In this chapter, we briefly discuss two main programming alternatives to the von Neumann style: functional programming and logic programming. We do not make a critical comparison between the traditional von Neumann style and nonconventional styles, but limit ourselves to justifying the choice adopted in this text, which has favoured the von Neumann approach, with the simple assertion that, except in very rare cases, it is the usual approach to introducing the neophyte to computer science.

26.1 An outline of functional programming

Functional programming is based on the fact that every problem can be formulated as a function to be calculated and, consequently, every program is a process that calculates a function. Indeed, all the programs discussed in this book, independently of the programming language used, carry out the task of calculating a function which, given a certain input, yields a certain output. Even when the effect of a computation is to update a database, this can be seen as the calculation of a function from the initial state to the final state of the database.

A functional program has the objective of uniquely defining the function to be calculated without specifying in detail the sequence of operations to be applied to the computer's memory in order to reach that objective.

Functional programming languages, which support the drafting of programs in this style, are therefore based on a classical mathematical formalism adopted for the definition of functions: **recursive functions**. See Chapter 8 for an introduction to recursion in the context of the C language.

Without attempting to give a rigorous and complete definition of a functional language, we shall nevertheless try to convey the basic idea through some examples.

EXAMPLE 26.1

Consider again the following C subroutine for recursively computing the factorial function (Example 8.2):

```
int     RecFact (int   n)
{
   int   result

   if (n == 0) result = 1;
   else result = n * RecFact(n - 1);
   return result;
}
```

It is not difficult to arrive at the following definition of the RecFact function which exhibits a functional style:

```
int     RecFact (int n)
        return (if (n == 0) 1; else (n * RecFact(n - 1)))
```

This definition consists of two parts: the first line defines the domain and range of RecFact using C syntax; the remainder defines the relation that links the independent variable of the function to the dependent variable, using a recursive formulation very similar to that of C.

The fundamental difference between the two formulations is that there is no assignment instruction in the second one: n and RecFact(n) are now two variables in the mathematical sense of the term, whereas in the previous formulation they and result are memory cells that are assigned different values during computation.

EXAMPLE 26.2

Using the same notation inspired by C, but without assignment instructions, we can define the Greatest Common Divisor (GCD) between two positive integers m, n:

```
int     GCD(int m, int n)
return  (if (m == n) n
        else if (m > n) GCD(m - n, n)
             else GCD(m, n - m))
```

In this case also, it is easy to see the similarity to the corresponding recursive formulation of Euclid's algorithm coded in C. Note, however, that whereas recursion is an add-on tool in the von Neumann style, it becomes the main tool in the functional programming style: in a 'pure' functional language, each function is defined using *only* the **if-else** construct and recursion.

EXAMPLE 26.3

Suppose the abstract type `List` has been defined, equipped with the following operations, among others:

- `EmptyList`: takes a list as its argument and returns as its result the value `TRUE` if the list is empty, `FALSE` otherwise.
- `Head`: takes a list as its argument and returns as its result the first element of the list. It returns an undefined value if the list is empty.
- `Tail`: takes a list as its argument and returns as its result the list remaining after deleting the first element of the input list. It returns an undefined value if applied to an empty list.
- `InsertAtTail`: takes as its arguments a list and a value of the type of the elements of the list, and returns as its result the list obtained by appending the second argument to the end of the first.

The following function defines the inversion of a list, using these basic operations:

```
List  Invert (List  L)
   return( if(EmptyList(L)) L
       else InsertAtTail(Invert(Tail(L)), Head(L)))
```

26.2 An outline of logic programming

While a functional program has the objective of defining a *function*, a logic program defines a *relation* between variables using formulas inspired by mathematical logic. A relation is a more general mathematical concept than a function: while a generic function $f(x)$ associates one and only one value with each value of the variable x, the relation $R(x, y)$ combines the values of x and the values of y in any possible way; thus, for each value of x there may be several values of y for which $R(x, y)$ holds and vice versa. Note that the equation $y = f(x)$ is a particular case of a relation.

In this case, too, we limit ourselves to giving an intuitive idea of logic programming via the definition of relations through simple examples.

EXAMPLE 26.4

The following formula defines the relation `Fact(n, m)`: it holds if and only if m is the factorial of n.

$$\text{Fact(n, m)} \quad \textbf{if} \ (n = 0 \ \textbf{and} \ m = 1) \ \textbf{or} \ (n > 0 \ \textbf{and} \ m > 0 \ \textbf{and} \qquad \textbf{(26.1)}$$
$$n = x + 1 \ \textbf{and} \ m = y \ * \ n \ \textbf{and} \ \text{Fact(x, y))}$$

Some comments and explanations will help understand (26.1) better.

First, (26.1), like the previous formulations of factorial, is based on the simple recursive characteristic $n! = n * (n - 1)!$ (for $n > 0$). Since here the objective is to define the conditions under which the relation `Fact(n, m)` holds, we adopt a slightly different syntax notation, aimed at emphasizing the conditions that must hold if we are to be able to deduce the validity of `Fact(n, m)`: *if* what is written to the right of the **if** is valid, *then* we can conclude that what is written to the left is valid. Our notation is close to the syntax of mathematical logic and that of the most popular logic programming language: Prolog.

Second, the fact that (26.1) defines a relation instead of a function considerably increases the generality of logic programming. Indeed, after defining the function `RecFact(n)`, it is possible to 'ask' the machine the value of that function for a certain value of n. In this case, however, it is possible to 'interrogate' the machine in various ways about whether the relation holds. We present some examples, taking further inspiration from the syntax of Prolog:

```
- Fact(3, 6)?
```

This question simply asks the machine if it is true that 6 is the factorial of 3. The machine answers:

```
YES.
```

```
- Fact(3, 8)?
```

The machine's answer to this question is:

```
NO.
```

```
- Fact(3, X)?
```

This question asks the machine to give the values of X such that X is the factorial of 3. Note that, *in general*, there may be different values of X satisfying a relation `Rel(k, X)`, for a given k. It is a particular characteristic of the `Fact` relation that there is only one X such that `Fact(3, X)` is true. The machine's answer to this question is:

```
YES: X = 6.
```

```
- Fact(X, 6)?
```

This question asks the machine to give the values of X such that 6 is the factorial of X. In this case, the relation is used in the reverse sense, that is, in such a way that the reverse function of factorial is calculated. The machine answers:

```
YES: X = 3.
```

```
- Fact(X, Y)?
```

This question asks the machine for the pairs `<X, Y>` such that Y is the factorial of X. The machine gives the following, *conceptually infinite* answer to this question:

```
YES: X = 0, Y = 1; X = 1, Y = 1; X = 2, Y = 2; X = 3, Y = 6; ...
```

EXAMPLE 26.5

The following formula defines the relation GCD(n, m, gcd): it holds if and only if GCD is the greatest common divisor of n and m.

```
GCD(n, m, gcd)   if (n = m and m = gcd) or
              (n > 0 and m > n and x = m − n and GCD(n, x, gcd)) or
              (n > 0 and n > m and x = n − m and GCD(x, m, gcd))
```

On the basis of this formula, the machine would answer the questions listed below in the following way:

- GCD(2, 3, 1)?
  YES

- GCD(2, 3, 4)?
  NO

- GCD(6, 9, X)?
  YES: X = 3

- GCD(6, X, 3)?
  YES: X = 3; X = 9; X = 15; X = 21; ...

A logic program can consist not just of a single formula, but also of a combination (logical 'and') of several formulas. Some may lack the keyword **if** and the part that follows it. In this case, the assertions have no conditions and are therefore also called *facts*. The following examples briefly illustrate their use.

EXAMPLE 26.6

The combination of the facts and the formula given in Table 26.1 allows a 'logic machine' to answer the following questions as indicated:

- mortal(hugh)?
    YES

- mortal(socrates)?
    YES

- mortal(Y)
    YES: Y = hugh; Y = stefano; Y = carla; Y = socrates

- mortal(aristotle)
  NO

Table 26.1 A combination of facts and logical formulas about properties of human beings.

```
human(hugh);
human(stefano);
human(carla);
human(socrates);
mortal (X) if human (X)
```

We adopt the Prolog convention that identifiers of constant non-numeric values begin with a lowercase letter, and those of variables begin with a capital.

Furthermore, observe that the negative answer to the last question derives from the fact that no information has been given to the machine for the constant aristotle. In this case, since it cannot deduce the feature mortal(aristotle) from its own 'knowledge' the machine answers 'NO'.

EXAMPLE 26.7

The combination of facts and formulas given in Table 26.2 allows a 'logic machine' to answer the following questions as indicated:

- distance(bologna, rome, D)?
    YES: D = 400

- distance(milan, venice, X)
    NO

- distance(milan, rome, D)?
    YES: D = 500; D = 600

Table 26.2 A combination of facts and logical formulas about geographic properties.

```
distance(milan, rome, 500);
distance(milan, bologna, 200);
distance(bologna, florence, 100);
distance(florence, rome, 300);
distance(X, Y, D) if (distance(X, W, D1) and distance(W, Y, D2)
                                         and D = D1 + D2)
```

Note that the machine gives two positive answers to the last question: for the first, it directly finds the fact that milan and rome are 500 (km) apart. However, it is also capable of independently constructing the distance 600 as the sum of the three parts 200, 100 and 300 km, respectively. Obviously, the machine has no information that would allow it to conclude that it is not possible for the distance between two towns to have more than one value. Indeed, the assertions in Table 26.2 must be interpreted as distances by road, not as absolute distances.

The evolution of computer science

27

Computer science is a constantly evolving discipline that increasingly influences every aspect of our individual lives and of our society. It is therefore not easy, even for specialists in the field, to evaluate the impact that its development has already had on everyday life, and even more difficult to foresee its future developments and their consequences. Indeed, the history of computer science is full of forecasts that turned out to be wrong, so we do not wish to take any risk by predicting the future.

This chapter aims at completing the reader's computer science education by giving a brief historical retrospective of the evolution of computer science and a short analysis of how it currently influences and is influenced by the organization of our society.

The chapter is divided into two main sections: the first presents a historical outline of the evolution of computer science; the second analyses the impact of this discipline on the organization of modern society.

27.1 A brief history of computer science

The history of computer science is characterized by the sheer speed at which it has taken place; it is therefore rather difficult to put its development into a well-organized framework. As a first approximation, it is possible to subdivide the evolutionary phases of computer science into decades, starting from the 1950s and ending with the 1990s. It is also useful to take into account three perspectives from which the phenomenon should be observed:

- the evolution of the concepts, methods and theoretical models that are the foundation of the discipline;
- the evolution of tools, including not only the hardware (the computer, the communication networks, input/output devices, ...) but also the software

613

(programming languages, compilers, editors, debuggers, development tools for analysis, specification and design, ...);

• the evolution of computer science applications of all types.

Using decades as staging posts introduces a certain artificiality: the roots of a phenomenon that becomes important in a certain period almost always have to be sought in earlier, sometimes even remote periods; but we cannot go any deeper into this analysis.

27.1.1 The prehistory of computer science

It is traditional and natural to assume that computer science began with the advent of its fundamental tool, the computer, which, in the form given it by von Neumann and other contemporary pioneers, was produced at the end of the Second World War.

However, since computer science is also the discipline of rigorous and precise processing of information, it is obvious that it has much deeper roots in the history of human thought: elements of computer science can be found in mathematics (in particular, in arithmetic) and also in logic (especially Aristotelian logic).

The first aim of arithmetic is to represent numerical information and find methods for processing it: executing operations. From this point of view, it is very interesting to compare the Greek and Roman number systems with the method used by the Arabs, which is still used by us today. We have also seen in Chapter 3 the richness, in terms of computer science insight, of Euclid's algorithm for calculating the greatest common divisor of two numbers.

Note also that the famous Aristotelian syllogism 'All humans are mortal, Socrates is a human, therefore Socrates is mortal' is a form of application of computer science rules that allow us to arrive at the conclusion 'Socrates is mortal', starting from the two preceding hypotheses. Thus, it is easy to identify elements of computer science in the very much longer history of mathematics.

Such elements assume sharper outlines from the end of the nineteenth century when Giuseppe Peano constructed his axiomatization of arithmetic (thus contributing to the foundations of modern mathematical logic) and George Boole developed the algebra that bears his name (and that later constituted the mathematical foundation of digital technology).

Mathematical logic and the theory of computation, which is closely related to mathematical logic, received a considerable boost in the early twentieth century (especially in the 1930s). It is surprising how, at almost the same time, pioneers such as Alonzo Church, Alan Turing, Kurt Gödel, Andrei Andreevich Markov and Stephen Cole Kleene, well before automatic computation became a reality, supplied an extremely precise characterization of it, and also identified its ultimate limits.

Each of these scientists arrived in an autonomous and original manner at a precise and abstract formulation of the concept of the algorithm, using a special mathematical notation or an abstract model of a calculator. We would like to mention particularly the Turing machine and Church's thesis.

The **Turing machine** is, perhaps, the simplest and most fascinating model of a computer. A Turing machine consists of two different memory supports:

- The first memory support is an infinite **tape**, partitioned into cells similar to those of the von Neumann machine, but each cell contains even more elementary information, namely a **single symbol** from a finite alphabet (such as a letter of the English alphabet or a decimal digit). Furthermore, the tape functions as the *data input support* (thus, it contains data to be processed which was recorded before the beginning of the computation), as the *memory support* (thus, it is possible not only to read the cells but also to change their contents), and as the *output support* (the result of the computation is part of what remains on the tape when execution terminates).

- The second memory support is finite and consists of a single cell that contains an element of a finite set, called the **state** in the jargon.

A Turing machine operation:

- reads a datum from the tape by means of a reading head similar to that of the von Neumann machine;

- reads its state;

and on the basis of the two readings:

- writes a new symbol to the tape in lieu of the one read (there is nothing to prevent the same symbol as before being written);

- writes a new symbol into the state cell (in other words, changes state);

- moves the read/write head one position to the right (R) or left (L), or leaves it where it is (N – for 'none').

Alternatively, the machine may not execute any further movement, that is, it **halts**: at this point, computation is terminated. Figure 27.1 gives an intuitive idea of how a Turing machine works.

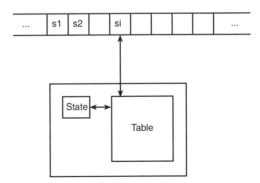

Figure 27.1   The Turing machine.

State \ s	–	l
s1	<l,s2,R>	<l,s1,R>
s2		

Figure 27.2 The table of a Turing machine for the computation of $n + 1$ coded in unary.

The language of the Turing machine is so simple that a program is simply a rectangular table in which the rows indicate the symbols that can be read from the tape, the columns indicate the possible states, and the cells indicate the move to be executed according to the symbol read and the state: the move is described by the three elements <symbol to be written to the tape, new state, movement of head (R, L, N)>; an empty cell indicates that the machine must stop.

Figure 27.2 describes, as an example, a simple machine whose tape alphabet consists of just two symbols: 'l' and '_', and whose set of states is constituted by the two states s1 and s2. Assuming that initially the state is s1, the tape contains a number n of consecutive 'l' with all other cells containing '_'[1], and the head is positioned on the first bar to the left. Then, at the end of the computation, there are $n + 1$ bars on the tape; in other words, the machine calculates $n + 1$ from n on the basis of a unary encoding.

Now, it can be rigorously proved that a Turing machine, in all its simplicity, is *capable of executing all the algorithms that can be executed by any existing computer*. Moreover, **Church's thesis** states that there is no more powerful computing architecture than the Turing machine and other equivalent formalisms; in other words, the class of problems that can be solved by algorithms is not influenced by the means of calculation adopted. Conceptually, if a problem can be solved by a modern supercomputer, it can also be solved by a simple PC, or even by the most modest Turing machine.

The founders of the theory of computation did not limit themselves to formalizing, in a simple and precise way, the concept of automatic calculation: they also identified its ultimate limits, showing that there is a vast category of problems that cannot and will never be solved by a mechanical instrument. The most representative element of this category is the **halt problem** of the Turing machine: 'Given a generic Turing machine and a generic input supplied to it, is it possible to establish whether its computation, applied to the input, will terminate in a finite time or will never terminate at all?' Now, the theory of computation shows that this question cannot be answered by means of an algorithm.

The impact of this statement goes much further than the mathematical formulation of the Turing machine halt problem: in fact, an immediate consequence

---

[1] In the theory of the Turing machine it is normal practice that one symbol may appear an infinite number of times on the tape: very naturally, this symbol is called 'blank' or 'space'.

is the impossibility of solving automatically a vast category of problems of practical interest, such as the termination of real programs written in any programming language, or their correctness, their equivalence and so on[2].

From the beginning, scientists have been tempted to associate algorithms for processing (typically numerical) information with instruments capable of executing those algorithms mechanically. The prototypes realized by Blaise Pascal and improved by Gottfried Leibniz in the seventeenth century are well known: they were mechanical calculators in the literal sense of the term, capable of executing arithmetic operations.

In the nineteenth century, Charles Babbage constructed the first calculator capable – potentially – of executing complex calculations (for astronomical applications). It made use of the recent availability of the steam engine, but its complexity undermined its reliability and made its use impossible in practice.

At the beginning of the twentieth century, the first electromechanical calculators were developed employing the electronic technology based on thermionic valves. Finally, in 1946, driven by the military requirements dictated by the Second World War (precisely, by the necessity of executing ballistic calculations in real time), John von Neumann developed the ENIAC (Electronic Numerical Integrator and Computer). ENIAC is considered to be the first modern computer and therefore forms the borderline between the prehistory and the history of computer science.

From the beginning, human thought did not limit itself to investigating the fundamental principles of automatic calculation and producing mechanisms capable of getting them to work, but has also tried to outline possible applications beyond the natural ones of numerical processing. It is therefore not surprising that some themes and challenges typical of artificial intelligence were already being addressed in the prehistory of computer science.

Among these, it is worth looking at the exciting **Turing test,** which is still adopted today, in spite of all its controversial aspects, as a typical 'test bed' for artificial intelligence. Without attempting to define the terms 'intelligence' or 'artificial intelligence', Turing proposed the following experiment to verify whether a machine had achieved 'intelligent behaviour': Let a person communicate with other interlocutors without specifying whether these are persons or machines. If the subject of the experiment cannot determine whether he/she is communicating with a human or mechanical interlocutor, then the machine is 'intelligent'.

Many studies of a technical and philosophical character would be needed to judge correctly this experiment and the results it has produced on the many occasions it has been carried out. Let us limit ourselves to admiring Turing's foresight, since he conceived the experiment long before it could be realized.

---

[2] The reader should not be worried at the impossibility of giving an algorithmic solution to certain problems. In reality, when an 'unsolvable' problem is important, it is often possible to find particular cases which determine acceptable solutions at application level. In other cases, support tools can be constructed which, although they do not solve the problem automatically, can facilitate the human analysis of the problem, complementing the user's intuition and experience. Such tools are often called 'semi-automatic'. It is important, however, to understand the limits of approximate or partial solutions in each case.

In conclusion, the prehistory of computer science shows that many of its principles have long been present in the minds of its pioneers, and that, from the beginning, its pioneers never neglected the importance of constructing instruments and investigating their application potential in all sectors of human knowledge.

27.1.2 Computer science in the 1950s

The history of computer science in its first decade – the 1950s – was dominated by the development of the computer itself, with the aim of improving its power in its principal application: the execution of a huge amount of numerical computations for scientific processing.

In order to achieve this goal, computers reached enormous dimensions, requiring a great deal of space, which led to the construction of special computer centres. A physical limit to the development of these first generation machines was imposed by the electronic valve technology which limited their size and reliability. Note that the average lifetime of a valve is relatively low; therefore, in a system containing a very large number of these components, the probability of a failure was extremely high.

As the use of computers became more widespread, the problem of the language in which to program them arose, as the inconvenience of programming in machine language became evident quickly.

Thus, assembler languages and their translators which allowed the use of symbolic identifiers were developed. Also, users wanted a language that would allow them to program at a higher level, more closely connected to the description of the problem (at that time mainly of a mathematical nature) than to the sequence of operations executed by the machine. The challenge was met by the Fortran language and its first compilers which emerged towards the end of the decade.

As we have said, for the whole decade, the main application of automatic computation was the processing of numerical data. There was, however, no lack of stimuli relating to the ever-fascinating challenge of artificial intelligence. Among these, particular attention was devoted to the problem of automatic translation of natural languages. This problem, which was also originally generated by wartime requirements, had initially been underrated, as it seemed that it could be reduced to consulting a dictionary automatically, but in reality it implied the much more difficult task of understanding the natural language.

This stimulated the development of new theoretical models aimed at formalizing the description of languages, whether natural or artificial. Independently of one another, Noam Chomsky (one of the fathers of mathematical linguistics) and John Backus (one of the developers of the first Fortran compilers), together with Peter Naur, invented the fundamental model of context-free grammar, also called Backus–Naur Form (BNF).

Towards the end of the decade, attention began to focus on other types of application. Among these, the different forms of processing stimulated by artificial intelligence research (the official introduction of this term occurred between the

1950s and 1960s) showed the necessity of handling symbolic information and led to the advent of Lisp. In a completely different way, requirements began to emerge for the treatment of management-type information, which led to the development of Cobol.

In conclusion, the development of this decade is characterized by the stimulus to improve the tools (first hardware, then software) required by the applications of the time, which were still limited but already quite diversified.

27.1.3 Computer science in the 1960s

The developments during the 1960s were extremely important from all three points of view.

The theoretical and conceptual study of the principles and models of computer science was approached in a systematic way. Initially, the theory of automata and the theory of formal languages developed vigorously, principally motivated by the wish to rationalize and optimize both the synthesis of hardware circuits and the construction of compilers. In both sectors, results of great conceptual importance and practical impact were achieved.

Later, attention turned to design methods, since it was discovered that an approach based on the inventiveness of a single person became inadequate when projects of vast dimensions had to be dealt with[3]. This requirement became particularly evident in the software sector and led to the advent of software engineering, a concept opposed to but not excluding the art of programming. Among the first results of the new discipline we find the identification of rigorous methods of programming which were given the name 'structured programming'.

The computer itself received a considerable impetus from the advent of semiconductor technology, initially using discrete components, then integrated circuits. This allowed both a reduction in the physical size of the computer and an increase in its reliability.

Programming languages increased considerably in number, but did not have great success, so that most of them were abandoned without succeeding in supplanting the already popular Fortran and Cobol. We would like to mention Algol 60 (in reality conceived in the previous decade) for the influence it had on many other later languages, including Pascal, defined and realized by Niklaus Wirth at the end of the decade, developed in an academic context with didactic aims.

Operating systems were developed in this period. Initially, the machine was handled directly by the user who was also its programmer and operator. In addition to preparing the programs, the user also loaded them into the machine and ran them.

With the increase in power of the machines, the problem of how to manage them arose; it was initially solved outside the machine by means of booking sheets and similar mechanisms. Very quickly, however, people realized the inefficiency of

---

[3] The culmination of the pioneer era of computer science is undoubtedly represented by Donald Knuth's monumental work, *The Art of Computer Programming*.

such a system, and began to understand how the computer could be used to manage itself: the operating system was thus developed as an automatic substitute for the operator.

The first operating systems were concerned only with organizing the execution of programs in the usual sequence: input of the program, compilation, loading and execution; in those days, the main input was packs of punched cards, easily loaded into the mechanical card reader. In this way, a program was executed immediately after the end of the preceding one (batch processing).

Subsequently, with the increase in I/O operations and, in general, in the interaction with the environment, the considerable amount of time lost by the machine became evident, caused by it having to wait for relatively slow operations compared to the speed of the CPU. This led to the concept of multitasking, that is, the simultaneous servicing of several tasks initiated by different users, thus introducing for the first time the concept of parallel processing (at least at logical level) and laying the foundations for the later introduction of physical parallelism and distributed processing.

On the application side, management applications became the principal sector of interest, owing to the considerable economic impact of automation, especially in the banking sector. This explosion led to the development of Database Management Systems (DBMS), software systems specifically designed for managing data.

Less conventional applications, such as artificial intelligence, continued to receive attention, largely in an academic context.

27.1.4 Computer science in the 1970s

From a conceptual point of view, the 1970s were characterized by close attention to design methods, in both hardware and software. While hardware achieved a good level of consolidation and success, owing to the design of integrated circuits, software engineering continued (and still continues) to leave the experts dissatisfied.

The more exquisitely theoretical elements of computer science experienced a rapid obsolescence: results found practical application in only a very few cases, which contributed to creating a certain lack of confidence in theoretical computer science. The traditional theory of automata and of formal languages was joined by various formal methods aimed at a more rigorous definition of the goals of a data processing product and a more reliable verification of its correctness. The practical usefulness of the resulting formal methods has never fully convinced the majority of experts and is still the object of fiery debates today.

Computer hardware continued to be improved in quite a surprising way, thanks to the enormous progress of integrated circuit technology. These improvements allowed the construction of machines of considerable power and ever-reducing size and cost, leading at the end of the 1970s to the advent of the **personal computer**. This had the natural consequence of enlarging the size of the data processing market and stimulating very many new applications. Together with the personal computer, a few personal productivity tools also became available.

At the same time, great progress was made in the telecommunications sector, permitting the transmission of data in a relatively limited time even over great distances. This laid the foundation for the construction of computer networks of various sizes.

Programming languages continued to experience obstacles and showed considerable inertia, mainly due to the huge financial investments in the software produced in the preceding years. The advent of C certainly deserves mention. C had been designed initially in close connection with the development of the UNIX operating system, but it spread rapidly into several application fields. Together with Pascal, it is one of the few successful products that originated in the research environment. Ada is the result of an initiative launched by the American Department of Defense in order to obtain for its own use a language more consistent with the requirements of modern software development. Notwithstanding the huge effort invested, it is still not clear even now whether and to what extent Ada has achieved success.

In this decade, development support tools started to become popular, for both hardware and software. In particular, the simple compiler began to be integrated with tools such as syntax-driven editors and debuggers. Also, a considerable contribution was made by UNIX, which provided a widely used platform on which new tools, sometimes just in the form of prototypes, were installed and made available to a vast public.

Applications began to go beyond the traditional sectors in a significant way, particularly because of the availability of personal tools and the possibility of accessing information distributed over vast geographic territories. In a certain sense, computer science has often inverted the saying 'Necessity is the mother of invention': sometimes, the availability of new tools has forced people to consider how to exploit them to their best advantage.

At the other extreme, the availability of enormous computing power produced supercomputers and stimulated attempts to transfer the ideas and ambitions of artificial intelligence to the real world. Among such initiatives, the so-called 'Fifth Generation Project' deserves to be mentioned; this was a project launched in Japan at the end of the decade and developed at the beginning of the next, with particular emphasis on deduction and natural language understanding. It is doubtful, however, whether the initiative has reached its objectives.

27.1.5 Computer science in the 1980s

Developments during the 1980s were substantially a confirmation and continuation of the evolution of the previous decade. Design methods in the various sectors continued to receive much attention and, especially in the software sector, a great many new methods were proposed. But this has to be seen as an index of substantial dissatisfaction with the state of the art and a persistent request for improvement. Methods based on formal approaches continued to be debated without the parties ever converging to a consolidated position.

New attention was focused on the theoretical computer science sector nearest to the traditional theory of computation, particularly because of interest in the complexity of calculation. Beyond the still open challenge of the computational treatability of certain algorithms, a considerable impetus for these problems came from the necessity of fully understanding the potential of parallel and distributed processing.

Development tools were enriched by a vast range which, according to their supporters, should allow each phase of both hardware and software development to be supported. The tools of hardware technology continued their growth, opening up new horizons of multimedia and distributed processing on various levels.

The programming languages sector saw the success of object-oriented languages as the fundamental tools for the development of higher-quality software, especially in terms of reliability and reusability. As often happens, it has to be observed that the cultural roots of object orientation are far older (the first object-oriented language is Simula 67 which owes its name to the year in which it was realized), but its final success or failure will be seen only in the future: object-oriented languages, too, are still the object of debate, although they have become widespread, especially C++.

The applications sector saw the definitive success of personal and distributed data processing. A deeper integration of computers and communication technology was developed, yielding a new discipline called telematics and the success of the client–server model of computation, especially for data management applications. There was also a growth in the level, at least at industrial level, of the expectations connected with artificial intelligence; we mention the success of expert systems capable of 'intelligent' behaviour in limited domains of expertise. Finally, there was a massive spread in data processing in the control of all kinds of industrial processes; from robotization of assembly lines to the control of whole plants, and to 'embedded' applications of computers, such as the electronic control centres in cars, planes, household appliances, and so on.

27.1.6 Computer science in the early 1990s

The early 1990s have seen the spread of computer science culture in society, encouraged by the falling costs and increasing performance of personal computers and by the growth of the Internet as a universal commodity. More than ever before, this era is characterized by the introduction, immediate popularity and rapid obsolescence of new hardware and software products. Among the emerging technologies, we quote the new Intel Pentium processor, the Windows 95 and Windows NT operating systems, the World Wide Web (WWW) technology on the Internet (and the development of tools for navigating the Internet, such as the Netscape browser) and the new programming language Java.

In spite of its continuous evolution and expansion, in the 1990s computer science has felt, for the first time, the repercussions of a worldwide economic crisis, especially in the personal computer sector (even though this sector has wide scope for future development). Without pretending to explain phenomena that are often obscure even to specialists, we observe that the origin of the crisis probably lies in the excessive speed of evolution of the technology. In the same way that it created problems for the designers of applications, causing an ever-increasing backlog of unsatisfied requests, this has also made end users insecure, because they have too often found themselves with a tool that is already obsolete when they buy it.

The past history of computer science makes us want to avoid the hazard of forecasting its future development: too often, even extremely competent forecasts have turned out to be completely unfounded. We quote the following facts as examples:

- At the dawn of the discipline, computer science was not thought to be economically viable, because a dozen of the computers then available would saturate the market. The analysis was correct with respect to the computing requirements that had been taken into account, but it neglected the fact that a greater availability of computers would lead to increased expectations and needs.

- Some expectations in the field of artificial intelligence (natural language understanding, 'the machine overtakes man') have turned out to be very difficult to pursue. (However, the distance between natural and artificial intelligence in the most classic battlefield of human–computer competition, namely the game of chess, is narrowing. In fact, it has now reached the point where artificial intelligence has overtaken its natural rival, with the defeat of the world's chess champion by Big Blue.)

- Repeated and frequent triumphalist forecasts about the success of new methods or languages have often not come true, and such methods and languages have quickly gone out of fashion.

- It has always been difficult to define and impose standards of any kind. There are many standards but they do not completely succeed in solving the problems of compatibility between computer systems.

This last point deserves a slightly deeper analysis. The creation and acceptance of standards is generally a symptom of the need for organizational coordination and of the maturity and stability of a technology. Observe, for example, how important it is that electricity is distributed with a standard voltage throughout a region, and how many disadvantages are created by the difference in these standards between America and Europe.

In the case of computer science, there is without doubt a great need for standards in many sectors (from programming languages to operating systems, from database languages to communication protocols), but rarely have efficient standards been defined. Often, the standards proposed by the relevant bodies (for example, by ISO: International Organization for Standardization) have not been adhered to, whereas 'de facto standards', such as HTML or Windows, have imposed themselves: often these are only partially standardized, and different versions that are not always entirely compatible with each other are produced.

Among the standards that can claim a certain success, we would like to quote the UNIX operating system, the ISO-OSI reference model (OSI is the acronym of Open Systems Interconnection), which defines a general structure for communication protocols, and the SQL database query language.

27.2 The impact of computer science on individuals and society

The evolution of computer science has had extraordinary effects on society, particularly because of the exponential growth of computer power. We have observed that many of the services available today were conceptually possible using the first computers (one could even imagine them being performed by a Turing machine), but in practice they became available only recently, when computers and communication technology were able to offer the necessary computing and communication power.

The principal effect of this technological revolution is that, whereas in the past computer science was exclusively a science for a few experts and therefore caused technical problems only for this 'small world', today it touches everyone, whether individually or as the member of various social groups (such as banks, public bodies or sports clubs). This fact has consequences that are not foreseen or well understood, and generates serious technical, organizational and social problems.

In this section, we analyse some of the main problems created by the rapid evolution of computer science and its applications.

27.2.1 Computers and safety

Today, 'embedded' applications include computerized components in nearly every type of machinery: from household appliances to cars, from aeroplanes to industrial plant. Many of these are highly critical for the safety of human beings: consider not only the consequences of an aeroplane crash or a nuclear power plant disaster, but also a failure in a car's ABS brake system.

Unfortunately, computer products have not yet reached the level of reliability of other engineering products. In particular, as we have emphasized in this book, software is often full of errors, even after being verified, installed and used in the field for some time.

This is due to a certain lack of ability, not only technical, to control the evolution of computer products and the resulting complexity of new requests for application software. Certainly, over the years, software production techniques have greatly improved, but not fast enough to manage the increased complexity of applications and the enormous power of computers. Perhaps, at the root of the problem, there is also a certain lack of organizational capacity (insofar as computer systems have a great impact on the organization of work), and an underestimation of the risks connected with certain applications and therefore insufficient resources dedicated to them. For example, we saw in Chapter 23 that software verification can be far more reliable if it is carried out systematically and with the aid of formal methods. This, however, entails high costs which are rarely included within the software manufacturers' budgets. This fact is a signal that safety problems must also be approached at an ethical and organizational level.

27.2.2 **Computers and security**

Very early in its evolution, computer science had a great economic and social impact, not only with respect to the costs and the benefits of computers, but also with respect to the importance of the information they could manage. The first case of this kind was banking applications. Here, the first problem is the security of the information managed, since there must be rigorous control over who has the right to access and modify data. Compare, for example, the limited operations that a customer can carry out at a bank cash dispenser with the greater discretion and complexity of the operations that an employee of the same bank can carry out inside the office.

The problem of security has become, with the passing of time, ever more critical, owing to distributed data processing. As we have seen, today practically every computer in the world can be connected to any other computer. This brings the benefits we have already mentioned: the possibility, for example, of being able to consult the most well-equipped library in the world on a certain subject, from one's own home. However, connections to the Internet of critical centres, such as bank or military computer systems, introduce a higher risk of incurring damage or fraud. Although in principle safety-critical systems should be well protected by authentication and authorization mechanisms – even when they are accessible via a network – in practice the possibility of intruders succeeding in connecting to these protected systems is quite high. Malicious users accessing protected data can cause serious damage. This shows the general weakness of computer systems with regard to the security requirements they are supposed to meet.

From a technological point of view, the problem can again be blamed on the inadequacy of the development of design techniques in the evolution of applications. In particular, the construction of wide area telecommunication networks was initially motivated by the need for cooperation: various scientists and professionals wanted to share their wealth of knowledge. Also, the UNIX operating system, which has played a major role in the development of large distributed systems, was originally intended to facilitate cooperation between its users rather than their protection from one another. The attempt to do something about this by subsequently introducing protection mechanisms into both networks and operating systems has obviously been less effective in achieving adequate security compared to what could have been achieved if the security problem had been properly addressed from the beginning.

However, there is no sense in tackling the problem exclusively from a technical viewpoint, pretending that totally impenetrable computer plants can be constructed:

there is always a margin of risk in the use of any security device and often, unfortunately, malefactors find themselves in an advantageous position vis-à-vis law-abiding citizens. Think, for example, of the use of cars, a modern convenience that can change into a social danger if badly used. The problem has social and ethical aspects: sometimes, drawbacks accrue both to the individual and to society from the use (and abuse) of tools conceived to increase the convenience and quality of life.

For example, electronic mail has contributed to exceptional improvements in the efficiency of interpersonal communication, replacing both traditional mail and phone calls, and often allowing expensive meetings to be avoided. On the other hand, it has also contributed to a further increase in the circulation of useless and disturbing information ('electronic junk'). Similarly, the possibility of connecting via a modem, from any private site, to any computer system has also reduced the 'private sphere' of the individual.

Once again, the necessity of controlling the results of technological evolution from a social point of view becomes apparent.

27.2.3 Computers and ethics

As is already evident from the previous sections, while the rapid evolution of computer science meant that it gradually left the restricted and 'protected' context of scientific research and entered ever-wider social classes, problems of social organization and therefore of law have emerged which often have not been approached and solved in a timely manner.

Let us briefly examine the main problems.

(1) *Technical competence and responsibility caused by malfunctioning*
    We have already seen that much, sometimes serious, damage to persons and things has occurred because of the malfunctioning of data processing components; this malfunctioning is often caused by design errors. Unlike standard practice in other sectors of engineering, the person or institution responsible for the error is seldom called to account, even assuming that those responsible can be found.

    Society does not provide the defences traditionally found in other sectors:

    (a) Preventively, by means of *verification* and *certification* of the capabilities of the designers (for example, via special registers of chartered designers).

    (b) When a product is released, by means of *warranties*: nobody would buy a car today without an adequate warranty, but the release of any software product is almost always accompanied by a 'disclaimer' that explicitly disclaims any responsibility for damage caused by malfunctioning of the product.

    Just recently, initiatives have been taken to certify the professionalism of an organization engaged in the production of software. One of the most important is the Software Engineering Institute at Carnegie Mellon University which set itself the goal of defining quality standards in the software production process and of awarding certificates to those that meet the standards. Similar initiatives concerning quality and its certification are undertaken by the ISO.

(2) *Protection of confidential information*
This problem has already been mentioned in the previous section; confidential information concerning a person's clinical records, economic situation, even grades at school, should not be used improperly by organizations or individuals (that is, for uses other than those for which such information is collected). Let us add that very often society has found itself unprepared not only to identify the guilty but also to apply the appropriate sanctions.

Also note that, even when the above-mentioned information is used in a perfectly legal way by the public authorities concerned, data processing poses difficult regulatory problems. For example, the collection of data on the behaviour of citizens could be useful in preventing illegal behaviour such as tax evasion. The same information, however, could violate citizens' civil liberties.

(3) *Culpable or malicious damage to someone else's data or to public data*
This problem has technical aspects similar to the previous one. The classic example is the virus, a deliberately constructed software defect which propagates itself on all systems with which it comes into contact. Once again, the vast number of network connections has the unpleasant effect of enormously amplifying the damage caused by this problem. What is surprising and should make one think is the fact that, in many cases, this damage is inflicted 'for fun'.

(4) *Copyright protection*
The dizzying growth of the data processing market and, above all, its 'invasion' of the individual sphere has posed serious problems in protecting the intellectual property invested in products. It is clear that the problems of managing and protecting the intellectual property of a library of scientific programs in a big university computer centre are quite different from those involving the intellectual property of software tools, such as word processors and spreadsheets, developed by a software producer in order to earn money from sales and royalties. In the latter case, mass production and distribution runs the risk of illegal copying.

Similar problems occur when a designer leaves a company and reuses the results of the work carried out there; who is the owner of these results, the designer or the company? It is clear that the intangible nature of software makes it much more difficult to answer such a question than in other cases: software is clearly not just the code, but also the design that precedes it.

For these reasons, software has more recently been likened to the products of the mind, like a piece of art or a book, rather than to industrial goods. Consequently, it is better protected by copyright than by patents.

As with other copyright-protected objects, however, it is very easy to infringe the law: copying a disk is as easy as photocopying a book. Attempts to prevent the infringement of the law by technical means turned out to be inadequate: software protection can easily be overcome, and often people pride themselves on having succeeded in breaking it.

All the above observations show that it is totally insufficient to tackle certain problems solely from a technical angle and not from a legal and ethical point of view as well: *first and foremost, the impact of computer science on the individual and on social life raises ethical problems.*

Too often we hear about individuals boasting of their ability to break into their own company's or someone else's computer security system. Instead of being publicly denigrated within their companies or social groups, these individuals are often highly regarded. Similarly, we hear of people who are proud of their success in accessing or copying protected information: the intellectual challenge prevails over the morals of people who in other contexts exhibit perfectly normal behaviour. Too often, individuals who would never dream of picking someone else's pocket have no scruples about copying books and disks.

The new term 'hacker' has been invented to denote computer experts who are capable of very sophisticated interaction with computer systems, but in many cases are not too careful about possessing the appropriate rights to such interaction. It must be emphasized that technical ability should never be confused with fraud.

As in all other areas of social life, it is impossible to solve problems solely by technology or by applying punitive laws: above all, awareness must be created in the citizen. In conclusion, mastering a computer system is not the only objective of a good education in computer science; society (and in particular the population of students and instructors of computer science, to whom this book is dedicated) also needs a specific awareness of the ethical and social problems raised by computer technology.

Further reading

Interested readers can complement the basic notions given in this text by selected reading from the huge amount of literature devoted to computer science. Here, we provide a few suggestions covering all the main topics addressed by this book.

Introductory books

As we stated in the preface, there are plenty of introductory texts on computer science: in general they are organized very differently.

Most introductory texts are still strongly biased towards programming. Some of them are also deeply committed to their choice of 'carrier' programming language. For instance, Roberts (1995) is based on C whereas Pinson *et al.* (1987) is based on Modula-2.

Other books tend to de-emphasize programming language dependence, though only a few of them go to the extreme position of not using any 'real' language at all and replacing it with suitable 'pseudocode'. For instance Pratt (1990) pays most attention to software design issues, by going deeper into topics that are traditionally taught in more advanced software engineering courses; it uses Pascal as the carrier language but does not focus on teaching language features. Aho and Ullman (1992) provide an introductory view of computer science with a strong emphasis on its theoretical fundamentals, whereas Norton (1996) helps the end user to approach the discipline through figures, tables and application examples. Brookshear (1997) gives a fairly comprehensive and up-to-date view of the whole computer science field with a descriptive style and without really aiming to teach programming. Books in this latter category must necessarily be complemented by suitable descriptions of a programming language if the reader wishes to experiment in practice with the concepts exposed in the text.

Finally, Abelson *et al.* (1996) is a text which teaches computer science in a 'non von Neumann style' from the very beginning and exploits Scheme, a subset of Lisp.

Abelson H., Sussman G. and Sussman J. (1996). *Structure and Interpretation of Computer Programs*. 2nd edn. McGraw-Hill

Aho A. D. and Ullman J. (1992). *Foundations of Computer Science*. Freeman and Company

Brookshear J. G. (1997). *Computer Science. An Overview* 5th edn. Addison-Wesley

Norton P. (1996). *Peter Norton's Introduction to Computers*. 2nd edn. Glencoe Macmillan/McGraw-Hill

Pinson L., Sincovec R. and Wiener R. (1987). *A First Course in Computer Science with Modula-2*. John Wiley & Sons

Pratt T. (1990). *Pascal. A New Introduction to Computer Science*. Prentice-Hall

Roberts E. S. (1995). *The Art and Science of C. A Library-based Introduction to Computer Science*. Addison-Wesley

Programming concepts

Dijkstra (1976) and the other books listed in the following concentrate exclusively on the conceptual bases of the programming discipline. Two classic texts that cover algorithms and data structure design and analysis are Aho *et al.* (1983) and Wirth (1976), while a text that provides a thorough comparison and evaluation of programming languages is Ghezzi and Jazayeri (1997).

Aho A. V., Hopcroft J. E. and Ullman J. (1983). *The Design and Analysis of Computer Algorithms* 2nd edn. Addison-Wesley

Dijkstra E. W. (1976). *A Discipline of Programming*. Prentice-Hall

Ghezzi C. and Jazayeri M. (1997). *Programming Language Concepts* 3rd edn. John Wiley & Sons

Wirth N. (1976). *Algorithms + Data Structures = Programs*. Prentice-Hall

Programming in C

Kelley and Pohl (1995) and Schildt (1995) are good references to the ANSI C standard. The first is also a comprehensive and well-structured tutorial: the underlying logic of programming is clearly described with numerous examples. Kernighan and Ritchie (1989) is a classic but not so easy presentation of the ANSI version of the C language, while in Schildt (1992) the reader can find a complete reference to the Turbo C/C++ programming environment with its library functions. More emphasis on data structures, algorithm analysis and program design in C can be found in Hanly *et al.* (1996), Kruse *et al.* (1996) and Weiss (1996).

Hanly J. R., Koffman E. B. and Friedman F. L. (1996). *Problem Solving and Program Design in C* 2nd edn. Addison-Wesley

Kelley A. and Pohl I. (1995). *A Book on C* 3rd edn. Benjamin/Cummings.

Kernighan B. W. and Ritchie D. M. (1989). *The C Programming Language* 2nd edn. Prentice-Hall.

Kruse R. L., Leung B. P. and Tondo C. L. (1996). *Data Structures and Program Design in C*. 2nd edn. Prentice-Hall

Schildt H. (1992). *Turbo C/C++: The Complete Reference*. McGraw-Hill

Schildt H. (1995). *C: The Complete Reference* 3rd edn. McGraw-Hill

Weiss M. A. (1996). *Data Structures and Algorithm Analysis in C*. 2nd edn. Benjamin/
    Cummings

Theoretical aspects

Hopcroft and Ullman (1979) is a classic text concentrating on the theory of
computation. Harel (1992) discusses computation and complexity theory in a fairly
intuitive way. The theoretical roots of computer science are described in depth in
Mandrioli and Ghezzi (1987).

Harel D. (1992). *Algorithmics. The Spirit of Computing* 2nd edn. Addison-Wesley
Hopcroft J. E. and Ullman J. D. (1979). *Introduction to Automata Theory, Languages and
    Computation*. Addison-Wesley
Mandrioli D. and Ghezzi C. (1987). *Theoretical Foundations of Computer Science*.
    John Wiley & Sons

Computer architectures

A comprehensive description and comparison of different computer architectures
can be found in Tanenbaum (1990). The author emphasizes a structural approach to
the construction of computing machines. A more technical description of different
computer architectures can be found in Patterson and Hennessy (1994) and Hennessy
and Patterson (1996). The first book presents the relationship between hardware
and software in modern computer architectures, while the second one analyses
architectural choices in relation to performance. More information on the synthesis
and optimization of digital circuits and on VLSI design can be found in De Micheli
(1994) and in Einspruch (1985).

De Micheli G. (1994). *Synthesis and Optimization of Digital Circuits*. McGraw-Hill
Einspruch N. G. (1985). *VLSI Handbook*. Academic-Press
Hennessy J. L. and Patterson D. A. (1996). *Computer Architecture: A Quantitative Approach*.
    2nd edn. Morgan Kaufmann
Patterson D. A. and Hennessy J. L. (1994). *Computer Organization and Design.
    The Hardware/Software Interface*. Morgan Kaufmann
Tanenbaum A. S. (1990). *Structured Computer Organization* . 3rd edn. Prentice-Hall

Operating systems and internetworking

Fundamentals of operating systems are given in Tanenbaum (1992) and in Silberschatz *et al.* (1994). Many books describe the user-level interface of the UNIX
operating system; Kernighan and Pike (1984) describes the programming interface
and Bach (1986) describes the internal algorithms and data structures that form the
basis of the UNIX operating system and their relationships to the programmer
interface. Concepts and design of distributed systems and distributed operating
systems are specifically treated in Coulouris *et al.* (1994) and in Tanenbaum (1995).
Renaud (1996) is focused on building applications on a client–server architecture.

Comer (1995) is a very readable introduction and an up-to-date overview of the TCP/IP protocol. While the book is specifically about the TCP/IP protocol suite, it is a good book for learning about computer communication protocols in general.

Bach M. J. (1986). *The Design of the UNIX Operating System*. Prentice-Hall
Comer D. E. (1995). *Internetworking with TCP/IP* Vol. I, 3rd edn. Prentice-Hall
Coulouris G., Dollimore J. and Kindberg T. (1994). *Distributed Systems. Concepts and Design* 2nd edn. Addison-Wesley
Kernighan B. W. and Pike R. (1984). *The UNIX Programming Environment*. Prentice-Hall
Renaud P. E. (1996). *Introduction to Client/Server Systems, A Practical Guide for Systems Professionals*. 2nd edn. John Wiley & Sons
Silberschatz A., Peterson J. L. and Galvin P. (1994). *Operating System Concepts* 4th edn. Addison-Wesley
Tanenbaum A. S. (1992). *Modern Operating Systems. Design and Implementation*. Prentice-Hall
Tanenbaum A. S. (1995). *Distributed Operating Systems*. Prentice-Hall

Databases

Navathe and Elmasri (1994) provides a well-organized and complete introduction to database management systems; Ullman (1988, 1989) describes data and knowledge bases with an emphasis on the theory of databases and on the use of rules. Batini *et al.* (1992) focuses on the process of designing database applications. Melton and Simon (1993) is a good guide to SQL2, the SQL standard approved by ANSI in 1992.

Batini C., Ceri S. and Navathe S. B. (1992). *Conceptual Database Design*. Benjamin/Cummings
Elmasri R. and Navathe S. B. (1994). *Fundamentals of Database Systems* 2nd edn. Benjamin/Cummings
Melton J. and Simon A. R. (1993). *Understanding the New SQL: A Complete Guide*. Morgan Kaufmann
Ullman J. D. (1988, 1989). *Principles of Database and Knowledge-base Systems* Vols. I, II. Computer Science Press

Object orientation and C++

Object-oriented design is treated in depth by Meyer (1997) and by Booch (1994). Budd (1995) presents classic data structures from an object-oriented perspective using the language C++, Schildt (1995) gives a complete reference to this popular object-oriented language, and Friedman and Koffman (1996) use C++ to teach introductory programming material.

Booch G. (1994). *Object-Oriented Analysis and Design. With Applications* 2nd edn. Benjamin/Cummings
Budd T. A. (1995). *Classic Data Structures in C++*. Addison-Wesley
Friedman F. L. and Koffman E. B. (1996). *Problem Solving, Abstraction and Design Using C++*. 2nd edn. Addison-Wesley

Meyer B. (1997). *Object-oriented Software Construction*. 2nd edn. Prentice-Hall
Schildt H. (1995). *C++: The Complete Reference* 3rd edn. McGraw-Hill

Software engineering

Part III of this text has been mainly based on Ghezzi *et al.* (1992). Other classic and somewhat complementary texts on software engineering are Pressman (1996) and Sommerville (1996).

Ghezzi C., Jazayeri M. and Mandrioli D. (1992). *Fundamentals of Software Engineering*. Prentice-Hall
Pressman R. S. (1996). *Software Engineering: A Practitioner's Approach*. 4th edn. McGraw-Hill
Sommerville I. (1996). *Software Engineering* 5th edn. Addison-Wesley

Other specialist subjects

We conclude this reading list with some specialist (and more advanced) texts.

Human–computer interface

Preece J. (1994). *Human-Computer Interaction*. Addison-Wesley
Thimbleby H. (1990). *User Interface Design*. Addison-Wesley

Multimedia

Gibbs S. J. and Tsichritzis D. C. (1995). *Multimedia Programming*. Addison-Wesley
Koegel Buford J. F. (1994). *Multimedia Systems*. Addison-Wesley

Artificial intelligence and expert systems

Buchanan B. G. and Shortliffe E. H. (1984). *Rule-Based Expert Systems: The Mycin Experiments of the Stanford Heuristic Programming Project*. Addison-Wesley
Rich E. and Knight K. (1991). *Artificial Intelligence* 2nd edn. McGraw-Hill
Winston P. H. (1992). *Artificial Intelligence* 3rd edn. Addison-Wesley

Logic programming

Clocksin W. and Mellish C. (1994). *Programming in PROLOG*. 4th edn. Springer-Verlag

Functional programming

Abelson H., Sussman G. and Sussman J. (1996). *Structure and Interpretation of Computer Programs*. 2nd edn. McGraw-Hill
Winston P. H. and Horn B. K. P. (1988). *Lisp*. 3rd edn. Addison-Wesley

The ASCII code

Dec	Hex	ASCII symbol	Control code	CTRL key	Dec	Hex	ASCII symbol	Control code	CTRL key
0	00		NUL	^@	16	10	►	DLE	^P
1	01	☺	SOH	^A	17	11	◄	DC1	^Q
2	02	☻	STX	^B	18	12	↕	DC2	^R
3	03	♥	ETX	^C	19	13	‼	DC3	^S
4	04	♦	EOT	^D	20	14	¶	DC4	^T
5	05	♣	ENQ	^E	21	15	§	NAK	^U
6	06	♠	ACK	^F	22	16	▬	SYN	^V
7	07	●	BEL	^G	23	17	↨	ETB	^W
8	08	◘	BS	^H	24	18	↑	CAN	^X
9	09	○	HT	^I	25	19	↓	EM	^Y
10	0A	◙	LF	^J	26	1A	→	SUB	^Z
11	0B	♂	VT	^K	27	1B	←	ESC	^[
12	0C	♀	FF	^L	28	1C	∟	FS	^\
13	0D	♪	CR	^M	29	1D	↔	GS	^]
14	0E	♫	SO	^N	30	1E	▲	RS	^^
15	0F	☼	SI	^O	31	1F	▼	US	^_

Dec	Hex	ASCII symbol	Dec	Hex	ASCII symbol
32	20		38	26	&
33	21	!	39	27	'
34	22	"	40	28	(
35	23	#	41	29	)
36	24	$	42	2A	*
37	25	%	43	2B	+

Dec	Hex	ASCII symbol	Dec	Hex	ASCII symbol
44	2C	,	87	57	W
45	2D	-	88	58	X
46	2E	.	89	59	Y
47	2F	/	90	5A	Z
48	30	0	91	5B	[
49	31	1	92	5C	\
50	32	2	93	5D	]
51	33	3	94	5E	^
52	34	4	95	5F	_
53	35	5	96	60	'
54	36	6	97	61	a
55	37	7	98	62	b
56	38	8	99	63	c
57	39	9	100	64	d
58	3A	:	101	65	e
59	3B	;	102	66	f
60	3C	<	103	67	g
61	3D	=	104	68	h
62	3E	>	105	69	i
63	3F	?	106	6A	j
64	40	@	107	6B	k
65	41	A	108	6C	l
66	42	B	109	6D	m
67	43	C	110	6E	n
68	44	D	111	6F	o
69	45	E	112	70	p
70	46	F	113	71	q
71	47	G	114	72	r
72	48	H	115	73	s
73	49	I	116	74	t
74	4A	J	117	75	u
75	4B	K	118	76	v
76	4C	L	119	77	w
77	4D	M	120	78	x
78	4E	N	121	79	y
79	4F	O	122	7A	z
80	50	P	123	7B	{
81	51	Q	124	7C		
82	52	R	125	7D	}
83	53	S	126	7E	~
84	54	T	127	7F	⌂
85	55	U	128	80	Ç
86	56	V	129	81	ü

Dec	Hex	ASCII symbol	Dec	Hex	ASCII symbol
130	82	é	173	AD	¡
131	83	â	174	AE	«
132	84	ä	175	AF	»
133	85	à	176	B0	░
134	86	å	177	B1	▒
135	87	ç	178	B2	▓
136	88	ê	179	B3	│
137	89	ë	180	B4	┤
138	8A	è	181	B5	╡
139	8B	ï	182	B6	╢
140	8C	î	183	B7	╖
141	8D	ì	184	B8	╕
142	8E	Ä	185	B9	╣
143	8F	Å	186	BA	║
144	90	É	187	BB	╗
145	91	æ	188	BC	╝
146	92	Æ	189	BD	╜
147	93	ô	190	BE	╛
148	94	ö	191	BF	┐
149	95	ò	192	C0	└
150	96	û	193	C1	┴
151	97	ù	194	C2	┬
152	98	ÿ	195	C3	├
153	99	Ö	196	C4	─
154	9A	Ü	197	C5	┼
155	9B	¢	198	C6	╞
156	9C	£	199	C7	╟
157	9D	¥	200	C8	╚
158	9E	Pt	201	C9	╔
159	9F	ƒ	202	CA	╩
160	A0	á	203	CB	╦
161	A1	í	204	CC	╠
162	A2	ó	205	CD	═
163	A3	ú	206	CE	╬
164	A4	ñ	207	CF	╧
165	A5	Ñ	208	D0	╨
166	A6	ª	209	D1	╤
167	A7	º	210	D2	╥
168	A8	¿	211	D3	╙
169	A9	⌐	212	D4	╘
170	AA	¬	213	D5	╒
171	AB	½	214	D6	╓
172	AC	¼	215	D7	╫

Dec	Hex	ASCII symbol	Dec	Hex	ASCII symbol
216	D8	÷	236	EC	∞
217	D9	⌐	237	ED	∅
218	DA	⌐	238	EE	∈
219	DB	■	239	EF	∩
220	DC	▬	240	F0	≡
221	DD	▌	241	F1	±
222	DE	▐	242	F2	≥
223	DF	▬	243	F3	≤
224	E0	α	244	F4	$\int$
225	E1	β	245	F5	$\int$
226	E2	Γ	246	F6	÷
227	E3	π	247	F7	≈
228	E4	Σ	248	F8	°
229	E5	σ	249	F9	•
230	E6	μ	250	FA	·
231	E7	τ	251	FB	√
232	E8	ϕ	252	FC	η
233	E9	θ	253	FD	^{2}
234	EA	Ω	254	FE	■
235	EB	δ	255	FF	

ANSI C operators

ANSI C operators are formed into groups. During the evaluation of an expression containing operators from different groups, those in the group with the higher precedence are evaluated before those in the lower precedence group. When the expression contains more than one operator from the same group the associativity of the operator determines whether these operations are performed from left to right or from right to left. The order of precedence can always be changed by the use of parentheses, and parentheses can also be used to make the expression more readable.

Table B.1 sets out all the ANSI C operators in groups with the highest precedence at the top and the lowest precedence at the bottom. The associativity within each group is shown to the right of the table.

Table B.1 ANSI C operators (highest precedence at the top, lowest precedence at the bottom)

Group	Operators	Associativity
postfix	( ) [ ] . ->	left to right
unary	! ~ ++ -- + - * & (*type*) **sizeof**	right to left
multiplicative	* / %	left to right
additive	+ -	left to right
shifting	>> <<	left to right
relational	< <= > >=	left to right
equality	== !=	left to right
bitwise and	&	left to right
bitwise complement	^	left to right
bitwise or	|	left to right
logical and	&&	left to right
logical or	||	left to right
conditional	?:	right to left
assignment	= += -= *= /= %= &= ^= |= <<= >>=	right to left
sequence	,	left to right

The concepts of precedence and associativity, defined by the language, make the evaluation of an expression unambiguous, and also make it simpler to write, as shown in the following conditional statement:

```
if ( x + y - 1 <= 10 && z > num - 1) ...
```

which is evaluated, using precedence and associativity rules, as the following parenthesized expression:

```
if ((((x + y) - 1) <= 10) && (z > (num - 1))) ...
```

ANSI C keywords and predefined identifiers

C.1 Keywords

auto	extern	sizeof
break	float	static
case	for	struct
char	goto	switch
const	if	typedef
continue	int	unsigned
default	long	void
do	register	volatile
double	return	while
else	short	
enum	signed	

C.2 Predefined identifiers

C.2.1 In <assert.h>

Functions

abort
assert

Macros

NDEBUG

C.2.2   In <ctype.h>

Functions

isalnum
isalpha
iscntrl

isdigit
isgraph
islower
isprint
ispunct

isspace
isupper
isxdigit

C.2.3   In <float.h>

Macros

DBL_MANT_DIG
DBL_DIG
DBL_EPSILON
DBL_MIN_EXP
DBL_MIN_10_EXP
DBL_MAX_EXP
DBL_MAX
DBL_MAX_10_EXP
EDOM

ERANGE
FLT_EPSILON
FLT_DIG
FLT_MANT_DIG
FLT_MAX
FLT_MAX_EXP
FLT_MAX_10_EXP
FLT_MIN
FLT_MIN_EXP
FLT_MIN_10_EXP
FLT_RADIX

FLT_ROUNDSLDBL_DIG
LDBL_EPSILON
LDBL_MANT_DIG
LDBL_MAX
LDBL_MAX_EXP
LDBL_MAX_10_EXP
LDBL_MIN
LDBL_MIN_EXP
LDBL_MIN_EXP
LDBL_MIN_10_EXP

C.2.4   In <limits.h>

Macros

CHAR_BIT
CHAR_MAX
CHAR_MIN
INT_MAX

INT_MIN
LONG_MAX
LONG_MIN
SCHAR_MAX
SCHAR_MIN
SHRT_MAX

SHRT_MIN
UCHAR_MAX
UINT_MAX
ULONG_MAX
USHRT_MAX

C.2.5   In <locale.h>

Functions

setlocale

C.2.6 In `<math.h>`

Functions

acos	fabs	sin
asin	floor	sinh
atan	fmod	sqrt
atan2	frexp	tan
ceil	labs	tanh
cos	ldexp	
cosh	log	
exp	log10	**Macros**
	modf	
	pow	HUGE_VAL

C.2.7 In `<setjmp.h>`

Functions

longjmp
setjmp

Types

JMP_BUF

C.2.8 In `<signal.h>`

Functions

raise
signal

Types

SIG_ATOMIC_T

Macros

SIG_DFL
SIG_ERR
SIG_IGN
SIGABRT
SIGFPE
SIGILL
SIGINT
SIGSEGV
SIGTERM

C.2.9 In `<stdargs.h>`

Functions

va_end

Types

va_list

Macros

va_arg
va_start

C.2.10   In <stddef.h>

Types

ptrdiff_t
size_t

Macros

errno
NULL

offsetof
wchar_t

C.2.11   In <stdio.h>

Functions

clearerr
fclose
feof
ferror
fflush
fgetc
fgetpos
fgets
fopen
fprintf
fputc
fputs
fread
freopen
fscanf
fseek
fsetpos
ftell
fwrite
getc
getchar
gets
perror
printf
putc
putchar
puts
remove
rename
rewind
setbuf
setvbuf
sprintf
sscanf
tmpfile
tmpnam
ungetc
vfprintf
vprintf
vsprintf

Types

FILE
fpos_t

Macros

BUFSIZ
EOF
L_tmpnam
OPEN_MAX
sseek_CUR
SEEK_END
SEEK_SET
TMP_MAX

C.2.12   In <stdlib.h>

Functions

abs
atexit
atof
atoi
atol
bsearch
calloc
exit
free
getenv
gmtime
ldiv
malloc
qsort
rand
realloc
srand
system

Types

div_t
ldiv_t

Macros

RAND_MAX

C.2.13 In <string.h>

Functions

	strcmp	strpbrk
	strcoll	strrchr
memchr	strcpy	strspn
memcmp	strcspn	strstr
memcpy	strerror	strtod
memmove	strlen	strtok
memset	strncat	strtol
strcat	strncmp	strtoul
strchr	strncpy	

C.2.14 In <time.h>

Functions

	strftime	**Macros**
	time	
asctime		CLOCKS_PER_SEC
clock	**Types**	
ctime		
difftime	clock_t	
localtime	time_t	
mktime	tm	

C.2.15 Macros defined by the specific implementation

DATE	_IOLBF	_STCD_
FILE	_IONBF	_TIME_
_IOFBF	_LINE_	

C.2.16 Pointers to file defined by the specific implementation

stderr	stdin	stdout

C.2.17 Preprocessor operations

define	error	ifndef
include	pragma	elif
undef	if	else
line	ifdef	endif

The formal syntax of ANSI C

Every language, whether natural or artificial, is defined through a syntax and a semantics. A **syntax** is a collection of rules that describe how to compose language sentences (in the case of programming languages, language sentences are programs or fragments of programs). A **semantics** is a collection of rules that define the meaning of sentences. For instance, in the case of C the syntax and semantics defining an assignment statement can be summarized as follows:

Syntax: an assignment statement consists of a variable identifier followed by the symbol '=' followed by an expression.

Semantics: the effect of an assignment statement consists of storing the value of the expression on the right-hand side of the symbol '=' into the variable identified by the left-hand side of the symbol '='.

The syntax and semantics of natural languages often exhibit a certain lack of precision and some ambiguity. Programming languages must be defined in an absolutely precise way. For this reason their syntax and semantics are often defined formally, that is, with the help of some mathematical notation.

In particular, a formal (yet at the same time simple and natural) notation is widely used to define the syntax of programming languages[1]. This is usually known as **context-free grammar**, or **Backus–Naur Form** (BNF) from the names of its inventors. Thanks to its precision and compactness, BNF usefully complements informal syntactic definitions such as those that we have proposed in this text.

In this appendix we provide a short introduction to BNF and we explain its use by briefly revisiting a few fundamental syntactic definitions of the C language that were informally introduced throughout this text. Then, we give the official ANSI BNF of the full language (with the warning that it includes several language features that have not been discussed in this text and the reader must therefore resort to language manuals for their semantics).

---

[1] There are also several formalisms to define language semantics, but these are more complex than syntactic formalisms and less standardized. Thus, they are adopted only by specialized users (language designers and implementers, highly sophisticated programmers).

D.1 The Backus–Naur Form of programming languages

The BNF of a language consists of the following elements:

- A finite set of symbols or characters, called the **terminal alphabet** (or **vocabulary**).

- A finite set of symbols or characters, disjoint from the previous set, called the **nonterminal alphabet** (or **vocabulary**). In order to avoid confusion, the elements of the nonterminal alphabet are written in italic whereas terminal symbols are written as plain text. Keywords are considered to be special terminal characters and are written in boldface, as usual.

- A finite set of **syntactic rules** (or **productions**) of the type

  $A ::= \alpha$

  where A is a nonterminal, that is, an element of the nonterminal vocabulary, ::= is a reserved symbol, and α is a string of terminals and nonterminals. In particular, α may contain no element. In that case, it is called the **empty string** and it is denoted by the symbol ε.

  A is called the **left-hand part** of the production and α is called the **right-hand part**.

- A distinguished element of the nonterminal vocabulary, called the **axiom** or **initial symbol**.

Given a BNF, we can use it to derive language sentences in the following way. First we write the axiom of the BNF, say S; then we replace S by a string α such that $S ::= \alpha$ is in the set of productions; in general, α will contain both terminals and nonterminals. We choose any nonterminal, say B, occurring in α and we replace it by any string β such that $B ::= \beta$ is in the production set; we obtain a new string γ. We iterate the procedure until we obtain a string that consists exclusively of terminals. At this point the rewriting process terminates and the string is by definition a string that belongs to the language **generated** by the BNF.

EXAMPLE D.1

The following BNF G generates the language L whose terminal alphabet contains only the characters 'a' and 'b', and whose sentences are strings composed of a number $n \geq 0$ of 'a's followed by the same number of 'b's:

- The terminal alphabet of G is {a, b}.
- The nonterminal alphabet of G is {S}, that is, the sole axiom S.

- The productions of G are:

  $S ::= a \, S \, b$
  $S ::= \varepsilon$

A first string of L is the empty string ε, which is simply obtained from the axiom by applying the second production.

If we rewrite S by applying the first production, we obtain a S b, which is not a string of the language because it contains a nonterminal. We can obtain the string ab from it, however, by rewriting S as ε, via the second production (rewriting a character as ε means deleting it).

In general, we can state that by applying the first syntax rule n times, and by 'closing' the rewriting process via the second rule, we obtain strings consisting of n 'a's followed by the same number of 'b's.

To help the reader become familiar with the use of BNF, in the next section we apply it to define some of the main C syntactic rules that have been presented throughout this text. First, however, we introduce some short notations that will help make C's BNF more compact.

- The notation

  $A ::= \alpha \mid \beta \mid \gamma$

is an abbreviation for the rules

  $A ::= \alpha$
  $A ::= \beta$
  $A ::= \gamma$

that is, A can be rewritten as either α or β or γ.

- The notation $\{\alpha\}_{1+}$ denotes the possibility of writing, during the derivation of language sentences, one or more occurrences of the string α. It is formally defined as follows: whenever it occurs in the right-hand part of a production such as

  $A ::= \beta \, \{\alpha\}_{1+} \, \gamma$

it must be understood as an abbreviation for the following rules:

  $A ::= \beta \, B \, \gamma$
  $B ::= \alpha \mid \alpha \, B$

where B is a *new* nonterminal not otherwise used in the BNF.

- The notation $\{\alpha\}_{0+}$ denotes the possibility of writing, during the derivation of language sentences, zero or more occurrences of the string α. It is formalized in a similar way to $\{\alpha\}_{1+}$.

- The notation $\{\alpha\}_{opt}$ denotes the possibility of writing or not writing the string α, during the derivation of language sentences. It is formally defined as follows: whenever it occurs in the right-hand part of a production such as

$$A ::= \beta \, \{\alpha\}_{opt} \, \gamma$$

it must be understood as an abbreviation for the following rules:

$$A ::= \beta \, \alpha \, \gamma \, | \, \beta \, \gamma$$

The above symbols { and } should not be confused with C's terminal symbols **{** and **}** which are written in boldface. Also, for the sake of simplicity, if α consists of a single nonterminal symbol, the delimiters { and } can be omitted.

D.2 The BNF of a C subset

In this section we show how some of the informal syntactic rules that we used throughout this text to introduce the C language can be formalized through BNF productions. The reader is warned that the productions given below are *not* part of the official C BNF definition; rather, they closely correspond to (a sample of) the informal definitions given in Chapters 3 through 7; they correctly define a *subset* of C, however. For simplicity, this subset does not include pointers. A few non-essential elements are omitted and replaced by '...'. The complete, official BNF of ANSI C is given in Section D.3.

D.2.1 The structure of C programs

Initially, in Chapter 4, we stated that, at the very minimum, a C program *must* contain, in order:

- a **directives part**, which contains directives for the compiler;
- the predefined identifier `main` followed by the pair '`()`';
- two parts, syntactically enclosed by the pair '`{ }`':
  - the declarative part, and
  - the executable part.

Later, in Chapter 7, we stated that a **global declarative part** *may* be included between the directive part and the main program and a sequence of function definitions also *may* follow the main program.

Such informal rules are formalized by the following BNF production:

program ::=
    directive_part $\{global\_declarative\_part\}_{opt}$ `main ( )` *{declarative_part*
    executable_part} $\{function\_definition\}_{0+}$

D.2.2 C's identifiers

In Chapter 3 we stated that a C identifier is a sequence of alphabetic letters and digits headed by a letter. The special character '_' is treated as a digit. This rule is formalized as follows

> *identifier* ::= *letter* {*letter* | *digit* | _}$_{0+}$
> *letter* ::= a | b | ... A | B | ...
> *digit* ::= 0 | 1 | 2 | ...

D.2.3 Directives part

We have seen in Chapter 4 that the directive part of a program contains directives for the compiler. Two sample directives are file inclusion and constant definition. This is formalized by the following rules

> *directive_part* ::= {*preprocessing_directive*}$_{0+}$
> *preprocessing_directive* ::=
>   # include <*identifier*> | # define *identifier constant*

D.2.4 Declarative part

Recall from Chapters 4, 5 and 7 that the declarative part of a program consists of the *constant declaration* (through the **const** keyword, which is different from the **define** directive), the *type declaration*, the *variable declaration* and the *function declaration*. The rules below define precisely how such declarations can be built.

> *declarative_part* ::=
>   {*constant_declaration*}$_{0+}$ {*type_declaration*}$_{0+}$ {*variable declaration*}$_{0+}$
>   {*function_prototype*}$_{0+}$
> *constant_declaration* ::=
>   **const** *type_specifier identifier* = *constant_value* ;
> *constant_value* ::= *numeric_constant* | *character_constant*
> *numerical_constant* ::= ...
> *character_constant* ::= ...
>
> *type_declaration* ::= **typedef** *type_specifier type_identifier* ;
> *type_specifier* ::=
>   **float** | **int** | **char** | ... **void** | *enum_specifier* | *struct_specifier* | *type_identifier*
>   *type_ identifier* ::= *identifier* | *array_type_identifier*
> *array_type_identifier* ::= *identifier* [*numeric_constant*]
> *enum_specifier* ::= **enum** {*enumerator_list*}
> *enumerator_list* ::= *identifier* {, *identifier*}$_{0+}$
> *struct_specifier* ::= **struct** {*field_list*}

$field\_list ::= \{type\_specifier\ field\_identifier\ \{, field\_identifier\}_{0+}\ ;\}_{1+}$
$field\_\ identifier ::= identifier$

$variable\_declaration ::=$
$\qquad type\_specifier\ variable\_identifier\ \{, variable\_identifier\}_{0+}\ ;$
$variable\_\ identifier ::= identifier$

$function\_prototype ::= function\_header;$
$function\_header ::= ...$

D.2.5 Executable part

The executable part of a program consists of a sequence of statements. Each statement can be of several types: assignment statement (included here in the larger category of expression statements), iteration statement and so on. The precise rules to build the executable part of programs are given below.

$executable\_part ::= statement\_sequence$
$statement\_sequence ::= \{statement\}_{1+}$

$statement ::= expression\_statement\ |\ selection\_statement\ |$
$\qquad iteration\ \_statement\ |\ compound\_statement\ |$
$\qquad jump\_statement ...$
$expression\_statement ::= \{expression\}_{opt}\ ;$
$selection\_statement ::=$
$\qquad \textbf{if}\ (expression)\ statement\ \{\textbf{else}\ statement\}_{opt}\ |\ switch\_statement$
$switch\_statement ::= ...$
$iteration\_statement ::= while\_statement\ |\ do\_statement\ |\ for\_statement$
$while\_statement ::= \textbf{while}\ (expression)\ statement$
$do\_statement ::= \textbf{do}\ (statement)\ \textbf{while}\ (expression)$
$for\_statement ::= ...$
$jump\_statement ::= ...$
$compound\_statement ::= \{\{declarative\_part\}_{opt}\ statement\_sequence\ \}$

$expression ::= \quad constant\_value\ |\ l\_value\ |\ (expression)\ |$
$\qquad +\ expression\ |\ -\ expression\ |\ function\_expression\ |$
$\qquad assignment\_expression\ |\ relational\_expression\ |$
$\qquad arithmetic\_expression\ |\ logical\_expression$
$l\_value ::= variable\_identifier\ |\ l\_value.identifier\ |\ identifier\ [expression]$
$assignment\_expression ::= l\_value\ ass\_op\ expression$
$arithmetic\_expression ::= expression\ arith\_op\ expression$
$relational\_expression ::= expression\ rel\_op\ expression$
$logical\_expression ::= expression\ log\_op\ expression$
$function\_expression ::= function\_name\ (argument\_list)$

> *function_name* ::= ...
> *argument_list* ::= ...
> *ass_op* ::= =
> *arith_op* ::= * | / | % | + | −
> *rel_op* ::= < | <= | > | >= | == | !=
> *log_op* ::= ! | && | ||

D.2.6   Function definition

A function definition consists of a function header, which specifies the parameters and the result of the function, and a function body, which consists of a compound statement. This is formalized by the following rules.

> *function_definition* ::= *function_header compound_statement*
> *function_header* ::=
>   *type_specifier function_name* ({*parameter_declaration_list*}$_{opt}$)
> *parameter_declaration_list* ::= ...

D.3   The complete BNF of ANSI C

We are now ready to provide the complete ANSI C BNF.

D.3.1   Programs

> *program* ::= {*file*}$_{1+}$
> *file* ::= *decls_and_fct_definitions*
>
> *decls_and_fct_definitions* ::= {*declaration*}$_{1+}$ *decls_and_fct_definitions*$_{opt}$ |
>   {*function_definition*}$_{1+}$ *decls_and_fct_definitions*$_{opt}$

D.3.2   Function definition

> *function_definition* ::= {**extern** | **static**}$_{opt}$ *type_specifier*
>   *function_name* (*parameter_declaration_list*$_{opt}$)
>   *compound_statement*
>
> *function_name* ::= *identifier*
> *parameter_declaration_list* ::= *parameter_declaration*
>   {, *parameter_declaration*}$_{0+}$

D.3.3 Declarations

$declaration ::= declaration\_specifiers\ init\_declarator\_list_{opt}$

$declaration\_specifiers ::=$

        $storage\_class\_specifier\_or\_typedef\ declaration\_specifiers_{opt}\ |$

        $type\_specifier\ declaration\_specifiers_{opt}\ |$

        $type\_qualifier\ declaration\_specifiers_{opt}$

$storage\_class\_specifier\_or\_typedef ::=$ **auto** | **extern** | **register** |

        static | **typedef**

$type\_specifier ::=$ **char** | **double** | **float** | **int** | **long** | **short** |

        signed | **unsigned** | **void** |

        $enum\_specifier$ | $struct\_or\_union\_specifier$ | $typedef\_name$

$enum\_specifier ::=$ **enum** tag_{opt} { $enumerator\_list$ } | **enum** tag

$tag ::= identifier$

$enumerator\_list ::= enumerator$ { , $enumerator$ }$_{opt}$

$enumerator ::= enumeration\_constant$ { $= const\_integral\_expr$ }$_{opt}$

$enumeration\_constant ::= identifier$

$struct\_or\_union\_specifier ::= struct\_or\_union\ tag_{opt}$ { $struct\_declaration\_list$ } |

        $struct\_or\_union\ tag$

$struct\_or\_union ::=$ **struct** | **union**

$struct\_declaration\_list ::=$ { $struct\_declaration$ }$_{1+}$

$struct\_declaration ::= type\_specifier\_qualifier\_list\ \ struct\_declarator\_list$;

$type\_specifier\_qualifier\_list ::= type\_specifier\ \ type\_specifier\_qualifier\_list_{opt}\ |$

        $type\_qualifier\ type\_specifier\_qualifier\_list_{opt}$

$struct\_declarator\_list ::= struct\_declarator$ { , $struct\_declarator$ }$_{0+}$

$struct\_declarator ::= declarator$ | $declarator_{opt}$: $const\_integral\_expr$

$type\_qualifier ::=$ **const** | **volatile**

$declarator ::= pointer_{opt}\ \ direct\_declarator$

pointer ::= ***** | { *type_qualifier_list*$_{opt}$ }$_{1+}$

type_qualifier_list ::= { *type_qualifier* }$_{1+}$

direct_declarator ::= *identifier* | (*declarator*) |
                direct_declarator [*const_integral_expr*$_{opt}$] |
                direct_declarator (*parameter_type_list*) |
                direct_declarator (*identifier_list*$_{opt}$)

parameter_type_list ::= *parameter_list* | *parameter_list* , ...
parameter_list ::= *parameter_declaration* { , *parameter_declaration* }$_{0+}$
parameter_declaration ::= *declaration_specifiers* *declarator* |
                declaration_specifiers *abstract_declarator*$_{opt}$

abstract_declarator ::= *pointer* | *pointer*$_{opt}$ *direct_abstract_declarator*

direct_abstract_declarator ::= (*abstract_declarator*)
                | *direct_abstract_declarator*$_{opt}$ [*const_integral_expr*$_{opt}$]
                | *direct_abstract_declarator*$_{opt}$ (*parameter_type_list*$_{opt}$)

identifier_list ::= *identifier* { , *identifier* }$_{0+}$

typedef_name ::= *identifier*

init_declarator_list ::= *init_declarator* { , *init_declarator* }$_{opt}$

init_declarator ::= *declarator* | *declarator* = *initializer*

initializer ::= *assignment_expression* | { *initializer_list* } | { *initializer_list* , }

initializer_list ::= *initializer* { , *initializer* }$_{0+}$

D.3.4 Statements

statement ::= *compound_statement* | *expression_statement* | *iteration_statement* |
            jump_statement | *labelled_statement* | *selection_statement*

compound_statement ::= { *declaration_list*$_{opt}$ *statement_list*}$_{opt}$

declaration_list ::= { *declaration* }$_{1+}$

statement_list ::= { *statement* }$_{1+}$

expression_statement ::= *expression*$_{opt}$;

iteration statement ::= *while_statement* | *do_statement* | *for_statement*

while_statement ::= **while** (*expression*) *statement*

do_statement ::= **do** *statement* **while** (*expression*)

for_statement ::= **for** (*expression; expression; expression*) *statement*

jump_statement ::= **break** *;* | **continue** *;* | **goto** *identifier ;* | **return** *expression*$_{opt}$ *;*

labelled_statement ::= *identifier : statement* |
        case *const_integral_expr : statement* |
        default : *statement*

selection_statement ::= **if** (*expression*) *statement* |
        if (*expression*) *statement* **else** *statement* |
        switch_statement

switch_statement ::= **switch** (*integral_expression*) *switch_body*

switch_body ::= *case_statement* | **default** : *statement* | *switch_block*

case_statement ::= { **case** *const_integral_expr* : }$_{1+}$ *statement*

switch_block ::= { {*declaration_list*}$_{opt}$ *case_default_group* }

case_default_group ::= { *case_group* }$_{1+}$ |
        { *case_group* }$_{0+}$ *default_group* { *case_group* }$_{0+}$

case_group ::= { **case** *const_integral_expr* : }$_{1+}$ { *statement* }$_{1+}$

default_group ::= **default** : {*statement*}$_{1+}$

D.3.5 Expressions

expression ::= *constant* | *string_literal* | (*expression*) | *lvalue* |
      assignment_expression | *expression , expression* | + *expression* |
      – *expression* | *function_expression* | *relational_expression* |
      equality_expression | *logical _expression* |
      expression arithmetic_op expression | *bitwise_expression* |
      expression ? *expression* : *expression* | **sizeof** *expression* |
      sizeof (*type_name*) | (*type_name*) *expression*

lvalue ::= **&** *lvalue* | **++** *lvalue* | *lvalue* **++** | **--** *lvalue* | *lvalue* **--** |
     identifier | ***expression* | *lvalue* [*expression*] | (*lvalue*) |
     lvalue **.** *identifier* | *lvalue->identifier*

assignment_expression ::= *lvalue assignment_op expression*

assignment_op ::= **=** | **+=** | **-=** | ***=** | **/=** | **%=** | **&=** | **^=** | **|=** | **>>=** | **<<=**

arithmetic_op ::= **+** | **-** | ***** | **/** | **%**

relational_expression ::= *expression* **<** *expression* | *expression* **>** *expression* |
     expression **<=** *expression* | *expression* **>=** *expression*

equality_expression ::= *expression* **==** *expression* | *expression* **!=** *expression*

logical_expression ::= **!** *expression* | *expression* **||** *expression* |
     expression **&&** *expression*

bitwise_expression ::= **~** *expression* | **^** *expression* |
     expression **&** *expression* | *expression* **|** *expression* |
     expression **<<** *expression* | *expression* **>>** *expression*

function_expression ::= *function_name*(*argument_list*$_{opt}$) |
     (***pointer*) (*argument_list*$_{opt}$)

argument_list ::= *expression* **{ ,** *expression* **}**$_{0+}$

type_name ::= *type_specifier declarator*$_{opt}$

D.3.6 Constants

constant ::= *character_constant* | *enumeration_constant* | *floating_constant* |
     integer_constant

character_constant ::= **'** *c* **'** | **L'** *c* **'**

c ::= ... every character from the set of characters except **'** or **** or *newline* |
     escape_sequence

escape_sequence ::= **\'** | **\"** | **\?** | **** | **\a** | **\b** | **\f** | **\n** | **\r** | **\t** | **\v** |
     **** *octal_digit octal_digit*$_{opt}$ *octal_digit*$_{opt}$ |
     \x *hexadecimal_digit* {*hexadecimal_digit*}$_{0+}$

enumeration_constant ::= *identifier*

floating_constant ::= *fractional_constant exponential_part*$_{opt}$ *floating_suffix*$_{opt}$
                                digit_sequence exponential_part floating_suffix$_{opt}$

fractional_constant ::= *digit_sequence*$_{opt}$. *digit_sequence* | *digit_sequence* .

digit_sequence ::= { *digit* }$_{1+}$

digit ::= 0 | 1 | 2 | 3 | 4 | 5 | 6 | 7 | 8 | 9

exponential_part ::= *exponential_prefix* { + | − }$_{opt}$ *digit_sequence*

exponential_prefix ::= e | E

floating_suffix ::= f | F | l | L

integer_constant ::= *decimal_constant integer_suffix*$_{opt}$ |
                              octal_constant integer_suffix$_{opt}$ |
                              hexadecimal_constant integer_suffix$_{opt}$

decimal_constant ::= 0 | *nonzero_digit digit_sequence*

nonzero_digit ::= 1 | 2 | 3 | 4 | 5 | 6 | 7 | 8 | 9

octal_constant ::= 0 | {*octal_digit*}$_{0+}$

octal_digit ::= 0 | 1 | 2 | 3 | 4 | 5 | 6 | 7

hexadecimal_constant ::= *hexadecimal_prefix* { *hexadecimal_digit* }$_{1+}$

hexadecimal_prefix ::= 0x | 0X

hexadecimal_digit ::= 0 | 1 | 2 | 3 | 4 | 5 | 6 | 7 | 8 | 9 |
                               a | b | c | d | e | f | A | B | C | D | E | F

integer_suffix ::= *unsigned_suffix long_suffix*$_{opt}$ |
                           long_suffix unsigned_suffix$_{opt}$

unsigned_suffix ::= u | U

long_suffix ::= l | L

D.3.7 Strings of characters

string_literal ::= "*s_char_sequence*" I L "*s_char_sequence*"

s_char_sequence ::= { *sc* }$_{1+}$

sc ::= every character in the set of characters except " or \ or *newline* I
  escape_sequence

D.3.8 Preprocessor directives

preprocessing_directive ::= *control_line newline* I *if_section* I
  pp_token newline

control_line ::= #include { <*identifier*> I "*identifier*"} I
  #undef *identifier* I #line *pp_token* I #error *pp_token* I
  #pragma *pp_token* I
  #define *identifier* { (*identifier_list*) }$_{opt}$ { *pp_token* }$_{0+}$

pp_token ::= *identifier* I *constant* I *string_literal* I *operator* I *punctuator* I
  pp_token # # *pp_token* I # *identifier*

if_section ::= *if_group* { *elif_group* }$_{0+}$ { *else_group* }$_{opt}$ *end_if_line*

if_group ::= #if *const_integral_expr newline preprocessing_directive*$_{opt}$ I
  #ifdef *identifier newline* { *preprocessing_directive* }$_{opt}$ I
  #ifndef *identifier newline* { *preprocessing_directive* }$_{opt}$

elif_group ::= #elif *constant_expression newline* { *preprocessing_directive* }$_{opt}$

else_group ::= #else *newline* { *preprocessing_directive* }$_{opt}$

end_if_line ::= #endif *newline*

newline ::= ... the newline character ...

Solutions to selected exercises

1.1

Answer (a) can be considered as an algorithm because it is precise and detailed enough to be executed without needing 'common sense'.

1.2

Yes, the answer constitutes the initial part of an algorithm to reach the destination. However, the algorithm will be complete only if the further request receives in its turn an answer of algorithmic type suitable to reach the destination.

1.8

The new formulation of the problem does not alter its difficulty. Indeed, the algorithm of the extended example of Chapter 1 is based on the construction of *all* paths that start in c_d, trying to identify a posteriori those that arrive in c_a, and selecting the shortest path among them.

2.1

If the data bus is composed of a number of lines equal to the memory word length, it is possible to transfer an entire word in one single bus transfer (the bits that constitute the single word can be transferred in parallel during the same transfer operation). If the number of data bus lines is less, the transfer of a word requires more than one bus transfer operation.

2.3

In order to execute the comparison between two numbers $s1$ and $s2$, the machine under consideration executes, through its ALU, the difference between the two numbers and checks the *zero* bits of the status register, SR determining, whether the two numbers are equal (zero bit = 1) or different (zero bit = 0).

3.12

```
main()
{
   len = 0;
   scanf(ch);
   while (ch != '%' )
   {
      text[len] = ch;
      len = len + 1;
      scanf(ch);
   }

   scanf(n); scanf(m); scanf(p);

   if (n > m " m > len " p > len - (m - n))
      printf("error");

   if (p < n)
   {                                /*write the first p - 1 characters*/
      i = 0;
      while (i < p - 1)
      {
         printf(text[i]);
         i = i + 1;
      }
                                    /*write the characters between the n-th and
                                    the m-th position*/
      i = n - 1;
      while (i < m)
      {
         printf(text[i]);
         i = i + 1;
      }
                                    /*write the characters between the p-th and
                                    the n-th position*/
      i = p - 1;
      while (i < n - 1)
      {
         printf(text[i]);
         i = i + 1;
      }
                                    /*write the remaining characters*/
      i = m;
      while (i < len)
      {
         printf(text[i]);
         i = i + 1;
      }
   }
```

```
        else
        {
                                        /*write the first n-1 characters*/
            i = 0;
            while (i < n - 1)
            {
                printf(text[i]);
                i = i + 1;
            }
                                        /*write (p - n) characters starting from the
                                        (m + 1)-th position*/
            i = 0;
            while (i < p - n)
            {
                printf(text[m + i]);
                i = i + 1;
            }
                                        /*write the characters between the n-th and
                                        the m-th position*/
            i = n - 1;
            while (i < m)
            {
                printf(text[i]);
                i = i + 1;
            }
                                        /*write the remaining characters*/
            i = p + m - n;
            while (i < len)
            {
                printf(text[i]);
                i = i + 1;
            }
        }
    }
```

3.14

The following program makes use of the fact that $(m + 1)^2 = m^2 + 2 * m + 1$.

```
    main()                                          /*IntegerSquareRootAlgorithm*/
                                        /*we assume that n is a positive integer*/
    {
        scanf(n);
        m = 1; square = 1;
        while (square <= n)
        {
            square = square + m + m + 1;
            m = m + 1;
        }
        printf(m - 1);
    }
```

☞ 3.2

Let m > n and k be a common divisor of m and n, that is, m = k * d and n = k*s
for some positive integers d and s. Further, let m = h * n + r, 0 < r < n. Then
r = k * (d – h * s), as d – h * s is a positive integer in its turn. The reasoning
continues as before, concluding that n and r have every divisor in common and
therefore also the greatest.

```
main()
{
   scanf(m); scanf(n);
   if (m < n)
   {
      r = m; m = n; n = m;
   }
   while (n > 0)
   {
      r = m % n;
      m = n;
      n = r;
   }
   gcd = m;
   printf(gcd);
}
```

4.2

```
#include <stdio.h>
main()
{
   int a, b, sum;
   printf("Type the value of a (must be integer)\n");
   scanf("%d", &a);
   printf("Type the value of b (must be integer)\n");
   scanf("%d", &b);
   sum = a + b;
   printf("The sum of a + b is:\n%d \nBye!\n", sum);
}
```

5.1

No: the values of an enumerated type must be valid C identifiers; and integer
numbers are not.

5.3

`ColourList[5] = red`   is correct.
`ColourList[15] = white`   is not correct because:

(a) The index value is out of range.

(b) `white` is not a correct value of the `colours` type.

6.1

In those examples of Chapter 5 where we deal with scanning arrays, the use of the **for** statement is more convenient. For instance, we can rewrite Example 5.5:

```
#include <stdio.h>
main()
{
  int Counter;
  int Storage[100];

  for (Counter = 0; Counter < 100; Counter++)
    scanf("%d", &Storage[Counter]);
  for (Counter = Counter - 1; Counter >= 0; Counter--)
    printf("%d\n", Storage[Counter]);
}
```

In the cases of the Examples 5.1 and 5.2 there is no advantage.

6.4

```
for (i = 0; i < nRows; i++)
  for (j = 0; j < nColumns; j++)
    norm += mat[i][j] * mat[i][j];
```

7.4

The easiest way consists of transforming the proposed statement first into the sequence

```
w = f(x);   y = z + w
```

where w is a new auxiliary variable. Then, transform the instruction w = f(x) using the technique introduced in Section 7.5.9.

If in special cases f is always called in the context of instructions like the one indicated in the exercise, it could just as well be transformed into a procedure such as the following:

```
void    f(int par1, int par2, int *par3)
{
  ...
  *par3 = par2 + result;
}
```

and then called as follows:

```
f (x, z, &y)
```

8.7

The application of tail would produce as a side-effect the modification of the parameter of the procedure searchElem, a fact normally not desired during a search. It would therefore be advisable to apply the tail procedure to a temporary variable.

9.1

```
void order(TforOrd ar[], int num)
{
   int i, j;
   TforOrd temp;

   for (i = 0; i < num; i++)
      for (j = 1; j < num - i; j++)
         if (ar[j-1].key > ar[j].key)
         {
            temp = ar[j];
            ar[j] = ar[j-1];
            ar[j-1] = temp;
         }
}

int createIndex(TforOrd  toOrder[], int  maxnum, FILE  *fb)
{
   book   bk;
   int    num = 0;
   int    offset = 0;
   while (fread(&bk, sizeof(book), 1, fb))
   {
      if (num > maxnum)
         exit(0);

      toOrder[num].index = offset;
      toOrder[num].key = bk.catmark;
      num++;
      offset += sizeof(book);
   }

   order(toOrder, num);

   return num;
}

main()
{
   FILE    *fp;
   TforOrd Ar[MAX_NUM];
   int     num, i;
   book    bk;
                                                        /*open the file*/
   if ((fp = fopen("filename1", "rb")) == NULL)
      exit(0);

   num = createIndex(Ar, MAX_NUM, fp);
                                                        /*print*/
   for (i = 0; i < num; i++)
   {
      fseek(fp, Ar[i].index, SEEK_SET);
      fread(&bk, sizeof(book), 1, fp);
```

```
              printf("%d %s \n %s \n %s   %d \n\n",
                 bk.catmark, bk.author, bk.title, bk.publisher, bk.year);
         }
    }
```

9.7

A possible solution is to pass the `ServWaitList` function a structure containing the customer and flight data as a parameter.

From the main menu, the command 'W' activates a procedure that asks for the data and then calls `ServWaitList`:

```
case 'W':  AskForData(&data);
           ServWaitList(data);
           break;
```

The `ServBooking` procedure can now call the `ServWaitList` function without asking for data but passing it directly the data already obtained.

9.8

Files not ordered
Scan the file `Update` and, using linear search, search through the file `Employee`.

```
main()
{
    FILE       *f1, *f2;
    Employee   em;
    newSalary  ns;
    bool       end_of_update = false;

    if ((f1 = fopen("Employee", "rb+")) == NULL)
       exit(0);
    if ((f2 = fopen("Update", "rb")) == NULL)
       exit(0);

    fread(&ns, sizeof(newSalary), 1, f2);

    while (! end_of_update)
    {
       rewind(f1);
       fread(&em, sizeof(Employee), 1, f1);

       while (strcmp(em.lastName, ns.lastName) ||
              strcmp(em.firstName, em.firstName))
       {
          if (fread(&em, sizeof(Employee), 1, f1) == 0)
          {
             fprintf(stderr, "%s %s not found in file Employee",
                ns.lastName, ns.firstName);
             exit(1);
          }
       }
```

```
        fseek(f1, -sizeof(Employee), SEEK_CUR);
        em.salary = ns.salary;
        if (fwrite(&em, sizeof(Employee), 1, f1) == 0)
            fprintf(stderr, "ERROR: Can't write to the file Employee");
        fflush(f1);

        if (fread(&ns, sizeof(newSalary), 1, f2) == 0)
            end_of_update = true;
    }
    fclose(f1);
    fclose(f2);
}
```

Only the file Employee is ordered

Scan the file Update and, using binary search, scan the file Employee (using a
function BinSearch which operates directly on the file and returns the offset of
the record sought).

```
main()
{
    FILE        *f1, *f2;
    Employee    em;
    newSalary   ns;
    bool        end_of_update = false;
    int         numEmp;
    long        pos;

    if ((f1 = fopen("Employee", "rb+")) == NULL)
        exit(0);
    if ((f2 = fopen("Update", "rb")) == NULL)
        exit(0);

    fseek(f1, 0, SEEK_END);
    numEmp = ftell(f1)/sizeof(Employee);
    fread(&ns, sizeof(newSalary), 1, f2);

    while (! end_of_update)
    {                               /*find the correct record using BinSearch*/
        pos = BinSearch(f1, 0, numEmp, &ns);
        if (pos >= 0)
        {
            fseek(f1, pos, SEEK_SET);
            fread(&em, sizeof(Employee), 1, f1);
            fseek(f1, -sizeof(Employee), SEEK_CUR);
            em.salary = ns.salary;
            if (fwrite(&em, sizeof(Employee), 1, f1) == 0)
                fprintf(stderr, "ERROR: Can't write to the file Employee");
            fflush(f1);

        }
        if (fread(&ns, sizeof(newSalary), 1, f2) == 0)
            end_of_update = true;
    }
    fclose(f1);
    fclose(f2);
}
```

Ordered files

Scan both files in parallel.

```
main()
{
   FILE       *f1, *f2, *f3;
   Employee   em;
   newSalary  ns;
   bool       end_of_update = false;
   int        cfr, cfr1;

   if ((f1 = fopen("Employee", "rb+")) == NULL)
      exit(0);
   if ((f2 = fopen("Update", "rb")) == NULL)
      exit(0);

                                            /*both files are ordered*/

                                /*read the first 'record' of both files*/
   fread(&em, sizeof(Employee), 1, f1);
   fread(&ns, sizeof(newSalary), 1, f2);

   while (! end_of_update)
   {
      cfr  = strcmp(em.lastName, ns.lastName);
      cfr1 = strcmp(em.firstName, ns.firstName);

      if (cfr < 0 || cfr == 0 && cfr1 < 0)
      {
         if (fread(&em, sizeof(Emp), 1, f1) == 0)
         {
            fprintf(stderr, "ERROR: Update of a nonexistent Employee");
            exit(0);
         }
      }
      else
      {
         if (cfr > 0 || cfr == 0 && cfr1 > 0)
         {
            fprintf(stderr, "ERROR: Update of a nonexistent Employee");
            exit(0);
         }
         else
                                            /*cfr == 0 && cfr1 == 0*/
         {
            fseek(f1, -sizeof(Employee), SEEK_CUR);
            em.salary = ns.salary;
            if (fwrite(&em, sizeof(Employee), 1, f1) == 0)
               fprintf(stderr, "ERROR: Can't write to the file Employee");

            fflush(f1);

            if (fread(&ns, sizeof(newSalary), 1, f2) == 0)
               end_of_update = 1;
```

```
            else if (fread(&em, sizeof(Employee), 1, f1) == 0)
            {
                fprintf(stderr, "ERROR: Update of a nonexistent Employee");
                exit(0);
            }
        }
    }
}
fclose(f1);
fclose(f2);
}
```

9.11

Two files are used instead of writing back to the same file because if something goes wrong, everything is not lost.

```
typedef struct { int      Day;
                 int      Month;
                 int      Year;
               } Date;

typedef struct { String   Addressee;
                 int      Amount;
                 Date     IssueDate;
               } InvoiceDescription;

int dateCmp(Date d1, Date d2)
{
    if (d1.Year > d2.Year)
        return 1;
    else if (d1.Year < d2.Year)
        return -1;
    else if (d1.Month > d2.Month)
        return 1;
    else if (d1.Month < d2.Month)
        return -1;
    else if (d1.Day > d2.Day)
        return 1;
    else if (d1.Day < d2.Day)
        return -1;
    else
        return 0;
}

bool addInvoiceToFile(char fileName[], InvoiceDescription invoice)
{
    FILE               *f1, *f2;
    InvoiceDescription tmpInvoice;
    bool               added = false;

    if ((f1 = fopen(fileName, "rb+")) == NULL)
        return false;
```

```
if ((f2 = fopen("temp00", "wb+")) == NULL)
{
   fclose (f1);
   return false;
}

while (fread(&tmpInvoice, sizeof(InvoiceDescription), 1, f1))
{
   if (! added && dateCmp(tmpInvoice.IssueDate, invoice.IssueDate) > 0)
   {
      if (fwrite(&invoice, sizeof(InvoiceDescription), 1, f2))
         added = true;
      else
      {
         fclose(f1);
         fclose(f2);
         return false;
      }
   }

   if (! fwrite(&tmpInvoice, sizeof(InvoiceDescription), 1, f2))
   {
      fclose(f1);
      fclose(f2);
      return false;
   }
}

if (! added)
   if (! fwrite(&invoice, sizeof(InvoiceDescription), 1, f2))
   {
      fclose(f1);
      fclose(f2);
      return false;
   }

fclose(f1);
fclose(f2);
remove(fileName);
rename("temp00", fileName);
return true;
}
```

9.13

```
void parseFile(FILE *inputfp, FILE *outputfp)
{
      float   side1, side2, side3;
      char    word[50];

      while (!feof(fp))
      {
        if (fscanf(inputfp,"%s",word)==1)
```

```
{
  if (strcmp(word,"TRIANGLE")==0)
  {
    if (fscanf(inputfp,"%f %f %f\n", &side1, &side2,
             &side3)==3)
      fprintf(outputfp,"The Perimeter of the triangle is:
                    %f\n", side1+side2+side3);
  }
  else if (strcmp(word,"RECTANGLE")==0)
  {
    if (fscanf(inputfp,"%f %f\n", &side1, &side2)==2)
      fprintf(outputfp,"The Perimeter of the rectangle is:
                    %f\n", side1*2+side2*2);
  }
  else if (strcmp(word,"SQUARE")==0)
  {
    if (fscanf(inputfp,"%f\n",&side1)==1)
      fprintf(outputfp, "The Perimeter of the square is:
                    %f\n", side1*4);
  }
}
  }
  }
}
```

10.5

The only difference is in the last instruction:

```
else  InsertAtTail(&(TailOfList(*List),Elem);
```

Let us examine what happened using the function `TailOfList`: the first parameter is not the address of the `Next` field (like in the version presented in Section 10.2), but that of a temporary variable (returned by the function `TailOfList`) pointing to the element pointed to by the `Next` field.

When used: &((*List)->Next)

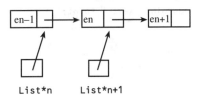

When used: &(TailOfList(List))

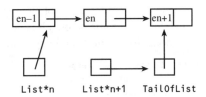

Thus, as result of the assignment *List = Point, the final situation is:

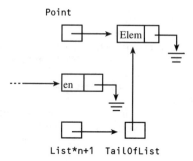

Point

List*n+1   TailOfList

where it is possible to see that the list remains unmodified.

10.6

```
void InsertInOrder (ListOfElements *List, ElementType Elem)
{
    ElemOfList *Point, *CurrentPoint, *PreviousPoint;

    PreviousPoint = NULL;
    CurrentPoint = *List;
    while (CurrentPoint != NULL && Elem > CurrentPoint->Info)
    {
        PreviousPoint = CurrentPointl
        CurrentPoint = CurrentPoint->Next;
    }
    if (CurrentPoint == NULL || Elem != CurrentPoint->Info)
                                        /*this is the added condition*/
    {
        Point = malloc(sizeof(ElemLista));
        Point->Info = Elem;
        Point->Next = CurrentPoint;
        if (PreviousPoint != NULL)
            PreviousPoint->Next = Point;
    }
    else
        *List = Point;
}
```

11.1

If the contents of the node of a graph are not sufficient to identify the node itself (for example, if they denote the colour of the object represented by the node but more than one node can have the same colour) it is necessary to add a field that uniquely identifies the node, for example an integer number.

```
typedef struct A {  int        key;
                    struct A   *Succ;
                 } Adjacent;
```

```
typedef struct NG  {  int       key;
                       Element   Info;
                       struct NG SuccNode;
                       Adjacent  *ListOfAdjacents;
                    } GraphNode, *GraphOfElem;
```

11.3

If the adjacency matrix is used to represent the graph, the most natural solution consists in changing the type of the elements of the array: they could then contain the label associated with the arc they represent; an empty element would indicate the absence of the corresponding arc.

Similarly, if a list representation is used, each node of type `Adjacent` (with reference to the declaration exemplified in Section 11.1.1) can be enriched with a suitable `Label` field; the same applies to the scheme exemplified by Figure 11.6 (the field must be added to the type of the second array).

11.14

With reference to the abstract operations defined for the stack, independently of how it is represented, a simple algorithm for the recognition of palindromic strings is as follows.

We assume that the type `StackOfElem` is defined together with the corresponding operations as described in the text.

```
typedef char Element;

main()
{
   StackOfElem   st;
   Element       ch;
   bool          error;
   FILE          *fp;
                                                      /*open the file*/
   if ((fp = fopen("filename", "r")) == NULL)
      exit(0);

   Initialize(&st);

   while ((ch = getc(fp)) != '%' )
      Push (&st, ch);

   error = false;

   while ((! error) && (ch = getc(fp)) != EOF) && (! Empty(st)))
   {
      if (Top(st) != ch)
         error = true;
      else
         Pop (&st);
   }
```

```
if ( error || ! Empty(st)  ||  ch != EOF)
   puts("This is not a palindrome");
else
   puts("This is a palindrome");
}
```

11.17

The easiest and most natural way to build a queue using pointers is to use a list with a pointer to the last element, as shown in Figure E.11.17.

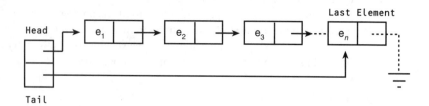

Figure E.11.17 Implementation of a queue using pointers.

In this way it is straightforward to realize all operations on the queue: for example, insertion into the queue involves creating a new element, pointing the previous last element (pointed to by the value of Tail) to the new element, and updating the value of Tail so that it points to the new element.

Note that each abstract operation on the queue can be executed in time $\Theta(1)$ for both implementation techniques.

We define the structure and three operations.

```
typedef struct s_ElQueue {  ElType           Info;
                            struct s_ElQueue  *Prox;
                         } ElQueue;

typedef struct s_Queue    {  ElQueue  *Head;
                             ElQueue  *Tail;
                          } Queue;

void InsertInQueue(Queue  *q, ElType  el)
{
   ElQueue  *tmp;

   if (q->Head == NULL)                           /*empty queue*/
   {
      q->Head = q->Tail = malloc(sizeof(ElQueue));
      q->Head->Info = el;
      q->Head->Prox = NULL;
   }
```

```
      else
      {
         tmp = q->Tail;
         q->Tail = malloc(sizeof(ElQueue));
         q->Tail->Info = el;
         q->Tail->Prox = NULL;
         tmp->Prox = q->Tail;
      }
   }

   void Extract(Queue *q)
   {
      ElQueue *tmp;

      if (q->Head == NULL)                              /*empty queue*/
         return;
      else
      {
         tmp = q->Head;
         q->Head = q->Head->Prox;
         free(tmp);
      }
   }
   void Front(Queue *q, ElType *el)
   {
      if (q->Head == NULL)                              /*empty queue*/
         el = NULL;
      else
         *el = q->Head->Info;
   }
```

11.18

The queue structure is the natural data structure to use whenever data has to be 'processed' in the same order in which it has been created (FIFO: First In, First Out). This occurs in numerous cases: for example if one wants to simulate the service of a cash till in a supermarket.

An interesting special case is given by the breadth-first visit of a tree: in this type of visit, instead of going from parent to child as in all types of visit discussed previously (also called depth-first), the visit proceeds from left to right through nodes of the same level, that is, of the same distance from the root. To obtain such a type of visit it is natural to use a queue structure: after having visited a node, it must be eliminated from the head of the queue and its children must be inserted at the tail.

12.17

An algorithm to balance an ordered tree is the following:

(1)   Visit the tree in order (left or right according to its ordering) and produce an ordered array of pointers to the nodes of the tree (crArray).

(2) Recursively construct a new tree that contains the elements of the array as follows:

(a) The (sub)procedure receives as a parameter the indexes of the first and last element of the array; it calculates their median value (obviously rounding it if the number *n* of elements is even).

(b) It creates a node that contains the element of the array which corresponds to the median index and returns it as the root of the tree produced.

(c) It recursively calls itself twice, passing itself as parameters the first of the parameters received as input and the calculated median value, and the median value and the second of the parameters received as input, respectively.

(d) It ties the values obtained as results to the previously produced node as its left-hand and right-hand child, respectively.

Even without completely coding such a balancing algorithm, it is evident that it produces a balanced tree and that its complexity is $\Theta(n)$. In the worst case, it is not possible to obtain a better order of magnitude of the complexity. However, there are algorithms much more sophisticated than the one suggested here.

```
                                        /*Principal subroutine*/
void balanceTree(ElTree **root)
{
    ElTree   *list[MAX_NODES];
    int      numNode = 0;

    crArray(list, *root, &numNode);
    *root = btree(list, list + numNode);
}

void crArray(ElTree *l[ ], ElTree *el, int *num)
{
    if (el->left)
        crArray(l, el->left, num);

    l[(*num)++] = el;

    if (el->right)
        crArray(l, el->right, num);
}

ElTree *btree(ElTree **first, ElTree **last)
{
    ElTree **median;
    if (last >= first)
    {
        median = first + (last - first)/2;
        *(median)->left = btree(first, median -1);
        *(median)->right = btree(median + 1, last);
        return (*median);
    }
    return NULL;
}
```

12.22

The simplest algorithm for the calculation of the product of two matrices consists in a simple coding of the formula that defines it:

$$c[i,j] = \sum_{k=1}^{n} a[i,k] \cdot b[k,j]$$

using three nested 'for' cycles. From this we can easily derive that the complexity of such an algorithm is $\Theta(n^3)$.

There are, however, more sophisticated algorithms with better complexities.

```c
typedef struct{ int     rows;
                int     cols;
                double  *mem;
              } matrix, *matrixptr;

double  *at(matrixptr  A,  int  r,  int  c)
{
   return (A->mem+r * (A->cols)+c);
}

int mult(matrixptr m1, matrixptr m2, matrixptr dm)
{
   int     i, j, k;
   double  cellval;
   if ((m1->cols != m2->rows) || (m2->cols != dm->cols) ||
       (m1->rows != dm->rows))
     return 0;
   for (i = 0;i < m1->rows; i++)
   {
      for (j = 0; j < m2->cols; j++)
      {
         cellval = 0.0;
         for (k = 0; k< m1->cols; k++)
            cellval += *at(m1, i, k) * (*at(m2, k, j));
         *at(dm, i, j) = cellval;
      }
   }
   return 1;
}

main()
{
   int     i, j;

   double  A[2][3] = {1, 2, 3,
                      4, 5, 6};

   double  B[3][4] = {1, 2, 3, 4,
                      5, 6, 7, 8,
                      9, 0, 1, 2};
```

```
double   C[2][4];

matrix   mA = {2, 3, &A[0][0]};
matrix   mB = {3, 4, &B[0][0]};
matrix   mC = {2, 4, &C[0][0]};

if (mult(&mA, &mB, &mC))
   for (i = 0; i < mC.rows; i++)
   {
      for (j = 0; j < mC.cols; j++)
         printf("%g",C[i][j]);
      putchar("\n");
   }
}
```

12.23

Calculating the determinant of an $n \times n$ matrix using the procedure of the example requires calculating the determinant of $(n-1) \times (n-1)$ matrices n times. This leads to the equation

$$f(n) = c_1 \cdot n + c_2 \cdot n^2 + n \cdot f(n-1) \qquad \text{(E.1)}$$

where the linear and square terms in n are due to the auxiliary operations executed within the cycle (mainly the extraction of the submatrices).

It is easy to state that the solutions of (E.1) are of the type

$$f(n) = n! + g(n)$$

with $g(n)$ being a polynomial function. Consequently, the complexity of the procedure is $\Theta(n!)$.

12.26

First, we represent the geographical map as an array of regions (for simplicity, we assume that each region is identified by an integer number between 0 and $n-1$). Further, we assume that the type colour has been declared as in Section 5.4.2.

The coloration of the map can therefore be represented as an array of colours:

```
colours Coloration[NR]
```

where NR is a constant that indicates the number of regions (+1).

When there are no particular criteria for constructing the coloration, the simplest way to achieve it is to assign the colours to the regions in the same order as they are found: the first colour to the first region, the second to the second and so on.

To realize this simple choice it is sufficient to check in advance that the number of colours is not less than the number of regions; then, take advantage of the fact that in C the explicit enumeration of values of one type via the enum construction is nothing other than the establishment of a unique correspondence between the identifiers of the type's values and the numbers 0, 1, ..., NR.

```
if (NR > NumAvailableColours)
{
   printf("problem too hard ... for me\n");
   if (NumAvailableColours < 4)
      printf("... and perhaps impossible...\n");
   else
      printf("try with the solution of the next exercise.\n");
}
else
   for (count = 0; count < NR; count++)
      Coloration[count] = count;
```

12.27

First, we represent the geographical map as an array of regions (for simplicity, we assume that each region is identified by an integer number between 0 and $n - 1$). A further array of records describes the adjacencies between regions: region R1 is adjacent to region R2 if and only if the pair <R1, R2> belongs to the array. Let Region be the identifier of the first array and Adjacency the identifier of the second. (Note that the technique used for the representation of the regions and their adjacencies implicitly assumes that the set of regions and the adjacency relation between them is a graph and uses one of the techniques to describe such a structure briefly introduced in Chapter 11.) Given that the adjacency relation is symmetrical, it is sufficient that in the array we find (any) one of the pairs <R1, R2>, <R2, R1>.

The result of the coloration is also represented as an array of pairs <region, colour>.

Having said this, a conceptually very simple, but also extremely inefficient way to solve the problem is the following:

(1)   Having established the set of available colours, for example C1, C2, C3, C4, we enumerate all possible colorations (which are 4^n, if 4 is the number of colours and n the number of regions). A simple enumeration technique is shown in Figure E.12.27.

(2)   For each coloration we verify whether it satisfies the condition that two adjacent regions must not be coloured with the same colour: this can be easily realized by scanning the Adjacency array and checking the colour assigned to each element of each pair of the coloration array under consideration.

As soon as a coloration has been found that satisfies the condition, the search is interrupted and the coloration produced. The famous four colour theorem, mentioned in the text of the exercise, guarantees that at least one of the possible colorations satisfies the condition.

There are techniques to solve the exercise in a better way. It should, however, be kept in mind that particularly efficient algorithms for the solution of this problem are not known.

The algorithm outlined above can be easily transformed into the following C program, when we establish that a suitable array, named coloration, contains the coloration under consideration.

> C1, C1, ..., C1, C1   /*C1 repeated *n* times: each region is coloured with C1*/
>
> C1, C1, ..., C1, C2
> C1, C1, ..., C1, C3
> C1, C1, ..., C1, C4
> C1, C1, ..., C2, C1
> C1, C1, ..., C2, C2
>
> ...
>
> C4, C4, ..., C4, C4

Figure E.12.27   Enumeration of all possible colorations of *n* regions with four colours.

```
typedef enum {C1, C2, C3, C4} colour;

typedef int    region;
typedef struct  { region  fst;
                  region  snd;
                } pair;

bool colourMap(colour coloration[], pair adjacency[], int n, int m)
{
   int     i;
   bool    found, OKAdj;

   found = false;

   for (i = 0; i < n; i++)
      coloration[i] = C1 ;

   while ( ! found )
   {
      OKAdj = true;

      for (i = 0; i < m; i++)
         if (coloration[adjacency[i].fst] == coloration[adjacency[i].snd])
         {
            OKAdj = false;
            break;
         }
      if (OKAdj)
         found = true;
      else
      {
         i = n - 1;
         while (i >= 0 && coloration[i] == C4)
            coloration[i!!!] = C1;

         if (i < 0)
         {
            puts("ERROR: No other combination...");
            break;
         }
```

```
                coloration[i]++;
        }
    }
    return found;
}

main()
{
    pair    adj[MAX_NUM_ADJ];
    colour  col[MAX_NUM_REG];
    int     numAdj, numRegions;
    int     i;

                                /*initialize adj, numRegions and numAdj*/

    if (colourMap(col, adj, numRegions, numAdj))
                                                          /*output*/

    else
        puts("The adjacency matrix cannot represent a real map");
}
```

☞ 12.3

Instead of the constant k_3 the following expression should be used:

> **if** Elem $\in$ Sequence **then** k_3 **else** 0.

It is clear, however, that this specification does not alter the substance of the complexity of the algorithm.

☞ 12.8

The substance of the binary search algorithm can be maintained even when the list is realized using pointers. In this case, however, access to the generic ith element of the list requires a time $\Theta(i)$ instead of the constant time needed when the list is realized using arrays. Consequently, the overall time in the worst case will be $\Theta(n.\log(n))$.

```
bool BinSearch(List ls, int num, ElType el)
                /*ls is a pointer to the first element of the list,
                 num is the number of the element in the list,
                 el is the element to be found*/
{
    List  tmp;
    int   i;

    tmp = ls;

    if (num == 0)
        return false;
                                        /*search of the median element*/
    for (i = 0; i < num/2; i++)
        tmp = tmp->Prox;
```

```
    if (tmp->Info == el)
        return true;
    else if (tmp->Info < el)
        return  BinSearch(tmp->Prox, (num - 1)/2, el);
    else
        return  BinSearch(ls, num/2, el);
}
```

13.1

$$10011100101_2 = 2345_8 = 4E5_{16} = 1253_{10}$$
$$10010101111_2 = 2257_8 = 4AF_{16} = 1199_{10}$$
$$1010111010_2 = 1272_8 = 2BA_{16} = 698_{10}$$

$$64752_8 = 110100111101010_2 = 69EA_{16} = 27114_{10}$$
$$34251_8 = 011100010101001_2 = 38A9_{16} = 14505_{10}$$
$$536777_8 = 101011110111111111_2 = 2BDFF_{16} = 179711_{10}$$

$$45_{10} = 101101_2 = 55_8 = 2D_{16}$$
$$56789_{10} = 1101110111010101_2 = 156725_8 = DDD5_{16}$$
$$2453_{10} = 100110010101_2 = 4625_8 = 995_{16}$$
$$500012_{10} = 111\ 1010\ 0001\ 0010\ 1100_2 = 1720454_8 = 7A12C_{16}$$

$$1E59_{16} = 1111001011001_2 = 17131_8 = 7769_{10}$$
$$AB45_{16} = 1010101101000101_2 = 125505_8 = 43845_{10}$$
$$C5E7_{16} = 1100010111100111_2 = 142747_8 = 50663_{10}$$

13.4

	(a)	(b)	(c)	(d)
real num	float point $p=b=10$	fixed point base 2	float point $p=b=2$	float point $p=10, b=2$
67.56	$0.67560000 \times 10^{(2)}$	01000011.10001111010111	$.10000111000111 \times 2^{(000111)}$	$.10101100111101 \times 10^{(000010)}$
0.000787	$0.78700000 \times 10^{(-2)}$	0.00000010000000	$.10000000111100 \times 2^{(111010)}$	$.11001001011110 \times 10^{(111110)}$
2.78	$0.27800000 \times 10^{(1)}$	010.11000111101011	$.10110001111010 \times 2^{(000010)}$	$.01000111001010 \times 10^{(000001)}$
564000.56	$0.56400056 \times 10^{(6)}$	010001001101100000000 .10001111010111	$10001001101100 \times 2^{(010100)}$	$.10010000011000 \times 10^{(000110)}$

13.5

```
+54      0 110110
+ 3      0 000011
─────────────────
+57      0 111001


-54      1 001010
- 3      1 111101
─────────────────
-57    (1)1 000111
```

```
-54        1  001010
-32        1  100000
─────────────────────────
-86[1]   (1)0  101010


+32        0  100000
-  6       1  111010
─────────────────────────
+26      (1)0  011010


-32        1  100000
+ 6        0  000110
─────────────────────────
-26        1  100110
```

13.7

F = (A OR B) OR NOT (A AND B)

A B	(A OR B)	(A AND B)	F
0 0	0	0	1
0 1	1	0	1
1 0	1	0	1
1 1	1	1	1

F = NOT (A OR B OR C)

A	B	C	(A OR B OR C)	F
0	0	0	0	1
0	0	1	1	0
0	1	0	1	0
0	1	1	1	0
1	0	0	1	0
1	0	1	1	0
1	1	0	1	0
1	1	1	1	0

F = ((A AND NOT C) OR B) OR (A AND C)

A	B	C	(A AND NOT C)	(A AND NOT C) OR B	(A AND C)	F
0	0	0	0	0	0	0
0	0	1	0	0	0	0
0	1	0	0	1	0	1
0	1	1	0	1	0	1
1	0	0	1	1	0	1
1	0	1	0	0	1	1
1	1	0	1	1	0	1
1	1	1	0	1	1	1

13.8

A tautology:

F1 = (A OR B) OR NOT (A AND B)

A contradiction:

F2 = ((A AND B) AND NOT B) OR (NOT A AND (A AND B))

13.9

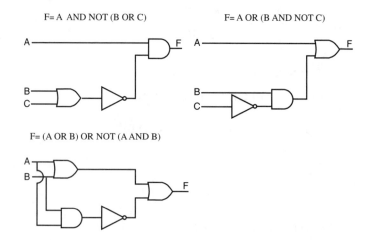

F= A AND NOT (B OR C)

F= A OR (B AND NOT C)

F= (A OR B) OR NOT (A AND B)

14.1

A simplified solution of this exercise avoids considering the carry and the overflow bits. If we name the zero and sign bits of the SR register as Z and N, respectively, and keep in mind that Z is set to 1 when A contains a zero and N is set to 1 when A contains a negative value, then

(a) the execution of the `jumpgtz ind1` instruction involves the following micro-instruction:

if (Z == 0 AND N == 0) OP(CIR) → PC

(b) the execution of the `jumpgez ind1` instruction involves the following micro-instruction:

if (Z == 1 OR N == 0) OP(CIR) → PC

(c) the execution of the `jumpltz ind1` instruction involves the following micro-instruction:

if (Z == 0 AND N == 1) OP(CIR) → PC

(d) the execution of the `jumplez ind1` instruction involves the following micro-instruction:

if (Z == 1 OR N == 1) OP(CIR) → PC

14.2

If we name OP1(CIR), OP2(CIR) and OP3(CIR), respectively, the contents of the first operand, second operand and third operand fields of the current instruction register, and take into account what has been shown in the solution to Exercise 2.3, the execution of the `jumpgt ind1 ind2 ind3` instruction involves the following micro-instructions:

OP1(CIR) $\rightarrow$ AR
MEM[AR] $\rightarrow$ A
OP2(CIR) $\rightarrow$ AR
MEM[AR] $\rightarrow$ B
DIF
if (Z == 0 AND N == 0) OP3(CIR) $\rightarrow$ PC

14.6

	LOADA	#0
	STOREA	COUNT
LOOP1	READ	NUM
	LOADA	NUM
	JUMPZ	LOOP2
	LOADI	COUNT
	STOREA	MEMO(I)
	LOADA	COUNT
	LOADB	#1
	ADD	
	STOREA	COUNT
	JUMP	LOOP1
LOOP2	LOADA	COUNT
	LOADB	#1
	DIF	
	STOREA	COUNT
	JUMPLT	END
	LOADI	COUNT
	WRITE	MEMO(I)
	JUMP	LOOP2
END	HALT	
COUNT	INT	
NUM	INT	
MEMO	INT	
MEMO+1	INT	
...		
MEMO+99	INT	

14.10

	READ	MAX
	LOADA	TEN
	LOADB	ONE
	DIF	
	STOREA	N
CYCLE	READ	NUM
	LOADA	MAX
	LOADB	NUM
	DIF	
	JUMPGEZ	NOCHANGE
	STOREB	MAX
NOCHANGE	LOADA	N
	LOADB	ONE
	DIF	
	STOREA	N
	JUMPGTZ	CYCLE
	WRITE	MAX
	HALT	
TEN	10	
ONE	1	
N	INT	
MAX	INT	
NUM	INT	

15.4 and 15.6

In order to solve the problems proposed by the two exercises, we might hypothesize that the memory handler of the operating system handles a Page Table composed of the following columns:

Process Identifier (PID – in binary coding)

Logical Page Number (LPN – in binary coding)

Present in main memory (PM – takes the value 1 if the logical page is present in main memory, 0 otherwise)

Physical Page Number (PPN – in binary coding)

Mass Memory Address (MMA – in binary coding)

Reference (R – takes the value 1 if the page has been accessed during the last time interval, 0 otherwise)

Ageing (A – signals the number of time intervals since the page was accessed)

Update (U – takes the value 1 if the page has been written to during the last time interval, 0 otherwise)

We also assume that all logical pages of the active processes on the machine are present in memory (in execution, ready, or wait state).

During a predefined time interval, each time that the process in execution requires access to a logical page, the handler sets

R = 1
U = 1

if the operation requested for the page is the updating of its contents (in the row of the page table corresponding to the particular process and the particular logical page).

At the end of the predefined time interval, the handler scans the table and:

- increments by 1 the contents of A in each row where R equals 0 and the page is 'ageing' (a page is not being accessed);
- resets to 0 all values of R.

When the process in execution requests access to a memory address, the handler

- considers the address to be expressed in terms of 'logical page number and offset within the page',
- consults the page table in an associative way (searching the row corresponding to that process and that page by scanning the table and consulting columns PID and LPN) and identifies the row in the table to be considered,
- checks (consulting PM) whether the logical page is present in memory.

If the logical page is not present in memory (PM == 0), if no free physical page is available, the handler

- identifies the logical page in memory that has not been accessed for the longest time (identifying the row in the table that has the highest value for A);
- discharges it from memory by performing the following operations:
  - sets PM = 0
  - if U == 1, copies to mass storage at address MMA the contents of the physical page that has to be freed (U == 1 indicates that the logical page has been modified during its stay in main memory and that these modifications must be stored in mass storage);
  - stores the physical page number that has thus become free.

Once a free physical page has been identified (or created), the handler

- loads the logical page in question into main memory by copying the contents of mass storage, taking into account the mass memory address (MMA) from where the logical page in question has to be copied and the number of the physical page that has been found (or freed for the purpose)

- sets PM = 1,
- sets the PPN field to the number of the physical page into which the logical page has been loaded.

15.7

The arrival of an external interrupt sets the value of one bit of the INTR register to 1; more than one bit could be 1, indicating that the interrupt handler has to handle more than one interrupt, in the appropriate order. The fetch cycle can be modified in the following way:

```
                              /*supplementary part needed for interrupt handling*/
    if (at least one of the bits of the INTR register equals 1)
        then
            DIS
            50 → AR
            SR → MEM[AR]
            51 → AR
            PC → MEM[AR]
            100 → PC
                              /*micro-instructions executed independently
                              of the occurrence of an interrupt*/
    PC → AR
    MEM[AR] → DR
    DR → CIR
    PC + 1 → PC
```

15.8

```
                              /*for saving the context of the active
                              process at the moment of the call to the
                              interrupt handler, we must save in order the
                              values of registers A and B and the values
                              of registers SR and PC (which had been saved
                              by the micro-instructions of the fetch cycle
                              into addresses 50 and 51, respectively,
                              before the call to the interrupt handler -
                              see the solution to Exercise 15.5)*/

    STOREA   1000             /*save the contents of register A into cell
                              1000*/
    STOREB   1001             /*save the contents of register B into cell
                              1001*/
    LOADA    50               /*copy into register A the value of SR that
                              the process had at the moment of the call to
                              the interrupt handler, available in memory
                              cell address 50*/
    LOADB    51               /*copy into register B the value of PC that
                              the process had at the moment of the call to
                              the interrupt handler, available in memory
                              cell address 51*/
```

```
STOREA    1002        /*save the SR value of the suspended process
                      into cell 1002*/
STOREB    1003        /*save the PC value of the suspended process
                      into cell 1003*/

                      /*for restoring the context of the program
                      that was suspended in order to handle the
                      interrupts, we assume that the assembler
                      language includes the instructions LOADSR
                      ind and LOADPC ind which assign the
                      registers SR and PC the value contained in
                      the cell with address ind*/

LOADA     1000
LOADB     1001
LOADRS    1002
LOADPC    1003
ENABLE                /*re-enabling of interrupts*/
```

16.1

| 1 | 3 | 4 | | 6 | 7 | 9 | 10 | | 13 | 15 | | 18 | 20 | 23 | 30 | | 33 | 35 | | 40 | 42 | 50 | | 54 | | 60 | 74 |

$$\frac{21}{28} = 0.75$$

(a) The binary search has to be modified insofar as it is possible that the median element does not contain any value. In the worst case, the complexity of the search is *linear* in the number of physical blocks allocated to the file.

(b) Inserting the number 14 (by moving the 15)

we obtain

| 1 | 3 | 4 | | 6 | 7 | 9 | 10 | | 13 | 14 | 15 | 18 | 20 | 23 | 30 | | 33 | 35 | | 40 | 42 | 50 | | 54 | | 60 | 74 |

In the same way, inserting the numbers 32, 41, 2

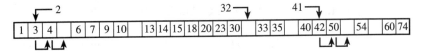

we obtain

| 1 | 2 | 3 | 4 | 6 | 7 | 9 | 10 | | 13 | 14 | 15 | 18 | 20 | 23 | 30 | 32 | 33 | 35 | | 40 | 41 | 42 | 50 | 54 | | 60 | 74 |

In order to perform the four insertions, five moves had to be made.

16.2

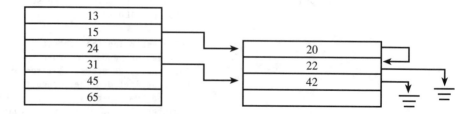

The search procedure can be decomposed into two phases.

During the first phase, a binary search is performed on the sequential archive.

Should this fail, the binary search nevertheless returns the cell that contains the element immediately preceding the one being searched; following its pointer to the overflow chain, a sequential search is then performed on the chain itself. The complexity of the search is therefore

$$\log(n) + m$$

where

- n is the length of the sequential archive,
- m is the maximum length of the overflow chains.

16.6

The key of STUDENT is REG-NUMBER (assuming each REG-NUMBER unique); the key of COURSE is CODE-COURSE (assuming that each course has a different code); the key of EXAM is the pair CODE-COURSE, REG-STUD (assuming that each student sits each exam just once: to allow storage of more marks, for example to include a 'failed' mark, we would need the triple CODE-COURSE, REG-STUD, DATE).

16.9

(SQL only)

(a) SELECT CODE-COURSE, LECTURER
     FROM COURSE
     WHERE TITLE = 'Foundations of Computer Science'
         OR TITLE = 'Analysis 1'

(b) SELECT NAME
     FROM STUDENT
     WHERE COURSE-STUD = 'Aeronautics'
         AND (COURSE-YEAR = 3 OR COURSE-YEAR = 4)

(c) SELECT NAME, REG-NUMBER
FROM STUDENT, COURSE, EXAM
WHERE STUDENT.REG-NUMBER = EXAM.REG-NUMBER
AND EXAM.CODE-COURSE = COURSE.CODE-COURSE
AND TITLE = 'Analysis'
AND MARK > 28
AND DATE = 10-1-93

(d) SELECT REG-NUMBER, NAME, MARK
FROM STUDENT, COURSE, EXAM
WHERE STUDENT.REG-NUMBER = EXAM.REG-NUMBER
AND EXAM.CODE-COURSE = COURSE.CODE-COURSE
AND (LECTURER = 'Jones' OR LECTURER = 'Smith')

(e) (SELECT REG-NUMBER
FROM EXAM, COURSE
WHERE EXAM.CODE-COURSE = COURSE.CODE-COURSE
AND TITLE = 'Analysis 1')
MINUS
(SELECT REG-NUMBER
FROM EXAM, COURSE
WHERE EXAM.CODE-COURSE = COURSE.CODE-COURSE
AND TITLE = 'Foundations of Computer Science')

(f) SELECT LECTURER
FROM STUDENT, COURSE, EXAM
WHERE STUDENT.REG-NUMBER = EXAM.REG-NUMBER
AND EXAM.CODE-COURSE = COURSE.CODE-COURSE
AND NAME = 'Phil Jones' AND MARK > 25

16.12

(a) INSERT INTO STUDENT: <'56765', 'Phil Jones', 8-1-75, 1, 'I'>
INSERT INTO EXAM: <'AG5067', '56765', 1-7-95, 28>

(b) DELETE FROM STUDENT   Overflow zone
WHERE REG-NUMBER = '67578'
DELETE FROM EXAM
WHERE REG-NUMBER = '67578'

(c) UPDATE COURSE
SET TITLE = 'Foundations of Computer Science'
WHERE TITLE = 'Computer Programming'
OR TITLE = 'Elements of Computer Science'

(d) UPDATE EXAM
SET MARK = MARK + 1
WHERE CODE-COURSE = 'AG0010'
AND DATE = 15-6-92

16.13

(a) The keys are:

for $R1$: A, B

for $R2$: C, D

for $R3$: F

for $R4$: I

(b) $R1$ is in first normal form

$R2$ is in first normal form

$R3$ is in second normal form

$R4$ is in third normal form

(c) We decompose $R1$ and $R2$, which are not in second normal form, into:

$R11(A, B, C)$, $R12(B, D)$

$R21(C, D, G)$, $R22(D, E, F)$

Resulting relations are in third normal form, therefore $R11$, $R12$, $R21$, $R22$, $R3$, $R4$ is a scheme in second normal form

We finally decompose $R3$, which is not in third normal form, into $R21(FH)$ and $R32(H1)$: these relations are in third normal form, therefore $R11$, $R12$, $R21$, $R22$, $R31$, $R32$, $R4$ is a scheme in third normal form.

16.14

Scheme in third normal form:

> PATIENT(NHS-CODE, NAME, ADDRESS) – key: NHS-CODE
> STAY(NCC, NHS-CODE, DATE-ADM, DEPARTMENT,
> DATE-DIS) – key: NCC
> DEPARTMENT(NAME-DEP, PATHOLOGY, CONSULTANT,
> TOTAL-BEDS) – key: NAME-DEP
> PERSONNEL(NAME-DEP, NAME-PERS, QUALIFICATION)
> – key: NAME-DEP, NAME-PERS
> BED(NAME-DEP, NUM-BED, STATE, NHS-CODE)
> – key: NAME-DEP, NUM-BED

17.1

(a) We construct a network with a cubic topology (the eight corners of the cube are the eight nodes).

Each node is assigned a binary coding (three binary digits) such that two corners connected by a side differ only by one digit (intuitively, the dimension along which we have moved).

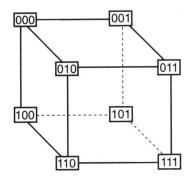

Not only is the property satisfied that from each node there is more than one path to its successor, but we can also see that each node is connected to each of the others by a path of maximum three steps.

(b)   It is possible to define a local routing algorithm that is valid for all nodes (taking advantage of the symmetry of the network).

```
if the node in question is XYZ and the destination node is xyz
then
    if X is different from x
       send the message to xYZ
    otherwise
       if Y is different from y
          send the message to XyZ (that is, xyZ)
       otherwise
          if Z is different from z
             send the message to XYz (that is, xyz, the addressee)
          otherwise
             I am the addressee XYZ = xyz
```

(c)   Node 2, in order to send a message to node 5, opens a dialogue session (level 5), then, following the routing policy, sends the message to node 6. Node 6 receives the message and, still following the routing algorithm, selects the next node, that is, node 4, which then sends the message to node 5 (the addressee). Node 5 takes care of closing the session.

(d)   The procedure differs from the previous one insofar as the file can be segmented into different messages. This happens on level 4. At this point, node 2 sends different messages to node 6 which, through node 4, forwards them to destination node 5. Here we go back to level 4 where the file is recomposed.

17.4

(a)   The warm restart handles malfunctions where loss of main memory occurs but mass storage is left intact.

(b)   Transaction T3 has to be redone and transactions T2 and T4 have to be undone, whereas transaction T1 is complete.

(c)   Redoing T3 corresponds to assigning datum D3 the value A3; undoing T2 and T4 corresponds to assigning D2 the value B2 and D4 the value B4.

20.1

If the user of the software product is the end user, reusability is normally an internal quality: it is typical of *components* that are sufficiently general to be easily inserted into different contexts. The task of integrating such components into a complete application is, however, the designer's, not the user's, task. It should be noted, however, that the *user* could be the designer of personalized applications, and as such make use of suitable, commercially distributed libraries: in that case, reusability is an external quality of the product *library* that serves the designer of personalized applications – the end user.

20.2

With the increasing diffusion of distributed and heterogeneous systems, resident on different computers that may be distant from each other, and based on often different base software and applications, the quality of interoperability becomes more and more important, understood as the ease with which a software component can communicate with and be integrated with other software: for example, network management software must be able to make different machines communicate with each other.

Interoperability refers to the product. It can be an external quality if the user of the application is interested in constructing composite systems; it is internal if the user is only interested in the overall system independently of the architecture used to realize it (centralized or distributed).

Another external quality which is often of the utmost importance is that the software should be easy to use and learn: the so-called 'user-friendliness'.

21.1

Some other typical requirements of an automated teller machine are the following:

- A user can carry out the following operations:
  - Enquiry about the overall balance of the user's own current account (checking account).
  - Withdrawal of a certain quantity of cash from the user's own current account. The withdrawal cannot be higher than the balance of the current account and in any case cannot exceed a predetermined maximum value.
  - Enquiry about recent movements of the current account. In this case, the machine must ask the user for the dates between which the movements in question took place. For each movement the date and amount have to be indicated.

– Paying in cash and/or cheques into the current account.

• The use of the teller machine is enabled only after the user has inserted a magnetic card and entered the correct PIN. In case of an incorrect PIN, the user may re-enter the code a certain number of times, after which access to the terminal will be denied (and the existence of a suspect user signalled to the control personnel).

• Another requirement which many users would like but which is unfortunately not satisfied by any of the systems the authors know of, is to be able to signal malfunctions that occur and ask for the intervention of service personnel (by phone if outside bank opening hours).

22.1

(a)

```
definition module TypeWord

typedef hidden   Word;
typedef enum     {greater, equal, less} compareResult;

bool    ReadWord(Word  *w, FILE  *f);
                        /*reads the word w from the file f
                        Returns the success of the operation*/

bool    WriteWord(Word  *st, FILE  *f);
                        /*writes the word w to the file f
                        Returns the success of the operation*/

        compareResult   CompareWords(Word w1, Word w2);
                        /*compares words w1 and w2*/

end.                    /*TypeWord definition module*/
```

```
definition module TypeSetOfWords

typedef hidden   SetOfWords;

void Initialize(SetOfWords *set);
                        /*initialize an empty Set*/

void Add(SetOfWords  *set, Word  w, bool  *inserted);
                        /*adds the word w to the set.
                        inserted is set to true if the word
                        was not already in the set*/

void Remove(SetOfWords  *set, Word  w, bool  *deleted);
                        /*removes the word w from the set
                        deleted is set to true if the word
                        was in the set*/

bool Belong(Word  w, SetOfWords  *set);
                        /*tests if the word w belongs to the set*/
```

```
void Union(SetOfWords  *set1, SetOfWords  *set2);
                           /*set1 is set to the union of the two sets*/


bool Empty(SetOfWords  set);
                                    /*tests if the set is empty*/


end.                           /*TypeSetOfWords definition module*/
```

(b)
```
definition module TypeQuadrilateral

typedef hidden  Quadrilateral;

void InitSquare (Quadrilateral  *q, double  side);
                                         /*initialize a square*/

void InitRectangle (Quadrilateral  *q, double  base,
                       double height);
                                      /*initialize a rectangle*/

void InitRhombus (Quadrilateral  *q, double  minorDiagonal,
                    double majorDiagonal);
                                       /*initialize a rhombus*/

double  perimeter (Quadrilateral  q);
                           /*calculates and returns the perimeter*/

double  area (Quadrilateral q);
                             /*calculates and returns the area*/

end.                       /*TypeQuadrilateral definition module*/
```

```
implementation module TypeQuadrilateral

import  sqrt from math;

typedef enum {square, rectangle, rhombus} Shape;

typedef struct  { double   side1;
                  double   side2;
                  double   side3;
                  double   side4;
                  double   diag1;
                  double   diag2;
                  Shape    shp;
                } Quadrilateral;

void InitSquare (Quadrilateral *q, double side)
{
   q->shp   = square;
   q->side1 = q->side2 = q->side3 = q->side4 = side;
   q->diag1 = q->diag2 = side*sqrt(2);
}
```

```
void InitRectangle (Quadrilateral *q, double base, double height)
{
   q->shp  = rectangle;
   q->side1 = q->side3 = base;
   q->side2 = q->side4 = height;
   q->diag1 = q->diag2 = sqrt(base^2 + height^2);
}

void InitRhombus (Quadrilateral *q, double minorDiagonal,
                   double majorDiagonal)
{
   q->shp   = rhombus;
   q->side1 = sqrt(minorDiagonal^2 + majorDiagonal^2)/2;
   q->side2 = q->side4 = q->side4 = q->side1;
   q->diag1 = minorDiagonal;
   q->diag2 = majorDiagonal;
}

double  perimeter (Quadrilateral q)
{
   if (q.shp  == square || q.shp  == rhombus)
     return side1*4;
   else if (q.shp  == rectangle)
     return 2*(side1+side2);
   else
     return (side1+side2+side3+side4);
}

double  area (Quadrilateral q)
{
   if (q.shp == square || q.shp  == rectangle)
     return side1*side2;
   else if (q.shp  == rhombus)
     return (diag1*diag2)/2
   else
     return  -1.0;
}

end.                   /*TypeQuadrilateral implementation module*/
```

22.2

```
definition module TypeStack

import  ElemType   from TypeElem

typedef hidden  Stack;

void    Initialize(Stack  *st);
                                     /*initializes an empty stack*/

void    Push(Stack  *st, ElemType info, bool  *result);
                                /*pushes an element on the stack;
                  result is set to false if the operation aborts*/
```

```
void        Pop(Stack *st);
                   /*deletes the element on the head of the stack*/

ElemType    Top(Stack st, bool *result);
                   /*returns the element on the head of the stack;
                   result is set to false if the stack is empty*/

bool    Empty(Stack st);
                                /*tests if the stack is empty*/

end.                            /*TypeStack definition module*/
```

First implementation

```
implementation module TypeStack

import ElemType from TypeElem

const    maxElem = 1000;

typedef struct { ElemType
Info[maxElem];
                int        pos;
            } Stack;



void    Initialize(Stack *st)
{
   st->pos = 0;
}

void    Push(Stack *st, ElemType info,
             bool*result)
{
   if (st->pos < maxElem)
   {
       st->Info[st->pos++] = info;
       *result = true;
   }
   else
       *result = false;
}

void    Pop(Stack *st)
{
   if (st->pos > 0)  /*stack not empty*/
      st->pos=st->pos-1;
}
```

Second implementation

```
implementation module TypeStack

import malloc, free from MemAllocation
import ElemType      from TypeElem

typedef struct s_ElStack {
                    ElemType        Info;
                    struct s_ElStack *Prox;
                 } ElStack;

typedef struct { ElStack    *head;
             } Stack;

void    Initialize(Stack *st)
{
    st->head = NULL;
}

void    Push(Stack *st, ElemType info,
             bool*result)
{
    ElStack *tmp;

    tmp = st->head;
    st->head = malloc(sizeof(ElStack));
    st->head->Info = info;
    st->head->Prox = tmp;
    *result = true;
}

void    Pop(Stack *st)
{
    ElStack *tmp;
    if (st->head != NULL)
                          /*stack not empty*/
    {
        tmp = st->head;
        st->head = tmp->Prox;
        free(tmp);
    }
}
```

First implementation	**Second implementation**
continued	*continued*

```
ElemType    Top(Stack st, bool *result)      ElemType    Top(Stack st, bool *result)
{                                             {
   ElemType el;                                  ElemType el;

   if (st.pos > 0)   /*Stack not empty*/      if (st-.head ! = NULL)
   {                                                               /*stack not empty*/
      el = st.Info[(st.pos)-1];                  {
      *result = true;                               el = st.head->Info;
   }                                                *result  = true;
   else                                          }
      *result = false;                          else
                                                   *result  = false;
   return el;                                     return el;
}                                             }

bool    Empty(Stack  st)                      bool    Empty(Stack  st)
{                                             {
   return (st.pos == 0);                         return (st-.head == ...);
}                                             }
end.                                          end.
        /*first implementation TypeStack*/            /*second implementation TypeStack*/
```

22.4

The definition module gtab.h should declare the types ContentType and TableType and the variable NameTable. This makes the variable visible to the program module but also unprotected because the variable can be modified by instructions or functions of the program module, independently of the functions belonging to the definition module gtab.h.

23.2

For Example 3.4 the program must be executed three times, for example with the following inputs:

> < w , w >
> < b , w >
> < w , b >

For Example 3.5 the program must be executed four times, for example with the following inputs:

> < 5, 5, 5 >
> < 5, 5, 8 >
> < 4, 5, 8 >
> < 10 , 2 , 3 >

For Example 3.5 the program must be executed once, for example with the following input:

< 1000 13 7 1996% >

25.1

File `figure.h`

```
class figure
{ private:
      int        numLines;
      double     Line[10];
   public:
      figure();
      figure(double lns[], int num);

      virtual void addLine(double line);
};

class closedFigure : public figure
{ public:
      closedFigure(double sides[], int num): (sides,num) {};

      virtual double getPerimeter();

      void changeFigure(double sides[], int num);

      virtual double addLine(double line)
      {
         printf("addLine: Not available for closedFigure class\n");
         return -1.0;
      }
};

class openFigure : public figure
{ public:
      double getLength();
};

class polygon : public closedFigure
{ public:
      void printInformation();

      virtual double getArea()
      {
         printf("No general formula to calculate area\n");
         return -1.0;
      }
};

class square : public polygon
{ public:
      square(double side);
```

```
        double getPerimeter();
        double getArea();
};


class rectangle : public polygon
{ public:
        double getPerimeter();
        double getArea();
};
```

File figure.cc

```
void polygon::printInformation()
{
    int i;
    printf("Number of sides: %d\n", numLines);
    for (i = 0; i <= numLines; i++)
        printf("Side-%d: %f\n", i, Line[i]);
    printf("Perimeter: %f\n", getPerimeter());
    printf("Area: %f\n", getArea());
}


double closedFigure::getPerimeter()
{
    double per  = 0.0;
    for (int i  = 0; i < numLines; i++)
        per += Line[i];
    return per;
}


double square::getPerimeter()
{
    return (4*Line[0]);
}


double square::getArea()
{
    return (Line[0])^2;
}


double rectangle::getPerimeter()
{
    return 2*(Line[0]+line[1]);
}


double rectangle::getArea()
{
    return (line[0]*line[1]);
}
```

25.3

Let us take as an example the function `printInformation` defined in the class `polygon` which uses the functions `virtual getArea` and `getPerimeter`. If they were not declared `virtual`, the compiler would link these calls to the implementations visible from the class `polygon`, namely `closedFigure::getPerimeter()` and `polygon::getArea()`. This leads to an error insofar as the method `printInformation` is called on an object, for example of type `square`. By defining the functions as `virtual`, the link is not made statically, but at run time the implementation that is visible from the class that effectively calls the method is chosen. In this way, the methods `square::getPerimeter()` and `square::getArea()` are called.

Index